Wendel All Together

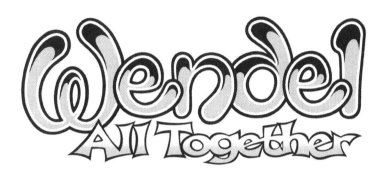

Wendel
All Together

by

Howard Cruse

OLMSTEAD
PRESS

Milford, CT

Copyright ©1982-90, 1992, 2001 Howard Cruse

All rights reserved. Except for the quotation of short passages for purposes of criticism and review, no part of this publication may be reproduced in whole or in part in any form.

Published in 2001 by Olmstead Press: Chicago, Illinois

The comic strips in this book were previously published by Gay Presses of New York, St. Martin's Press, Kitchen Sink Press, *The Advocate*, *Gay Comix*, and *The Village Voice*, Additional illustrations originally appeared in *Amazing Heroes*, *Gayellow Pages*, *Out/Look*, Volume 1 of Maurice Horn's *Contemporary Graphic Artists*, and the program for the 1989 San Diego Comic-Con International. The panel on page xii of the Introduction is excerpted from *Stuck Rubber Baby*, published by Paradox Press. *Stuck Rubber Baby* is a trademark of Paradox Press.

Cover designed by Howard Cruse. Book designed and typeset by Howard Cruse.

Library of Congress Card Number: 2001086932
ISBN: 1-58754-012-6

Editorial sales rights and permission inquiries should be addressed to:
Olmstead Press, 22 Broad Street, Suite 34, Milford, CT 06460

Email: Editor@lpcgroup.com

Manufactured in the United States of America
1 3 5 7 9 10 8 6 4 2

Substantial discounts on bulk quantities of Olmstead Press books are available to corporations, professional associations and other organizations.

If you are in the USA or Canada, contact:
LPC Group
Attn: Special Sales Department
1-800-626-4330, fax 1-800-334-3892, or email: sales@lpcgroup.com.

Acknowledgments

I'd like to express my heartfelt gratitude to Robert Boyd, my editor at Olmstead Press, who made this book possible; to Kathy Douglass, Olmstead's graphic production coordinator, who has helped to save me from the consequences of my many gaps in book-production skills; and to my agent, Mike Friedrich of Star*Reach Productions, who helped lay the contractual groundwork for this project.

This book couldn't exist had others not helped *Wendel* gain an audience in times past, so I'd like to thank them as well. First and foremost must be the late Robert I. McQueen, the editor-in-chief at *The Advocate* who gave the Strawhead a stage to play on, as well as Lenny Giteck and Stuart Kellogg, two successors to McQueen, who kept the door open after McQueen moved on. Thanks also to Felice Picano, the editor and (along with Terry Helbing and Larry Mitchell) a co-partner at Gay Presses of New York, who green-lighted the first *Wendel* book; Michael Denneny, the editor at St. Martin's Press who played the same role with the follow-up collection *Wendel on the Rebound*; and Denis Kitchen, founder and publisher of Kitchen Sink Comix/Kitchen Sink Press, who packaged some later episodes of my feature in comic-book form.

I'm also mindful of past contributions by others such as Fern Schwaber, who brought her professional skills to bear when *Wendel* had tricky legal rapids to negotiate, as well as David Groff, James Vance, Charlotte Sheedy, and Craig Nelson, all of whom tried at different times over a span of years to help *Wendel* reclaim some shelf space in the nation's bookstores.

I'd like to thank my fellow cartoonist Eric Orner, creator of *The Mostly Unfabulous Social Life of Ethan Green*, for letting me reprint "Two Toons Talking," the "jam" strip we co-created at *The Advocate*'s behest.

I'm grateful to Robert Triptow and Andy Mangels for offering cameo space to *Wendel* in *Gay Comix* during their respective editorships; to Reed Waller and Kate Worley, who gave *Wendel* a showcase in the back pages of *Omaha the Cat Dancer*; and to Jason Fairchild, who reprinted *Wendel* episodes for *All-Man* readers during the 1990s.

You may notice the frequent use I've made in this book of a type font that bears a suspicious resemblance to my own comic-book hand lettering. The font is called Loose Cruse, and Jess Latham helped me create it for his web site Blue Vinyl Fonts (www.bvfonts.com). Thanks, Jess.

And finally, I want to thank Ed Sedarbaum for the encouragement and support he has provided (along with invaluable editorial suggestions) for this and every other project I've undertaken during our twenty-one years as a couple. In my first book I echoed a phrase from *Wendel* in calling Eddie "my best friend, lover, and lifemate." Happily, he still is.

A Note About This Collection

Some discrepancies may be noticed between a few of the *Wendel* episodes in this book and their counterparts as originally published in *The Advocate*. Most of these reflect revisions made at the time of *Wendel on the Rebound*'s publication that I have chosen to retain. The same is true regarding a few small shifts I made in the ordering of episodes when putting together the St. Martin's Press collection.

Other Books by
Howard Cruse

Wendel

Wendel on the Rebound

Dancin' Nekkid with the Angels

Early Barefootz

Stuck Rubber Baby

My last chat with Wendel Trupstock was at a loud party in 1995. He was dancing the Macarena.

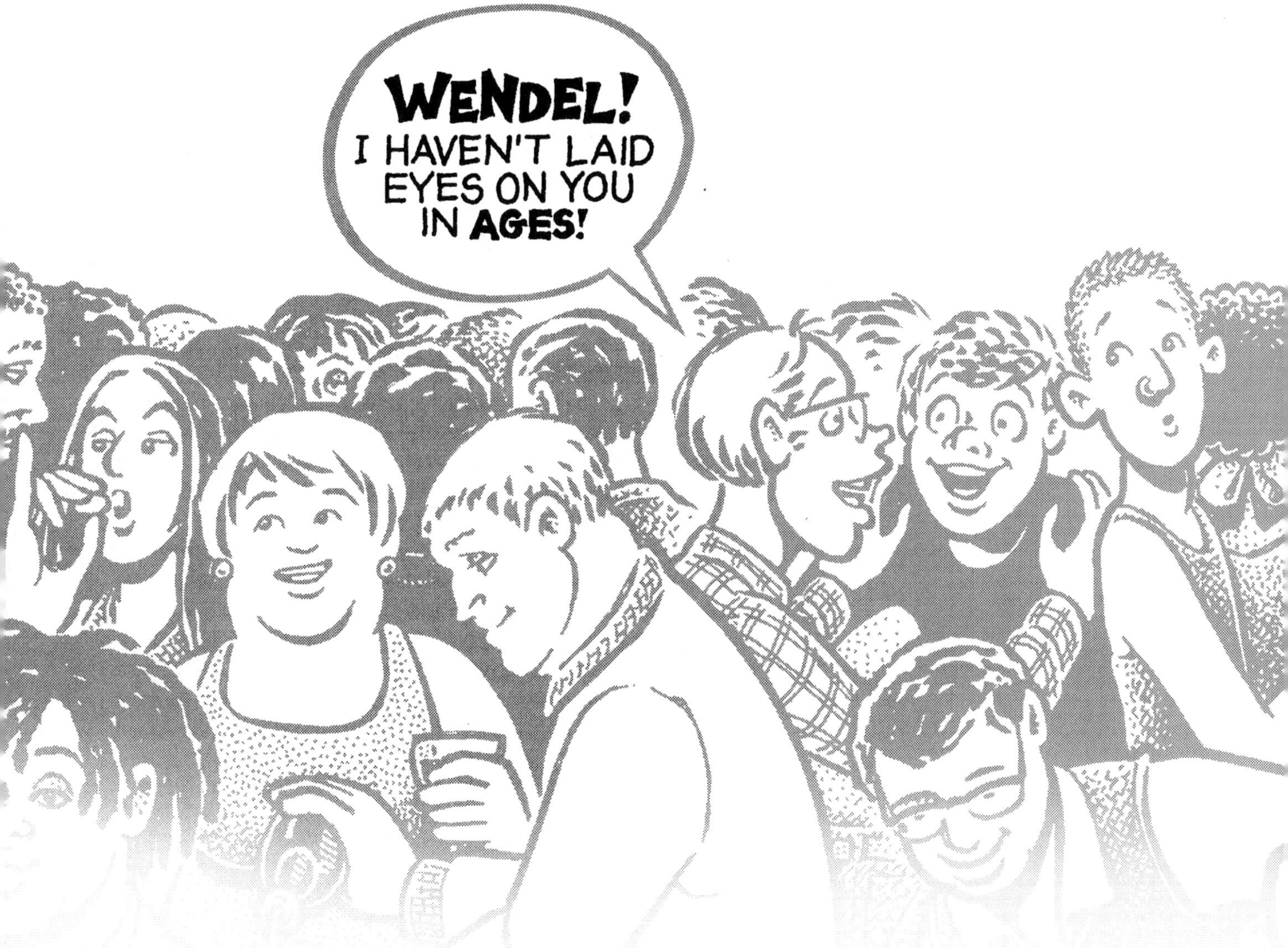
WENDEL!
I HAVEN'T LAID EYES ON YOU IN AGES!

Actually, it wasn't a *real* party. The party was in a dream. And it wasn't even a real *dream,* strictly speaking. It was a *fictional* dream

But everything *else* about the encounter was true.

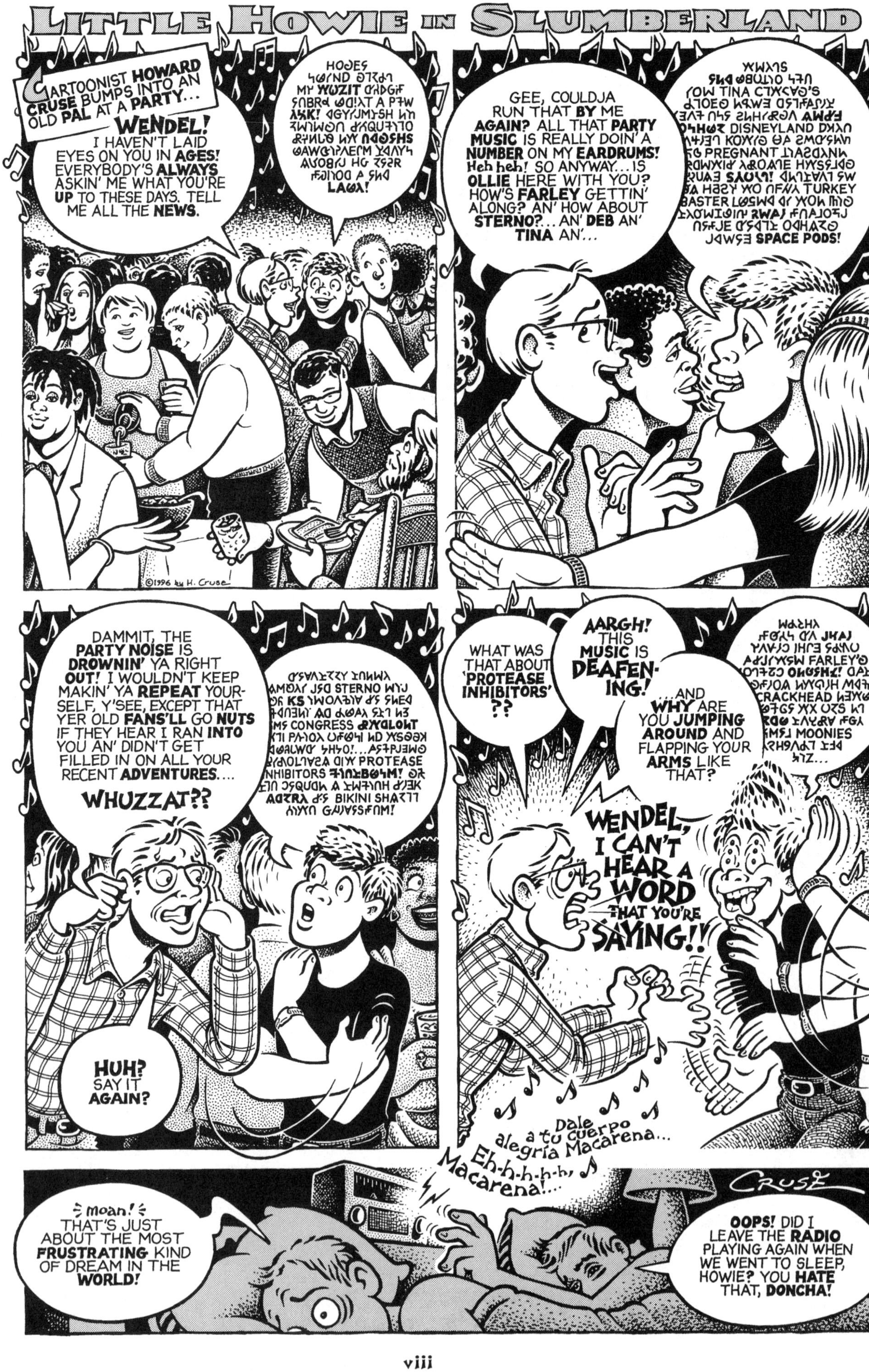

LITTLE HOWIE IN SLUMBERLAND
CARTOONIST HOWARD CRUSE BUMPS INTO AN OLD PAL AT A PARTY...
WENDEL! I HAVEN'T LAID EYES ON YOU IN AGES! EVERYBODY'S ALWAYS ASKIN' ME WHAT YOU'RE UP TO THESE DAYS. TELL ME ALL THE NEWS.
©1996 by H. Cruse
GEE, COULDJA RUN THAT BY ME AGAIN? ALL THAT PARTY MUSIC IS REALLY DOIN' A NUMBER ON MY EARDRUMS! Heh heh! SO ANYWAY... IS OLLIE HERE WITH YOU? HOW'S FARLEY GETTIN' ALONG? AN' HOW ABOUT STERNO?... AN' DEB AN' TINA AN'...
DAMMIT, THE PARTY NOISE IS DROWNIN' YA RIGHT OUT! I WOULDN'T KEEP MAKIN' YA REPEAT YOURSELF, Y'SEE, EXCEPT THAT YER OLD FANS'LL GO NUTS IF THEY HEAR I RAN INTO YOU AN' DIDN'T GET FILLED IN ON ALL YOUR RECENT ADVENTURES....
WHUZZAT??
HUH? SAY IT AGAIN?
WHAT WAS THAT ABOUT 'PROTEASE INHIBITORS'??
AARGH! THIS MUSIC IS DEAFENING!
...AND WHY ARE YOU JUMPING AROUND AND FLAPPING YOUR ARMS LIKE THAT?
WENDEL, I CAN'T HEAR A WORD THAT YOU'RE SAYING!!
Dale a tu cuerpo alegría Macarena... Eh-h-h-h-h, Macarena!...
CRUSE
moan! THAT'S JUST ABOUT THE MOST FRUSTRATING KIND OF DREAM IN THE WORLD!
OOPS! DID I LEAVE THE RADIO PLAYING AGAIN WHEN WE WENT TO SLEEP, HOWIE? YOU HATE THAT, DONCHA!

At left: My contribution to the special reunion issue of *Gay Comix* (#25).

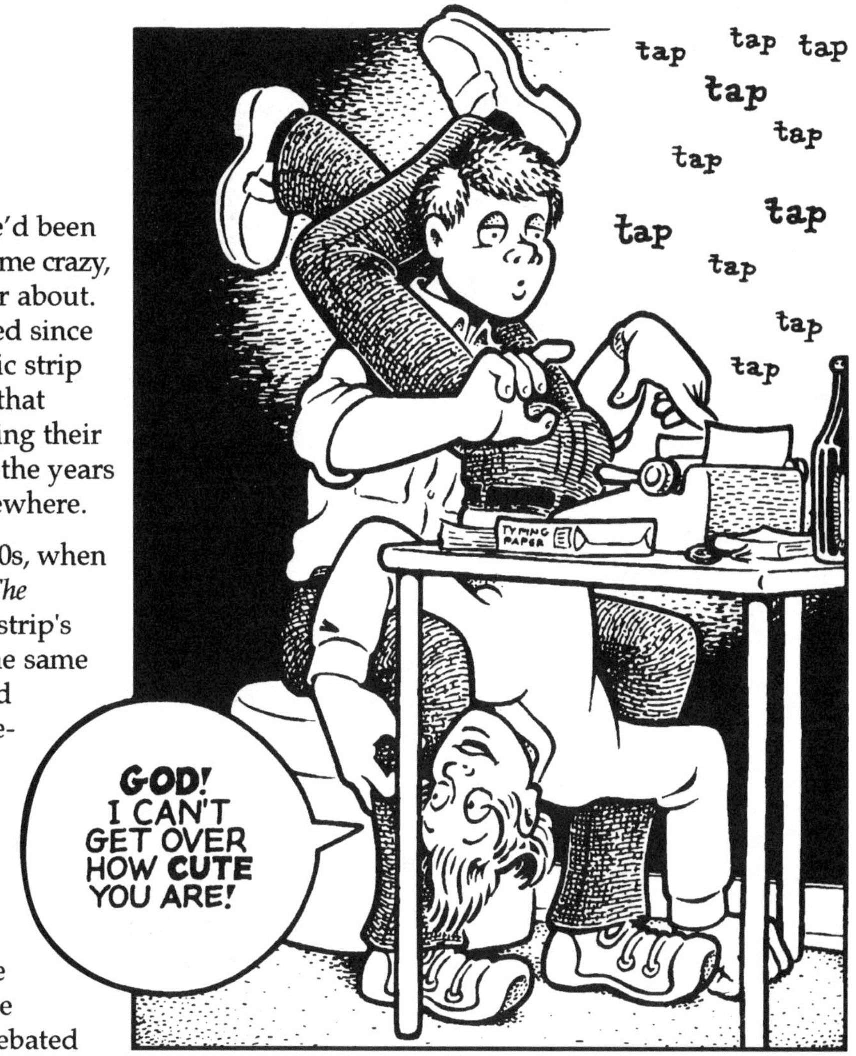
tap tap tap
tap
tap
tap
tap
tap
tap
tap
tap
TYPING PAPER
GOD! I CAN'T GET OVER HOW CUTE YOU ARE!

I asked "the Strawhead" what he'd been up to since I last drew him. Call me crazy, but that's something I often wonder about. Although a dozen years have passed since the curtain came down on the comic strip they starred in, I enjoy fantasizing that Wendel and Ollie have gone on living their lives with no help from me during the years when my attention was turned elsewhere.

It's a habit I got into during the 1980s, when *Wendel* ran as a regular feature in *The Advocate*. I always fancied that the strip's fictional characters were reading the same real-world news accounts that I and their fans read each morning. Sometimes they reacted the same way their flesh-and-blood counterparts did. When *Advocate* readers descended on the nation's capital for the 1987 March on Washington, Wendel and his friends did, too. Sometimes their activism was more inventive than ours. When the Pope traveled to San Francisco, Sterno debated him on *Nightline*.

Not that the strip was regularly tethered to big news events. More typically it was a comedic portrayal of everyday life. Of course, it's a measure of how disconnected from reality a lot of nongay Americans were in those days that to depict lesbians and gay guys as even *having* "everyday lives" was provocative. After all, according to a 1982 Moral Majority fundraising letter from Jerry Falwell, our main goal in life was to "legitimize perversion" so that "the very foundations of moral principle upon which this great nation was established [would] soon crumble." That's quite an undertaking for us queers. Who had time to do laundry?

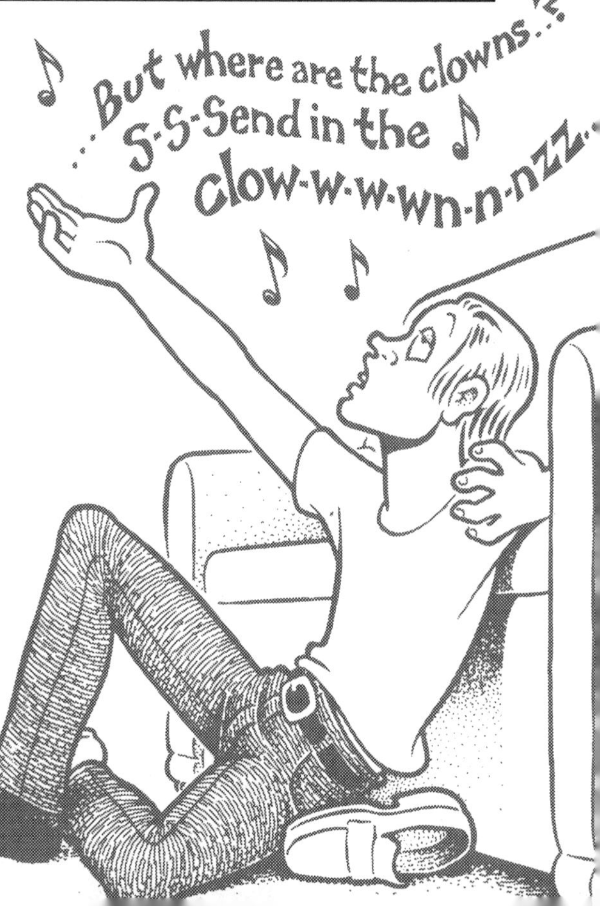
...But where are the clowns..?
S-S-Send in the
clow-w-w-wn-n-nzz..

Even for the uncloseted among us, leading a dual existence was a running theme for gays and lesbians (along with other unfavored minorities) during the years when the Moral Majority ruled. From the moment you slid out of bed in the morning you began operating on two planes. There were the regular tasks of life to take care of (picking up the mail; finding love). And there was crafting a response toward those who wanted you jettisoned from the planet, which meant concocting rapid-response strategies for use whenever their invective showed signs of becoming public policy.

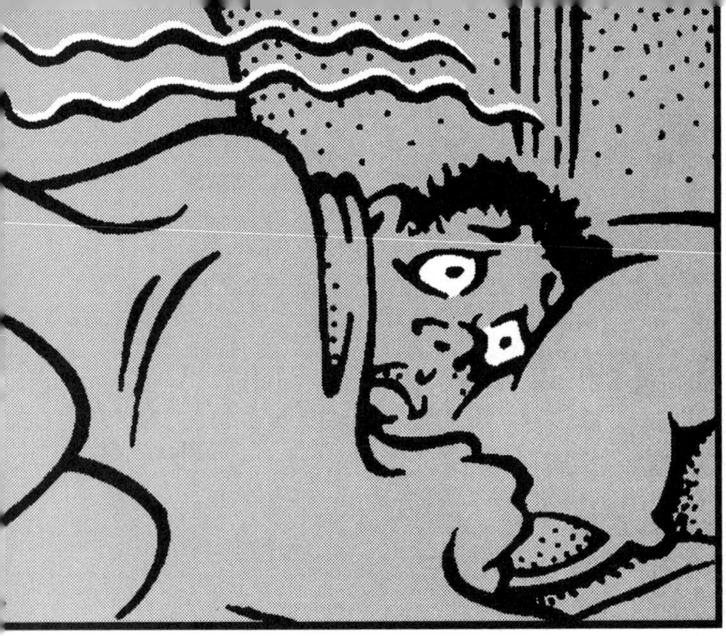

At left: Sterno in the wake of Reagan's re-election.

Life under Ronald Reagan was scary even before the AIDS epidemic took hold. Admittedly, Reagan's personal views about gay people were hard to read. By all reports he and Nancy had benign attitudes toward Rock Hudson and Roy Cohn and word was that you didn't have to be a het to do Nancy's hair. But the crowd that rode into Washington on Reagan's coattails wore hostility toward us homosexuals as a badge of honor. Any admonitions from Jesus about loving one's neighbors did not dampen the relish with which they stoked the fires of homophobia among the nation's citizenry. It was not a time for feeling safe.

Their callousness turned murderous, effectively, when AIDS struck and people began dying – by the dozens, hundreds, then thousands. Concern from on high was muted. Efforts to stop the spread were stymied by a queasy reluctance to talk frankly about sex. Medical care was administered stingily and with a big dose of stigma. It was clear, during that sad, angry era, that gay men (along with i.v. drug users and other marginalized populations) were viewed as expendable by those in power.

Movement-oriented gays, more than other groups hit hard by the virus, had already acquired a few skills in collective political action from the gay-liberation battles of the 1970s. So after reeling in shock and benumbed denial for a time while our friends fell sick around us, we began organizing. The fervor and ingenuity of ACT UP (AIDS Coalition To Unleash Power), in particular, began cutting shrilly through the national silence. When not brandishing placards in the streets gays created strategies for taking care of those who had been abandoned by traditional caregivers, learning more about drug protocols along the way than the medically untrained among us would have ever thought possible. Drama was high and rhetoric furious as we learned how to cry foul loudly and in large numbers.

And when the crowds had dispersed we would trudge home to the mildew that still waited to be scrubbed from our bathroom tiles.

I mention the pressures and dualities of that era for the benefit of those younger ones of you whose impressions of civil life in America have been formed during Bill Clinton's Presidency. While many crises continue to fester below the surface, it's indisputable that gay politics has been a quieter endeavor of late. For that reason, it may not be instantly apparent why protest marches and other forms of political activism ranked as high as they did among the priorities of Wendel and his friends.

You construct your life differently when you don't spend your time being scared. Bill Clinton disappointed his queer supporters in many ways, and even betrayed us on some important issues. But on remaining fronts he strove to validate us as citizens in both symbolic and concrete terms. Unlike any President before him, he portrayed himself publicly as a friend to lesbians and gay men. During his years in the White House the power of our political adversaries was blunted by countervailing powers that affirmed our value and accomplishments. In contrast to the eras of Reagan and Bush the Elder, we felt less endangered. It was a better environment for peace of mind, if also too fertile a ground for complacency.

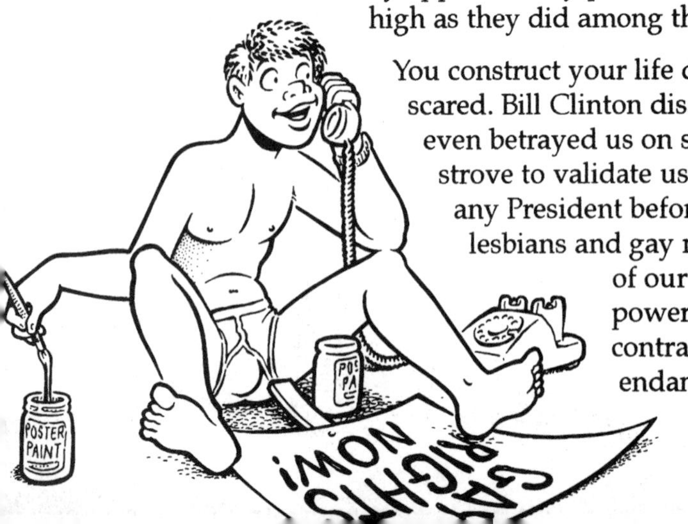
POSTER PAINT
GAY RIGHTS NOW!

More effective drug treatments led to a slowdown (arguably temporary) in the relentless march of death within the gay community. This has also led to less stridency in the streets.

As I write this no one knows where Bush the Younger will lead us from 2001 onward. Be that as it may, eight years under Clinton have undeniably led us to less overtly beseiged states of mind, allowing many to theorize that the worst is over. In such a context, the commitment of Wendel and his friends to political activism may well come across as quaint. Perhaps some of you will view the Wendel on view in these pages as too much a creature of the 1980s to remain relevant in the 21st century.

But complacency is not the only option when times change and tensions ease. Issues of justice that are broader than the home team's welfare always wait in the wings. Freedom from more pressing fears can give us time to attend to such concerns. The Wendel of my imagination has not been idle since he retired from active comic-strip duty. His upbringing and basic character will never allow him to be.

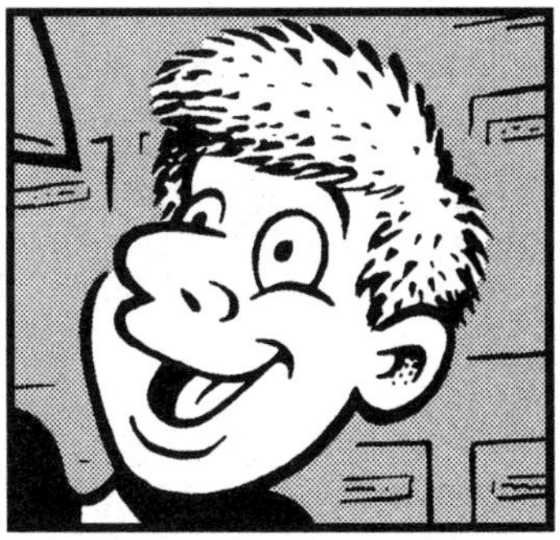

Wendel Trupstock was young, green, and naïve when I began drawing him and a flush of innocence still lingered in his cheeks when I stopped. His comic strip debuted as sex farce, as befitted a feature whose early installments were nestled in *The Advocate*'s pink-tinted classified-ad supplement next to heavy-breathing pitches for penis enlargers and erotic telephone services. When first seen, he was aggressively goofy in appearance, looking a lot like the 1950s comic-book version of Jerry Lewis (their dissimilar hairstyles aside). To my surprise, my comic strip and its namesake quickly moved beyond sexplay as the Strawhead came to life in my mind. I watched him fall for Ollie and found myself falling for him.

Below: When Wendel met Ollie.

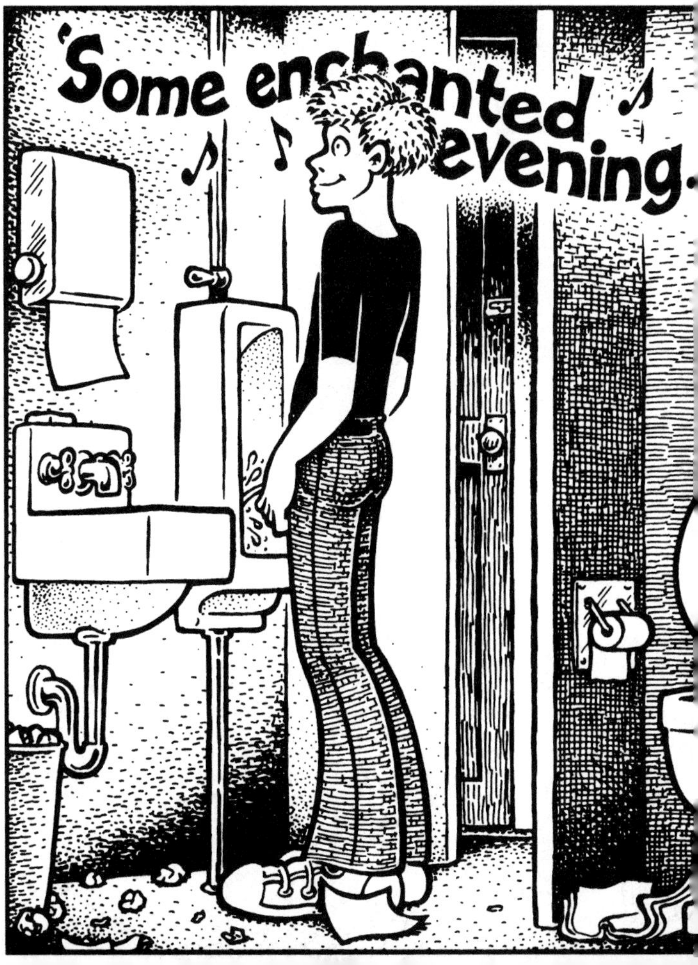
'Some enchanted evening...

Enthralled as I became with Wendel's embodiment of my own more idealistic side, the cartooning strokes with which I rendered him became kinder. His face grew more vulnerable, his body a touch sexier. Ollie, the standard-bearer for my more battered self, stepped in to offset the Strawhead's guilelessness with bruised life experience.

I had drawn the first episode with no assurance that space would ever be offered for a second one. But *The Advocate* soliticited one additional episode after another and readers seemed pleased that the feature was there. Irregular appearances eventually gave way to a guaranteed spot in the magazine's more "respectable" white pages. The series ended in 1985 when a change in *The Advocate*'s format presented me with pages too small for *Wendel*'s unhurried narrative pace, but a year later the series returned as a two-page feature, settling in as the magazine's closing feature through the rest of the decade.

Through all of this I was trying to give the feature ever more elasticity. The gay life I aimed at reflecting had too many facets to be portrayed with a single tonality. I wanted to be funny, but not to be blind to pain. I needed my characters to be made of rubber one week, of flesh the next. Would readers buy it? I could never be certain, but the ongoing experiment kept the project interesting.

My goals evolved gradually. My stories (once the strip earned a regular spot in each issue) barely outpaced their biweekly deadline, which meant that I could rarely have told you where a particular storyline was heading. The fact that narrative uncertainty was so much a part of creating *Wendel* is more striking to me now than it was at the time, because of what has happened since.

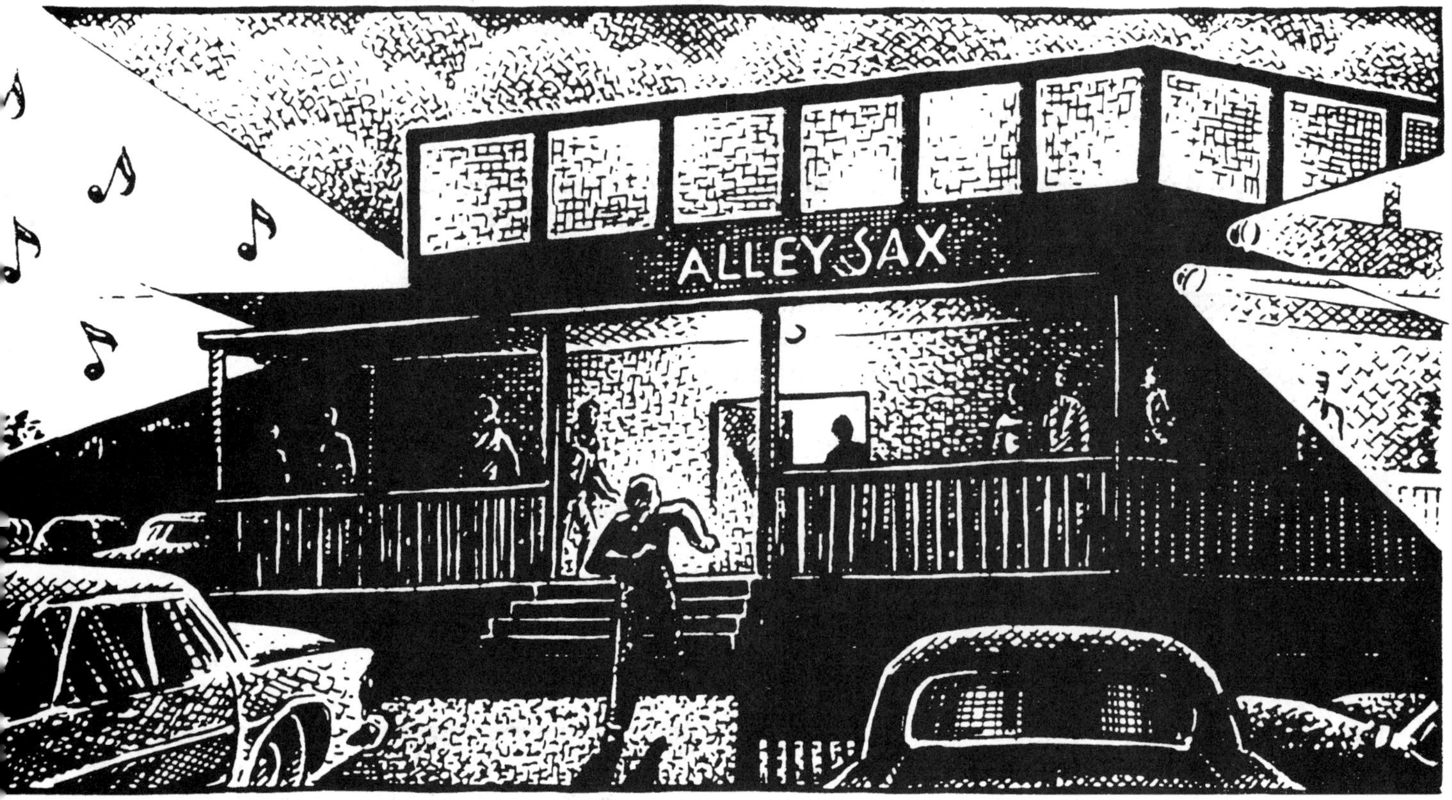
ALLEY SAX

Above: Toland Polk flees his demons in *Stuck Rubber Baby*.

My major creative project during the years after *Wendel* ended was writing and drawing a 210-page graphic novel called *Stuck Rubber Baby*. While also a "comic," this latter endeavor was created quite differently from the series that had gone before. It seems worthwhile to mention this difference up front, since enjoying a collection of *Wendel* strips will call for a mindset unlike the one you might bring to reading *Stuck Rubber Baby* – or any other novel.

It's a distinction that was initially missed by a friend of mine who told me in 1988 that *Wendel on the Rebound* was "really a *novel*." Since producing a novel sounds loftier than assembling a bunch of comic strips, I was pleased by the implied compliment and refrained from denying that, simply by virtue of its length and multiplicity of incidents, *Wendel* episodes strung one after the other could claim some novelistic qualities.

But here's the difference: not a panel of *Stuck Rubber Baby* was drawn until a working script for the entire book was drafted. This took five months and as much pacing and muttering as actual typing. Several versions of the book's events and the words spoken by its characters had to materialize before I arrived at a story that felt cohesive. Then came four years of drawing, during which midcourse corrections in one tricky section would lead to compensating alterations in sequences destined to be drawn two years thereafter. In other words, I had a blueprint for the whole book from the day I began drawing, with lots of time remaining to refine that blueprint as I went along.

By contrast, the story of Wendel Trupstock that you'll find in the following pages was improvised on the run. Now and then I had story developments mapped out two or three episodes in advance, but that was rare. Usually the strip's biweekly deadline kept the creative process too frantic for narrative elegance. Fortunately, having quite a few years of cartooning under my belt, I had confidence in my ability to dig myself out of whatever holes I might unwittingly shove myself into. It's all part of the serialization craft.

Making a story up as you go along is fun in a chaotic kind of way. It keeps things lively. By leaving the characters' futures unplanned, you reserve space for unexpected developments, some of which arrive as pure inspirations from the Muse while others are prompted by serendipitous real-world stimuli. The downside of this mode of storytelling is suffering through the weeks when you feel blocked. But there are ways to deal with that.

Yes, even in the realm of improvisation, there are tricks of the trade. The best insurance against finding yourself stranded without story ideas is to make a habit of strewing the landscape with potential plot options – Sterno's impulse to take camera in hand, say, or Wendel's tryst with a closeted celebrity. These throwaway storylets may lie unused in the underbrush forever, but in the back of your mind you know they're there. That knowledge is reassuring, since pure inspiration is too unreliable a resource for most artists' nerves – particularly artists who have made contractual promises to produce.

Preparing this book has let me review the *Wendel* series in its entirety from a distance of years. Since I also remember the anxieties and thrills that came with writing and drawing the series, re-experiencing the results of my long-ago labors involves yet another form of dual existence. I watch myself from within and from without, smiling knowingly at my younger self as he deposits backup plot elements where they can easily be found if needed. Some of these did serious duty; Newton Blowright's Space Pods and Ollie's hunger for the stage come to mind. Other undercurrents surfaced more fleetingly but still produced pungent moments, like the lust that distracted Ollie and Lyle from their actorly duties or the signs that a rebellion may have been brewing inside Farley as he inched toward puberty.

I see characters clearly inserted with an eye to further development who never got to claim the spotlight. I still regret some of those missed opportunities. Deb's hostile ex-lover Lucy, referred to only twice, could have ignited lively sparks had I brought her in from the cold. Unfortunately, Lucy's presence remained limited to snipes at Deb that she posted periodically in *Gayblaze*. Ollie's twice-born brother Carl could have generated useful energy, particularly if he had joined forces with the First Holy Church of the Bellicose Rapture.

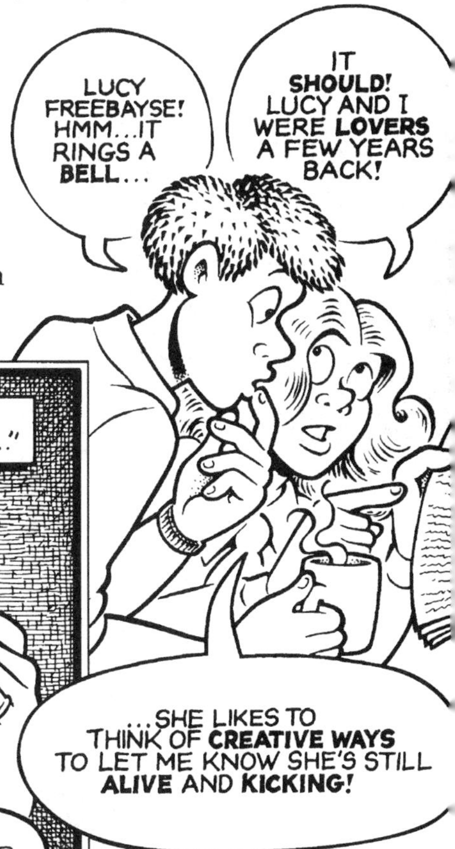
LUCY FREEBAYSE! HMM...IT RINGS A BELL...
IT SHOULD! LUCY AND I WERE LOVERS A FEW YEARS BACK!
...SHE LIKES TO THINK OF CREATIVE WAYS TO LET ME KNOW SHE'S STILL ALIVE AND KICKING!

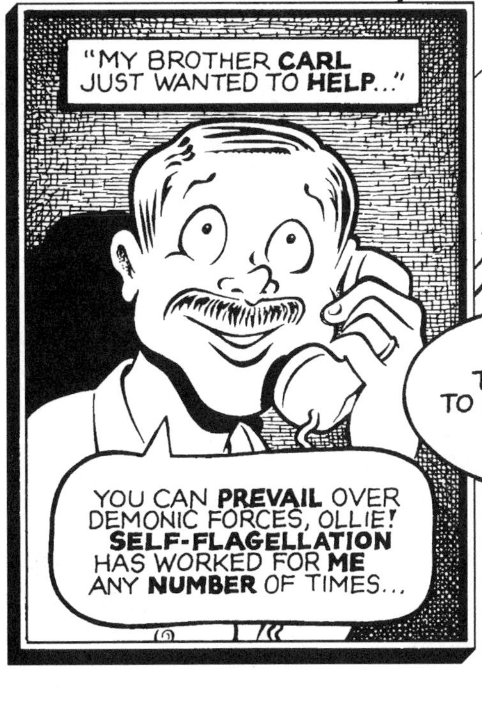
"MY BROTHER CARL JUST WANTED TO HELP..."
YOU CAN PREVAIL OVER DEMONIC FORCES, OLLIE! SELF-FLAGELLATION HAS WORKED FOR ME ANY NUMBER OF TIMES...

Above and at left: Lucy and Carl waited patiently in the wings but never made it to center stage.

Why would I, a nonsmoker, have made Wendel's Mom a nicotine addict had I not been harboring plans to someday put her through a humorously arduous battle to quit the

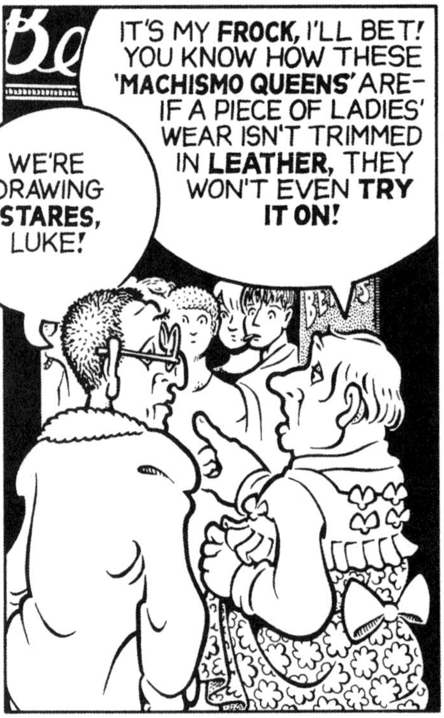
IT'S MY **FROCK,** I'LL BET! YOU KNOW HOW THESE **'MACHISMO QUEENS'** ARE– IF A PIECE OF LADIES' WEAR ISN'T TRIMMED IN **LEATHER,** THEY WON'T EVEN **TRY IT ON!**
WE'RE DRAWING **STARES,** LUKE!

Above: Wendel's randy uncles prowl the night in "Dirty old Lovers."

Below: Wendel ponders his place in the cosmos.

habit? Then there were throwaway bits of foreshadowing, some very dark, such as the panel in which Ramon wordlessly inspects an ominous blemish on his face while his lover, Sawyer, chats on the phone with Wendel. How many of us monitored every skin blemish in those days with mortality justifiably on our minds?

The outrageous banter that volleyed between Luke and Clark (imported wholesale from their stand-alone story "Dirty Old Lovers" in *Gay Comix* #3) wrote itself so effortlessly once Wendel arrived at their door that I cursed myself for not introducing them earlier in the series, and for placing them in a faraway city instead of just down the street. The bawdiness of Luke and Clark's seasoned relationship served as a perfect counterpoint to the tender newness of Wendel and Ollie's couplehood. How silly not to have placed these guys within easy reach. Sawyer and Ramon also lived an airplane ride away from Wendel and the gang. Such are the drawbacks of creating art without planning. I made the same mistake with Sterno when he made his first appearance. Quickly realizing that his was too incandescent a personality to serve merely as a walk-on, I had to quickly concoct a reason for him to move to Wendel's city. (His parents threw him out.)

Improvisation is not the friend of logic, and my strip's biweekly schedule did weird things to the temporal logic of Wendel's continuity. Sawyer's visit to Wendel's berg unaccountably expanded to a half-year's duration before he said his goodbyes, thanks to all the other plotlines I was keeping in play between the episode that depicted his arrival and the one in which he departed. Such time warps pass unnoticed in a series consumed in biweekly bites. Read end-to-end in book form, however, a few of them may require indulgence from the reader.

Other "backstories" that I squirreled away in *Wendel*'s nooks and crannies would surely have come to the fore eventually had the series spun on for additional years. Some of them promised fascinating complications. For that reason, a part

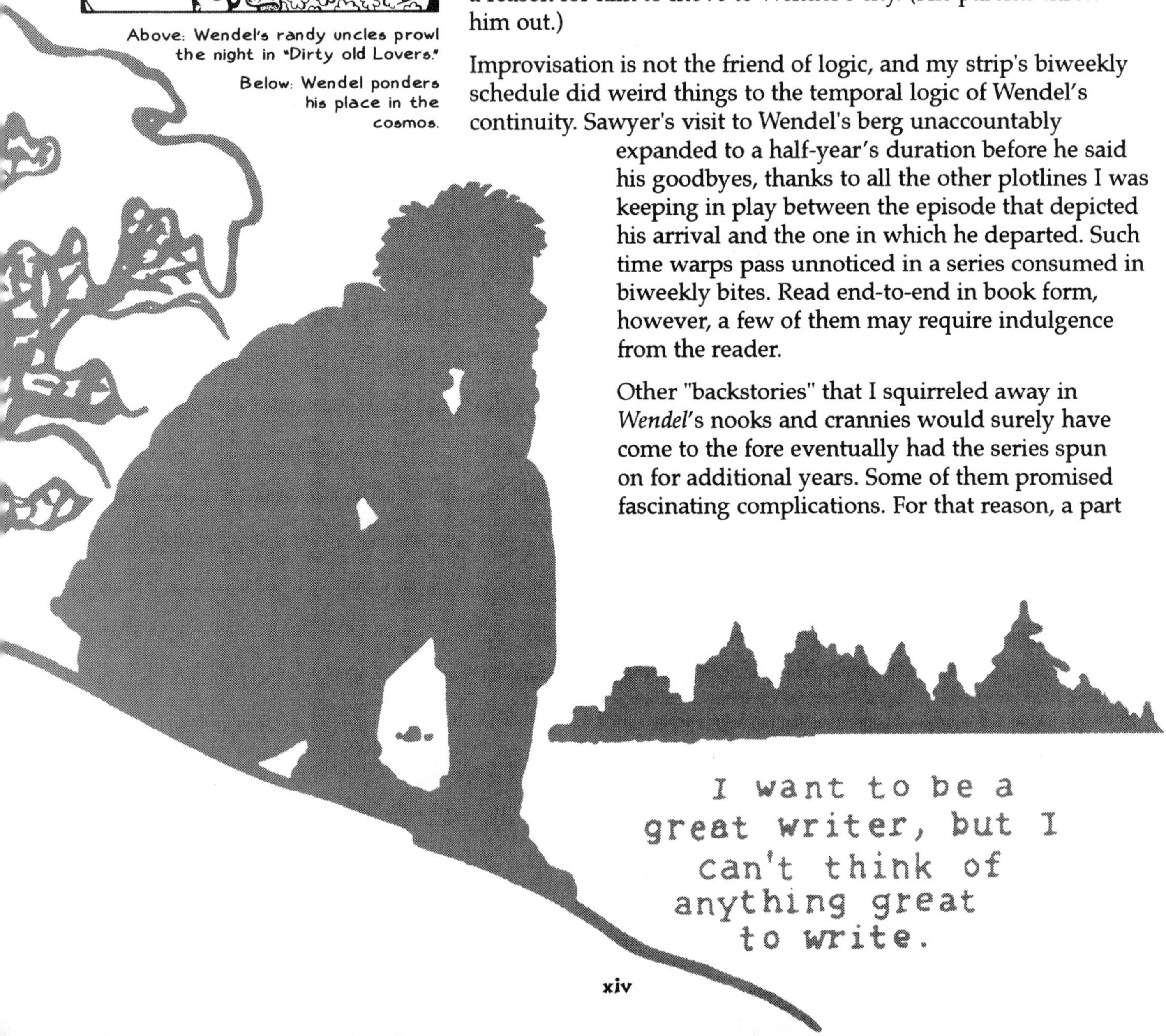
I want to be a great writer, but I can't think of anything great to write.

of me will always be unsatisfied when I revisit the strips in this book. But I recognize that such assymetries of story-telling are bound up inevitably in the act of serialization. And with or without blueprints in hand, creating characters usually means abandoning them eventually, unless one adopts the Charles M. Schulz model and sticks with a single character until claimed by the grave. I've chosen not to take that road, so it's by my own decision that saying good-bye to characters I care about is a recurrent ritual of my life.

Leaving characters behind means turning loose of what-ifs. This is why it's such an enjoyable fantasy to imagine that characters created for a limited run will continue to have a form of afterlife, in my own imagination and and also the imaginations of readers who learned to care about them during their time in print. And for all I know, Wendel may engage in more intriguing adventures in your mind, once you've read this book, than he will in mine.

So in that spirit I present you with Wendel Trupstock and his friends, fresh from the harrowing 1980s. May you enjoy their company as much as I did (and do).

Howard Cruse
January 2001

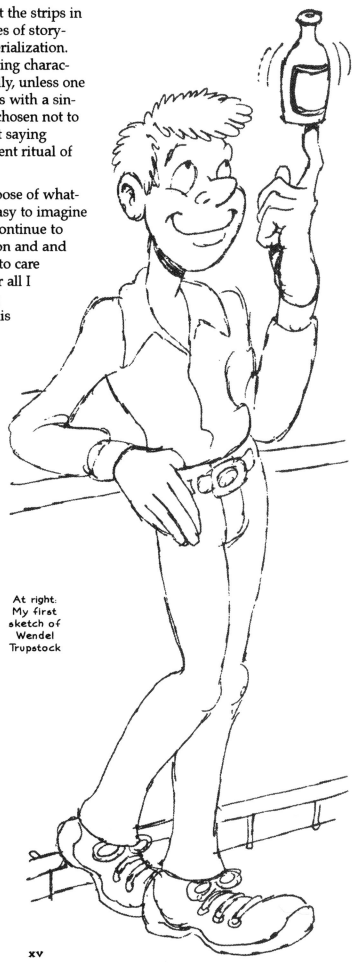

At right:
My first
sketch of
Wendel
Trupstock

WHY is PART of this book PRINTED SIDEWAYS???

The Advocate didn't always look the way it does now. In fact, it changed its size and shape radically midway through *Wendel*'s run. When my strip was launched the magazine was a tabloid with large, roomy pages. Then in 1985 its current, smaller format was adopted.

At left and below: The Advocate and my comic strip before and after the big change.

Thanks to this mid-course redesign, Wendel's adventures come in two distinct parts. Episodes from the First Series were drawn for a single large page. Later episodes were spread across two facing pages.

This makes it tricky to compile the whole series in a single book, since books can't change their page sizes halfway through just because the comics in them do.

So that's why we're running the early strips sideways. It lets them stay big and easy to read — the way I _meant_ for them to be when I first began drawing them in '83.

Got the picture? Good!

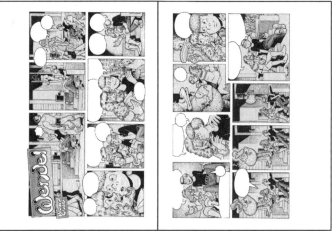

Now on with the show...

The FIRST SERIES

1

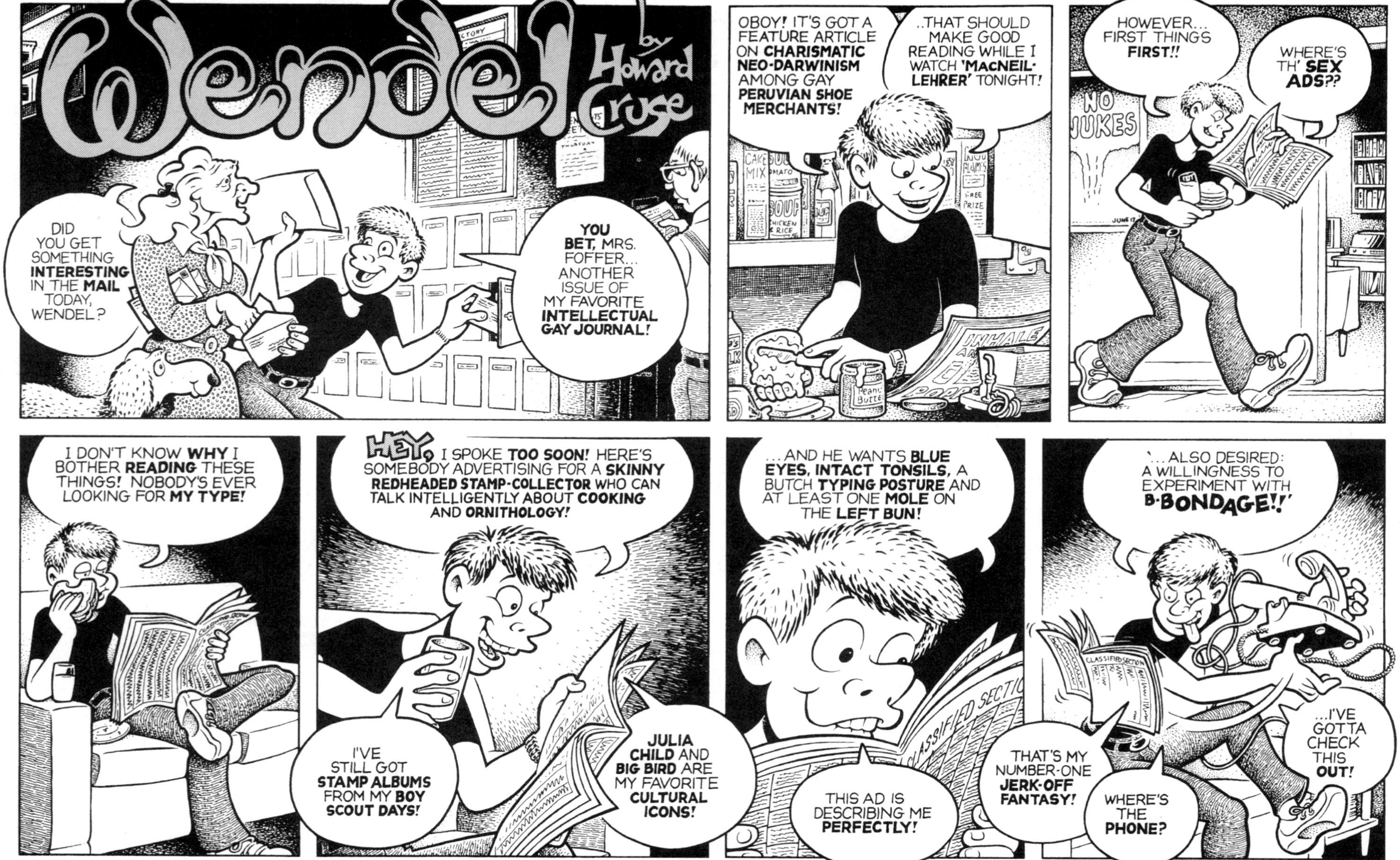
Wendel
by Howard Cruse
DID YOU GET SOMETHING INTERESTING IN THE MAIL TODAY, WENDEL?
YOU BET, MRS. FOFFER... ANOTHER ISSUE OF MY FAVORITE INTELLECTUAL GAY JOURNAL!
OBOY! IT'S GOT A FEATURE ARTICLE ON CHARISMATIC NEO-DARWINISM AMONG GAY PERUVIAN SHOE MERCHANTS!
..THAT SHOULD MAKE GOOD READING WHILE I WATCH 'MacNEIL-LEHRER' TONIGHT!
HOWEVER... FIRST THING'S FIRST!!
WHERE'S TH' SEX ADS??
NO JUKES
I DON'T KNOW WHY I BOTHER READING THESE THINGS! NOBODY'S EVER LOOKING FOR MY TYPE!
HEY, I SPOKE TOO SOON! HERE'S SOMEBODY ADVERTISING FOR A SKINNY REDHEADED STAMP-COLLECTOR WHO CAN TALK INTELLIGENTLY ABOUT COOKING AND ORNITHOLOGY!
I'VE STILL GOT STAMP ALBUMS FROM MY BOY SCOUT DAYS!
JULIA CHILD AND BIG BIRD ARE MY FAVORITE CULTURAL ICONS!
...AND HE WANTS BLUE EYES, INTACT TONSILS, A BUTCH TYPING POSTURE AND AT LEAST ONE MOLE ON THE LEFT BUN!
THIS AD IS DESCRIBING ME PERFECTLY!
'...ALSO DESIRED: A WILLINGNESS TO EXPERIMENT WITH B-BONDAGE!!'
THAT'S MY NUMBER-ONE JERK-OFF FANTASY!
WHERE'S THE PHONE?
...I'VE GOTTA CHECK THIS OUT!

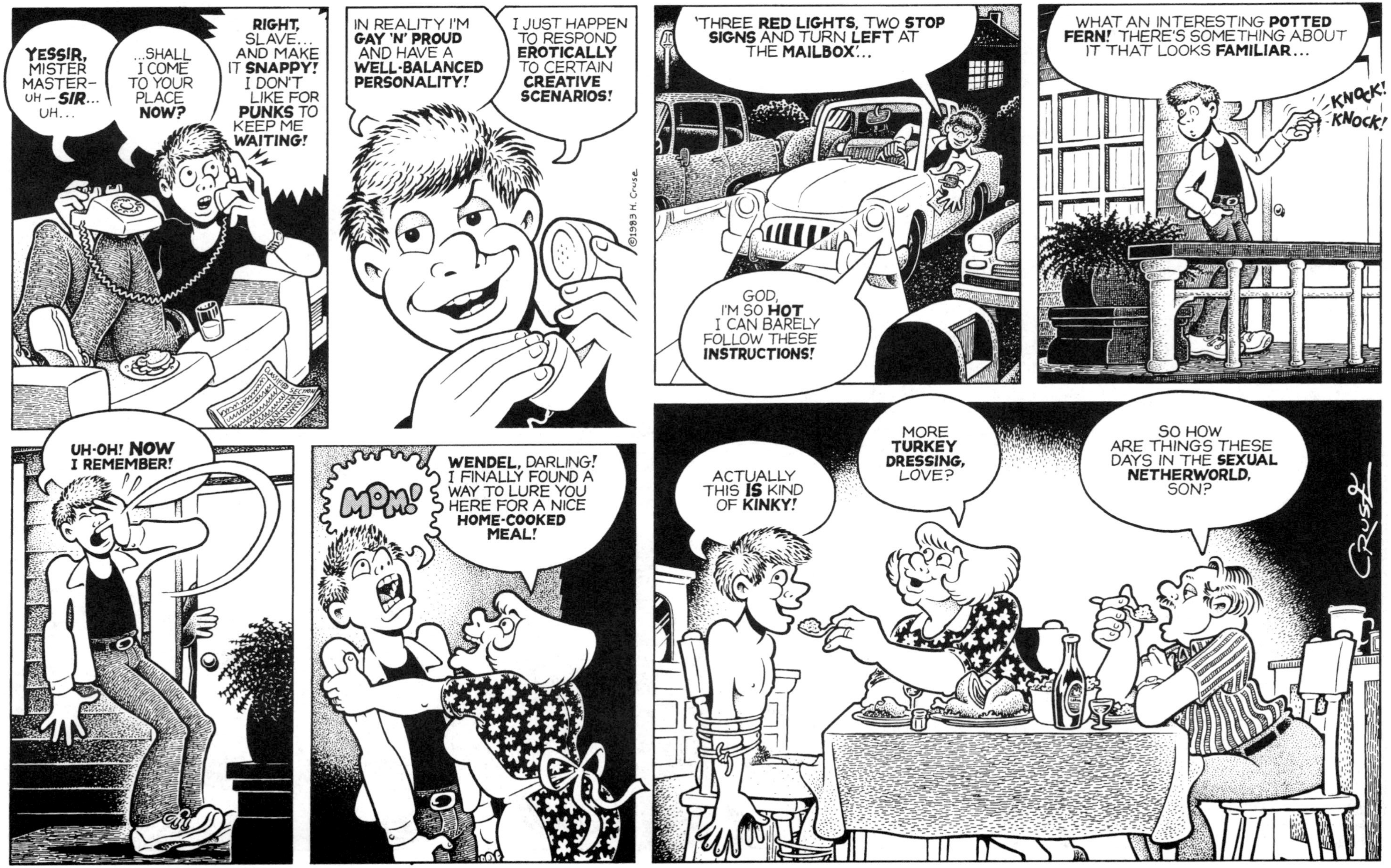
YESSIR, MISTER MASTER— UH — SIR... UH...
...SHALL I COME TO YOUR PLACE NOW?
RIGHT, SLAVE... AND MAKE IT SNAPPY! I DON'T LIKE FOR PUNKS TO KEEP ME WAITING!
CLASSIFIED SECTION
IN REALITY I'M GAY 'N' PROUD AND HAVE A WELL-BALANCED PERSONALITY!
I JUST HAPPEN TO RESPOND EROTICALLY TO CERTAIN CREATIVE SCENARIOS!
©1983 H. CRUSE
'THREE RED LIGHTS, TWO STOP SIGNS AND TURN LEFT AT THE MAILBOX'...
GOD, I'M SO HOT I CAN BARELY FOLLOW THESE INSTRUCTIONS!
WHAT AN INTERESTING POTTED FERN! THERE'S SOMETHING ABOUT IT THAT LOOKS FAMILIAR...
KNOCK! KNOCK!
UH-OH! NOW I REMEMBER!
MOM!
WENDEL, DARLING! I FINALLY FOUND A WAY TO LURE YOU HERE FOR A NICE HOME-COOKED MEAL!
ACTUALLY THIS IS KIND OF KINKY!
MORE TURKEY DRESSING, LOVE?
SO HOW ARE THINGS THESE DAYS IN THE SEXUAL NETHERWORLD, SON?
CRUSE

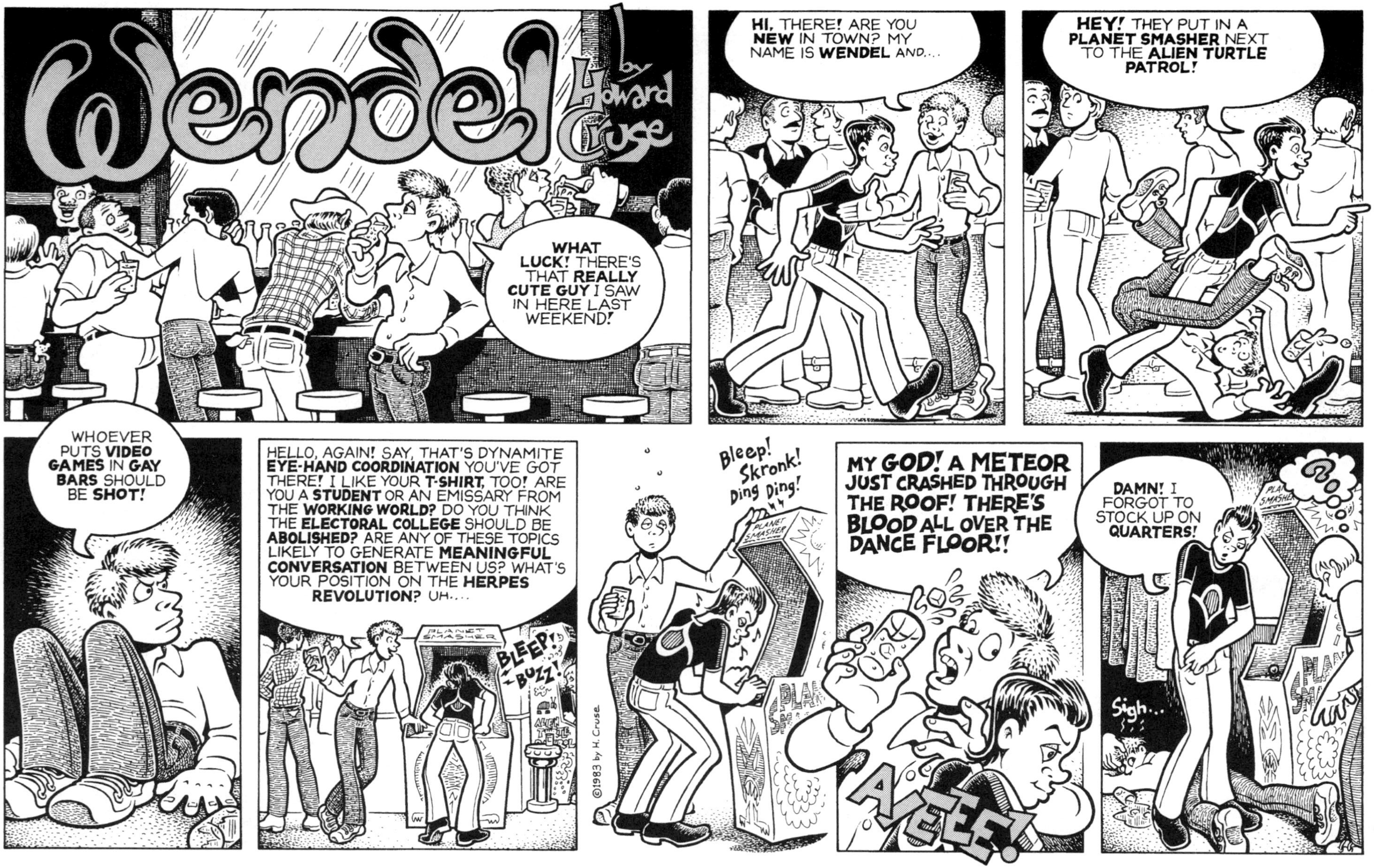
Wendel
by Howard Cruse
WHAT LUCK! THERE'S THAT REALLY CUTE GUY I SAW IN HERE LAST WEEKEND!
HI, THERE! ARE YOU NEW IN TOWN? MY NAME IS WENDEL AND...
HEY! THEY PUT IN A PLANET SMASHER NEXT TO THE ALIEN TURTLE PATROL!
WHOEVER PUTS VIDEO GAMES IN GAY BARS SHOULD BE SHOT!
HELLO, AGAIN! SAY, THAT'S DYNAMITE EYE-HAND COORDINATION YOU'VE GOT THERE! I LIKE YOUR T-SHIRT, TOO! ARE YOU A STUDENT OR AN EMISSARY FROM THE WORKING WORLD? DO YOU THINK THE ELECTORAL COLLEGE SHOULD BE ABOLISHED? ARE ANY OF THESE TOPICS LIKELY TO GENERATE MEANINGFUL CONVERSATION BETWEEN US? WHAT'S YOUR POSITION ON THE HERPES REVOLUTION? UH...
PLANET SMASHER
BLEEP! BUZZ!
©1983 by H. Cruse
Bleep! Skronk! Ding Ding!
PLANET SMASHER
MY GOD! A METEOR JUST CRASHED THROUGH THE ROOF! THERE'S BLOOD ALL OVER THE DANCE FLOOR!!
AEEE!
DAMN! I FORGOT TO STOCK UP ON QUARTERS!
Sigh...

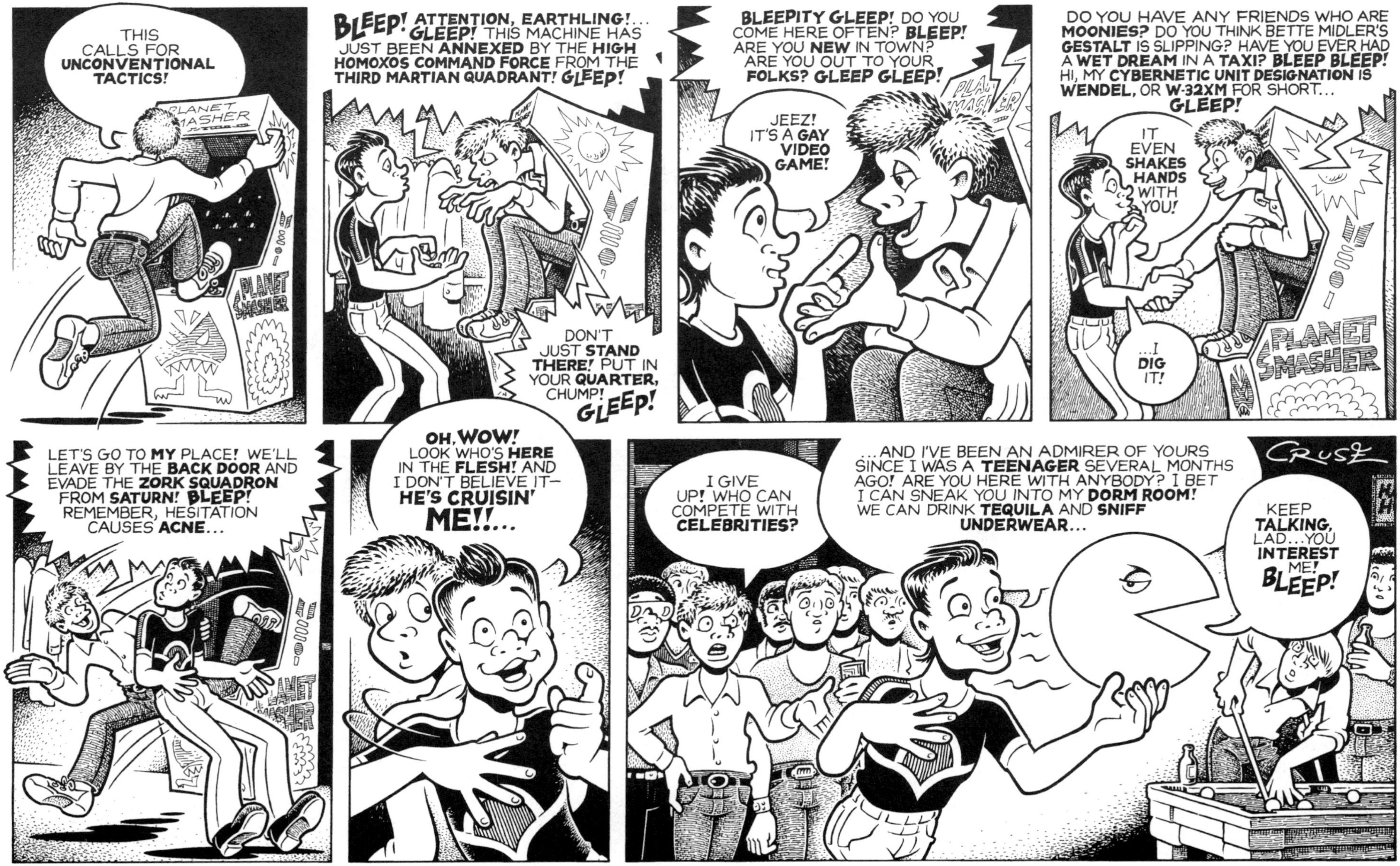
THIS CALLS FOR UNCONVENTIONAL TACTICS!
PLANET SMASHER
BLEEP! ATTENTION, EARTHLING!... GLEEP! THIS MACHINE HAS JUST BEEN ANNEXED BY THE HIGH HOMOXOS COMMAND FORCE FROM THE THIRD MARTIAN QUADRANT! GLEEP!
DON'T JUST STAND THERE! PUT IN YOUR QUARTER, CHUMP! GLEEP!
BLEEPITY GLEEP! DO YOU COME HERE OFTEN? BLEEP! ARE YOU NEW IN TOWN? ARE YOU OUT TO YOUR FOLKS? GLEEP GLEEP!
JEEZ! IT'S A GAY VIDEO GAME!
DO YOU HAVE ANY FRIENDS WHO ARE MOONIES? DO YOU THINK BETTE MIDLER'S GESTALT IS SLIPPING? HAVE YOU EVER HAD A WET DREAM IN A TAXI? BLEEP BLEEP! HI, MY CYBERNETIC UNIT DESIGNATION IS WENDEL, OR W-32XM FOR SHORT... GLEEP!
IT EVEN SHAKES HANDS WITH YOU!
...I DIG IT!
PLANET SMASHER
LET'S GO TO MY PLACE! WE'LL LEAVE BY THE BACK DOOR AND EVADE THE ZORK SQUADRON FROM SATURN! BLEEP! REMEMBER, HESITATION CAUSES ACNE...
OH, WOW! LOOK WHO'S HERE IN THE FLESH! AND I DON'T BELIEVE IT— HE'S CRUISIN' ME!!...
I GIVE UP! WHO CAN COMPETE WITH CELEBRITIES?
...AND I'VE BEEN AN ADMIRER OF YOURS SINCE I WAS A TEENAGER SEVERAL MONTHS AGO! ARE YOU HERE WITH ANYBODY? I BET I CAN SNEAK YOU INTO MY DORM ROOM! WE CAN DRINK TEQUILA AND SNIFF UNDERWEAR...
KEEP TALKING, LAD...YOU INTEREST ME! BLEEP!
CRUSE

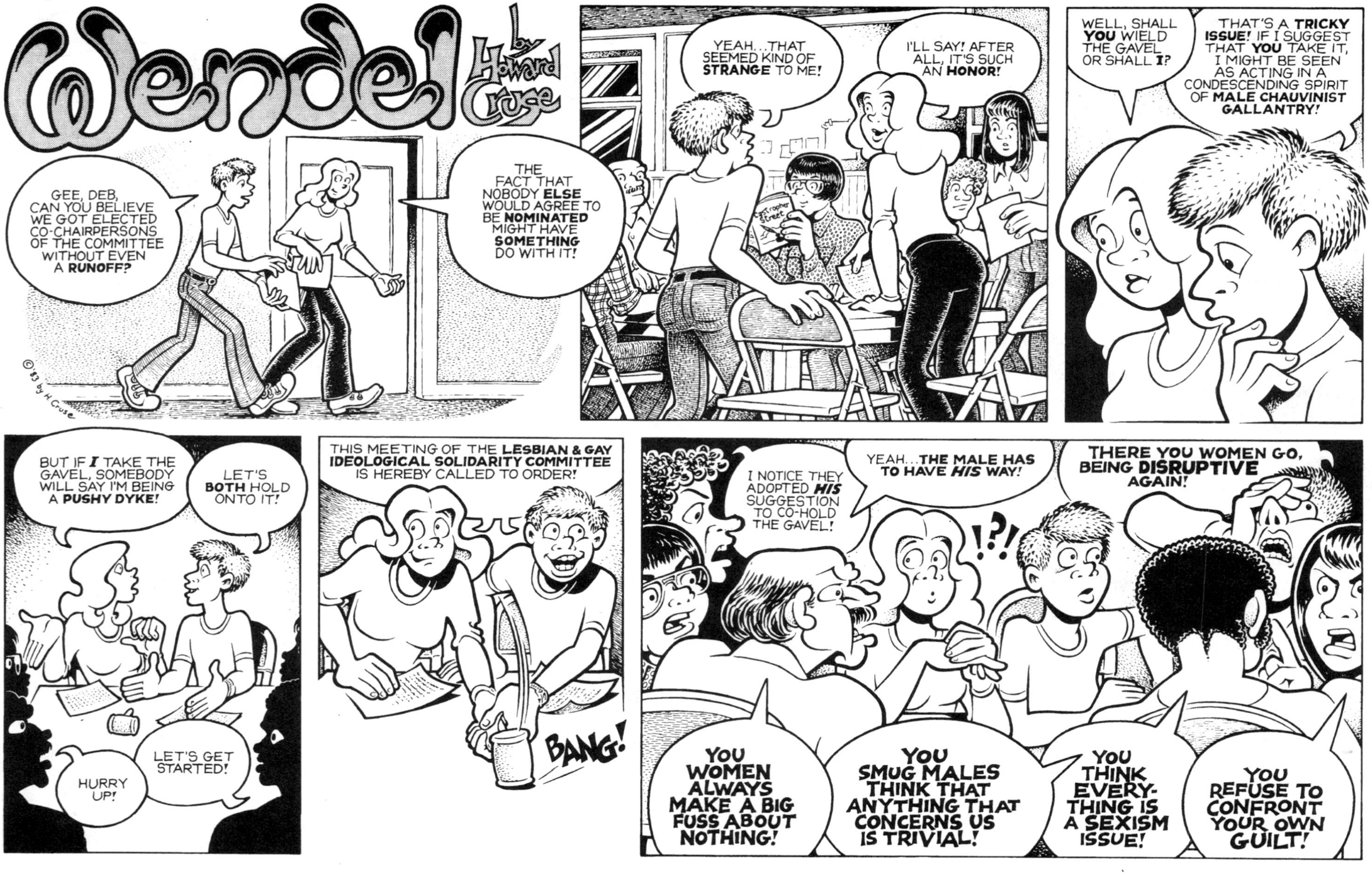

Wendel
by Howard Cruse
GEE, DEB, CAN YOU BELIEVE WE GOT ELECTED CO-CHAIRPERSONS OF THE COMMITTEE WITHOUT EVEN A **RUNOFF?**
THE FACT THAT NOBODY **ELSE** WOULD AGREE TO BE **NOMINATED** MIGHT HAVE **SOMETHING** DO WITH IT!
©'83 by H. Cruse
YEAH...THAT SEEMED KIND OF **STRANGE** TO ME!
I'LL SAY! AFTER ALL, IT'S SUCH AN **HONOR!**
Christopher Street
WELL, SHALL **YOU** WIELD THE GAVEL OR SHALL **I?**
THAT'S A **TRICKY ISSUE!** IF I SUGGEST THAT **YOU** TAKE IT, I MIGHT BE SEEN AS ACTING IN A CONDESCENDING SPIRIT OF **MALE CHAUVINIST GALLANTRY!**
BUT IF ***I*** TAKE THE GAVEL, SOMEBODY WILL SAY I'M BEING A **PUSHY DYKE!**
LET'S **BOTH** HOLD ONTO IT!
LET'S GET STARTED!
HURRY UP!
THIS MEETING OF THE **LESBIAN & GAY IDEOLOGICAL SOLIDARITY COMMITTEE** IS HEREBY CALLED TO ORDER!
BANG!
I NOTICE THEY ADOPTED ***HIS*** SUGGESTION TO CO-HOLD THE GAVEL!
YEAH...**THE MALE HAS TO HAVE *HIS* WAY!**
!?!
THERE YOU WOMEN GO, BEING **DISRUPTIVE** AGAIN!
YOU WOMEN ALWAYS MAKE A BIG FUSS ABOUT NOTHING!
YOU SMUG MALES THINK THAT ANYTHING THAT CONCERNS US IS TRIVIAL!
YOU THINK EVERY-THING IS A **SEXISM** ISSUE!
YOU REFUSE TO CONFRONT YOUR OWN GUILT!

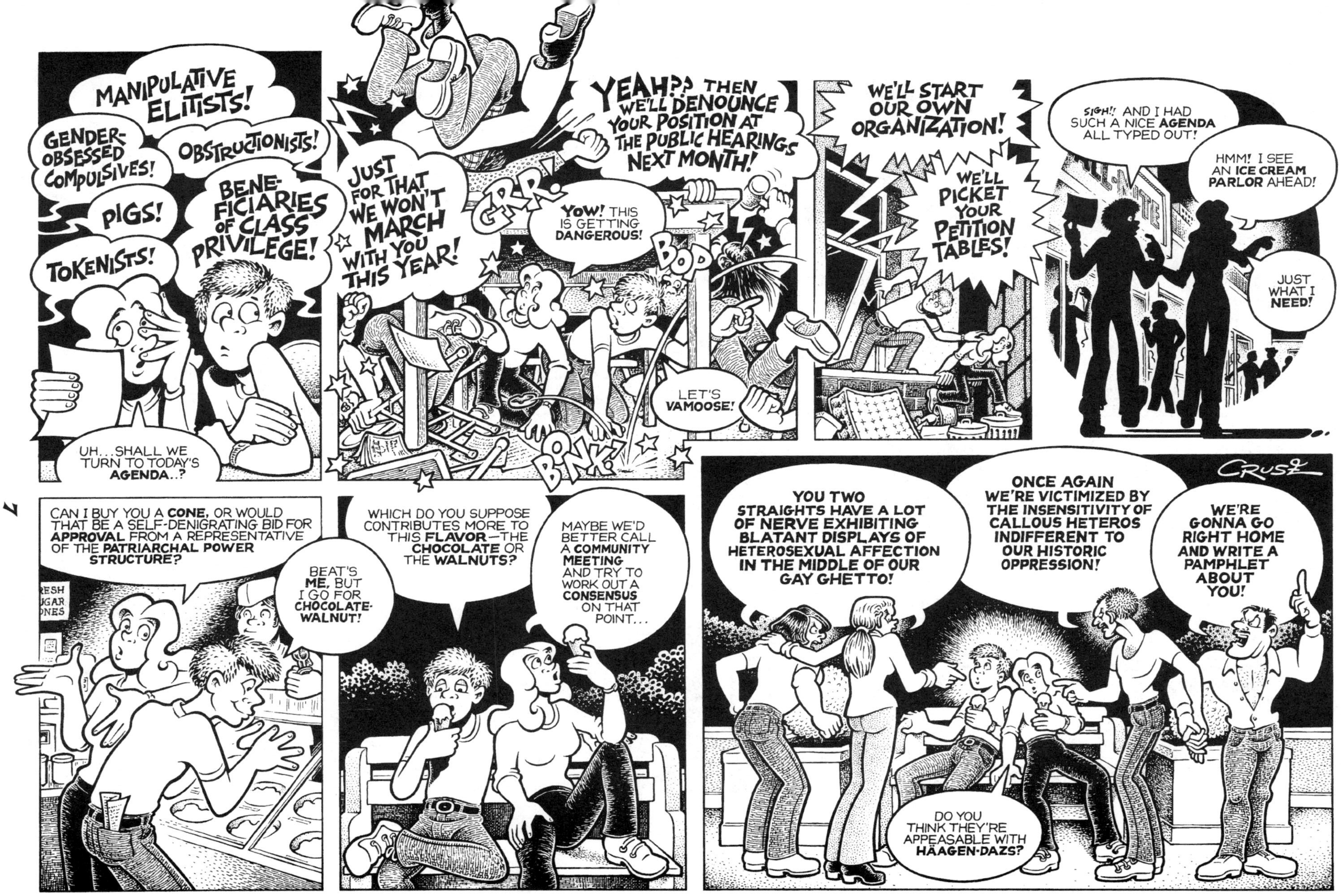
MANIPULATIVE ELITISTS!
GENDER-OBSESSED COMPULSIVES!
OBSTRUCTIONISTS!
PIGS!
BENE-FICIARIES OF CLASS PRIVILEGE!
TOKENISTS!
UH...SHALL WE TURN TO TODAY'S AGENDA..?
JUST FOR THAT WE WON'T MARCH WITH YOU THIS YEAR!
YEAH?? THEN WE'LL DENOUNCE YOUR POSITION AT THE PUBLIC HEARINGS NEXT MONTH!
GRR!
YOW! THIS IS GETTING DANGEROUS!
BOP
LET'S VAMOOSE!
BONK!
WE'LL START OUR OWN ORGANIZATION!
WE'LL PICKET YOUR PETITION TABLES!
SIGH!! AND I HAD SUCH A NICE AGENDA ALL TYPED OUT!
HMM! I SEE AN ICE CREAM PARLOR AHEAD!
JUST WHAT I NEED!
CAN I BUY YOU A CONE, OR WOULD THAT BE A SELF-DENIGRATING BID FOR APPROVAL FROM A REPRESENTATIVE OF THE PATRIARCHAL POWER STRUCTURE?
BEAT'S ME, BUT I GO FOR CHOCOLATE-WALNUT!
WHICH DO YOU SUPPOSE CONTRIBUTES MORE TO THIS FLAVOR—THE CHOCOLATE OR THE WALNUTS?
MAYBE WE'D BETTER CALL A COMMUNITY MEETING AND TRY TO WORK OUT A CONSENSUS ON THAT POINT...
CRUSE
YOU TWO STRAIGHTS HAVE A LOT OF NERVE EXHIBITING BLATANT DISPLAYS OF HETEROSEXUAL AFFECTION IN THE MIDDLE OF OUR GAY GHETTO!
ONCE AGAIN WE'RE VICTIMIZED BY THE INSENSITIVITY OF CALLOUS HETEROS INDIFFERENT TO OUR HISTORIC OPPRESSION!
WE'RE GONNA GO RIGHT HOME AND WRITE A PAMPHLET ABOUT YOU!
DO YOU THINK THEY'RE APPEASABLE WITH HÄAGEN-DAZS?

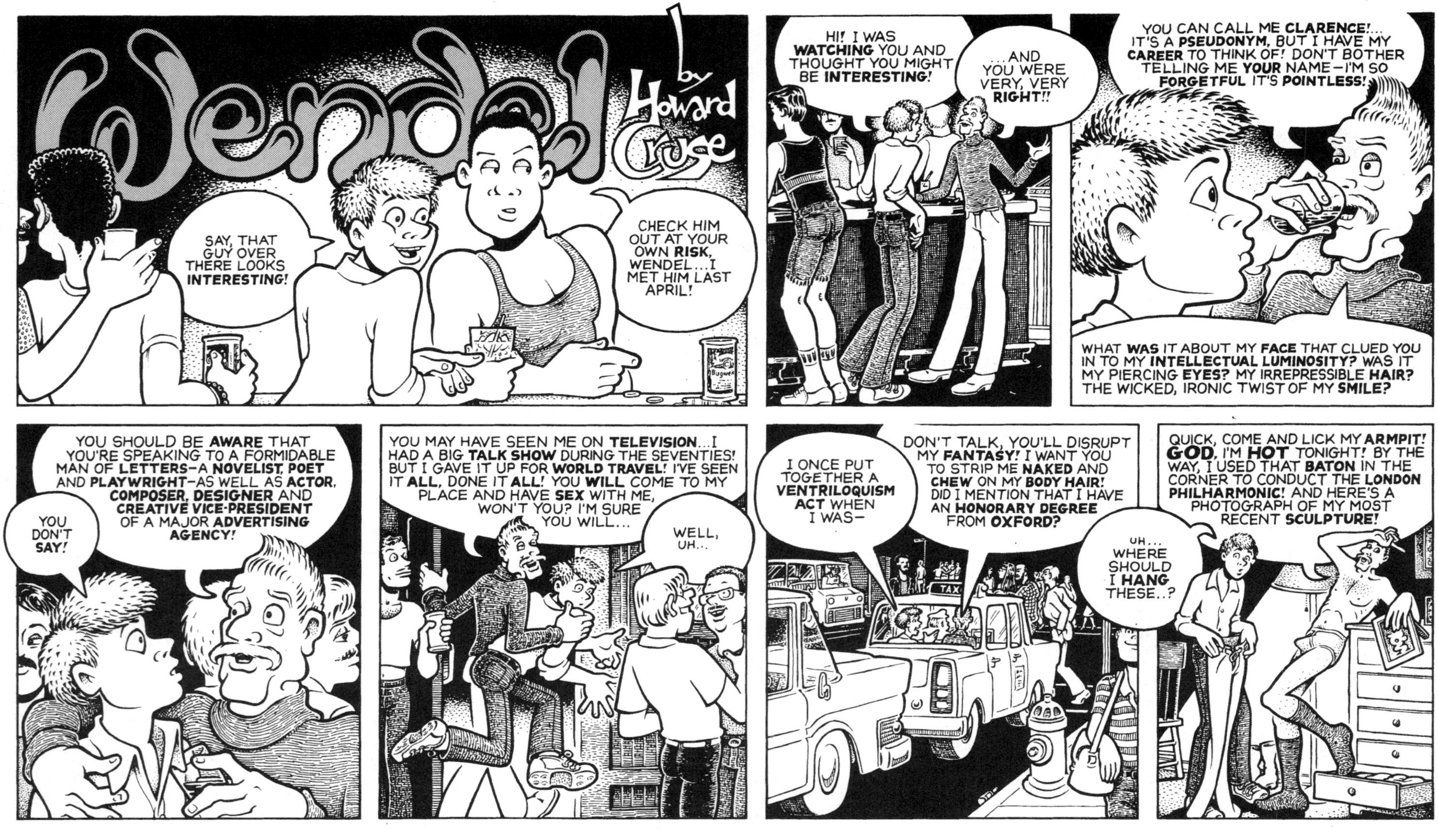
Wendel
by Howard Cruse
SAY, THAT GUY OVER THERE LOOKS **INTERESTING**!
CHECK HIM OUT AT YOUR OWN **RISK**, WENDEL...I MET HIM LAST APRIL!
HI! I WAS **WATCHING** YOU AND THOUGHT YOU MIGHT BE **INTERESTING**!
...AND YOU WERE VERY, VERY **RIGHT**!!
YOU CAN CALL ME **CLARENCE**!... IT'S A **PSEUDONYM**, BUT I HAVE MY **CAREER** TO THINK OF! DON'T BOTHER TELLING ME **YOUR** NAME—I'M SO **FORGETFUL** IT'S **POINTLESS**!
WHAT **WAS** IT ABOUT MY **FACE** THAT CLUED YOU IN TO MY **INTELLECTUAL LUMINOSITY?** WAS IT MY PIERCING **EYES?** MY IRREPRESSIBLE **HAIR?** THE WICKED, IRONIC TWIST OF MY **SMILE?**
YOU SHOULD BE **AWARE** THAT YOU'RE SPEAKING TO A FORMIDABLE MAN OF **LETTERS**—A **NOVELIST, POET** AND **PLAYWRIGHT**—AS WELL AS **ACTOR, COMPOSER, DESIGNER** AND **CREATIVE VICE-PRESIDENT** OF A MAJOR **ADVERTISING AGENCY**!
YOU DON'T **SAY**!
YOU MAY HAVE SEEN ME ON **TELEVISION**...I HAD A BIG **TALK SHOW** DURING THE SEVENTIES! BUT I GAVE IT UP FOR **WORLD TRAVEL**! I'VE SEEN IT **ALL**, DONE IT **ALL**! YOU **WILL** COME TO MY PLACE AND HAVE **SEX** WITH ME, WON'T YOU? I'M SURE YOU WILL...
WELL, UH...
I ONCE PUT TOGETHER A **VENTRILOQUISM ACT** WHEN I WAS—
DON'T TALK, YOU'LL DISRUPT MY **FANTASY**! I WANT YOU TO STRIP ME **NAKED** AND **CHEW** ON MY **BODY HAIR**! DID I MENTION THAT I HAVE AN **HONORARY DEGREE** FROM **OXFORD?**
TAXI
QUICK, COME AND LICK MY **ARMPIT**! **GOD**, I'M **HOT** TONIGHT! BY THE WAY, I USED THAT **BATON** IN THE CORNER TO CONDUCT THE **LONDON PHILHARMONIC**! AND HERE'S A PHOTOGRAPH OF MY MOST RECENT **SCULPTURE**!
UH... WHERE SHOULD I **HANG** THESE..?

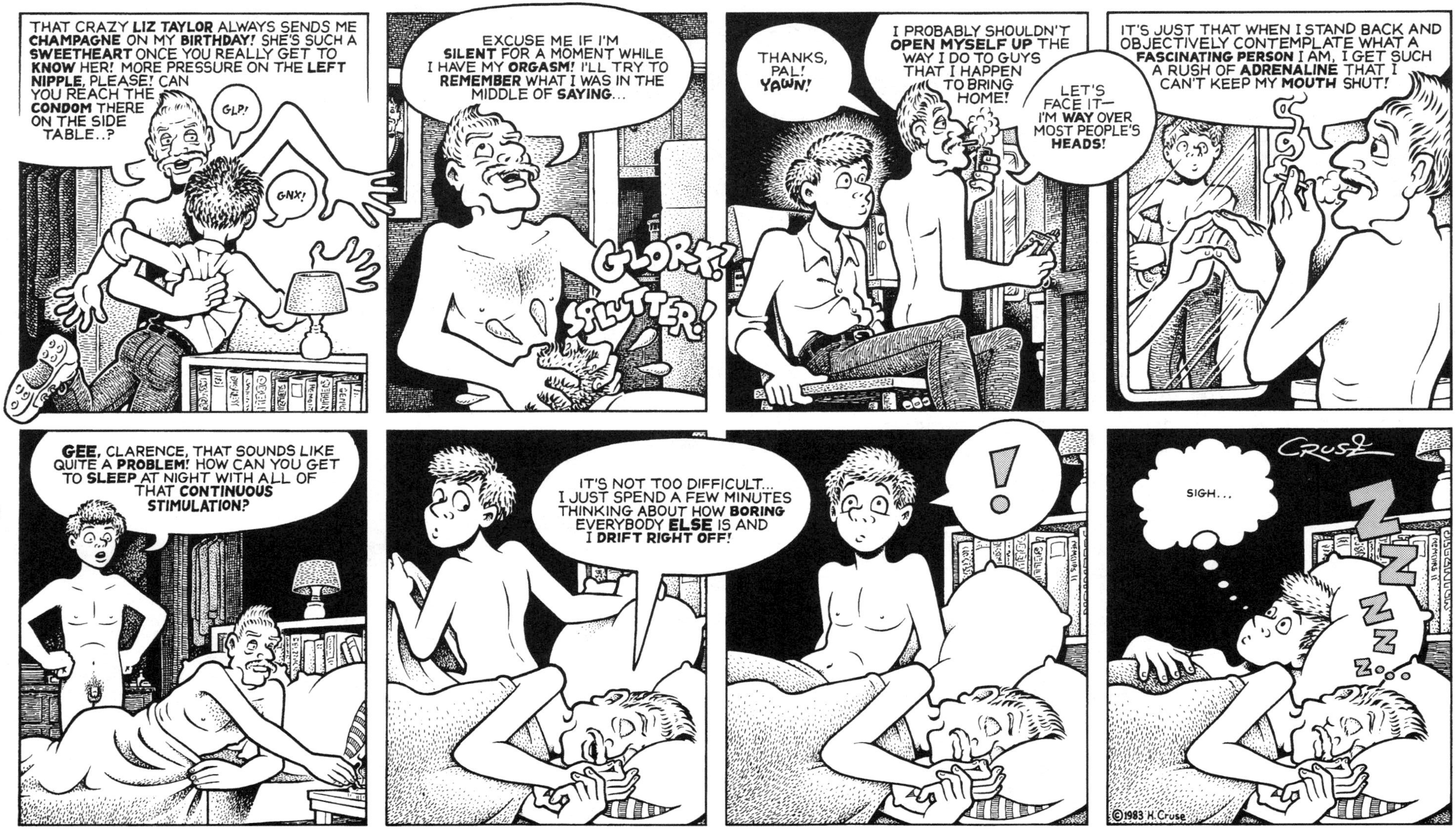
THAT CRAZY LIZ TAYLOR ALWAYS SENDS ME CHAMPAGNE ON MY BIRTHDAY! SHE'S SUCH A SWEETHEART ONCE YOU REALLY GET TO KNOW HER! MORE PRESSURE ON THE LEFT NIPPLE, PLEASE! CAN YOU REACH THE CONDOM THERE ON THE SIDE TABLE..?
GLP!
GNX!
EXCUSE ME IF I'M SILENT FOR A MOMENT WHILE I HAVE MY ORGASM! I'LL TRY TO REMEMBER WHAT I WAS IN THE MIDDLE OF SAYING...
GLORK!
SPLUTTER!
THANKS, PAL! YAWN!
I PROBABLY SHOULDN'T OPEN MYSELF UP THE WAY I DO TO GUYS THAT I HAPPEN TO BRING HOME!
LET'S FACE IT— I'M WAY OVER MOST PEOPLE'S HEADS!
IT'S JUST THAT WHEN I STAND BACK AND OBJECTIVELY CONTEMPLATE WHAT A FASCINATING PERSON I AM, I GET SUCH A RUSH OF ADRENALINE THAT I CAN'T KEEP MY MOUTH SHUT!
GEE, CLARENCE, THAT SOUNDS LIKE QUITE A PROBLEM! HOW CAN YOU GET TO SLEEP AT NIGHT WITH ALL OF THAT CONTINUOUS STIMULATION?
IT'S NOT TOO DIFFICULT... I JUST SPEND A FEW MINUTES THINKING ABOUT HOW BORING EVERYBODY ELSE IS AND I DRIFT RIGHT OFF!
!
CRUSE
SIGH...
ZZZZ...
©1983 H. Cruse

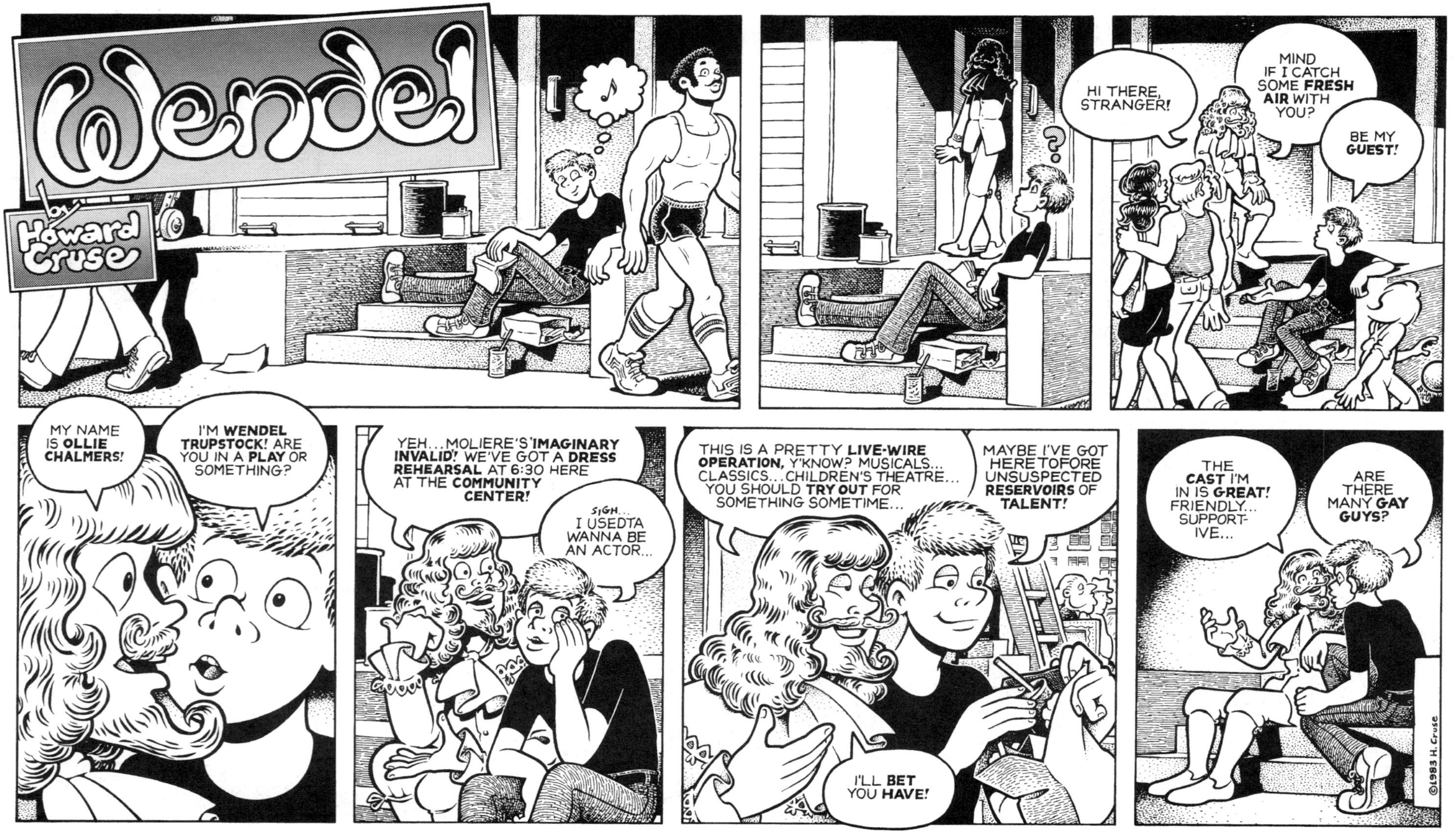

Wendel
by Howard Cruse
HI THERE, STRANGER!
MIND IF I CATCH SOME FRESH AIR WITH YOU?
BE MY GUEST!
MY NAME IS OLLIE CHALMERS!
I'M WENDEL TRUPSTOCK! ARE YOU IN A PLAY OR SOMETHING?
YEH...MOLIERE'S 'IMAGINARY INVALID'! WE'VE GOT A DRESS REHEARSAL AT 6:30 HERE AT THE COMMUNITY CENTER!
SIGH... I USEDTA WANNA BE AN ACTOR...
THIS IS A PRETTY LIVE-WIRE OPERATION, Y'KNOW? MUSICALS... CLASSICS... CHILDREN'S THEATRE... YOU SHOULD TRY OUT FOR SOMETHING SOMETIME...
MAYBE I'VE GOT HERETOFORE UNSUSPECTED RESERVOIRS OF TALENT!
I'LL BET YOU HAVE!
THE CAST I'M IN IS GREAT! FRIENDLY... SUPPORT-IVE...
ARE THERE MANY GAY GUYS?
©1983 H. Cruse

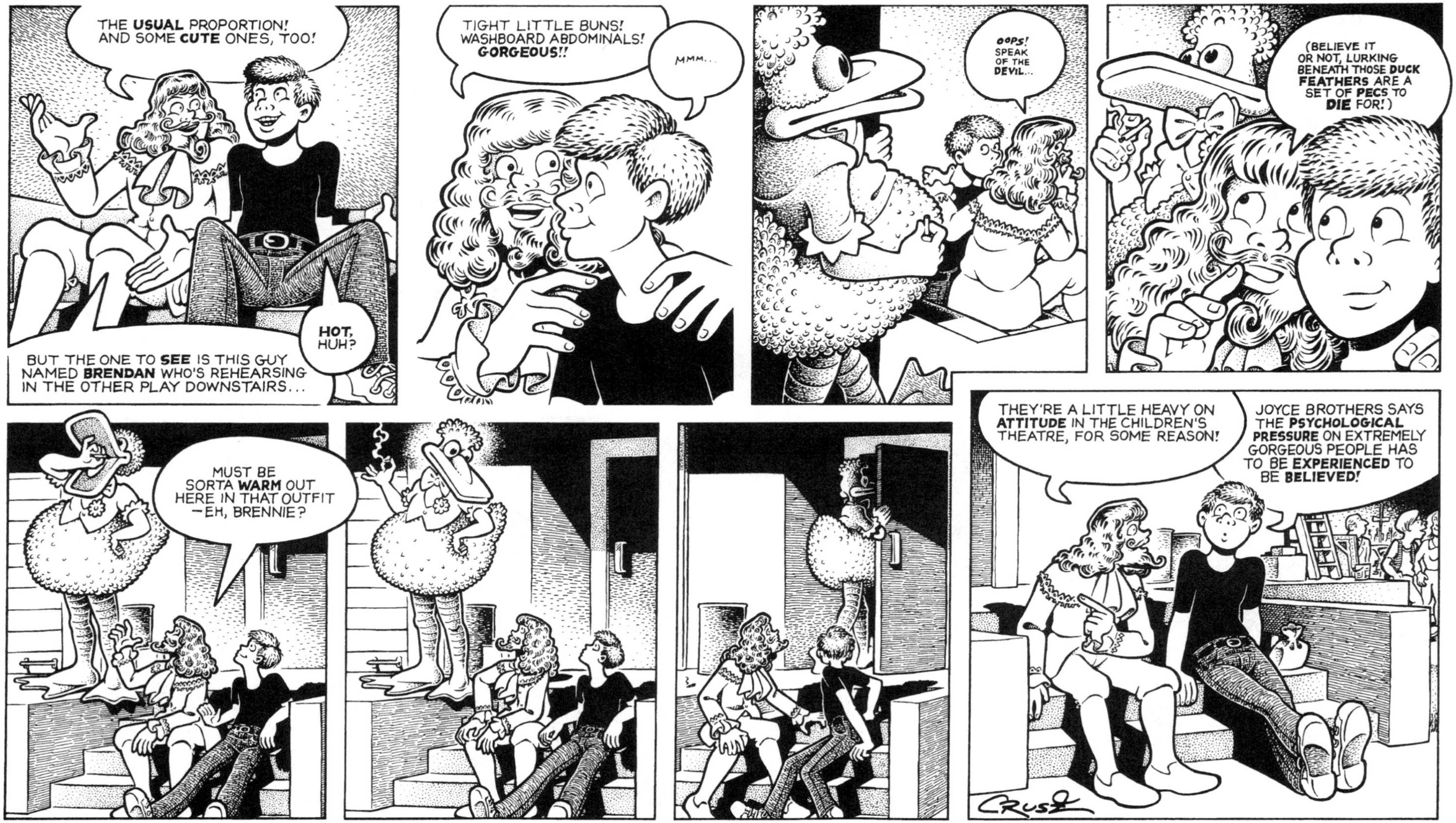

THE **USUAL** PROPORTION! AND SOME **CUTE** ONES, TOO!
HOT, HUH?
BUT THE ONE TO **SEE** IS THIS GUY NAMED **BRENDAN** WHO'S REHEARSING IN THE OTHER PLAY DOWNSTAIRS...
TIGHT LITTLE BUNS! WASHBOARD ABDOMINALS! **GORGEOUS!!**
MMM...
OOPS! SPEAK OF THE **DEVIL**...
(BELIEVE IT OR NOT, LURKING BENEATH THOSE **DUCK FEATHERS** ARE A SET OF **PECS** TO **DIE** FOR!)
MUST BE SORTA **WARM** OUT HERE IN THAT OUTFIT —EH, BRENNIE?
THEY'RE A LITTLE HEAVY ON **ATTITUDE** IN THE CHILDREN'S THEATRE, FOR SOME REASON!
JOYCE BROTHERS SAYS THE **PSYCHOLOGICAL PRESSURE** ON EXTREMELY GORGEOUS PEOPLE HAS TO BE **EXPERIENCED** TO BE **BELIEVED!**
CRUSE

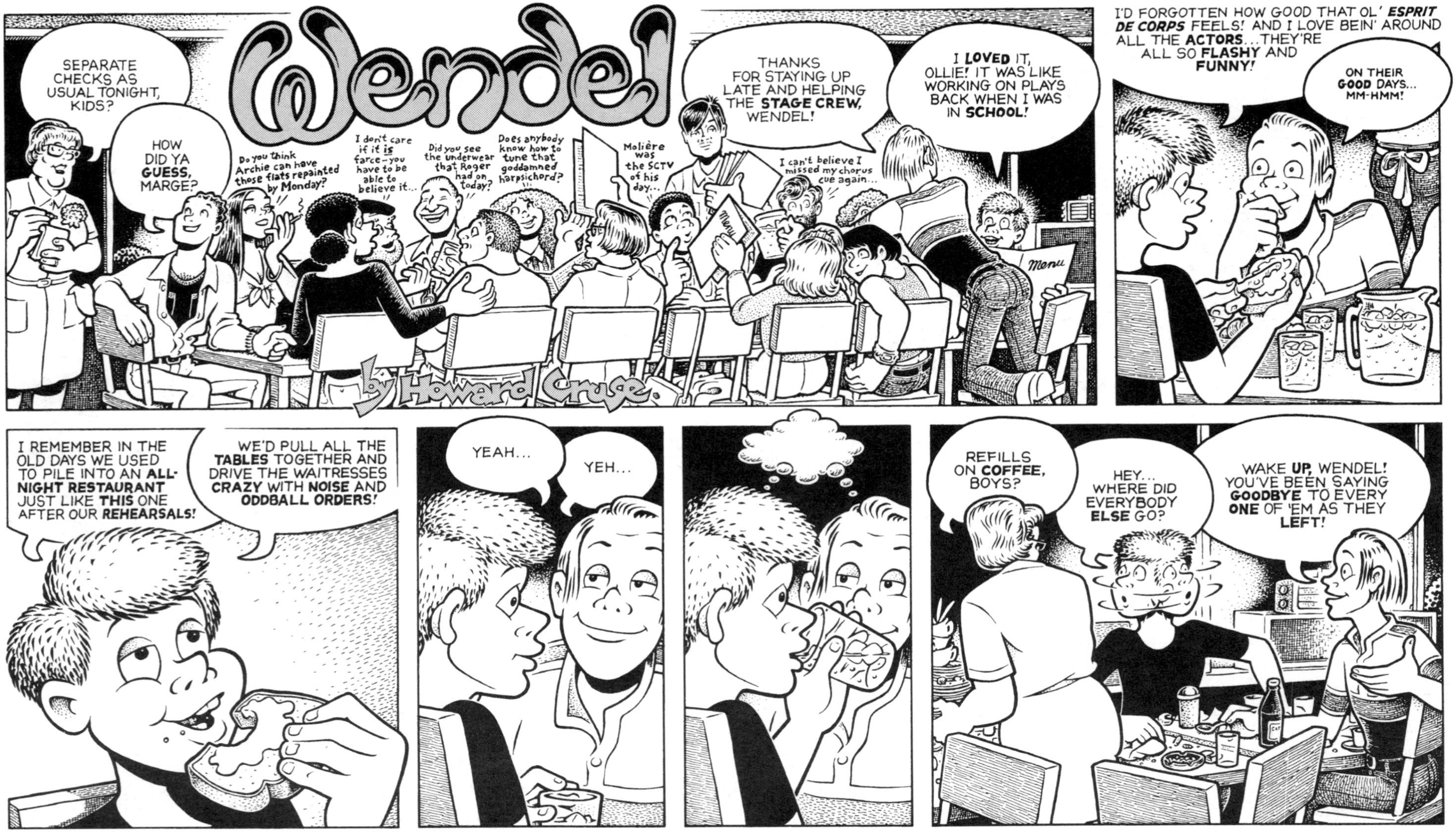
Wendel
by Howard Cruse
SEPARATE CHECKS AS USUAL TONIGHT, KIDS?
HOW DID YA GUESS, MARGE?
Do you think Archie can have those flats repainted by Monday?
I don't care if it is farce—you have to be able to believe it...
Did you see the underwear that Roger had on today?
Does anybody know how to tune that goddamned harpsichord?
Molière was the SCTV of his day...
THANKS FOR STAYING UP LATE AND HELPING THE STAGE CREW, WENDEL!
I can't believe I missed my chorus cue again...
I LOVED IT, OLLIE! IT WAS LIKE WORKING ON PLAYS BACK WHEN I WAS IN SCHOOL!
Menu
I'D FORGOTTEN HOW GOOD THAT OL' ESPRIT DE CORPS FEELS! AND I LOVE BEIN' AROUND ALL THE ACTORS... THEY'RE ALL SO FLASHY AND FUNNY!
ON THEIR GOOD DAYS... MM-HMM!
I REMEMBER IN THE OLD DAYS WE USED TO PILE INTO AN ALL-NIGHT RESTAURANT JUST LIKE THIS ONE AFTER OUR REHEARSALS!
WE'D PULL ALL THE TABLES TOGETHER AND DRIVE THE WAITRESSES CRAZY WITH NOISE AND ODDBALL ORDERS!
YEAH...
YEH...
REFILLS ON COFFEE, BOYS?
HEY... WHERE DID EVERYBODY ELSE GO?
WAKE UP, WENDEL! YOU'VE BEEN SAYING GOODBYE TO EVERY ONE OF 'EM AS THEY LEFT!

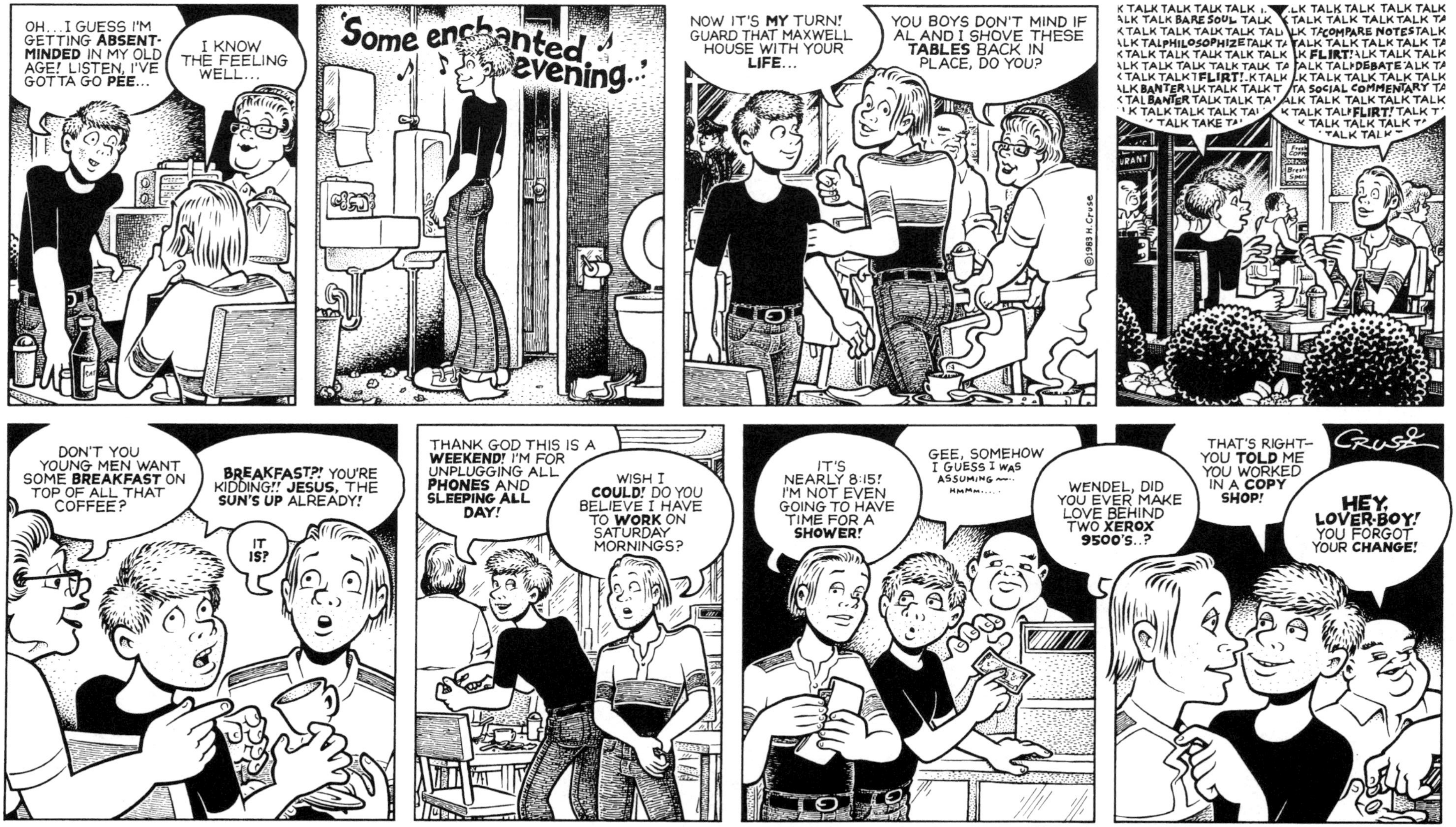
OH... I GUESS I'M GETTING **ABSENT-MINDED** IN MY OLD AGE! LISTEN, I'VE GOTTA GO **PEE**...
I KNOW THE FEELING WELL...
'Some enchanted evening...'
NOW IT'S **MY** TURN! GUARD THAT MAXWELL HOUSE WITH YOUR **LIFE**...
YOU BOYS DON'T MIND IF AL AND I SHOVE THESE **TABLES** BACK IN PLACE, DO YOU?
©1983 H. Cruse
TALK TALK TALK TALK BARE SOUL TALK PHILOSOPHIZE FLIRT! BANTER
TALK TALK COMPARE NOTES FLIRT! DEBATE SOCIAL COMMENTARY FLIRT! TALK
DON'T YOU YOUNG MEN WANT SOME **BREAKFAST** ON TOP OF ALL THAT COFFEE?
BREAKFAST?! YOU'RE KIDDING!! **JESUS,** THE **SUN'S UP** ALREADY!
IT IS?
THANK GOD THIS IS A **WEEKEND!** I'M FOR UNPLUGGING ALL **PHONES** AND **SLEEPING ALL DAY!**
WISH I **COULD!** DO YOU BELIEVE I HAVE TO **WORK** ON SATURDAY MORNINGS?
IT'S NEARLY 8:15! I'M NOT EVEN GOING TO HAVE TIME FOR A **SHOWER!**
GEE, SOMEHOW I GUESS I WAS ASSUMING... HMMM.....
WENDEL, DID YOU EVER MAKE LOVE BEHIND TWO **XEROX 9500'S**..?
THAT'S RIGHT— YOU **TOLD** ME YOU WORKED IN A **COPY SHOP!**
CRUSE
HEY, LOVER-BOY! YOU FORGOT YOUR **CHANGE!**

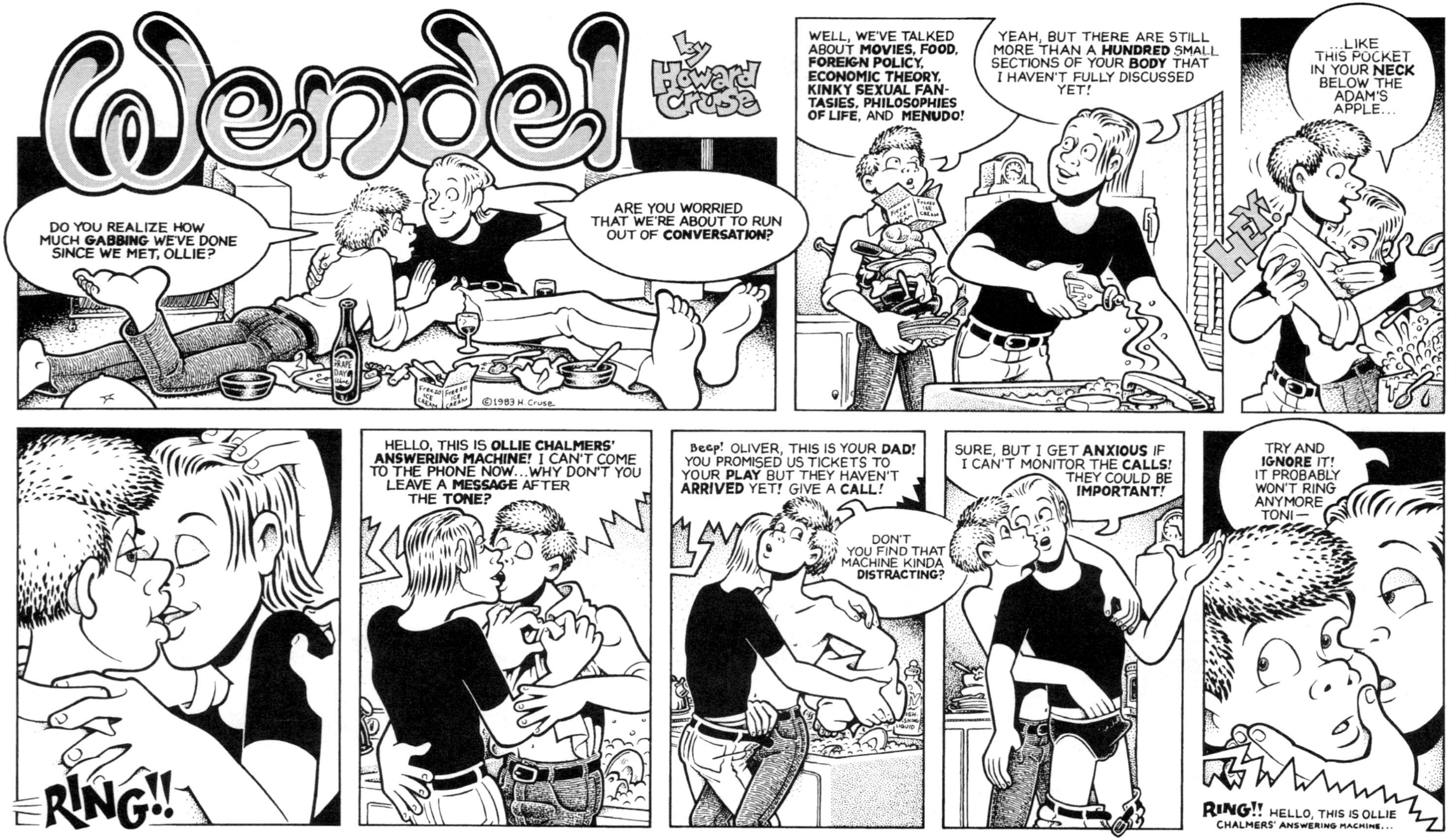
Wendel
by Howard Cruse
DO YOU REALIZE HOW MUCH GABBING WE'VE DONE SINCE WE MET, OLLIE?
ARE YOU WORRIED THAT WE'RE ABOUT TO RUN OUT OF CONVERSATION?
FREEZO ICE CREAM
©1983 H. Cruse
WELL, WE'VE TALKED ABOUT MOVIES, FOOD, FOREIGN POLICY, ECONOMIC THEORY, KINKY SEXUAL FANTASIES, PHILOSOPHIES OF LIFE, AND MENUDO!
YEAH, BUT THERE ARE STILL MORE THAN A HUNDRED SMALL SECTIONS OF YOUR BODY THAT I HAVEN'T FULLY DISCUSSED YET!
HEY!
...LIKE THIS POCKET IN YOUR NECK BELOW THE ADAM'S APPLE...
RING!!
HELLO, THIS IS OLLIE CHALMERS' ANSWERING MACHINE! I CAN'T COME TO THE PHONE NOW...WHY DON'T YOU LEAVE A MESSAGE AFTER THE TONE?
Beep! OLIVER, THIS IS YOUR DAD! YOU PROMISED US TICKETS TO YOUR PLAY BUT THEY HAVEN'T ARRIVED YET! GIVE A CALL!
DON'T YOU FIND THAT MACHINE KINDA DISTRACTING?
SURE, BUT I GET ANXIOUS IF I CAN'T MONITOR THE CALLS! THEY COULD BE IMPORTANT!
TRY AND IGNORE IT! IT PROBABLY WON'T RING ANYMORE TONI—
RING!! HELLO, THIS IS OLLIE CHALMERS' ANSWERING MACHINE...

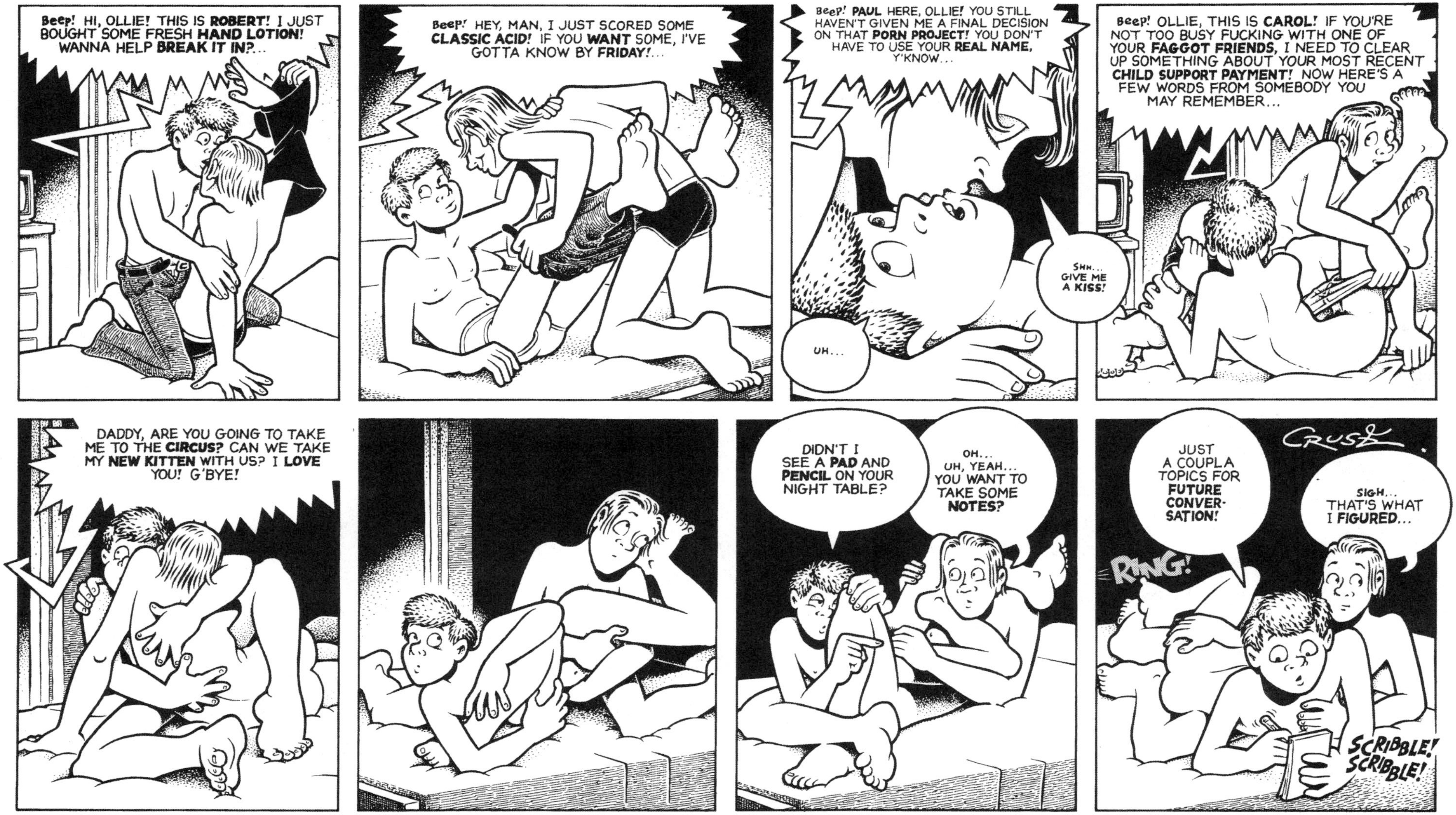
Beep! HI, OLLIE! THIS IS ROBERT! I JUST BOUGHT SOME FRESH HAND LOTION! WANNA HELP BREAK IT IN?...
Beep! HEY, MAN, I JUST SCORED SOME CLASSIC ACID! IF YOU WANT SOME, I'VE GOTTA KNOW BY FRIDAY!...
Beep! PAUL HERE, OLLIE! YOU STILL HAVEN'T GIVEN ME A FINAL DECISION ON THAT PORN PROJECT! YOU DON'T HAVE TO USE YOUR REAL NAME, Y'KNOW...
UH...
SHH... GIVE ME A KISS!
Beep! OLLIE, THIS IS CAROL! IF YOU'RE NOT TOO BUSY FUCKING WITH ONE OF YOUR FAGGOT FRIENDS, I NEED TO CLEAR UP SOMETHING ABOUT YOUR MOST RECENT CHILD SUPPORT PAYMENT! NOW HERE'S A FEW WORDS FROM SOMEBODY YOU MAY REMEMBER...
DADDY, ARE YOU GOING TO TAKE ME TO THE CIRCUS? CAN WE TAKE MY NEW KITTEN WITH US? I LOVE YOU! G'BYE!
DIDN'T I SEE A PAD AND PENCIL ON YOUR NIGHT TABLE?
OH... UH, YEAH... YOU WANT TO TAKE SOME NOTES?
RING!
JUST A COUPLA TOPICS FOR FUTURE CONVER-SATION!
SIGH... THAT'S WHAT I FIGURED...
SCRIBBLE! SCRIBBLE!
CRUSE

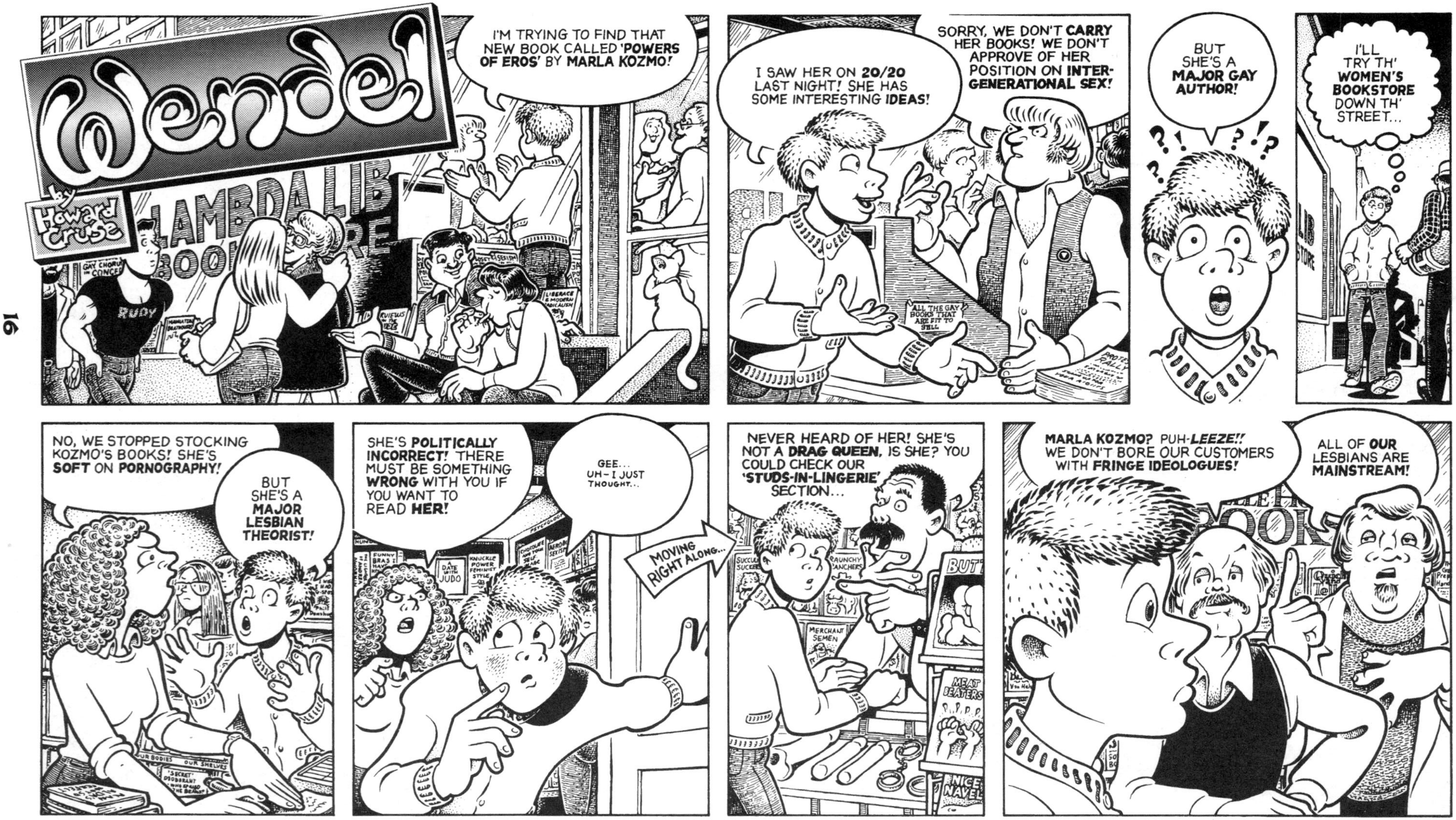
Wendel
by Howard Cruse
LAMBDA LIB BOOKSTORE
I'M TRYING TO FIND THAT NEW BOOK CALLED 'POWERS OF EROS' BY MARLA KOZMO!
I SAW HER ON 20/20 LAST NIGHT! SHE HAS SOME INTERESTING IDEAS!
SORRY, WE DON'T CARRY HER BOOKS! WE DON'T APPROVE OF HER POSITION ON INTER-GENERATIONAL SEX!
ALL THE GAY BOOKS THAT ARE FIT TO SELL
BUT SHE'S A MAJOR GAY AUTHOR!
?!?!?!?
I'LL TRY TH' WOMEN'S BOOKSTORE DOWN TH' STREET...
NO, WE STOPPED STOCKING KOZMO'S BOOKS! SHE'S SOFT ON PORNOGRAPHY!
BUT SHE'S A MAJOR LESBIAN THEORIST!
SHE'S POLITICALLY INCORRECT! THERE MUST BE SOMETHING WRONG WITH YOU IF YOU WANT TO READ HER!
GEE... UH-I JUST THOUGHT...
MOVING RIGHT ALONG...
NEVER HEARD OF HER! SHE'S NOT A DRAG QUEEN, IS SHE? YOU COULD CHECK OUR 'STUDS-IN-LINGERIE' SECTION...
MARLA KOZMO? PUH-LEEZE!! WE DON'T BORE OUR CUSTOMERS WITH FRINGE IDEOLOGUES!
ALL OF OUR LESBIANS ARE MAINSTREAM!

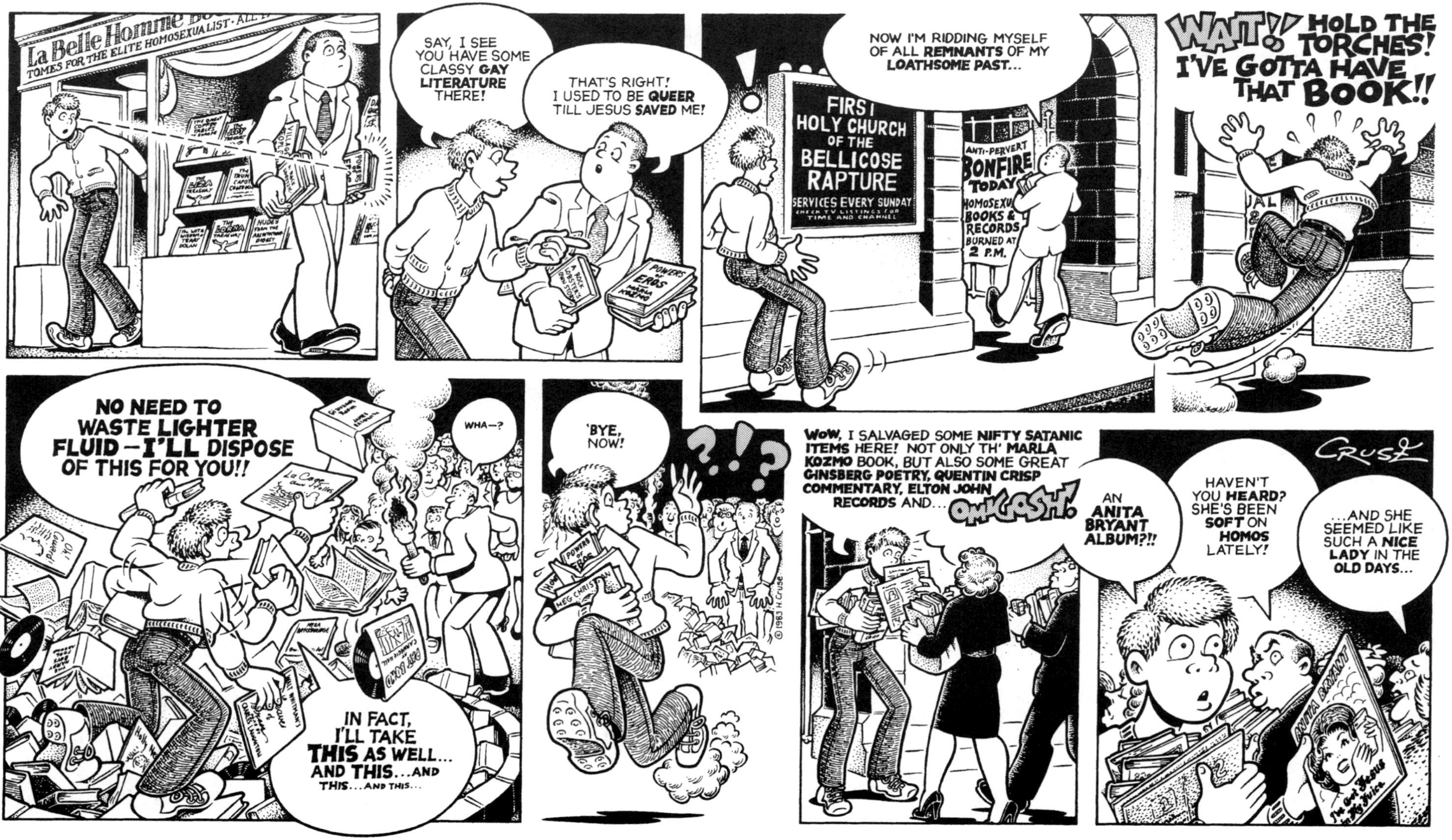

La Belle Homme
TOMES FOR THE ELITE HOMOSEXUALIST · ALL
SAY, I SEE YOU HAVE SOME CLASSY **GAY LITERATURE** THERE!
THAT'S RIGHT! I USED TO BE **QUEER** TILL JESUS **SAVED** ME!
POWERS OF EROS MARLA KOZMO
!
NOW I'M RIDDING MYSELF OF ALL **REMNANTS** OF MY **LOATHSOME PAST...**
FIRST HOLY CHURCH OF THE BELLICOSE RAPTURE
SERVICES EVERY SUNDAY
CHECK TV LISTINGS FOR TIME AND CHANNEL
ANTI-PERVERT BONFIRE TODAY
HOMOSEXU BOOKS & RECORDS BURNED AT 2 P.M.
WAIT!! HOLD THE TORCHES! I'VE GOTTA HAVE THAT BOOK!!
NO NEED TO WASTE LIGHTER FLUID — **I'LL** DISPOSE OF THIS FOR YOU!!
WHA—?
IN FACT, I'LL TAKE **THIS** AS WELL... AND **THIS**...AND THIS...AND THIS...
'BYE, NOW!
?!?
© 1983 H. Cruse
WOW, I SALVAGED SOME **NIFTY SATANIC ITEMS** HERE! NOT ONLY TH' **MARLA KOZMO** BOOK, BUT ALSO SOME GREAT **GINSBERG POETRY, QUENTIN CRISP COMMENTARY, ELTON JOHN RECORDS** AND... OH-GOSH!
AN **ANITA BRYANT ALBUM?!!**
HAVEN'T YOU **HEARD?** SHE'S BEEN **SOFT** ON **HOMOS** LATELY!
...AND SHE SEEMED LIKE SUCH A **NICE LADY** IN THE **OLD DAYS...**
ANITA BRYANT
CRUSE

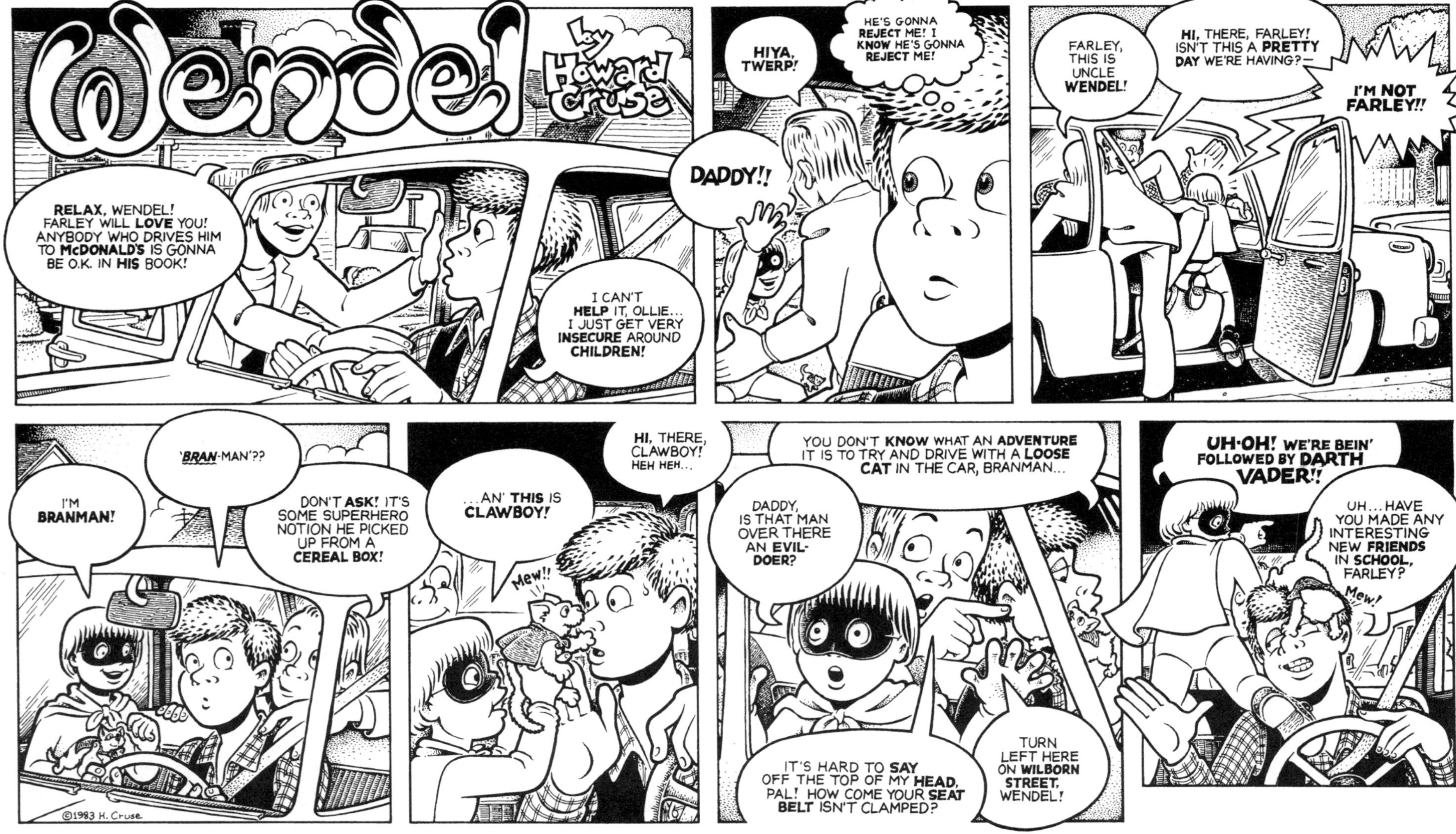
Wendel!
by Howard Cruse
RELAX, WENDEL! FARLEY WILL LOVE YOU! ANYBODY WHO DRIVES HIM TO McDONALD'S IS GONNA BE O.K. IN HIS BOOK!
I CAN'T HELP IT, OLLIE... I JUST GET VERY INSECURE AROUND CHILDREN!
DADDY!!
HIYA, TWERP!
HE'S GONNA REJECT ME! I KNOW HE'S GONNA REJECT ME!
FARLEY, THIS IS UNCLE WENDEL!
HI, THERE, FARLEY! ISN'T THIS A PRETTY DAY WE'RE HAVING?—
I'M NOT FARLEY!!
I'M BRANMAN!
'BRAN-MAN'??
DON'T ASK! IT'S SOME SUPERHERO NOTION HE PICKED UP FROM A CEREAL BOX!
...AN' THIS IS CLAWBOY!
Mew!!
HI, THERE, CLAWBOY! HEH HEH...
YOU DON'T KNOW WHAT AN ADVENTURE IT IS TO TRY AND DRIVE WITH A LOOSE CAT IN THE CAR, BRANMAN...
DADDY, IS THAT MAN OVER THERE AN EVIL-DOER?
IT'S HARD TO SAY OFF THE TOP OF MY HEAD, PAL! HOW COME YOUR SEAT BELT ISN'T CLAMPED?
TURN LEFT HERE ON WILBORN STREET, WENDEL!
UH-OH! WE'RE BEIN' FOLLOWED BY DARTH VADER!!
UH... HAVE YOU MADE ANY INTERESTING NEW FRIENDS IN SCHOOL, FARLEY?
Mew!
©1983 H. Cruse

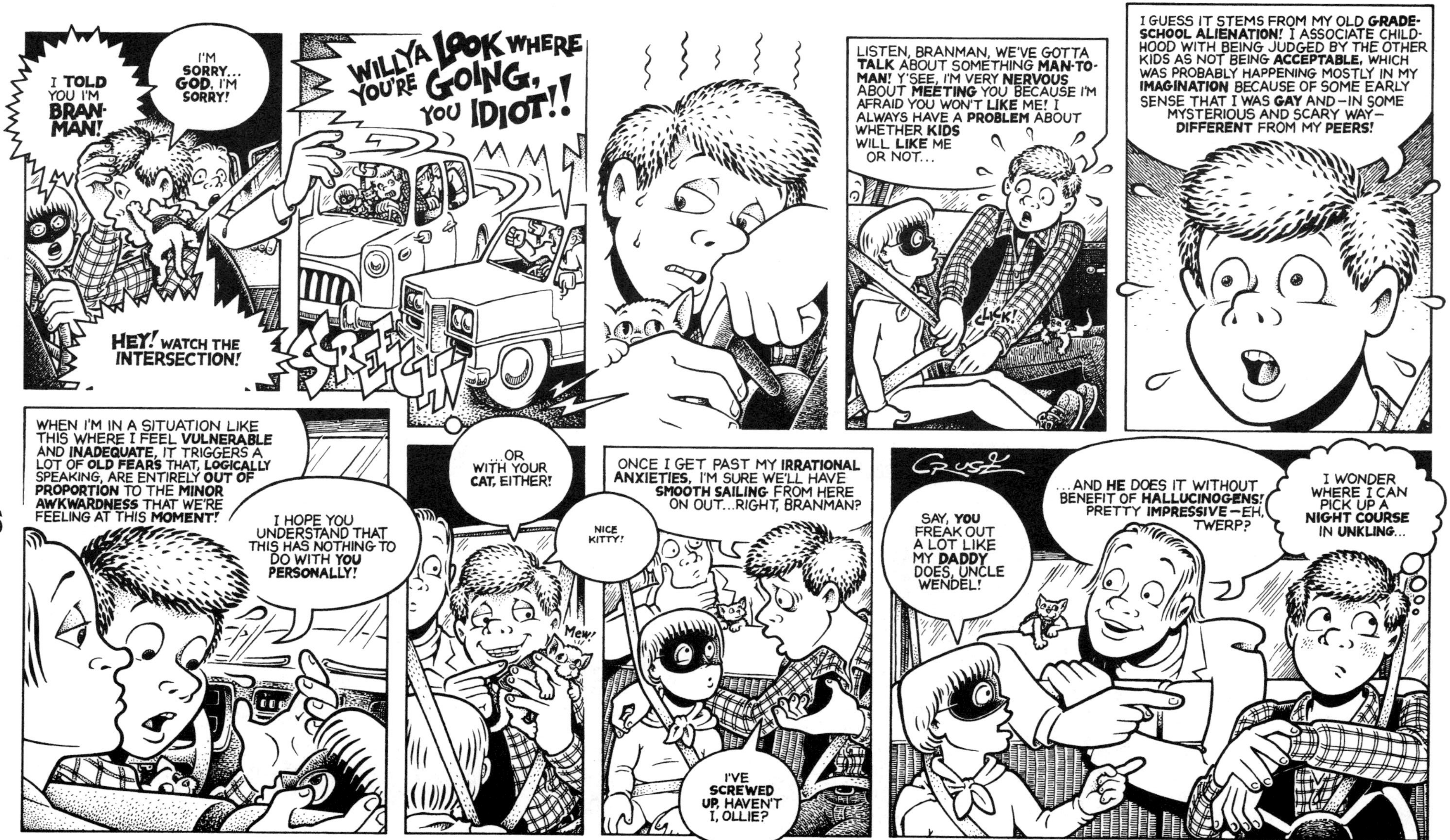
I TOLD YOU I'M BRAN-MAN!
I'M SORRY... GOD, I'M SORRY!
HEY! WATCH THE INTERSECTION!
WILLYA LOOK WHERE YOU'RE GOING, YOU IDIOT!!
SCREECH!
LISTEN, BRANMAN, WE'VE GOTTA TALK ABOUT SOMETHING MAN-TO-MAN! Y'SEE, I'M VERY NERVOUS ABOUT MEETING YOU BECAUSE I'M AFRAID YOU WON'T LIKE ME! I ALWAYS HAVE A PROBLEM ABOUT WHETHER KIDS WILL LIKE ME OR NOT...
CLICK!
I GUESS IT STEMS FROM MY OLD GRADE-SCHOOL ALIENATION! I ASSOCIATE CHILDHOOD WITH BEING JUDGED BY THE OTHER KIDS AS NOT BEING ACCEPTABLE, WHICH WAS PROBABLY HAPPENING MOSTLY IN MY IMAGINATION BECAUSE OF SOME EARLY SENSE THAT I WAS GAY AND—IN SOME MYSTERIOUS AND SCARY WAY—DIFFERENT FROM MY PEERS!
WHEN I'M IN A SITUATION LIKE THIS WHERE I FEEL VULNERABLE AND INADEQUATE, IT TRIGGERS A LOT OF OLD FEARS THAT, LOGICALLY SPEAKING, ARE ENTIRELY OUT OF PROPORTION TO THE MINOR AWKWARDNESS THAT WE'RE FEELING AT THIS MOMENT!
I HOPE YOU UNDERSTAND THAT THIS HAS NOTHING TO DO WITH YOU PERSONALLY!
...OR WITH YOUR CAT, EITHER!
NICE KITTY!
Mew!
ONCE I GET PAST MY IRRATIONAL ANXIETIES, I'M SURE WE'LL HAVE SMOOTH SAILING FROM HERE ON OUT...RIGHT, BRANMAN?
I'VE SCREWED UP, HAVEN'T I, OLLIE?
CRUSE
SAY, YOU FREAK OUT A LOT LIKE MY DADDY DOES, UNCLE WENDEL!
...AND HE DOES IT WITHOUT BENEFIT OF HALLUCINOGENS! PRETTY IMPRESSIVE—EH, TWERP?
I WONDER WHERE I CAN PICK UP A NIGHT COURSE IN UNKLING...

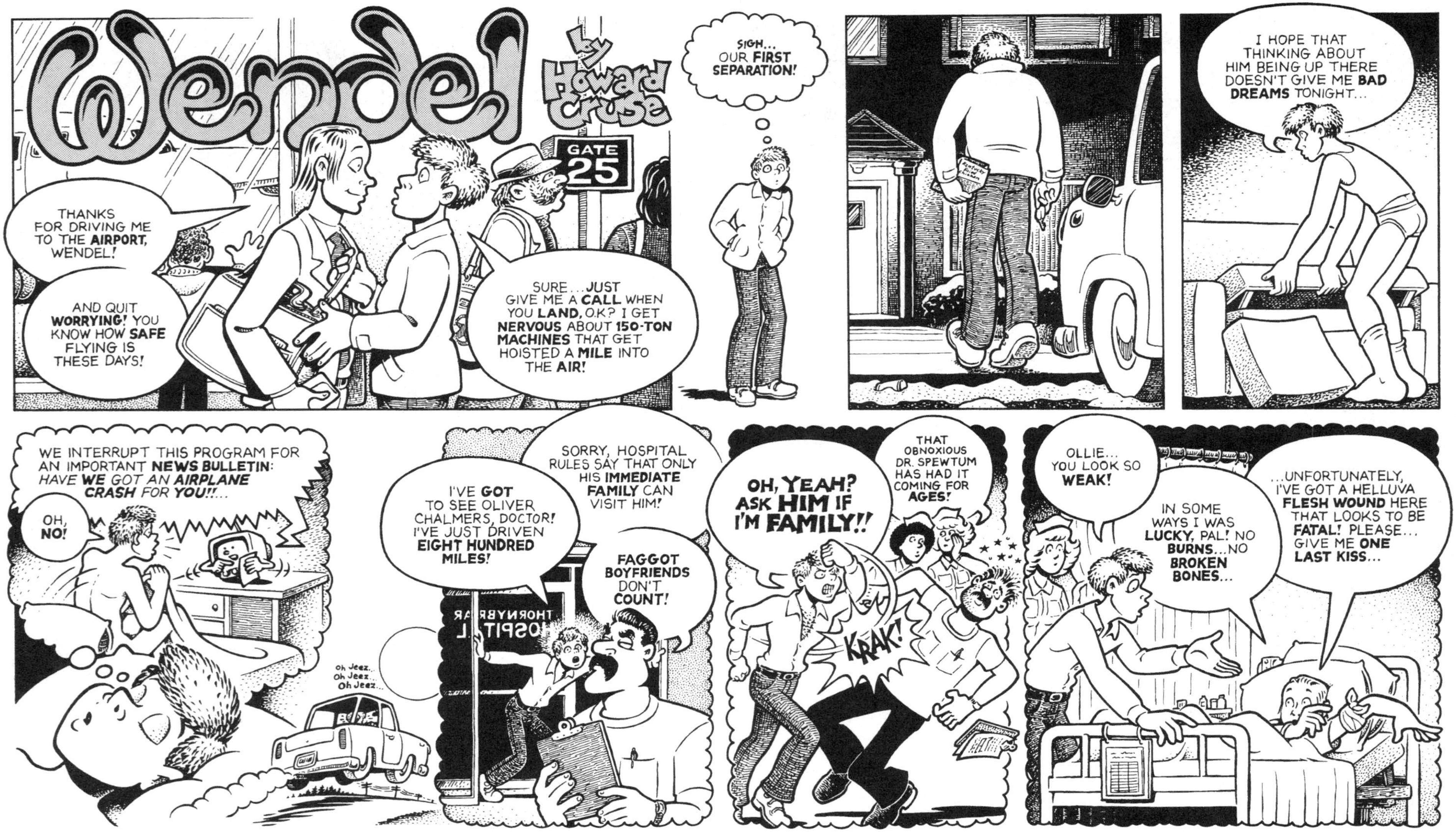
Wendel
by Howard Cruse
THANKS FOR DRIVING ME TO THE AIRPORT, WENDEL!
AND QUIT WORRYING! YOU KNOW HOW SAFE FLYING IS THESE DAYS!
GATE 25
SURE... JUST GIVE ME A CALL WHEN YOU LAND, O.K? I GET NERVOUS ABOUT 150-TON MACHINES THAT GET HOISTED A MILE INTO THE AIR!
SIGH... OUR FIRST SEPARATION!
I HOPE THAT THINKING ABOUT HIM BEING UP THERE DOESN'T GIVE ME BAD DREAMS TONIGHT...
WE INTERRUPT THIS PROGRAM FOR AN IMPORTANT NEWS BULLETIN: HAVE WE GOT AN AIRPLANE CRASH FOR YOU!!...
OH, NO!
Oh Jeez.. Oh Jeez.. Oh Jeez...
I'VE GOT TO SEE OLIVER CHALMERS, DOCTOR! I'VE JUST DRIVEN EIGHT HUNDRED MILES!
SORRY, HOSPITAL RULES SAY THAT ONLY HIS IMMEDIATE FAMILY CAN VISIT HIM!
FAGGOT BOYFRIENDS DON'T COUNT!
OH, YEAH? ASK HIM IF I'M FAMILY!!
THAT OBNOXIOUS DR. SPEWTUM HAS HAD IT COMING FOR AGES!
KRAK!
OLLIE... YOU LOOK SO WEAK!
IN SOME WAYS I WAS LUCKY, PAL! NO BURNS...NO BROKEN BONES...
...UNFORTUNATELY, I'VE GOT A HELLUVA FLESH WOUND HERE THAT LOOKS TO BE FATAL! PLEASE... GIVE ME ONE LAST KISS...

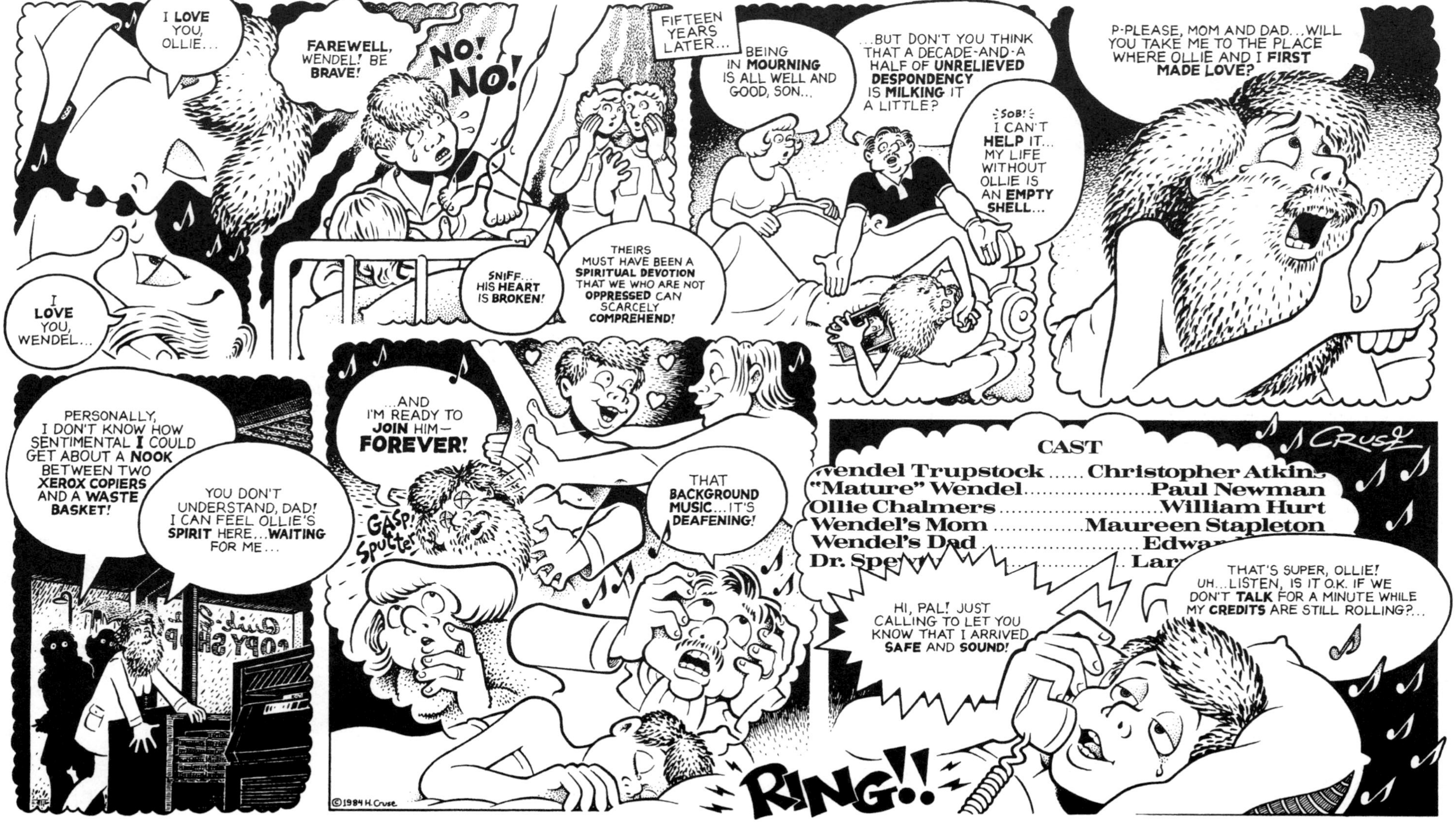
I LOVE YOU, OLLIE...
I LOVE YOU, WENDEL...
FAREWELL, WENDEL! BE BRAVE!
NO! NO!
SNIFF... HIS HEART IS BROKEN!
THEIRS MUST HAVE BEEN A SPIRITUAL DEVOTION THAT WE WHO ARE NOT OPPRESSED CAN SCARCELY COMPREHEND!
FIFTEEN YEARS LATER...
BEING IN MOURNING IS ALL WELL AND GOOD, SON...
...BUT DON'T YOU THINK THAT A DECADE-AND-A HALF OF UNRELIEVED DESPONDENCY IS MILKING IT A LITTLE?
SOB! I CAN'T HELP IT... MY LIFE WITHOUT OLLIE IS AN EMPTY SHELL...
P-PLEASE, MOM AND DAD... WILL YOU TAKE ME TO THE PLACE WHERE OLLIE AND I FIRST MADE LOVE?
PERSONALLY, I DON'T KNOW HOW SENTIMENTAL I COULD GET ABOUT A NOOK BETWEEN TWO XEROX COPIERS AND A WASTE BASKET!
YOU DON'T UNDERSTAND, DAD! I CAN FEEL OLLIE'S SPIRIT HERE... WAITING FOR ME...
COPY SHOP
...AND I'M READY TO JOIN HIM— FOREVER!
GASP! SPUTTER
THAT BACKGROUND MUSIC... IT'S DEFAENING!
©1984 H. Cruse
CAST
Wendel Trupstock ...... Christopher Atkin
"Mature" Wendel ...... Paul Newman
Ollie Chalmers ...... William Hurt
Wendel's Mom ...... Maureen Stapleton
Wendel's Dad ...... Edwa
Dr. Spe ...... Lar
CRUSE
HI, PAL! JUST CALLING TO LET YOU KNOW THAT I ARRIVED SAFE AND SOUND!
THAT'S SUPER, OLLIE! UH... LISTEN, IS IT O.K. IF WE DON'T TALK FOR A MINUTE WHILE MY CREDITS ARE STILL ROLLING?...
RING!!

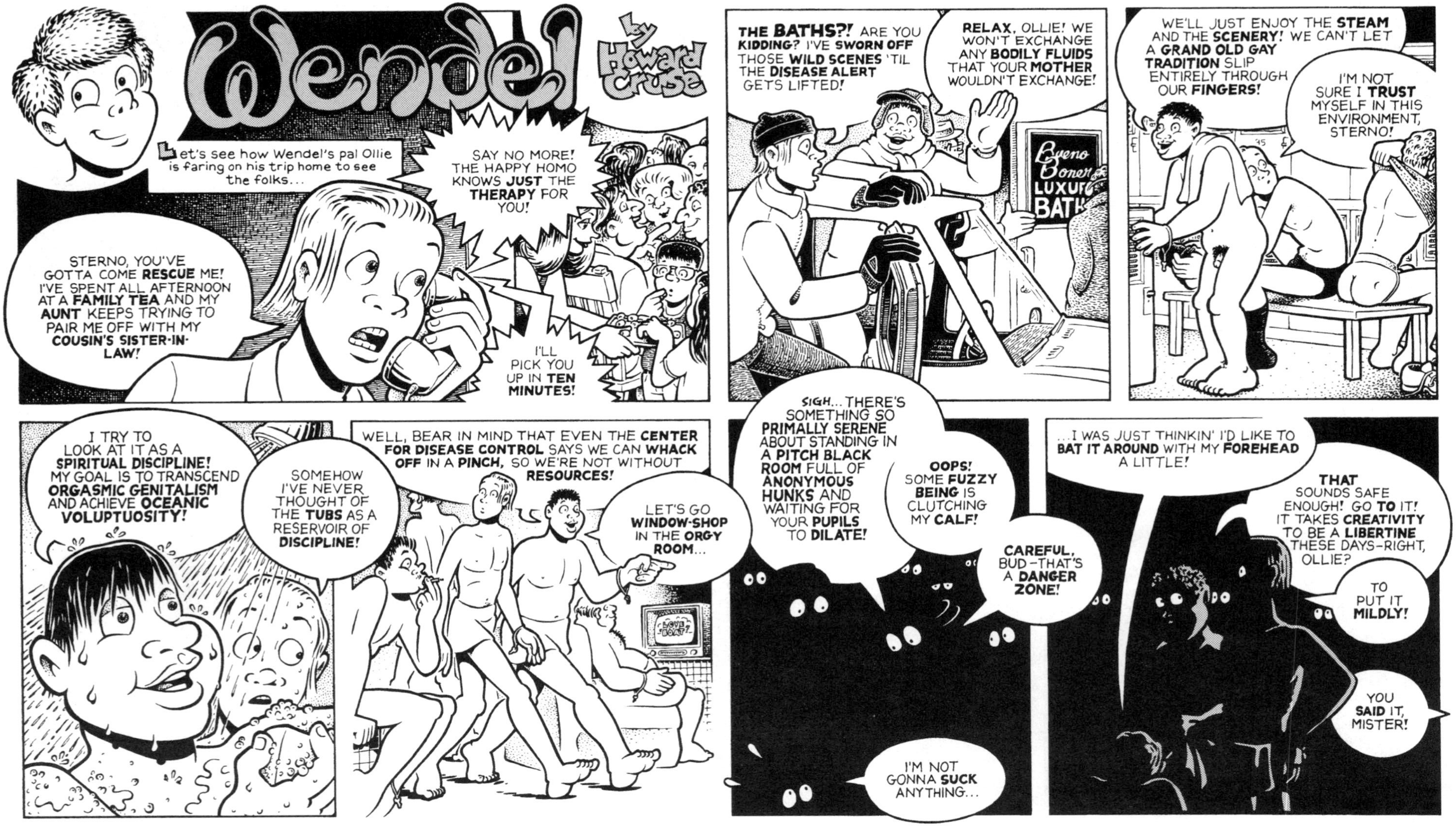
Wendel
by Howard Cruse
Let's see how Wendel's pal Ollie is faring on his trip home to see the folks...
STERNO, YOU'VE GOTTA COME RESCUE ME! I'VE SPENT ALL AFTERNOON AT A FAMILY TEA AND MY AUNT KEEPS TRYING TO PAIR ME OFF WITH MY COUSIN'S SISTER-IN-LAW!
SAY NO MORE! THE HAPPY HOMO KNOWS JUST THE THERAPY FOR YOU!
I'LL PICK YOU UP IN TEN MINUTES!
THE BATHS?! ARE YOU KIDDING? I'VE SWORN OFF THOSE WILD SCENES 'TIL THE DISEASE ALERT GETS LIFTED!
RELAX, OLLIE! WE WON'T EXCHANGE ANY BODILY FLUIDS THAT YOUR MOTHER WOULDN'T EXCHANGE!
Bueno Boner LUXURY BATH
WE'LL JUST ENJOY THE STEAM AND THE SCENERY! WE CAN'T LET A GRAND OLD GAY TRADITION SLIP ENTIRELY THROUGH OUR FINGERS!
I'M NOT SURE I TRUST MYSELF IN THIS ENVIRONMENT, STERNO!
I TRY TO LOOK AT IT AS A SPIRITUAL DISCIPLINE! MY GOAL IS TO TRANSCEND ORGASMIC GENITALISM AND ACHIEVE OCEANIC VOLUPTUOSITY!
SOMEHOW I'VE NEVER THOUGHT OF THE TUBS AS A RESERVOIR OF DISCIPLINE!
WELL, BEAR IN MIND THAT EVEN THE CENTER FOR DISEASE CONTROL SAYS WE CAN WHACK OFF IN A PINCH, SO WE'RE NOT WITHOUT RESOURCES!
LET'S GO WINDOW-SHOP IN THE ORGY ROOM...
LOVE BOAT
SIGH... THERE'S SOMETHING SO PRIMALLY SERENE ABOUT STANDING IN A PITCH BLACK ROOM FULL OF ANONYMOUS HUNKS AND WAITING FOR YOUR PUPILS TO DILATE!
OOPS! SOME FUZZY BEING IS CLUTCHING MY CALF!
CAREFUL, BUD–THAT'S A DANGER ZONE!
I'M NOT GONNA SUCK ANYTHING...
...I WAS JUST THINKIN' I'D LIKE TO BAT IT AROUND WITH MY FOREHEAD A LITTLE!
THAT SOUNDS SAFE ENOUGH! GO TO IT! IT TAKES CREATIVITY TO BE A LIBERTINE THESE DAYS–RIGHT, OLLIE?
TO PUT IT MILDLY!
YOU SAID IT, MISTER!

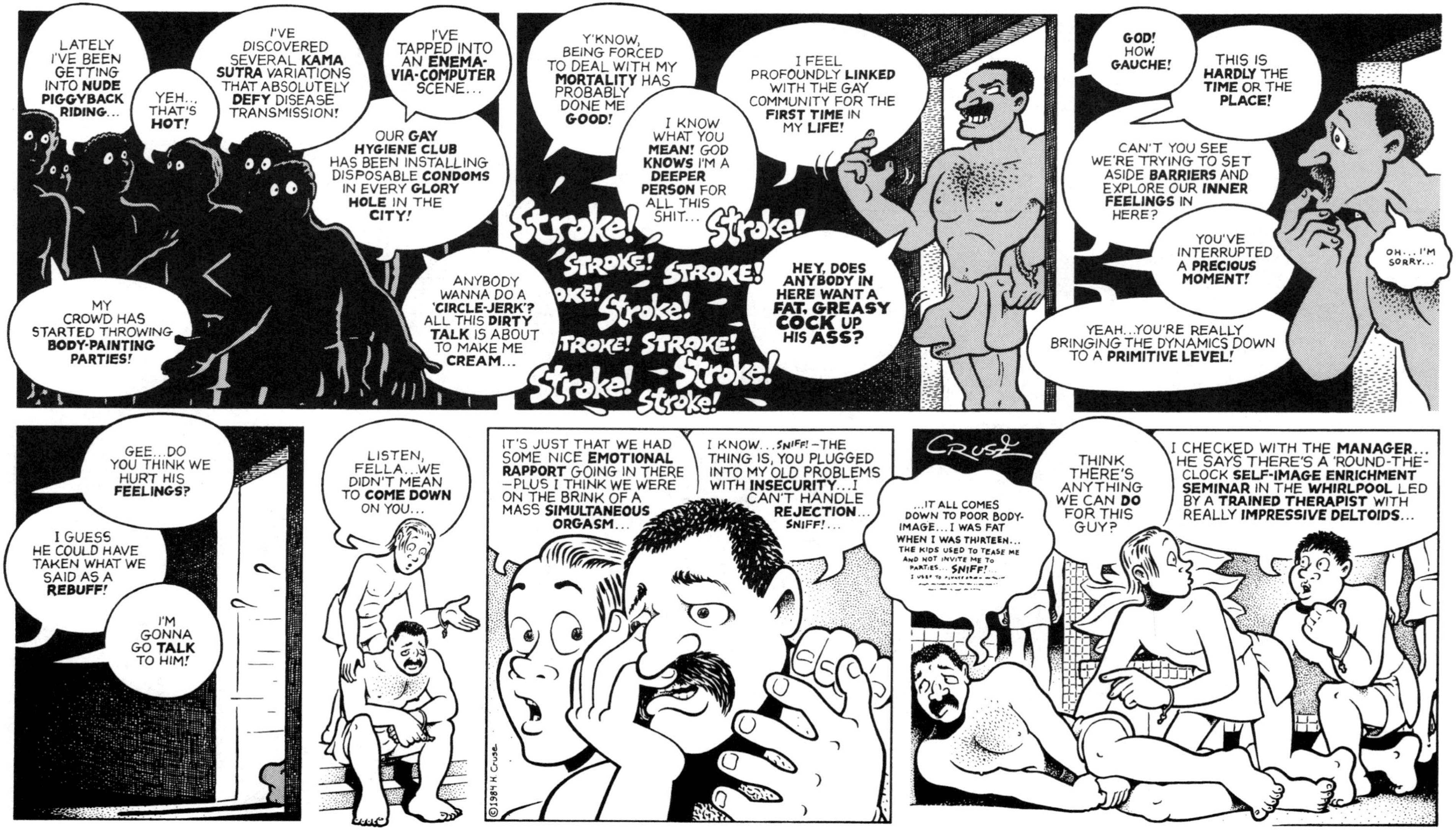
LATELY I'VE BEEN GETTING INTO NUDE PIGGYBACK RIDING...
YEH... THAT'S HOT!
I'VE DISCOVERED SEVERAL KAMA SUTRA VARIATIONS THAT ABSOLUTELY DEFY DISEASE TRANSMISSION!
I'VE TAPPED INTO AN ENEMA-VIA-COMPUTER SCENE...
OUR GAY HYGIENE CLUB HAS BEEN INSTALLING DISPOSABLE CONDOMS IN EVERY GLORY HOLE IN THE CITY!
MY CROWD HAS STARTED THROWING BODY-PAINTING PARTIES!
ANYBODY WANNA DO A 'CIRCLE-JERK'? ALL THIS DIRTY TALK IS ABOUT TO MAKE ME CREAM...
Y'KNOW, BEING FORCED TO DEAL WITH MY MORTALITY HAS PROBABLY DONE ME GOOD!
I KNOW WHAT YOU MEAN! GOD KNOWS I'M A DEEPER PERSON FOR ALL THIS SHIT...
I FEEL PROFOUNDLY LINKED WITH THE GAY COMMUNITY FOR THE FIRST TIME IN MY LIFE!
Stroke! Stroke! STROKE! STROKE! Stroke! STROKE! STROKE! Stroke! Stroke! Stroke!
HEY, DOES ANYBODY IN HERE WANT A FAT, GREASY COCK UP HIS ASS?
GOD! HOW GAUCHE!
THIS IS HARDLY THE TIME OR THE PLACE!
CAN'T YOU SEE WE'RE TRYING TO SET ASIDE BARRIERS AND EXPLORE OUR INNER FEELINGS IN HERE?
YOU'VE INTERRUPTED A PRECIOUS MOMENT!
OH... I'M SORRY...
YEAH... YOU'RE REALLY BRINGING THE DYNAMICS DOWN TO A PRIMITIVE LEVEL!
GEE... DO YOU THINK WE HURT HIS FEELINGS?
I GUESS HE COULD HAVE TAKEN WHAT WE SAID AS A REBUFF!
I'M GONNA GO TALK TO HIM!
LISTEN, FELLA... WE DIDN'T MEAN TO COME DOWN ON YOU...
IT'S JUST THAT WE HAD SOME NICE EMOTIONAL RAPPORT GOING IN THERE —PLUS I THINK WE WERE ON THE BRINK OF A MASS SIMULTANEOUS ORGASM...
I KNOW... SNIFF! —THE THING IS, YOU PLUGGED INTO MY OLD PROBLEMS WITH INSECURITY... I CAN'T HANDLE REJECTION... SNIFF!...
©1984 H. Cruse
CRUSE
...IT ALL COMES DOWN TO POOR BODY-IMAGE... I WAS FAT WHEN I WAS THIRTEEN... THE KIDS USED TO TEASE ME AND NOT INVITE ME TO PARTIES... SNIFF!
THINK THERE'S ANYTHING WE CAN DO FOR THIS GUY?
I CHECKED WITH THE MANAGER... HE SAYS THERE'S A 'ROUND-THE-CLOCK SELF-IMAGE ENRICHMENT SEMINAR IN THE WHIRLPOOL LED BY A TRAINED THERAPIST WITH REALLY IMPRESSIVE DELTOIDS...

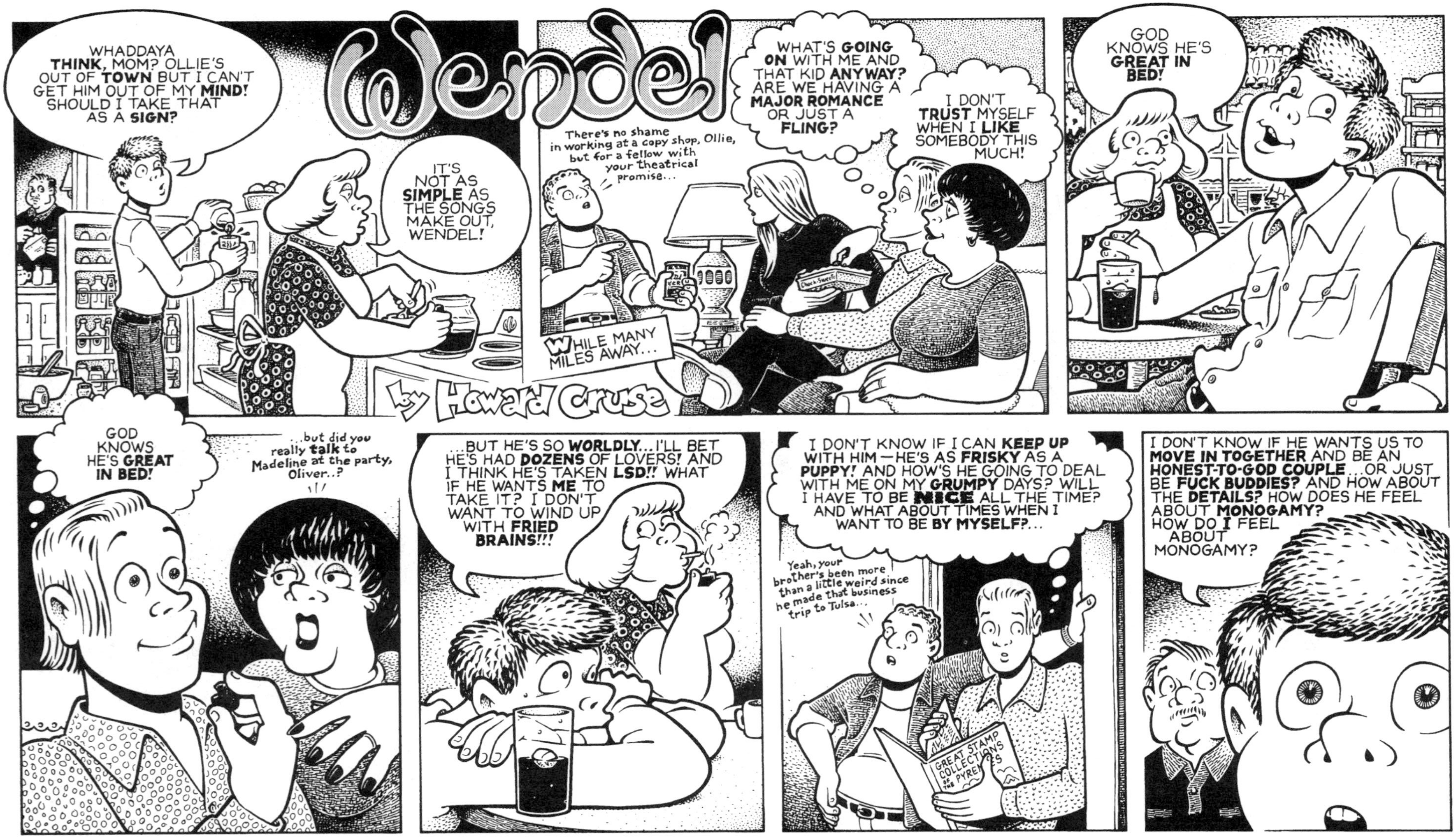
Wendel
by Howard Cruse
WHADDAYA THINK, MOM? OLLIE'S OUT OF TOWN BUT I CAN'T GET HIM OUT OF MY MIND! SHOULD I TAKE THAT AS A SIGN?
IT'S NOT AS SIMPLE AS THE SONGS MAKE OUT, WENDEL!
WHILE MANY MILES AWAY...
There's no shame in working at a copy shop, Ollie, but for a fellow with your theatrical promise...
WHAT'S GOING ON WITH ME AND THAT KID ANYWAY? ARE WE HAVING A MAJOR ROMANCE OR JUST A FLING?
I DON'T TRUST MYSELF WHEN I LIKE SOMEBODY THIS MUCH!
GOD KNOWS HE'S GREAT IN BED!
GOD KNOWS HE'S GREAT IN BED!
...but did you really talk to Madeline at the party, Oliver..?
...BUT HE'S SO WORLDLY... I'LL BET HE'S HAD DOZENS OF LOVERS! AND I THINK HE'S TAKEN LSD!! WHAT IF HE WANTS ME TO TAKE IT? I DON'T WANT TO WIND UP WITH FRIED BRAINS!!!
I DON'T KNOW IF I CAN KEEP UP WITH HIM—HE'S AS FRISKY AS A PUPPY! AND HOW'S HE GOING TO DEAL WITH ME ON MY GRUMPY DAYS? WILL I HAVE TO BE NICE ALL THE TIME? AND WHAT ABOUT TIMES WHEN I WANT TO BE BY MYSELF?...
Yeah, your brother's been more than a little weird since he made that business trip to Tulsa...
GREAT STAMP COLLECTIONS OF THE PYRENEES
I DON'T KNOW IF HE WANTS US TO MOVE IN TOGETHER AND BE AN HONEST-TO-GOD COUPLE...OR JUST BE FUCK BUDDIES? AND HOW ABOUT THE DETAILS? HOW DOES HE FEEL ABOUT MONOGAMY? HOW DO I FEEL ABOUT MONOGAMY?

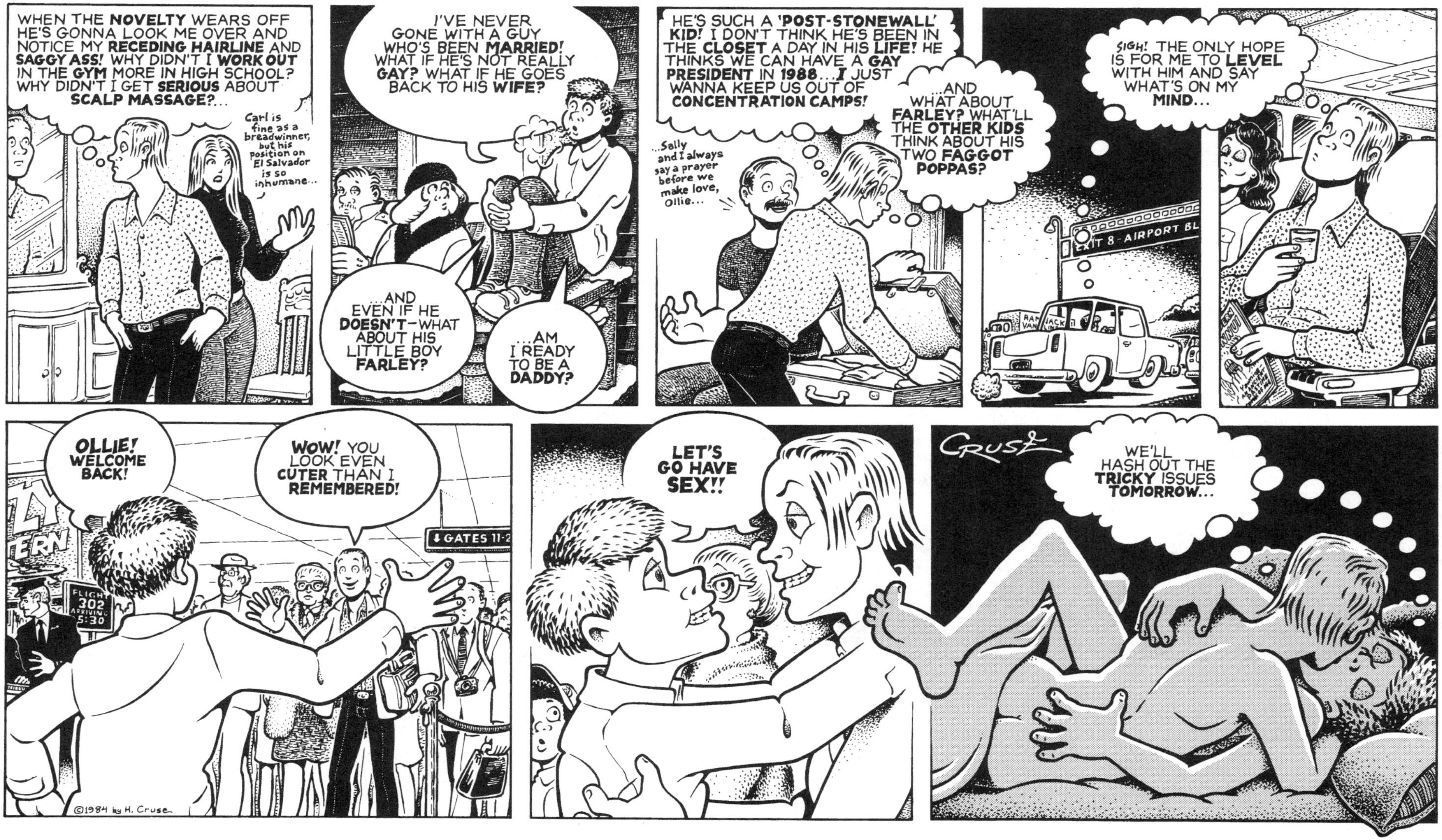
WHEN THE NOVELTY WEARS OFF HE'S GONNA LOOK ME OVER AND NOTICE MY RECEDING HAIRLINE AND SAGGY ASS! WHY DIDN'T I WORK OUT IN THE GYM MORE IN HIGH SCHOOL? WHY DIDN'T I GET SERIOUS ABOUT SCALP MASSAGE?...
Carl is fine as a breadwinner, but his position on El Salvador is so inhumane...
I'VE NEVER GONE WITH A GUY WHO'S BEEN MARRIED! WHAT IF HE'S NOT REALLY GAY? WHAT IF HE GOES BACK TO HIS WIFE?
...AND EVEN IF HE DOESN'T—WHAT ABOUT HIS LITTLE BOY FARLEY?
...AM I READY TO BE A DADDY?
HE'S SUCH A 'POST-STONEWALL' KID! I DON'T THINK HE'S BEEN IN THE CLOSET A DAY IN HIS LIFE! HE THINKS WE CAN HAVE A GAY PRESIDENT IN 1988...I JUST WANNA KEEP US OUT OF CONCENTRATION CAMPS!
...Sally and I always say a prayer before we make love, Ollie...
...AND WHAT ABOUT FARLEY? WHAT'LL THE OTHER KIDS THINK ABOUT HIS TWO FAGGOT POPPAS?
EXIT 8 - AIRPORT BL
SIGH! THE ONLY HOPE IS FOR ME TO LEVEL WITH HIM AND SAY WHAT'S ON MY MIND...
OLLIE! WELCOME BACK!
WOW! YOU LOOK EVEN CUTER THAN I REMEMBERED!
↓GATES 11-2
FLIGHT 302 ARRIVING 5:30
©1984 by H. Cruse
LET'S GO HAVE SEX!!
CRUSE
WE'LL HASH OUT THE TRICKY ISSUES TOMORROW...

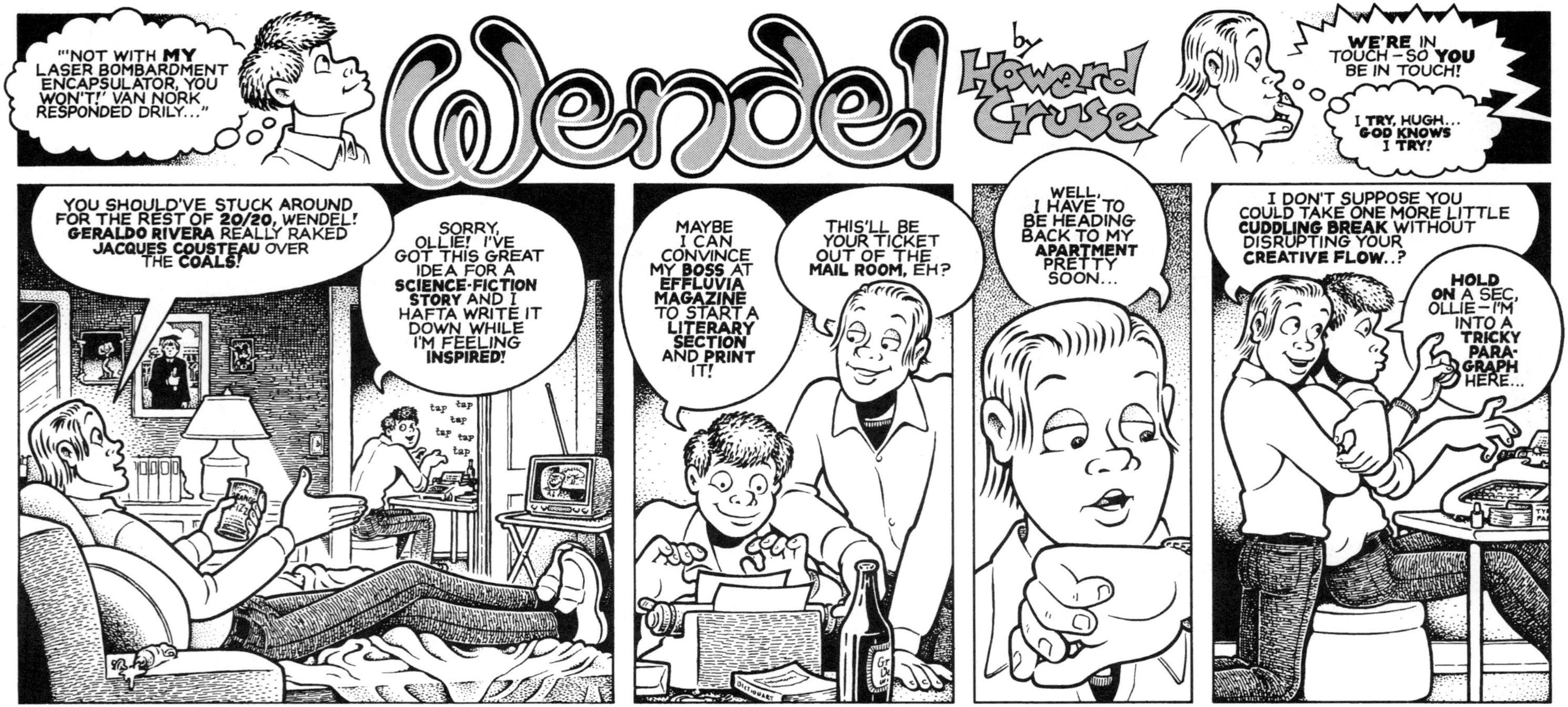

"'NOT WITH MY LASER BOMBARDMENT ENCAPSULATOR, YOU WON'T!' VAN NORK RESPONDED DRILY..."
Wendel
by Howard Cruse
WE'RE IN TOUCH—SO YOU BE IN TOUCH!
I TRY, HUGH... GOD KNOWS I TRY!
YOU SHOULD'VE STUCK AROUND FOR THE REST OF 20/20, WENDEL! GERALDO RIVERA REALLY RAKED JACQUES COUSTEAU OVER THE COALS!
SORRY, OLLIE! I'VE GOT THIS GREAT IDEA FOR A SCIENCE-FICTION STORY AND I HAFTA WRITE IT DOWN WHILE I'M FEELING INSPIRED!
tap tap tap tap tap tap
MAYBE I CAN CONVINCE MY BOSS AT EFFLUVIA MAGAZINE TO START A LITERARY SECTION AND PRINT IT!
THIS'LL BE YOUR TICKET OUT OF THE MAIL ROOM, EH?
WELL, I HAVE TO BE HEADING BACK TO MY APARTMENT PRETTY SOON...
I DON'T SUPPOSE YOU COULD TAKE ONE MORE LITTLE CUDDLING BREAK WITHOUT DISRUPTING YOUR CREATIVE FLOW..?
HOLD ON A SEC, OLLIE—I'M INTO A TRICKY PARA-GRAPH HERE...

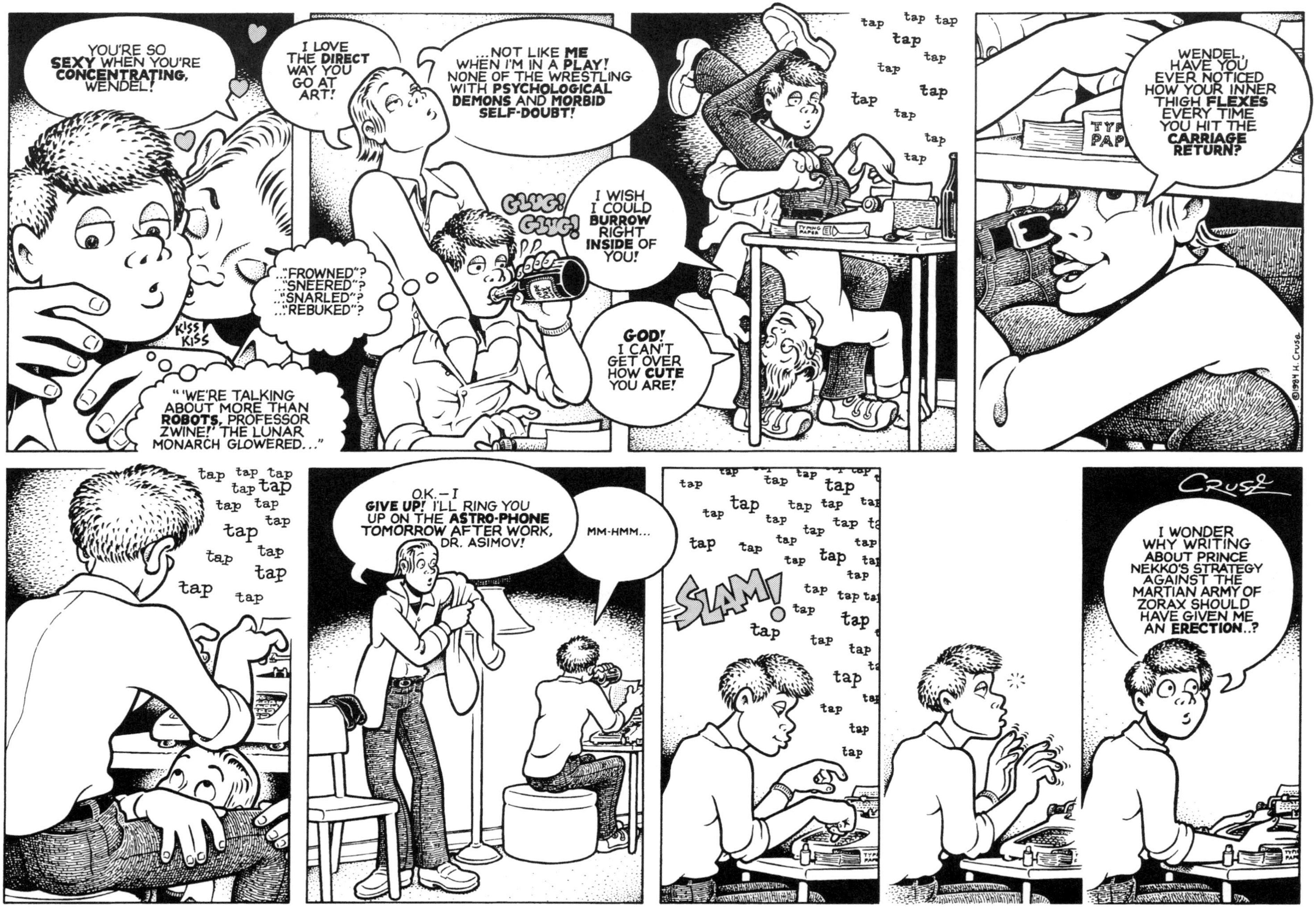
YOU'RE SO **SEXY** WHEN YOU'RE **CONCENTRATING,** WENDEL!
KISS KISS
"'WE'RE TALKING ABOUT MORE THAN **ROBOTS,** PROFESSOR ZWINE!' THE LUNAR MONARCH GLOWERED..."
..."FROWNED"? ..."SNEERED"? ..."SNARLED"? ..."REBUKED"?
I LOVE THE **DIRECT** WAY YOU GO AT ART!
...NOT LIKE **ME** WHEN I'M IN A **PLAY!** NONE OF THE WRESTLING WITH **PSYCHOLOGICAL DEMONS** AND **MORBID SELF-DOUBT!**
GLUG! GLUG!
I WISH I COULD **BURROW** RIGHT **INSIDE** OF YOU!
GOD! I CAN'T GET OVER HOW **CUTE** YOU ARE!
tap tap tap tap tap tap tap tap tap tap tap
TYPING PAPER
WENDEL, HAVE YOU EVER NOTICED HOW YOUR INNER THIGH **FLEXES** EVERY TIME YOU HIT THE **CARRIAGE RETURN?**
©1984 H. Cruse
tap tap tap tap tap tap tap tap tap tap tap tap tap
O.K.—I **GIVE UP!** I'LL RING YOU UP ON THE **ASTRO-PHONE TOMORROW** AFTER WORK, DR. ASIMOV!
MM-HMM...
SLAM!
tap tap tap tap tap tap tap tap tap tap
CRUSE
I WONDER WHY WRITING ABOUT PRINCE NEKKO'S STRATEGY AGAINST THE MARTIAN ARMY OF ZORAX SHOULD HAVE GIVEN ME AN **ERECTION**..?

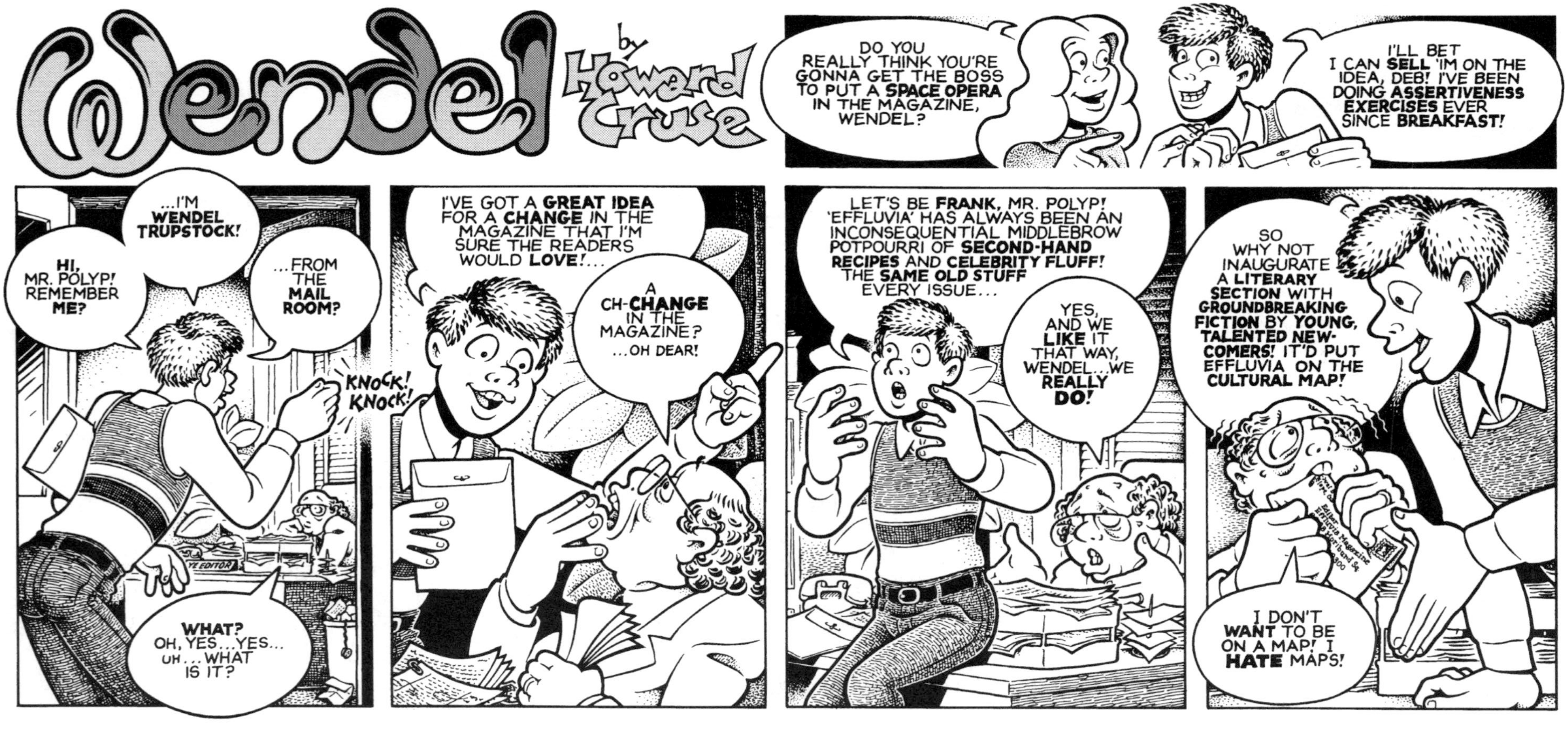
Wendel
by Howard Cruse
DO YOU REALLY THINK YOU'RE GONNA GET THE BOSS TO PUT A SPACE OPERA IN THE MAGAZINE, WENDEL?
I'LL BET I CAN SELL 'IM ON THE IDEA, DEB! I'VE BEEN DOING ASSERTIVENESS EXERCISES EVER SINCE BREAKFAST!
HI, MR. POLYP! REMEMBER ME?
...I'M WENDEL TRUPSTOCK!
...FROM THE MAIL ROOM?
KNOCK! KNOCK!
WHAT? OH, YES...YES... UH...WHAT IS IT?
I'VE GOT A GREAT IDEA FOR A CHANGE IN THE MAGAZINE THAT I'M SURE THE READERS WOULD LOVE!...
A CH-CHANGE IN THE MAGAZINE? ...OH DEAR!
LET'S BE FRANK, MR. POLYP! 'EFFLUVIA' HAS ALWAYS BEEN AN INCONSEQUENTIAL MIDDLEBROW POTPOURRI OF SECOND-HAND RECIPES AND CELEBRITY FLUFF! THE SAME OLD STUFF EVERY ISSUE...
YES, AND WE LIKE IT THAT WAY, WENDEL...WE REALLY DO!
SO WHY NOT INAUGURATE A LITERARY SECTION WITH GROUNDBREAKING FICTION BY YOUNG, TALENTED NEW-COMERS! IT'D PUT EFFLUVIA ON THE CULTURAL MAP!
I DON'T WANT TO BE ON A MAP! I HATE MAPS!

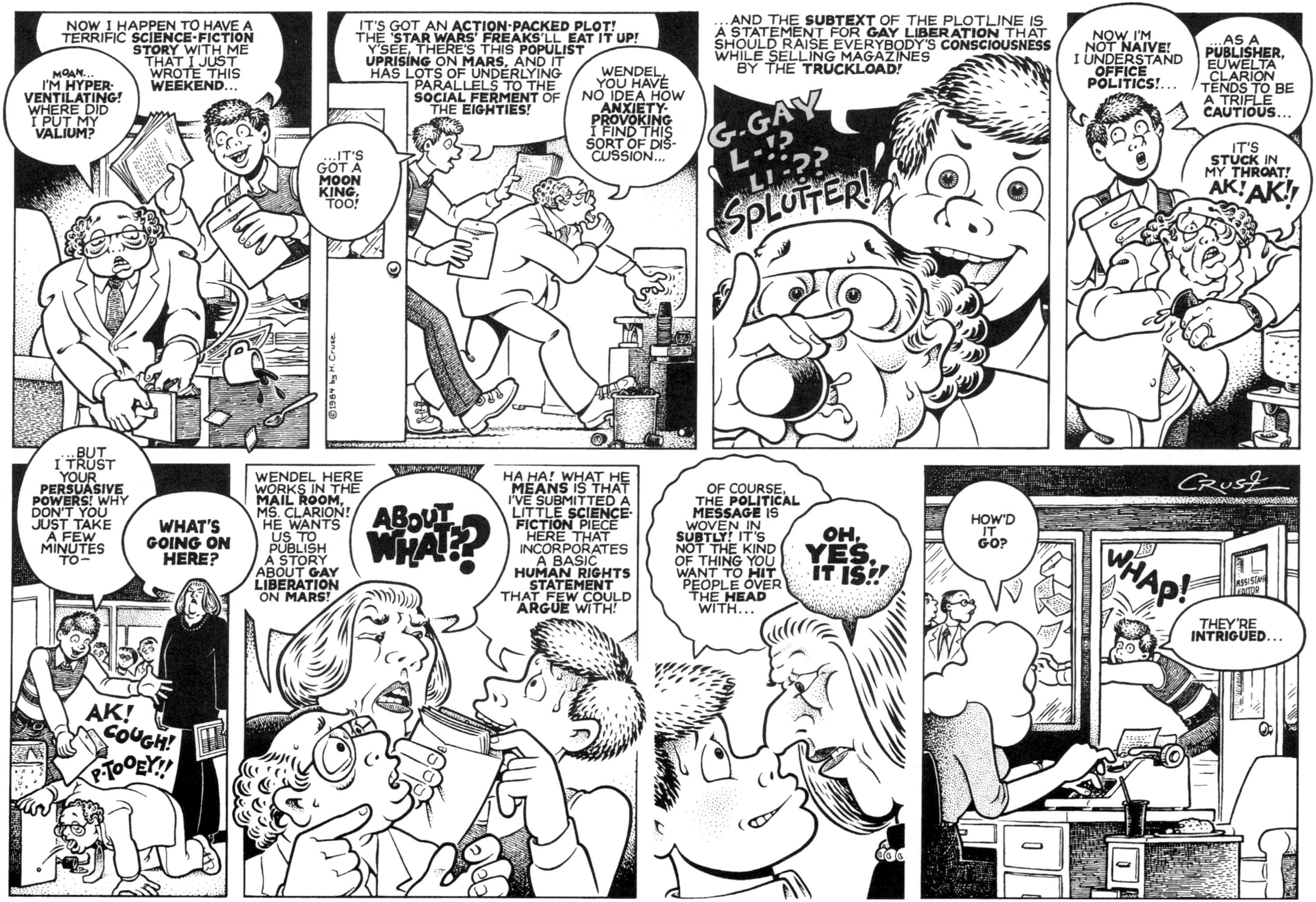
NOW I HAPPEN TO HAVE A TERRIFIC SCIENCE-FICTION STORY WITH ME THAT I JUST WROTE THIS WEEKEND...
MOAN... I'M HYPER-VENTILATING! WHERE DID I PUT MY VALIUM?
IT'S GOT AN ACTION-PACKED PLOT! THE 'STAR WARS' FREAKS'LL EAT IT UP! Y'SEE, THERE'S THIS POPULIST UPRISING ON MARS, AND IT HAS LOTS OF UNDERLYING PARALLELS TO THE SOCIAL FERMENT OF THE EIGHTIES!
...IT'S GOT A MOON KING, TOO!
WENDEL, YOU HAVE NO IDEA HOW ANXIETY-PROVOKING I FIND THIS SORT OF DIS-CUSSION...
©1984 by H. Cruse.
...AND THE SUBTEXT OF THE PLOTLINE IS A STATEMENT FOR GAY LIBERATION THAT SHOULD RAISE EVERYBODY'S CONSCIOUSNESS WHILE SELLING MAGAZINES BY THE TRUCKLOAD!
G-GAY L-!? LI-?? SPLUTTER!
NOW I'M NOT NAIVE! I UNDERSTAND OFFICE POLITICS!...
...AS A PUBLISHER, EUWELTA CLARION TENDS TO BE A TRIFLE CAUTIOUS...
IT'S STUCK IN MY THROAT! AK! AK!
...BUT I TRUST YOUR PERSUASIVE POWERS! WHY DON'T YOU JUST TAKE A FEW MINUTES TO–
WHAT'S GOING ON HERE?
AK! COUGH! P-TOOEY!!
WENDEL HERE WORKS IN THE MAIL ROOM, MS. CLARION! HE WANTS US TO PUBLISH A STORY ABOUT GAY LIBERATION ON MARS!
ABOUT WHAT??
HA HA! WHAT HE MEANS IS THAT I'VE SUBMITTED A LITTLE SCIENCE-FICTION PIECE HERE THAT INCORPORATES A BASIC HUMAN RIGHTS STATEMENT THAT FEW COULD ARGUE WITH!
OF COURSE, THE POLITICAL MESSAGE IS WOVEN IN SUBTLY! IT'S NOT THE KIND OF THING YOU WANT TO HIT PEOPLE OVER THE HEAD WITH...
OH, YES, IT IS!!
CRUSE
HOW'D IT GO?
WHAP!
THEY'RE INTRIGUED...

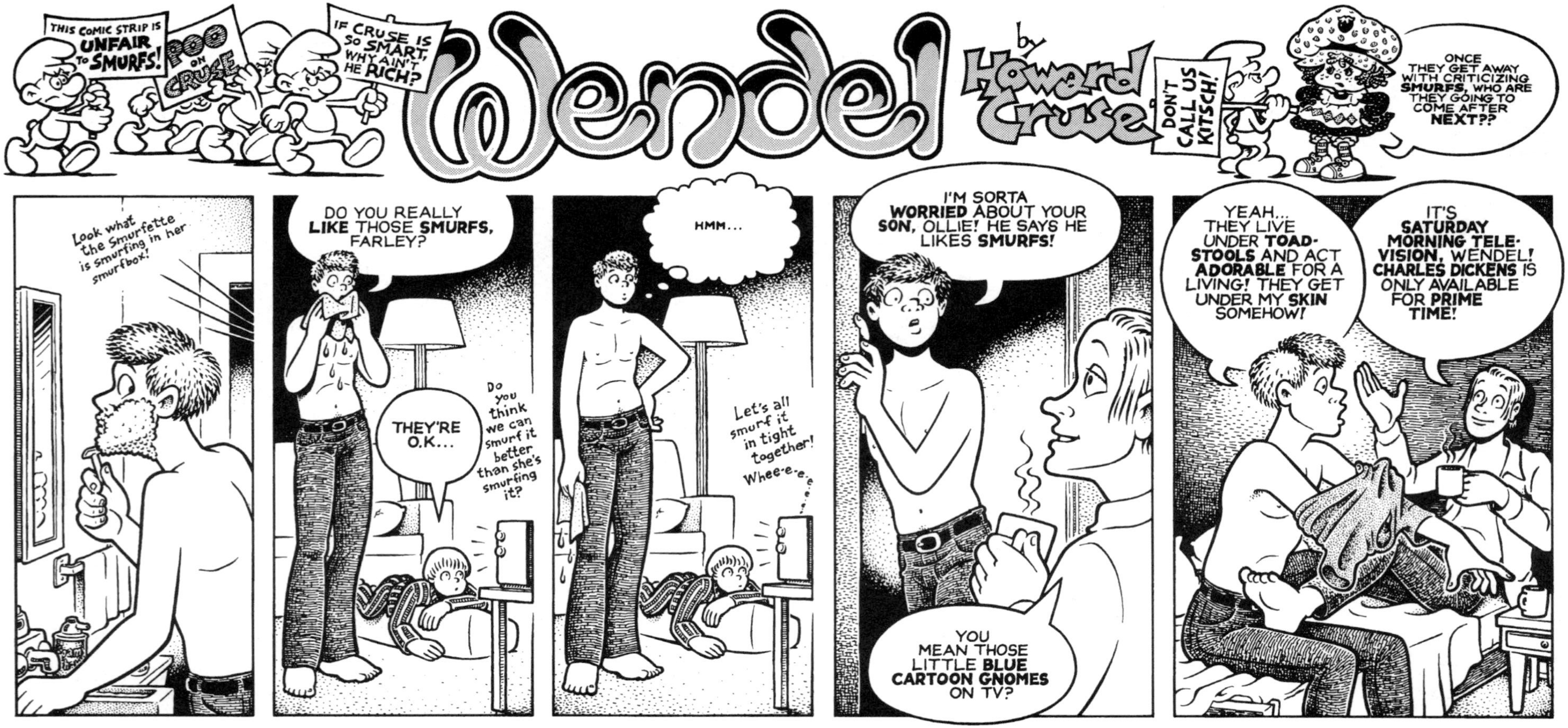
THIS COMIC STRIP IS UNFAIR TO SMURFS!
POO ON CRUSE
IF CRUSE IS SO SMART, WHY AIN'T HE RICH?
Wendel
by Howard Cruse
DON'T CALL US KITSCH!
ONCE THEY GET AWAY WITH CRITICIZING SMURFS, WHO ARE THEY GOING TO COME AFTER NEXT??
Look what the Smurfette is smurfing in her smurfbox!
DO YOU REALLY LIKE THOSE SMURFS, FARLEY?
THEY'RE O.K...
Do you think we can smurf it better than she's smurfing it?
HMM...
Let's all smurf it in tight together!
Whee-e-e-e-e...
I'M SORTA WORRIED ABOUT YOUR SON, OLLIE! HE SAYS HE LIKES SMURFS!
YOU MEAN THOSE LITTLE BLUE CARTOON GNOMES ON TV?
YEAH... THEY LIVE UNDER TOAD-STOOLS AND ACT ADORABLE FOR A LIVING! THEY GET UNDER MY SKIN SOMEHOW!
IT'S SATURDAY MORNING TELE-VISION, WENDEL! CHARLES DICKENS IS ONLY AVAILABLE FOR PRIME TIME!

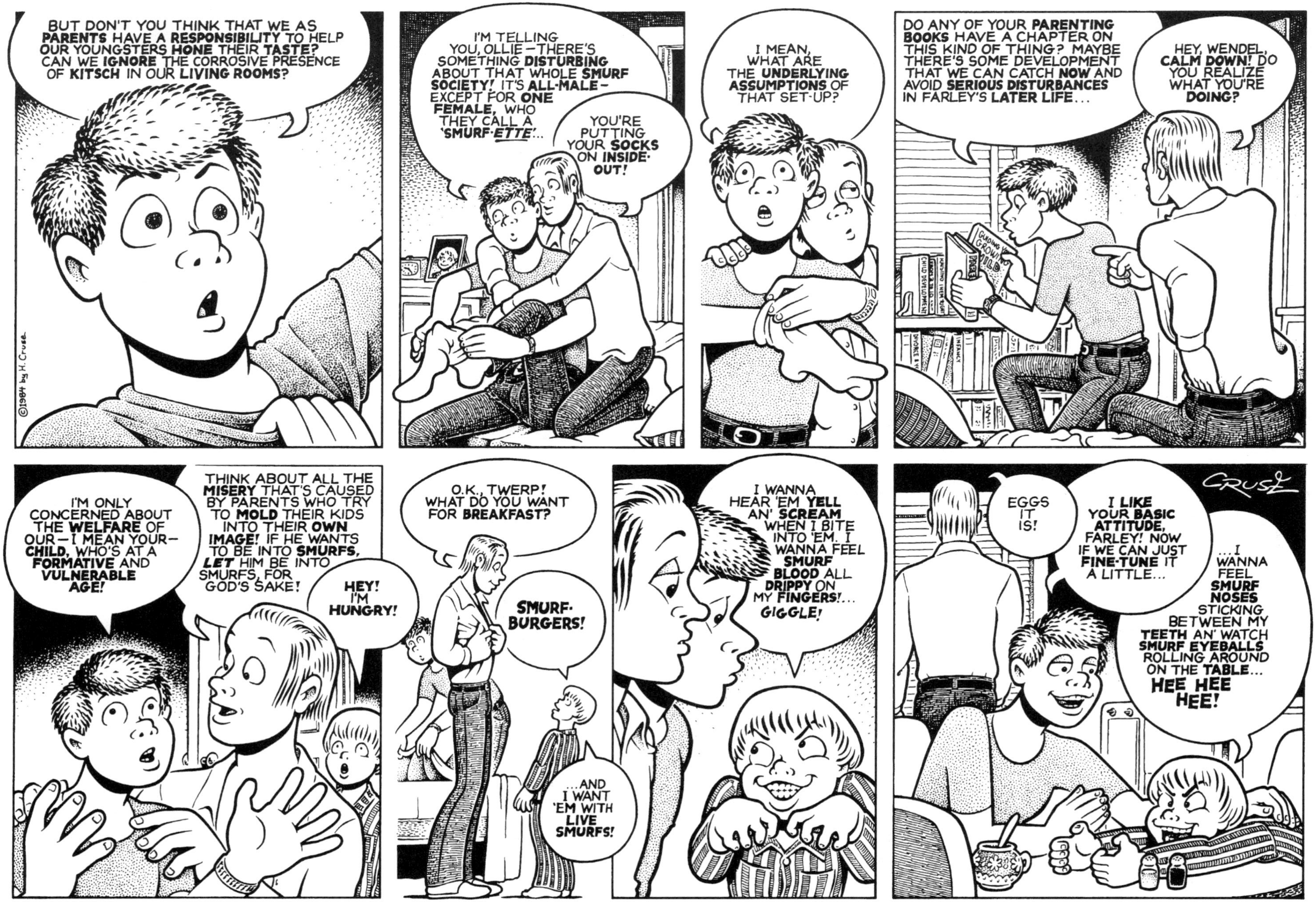
BUT DON'T YOU THINK THAT WE AS PARENTS HAVE A RESPONSIBILITY TO HELP OUR YOUNGSTERS HONE THEIR TASTE? CAN WE IGNORE THE CORROSIVE PRESENCE OF KITSCH IN OUR LIVING ROOMS?
©1984 by H. Cruse
I'M TELLING YOU, OLLIE—THERE'S SOMETHING DISTURBING ABOUT THAT WHOLE SMURF SOCIETY! IT'S ALL-MALE—EXCEPT FOR ONE FEMALE, WHO THEY CALL A 'SMURF·ETTE'...
YOU'RE PUTTING YOUR SOCKS ON INSIDE·OUT!
I MEAN, WHAT ARE THE UNDERLYING ASSUMPTIONS OF THAT SET-UP?
DO ANY OF YOUR PARENTING BOOKS HAVE A CHAPTER ON THIS KIND OF THING? MAYBE THERE'S SOME DEVELOPMENT THAT WE CAN CATCH NOW AND AVOID SERIOUS DISTURBANCES IN FARLEY'S LATER LIFE...
HEY, WENDEL, CALM DOWN! DO YOU REALIZE WHAT YOU'RE DOING?
CHILD DEVELOPMENT
INFANCY
I'M ONLY CONCERNED ABOUT THE WELFARE OF OUR—I MEAN YOUR—CHILD, WHO'S AT A FORMATIVE AND VULNERABLE AGE!
THINK ABOUT ALL THE MISERY THAT'S CAUSED BY PARENTS WHO TRY TO MOLD THEIR KIDS INTO THEIR OWN IMAGE! IF HE WANTS TO BE INTO SMURFS, LET HIM BE INTO SMURFS, FOR GOD'S SAKE!
HEY! I'M HUNGRY!
O.K., TWERP! WHAT DO YOU WANT FOR BREAKFAST?
SMURF·BURGERS!
...AND I WANT 'EM WITH LIVE SMURFS!
I WANNA HEAR 'EM YELL AN' SCREAM WHEN I BITE INTO 'EM. I WANNA FEEL SMURF BLOOD ALL DRIPPY ON MY FINGERS!... GIGGLE!
CRUSE
EGGS IT IS!
I LIKE YOUR BASIC ATTITUDE, FARLEY! NOW IF WE CAN JUST FINE·TUNE IT A LITTLE...
...I WANNA FEEL SMURF NOSES STICKING BETWEEN MY TEETH AN' WATCH SMURF EYEBALLS ROLLING AROUND ON THE TABLE... HEE HEE HEE!

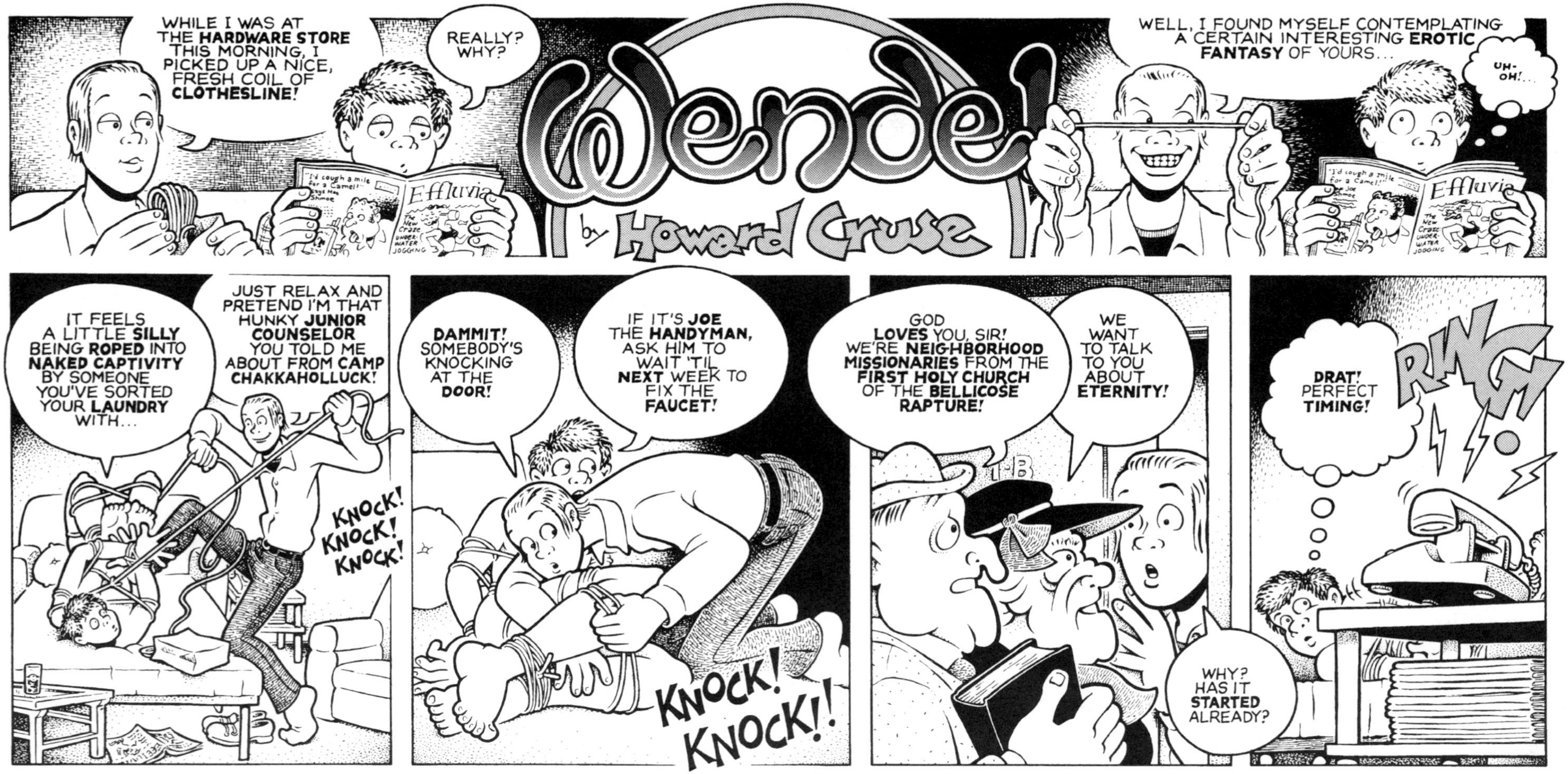
WHILE I WAS AT THE **HARDWARE STORE** THIS MORNING, I PICKED UP A NICE, FRESH COIL OF **CLOTHESLINE**!
REALLY? WHY?
Wendel
by Howard Cruse
WELL, I FOUND MYSELF CONTEMPLATING A CERTAIN INTERESTING **EROTIC FANTASY** OF YOURS...
UH-OH!...
Effluvia
IT FEELS A LITTLE **SILLY** BEING **ROPED** INTO **NAKED CAPTIVITY** BY SOMEONE YOU'VE SORTED YOUR **LAUNDRY** WITH...
JUST RELAX AND PRETEND I'M THAT HUNKY **JUNIOR COUNSELOR** YOU TOLD ME ABOUT FROM **CAMP CHAKKAHOLLUCK**!
KNOCK! KNOCK! KNOCK!
DAMMIT! SOMEBODY'S KNOCKING AT THE **DOOR**!
IF IT'S **JOE** THE **HANDYMAN**, ASK HIM TO WAIT 'TIL **NEXT** WEEK TO FIX THE **FAUCET**!
KNOCK! KNOCK!!
GOD **LOVES** YOU, SIR! WE'RE **NEIGHBORHOOD MISSIONARIES** FROM THE **FIRST HOLY CHURCH** OF THE **BELLICOSE RAPTURE**!
WE WANT TO TALK TO YOU ABOUT **ETERNITY**!
WHY? HAS IT **STARTED** ALREADY?
DRAT! PERFECT **TIMING!**
RING!

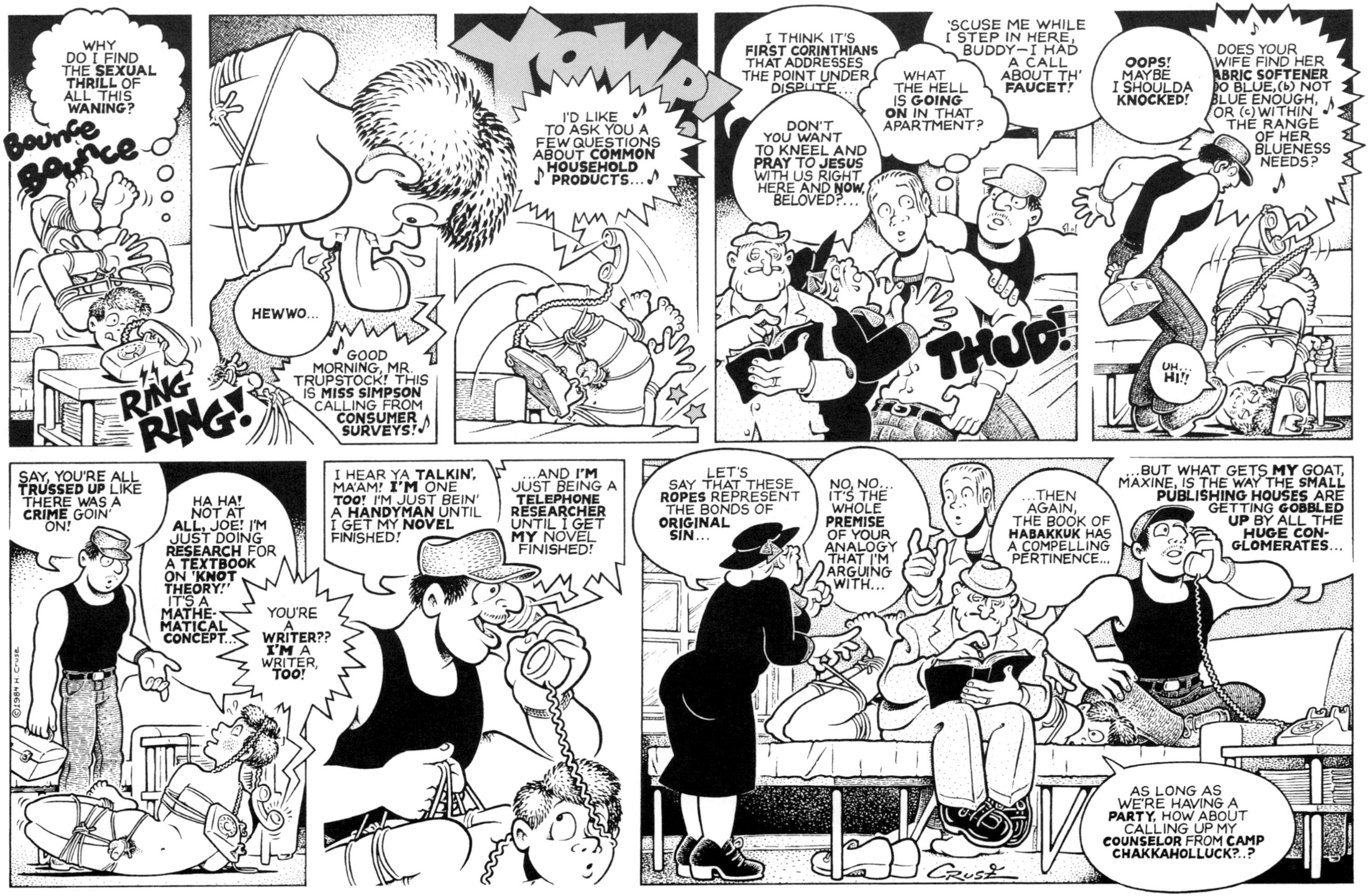
WHY DO I FIND THE **SEXUAL THRILL** OF ALL THIS **WANING**?
Bounce Bounce
RING RING!
HEWWO...
GOOD MORNING, MR. TRUPSTOCK! THIS IS **MISS SIMPSON** CALLING FROM **CONSUMER SURVEYS**!
I'D LIKE TO ASK YOU A FEW QUESTIONS ABOUT **COMMON HOUSEHOLD PRODUCTS**...
YOWP!
I THINK IT'S **FIRST CORINTHIANS** THAT ADDRESSES THE POINT UNDER DISPUTE...
DON'T YOU WANT TO KNEEL AND **PRAY TO JESUS** WITH US RIGHT HERE AND **NOW**, BELOVED?...
WHAT THE HELL IS **GOING ON** IN THAT APARTMENT?
'SCUSE ME WHILE I STEP IN HERE, BUDDY—I HAD A CALL ABOUT TH' **FAUCET**!
THUD!
OOPS! MAYBE I SHOULDA **KNOCKED!**
DOES YOUR WIFE FIND HER **FABRIC SOFTENER** (a) TOO BLUE, (b) NOT BLUE ENOUGH, OR (c) WITHIN THE RANGE OF HER BLUENESS NEEDS?
UH... **HI!!**
SAY, YOU'RE ALL **TRUSSED UP** LIKE THERE WAS A **CRIME** GOIN' ON!
HA HA! NOT AT **ALL**, JOE! I'M JUST DOING **RESEARCH** FOR A **TEXTBOOK** ON **'KNOT THEORY.'** IT'S A **MATHEMATICAL CONCEPT**...
YOU'RE A **WRITER??** **I'M** A WRITER, **TOO!**
©1984 H. CRUSE.
I HEAR YA **TALKIN'**, MA'AM! **I'M** ONE **TOO!** I'M JUST BEIN' A **HANDYMAN** UNTIL I GET MY **NOVEL** FINISHED!
...AND **I'M** JUST BEING A **TELEPHONE RESEARCHER** UNTIL I GET **MY** NOVEL FINISHED!
LET'S SAY THAT THESE **ROPES** REPRESENT THE BONDS OF **ORIGINAL SIN**...
NO, NO... IT'S THE WHOLE **PREMISE** OF YOUR ANALOGY THAT I'M ARGUING WITH...
...THEN AGAIN, THE BOOK OF **HABAKKUK** HAS A COMPELLING PERTINENCE...
...BUT WHAT GETS **MY** GOAT, MAXINE, IS THE WAY THE **SMALL PUBLISHING HOUSES** ARE GETTING **GOBBLED UP** BY ALL THE **HUGE CONGLOMERATES**...
AS LONG AS WE'RE HAVING A **PARTY**, HOW ABOUT CALLING UP MY **COUNSELOR** FROM **CAMP CHAKKAHOLLUCK?**..?
CRUSE

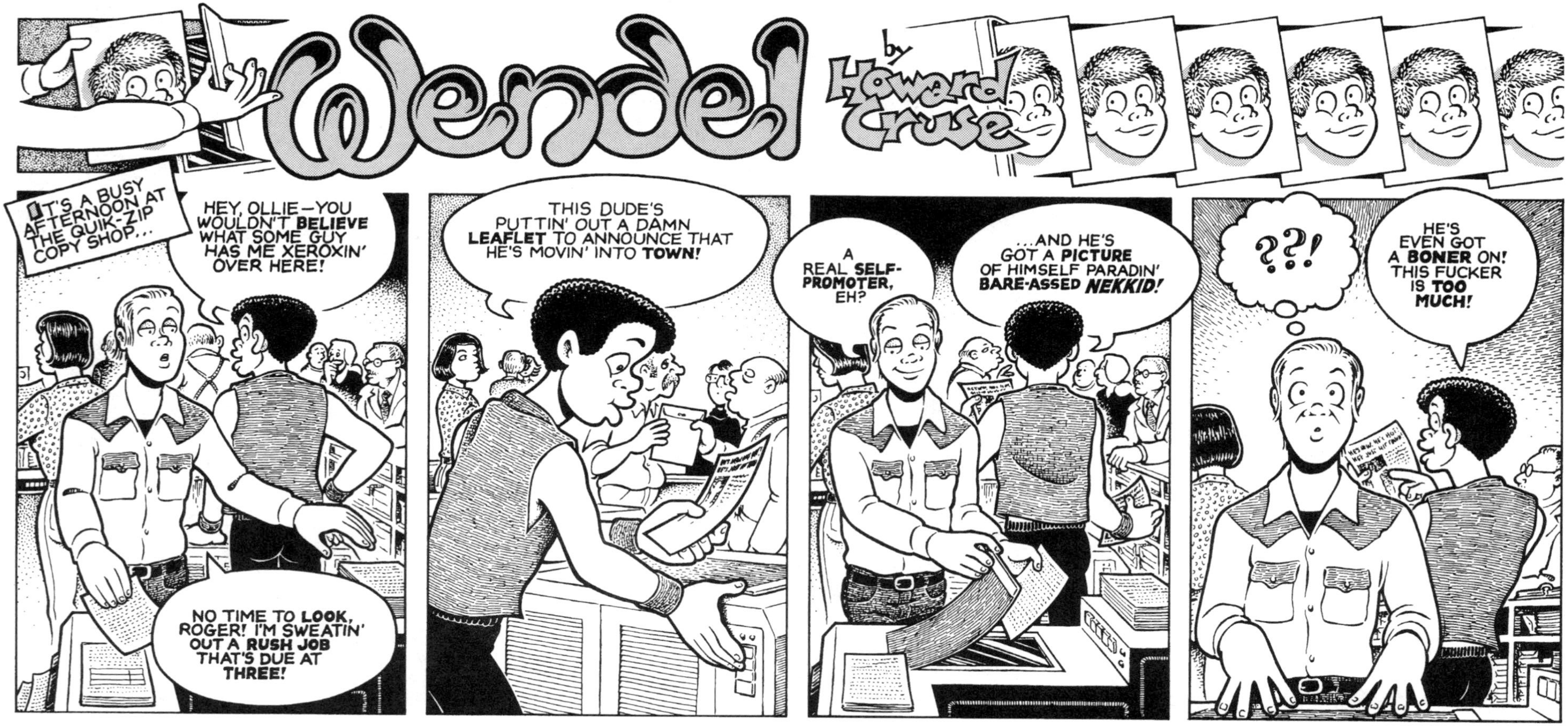
Wendel
by Howard Cruse
IT'S A BUSY AFTERNOON AT THE QUIK-ZIP COPY SHOP...
HEY, OLLIE—YOU WOULDN'T **BELIEVE** WHAT SOME GUY HAS ME XEROXIN' OVER HERE!
NO TIME TO **LOOK**, ROGER! I'M SWEATIN' OUT A **RUSH JOB** THAT'S DUE AT **THREE!**
THIS DUDE'S PUTTIN' OUT A DAMN **LEAFLET** TO ANNOUNCE THAT HE'S MOVIN' INTO **TOWN!**
A REAL **SELF-PROMOTER**, EH?
...AND HE'S GOT A **PICTURE** OF HIMSELF PARADIN' **BARE-ASSED *NEKKID!***
??!
HE'S EVEN GOT A **BONER** ON! THIS FUCKER IS **TOO MUCH!**

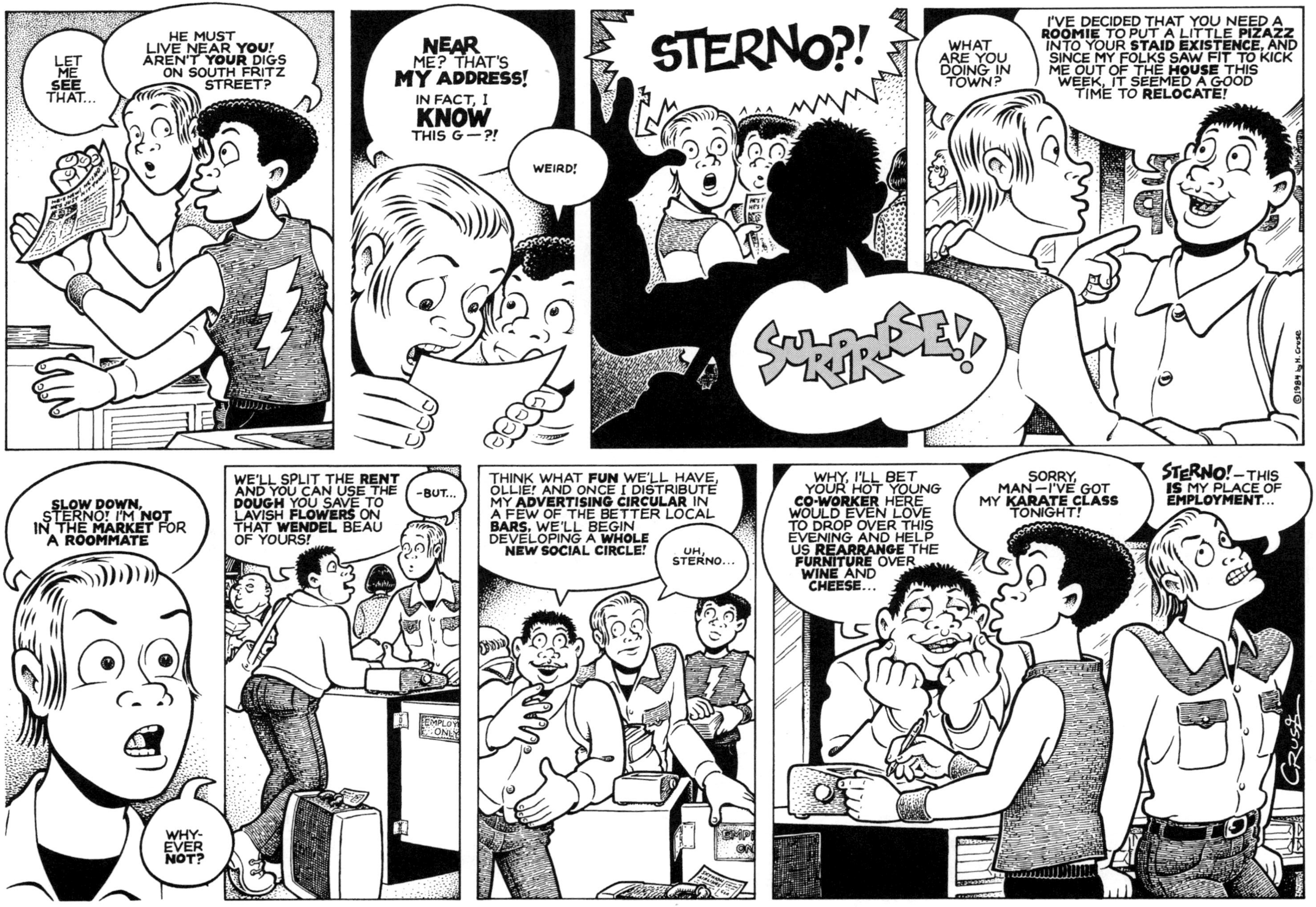
LET ME SEE THAT...
HE MUST LIVE NEAR YOU! AREN'T YOUR DIGS ON SOUTH FRITZ STREET?
NEAR ME? THAT'S MY ADDRESS! IN FACT, I KNOW THIS G—?!
WEIRD!
STERNO?!
SURPRISE!!
WHAT ARE YOU DOING IN TOWN?
I'VE DECIDED THAT YOU NEED A ROOMIE TO PUT A LITTLE PIZAZZ INTO YOUR STAID EXISTENCE, AND SINCE MY FOLKS SAW FIT TO KICK ME OUT OF THE HOUSE THIS WEEK, IT SEEMED A GOOD TIME TO RELOCATE!
©1984 by H. Cruse
SLOW DOWN, STERNO! I'M NOT IN THE MARKET FOR A ROOMMATE
WHY-EVER NOT?
WE'LL SPLIT THE RENT AND YOU CAN USE THE DOUGH YOU SAVE TO LAVISH FLOWERS ON THAT WENDEL BEAU OF YOURS!
-BUT...
THINK WHAT FUN WE'LL HAVE, OLLIE! AND ONCE I DISTRIBUTE MY ADVERTISING CIRCULAR IN A FEW OF THE BETTER LOCAL BARS, WE'LL BEGIN DEVELOPING A WHOLE NEW SOCIAL CIRCLE!
UH, STERNO...
WHY, I'LL BET YOUR HOT YOUNG CO-WORKER HERE WOULD EVEN LOVE TO DROP OVER THIS EVENING AND HELP US REARRANGE THE FURNITURE OVER WINE AND CHEESE...
SORRY, MAN—I'VE GOT MY KARATE CLASS TONIGHT!
STERNO!—THIS IS MY PLACE OF EMPLOYMENT...
CRUSE

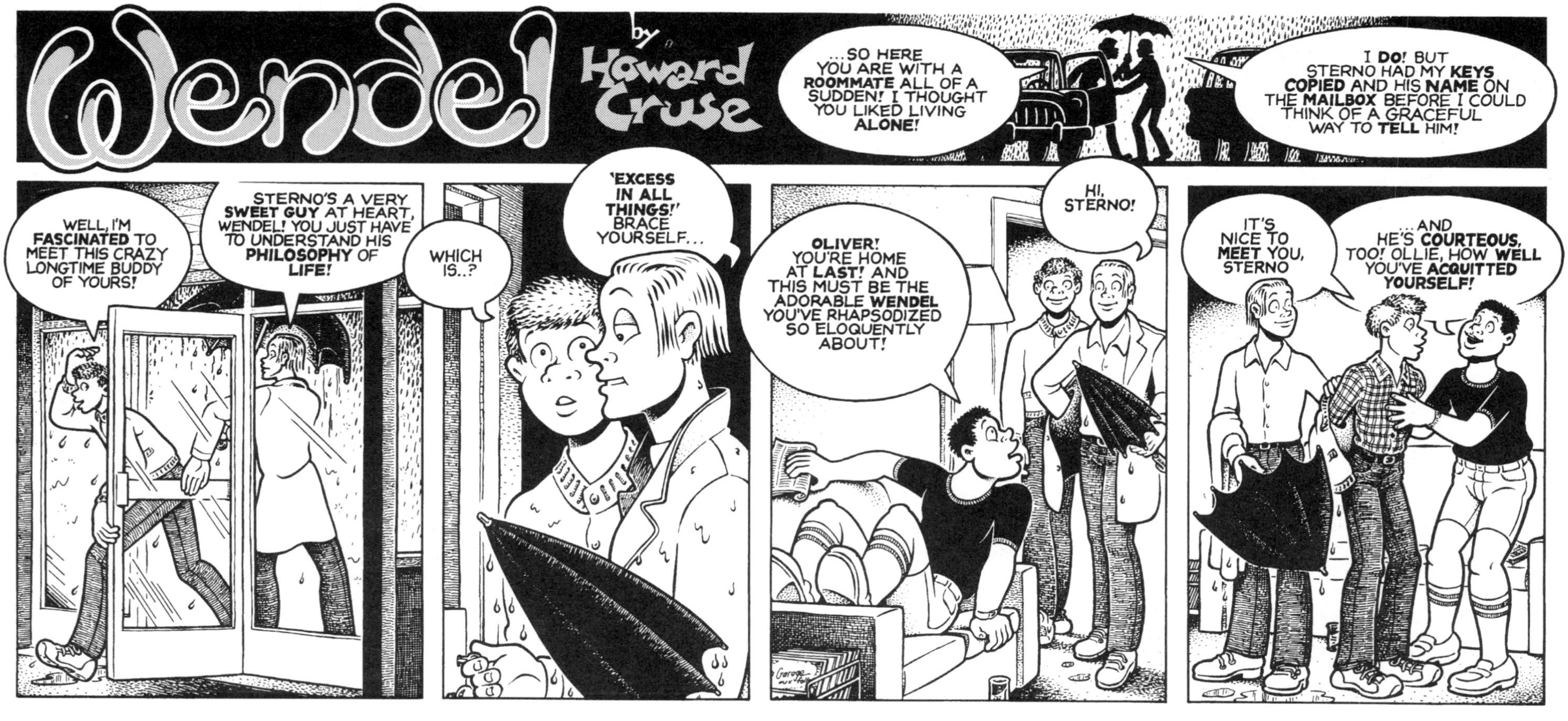
Wendel
by Howard Cruse
...SO HERE YOU ARE WITH A **ROOMMATE** ALL OF A SUDDEN! I THOUGHT YOU LIKED LIVING **ALONE**!
I **DO**! BUT STERNO HAD MY **KEYS COPIED** AND HIS **NAME** ON THE **MAILBOX** BEFORE I COULD THINK OF A GRACEFUL WAY TO **TELL** HIM!
WELL, I'M **FASCINATED** TO MEET THIS CRAZY LONGTIME BUDDY OF YOURS!
STERNO'S A VERY **SWEET GUY** AT HEART, WENDEL! YOU JUST HAVE TO UNDERSTAND HIS **PHILOSOPHY** OF **LIFE**!
WHICH IS..?
'EXCESS IN ALL THINGS!' BRACE YOURSELF...
OLIVER! YOU'RE HOME AT **LAST**! AND THIS MUST BE THE ADORABLE **WENDEL** YOU'VE RHAPSODIZED SO ELOQUENTLY ABOUT!
HI, STERNO!
IT'S NICE TO **MEET** YOU, STERNO
...AND HE'S **COURTEOUS**, TOO! OLLIE, HOW **WELL** YOU'VE **ACQUITTED YOURSELF**!

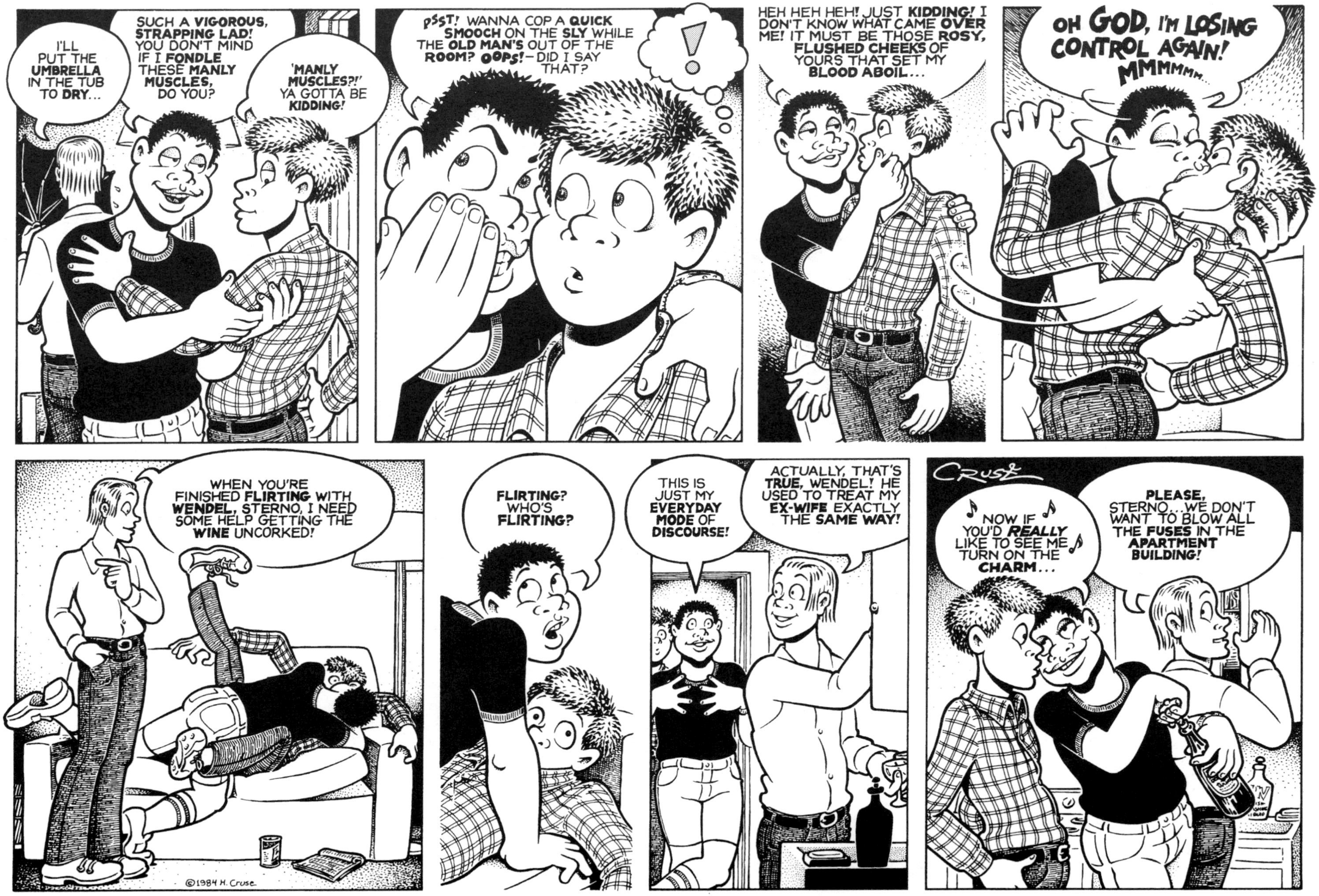
I'LL PUT THE **UMBRELLA** IN THE TUB TO **DRY**...
SUCH A **VIGOROUS, STRAPPING LAD!** YOU DON'T MIND IF I **FONDLE** THESE **MANLY MUSCLES,** DO YOU?
'MANLY MUSCLES?!' YA GOTTA BE **KIDDING!**
PSST! WANNA COP A **QUICK SMOOCH** ON THE **SLY** WHILE THE **OLD MAN'S** OUT OF THE **ROOM? OOPS!**—DID I SAY THAT?
!
HEH HEH HEH! JUST **KIDDING!** I DON'T KNOW WHAT CAME **OVER** ME! IT MUST BE THOSE **ROSY, FLUSHED CHEEKS** OF YOURS THAT SET MY **BLOOD ABOIL**...
OH **GOD,** I'M **LOSING CONTROL AGAIN!** MMMMMM...
WHEN YOU'RE FINISHED **FLIRTING** WITH **WENDEL,** STERNO, I NEED SOME HELP GETTING THE **WINE** UNCORKED!
©1984 H. Cruse
FLIRTING? WHO'S **FLIRTING?**
THIS IS JUST MY **EVERYDAY MODE** OF **DISCOURSE!**
ACTUALLY, THAT'S **TRUE,** WENDEL! HE USED TO TREAT MY **EX-WIFE** EXACTLY THE **SAME WAY!**
CRUSE
♪ NOW IF YOU'D ***REALLY*** LIKE TO SEE ME TURN ON THE **CHARM**... ♪
PLEASE, STERNO...WE DON'T WANT TO BLOW ALL THE **FUSES** IN THE **APARTMENT BUILDING!**

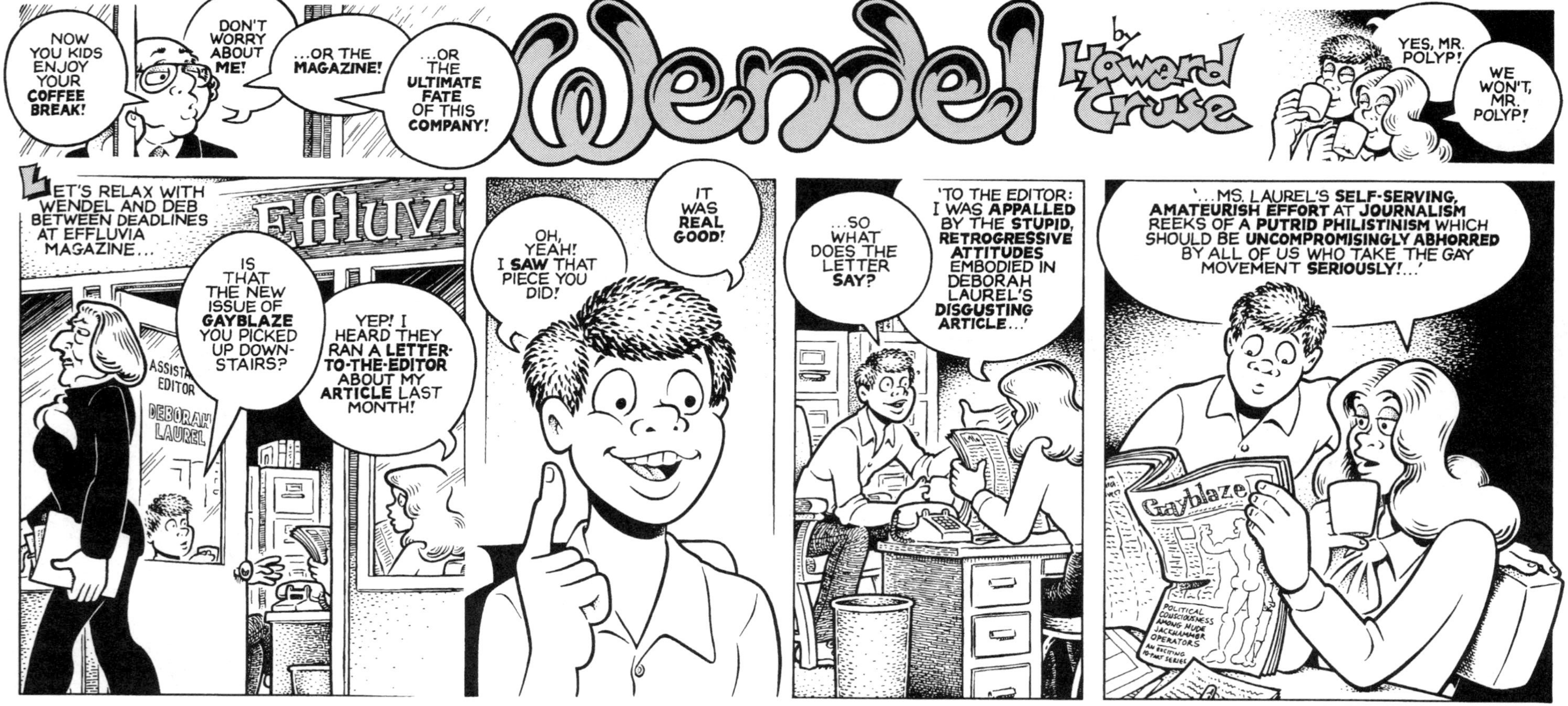
NOW YOU KIDS ENJOY YOUR COFFEE BREAK!
DON'T WORRY ABOUT ME!
...OR THE MAGAZINE!
...OR THE ULTIMATE FATE OF THIS COMPANY!
Wendel
by Howard Cruse
YES, MR. POLYP!
WE WON'T, MR. POLYP!
LET'S RELAX WITH WENDEL AND DEB BETWEEN DEADLINES AT EFFLUVIA MAGAZINE...
Effluvi
ASSISTA EDITOR
DEBORAH LAUREL
IS THAT THE NEW ISSUE OF GAYBLAZE YOU PICKED UP DOWN-STAIRS?
YEP! I HEARD THEY RAN A LETTER-TO-THE-EDITOR ABOUT MY ARTICLE LAST MONTH!
OH, YEAH! I SAW THAT PIECE YOU DID!
IT WAS REAL GOOD!
...SO WHAT DOES THE LETTER SAY?
'TO THE EDITOR: I WAS APPALLED BY THE STUPID, RETROGRESSIVE ATTITUDES EMBODIED IN DEBORAH LAUREL'S DISGUSTING ARTICLE...'
'...MS. LAUREL'S SELF-SERVING, AMATEURISH EFFORT AT JOURNALISM REEKS OF A PUTRID PHILISTINISM WHICH SHOULD BE UNCOMPROMISINGLY ABHORRED BY ALL OF US WHO TAKE THE GAY MOVEMENT SERIOUSLY!...'
Gayblaze
POLITICAL CONSCIOUSNESS AMONG NUDE JACKHAMMER OPERATORS
AN EXCITING 10-PART SERIES

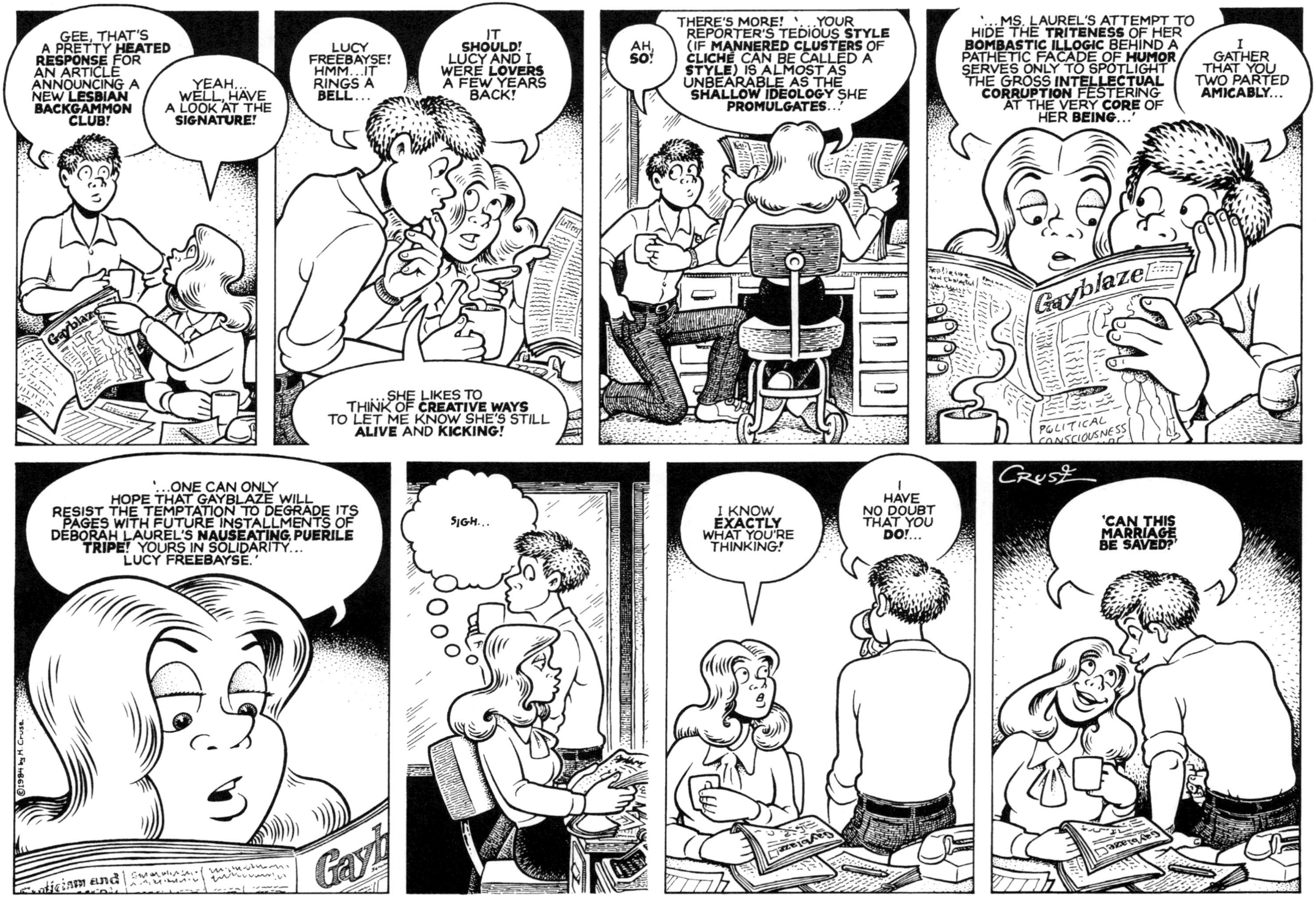
GEE, THAT'S A PRETTY HEATED RESPONSE FOR AN ARTICLE ANNOUNCING A NEW LESBIAN BACKGAMMON CLUB!
YEAH... WELL, HAVE A LOOK AT THE SIGNATURE!
Gayblaze
LUCY FREEBAYSE! HMM...IT RINGS A BELL...
IT SHOULD! LUCY AND I WERE LOVERS A FEW YEARS BACK!
...SHE LIKES TO THINK OF CREATIVE WAYS TO LET ME KNOW SHE'S STILL ALIVE AND KICKING!
AH, SO!
THERE'S MORE! '...YOUR REPORTER'S TEDIOUS STYLE (IF MANNERED CLUSTERS OF CLICHÉ CAN BE CALLED A STYLE) IS ALMOST AS UNBEARABLE AS THE SHALLOW IDEOLOGY SHE PROMULGATES...'
'...MS. LAUREL'S ATTEMPT TO HIDE THE TRITENESS OF HER BOMBASTIC ILLOGIC BEHIND A PATHETIC FACADE OF HUMOR SERVES ONLY TO SPOTLIGHT THE GROSS INTELLECTUAL CORRUPTION FESTERING AT THE VERY CORE OF HER BEING...'
I GATHER THAT YOU TWO PARTED AMICABLY...
Gayblaze
POLITICAL CONSCIOUSNESS
'...ONE CAN ONLY HOPE THAT GAYBLAZE WILL RESIST THE TEMPTATION TO DEGRADE ITS PAGES WITH FUTURE INSTALLMENTS OF DEBORAH LAUREL'S NAUSEATING, PUERILE TRIPE! YOURS IN SOLIDARITY... LUCY FREEBAYSE.'
©1984 by H. Cruse
SIGH...
I KNOW EXACTLY WHAT YOU'RE THINKING!
I HAVE NO DOUBT THAT YOU DO!...
CRUSE
'CAN THIS MARRIAGE BE SAVED?'

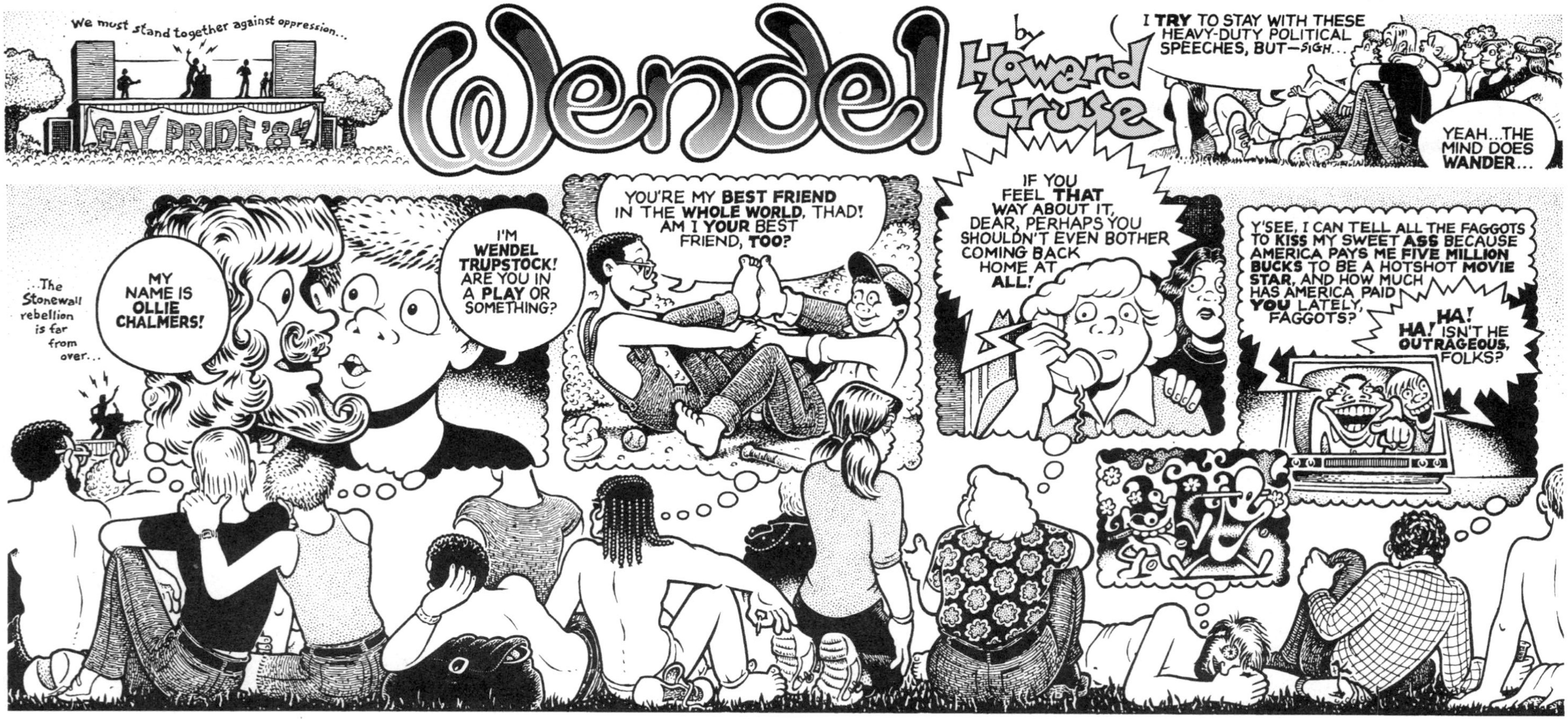
We must stand together against oppression...
GAY PRIDE '84
Wendel
by Howard Cruse
I TRY TO STAY WITH THESE HEAVY-DUTY POLITICAL SPEECHES, BUT—SIGH...
YEAH...THE MIND DOES WANDER...
...The Stonewall rebellion is far from over...
MY NAME IS OLLIE CHALMERS!
I'M WENDEL TRUPSTOCK! ARE YOU IN A PLAY OR SOMETHING?
YOU'RE MY BEST FRIEND IN THE WHOLE WORLD, THAD! AM I YOUR BEST FRIEND, TOO?
IF YOU FEEL THAT WAY ABOUT IT, DEAR, PERHAPS YOU SHOULDN'T EVEN BOTHER COMING BACK HOME AT ALL!
Y'SEE, I CAN TELL ALL THE FAGGOTS TO KISS MY SWEET ASS BECAUSE AMERICA PAYS ME FIVE MILLION BUCKS TO BE A HOTSHOT MOVIE STAR, AND HOW MUCH HAS AMERICA PAID YOU LATELY, FAGGOTS?
HA! HA! ISN'T HE OUTRAGEOUS, FOLKS?

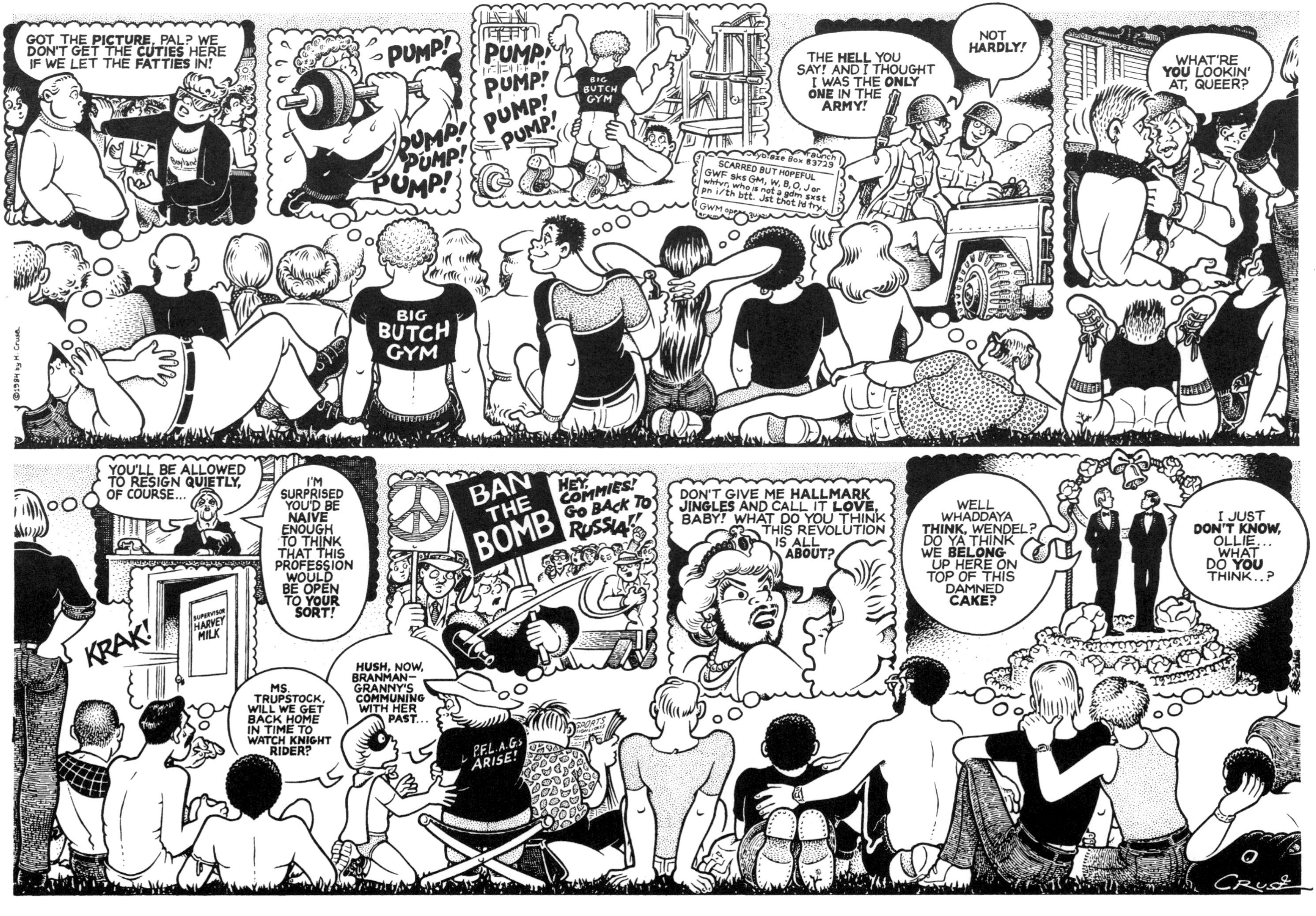
GOT THE PICTURE, PAL? WE DON'T GET THE CUTIES HERE IF WE LET THE FATTIES IN!
Boyland
PUMP!
PUMP! PUMP! PUMP!
PUMP! PUMP! PUMP! PUMP!
BIG BUTCH GYM
SCARRED BUT HOPEFUL
GWF sks GM, W, B, O, J or whtvr, who is not a gdm sxst pn i/'th btt. Jst thot I'd try.
Box 83729
THE HELL YOU SAY! AND I THOUGHT I WAS THE ONLY ONE IN THE ARMY!
NOT HARDLY!
WHAT'RE YOU LOOKIN' AT, QUEER?
BIG BUTCH GYM
©1984 by H. Cruse
YOU'LL BE ALLOWED TO RESIGN QUIETLY, OF COURSE...
I'M SURPRISED YOU'D BE NAIVE ENOUGH TO THINK THAT THIS PROFESSION WOULD BE OPEN TO YOUR SORT!
SUPERVISOR HARVEY MILK
KRAK!
BAN THE BOMB
HEY, COMMIES! GO BACK TO RUSSIA!!
MS. TRUPSTOCK, WILL WE GET BACK HOME IN TIME TO WATCH KNIGHT RIDER?
HUSH, NOW, BRANMAN— GRANNY'S COMMUNING WITH HER PAST...
P.F.L.A.G.s ARISE!
SPORTS
DON'T GIVE ME HALLMARK JINGLES AND CALL IT LOVE, BABY! WHAT DO YOU THINK THIS REVOLUTION IS ALL ABOUT?
WELL WHADDAYA THINK, WENDEL? DO YA THINK WE BELONG UP HERE ON TOP OF THIS DAMNED CAKE?
I JUST DON'T KNOW, OLLIE... WHAT DO YOU THINK..?
CRUSE

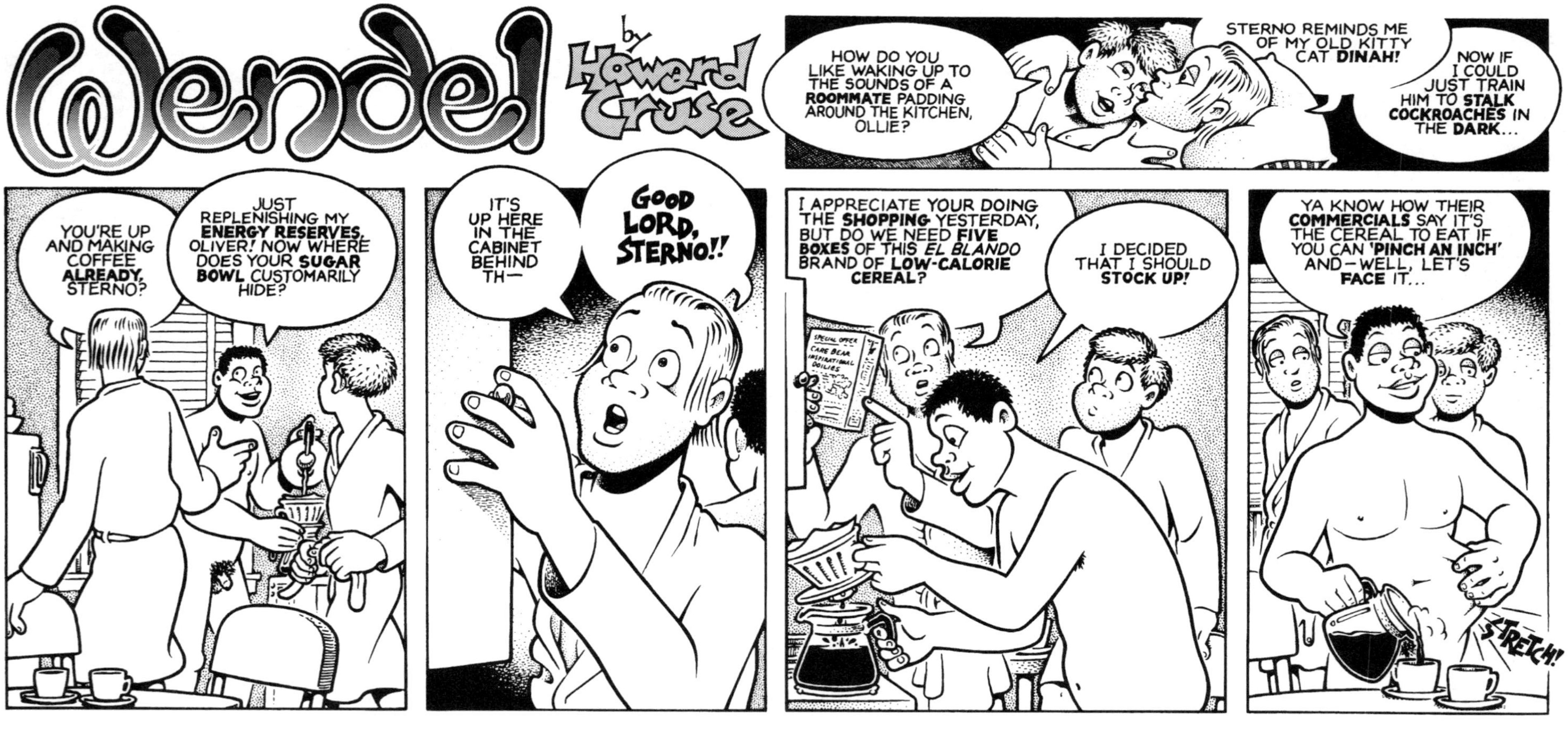
Wendel
by Howard Cruse
HOW DO YOU LIKE WAKING UP TO THE SOUNDS OF A **ROOMMATE** PADDING AROUND THE KITCHEN, OLLIE?
STERNO REMINDS ME OF MY OLD KITTY CAT **DINAH!**
NOW IF I COULD JUST TRAIN HIM TO **STALK COCKROACHES** IN THE **DARK**...
YOU'RE UP AND MAKING COFFEE **ALREADY,** STERNO?
JUST REPLENISHING MY **ENERGY RESERVES,** OLIVER! NOW WHERE DOES YOUR **SUGAR BOWL** CUSTOMARILY HIDE?
IT'S UP HERE IN THE CABINET BEHIND TH—
GOOD LORD, STERNO!!
I APPRECIATE YOUR DOING THE **SHOPPING** YESTERDAY, BUT DO WE NEED **FIVE BOXES** OF THIS *EL BLANDO* BRAND OF **LOW-CALORIE CEREAL?**
SPECIAL OFFER
CARE BEAR INSPIRATIONAL DOILIES
I DECIDED THAT I SHOULD **STOCK UP!**
YA KNOW HOW THEIR **COMMERCIALS** SAY IT'S THE CEREAL TO EAT IF YOU CAN **'PINCH AN INCH'** AND—WELL, LET'S **FACE** IT...
STRETCH!

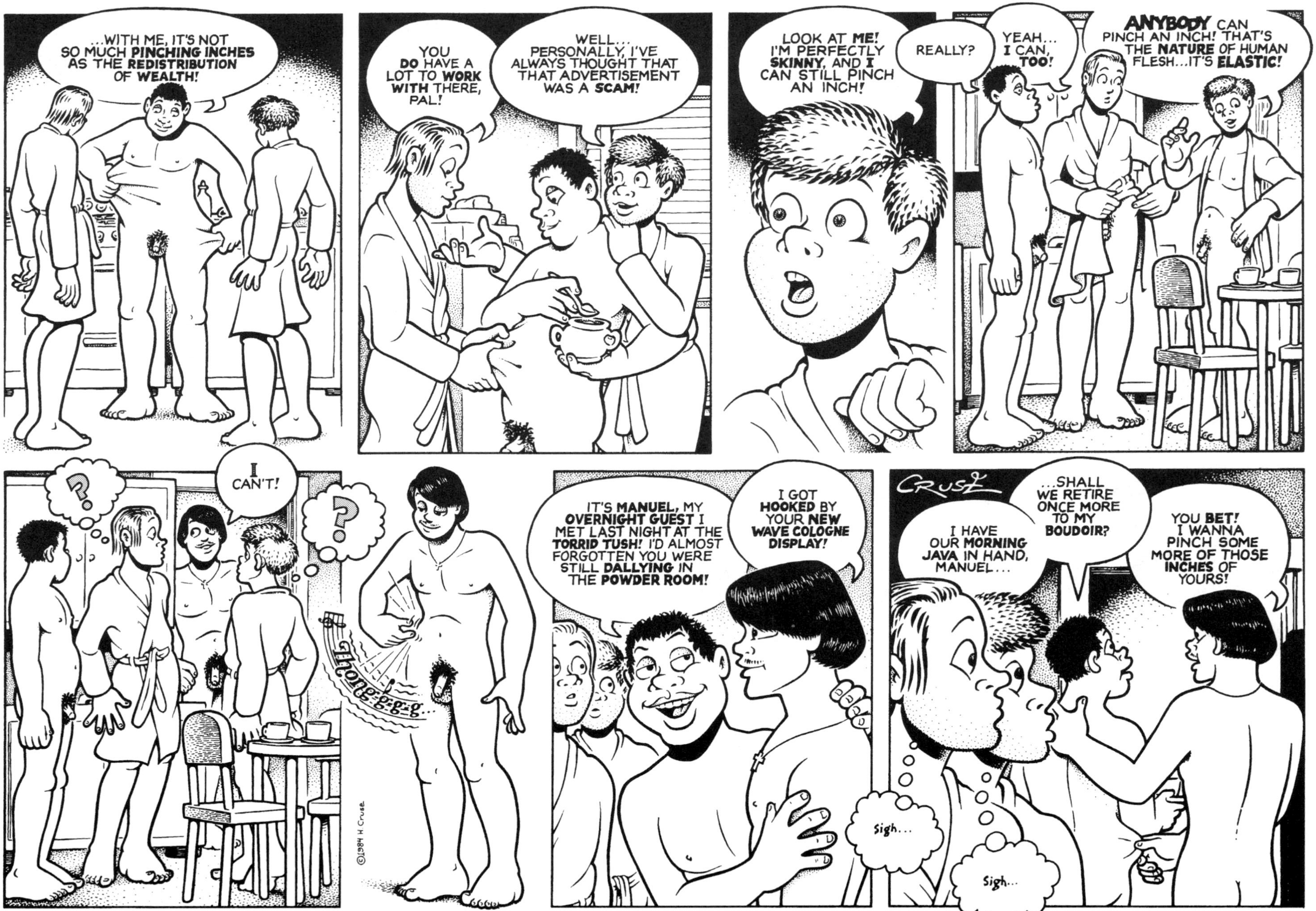

...WITH ME, IT'S NOT SO MUCH PINCHING INCHES AS THE REDISTRIBUTION OF WEALTH!
YOU DO HAVE A LOT TO WORK WITH THERE, PAL!
WELL... PERSONALLY, I'VE ALWAYS THOUGHT THAT THAT ADVERTISEMENT WAS A SCAM!
LOOK AT ME! I'M PERFECTLY SKINNY, AND I CAN STILL PINCH AN INCH!
REALLY?
YEAH... I CAN, TOO!
ANYBODY CAN PINCH AN INCH! THAT'S THE NATURE OF HUMAN FLESH...IT'S ELASTIC!
?
I CAN'T!
?
Thong-g-g-g...
©1984 H Cruse
IT'S MANUEL, MY OVERNIGHT GUEST I MET LAST NIGHT AT THE TORRID TUSH! I'D ALMOST FORGOTTEN YOU WERE STILL DALLYING IN THE POWDER ROOM!
I GOT HOOKED BY YOUR NEW WAVE COLOGNE DISPLAY!
CRUSE
I HAVE OUR MORNING JAVA IN HAND, MANUEL...
...SHALL WE RETIRE ONCE MORE TO MY BOUDOIR?
YOU BET! I WANNA PINCH SOME MORE OF THOSE INCHES OF YOURS!
Sigh...
Sigh...

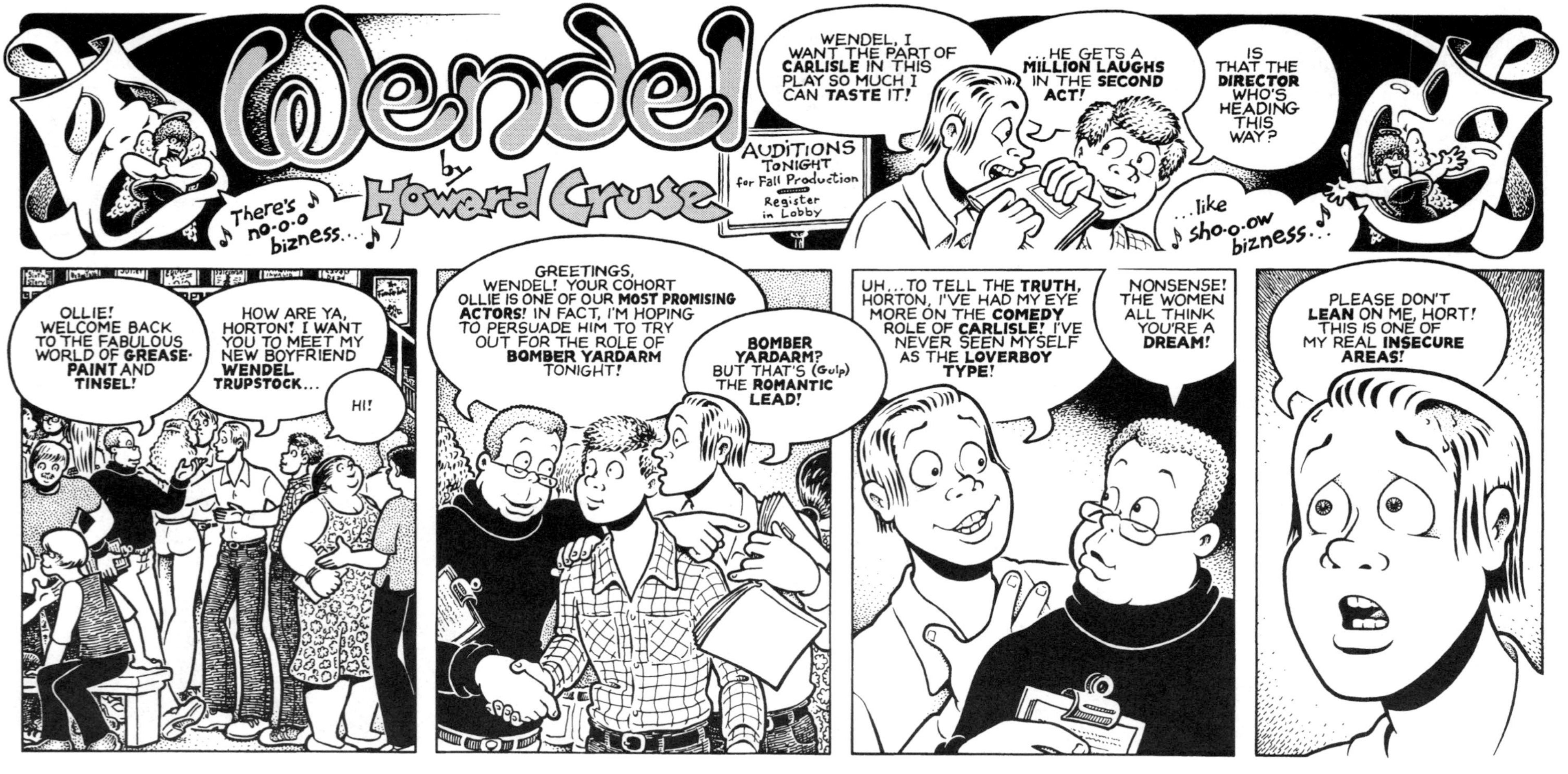
Wendel
by Howard Cruse
There's no-o-o bizness...
AUDITIONS TONIGHT for Fall Production
Register in Lobby
WENDEL, I WANT THE PART OF CARLISLE IN THIS PLAY SO MUCH I CAN TASTE IT!
...HE GETS A MILLION LAUGHS IN THE SECOND ACT!
IS THAT THE DIRECTOR WHO'S HEADING THIS WAY?
...like sho-o-ow bizness...
OLLIE! WELCOME BACK TO THE FABULOUS WORLD OF GREASE-PAINT AND TINSEL!
HOW ARE YA, HORTON! I WANT YOU TO MEET MY NEW BOYFRIEND WENDEL TRUPSTOCK...
HI!
GREETINGS, WENDEL! YOUR COHORT OLLIE IS ONE OF OUR MOST PROMISING ACTORS! IN FACT, I'M HOPING TO PERSUADE HIM TO TRY OUT FOR THE ROLE OF BOMBER YARDARM TONIGHT!
BOMBER YARDARM? BUT THAT'S (Gulp) THE ROMANTIC LEAD!
UH...TO TELL THE TRUTH, HORTON, I'VE HAD MY EYE MORE ON THE COMEDY ROLE OF CARLISLE! I'VE NEVER SEEN MYSELF AS THE LOVERBOY TYPE!
NONSENSE! THE WOMEN ALL THINK YOU'RE A DREAM!
PLEASE DON'T LEAN ON ME, HORT! THIS IS ONE OF MY REAL INSECURE AREAS!

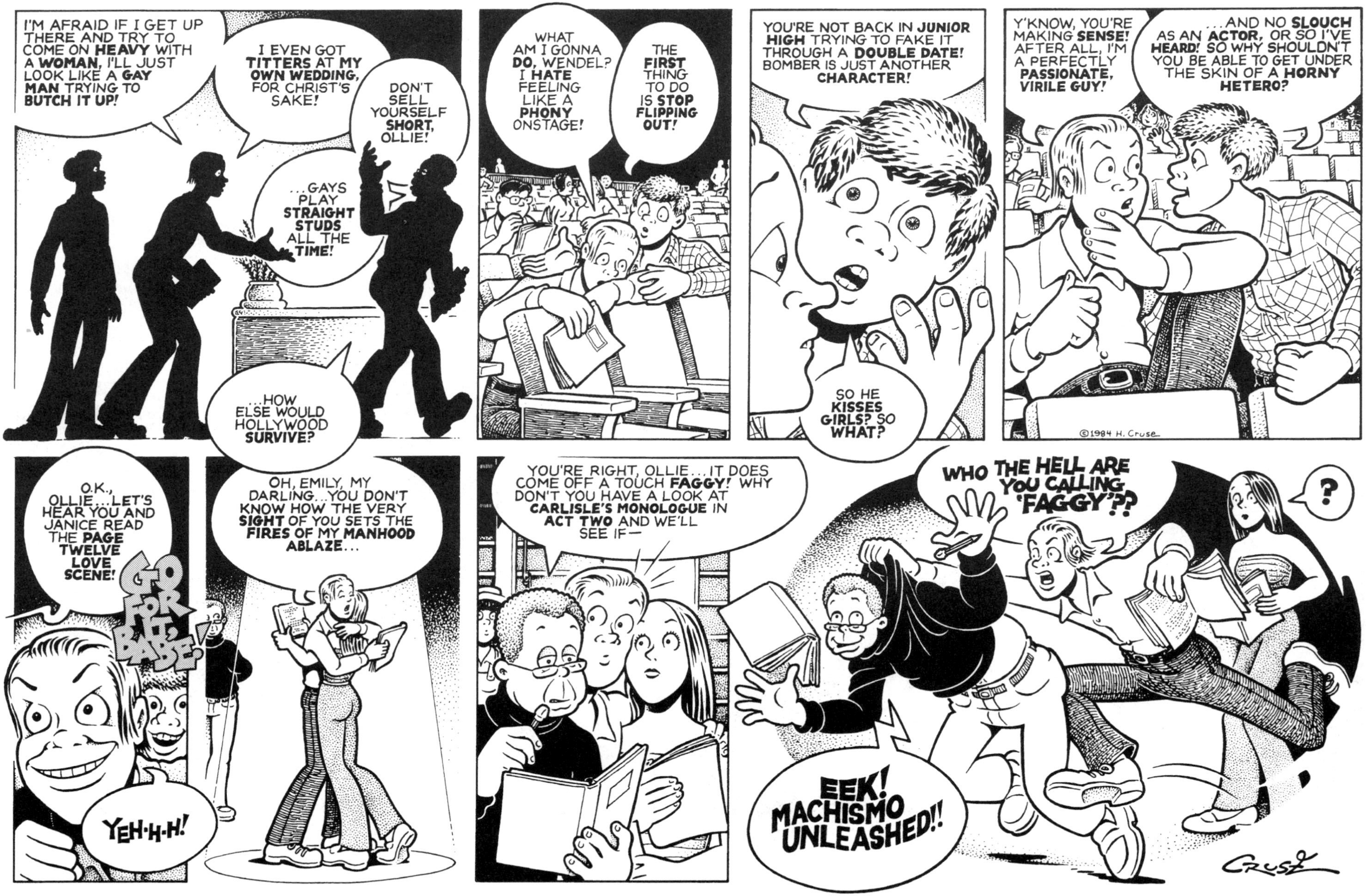
I'M AFRAID IF I GET UP THERE AND TRY TO COME ON **HEAVY** WITH A **WOMAN**, I'LL JUST LOOK LIKE A **GAY MAN** TRYING TO **BUTCH IT UP!**
I EVEN GOT **TITTERS AT MY OWN WEDDING**, FOR CHRIST'S SAKE!
DON'T SELL YOURSELF **SHORT**, OLLIE!
...GAYS PLAY **STRAIGHT STUDS** ALL THE **TIME!**
...HOW ELSE WOULD HOLLYWOOD **SURVIVE?**
WHAT AM I GONNA **DO**, WENDEL? **I HATE** FEELING LIKE A **PHONY** ONSTAGE!
THE **FIRST** THING TO DO IS **STOP FLIPPING OUT!**
YOU'RE NOT BACK IN **JUNIOR HIGH** TRYING TO FAKE IT THROUGH A **DOUBLE DATE!** BOMBER IS JUST ANOTHER **CHARACTER!**
SO HE **KISSES GIRLS?** SO **WHAT?**
Y'KNOW, YOU'RE MAKING **SENSE!** AFTER ALL, I'M A PERFECTLY **PASSIONATE, VIRILE GUY!**
...AND NO **SLOUCH** AS AN **ACTOR**, OR SO I'VE **HEARD!** SO WHY SHOULDN'T YOU BE ABLE TO GET UNDER THE SKIN OF A **HORNY HETERO?**
©1984 H. Cruse
O.K., OLLIE...LET'S HEAR YOU AND JANICE READ THE **PAGE TWELVE LOVE SCENE!**
GO FOR IT, BABE!
YEH-H-H!
OH, EMILY, MY DARLING...YOU DON'T KNOW HOW THE VERY **SIGHT** OF YOU SETS THE **FIRES OF MY MANHOOD ABLAZE**...
YOU'RE RIGHT, OLLIE...IT DOES COME OFF A TOUCH **FAGGY!** WHY DON'T YOU HAVE A LOOK AT **CARLISLE'S MONOLOGUE** IN **ACT TWO** AND WE'LL SEE IF—
WHO THE HELL ARE YOU CALLING 'FAGGY'??
?
EEK! MACHISMO UNLEASHED!!
CRUSE

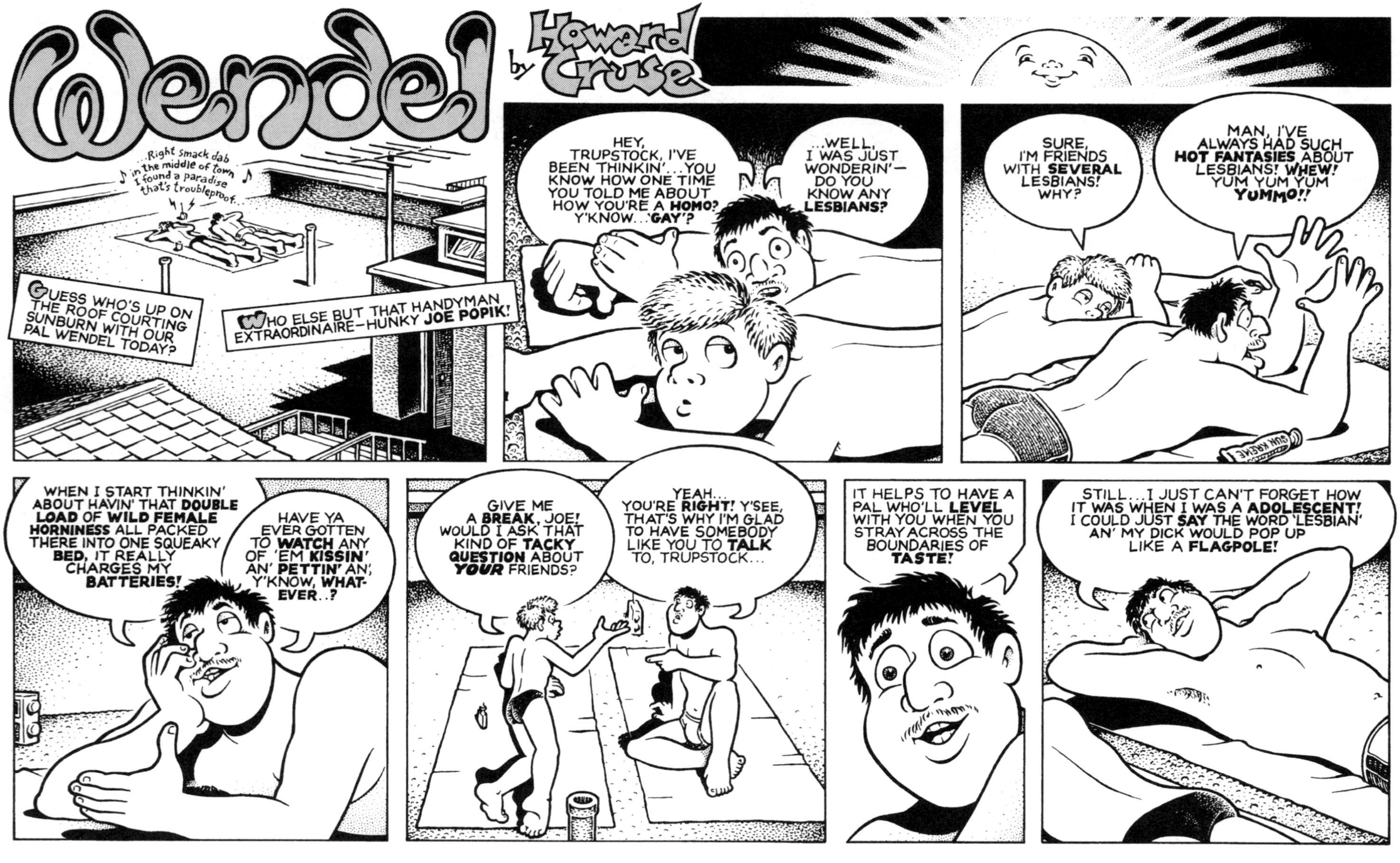
Wendel
by Howard Cruse
...Right smack dab in the middle of town I found a paradise that's troubleproof...
GUESS WHO'S UP ON THE ROOF COURTING SUNBURN WITH OUR PAL WENDEL TODAY?
WHO ELSE BUT THAT HANDYMAN EXTRAORDINAIRE—HUNKY JOE POPIK!
HEY, TRUPSTOCK, I'VE BEEN THINKIN'... YOU KNOW HOW ONE TIME YOU TOLD ME ABOUT HOW YOU'RE A HOMO? Y'KNOW... 'GAY'?
...WELL, I WAS JUST WONDERIN'— DO YOU KNOW ANY LESBIANS?
SURE, I'M FRIENDS WITH SEVERAL LESBIANS! WHY?
MAN, I'VE ALWAYS HAD SUCH HOT FANTASIES ABOUT LESBIANS! WHEW! YUM YUM YUM YUMMO!!
SUN KREME
WHEN I START THINKIN' ABOUT HAVIN' THAT DOUBLE LOAD OF WILD FEMALE HORNINESS ALL PACKED THERE INTO ONE SQUEAKY BED, IT REALLY CHARGES MY BATTERIES!
HAVE YA EVER GOTTEN TO WATCH ANY OF 'EM KISSIN' AN' PETTIN' AN', Y'KNOW, WHAT-EVER..?
GIVE ME A BREAK, JOE! WOULD I ASK THAT KIND OF TACKY QUESTION ABOUT YOUR FRIENDS?
YEAH... YOU'RE RIGHT! Y'SEE, THAT'S WHY I'M GLAD TO HAVE SOMEBODY LIKE YOU TO TALK TO, TRUPSTOCK...
IT HELPS TO HAVE A PAL WHO'LL LEVEL WITH YOU WHEN YOU STRAY ACROSS THE BOUNDARIES OF TASTE!
STILL... I JUST CAN'T FORGET HOW IT WAS WHEN I WAS A ADOLESCENT! I COULD JUST SAY THE WORD 'LESBIAN' AN' MY DICK WOULD POP UP LIKE A FLAGPOLE!

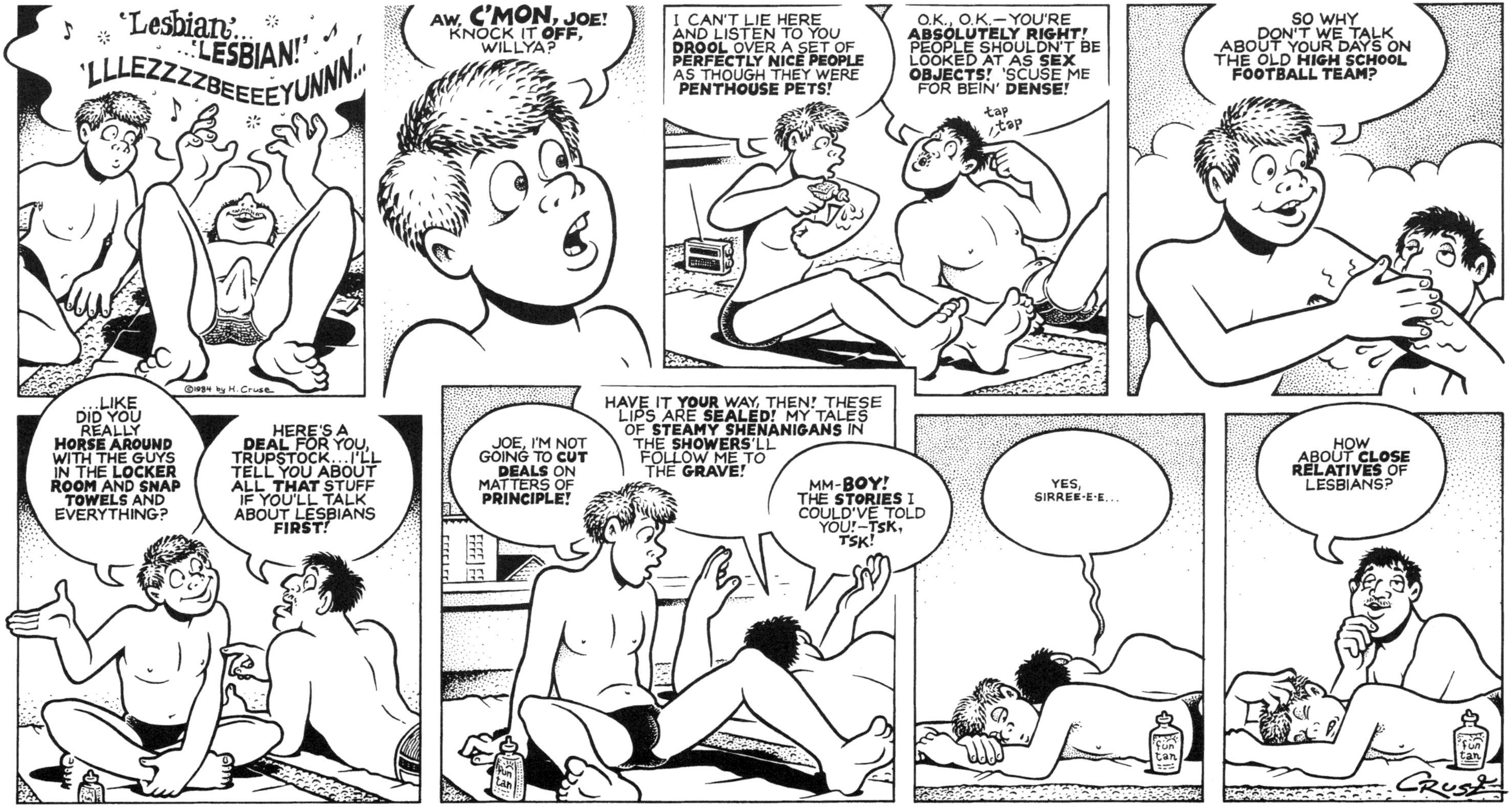

'Lesbian'... ...'LESBIAN!' 'LLLEZZZZZBEEEEYUNNN...'
©1984 by H. Cruse
AW, C'MON, JOE! KNOCK IT OFF, WILLYA?
I CAN'T LIE HERE AND LISTEN TO YOU DROOL OVER A SET OF PERFECTLY NICE PEOPLE AS THOUGH THEY WERE PENTHOUSE PETS!
O.K., O.K.—YOU'RE ABSOLUTELY RIGHT! PEOPLE SHOULDN'T BE LOOKED AT AS SEX OBJECTS! 'SCUSE ME FOR BEIN' DENSE!
tap tap
SO WHY DON'T WE TALK ABOUT YOUR DAYS ON THE OLD HIGH SCHOOL FOOTBALL TEAM?
...LIKE DID YOU REALLY HORSE AROUND WITH THE GUYS IN THE LOCKER ROOM AND SNAP TOWELS AND EVERYTHING?
HERE'S A DEAL FOR YOU, TRUPSTOCK...I'LL TELL YOU ABOUT ALL THAT STUFF IF YOU'LL TALK ABOUT LESBIANS FIRST!
JOE, I'M NOT GOING TO CUT DEALS ON MATTERS OF PRINCIPLE!
HAVE IT YOUR WAY, THEN! THESE LIPS ARE SEALED! MY TALES OF STEAMY SHENANIGANS IN THE SHOWERS'LL FOLLOW ME TO THE GRAVE!
MM-BOY! THE STORIES I COULD'VE TOLD YOU!—TSK, TSK!
fun tan
YES, SIRREE-E-E...
fun tan
HOW ABOUT CLOSE RELATIVES OF LESBIANS?
fun tan
CRUSE

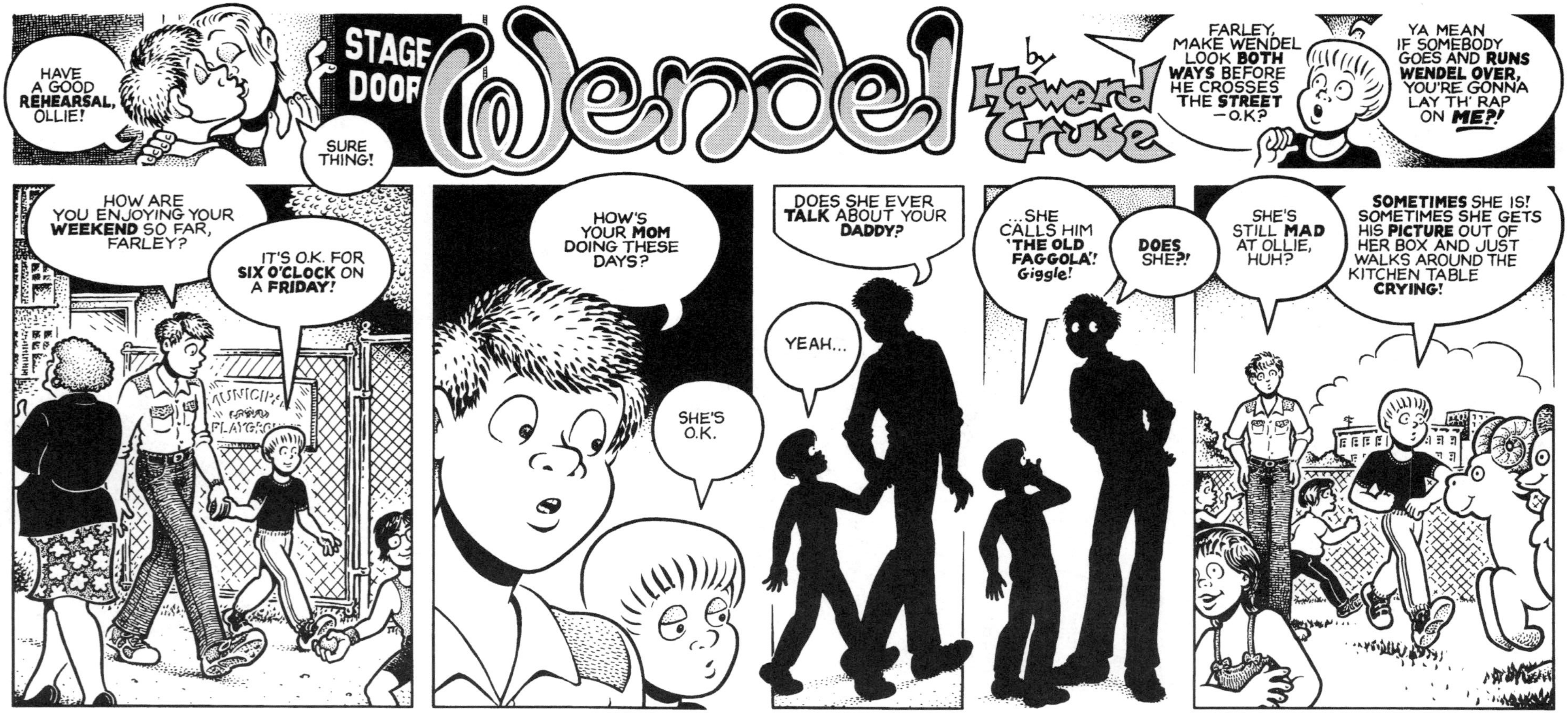
HAVE A GOOD **REHEARSAL,** OLLIE!
STAGE DOOR
SURE THING!
Wendel
by Howard Cruse
FARLEY, MAKE WENDEL LOOK **BOTH WAYS** BEFORE HE CROSSES THE **STREET** —O.K.?
YA MEAN IF SOMEBODY GOES AND **RUNS WENDEL OVER,** YOU'RE GONNA LAY TH' RAP ON **ME?!**
HOW ARE YOU ENJOYING YOUR **WEEKEND** SO FAR, FARLEY?
IT'S O.K. FOR **SIX O'CLOCK** ON A **FRIDAY!**
HOW'S YOUR **MOM** DOING THESE DAYS?
SHE'S O.K.
DOES SHE EVER **TALK** ABOUT YOUR **DADDY?**
YEAH...
...SHE CALLS HIM **'THE OLD FAGGOLA'!** *Giggle!*
DOES SHE?!
SHE'S STILL **MAD** AT OLLIE, HUH?
SOMETIMES SHE IS! SOMETIMES SHE GETS HIS **PICTURE** OUT OF HER BOX AND JUST WALKS AROUND THE KITCHEN TABLE **CRYING!**

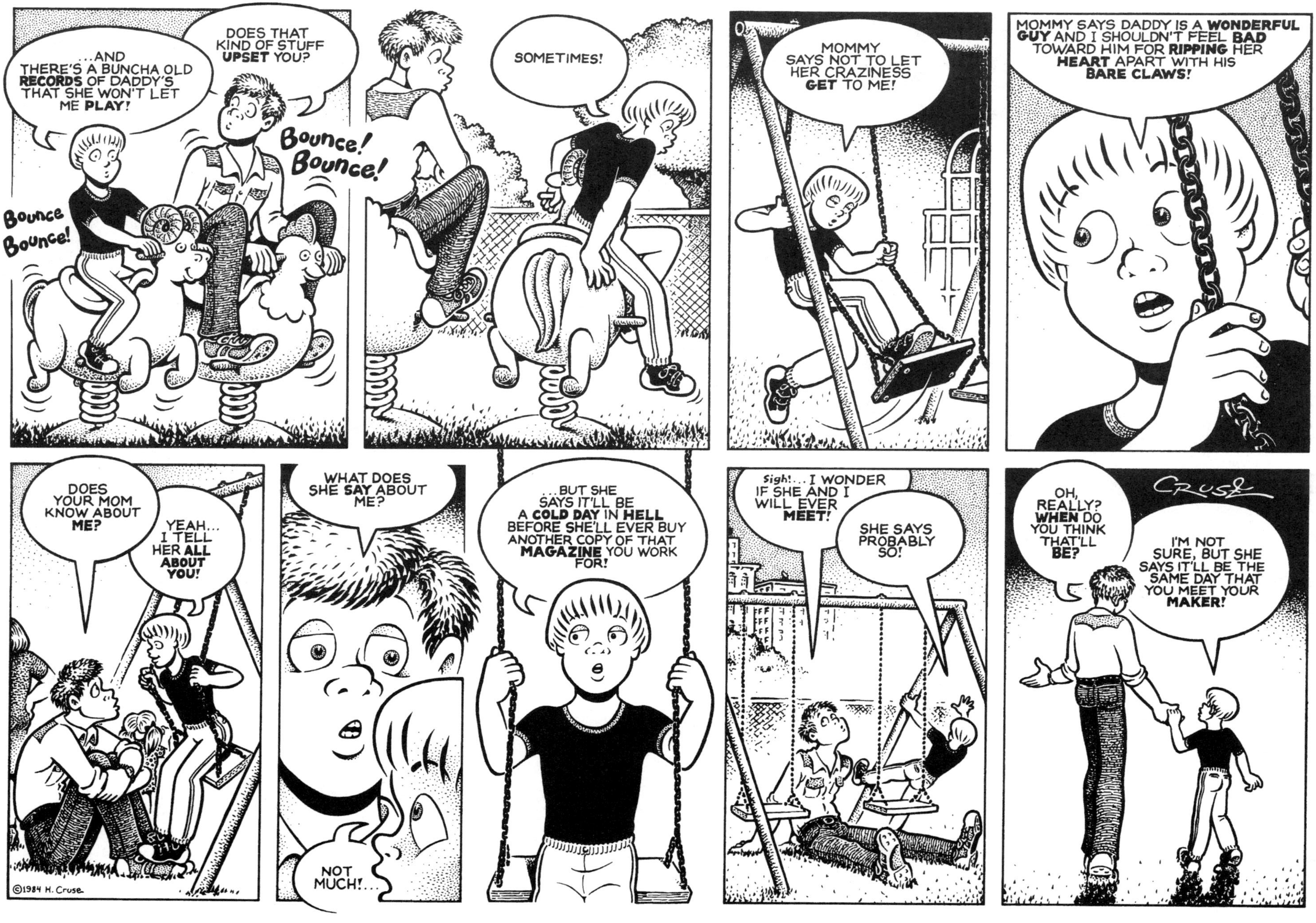
...AND THERE'S A BUNCHA OLD **RECORDS** OF DADDY'S THAT SHE WON'T LET ME **PLAY**!
DOES THAT KIND OF STUFF **UPSET** YOU?
Bounce Bounce!
Bounce! Bounce!
SOMETIMES!
MOMMY SAYS NOT TO LET HER CRAZINESS **GET** TO ME!
MOMMY SAYS DADDY IS A **WONDERFUL GUY** AND I SHOULDN'T FEEL **BAD** TOWARD HIM FOR **RIPPING** HER **HEART** APART WITH HIS **BARE CLAWS**!
DOES YOUR MOM KNOW ABOUT **ME?**
YEAH... I TELL HER **ALL ABOUT YOU**!
©1984 H. Cruse
WHAT DOES SHE **SAY** ABOUT ME?
NOT MUCH!...
...BUT SHE SAYS IT'LL BE A **COLD DAY** IN **HELL** BEFORE **SHE'LL** EVER BUY ANOTHER COPY OF THAT **MAGAZINE** YOU WORK FOR!
Sigh!... I WONDER IF SHE AND I WILL EVER **MEET**!
SHE SAYS PROBABLY SO!
CRUSE
OH, REALLY? **WHEN** DO YOU THINK THAT'LL **BE?**
I'M NOT SURE, BUT SHE SAYS IT'LL BE THE SAME DAY THAT YOU MEET YOUR **MAKER**!

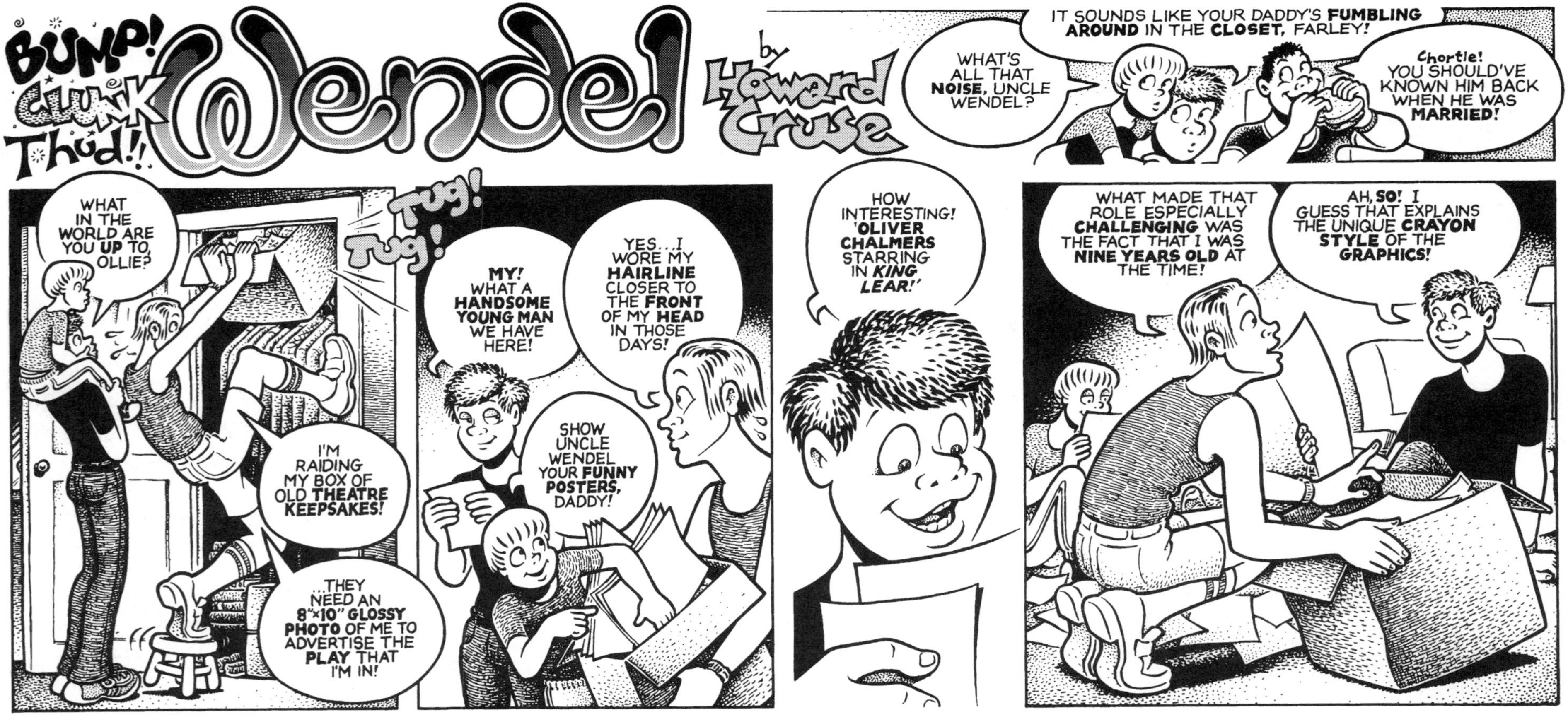
BUMP! CLUNK THUD!!
Wendel
by Howard Cruse
WHAT'S ALL THAT NOISE, UNCLE WENDEL?
IT SOUNDS LIKE YOUR DADDY'S FUMBLING AROUND IN THE CLOSET, FARLEY!
Chortle! YOU SHOULD'VE KNOWN HIM BACK WHEN HE WAS MARRIED!
WHAT IN THE WORLD ARE YOU UP TO, OLLIE?
I'M RAIDING MY BOX OF OLD THEATRE KEEPSAKES!
THEY NEED AN 8"×10" GLOSSY PHOTO OF ME TO ADVERTISE THE PLAY THAT I'M IN!
TUG! TUG!
MY! WHAT A HANDSOME YOUNG MAN WE HAVE HERE!
YES...I WORE MY HAIRLINE CLOSER TO THE FRONT OF MY HEAD IN THOSE DAYS!
SHOW UNCLE WENDEL YOUR FUNNY POSTERS, DADDY!
HOW INTERESTING! 'OLIVER CHALMERS STARRING IN KING LEAR!'
WHAT MADE THAT ROLE ESPECIALLY CHALLENGING WAS THE FACT THAT I WAS NINE YEARS OLD AT THE TIME!
AH, SO! I GUESS THAT EXPLAINS THE UNIQUE CRAYON STYLE OF THE GRAPHICS!

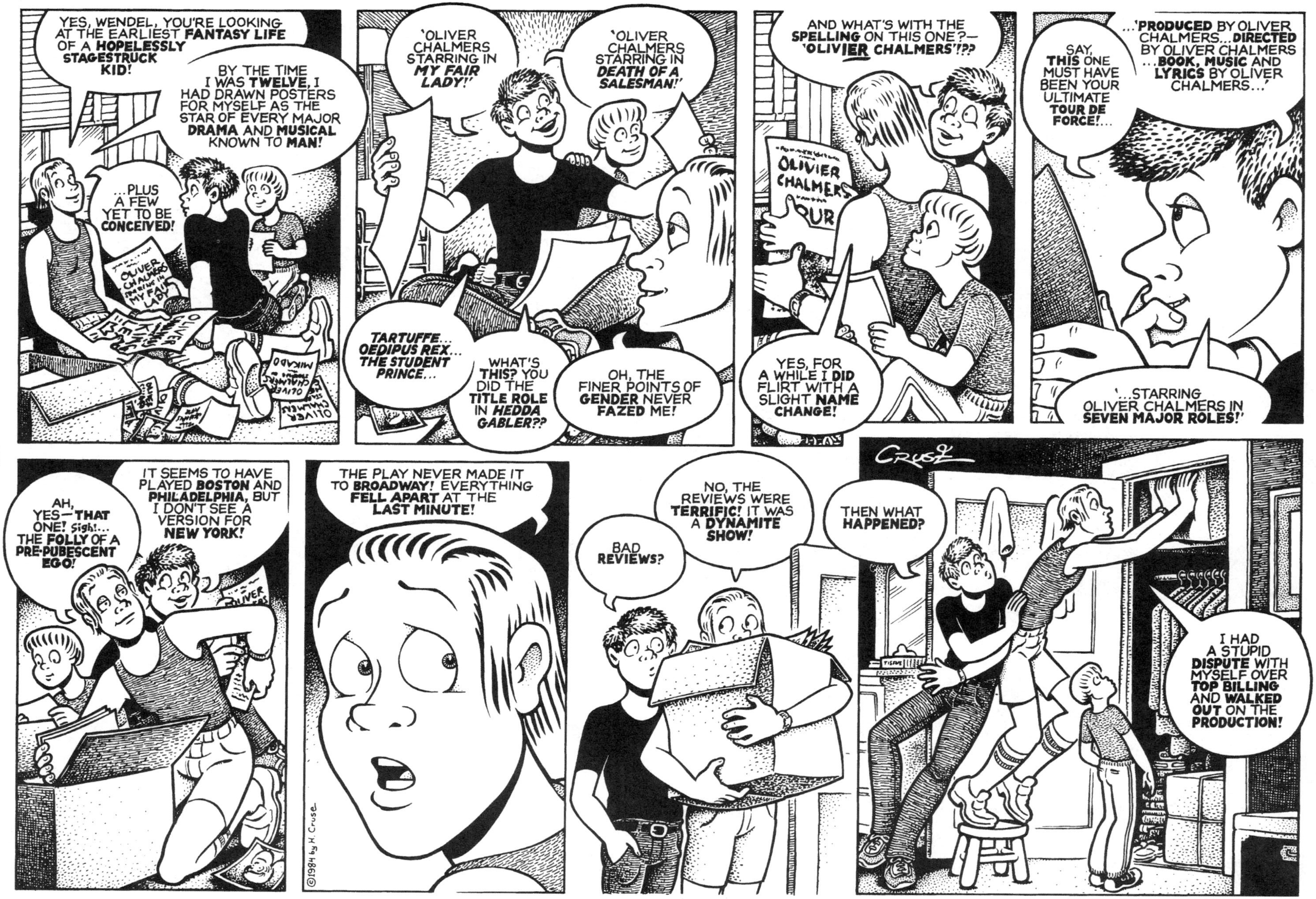
YES, WENDEL, YOU'RE LOOKING AT THE EARLIEST **FANTASY LIFE** OF A **HOPELESSLY STAGESTRUCK KID**!
BY THE TIME I WAS **TWELVE**, I HAD DRAWN POSTERS FOR MYSELF AS THE STAR OF EVERY MAJOR **DRAMA** AND **MUSICAL** KNOWN TO **MAN**!
...PLUS A FEW YET TO BE **CONCEIVED**!
OLIVER CHALMERS STARRING IN MY FAIR LADY
'OLIVER CHALMERS STARRING IN ***MY FAIR LADY***!'
'OLIVER CHALMERS STARRING IN ***DEATH OF A SALESMAN***!'
TARTUFFE... OEDIPUS REX... THE STUDENT PRINCE...
WHAT'S **THIS?** YOU DID THE **TITLE ROLE** IN ***HEDDA GABLER??***
OH, THE FINER POINTS OF **GENDER** NEVER **FAZED** ME!
AND WHAT'S WITH THE **SPELLING** ON THIS ONE?— **'OLIVIER CHALMERS'!??**
OLIVIER CHALMERS
YES, FOR A WHILE I **DID** FLIRT WITH A SLIGHT **NAME CHANGE**!
SAY, **THIS** ONE MUST HAVE BEEN YOUR ULTIMATE **TOUR DE FORCE**!...
...'**PRODUCED** BY OLIVER CHALMERS... **DIRECTED** BY OLIVER CHALMERS ...**BOOK, MUSIC** AND **LYRICS** BY OLIVER CHALMERS...'
'...STARRING OLIVER CHALMERS IN **SEVEN MAJOR ROLES**!'
IT SEEMS TO HAVE PLAYED **BOSTON** AND **PHILADELPHIA**, BUT I DON'T SEE A VERSION FOR **NEW YORK**!
AH, YES—**THAT** ONE! Sigh!... THE **FOLLY** OF A **PRE-PUBESCENT EGO**!
THE PLAY NEVER MADE IT TO **BROADWAY**! EVERYTHING **FELL APART** AT THE **LAST MINUTE**!
©1984 by H. Cruse
BAD **REVIEWS?**
NO, THE REVIEWS WERE **TERRIFIC**! IT WAS A **DYNAMITE SHOW**!
THEN WHAT **HAPPENED?**
CRUSE
I HAD A STUPID **DISPUTE** WITH MYSELF OVER **TOP BILLING** AND **WALKED OUT** ON THE **PRODUCTION**!

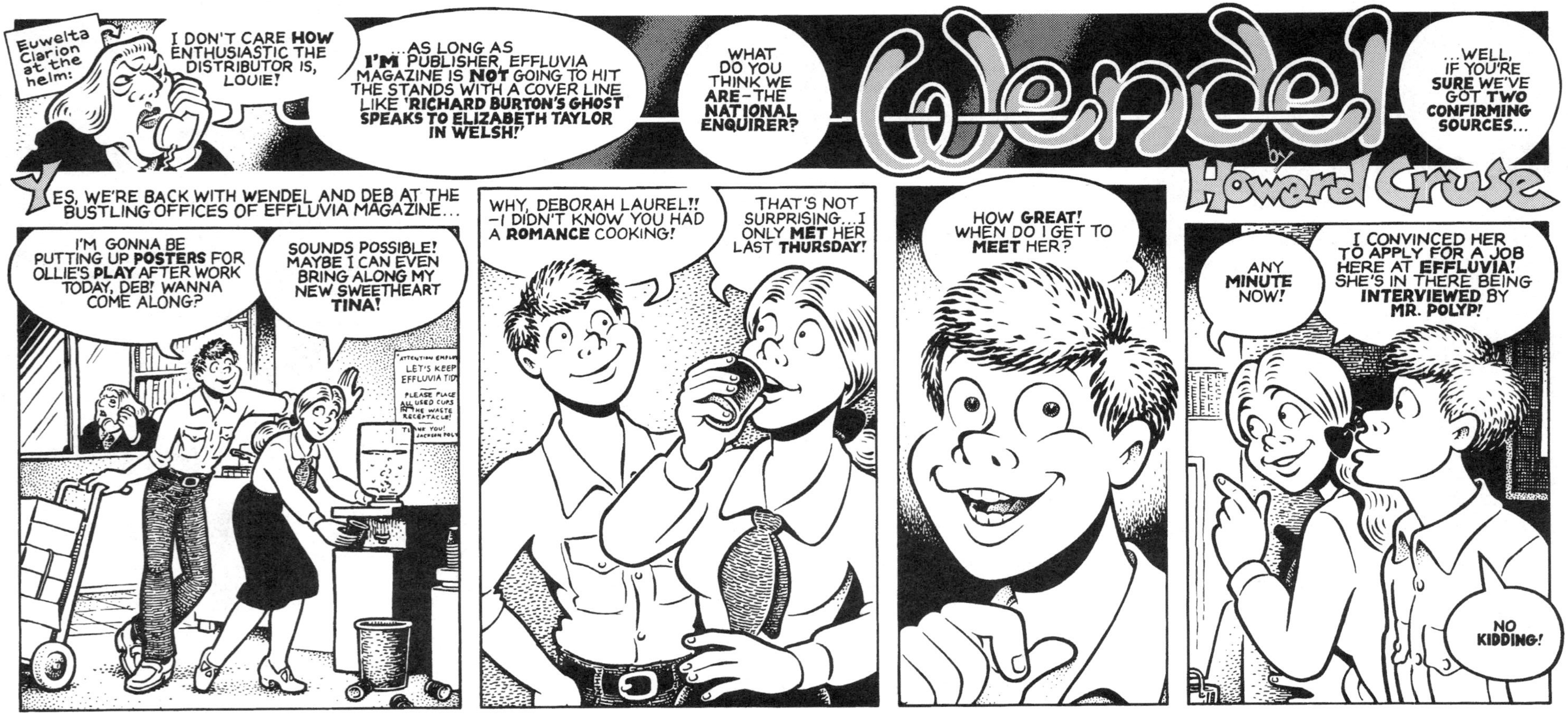
Euwelta Clarion at the helm:
I DON'T CARE HOW ENTHUSIASTIC THE DISTRIBUTOR IS, LOUIE!
...AS LONG AS I'M PUBLISHER, EFFLUVIA MAGAZINE IS NOT GOING TO HIT THE STANDS WITH A COVER LINE LIKE 'RICHARD BURTON'S GHOST SPEAKS TO ELIZABETH TAYLOR IN WELSH!'
WHAT DO YOU THINK WE ARE–THE NATIONAL ENQUIRER?
Wendel
by Howard Cruse
...WELL, IF YOU'RE SURE WE'VE GOT TWO CONFIRMING SOURCES...
YES, WE'RE BACK WITH WENDEL AND DEB AT THE BUSTLING OFFICES OF EFFLUVIA MAGAZINE...
I'M GONNA BE PUTTING UP POSTERS FOR OLLIE'S PLAY AFTER WORK TODAY, DEB! WANNA COME ALONG?
SOUNDS POSSIBLE! MAYBE I CAN EVEN BRING ALONG MY NEW SWEETHEART TINA!
WHY, DEBORAH LAUREL!! –I DIDN'T KNOW YOU HAD A ROMANCE COOKING!
THAT'S NOT SURPRISING... I ONLY MET HER LAST THURSDAY!
HOW GREAT! WHEN DO I GET TO MEET HER?
I CONVINCED HER TO APPLY FOR A JOB HERE AT EFFLUVIA! SHE'S IN THERE BEING INTERVIEWED BY MR. POLYP!
ANY MINUTE NOW!
NO KIDDING!

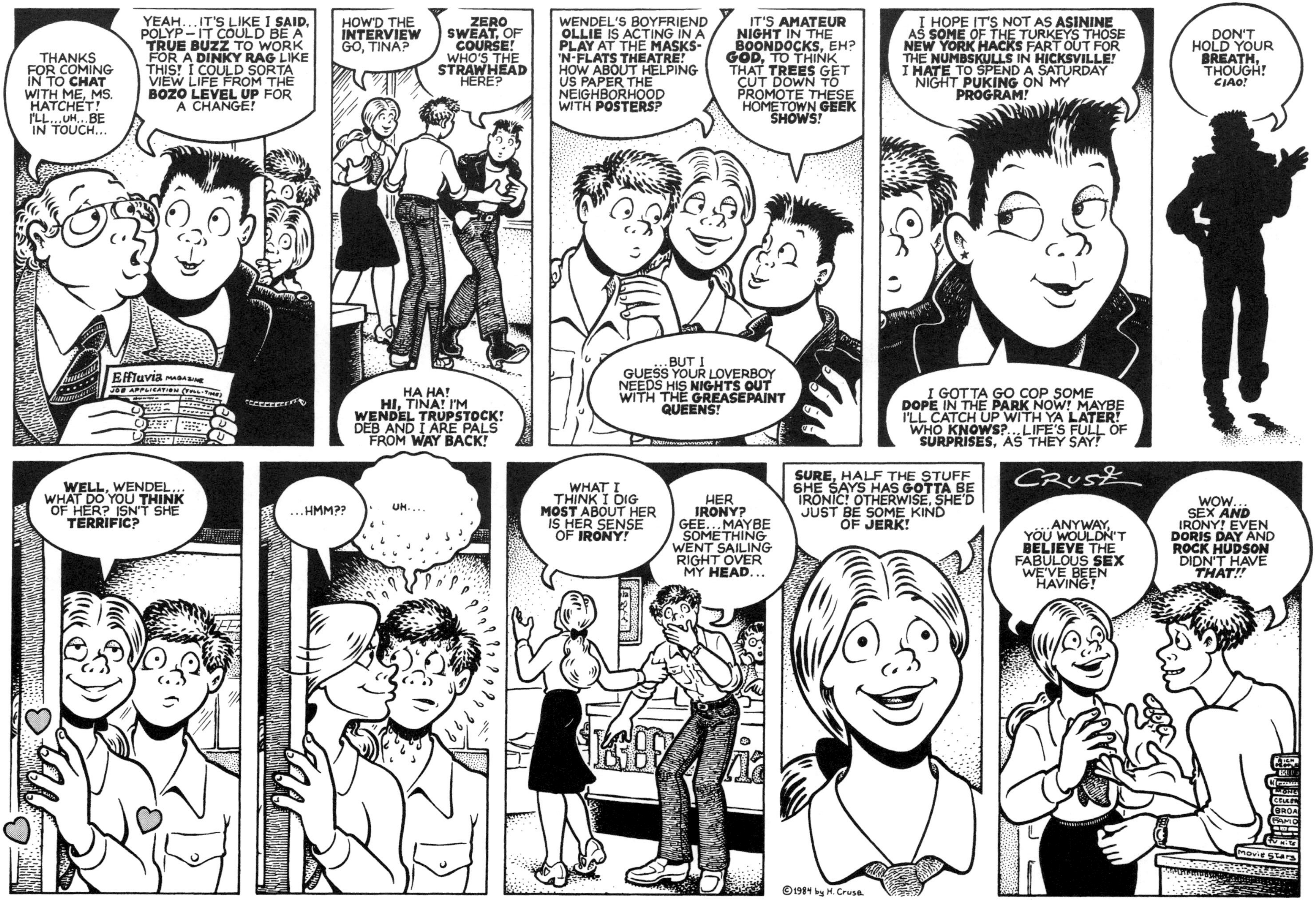
THANKS FOR COMING IN TO CHAT WITH ME, MS. HATCHET! I'LL...UH...BE IN TOUCH...
YEAH... IT'S LIKE I SAID, POLYP – IT COULD BE A TRUE BUZZ TO WORK FOR A DINKY RAG LIKE THIS! I COULD SORTA VIEW LIFE FROM THE BOZO LEVEL UP FOR A CHANGE!
Effluvia MAGAZINE
JOB APPLICATION (FULL-TIME)
HOW'D THE INTERVIEW GO, TINA?
ZERO SWEAT, OF COURSE! WHO'S THE STRAWHEAD HERE?
HA HA! HI, TINA! I'M WENDEL TRUPSTOCK! DEB AND I ARE PALS FROM WAY BACK!
WENDEL'S BOYFRIEND OLLIE IS ACTING IN A PLAY AT THE MASKS-'N-FLATS THEATRE! HOW ABOUT HELPING US PAPER THE NEIGHBORHOOD WITH POSTERS?
IT'S AMATEUR NIGHT IN THE BOONDOCKS, EH? GOD, TO THINK THAT TREES GET CUT DOWN TO PROMOTE THESE HOMETOWN GEEK SHOWS!
...BUT I GUESS YOUR LOVERBOY NEEDS HIS NIGHTS OUT WITH THE GREASEPAINT QUEENS!
I HOPE IT'S NOT AS ASININE AS SOME OF THE TURKEYS THOSE NEW YORK HACKS FART OUT FOR THE NUMBSKULLS IN HICKSVILLE! I HATE TO SPEND A SATURDAY NIGHT PUKING ON MY PROGRAM!
I GOTTA GO COP SOME DOPE IN THE PARK NOW! MAYBE I'LL CATCH UP WITH YA LATER! WHO KNOWS?...LIFE'S FULL OF SURPRISES, AS THEY SAY!
DON'T HOLD YOUR BREATH, THOUGH! CIAO!
WELL, WENDEL... WHAT DO YOU THINK OF HER? ISN'T SHE TERRIFIC?
...HMM??
UH....
WHAT I THINK I DIG MOST ABOUT HER IS HER SENSE OF IRONY!
HER IRONY? GEE...MAYBE SOMETHING WENT SAILING RIGHT OVER MY HEAD...
SURE, HALF THE STUFF SHE SAYS HAS GOTTA BE IRONIC! OTHERWISE, SHE'D JUST BE SOME KIND OF JERK!
©1984 by H. Cruse
CRUSE
...ANYWAY, YOU WOULDN'T BELIEVE THE FABULOUS SEX WE'VE BEEN HAVING!
WOW... SEX AND IRONY! EVEN DORIS DAY AND ROCK HUDSON DIDN'T HAVE THAT!!
Movie Stars

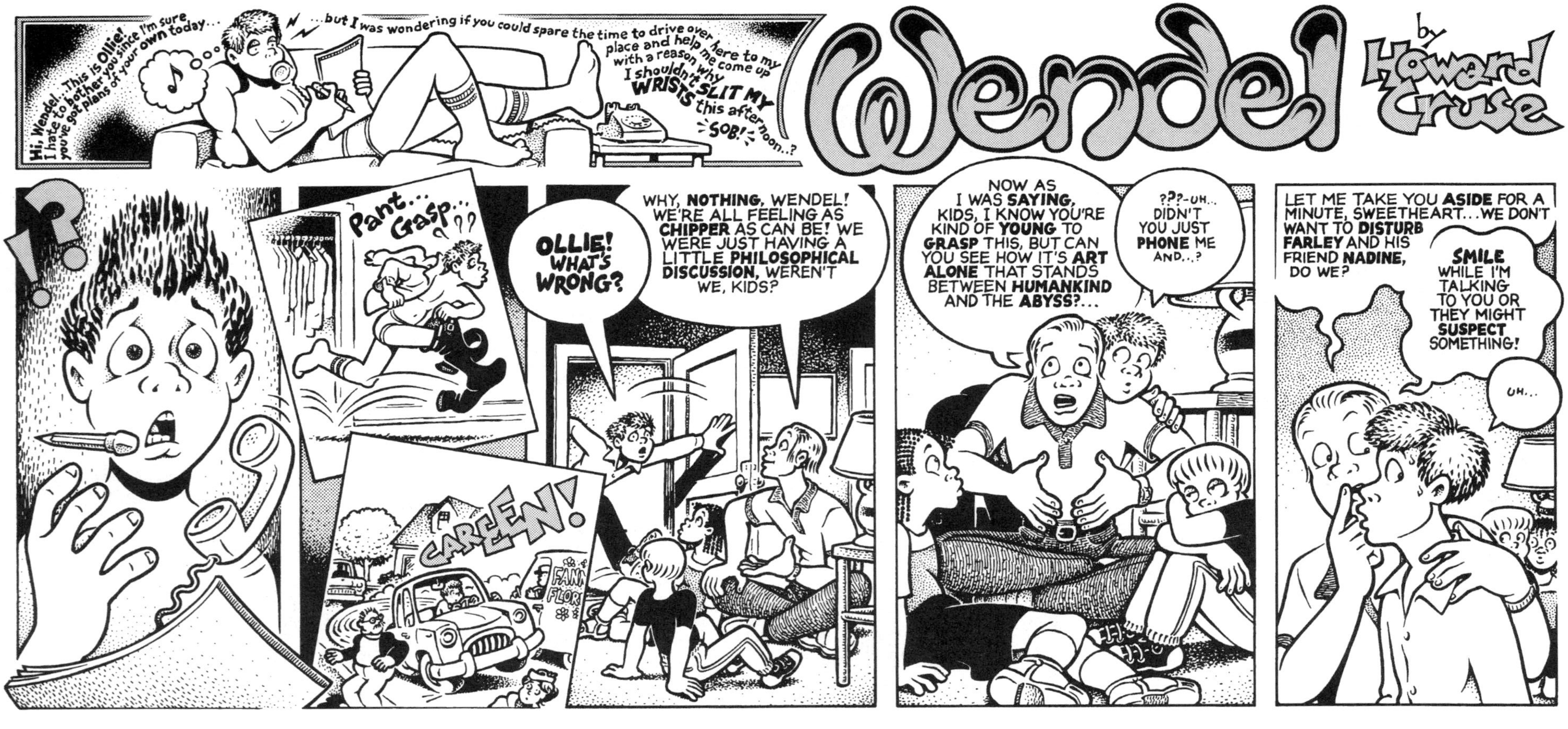
Wendel
by Howard Cruse
Hi, Wendel... This is Ollie! I hate to bother you since I'm sure you've got plans of your own today...
...but I was wondering if you could spare the time to drive over here to my place and help me come up with a reason why I shouldn't SLIT MY WRISTS this afternoon..?
SOB!
!?
Pant... Gasp...
CAREEN!
OLLIE! WHAT'S WRONG?
WHY, NOTHING, WENDEL! WE'RE ALL FEELING AS CHIPPER AS CAN BE! WE WERE JUST HAVING A LITTLE PHILOSOPHICAL DISCUSSION, WEREN'T WE, KIDS?
NOW AS I WAS SAYING, KIDS, I KNOW YOU'RE KIND OF YOUNG TO GRASP THIS, BUT CAN YOU SEE HOW IT'S ART ALONE THAT STANDS BETWEEN HUMANKIND AND THE ABYSS?...
???-UH... DIDN'T YOU JUST PHONE ME AND..?
LET ME TAKE YOU ASIDE FOR A MINUTE, SWEETHEART... WE DON'T WANT TO DISTURB FARLEY AND HIS FRIEND NADINE, DO WE?
SMILE WHILE I'M TALKING TO YOU OR THEY MIGHT SUSPECT SOMETHING!
UH...

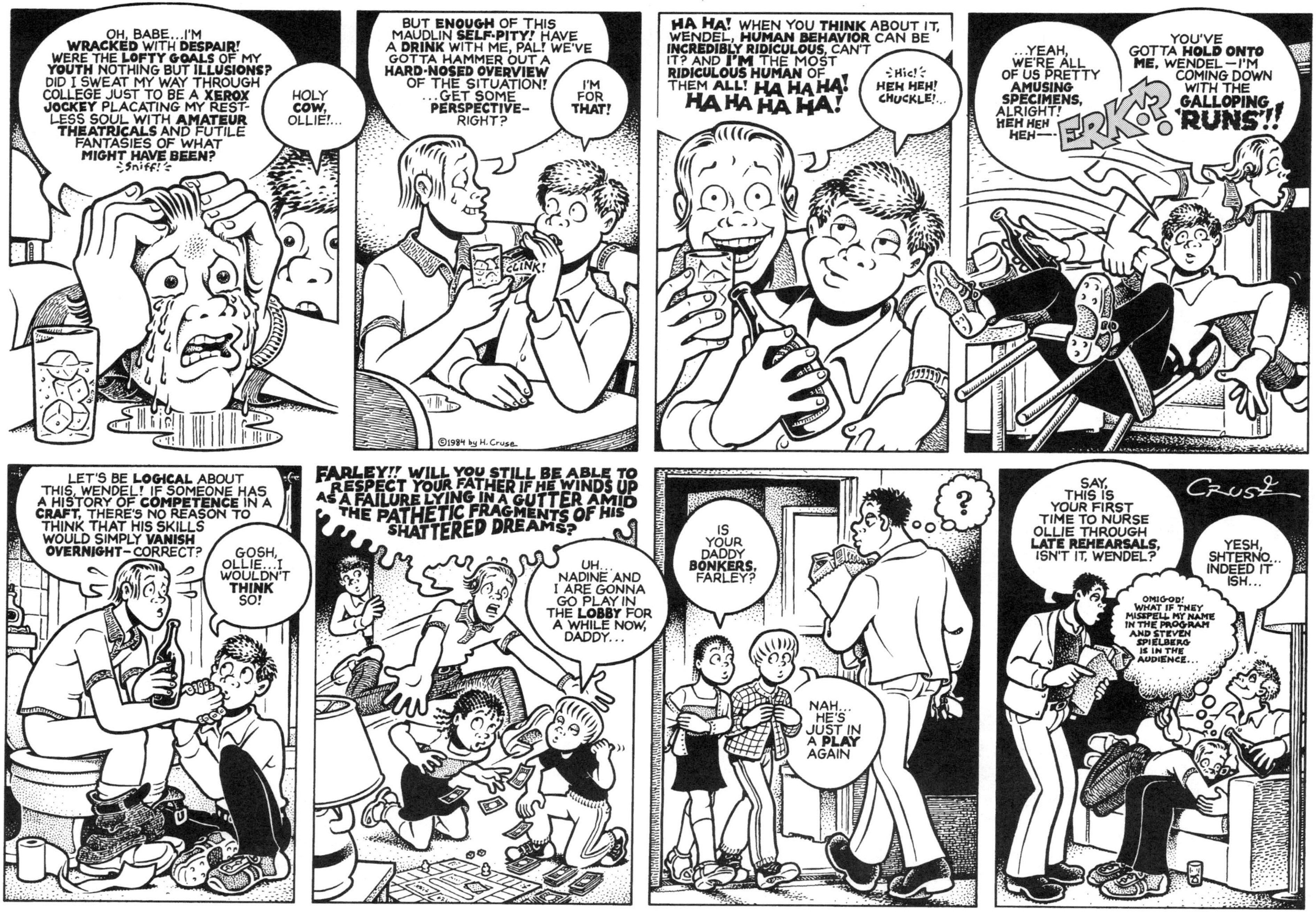
OH, BABE... I'M WRACKED WITH DESPAIR! WERE THE LOFTY GOALS OF MY YOUTH NOTHING BUT ILLUSIONS? DID I SWEAT MY WAY THROUGH COLLEGE JUST TO BE A XEROX JOCKEY PLACATING MY RESTLESS SOUL WITH AMATEUR THEATRICALS AND FUTILE FANTASIES OF WHAT MIGHT HAVE BEEN? Sniff!
HOLY COW, OLLIE!...
BUT ENOUGH OF THIS MAUDLIN SELF-PITY! HAVE A DRINK WITH ME, PAL! WE'VE GOTTA HAMMER OUT A HARD-NOSED OVERVIEW OF THE SITUATION! ...GET SOME PERSPECTIVE- RIGHT?
I'M FOR THAT!
CLINK!
©1984 by H. Cruse
HA HA! WHEN YOU THINK ABOUT IT, WENDEL, HUMAN BEHAVIOR CAN BE INCREDIBLY RIDICULOUS, CAN'T IT? AND I'M THE MOST RIDICULOUS HUMAN OF THEM ALL! HA HA HA! HA HA HA HA!
Hic! HEH HEH! CHUCKLE!...
...YEAH, WE'RE ALL OF US PRETTY AMUSING SPECIMENS, ALRIGHT! HEH HEH HEH—
ERK!?
YOU'VE GOTTA HOLD ONTO ME, WENDEL—I'M COMING DOWN WITH THE GALLOPING 'RUNS'!!
LET'S BE LOGICAL ABOUT THIS, WENDEL! IF SOMEONE HAS A HISTORY OF COMPETENCE IN A CRAFT, THERE'S NO REASON TO THINK THAT HIS SKILLS WOULD SIMPLY VANISH OVERNIGHT—CORRECT?
GOSH, OLLIE... I WOULDN'T THINK SO!
FARLEY!! WILL YOU STILL BE ABLE TO RESPECT YOUR FATHER IF HE WINDS UP AS A FAILURE LYING IN A GUTTER AMID THE PATHETIC FRAGMENTS OF HIS SHATTERED DREAMS?
UH... NADINE AND I ARE GONNA GO PLAY IN THE LOBBY FOR A WHILE NOW, DADDY...
IS YOUR DADDY BONKERS, FARLEY?
NAH... HE'S JUST IN A PLAY AGAIN
?
CRUSE
SAY, THIS IS YOUR FIRST TIME TO NURSE OLLIE THROUGH LATE REHEARSALS, ISN'T IT, WENDEL?
OMIGOD! WHAT IF THEY MISSPELL MY NAME IN THE PROGRAM AND STEVEN SPIELBERG IS IN THE AUDIENCE...
YESH, SHTERNO... INDEED IT ISH...

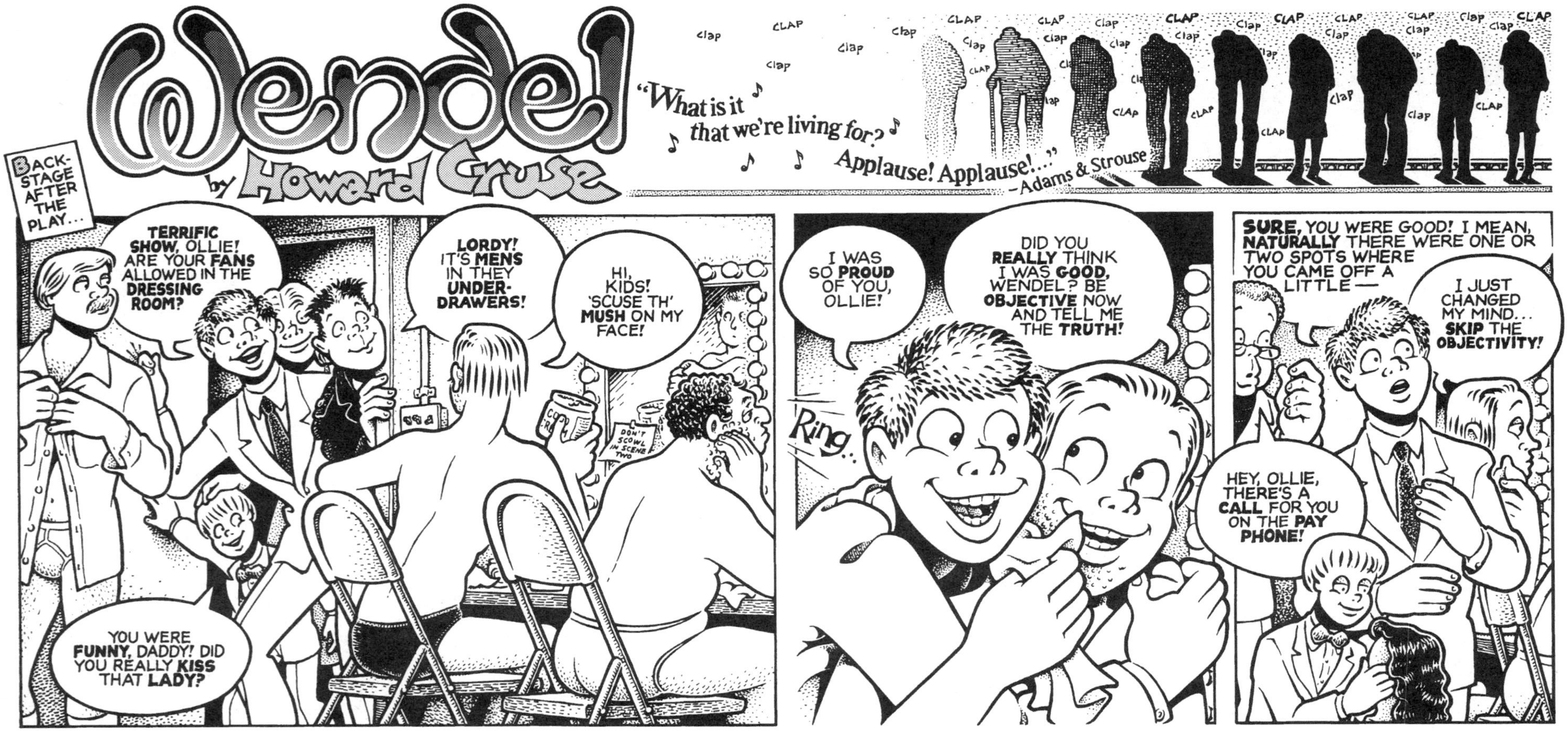
Wendel
by Howard Cruse
"What is it that we're living for? Applause! Applause!..." –Adams & Strouse
clap CLAP clap clap clap CLAP clap clap CLAP CLAP clap CLAP CLAP clap CLAP CLAP clap clap clap CLAP
BACKSTAGE AFTER THE PLAY...
TERRIFIC SHOW, OLLIE! ARE YOUR FANS ALLOWED IN THE DRESSING ROOM?
YOU WERE FUNNY, DADDY! DID YOU REALLY KISS THAT LADY?
LORDY! IT'S MENS IN THEY UNDER-DRAWERS!
HI, KIDS! 'SCUSE TH' MUSH ON MY FACE!
DON'T SCOWL IN SCENE TWO
I WAS SO PROUD OF YOU, OLLIE!
DID YOU REALLY THINK I WAS GOOD, WENDEL? BE OBJECTIVE NOW AND TELL ME THE TRUTH!
Ring...
SURE, YOU WERE GOOD! I MEAN, NATURALLY THERE WERE ONE OR TWO SPOTS WHERE YOU CAME OFF A LITTLE —
I JUST CHANGED MY MIND... SKIP THE OBJECTIVITY!
HEY, OLLIE, THERE'S A CALL FOR YOU ON THE PAY PHONE!

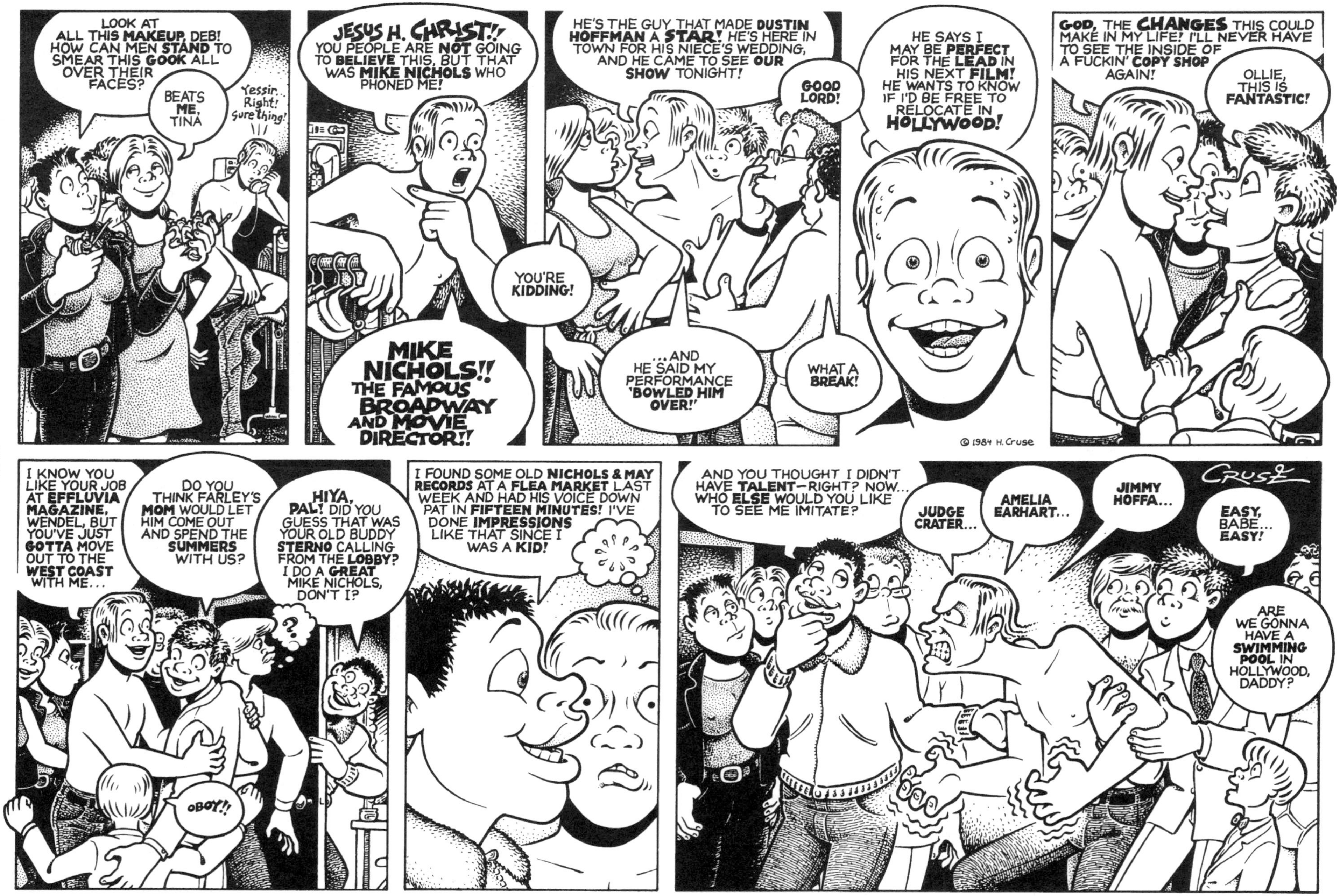

LOOK AT ALL THIS **MAKEUP**, DEB! HOW CAN MEN **STAND** TO SMEAR THIS **GOOK** ALL OVER THEIR FACES?
BEATS **ME**, TINA
Yessir.. Right! Sure thing!
JESUS H. CHRIST!! YOU PEOPLE ARE **NOT** GOING TO **BELIEVE** THIS, BUT THAT WAS **MIKE NICHOLS** WHO PHONED ME!
YOU'RE **KIDDING!**
MIKE NICHOLS!! THE FAMOUS BROADWAY AND MOVIE DIRECTOR!!
HE'S THE GUY THAT MADE **DUSTIN HOFFMAN** A **STAR!** HE'S HERE IN TOWN FOR HIS NIECE'S WEDDING, AND HE CAME TO SEE **OUR SHOW** TONIGHT!
GOOD LORD!
...AND HE SAID MY PERFORMANCE **'BOWLED HIM OVER!'**
WHAT A **BREAK!**
HE SAYS I MAY BE **PERFECT** FOR THE **LEAD** IN HIS NEXT **FILM!** HE WANTS TO KNOW IF I'D BE FREE TO RELOCATE IN **HOLLYWOOD!**
GOD, THE **CHANGES** THIS COULD MAKE IN MY LIFE! I'LL NEVER HAVE TO SEE THE INSIDE OF A FUCKIN' **COPY SHOP** AGAIN!
OLLIE, THIS IS **FANTASTIC!**
© 1984 H. Cruse
I KNOW YOU LIKE YOUR JOB AT **EFFLUVIA MAGAZINE**, WENDEL, BUT YOU'VE JUST **GOTTA** MOVE OUT TO THE **WEST COAST** WITH ME...
DO YOU THINK FARLEY'S **MOM** WOULD LET HIM COME OUT AND SPEND THE **SUMMERS** WITH US?
?
OBOY!!
HIYA, PAL! DID YOU GUESS THAT WAS YOUR OLD BUDDY **STERNO** CALLING FROM THE **LOBBY?** I DO A **GREAT** MIKE NICHOLS, DON'T I?
I FOUND SOME OLD **NICHOLS & MAY RECORDS** AT A **FLEA MARKET** LAST WEEK AND HAD HIS VOICE DOWN PAT IN **FIFTEEN MINUTES!** I'VE DONE **IMPRESSIONS** LIKE THAT SINCE I WAS A **KID!**
AND YOU THOUGHT I DIDN'T HAVE **TALENT**—RIGHT? NOW... WHO **ELSE** WOULD YOU LIKE TO SEE ME IMITATE?
JUDGE CRATER...
AMELIA EARHART...
JIMMY HOFFA...
EASY, BABE... **EASY!**
ARE WE GONNA HAVE A **SWIMMING POOL** IN HOLLYWOOD, DADDY?
CRUSE

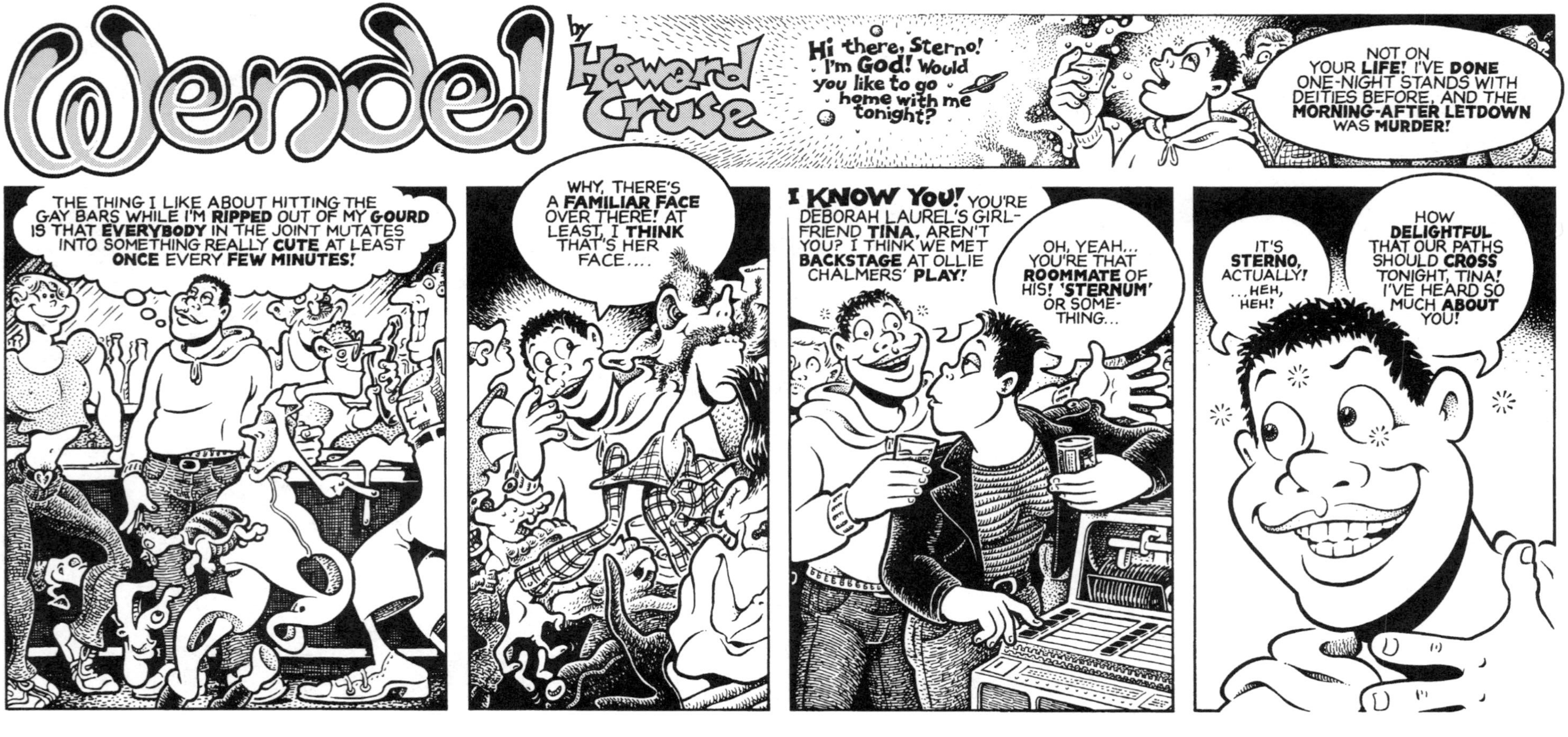
Wendel
by Howard Cruse
Hi there, Sterno! I'm God! Would you like to go home with me tonight?
NOT ON YOUR LIFE! I'VE DONE ONE-NIGHT STANDS WITH DEITIES BEFORE, AND THE MORNING-AFTER LETDOWN WAS MURDER!
THE THING I LIKE ABOUT HITTING THE GAY BARS WHILE I'M RIPPED OUT OF MY GOURD IS THAT EVERYBODY IN THE JOINT MUTATES INTO SOMETHING REALLY CUTE AT LEAST ONCE EVERY FEW MINUTES!
WHY, THERE'S A FAMILIAR FACE OVER THERE! AT LEAST, I THINK THAT'S HER FACE....
I KNOW YOU! YOU'RE DEBORAH LAUREL'S GIRL-FRIEND TINA, AREN'T YOU? I THINK WE MET BACKSTAGE AT OLLIE CHALMERS' PLAY!
OH, YEAH... YOU'RE THAT ROOMMATE OF HIS! 'STERNUM' OR SOME-THING...
HOW DELIGHTFUL THAT OUR PATHS SHOULD CROSS TONIGHT, TINA! I'VE HEARD SO MUCH ABOUT YOU!
IT'S STERNO, ACTUALLY! ...HEH, HEH!

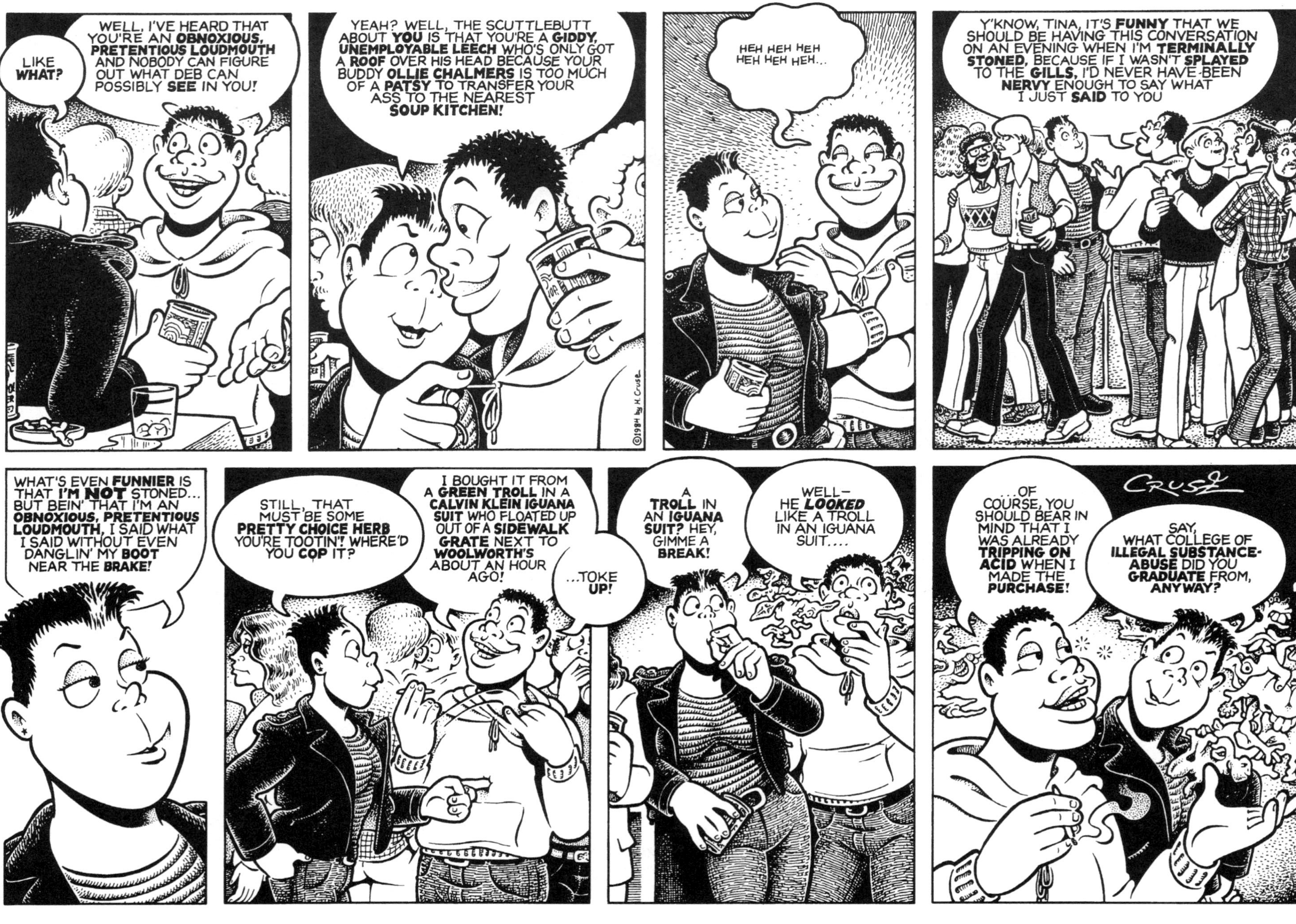
LIKE WHAT?
WELL, I'VE HEARD THAT YOU'RE AN OBNOXIOUS, PRETENTIOUS LOUDMOUTH AND NOBODY CAN FIGURE OUT WHAT DEB CAN POSSIBLY SEE IN YOU!
YEAH? WELL, THE SCUTTLEBUTT ABOUT YOU IS THAT YOU'RE A GIDDY, UNEMPLOYABLE LEECH WHO'S ONLY GOT A ROOF OVER HIS HEAD BECAUSE YOUR BUDDY OLLIE CHALMERS IS TOO MUCH OF A PATSY TO TRANSFER YOUR ASS TO THE NEAREST SOUP KITCHEN!
©1984 by H. Cruse
HEH HEH HEH HEH HEH HEH...
Y'KNOW, TINA, IT'S FUNNY THAT WE SHOULD BE HAVING THIS CONVERSATION ON AN EVENING WHEN I'M TERMINALLY STONED, BECAUSE IF I WASN'T SPLAYED TO THE GILLS, I'D NEVER HAVE BEEN NERVY ENOUGH TO SAY WHAT I JUST SAID TO YOU
WHAT'S EVEN FUNNIER IS THAT I'M NOT STONED... BUT BEIN' THAT I'M AN OBNOXIOUS, PRETENTIOUS LOUDMOUTH, I SAID WHAT I SAID WITHOUT EVEN DANGLIN' MY BOOT NEAR THE BRAKE!
STILL, THAT MUST BE SOME PRETTY CHOICE HERB YOU'RE TOOTIN'! WHERE'D YOU COP IT?
I BOUGHT IT FROM A GREEN TROLL IN A CALVIN KLEIN IGUANA SUIT WHO FLOATED UP OUT OF A SIDEWALK GRATE NEXT TO WOOLWORTH'S ABOUT AN HOUR AGO!
...TOKE UP!
A TROLL IN AN IGUANA SUIT? HEY, GIMME A BREAK!
WELL— HE LOOKED LIKE A TROLL IN AN IGUANA SUIT....
...OF COURSE, YOU SHOULD BEAR IN MIND THAT I WAS ALREADY TRIPPING ON ACID WHEN I MADE THE PURCHASE!
SAY, WHAT COLLEGE OF ILLEGAL SUBSTANCE-ABUSE DID YOU GRADUATE FROM, ANYWAY?
CRUSE

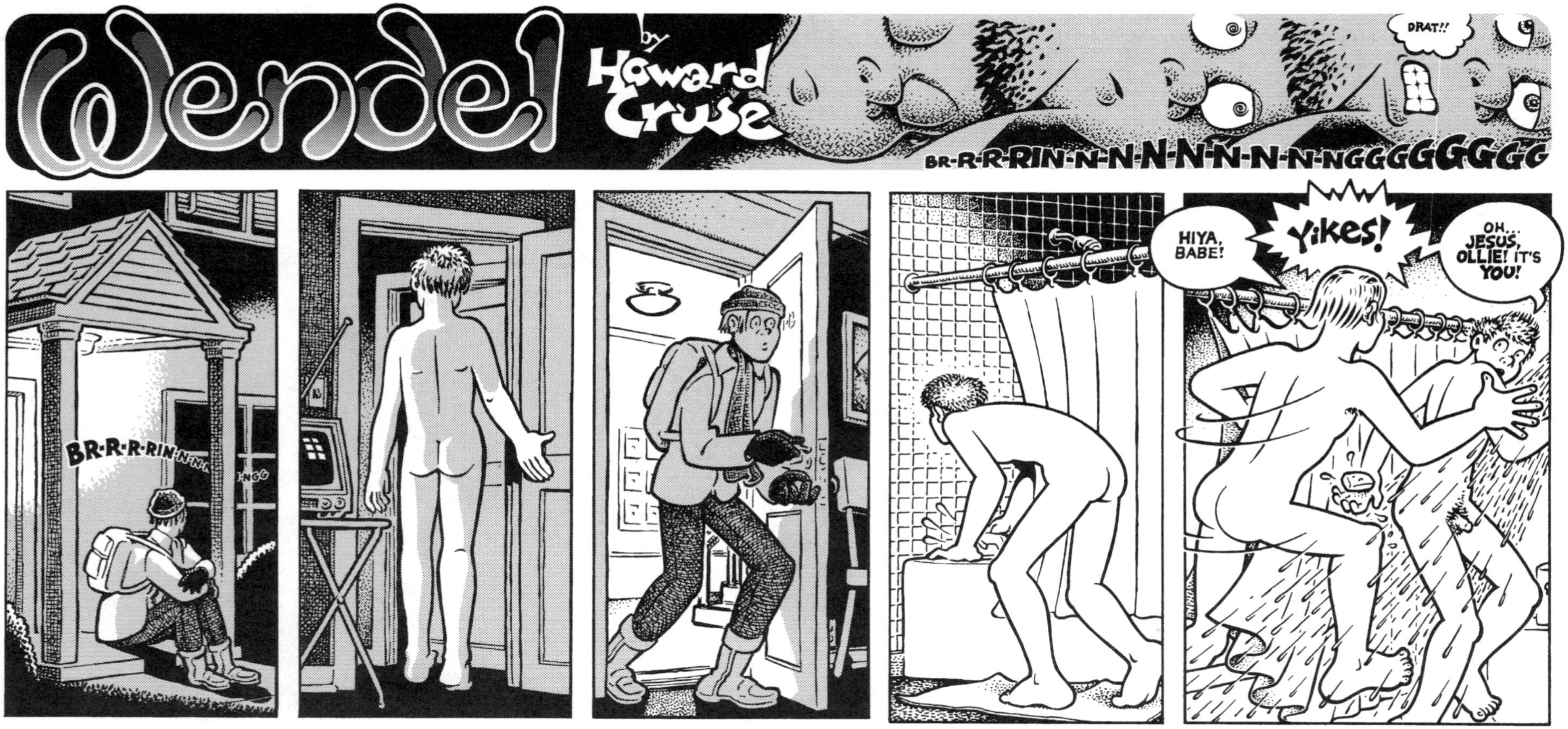
Wendel
by Howard Cruse
DRAT!!
BR-R-R-RIN-N-N-N-N-N-N-N-N-NGGGGGGGG
BR-R-R-RIN-N-N-
-NGG
HIYA, BABE!
YIKES!
OH... JESUS, OLLIE! IT'S YOU!

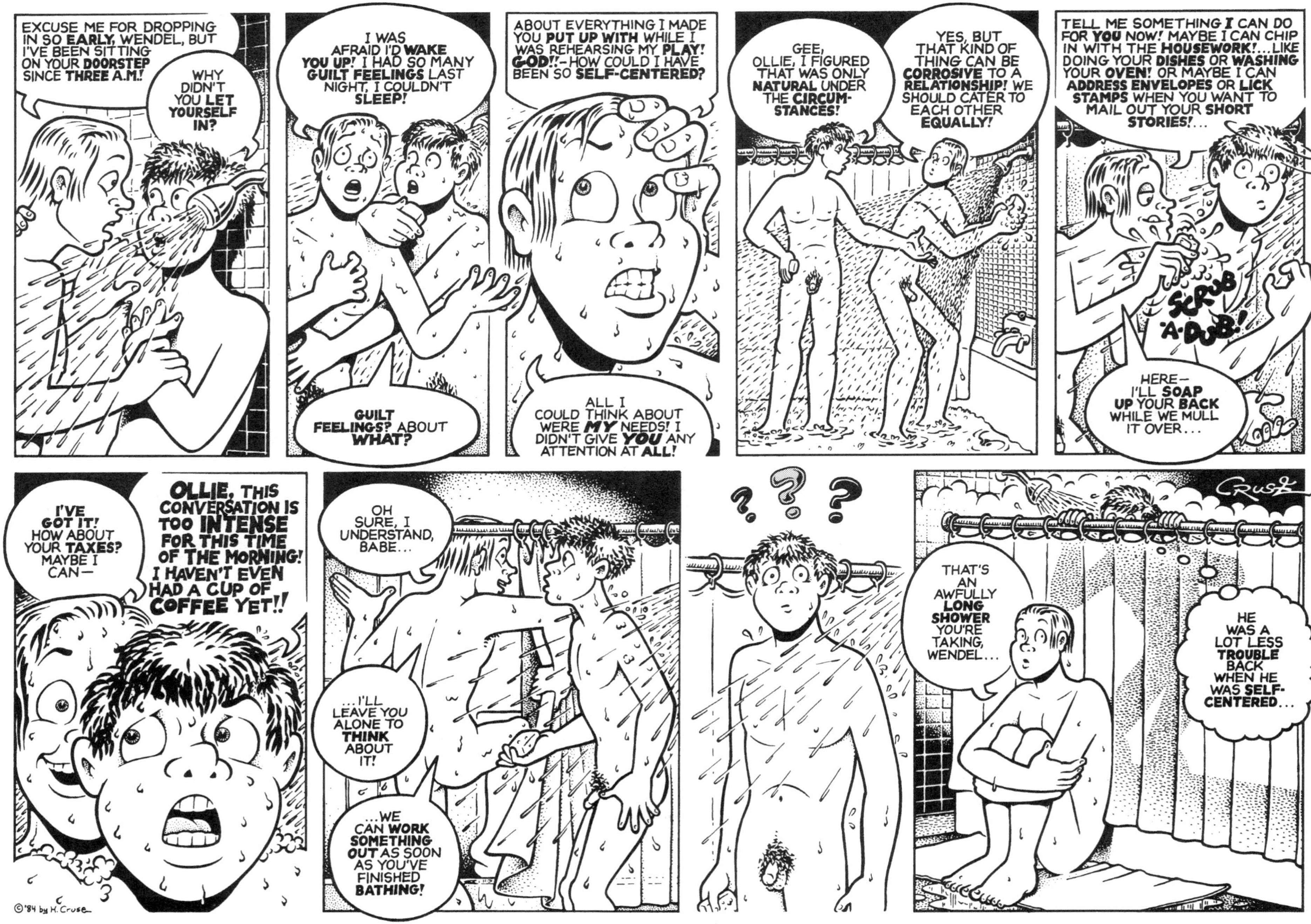

EXCUSE ME FOR DROPPING IN SO **EARLY**, WENDEL, BUT I'VE BEEN SITTING ON YOUR **DOORSTEP** SINCE **THREE A.M.!**
WHY DIDN'T YOU **LET YOURSELF IN?**
I WAS AFRAID I'D **WAKE YOU UP!** I HAD SO MANY **GUILT FEELINGS** LAST NIGHT, I COULDN'T **SLEEP!**
GUILT FEELINGS? ABOUT **WHAT?**
ABOUT EVERYTHING I MADE YOU **PUT UP WITH** WHILE I WAS REHEARSING MY **PLAY! GOD!!**–HOW COULD I HAVE BEEN SO **SELF-CENTERED?**
ALL I COULD THINK ABOUT WERE ***MY*** NEEDS! I DIDN'T GIVE ***YOU*** ANY ATTENTION AT **ALL!**
GEE, OLLIE, I FIGURED THAT WAS ONLY **NATURAL** UNDER THE **CIRCUM-STANCES!**
YES, BUT THAT KIND OF THING CAN BE **CORROSIVE** TO A **RELATIONSHIP!** WE SHOULD CATER TO EACH OTHER **EQUALLY!**
TELL ME SOMETHING ***I*** CAN DO FOR **YOU** NOW! MAYBE I CAN CHIP IN WITH THE **HOUSEWORK!**...LIKE DOING YOUR **DISHES** OR **WASHING** YOUR **OVEN!** OR MAYBE I CAN **ADDRESS ENVELOPES** OR **LICK STAMPS** WHEN YOU WANT TO MAIL OUT YOUR **SHORT STORIES!**...
SCRUB 'A-DUB!'
HERE– I'LL **SOAP UP** YOUR **BACK** WHILE WE MULL IT OVER...
I'VE GOT IT! HOW ABOUT YOUR **TAXES?** MAYBE I CAN—
OLLIE, THIS CONVERSATION IS TOO INTENSE FOR THIS TIME OF THE MORNING! I HAVEN'T EVEN HAD A CUP OF COFFEE YET!!
OH SURE, I UNDERSTAND, BABE...
...I'LL LEAVE YOU ALONE TO **THINK** ABOUT IT!
...WE CAN **WORK SOMETHING OUT** AS SOON AS YOU'VE FINISHED **BATHING!**
? ? ?
THAT'S AN AWFULLY **LONG SHOWER** YOU'RE TAKING, WENDEL...
HE WAS A LOT LESS **TROUBLE** BACK WHEN HE WAS **SELF-CENTERED**...
CRUSE
©'84 by H. Cruse

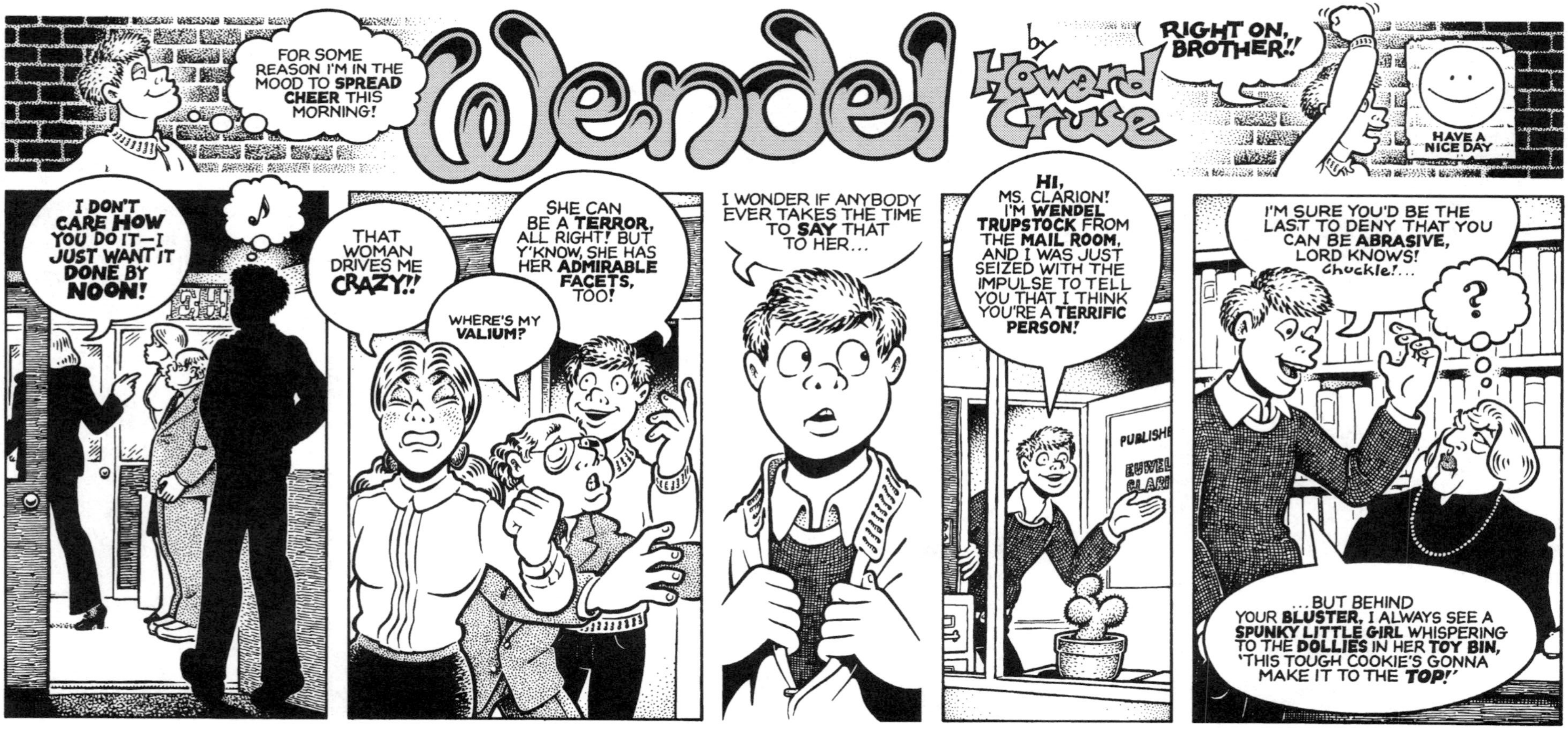
FOR SOME REASON I'M IN THE MOOD TO **SPREAD CHEER** THIS MORNING!
Wendel
by Howard Cruse
RIGHT ON, BROTHER!!
HAVE A NICE DAY
I DON'T CARE **HOW** YOU DO IT—I JUST WANT IT **DONE BY NOON!**
THAT WOMAN DRIVES ME **CRAZY!!**
WHERE'S MY **VALIUM?**
SHE CAN BE A **TERROR,** ALL RIGHT! BUT Y'KNOW, SHE HAS HER **ADMIRABLE FACETS,** TOO!
I WONDER IF ANYBODY EVER TAKES THE TIME TO **SAY** THAT TO HER...
HI, MS. CLARION! I'M **WENDEL TRUPSTOCK** FROM THE **MAIL ROOM,** AND I WAS JUST SEIZED WITH THE IMPULSE TO TELL YOU THAT I THINK YOU'RE A **TERRIFIC PERSON!**
PUBLISHE
I'M SURE YOU'D BE THE LAST TO DENY THAT YOU CAN BE **ABRASIVE,** LORD KNOWS! *Chuckle!...*
?
...BUT BEHIND YOUR **BLUSTER,** I ALWAYS SEE A **SPUNKY LITTLE GIRL** WHISPERING TO THE **DOLLIES** IN HER **TOY BIN,** 'THIS TOUGH COOKIE'S GONNA MAKE IT TO THE ***TOP!***'

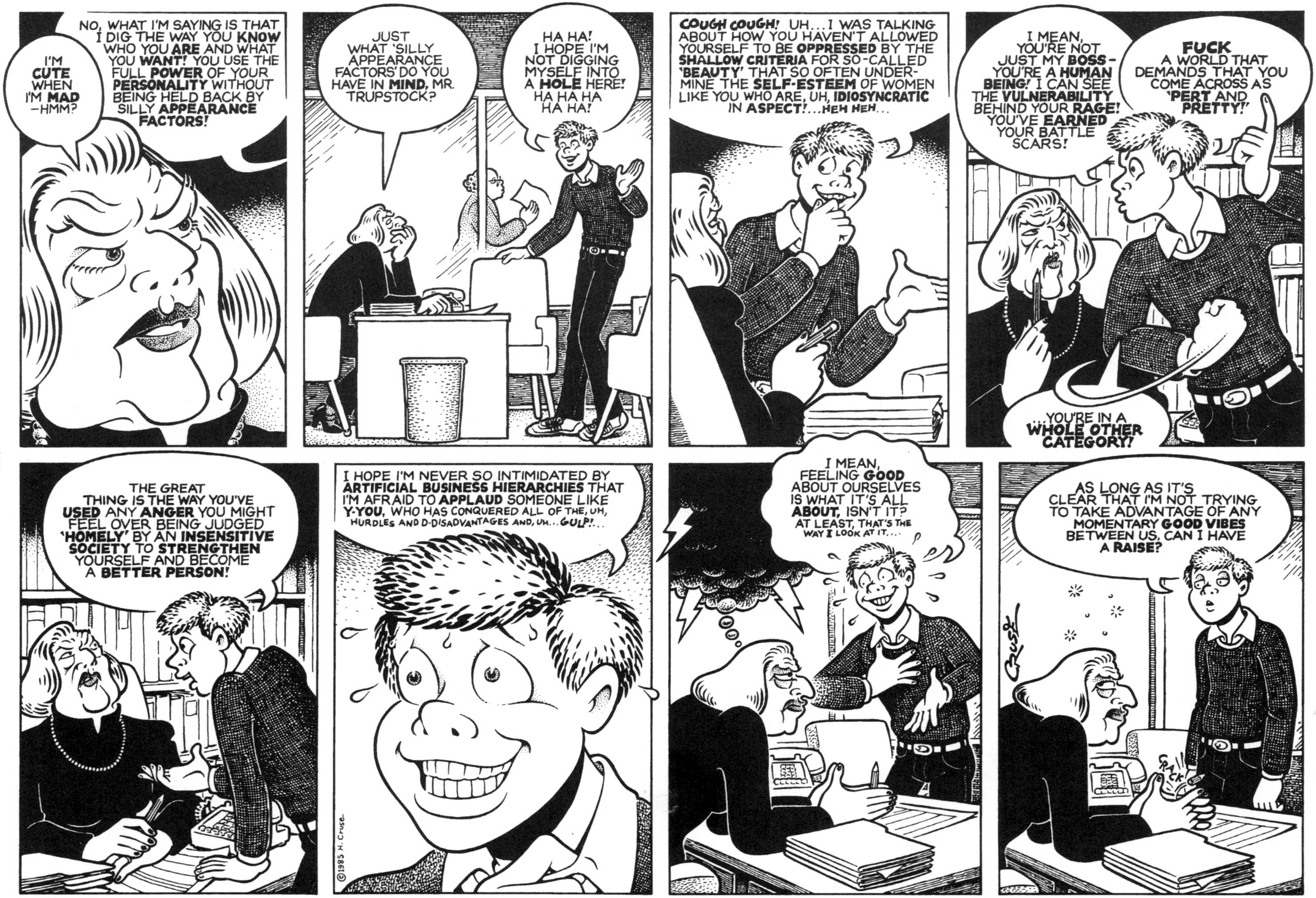
I'M CUTE WHEN I'M MAD —HMM?
NO, WHAT I'M SAYING IS THAT I DIG THE WAY YOU KNOW WHO YOU ARE AND WHAT YOU WANT! YOU USE THE FULL POWER OF YOUR PERSONALITY WITHOUT BEING HELD BACK BY SILLY APPEARANCE FACTORS!
JUST WHAT 'SILLY APPEARANCE FACTORS' DO YOU HAVE IN MIND, MR. TRUPSTOCK?
HA HA! I HOPE I'M NOT DIGGING MYSELF INTO A HOLE HERE! HA HA HA HA HA!
COUGH COUGH! UH... I WAS TALKING ABOUT HOW YOU HAVEN'T ALLOWED YOURSELF TO BE OPPRESSED BY THE SHALLOW CRITERIA FOR SO-CALLED 'BEAUTY' THAT SO OFTEN UNDERMINE THE SELF-ESTEEM OF WOMEN LIKE YOU WHO ARE, UH, IDIOSYNCRATIC IN ASPECT!...HEH HEH...
I MEAN, YOU'RE NOT JUST MY BOSS - YOU'RE A HUMAN BEING! I CAN SEE THE VULNERABILITY BEHIND YOUR RAGE! YOU'VE EARNED YOUR BATTLE SCARS!
FUCK A WORLD THAT DEMANDS THAT YOU COME ACROSS AS 'PERT AND PRETTY!'
...YOU'RE IN A WHOLE OTHER CATEGORY!
THE GREAT THING IS THE WAY YOU'VE USED ANY ANGER YOU MIGHT FEEL OVER BEING JUDGED 'HOMELY' BY AN INSENSITIVE SOCIETY TO STRENGTHEN YOURSELF AND BECOME A BETTER PERSON!
I HOPE I'M NEVER SO INTIMIDATED BY ARTIFICIAL BUSINESS HIERARCHIES THAT I'M AFRAID TO APPLAUD SOMEONE LIKE Y-YOU, WHO HAS CONQUERED ALL OF THE, UH, HURDLES AND D-DISADVANTAGES AND, UH... GULP!...
©1985 H. Cruse
I MEAN, FEELING GOOD ABOUT OURSELVES IS WHAT IT'S ALL ABOUT, ISN'T IT? AT LEAST, THAT'S THE WAY I LOOK AT IT...
AS LONG AS IT'S CLEAR THAT I'M NOT TRYING TO TAKE ADVANTAGE OF ANY MOMENTARY GOOD VIBES BETWEEN US, CAN I HAVE A RAISE?
CRACK
CRUSE

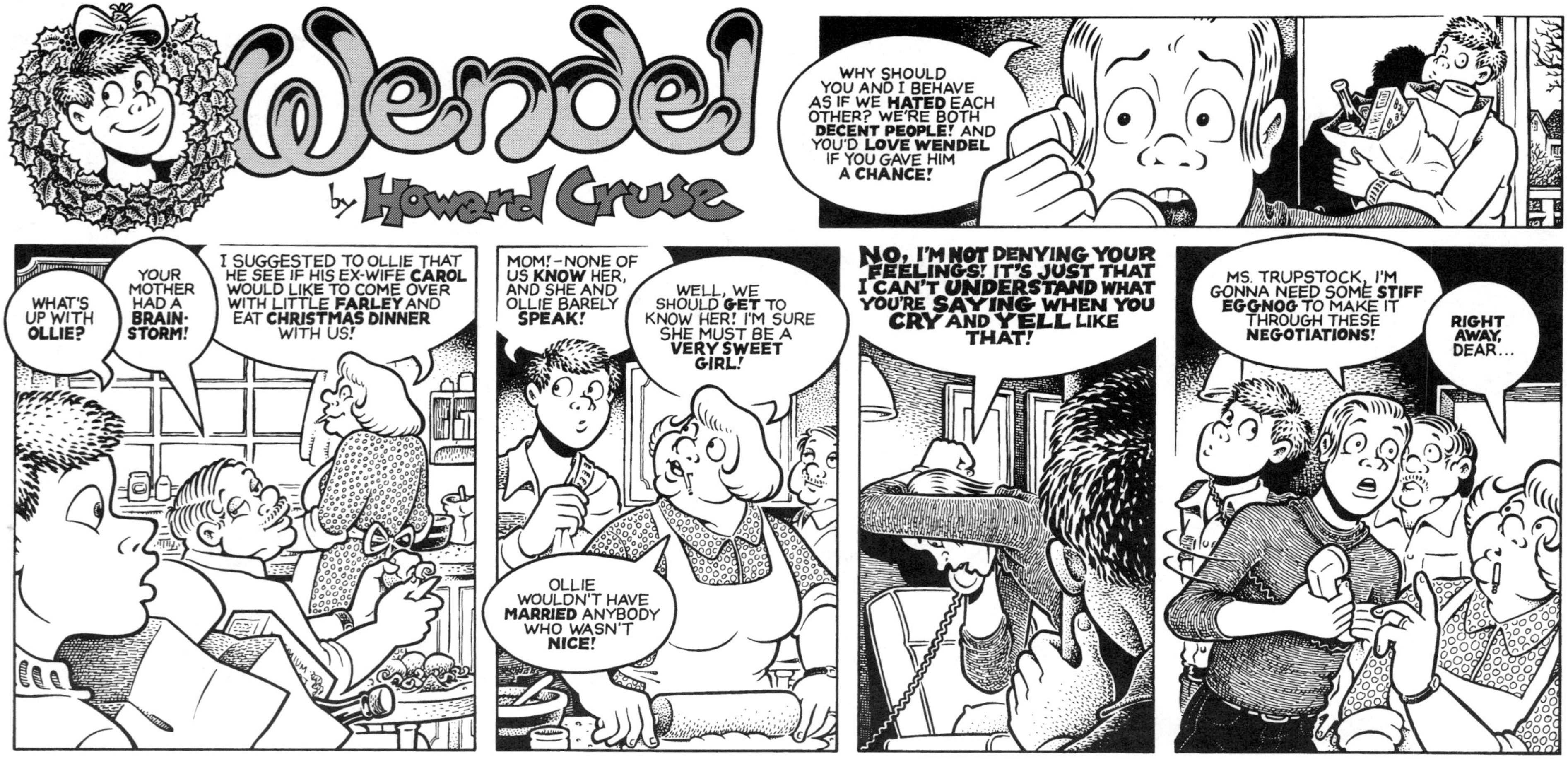
Wendel
by Howard Cruse
WHY SHOULD YOU AND I BEHAVE AS IF WE HATED EACH OTHER? WE'RE BOTH DECENT PEOPLE! AND YOU'D LOVE WENDEL IF YOU GAVE HIM A CHANCE!
WHAT'S UP WITH OLLIE?
YOUR MOTHER HAD A BRAIN-STORM!
I SUGGESTED TO OLLIE THAT HE SEE IF HIS EX-WIFE CAROL WOULD LIKE TO COME OVER WITH LITTLE FARLEY AND EAT CHRISTMAS DINNER WITH US!
MOM! –NONE OF US KNOW HER, AND SHE AND OLLIE BARELY SPEAK!
WELL, WE SHOULD GET TO KNOW HER! I'M SURE SHE MUST BE A VERY SWEET GIRL!
OLLIE WOULDN'T HAVE MARRIED ANYBODY WHO WASN'T NICE!
NO, I'M NOT DENYING YOUR FEELINGS! IT'S JUST THAT I CAN'T UNDERSTAND WHAT YOU'RE SAYING WHEN YOU CRY AND YELL LIKE THAT!
MS. TRUPSTOCK, I'M GONNA NEED SOME STIFF EGGNOG TO MAKE IT THROUGH THESE NEGOTIATIONS!
RIGHT AWAY, DEAR...

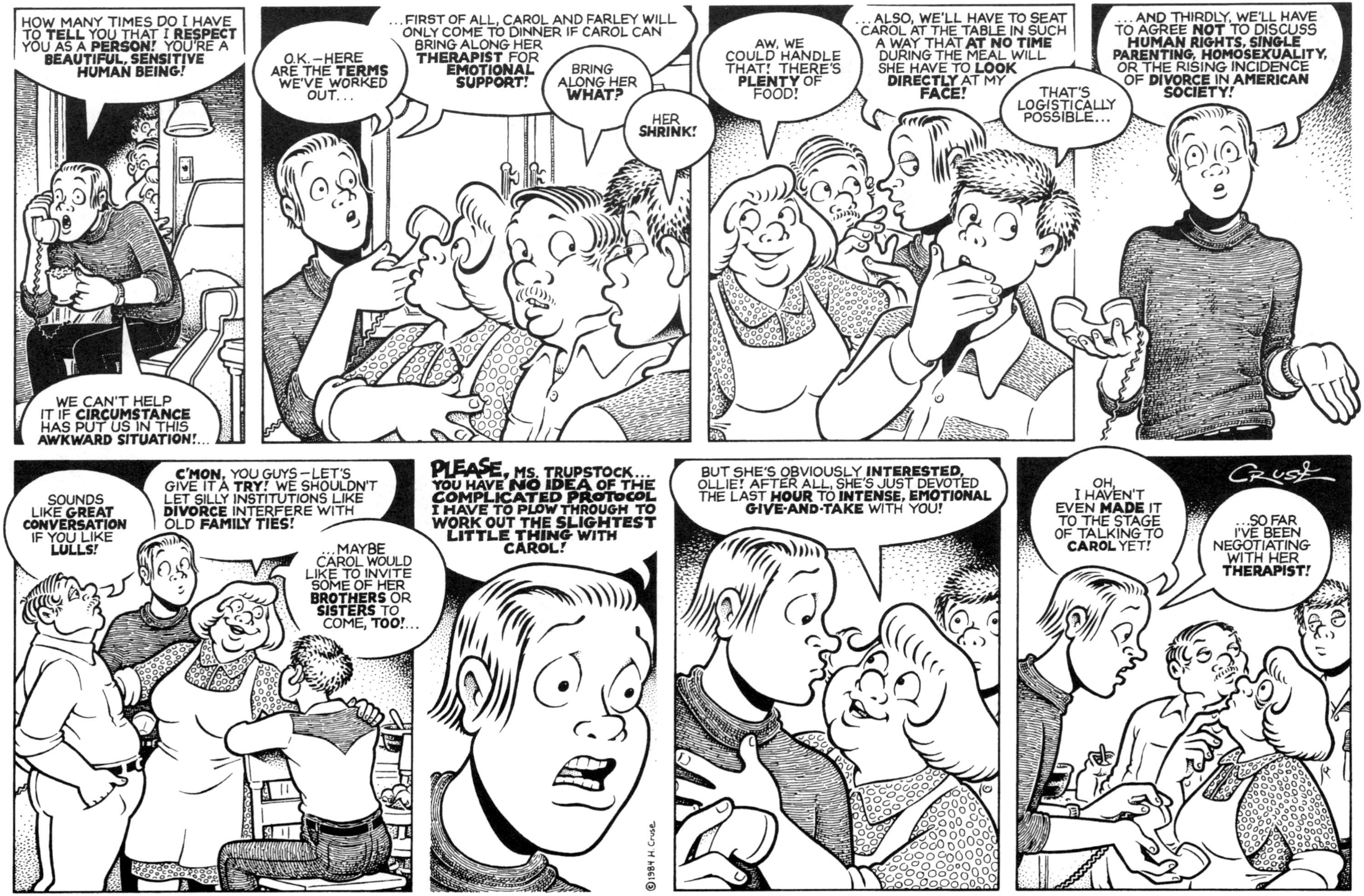
HOW MANY TIMES DO I HAVE TO **TELL** YOU THAT I **RESPECT** YOU AS A **PERSON!** YOU'RE A **BEAUTIFUL, SENSITIVE HUMAN BEING!**
WE CAN'T HELP IT IF **CIRCUMSTANCE** HAS PUT US IN THIS **AWKWARD SITUATION!**...
O.K.—HERE ARE THE **TERMS** WE'VE WORKED OUT...
...FIRST OF ALL, CAROL AND FARLEY WILL ONLY COME TO DINNER IF CAROL CAN BRING ALONG HER **THERAPIST** FOR **EMOTIONAL SUPPORT!**
BRING ALONG HER **WHAT?**
HER **SHRINK!**
AW, WE COULD HANDLE THAT! THERE'S **PLENTY** OF FOOD!
...ALSO, WE'LL HAVE TO SEAT CAROL AT THE TABLE IN SUCH A WAY THAT **AT NO TIME** DURING THE MEAL WILL SHE HAVE TO **LOOK DIRECTLY** AT MY **FACE!**
THAT'S LOGISTICALLY POSSIBLE...
...AND THIRDLY, WE'LL HAVE TO AGREE **NOT** TO DISCUSS **HUMAN RIGHTS, SINGLE PARENTING, HOMOSEXUALITY,** OR THE RISING INCIDENCE OF **DIVORCE** IN **AMERICAN SOCIETY!**
SOUNDS LIKE **GREAT CONVERSATION** IF YOU LIKE **LULLS!**
C'MON, YOU GUYS—LET'S GIVE IT A **TRY!** WE SHOULDN'T LET SILLY INSTITUTIONS LIKE **DIVORCE** INTERFERE WITH OLD **FAMILY TIES!**
...MAYBE CAROL WOULD LIKE TO INVITE SOME OF HER **BROTHERS** OR **SISTERS** TO COME, **TOO!**...
PLEASE, MS. TRUPSTOCK... **YOU HAVE NO IDEA OF THE COMPLICATED PROTOCOL I HAVE TO PLOW THROUGH TO WORK OUT THE SLIGHTEST LITTLE THING WITH CAROL!**
©1984 H. Cruse
BUT SHE'S OBVIOUSLY **INTERESTED,** OLLIE! AFTER ALL, SHE'S JUST DEVOTED THE LAST **HOUR** TO **INTENSE, EMOTIONAL GIVE-AND-TAKE** WITH YOU!
OH, I HAVEN'T EVEN **MADE** IT TO THE STAGE OF TALKING TO **CAROL** YET!
...SO FAR I'VE BEEN NEGOTIATING WITH HER **THERAPIST!**
CRUSE

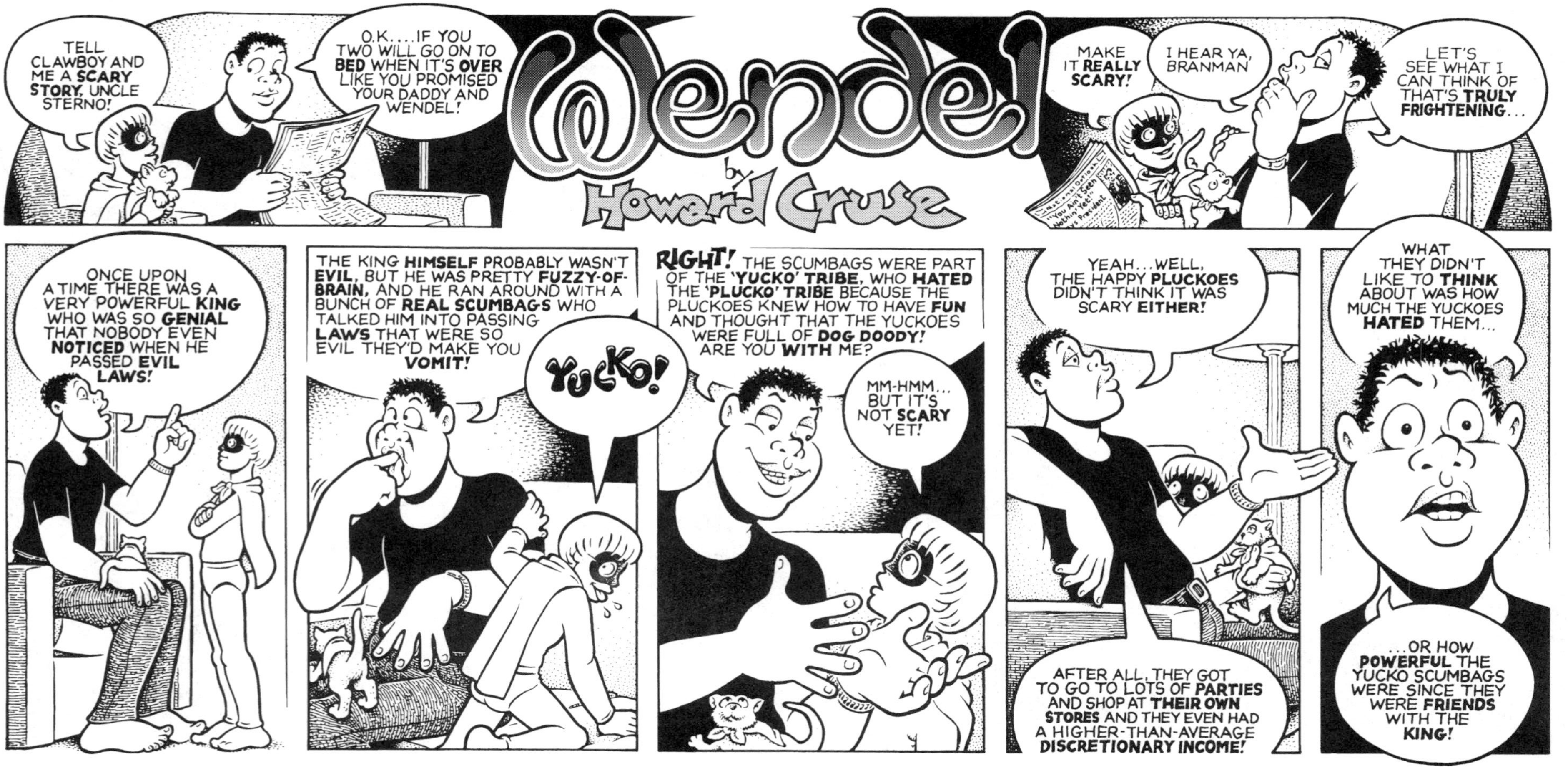
Wendel
by Howard Cruse
TELL CLAWBOY AND ME A SCARY STORY, UNCLE STERNO!
O.K.... IF YOU TWO WILL GO ON TO BED WHEN IT'S OVER LIKE YOU PROMISED YOUR DADDY AND WENDEL!
MAKE IT REALLY SCARY!
I HEAR YA, BRANMAN
LET'S SEE WHAT I CAN THINK OF THAT'S TRULY FRIGHTENING...
ONCE UPON A TIME THERE WAS A VERY POWERFUL KING WHO WAS SO GENIAL THAT NOBODY EVEN NOTICED WHEN HE PASSED EVIL LAWS!
THE KING HIMSELF PROBABLY WASN'T EVIL, BUT HE WAS PRETTY FUZZY-OF-BRAIN, AND HE RAN AROUND WITH A BUNCH OF REAL SCUMBAGS WHO TALKED HIM INTO PASSING LAWS THAT WERE SO EVIL THEY'D MAKE YOU VOMIT!
YUCKO!
RIGHT! THE SCUMBAGS WERE PART OF THE 'YUCKO' TRIBE, WHO HATED THE 'PLUCKO' TRIBE BECAUSE THE PLUCKOES KNEW HOW TO HAVE FUN AND THOUGHT THAT THE YUCKOES WERE FULL OF DOG DOODY! ARE YOU WITH ME?
MM-HMM... BUT IT'S NOT SCARY YET!
YEAH...WELL, THE HAPPY PLUCKOES DIDN'T THINK IT WAS SCARY EITHER!
AFTER ALL, THEY GOT TO GO TO LOTS OF PARTIES AND SHOP AT THEIR OWN STORES AND THEY EVEN HAD A HIGHER-THAN-AVERAGE DISCRETIONARY INCOME!
WHAT THEY DIDN'T LIKE TO THINK ABOUT WAS HOW MUCH THE YUCKOES HATED THEM...
...OR HOW POWERFUL THE YUCKO SCUMBAGS WERE SINCE THEY WERE FRIENDS WITH THE KING!

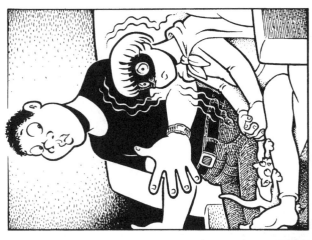

LITTLE CHILDREN WERE TAKEN AWAY FROM THEIR PLUCKO MOMS AND DADDIES...

PLUCKOES GOT SEPARATED FOREVER FROM THE OTHER PLUCKOES THAT THEY LOVED!

PRETTY SOON THE POLICE STARTED COMING AND ARRESTING THE PLUCKOES FOR MAYBE HAVING THE DISEASE!

NICE PLUCKOES WERE DRAGGED OFF TO HOSPITAL-PRISONS OR BEATEN UP BY MOBS!

©1985 by K. Cruse

NAH... SCARY STORIES DON'T BOTHER ME! G'NIGHT UNCLE STERNO!

NOW YOU'RE NOT GONNA HAVE TROUBLE SLEEPING TONIGHT, ARE YA?

G'NIGHT, FARLEY!

—THERE! WAS THAT SCARY ENOUGH FOR YOU?

YEAH, 'SPECIALLY THE LAST PART WITH THE SLIMY MONSTER!

NAMELY, BRANIMAN!!

JUST THEN A GIANT SLIMY MONSTER FROM MARS FLEW DOWN AND BIT OFF THE HEADS OF THE KING AND ALL THE YUCKOES AND PLUCKOES AND DRANK THEIR BLOOD AND TIED THEIR GUTS AROUND PARKING METERS UNTIL IT GOT KILLED BY THE ONLY REAL HERO WHO WAS STILL ALIVE IN THE WORLD!...

THE SCARY PART CAME WHEN THE KING MADE A LAW THAT ANYONE WHO WAS A MEMBER OF THE PLUCKO TRIBE MIGHT HAVE AN AWFUL DISEASE AND SO NONE OF THE PLUCKOES COULD BE FREE ANYMORE!

WHEN DOES IT GET SCARY?

67

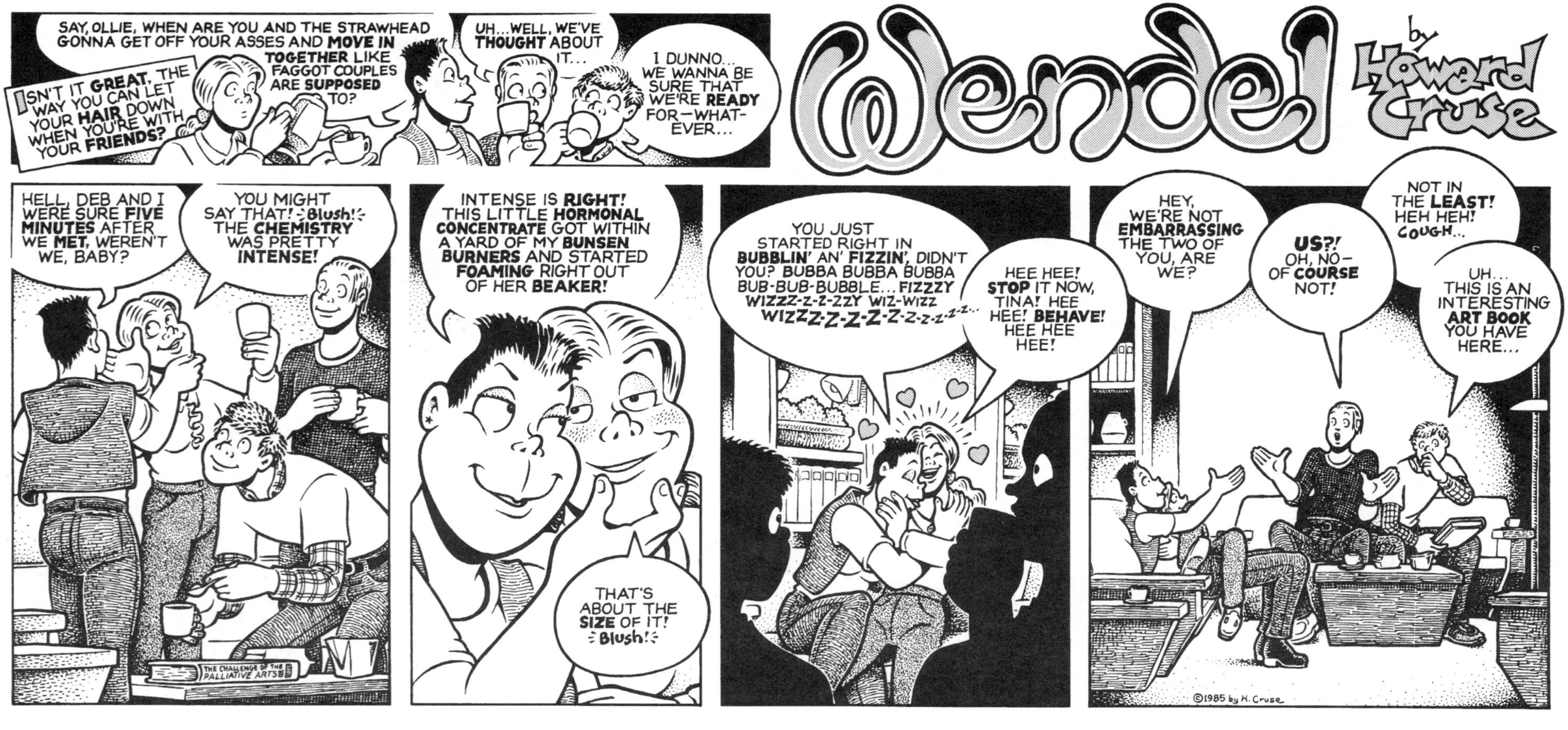
Wendel
by Howard Cruse
SAY, OLLIE, WHEN ARE YOU AND THE STRAWHEAD GONNA GET OFF YOUR ASSES AND **MOVE IN TOGETHER** LIKE FAGGOT COUPLES ARE **SUPPOSED** TO?
ISN'T IT **GREAT**, THE WAY YOU CAN LET YOUR **HAIR** DOWN WHEN YOU'RE WITH YOUR **FRIENDS?**
UH...WELL, WE'VE **THOUGHT** ABOUT IT...
I DUNNO... WE WANNA BE SURE THAT WE'RE **READY** FOR—WHAT-EVER...
HELL, DEB AND I WERE SURE **FIVE MINUTES** AFTER WE **MET**, WEREN'T WE, BABY?
YOU MIGHT SAY THAT! Blush! THE **CHEMISTRY** WAS PRETTY **INTENSE!**
THE CHALLENGE OF THE PALLIATIVE ARTS
INTENSE IS **RIGHT!** THIS LITTLE **HORMONAL CONCENTRATE** GOT WITHIN A YARD OF MY **BUNSEN BURNERS** AND STARTED **FOAMING** RIGHT OUT OF HER **BEAKER!**
THAT'S ABOUT THE **SIZE** OF IT! Blush!
YOU JUST STARTED RIGHT IN **BUBBLIN' AN' FIZZIN'**, DIDN'T YOU? BUBBA BUBBA BUBBA BUB-BUB-BUBBLE... **FIZZZY WIZZZ-Z-Z-ZZY** WIZ-WIZZ **WIZZZ-Z-Z-Z-Z**-Z-Z-Z-Z-Z...
HEE HEE! **STOP** IT NOW, TINA! HEE HEE! **BEHAVE!** HEE HEE HEE!
HEY, WE'RE NOT **EMBARRASSING** THE TWO OF YOU, ARE WE?
US?! OH, NO— OF **COURSE** NOT!
NOT IN THE **LEAST!** HEH HEH! COUGH...
UH... THIS IS AN INTERESTING **ART BOOK** YOU HAVE HERE...
©1985 by H. Cruse

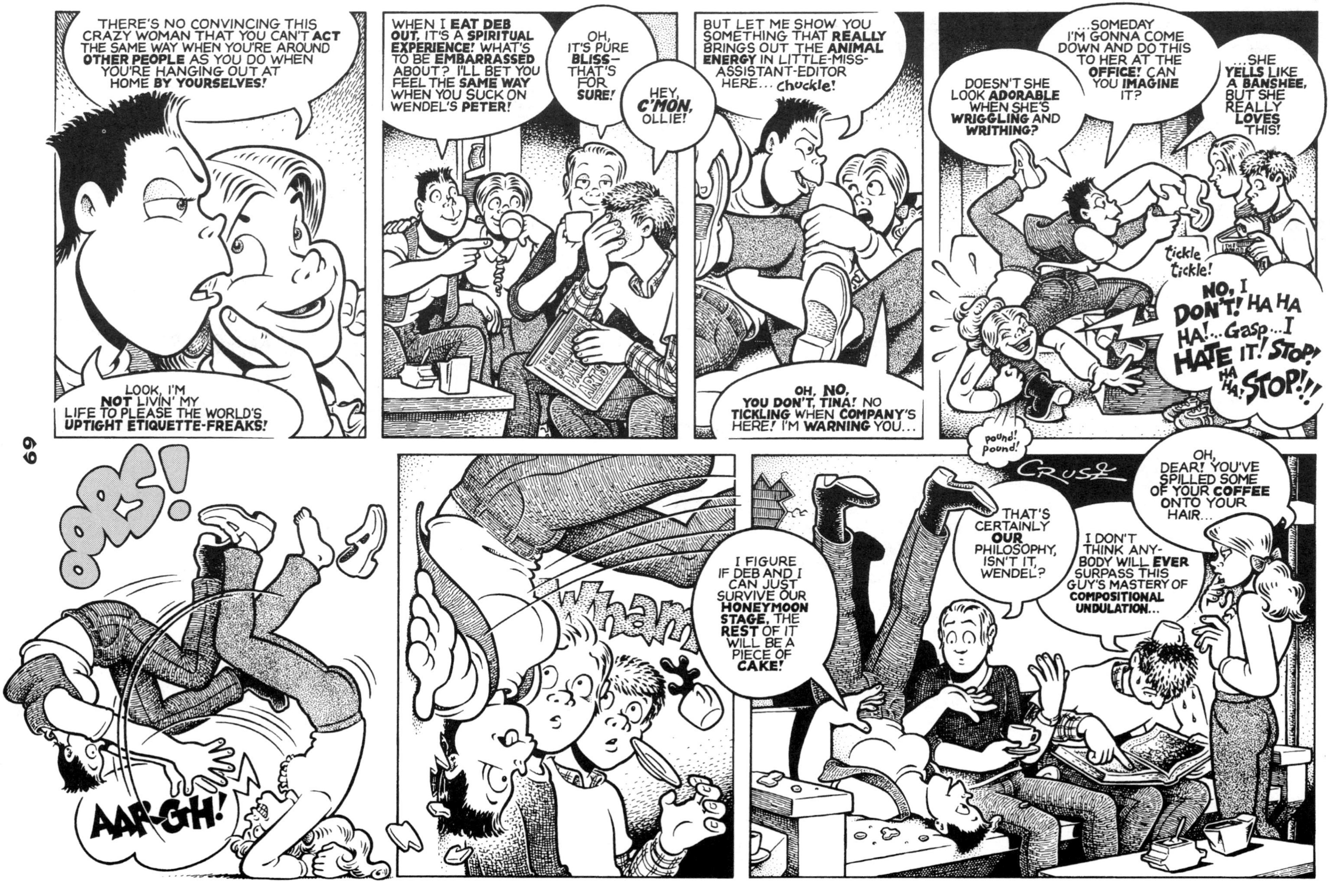
THERE'S NO CONVINCING THIS CRAZY WOMAN THAT YOU CAN'T ACT THE SAME WAY WHEN YOU'RE AROUND OTHER PEOPLE AS YOU DO WHEN YOU'RE HANGING OUT AT HOME BY YOURSELVES!
LOOK, I'M NOT LIVIN' MY LIFE TO PLEASE THE WORLD'S UPTIGHT ETIQUETTE-FREAKS!
WHEN I EAT DEB OUT, IT'S A SPIRITUAL EXPERIENCE! WHAT'S TO BE EMBARRASSED ABOUT? I'LL BET YOU FEEL THE SAME WAY WHEN YOU SUCK ON WENDEL'S PETER!
OH, IT'S PURE BLISS— THAT'S FOR SURE!
HEY, C'MON, OLLIE!
BUT LET ME SHOW YOU SOMETHING THAT REALLY BRINGS OUT THE ANIMAL ENERGY IN LITTLE-MISS-ASSISTANT-EDITOR HERE... chuckle!
OH, NO, YOU DON'T, TINA! NO TICKLING WHEN COMPANY'S HERE! I'M WARNING YOU...
DOESN'T SHE LOOK ADORABLE WHEN SHE'S WRIGGLING AND WRITHING?
...SOMEDAY I'M GONNA COME DOWN AND DO THIS TO HER AT THE OFFICE! CAN YOU IMAGINE IT?
...SHE YELLS LIKE A BANSHEE, BUT SHE REALLY LOVES THIS!
tickle tickle!
NO, I DON'T! HA HA HA!...Gasp...I HATE IT! STOP! HA HA! STOP!!!
pound! pound!
OOPS!
AAR-GH!
WHAM!
I FIGURE IF DEB AND I CAN JUST SURVIVE OUR HONEYMOON STAGE, THE REST OF IT WILL BE A PIECE OF CAKE!
CRUSE
THAT'S CERTAINLY OUR PHILOSOPHY, ISN'T IT, WENDEL?
I DON'T THINK ANY-BODY WILL EVER SURPASS THIS GUY'S MASTERY OF COMPOSITIONAL UNDULATION...
OH, DEAR! YOU'VE SPILLED SOME OF YOUR COFFEE ONTO YOUR HAIR...

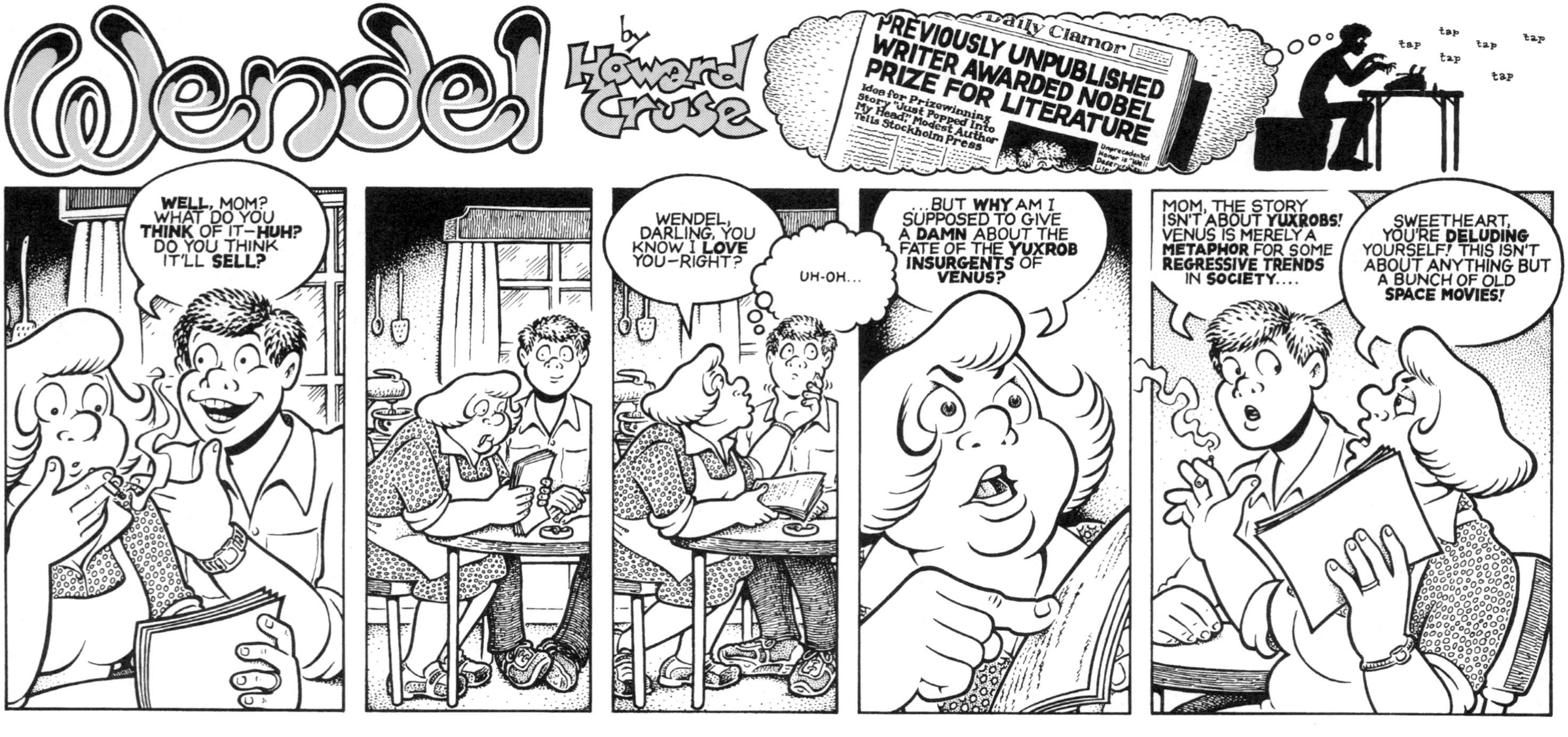
Wendel
by Howard Cruse
Daily Clamor
PREVIOUSLY UNPUBLISHED WRITER AWARDED NOBEL PRIZE FOR LITERATURE
Idea for Prizewinning Story "Just Popped Into My Head," Modest Author Tells Stockholm Press
tap tap tap tap tap tap
WELL, MOM? WHAT DO YOU THINK OF IT—HUH? DO YOU THINK IT'LL SELL?
WENDEL, DARLING, YOU KNOW I LOVE YOU—RIGHT?
UH-OH...
...BUT WHY AM I SUPPOSED TO GIVE A DAMN ABOUT THE FATE OF THE YUXROB INSURGENTS OF VENUS?
MOM, THE STORY ISN'T ABOUT YUXROBS! VENUS IS MERELY A METAPHOR FOR SOME REGRESSIVE TRENDS IN SOCIETY....
SWEETHEART, YOU'RE DELUDING YOURSELF! THIS ISN'T ABOUT ANYTHING BUT A BUNCH OF OLD SPACE MOVIES!

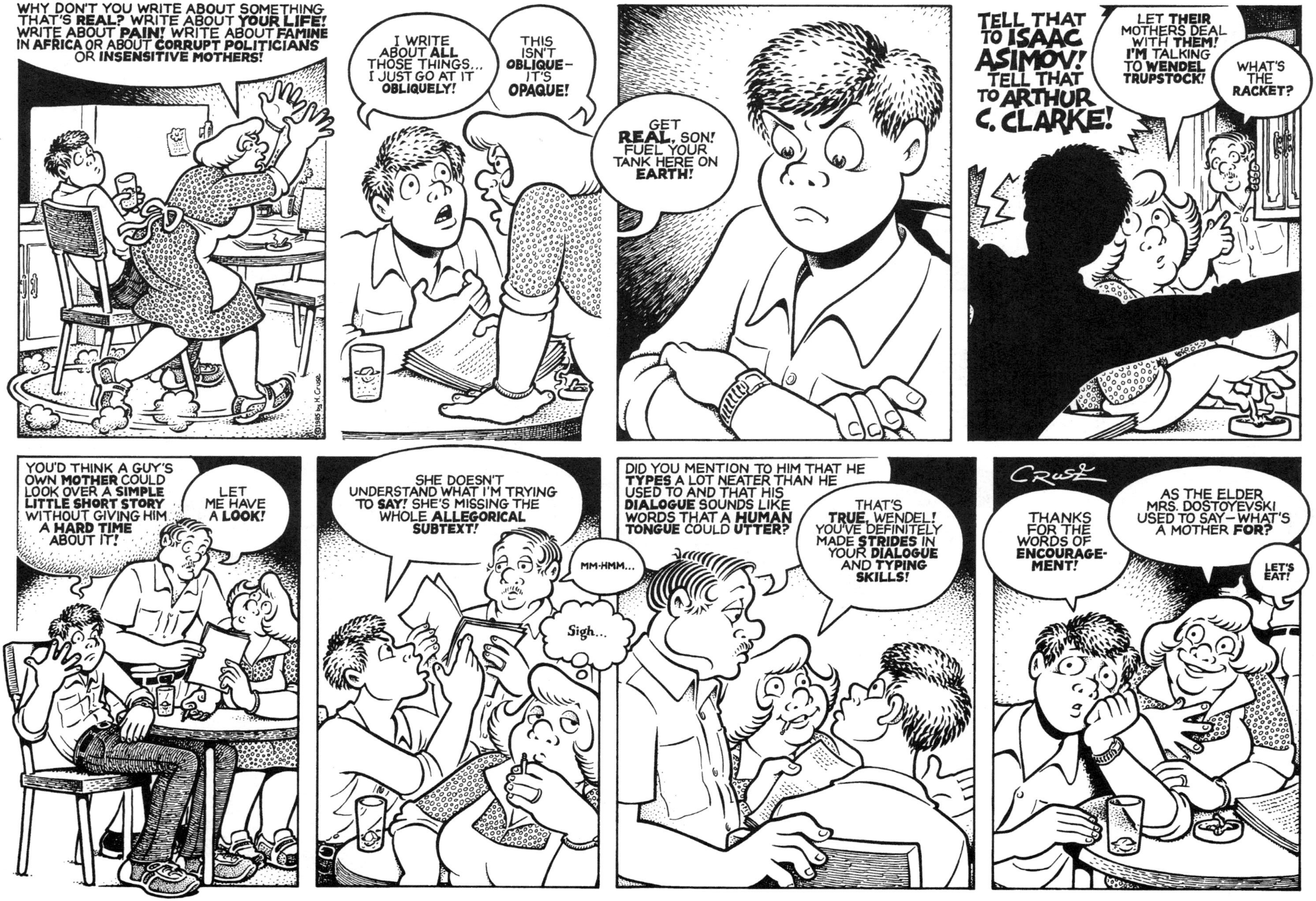

WHY DON'T YOU WRITE ABOUT SOMETHING THAT'S **REAL?** WRITE ABOUT **YOUR LIFE!** WRITE ABOUT **PAIN!** WRITE ABOUT **FAMINE** IN **AFRICA** OR ABOUT **CORRUPT POLITICIANS** OR **INSENSITIVE MOTHERS!**
©1985 by H. Cruse
I WRITE ABOUT **ALL** THOSE THINGS... I JUST GO AT IT **OBLIQUELY!**
THIS ISN'T **OBLIQUE**– IT'S **OPAQUE!**
GET **REAL**, SON! FUEL YOUR TANK HERE ON **EARTH!**
TELL THAT TO **ISAAC ASIMOV!** TELL THAT TO **ARTHUR C. CLARKE!**
LET **THEIR** MOTHERS DEAL WITH **THEM! I'M** TALKING TO **WENDEL TRUPSTOCK!**
WHAT'S THE **RACKET?**
YOU'D THINK A GUY'S OWN **MOTHER** COULD LOOK OVER A **SIMPLE LITTLE SHORT STORY** WITHOUT GIVING HIM A **HARD TIME** ABOUT IT!
LET ME HAVE A **LOOK!**
SHE DOESN'T UNDERSTAND WHAT I'M TRYING TO **SAY!** SHE'S MISSING THE WHOLE **ALLEGORICAL SUBTEXT!**
MM-HMM...
Sigh...
DID YOU MENTION TO HIM THAT HE **TYPES** A LOT NEATER THAN HE USED TO AND THAT HIS **DIALOGUE** SOUNDS LIKE WORDS THAT A **HUMAN TONGUE** COULD **UTTER?**
THAT'S **TRUE**, WENDEL! YOU'VE DEFINITELY MADE **STRIDES** IN YOUR **DIALOGUE** AND **TYPING SKILLS!**
CRUSE
THANKS FOR THE WORDS OF **ENCOURAGE-MENT!**
AS THE ELDER MRS. DOSTOYEVSKI USED TO SAY–WHAT'S A MOTHER **FOR?**
LET'S EAT!

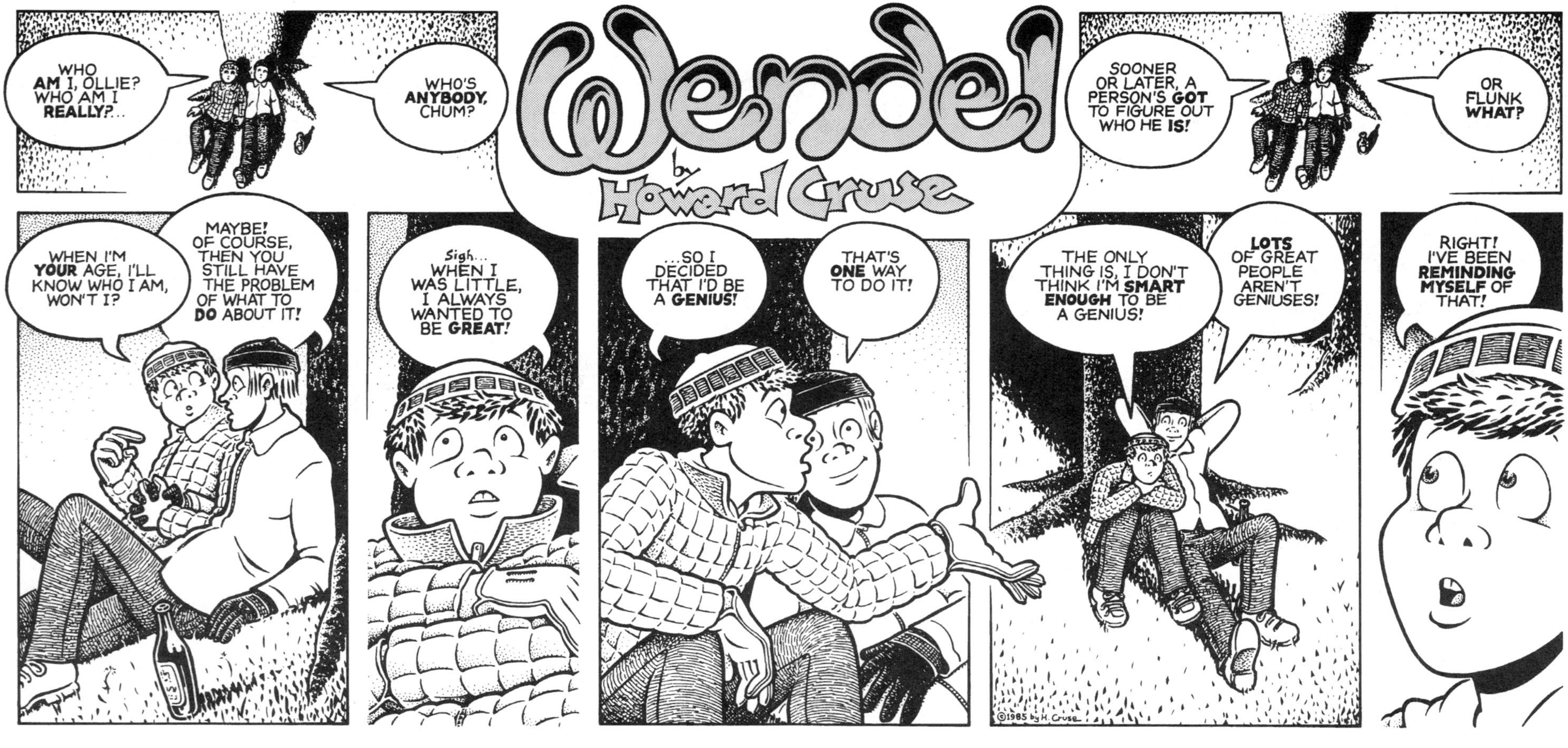
Wendel
by Howard Cruse
WHO AM I, OLLIE? WHO AM I REALLY?...
WHO'S ANYBODY, CHUM?
SOONER OR LATER, A PERSON'S GOT TO FIGURE OUT WHO HE IS!
OR FLUNK WHAT?
WHEN I'M YOUR AGE, I'LL KNOW WHO I AM, WON'T I?
MAYBE! OF COURSE, THEN YOU STILL HAVE THE PROBLEM OF WHAT TO DO ABOUT IT!
Sigh... WHEN I WAS LITTLE, I ALWAYS WANTED TO BE GREAT!
...SO I DECIDED THAT I'D BE A GENIUS!
THAT'S ONE WAY TO DO IT!
THE ONLY THING IS, I DON'T THINK I'M SMART ENOUGH TO BE A GENIUS!
LOTS OF GREAT PEOPLE AREN'T GENIUSES!
RIGHT! I'VE BEEN REMINDING MYSELF OF THAT!
©1985 by H. Cruse

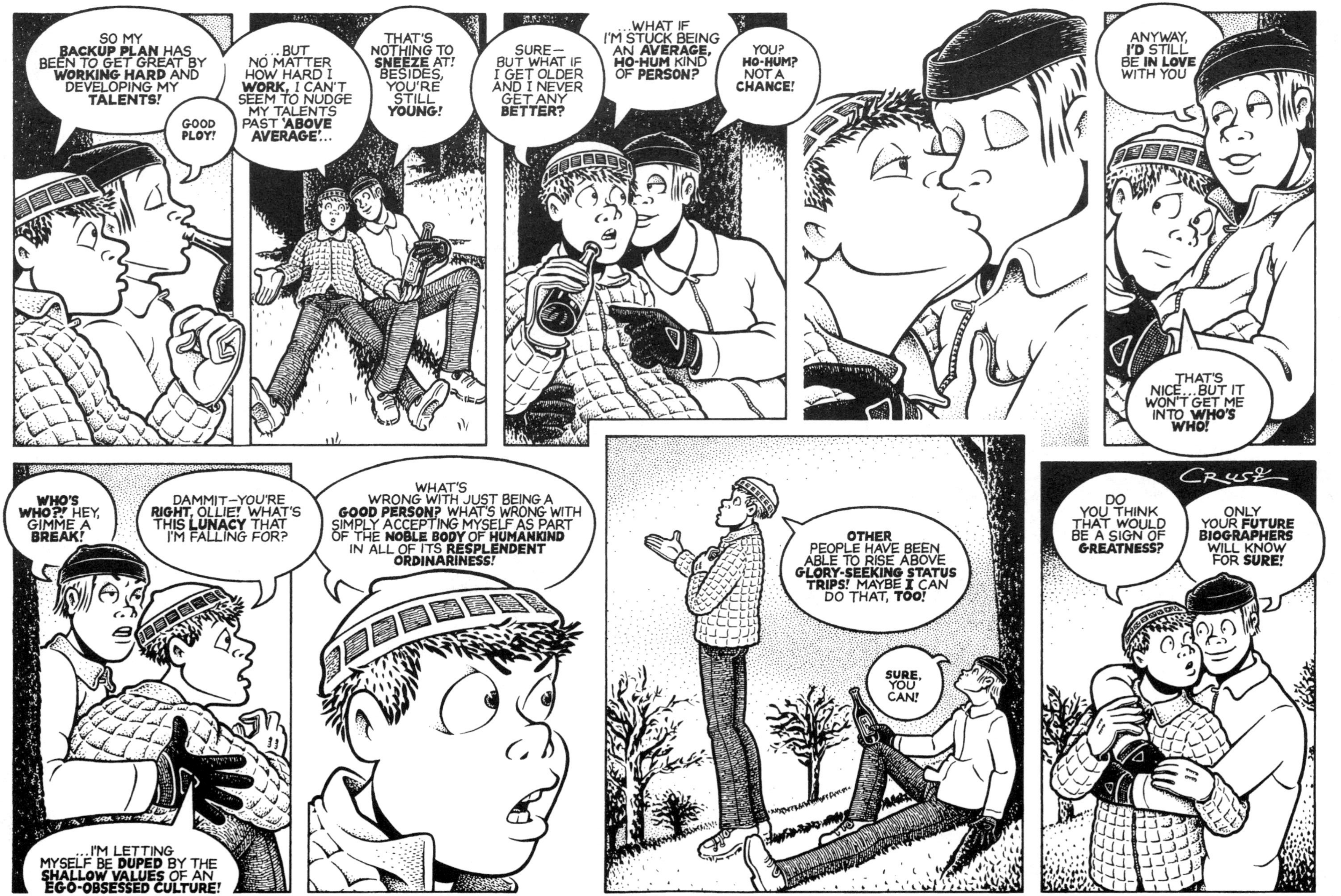
SO MY **BACKUP PLAN** HAS BEEN TO GET GREAT BY **WORKING HARD** AND DEVELOPING MY **TALENTS!**
GOOD PLOY!
...BUT NO MATTER HOW HARD I **WORK,** I CAN'T SEEM TO NUDGE MY TALENTS PAST **'ABOVE AVERAGE'...**
THAT'S NOTHING TO **SNEEZE** AT! BESIDES, YOU'RE STILL **YOUNG!**
SURE— BUT WHAT IF I GET OLDER AND I NEVER GET ANY **BETTER?**
...WHAT IF I'M STUCK BEING AN **AVERAGE, HO-HUM** KIND OF **PERSON?**
YOU? **HO-HUM?** NOT A **CHANCE!**
ANYWAY, **I'D** STILL BE **IN LOVE** WITH YOU
THAT'S NICE...BUT IT WON'T GET ME INTO **WHO'S WHO!**
WHO'S WHO?! HEY, GIMME A **BREAK!**
DAMMIT—YOU'RE **RIGHT, OLLIE!** WHAT'S THIS **LUNACY** THAT I'M FALLING FOR?
...I'M LETTING MYSELF BE **DUPED** BY THE **SHALLOW VALUES** OF AN **EGO-OBSESSED CULTURE!**
WHAT'S WRONG WITH JUST BEING A **GOOD PERSON?** WHAT'S WRONG WITH SIMPLY ACCEPTING MYSELF AS PART OF THE **NOBLE BODY** OF **HUMANKIND** IN ALL OF ITS **RESPLENDENT ORDINARINESS!**
OTHER PEOPLE HAVE BEEN ABLE TO RISE ABOVE **GLORY-SEEKING STATUS TRIPS!** MAYBE **I** CAN DO THAT, **TOO!**
SURE, YOU CAN!
DO YOU THINK THAT WOULD BE A SIGN OF **GREATNESS?**
ONLY YOUR **FUTURE BIOGRAPHERS** WILL KNOW FOR **SURE!**
CRUSE

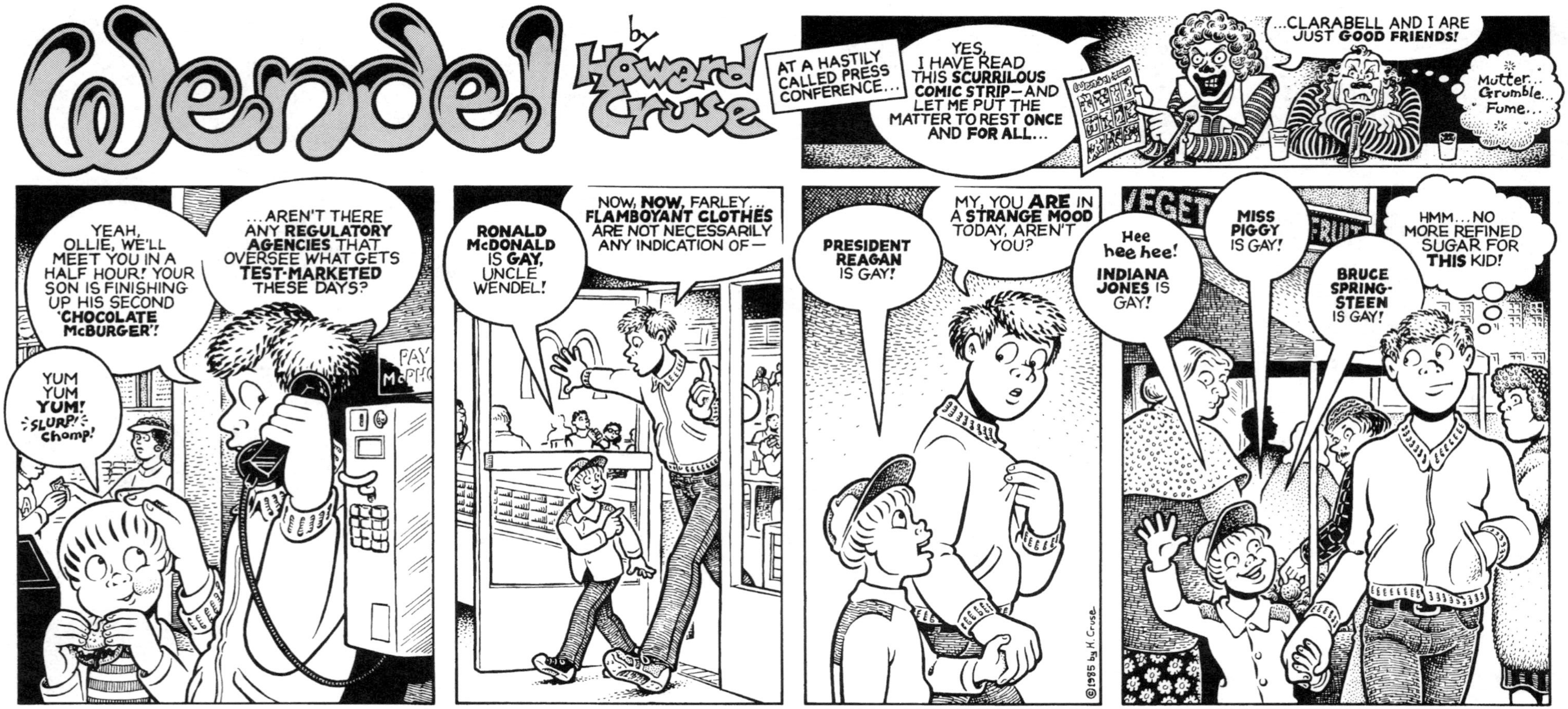
Wendel
by Howard Cruse
AT A HASTILY CALLED PRESS CONFERENCE...
YES, I HAVE READ THIS SCURRILOUS COMIC STRIP—AND LET ME PUT THE MATTER TO REST ONCE AND FOR ALL...
...CLARABELL AND I ARE JUST GOOD FRIENDS!
Mutter.. Grumble.. Fume..
YEAH, OLLIE, WE'LL MEET YOU IN A HALF HOUR! YOUR SON IS FINISHING UP HIS SECOND 'CHOCOLATE McBURGER'!
...AREN'T THERE ANY REGULATORY AGENCIES THAT OVERSEE WHAT GETS TEST-MARKETED THESE DAYS?
YUM YUM YUM! SLURP! Chomp!
RONALD McDONALD IS GAY, UNCLE WENDEL!
NOW, NOW, FARLEY... FLAMBOYANT CLOTHES ARE NOT NECESSARILY ANY INDICATION OF—
PRESIDENT REAGAN IS GAY!
MY, YOU ARE IN A STRANGE MOOD TODAY, AREN'T YOU?
©1985 by H. Cruse.
Hee hee hee! INDIANA JONES IS GAY!
MISS PIGGY IS GAY!
BRUCE SPRING-STEEN IS GAY!
HMM...NO MORE REFINED SUGAR FOR THIS KID!

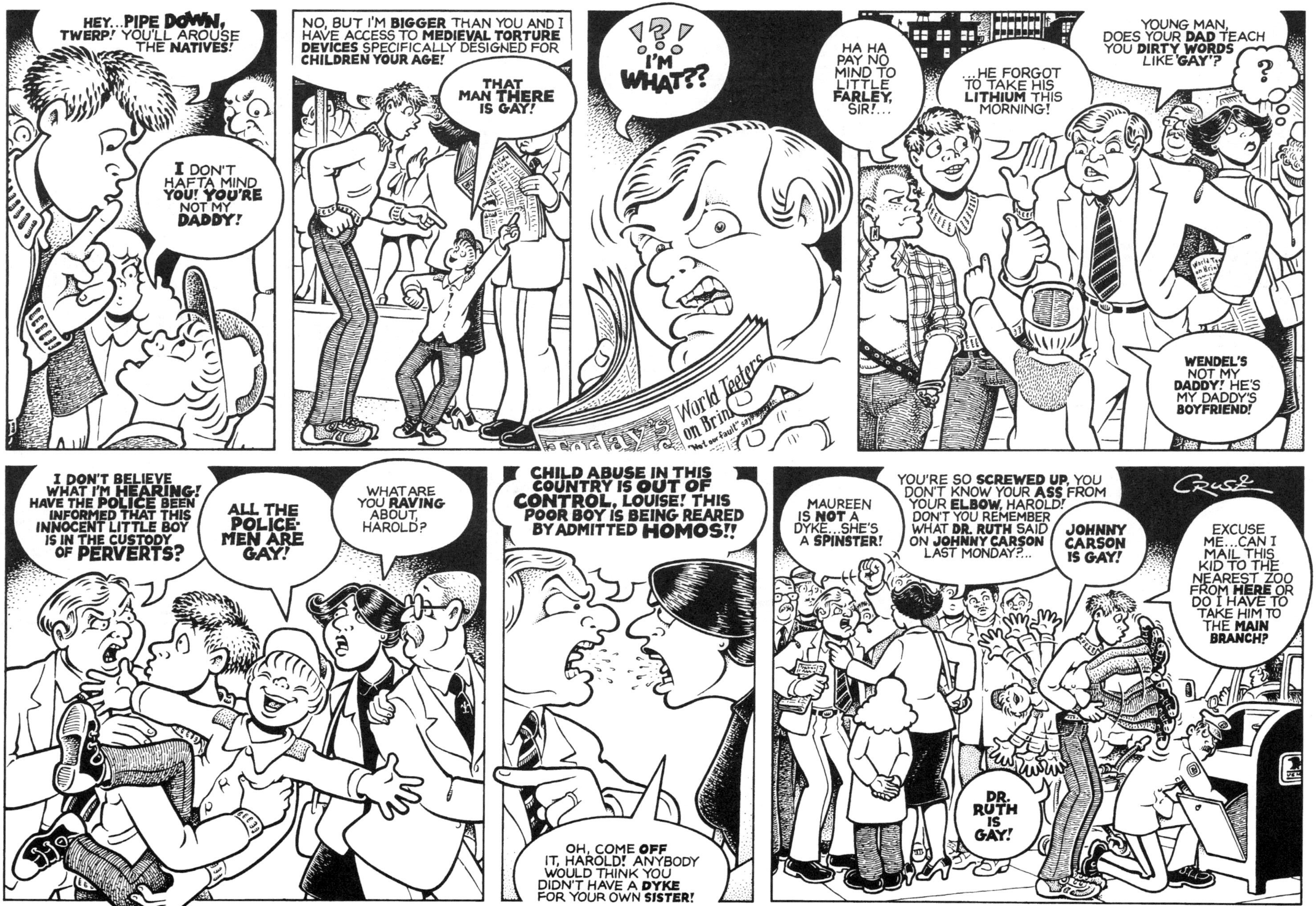
HEY...PIPE DOWN, TWERP! YOU'LL AROUSE THE NATIVES!
I DON'T HAFTA MIND YOU! YOU'RE NOT MY DADDY!
NO, BUT I'M BIGGER THAN YOU AND I HAVE ACCESS TO MEDIEVAL TORTURE DEVICES SPECIFICALLY DESIGNED FOR CHILDREN YOUR AGE!
THAT MAN THERE IS GAY!
!?! I'M WHAT??
World Teeters on Brink
"Not our fault," says
HA HA PAY NO MIND TO LITTLE FARLEY, SIR!...
...HE FORGOT TO TAKE HIS LITHIUM THIS MORNING!
YOUNG MAN, DOES YOUR DAD TEACH YOU DIRTY WORDS LIKE 'GAY'?
?
WENDEL'S NOT MY DADDY! HE'S MY DADDY'S BOYFRIEND!
I DON'T BELIEVE WHAT I'M HEARING! HAVE THE POLICE BEEN INFORMED THAT THIS INNOCENT LITTLE BOY IS IN THE CUSTODY OF PERVERTS?
ALL THE POLICE-MEN ARE GAY!
WHAT ARE YOU RAVING ABOUT, HAROLD?
CHILD ABUSE IN THIS COUNTRY IS OUT OF CONTROL, LOUISE! THIS POOR BOY IS BEING REARED BY ADMITTED HOMOS!!
OH, COME OFF IT, HAROLD! ANYBODY WOULD THINK YOU DIDN'T HAVE A DYKE FOR YOUR OWN SISTER!
CRUSE
MAUREEN IS NOT A DYKE...SHE'S A SPINSTER!
YOU'RE SO SCREWED UP, YOU DON'T KNOW YOUR ASS FROM YOUR ELBOW, HAROLD! DON'T YOU REMEMBER WHAT DR. RUTH SAID ON JOHNNY CARSON LAST MONDAY?...
JOHNNY CARSON IS GAY!
DR. RUTH IS GAY!
EXCUSE ME...CAN I MAIL THIS KID TO THE NEAREST ZOO FROM HERE OR DO I HAVE TO TAKE HIM TO THE MAIN BRANCH?

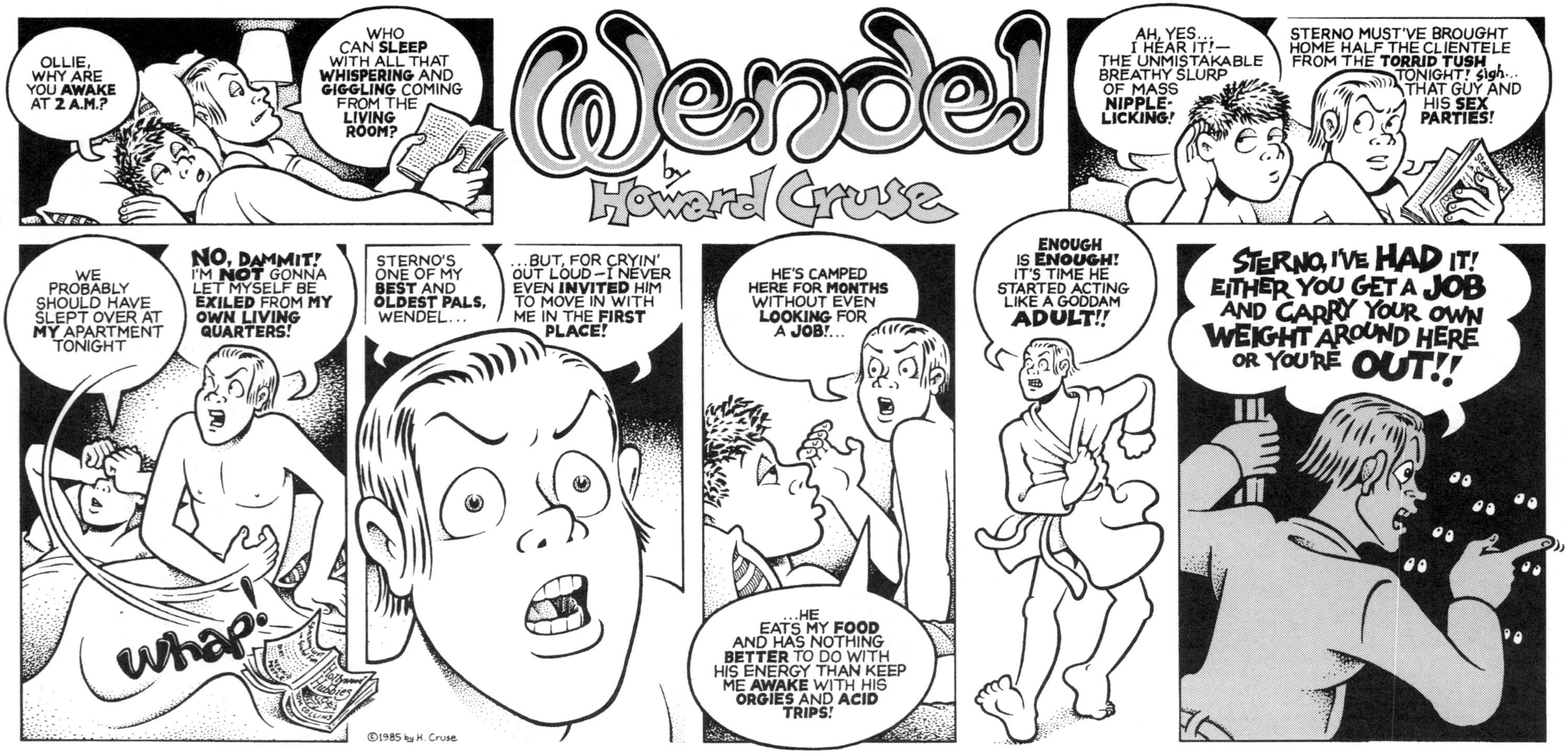
Wendel
by Howard Cruse
OLLIE, WHY ARE YOU AWAKE AT 2 A.M.?
WHO CAN SLEEP WITH ALL THAT WHISPERING AND GIGGLING COMING FROM THE LIVING ROOM?
AH, YES... I HEAR IT!— THE UNMISTAKABLE BREATHY SLURP OF MASS NIPPLE-LICKING!
STERNO MUST'VE BROUGHT HOME HALF THE CLIENTELE FROM THE TORRID TUSH TONIGHT! sigh... THAT GUY AND HIS SEX PARTIES!
WE PROBABLY SHOULD HAVE SLEPT OVER AT MY APARTMENT TONIGHT
NO, DAMMIT! I'M NOT GONNA LET MYSELF BE EXILED FROM MY OWN LIVING QUARTERS!
WHAP!
STERNO'S ONE OF MY BEST AND OLDEST PALS, WENDEL...
...BUT, FOR CRYIN' OUT LOUD—I NEVER EVEN INVITED HIM TO MOVE IN WITH ME IN THE FIRST PLACE!
HE'S CAMPED HERE FOR MONTHS WITHOUT EVEN LOOKING FOR A JOB!...
...HE EATS MY FOOD AND HAS NOTHING BETTER TO DO WITH HIS ENERGY THAN KEEP ME AWAKE WITH HIS ORGIES AND ACID TRIPS!
ENOUGH IS ENOUGH! IT'S TIME HE STARTED ACTING LIKE A GODDAM ADULT!!
STERNO, I'VE HAD IT! EITHER YOU GET A JOB AND CARRY YOUR OWN WEIGHT AROUND HERE OR YOU'RE OUT!!
©1985 by H. Cruse

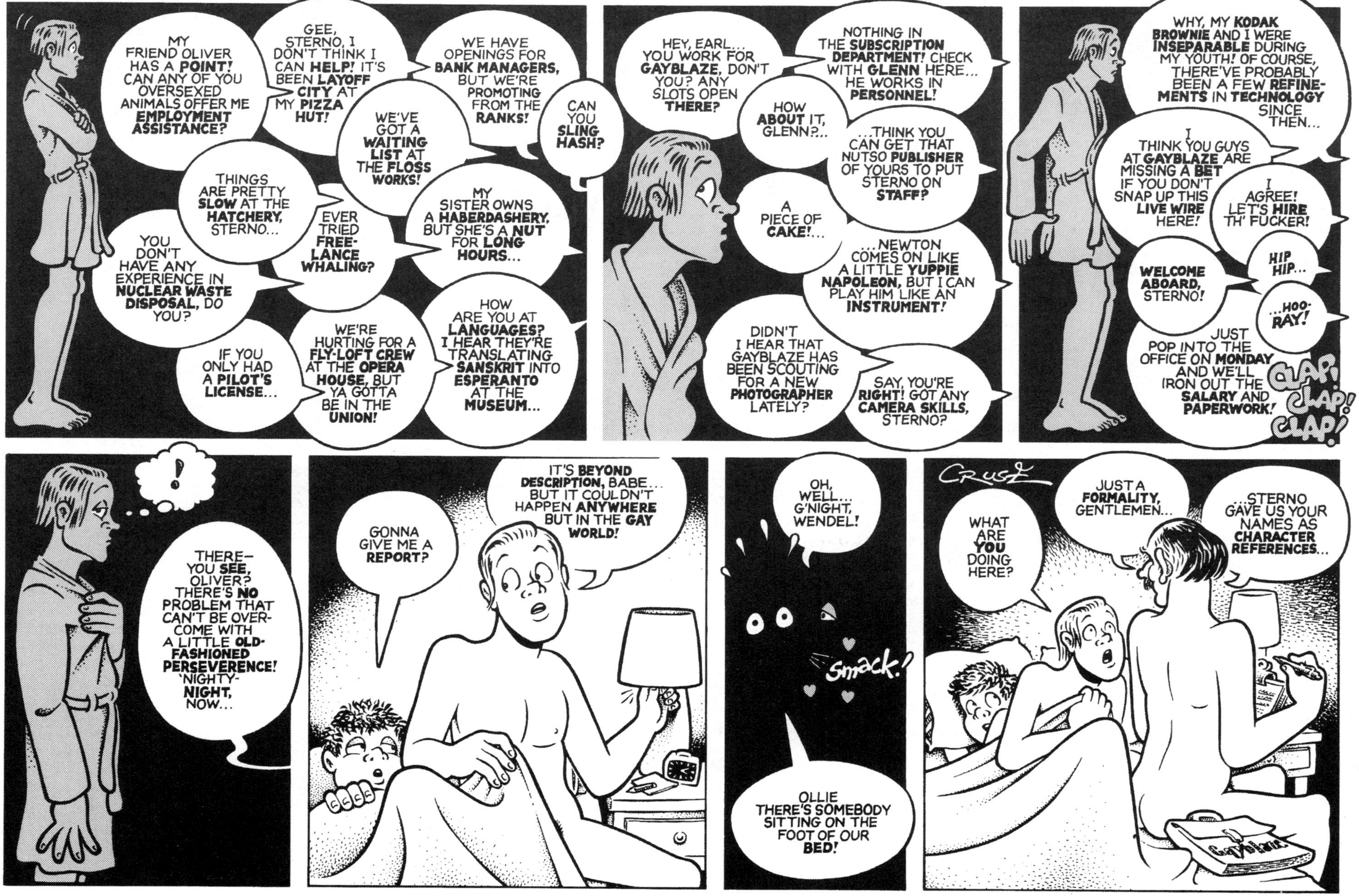
MY FRIEND OLIVER HAS A POINT! CAN ANY OF YOU OVERSEXED ANIMALS OFFER ME EMPLOYMENT ASSISTANCE?
GEE, STERNO, I DON'T THINK I CAN HELP! IT'S BEEN LAYOFF CITY AT MY PIZZA HUT!
WE HAVE OPENINGS FOR BANK MANAGERS, BUT WE'RE PROMOTING FROM THE RANKS!
CAN YOU SLING HASH?
WE'VE GOT A WAITING LIST AT THE FLOSS WORKS!
THINGS ARE PRETTY SLOW AT THE HATCHERY, STERNO...
EVER TRIED FREE-LANCE WHALING?
MY SISTER OWNS A HABERDASHERY, BUT SHE'S A NUT FOR LONG HOURS...
YOU DON'T HAVE ANY EXPERIENCE IN NUCLEAR WASTE DISPOSAL, DO YOU?
HOW ARE YOU AT LANGUAGES? I HEAR THEY'RE TRANSLATING SANSKRIT INTO ESPERANTO AT THE MUSEUM...
IF YOU ONLY HAD A PILOT'S LICENSE...
WE'RE HURTING FOR A FLY-LOFT CREW AT THE OPERA HOUSE, BUT YA GOTTA BE IN THE UNION!
HEY, EARL... YOU WORK FOR GAYBLAZE, DON'T YOU? ANY SLOTS OPEN THERE?
NOTHING IN THE SUBSCRIPTION DEPARTMENT! CHECK WITH GLENN HERE... HE WORKS IN PERSONNEL!
HOW ABOUT IT, GLENN?...
...THINK YOU CAN GET THAT NUTSO PUBLISHER OF YOURS TO PUT STERNO ON STAFF?
A PIECE OF CAKE!...
...NEWTON COMES ON LIKE A LITTLE YUPPIE NAPOLEON, BUT I CAN PLAY HIM LIKE AN INSTRUMENT!
DIDN'T I HEAR THAT GAYBLAZE HAS BEEN SCOUTING FOR A NEW PHOTOGRAPHER LATELY?
SAY, YOU'RE RIGHT! GOT ANY CAMERA SKILLS, STERNO?
WHY, MY KODAK BROWNIE AND I WERE INSEPARABLE DURING MY YOUTH! OF COURSE, THERE'VE PROBABLY BEEN A FEW REFINE-MENTS IN TECHNOLOGY SINCE THEN...
I THINK YOU GUYS AT GAYBLAZE ARE MISSING A BET IF YOU DON'T SNAP UP THIS LIVE WIRE HERE!
I AGREE! LET'S HIRE TH' FUCKER!
WELCOME ABOARD, STERNO!
HIP HIP...
...HOO-RAY!
JUST POP INTO THE OFFICE ON MONDAY AND WE'LL IRON OUT THE SALARY AND PAPERWORK!
CLAP! CLAP! CLAP!
!
THERE— YOU SEE, OLIVER? THERE'S NO PROBLEM THAT CAN'T BE OVER-COME WITH A LITTLE OLD-FASHIONED PERSEVERENCE! 'NIGHTY-NIGHT, NOW...
GONNA GIVE ME A REPORT?
IT'S BEYOND DESCRIPTION, BABE... BUT IT COULDN'T HAPPEN ANYWHERE BUT IN THE GAY WORLD!
OH, WELL... G'NIGHT, WENDEL!
SMACK!
OLLIE THERE'S SOMEBODY SITTING ON THE FOOT OF OUR BED!
CRUSE
WHAT ARE YOU DOING HERE?
JUST A FORMALITY, GENTLEMEN...
...STERNO GAVE US YOUR NAMES AS CHARACTER REFERENCES...

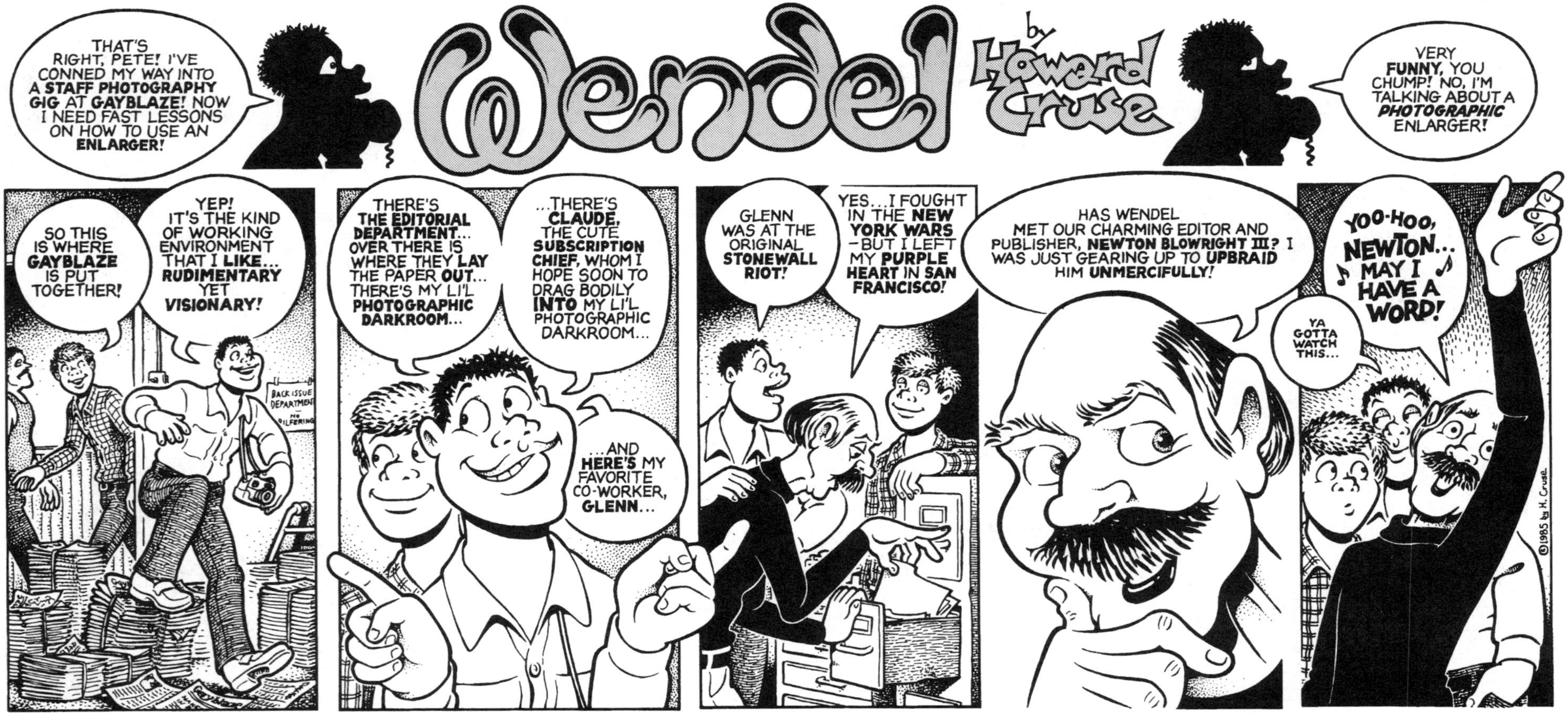
Wendel
by Howard Cruse
THAT'S RIGHT, PETE! I'VE CONNED MY WAY INTO A STAFF PHOTOGRAPHY GIG AT GAYBLAZE! NOW I NEED FAST LESSONS ON HOW TO USE AN ENLARGER!
VERY FUNNY, YOU CHUMP! NO, I'M TALKING ABOUT A PHOTOGRAPHIC ENLARGER!
SO THIS IS WHERE GAYBLAZE IS PUT TOGETHER!
YEP! IT'S THE KIND OF WORKING ENVIRONMENT THAT I LIKE... RUDIMENTARY YET VISIONARY!
BACK ISSUE DEPARTMENT
NO PILFERING
THERE'S THE EDITORIAL DEPARTMENT... OVER THERE IS WHERE THEY LAY THE PAPER OUT... THERE'S MY LI'L PHOTOGRAPHIC DARKROOM...
...THERE'S CLAUDE, THE CUTE SUBSCRIPTION CHIEF, WHOM I HOPE SOON TO DRAG BODILY INTO MY LI'L PHOTOGRAPHIC DARKROOM...
...AND HERE'S MY FAVORITE CO-WORKER, GLENN...
GLENN WAS AT THE ORIGINAL STONEWALL RIOT!
YES...I FOUGHT IN THE NEW YORK WARS —BUT I LEFT MY PURPLE HEART IN SAN FRANCISCO!
HAS WENDEL MET OUR CHARMING EDITOR AND PUBLISHER, NEWTON BLOWRIGHT III? I WAS JUST GEARING UP TO UPBRAID HIM UNMERCIFULLY!
YA GOTTA WATCH THIS...
YOO-HOO, NEWTON... MAY I HAVE A WORD!
©1985 by H. Cruse

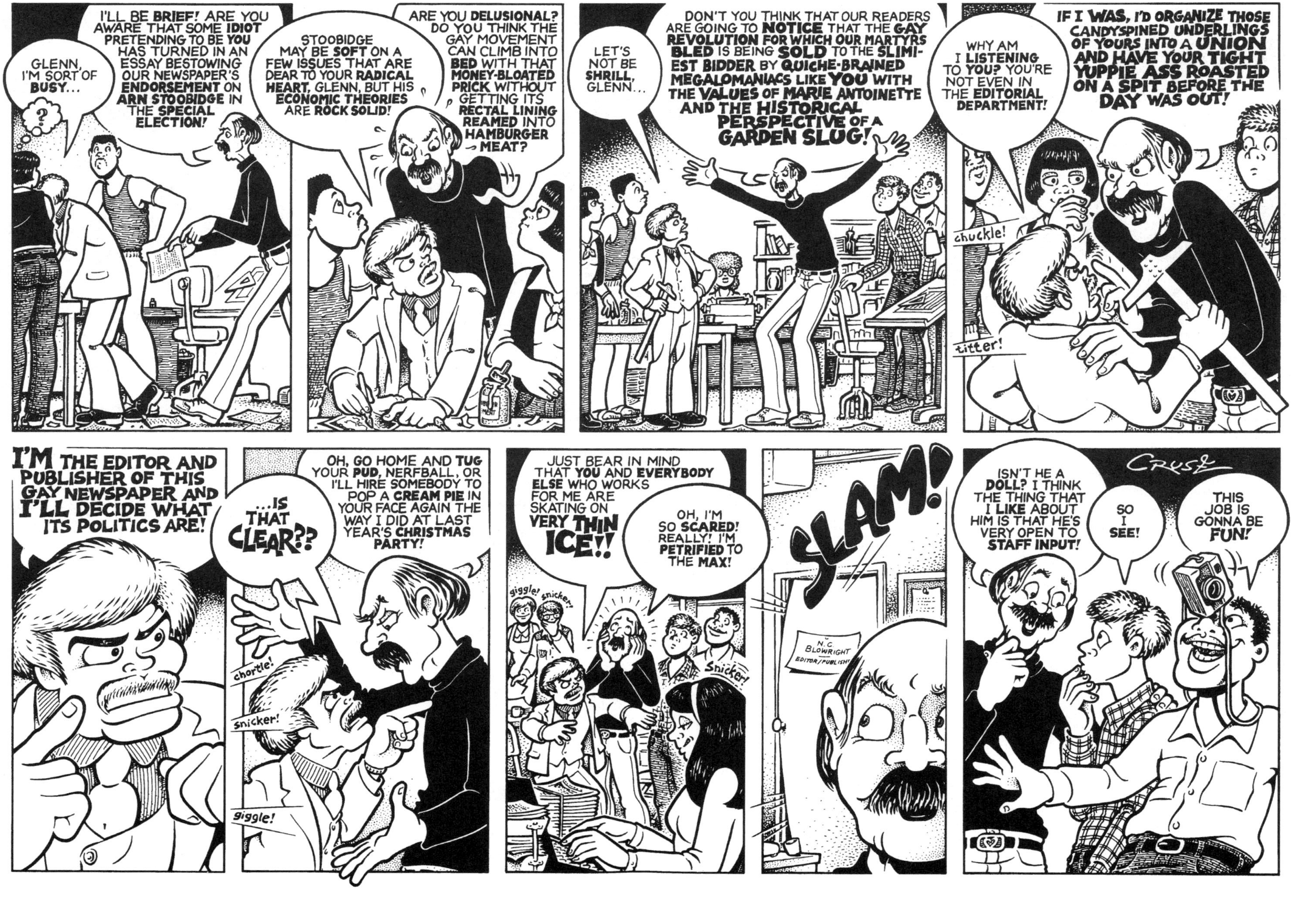
GLENN, I'M SORT OF BUSY...
?
I'LL BE BRIEF! ARE YOU AWARE THAT SOME IDIOT PRETENDING TO BE YOU HAS TURNED IN AN ESSAY BESTOWING OUR NEWSPAPER'S ENDORSEMENT ON ARN STOOBIDGE IN THE SPECIAL ELECTION!
STOOBIDGE MAY BE SOFT ON A FEW ISSUES THAT ARE DEAR TO YOUR RADICAL HEART, GLENN, BUT HIS ECONOMIC THEORIES ARE ROCK SOLID!
ARE YOU DELUSIONAL? DO YOU THINK THE GAY MOVEMENT CAN CLIMB INTO BED WITH THAT MONEY-BLOATED PRICK WITHOUT GETTING ITS RECTAL LINING REAMED INTO HAMBURGER MEAT?
LET'S NOT BE SHRILL, GLENN...
DON'T YOU THINK THAT OUR READERS ARE GOING TO NOTICE THAT THE GAY REVOLUTION FOR WHICH OUR MARTYRS BLED IS BEING SOLD TO THE SLIMIEST BIDDER BY QUICHE-BRAINED MEGALOMANIACS LIKE YOU WITH THE VALUES OF MARIE ANTOINETTE AND THE HISTORICAL PERSPECTIVE OF A GARDEN SLUG!
WHY AM I LISTENING TO YOU? YOU'RE NOT EVEN IN THE EDITORIAL DEPARTMENT!
chuckle!
titter!
IF I WAS, I'D ORGANIZE THOSE CANDYSPINED UNDERLINGS OF YOURS INTO A UNION AND HAVE YOUR TIGHT YUPPIE ASS ROASTED ON A SPIT BEFORE THE DAY WAS OUT!
I'M THE EDITOR AND PUBLISHER OF THIS GAY NEWSPAPER AND I'LL DECIDE WHAT ITS POLITICS ARE!
...IS THAT CLEAR??
OH, GO HOME AND TUG YOUR PUD, NERFBALL, OR I'LL HIRE SOMEBODY TO POP A CREAM PIE IN YOUR FACE AGAIN THE WAY I DID AT LAST YEAR'S CHRISTMAS PARTY!
chortle!
snicker!
giggle!
JUST BEAR IN MIND THAT YOU AND EVERYBODY ELSE WHO WORKS FOR ME ARE SKATING ON VERY THIN ICE!!
OH, I'M SO SCARED! REALLY! I'M PETRIFIED TO THE MAX!
giggle! snicker!
Snicker!
SLAM!
N.C. BLOWRIGHT
ISN'T HE A DOLL? I THINK THE THING THAT I LIKE ABOUT HIM IS THAT HE'S VERY OPEN TO STAFF INPUT!
SO I SEE!
THIS JOB IS GONNA BE FUN!
CRUSE

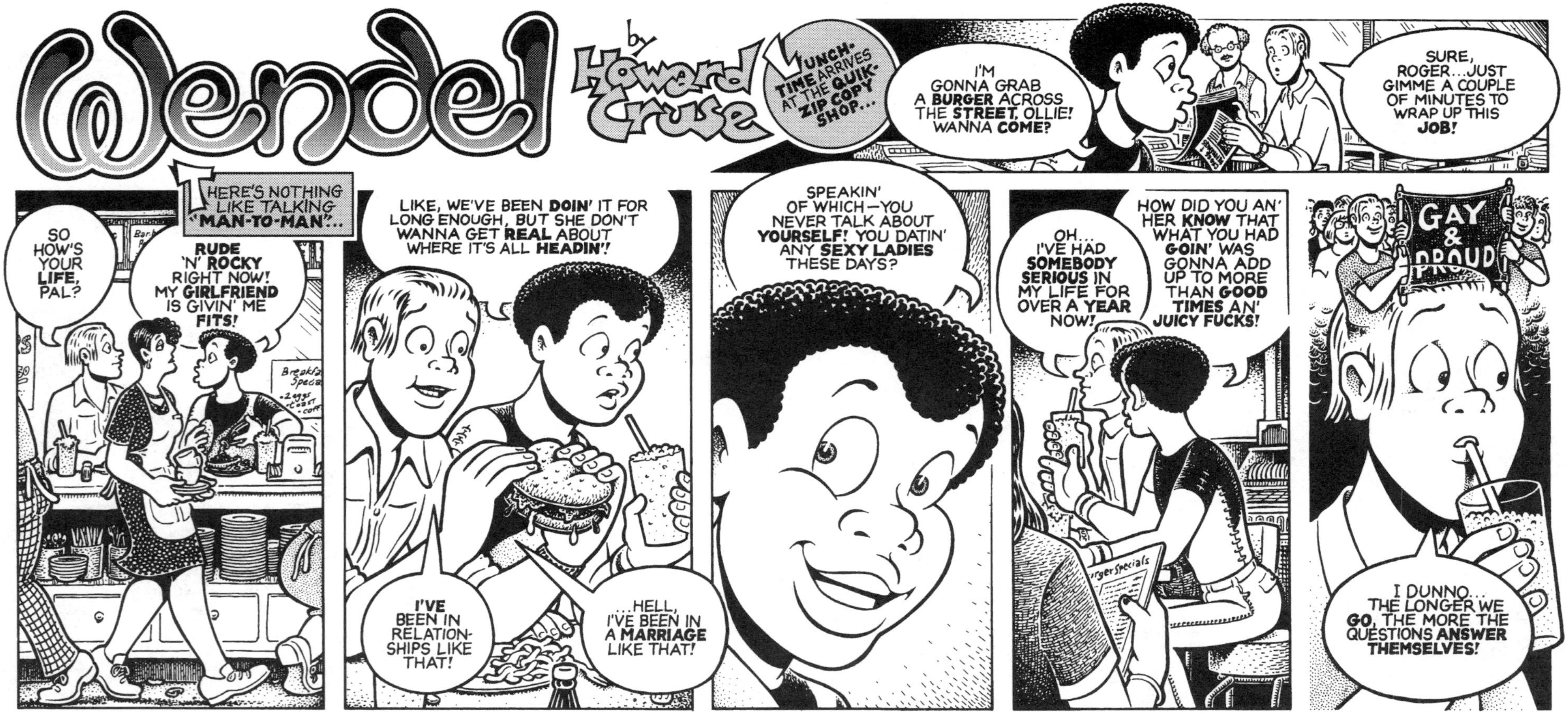
Wendel
by Howard Cruse
LUNCH-TIME ARRIVES AT THE QUIK-ZIP COPY SHOP...
I'M GONNA GRAB A BURGER ACROSS THE STREET, OLLIE! WANNA COME?
SURE, ROGER...JUST GIMME A COUPLE OF MINUTES TO WRAP UP THIS JOB!
THERE'S NOTHING LIKE TALKING "MAN-TO-MAN"...
SO HOW'S YOUR LIFE, PAL?
RUDE 'N' ROCKY RIGHT NOW! MY GIRLFRIEND IS GIVIN' ME FITS!
LIKE, WE'VE BEEN DOIN' IT FOR LONG ENOUGH, BUT SHE DON'T WANNA GET REAL ABOUT WHERE IT'S ALL HEADIN'!
I'VE BEEN IN RELATION-SHIPS LIKE THAT!
...HELL, I'VE BEEN IN A MARRIAGE LIKE THAT!
SPEAKIN' OF WHICH—YOU NEVER TALK ABOUT YOURSELF! YOU DATIN' ANY SEXY LADIES THESE DAYS?
OH... I'VE HAD SOMEBODY SERIOUS IN MY LIFE FOR OVER A YEAR NOW!
HOW DID YOU AN' HER KNOW THAT WHAT YOU HAD GOIN' WAS GONNA ADD UP TO MORE THAN GOOD TIMES AN' JUICY FUCKS!
GAY & PROUD
I DUNNO... THE LONGER WE GO, THE MORE THE QUESTIONS ANSWER THEMSELVES!

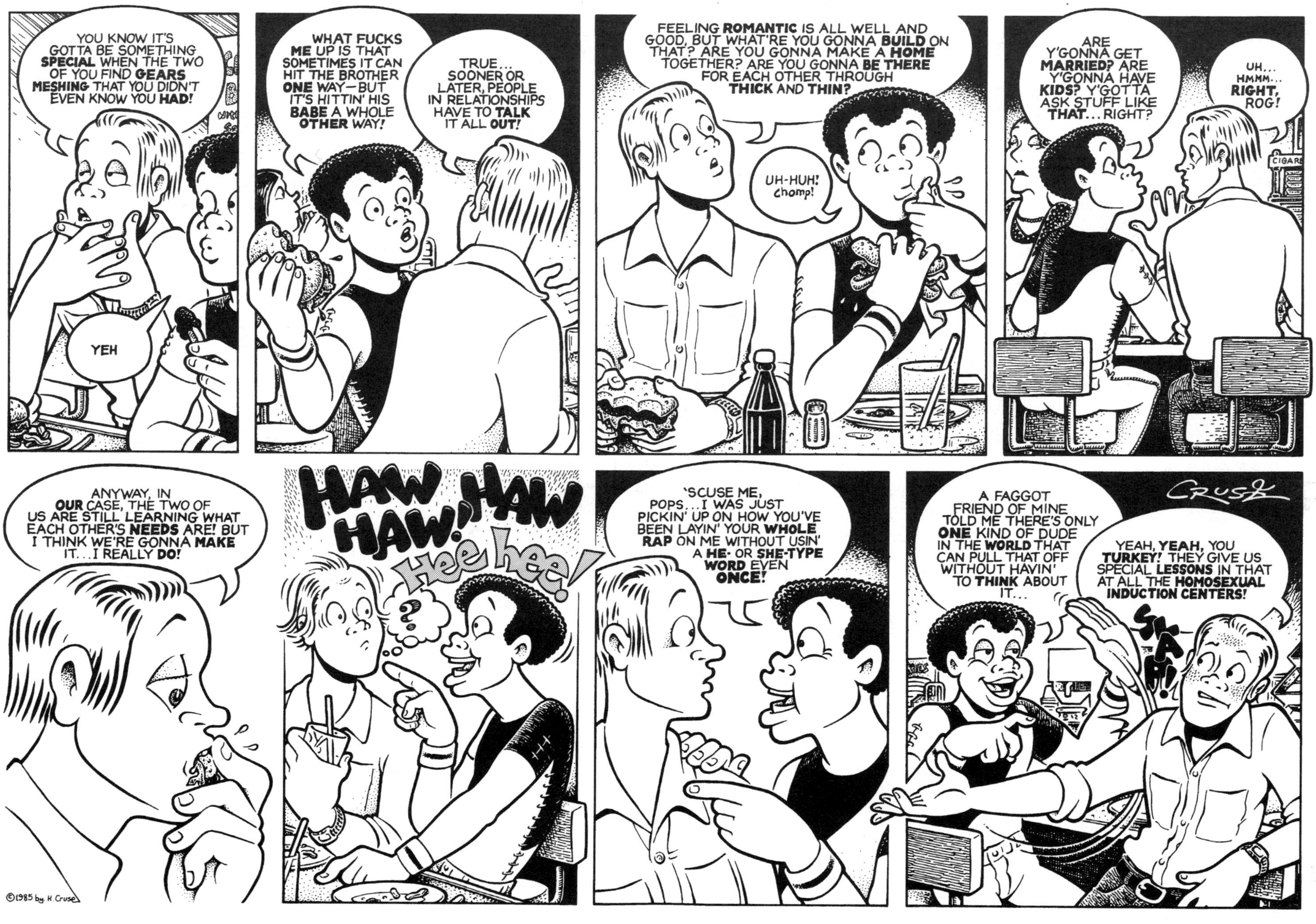
YOU KNOW IT'S GOTTA BE SOMETHING **SPECIAL** WHEN THE TWO OF YOU FIND **GEARS MESHING** THAT YOU DIDN'T EVEN KNOW YOU **HAD!**
YEH
WHAT FUCKS **ME** UP IS THAT SOMETIMES IT CAN HIT THE BROTHER **ONE** WAY—BUT IT'S HITTIN' HIS **BABE** A WHOLE **OTHER** WAY!
TRUE... SOONER OR LATER, PEOPLE IN RELATIONSHIPS HAVE TO **TALK** IT ALL **OUT!**
FEELING **ROMANTIC** IS ALL WELL AND GOOD, BUT WHAT'RE YOU GONNA **BUILD** ON THAT? ARE YOU GONNA MAKE A **HOME** TOGETHER? ARE YOU GONNA **BE THERE** FOR EACH OTHER THROUGH **THICK** AND **THIN?**
UH-HUH! chomp!
ARE Y'GONNA GET **MARRIED?** ARE Y'GONNA HAVE **KIDS?** Y'GOTTA ASK STUFF LIKE **THAT**... RIGHT?
UH... HMMM... **RIGHT,** ROG!
CIGAR
ANYWAY, IN **OUR** CASE, THE TWO OF US ARE STILL LEARNING WHAT EACH OTHER'S **NEEDS** ARE! BUT I THINK WE'RE GONNA **MAKE** IT... I REALLY **DO!**
©1985 by H. Cruse
HAW HAW HAW! HAW
Hee hee!
?
'SCUSE ME, POPS... I WAS JUST PICKIN' UP ON HOW YOU'VE BEEN LAYIN' YOUR **WHOLE RAP** ON ME WITHOUT USIN' A **HE-** OR **SHE-TYPE WORD** EVEN **ONCE!**
CRUSE
A FAGGOT FRIEND OF MINE TOLD ME THERE'S ONLY **ONE** KIND OF DUDE IN THE **WORLD** THAT CAN PULL THAT OFF WITHOUT HAVIN' TO **THINK** ABOUT IT...
YEAH, **YEAH,** YOU **TURKEY!** THEY GIVE US SPECIAL **LESSONS** IN THAT AT ALL THE **HOMOSEXUAL INDUCTION CENTERS!**
SWAP!

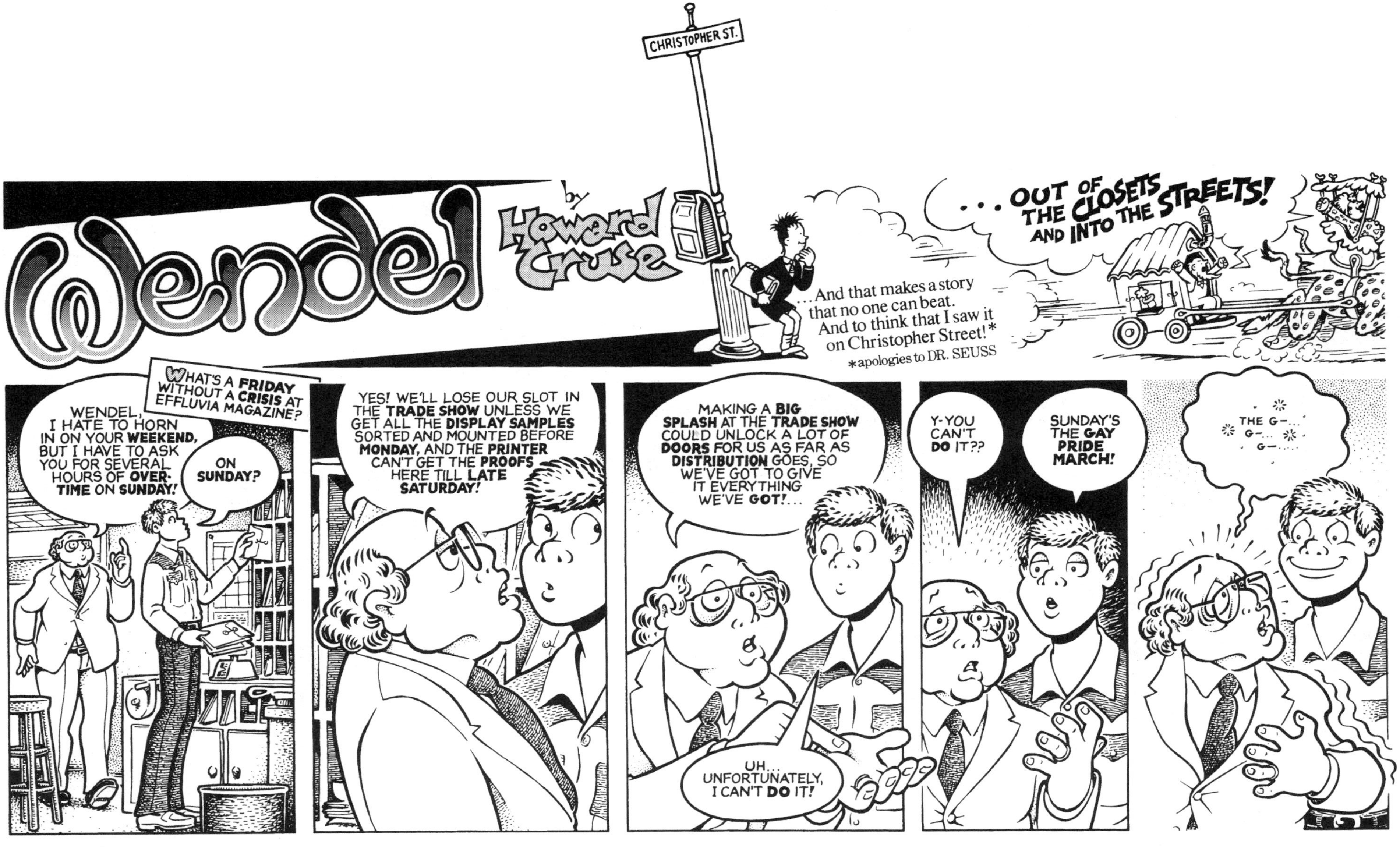
Wendel
by Howard Cruse
CHRISTOPHER ST.
...And that makes a story that no one can beat. And to think that I saw it on Christopher Street!*
*apologies to DR. SEUSS
...OUT OF THE CLOSETS AND INTO THE STREETS!
WHAT'S A FRIDAY WITHOUT A CRISIS AT EFFLUVIA MAGAZINE?
WENDEL, I HATE TO HORN IN ON YOUR WEEKEND, BUT I HAVE TO ASK YOU FOR SEVERAL HOURS OF OVER-TIME ON SUNDAY!
ON SUNDAY?
YES! WE'LL LOSE OUR SLOT IN THE TRADE SHOW UNLESS WE GET ALL THE DISPLAY SAMPLES SORTED AND MOUNTED BEFORE MONDAY, AND THE PRINTER CAN'T GET THE PROOFS HERE TILL LATE SATURDAY!
MAKING A BIG SPLASH AT THE TRADE SHOW COULD UNLOCK A LOT OF DOORS FOR US AS FAR AS DISTRIBUTION GOES, SO WE'VE GOT TO GIVE IT EVERYTHING WE'VE GOT!...
UH... UNFORTUNATELY, I CAN'T DO IT!
Y-YOU CAN'T DO IT??
SUNDAY'S THE GAY PRIDE MARCH!
THE G-... G-... G-...

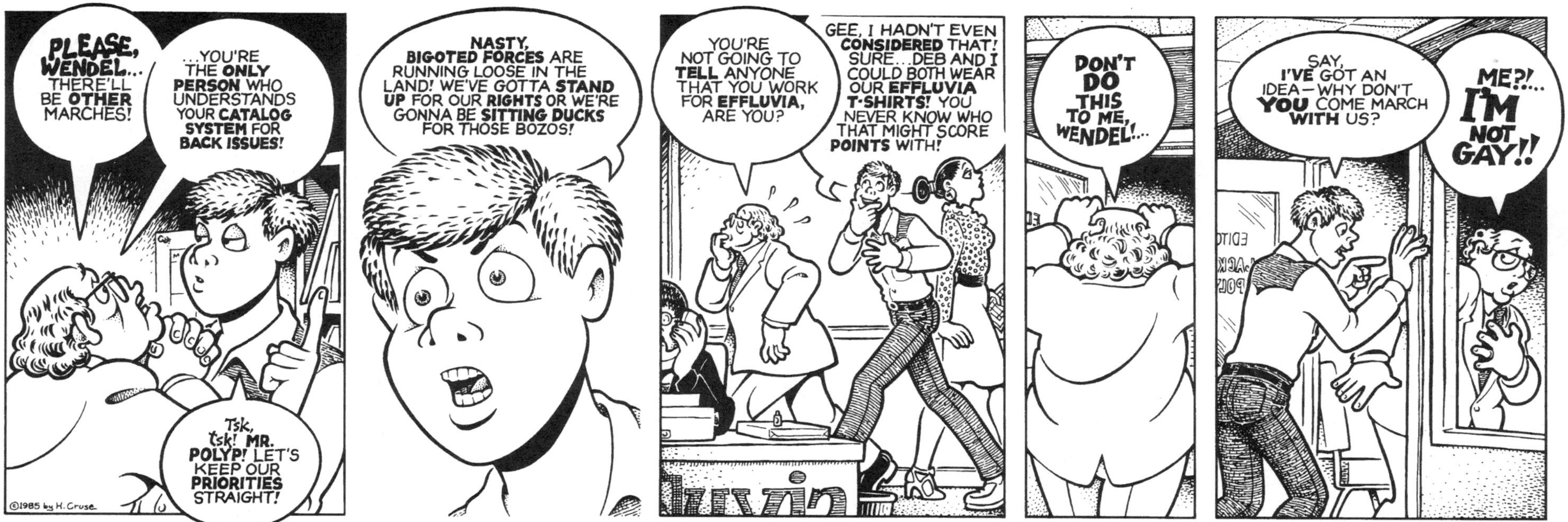
PLEASE, WENDEL... THERE'LL BE OTHER MARCHES!
...YOU'RE THE ONLY PERSON WHO UNDERSTANDS YOUR CATALOG SYSTEM FOR BACK ISSUES!
Tsk, tsk! MR. POLYP! LET'S KEEP OUR PRIORITIES STRAIGHT!
©1985 by H. Cruse
NASTY, BIGOTED FORCES ARE RUNNING LOOSE IN THE LAND! WE'VE GOTTA STAND UP FOR OUR RIGHTS OR WE'RE GONNA BE SITTING DUCKS FOR THOSE BOZOS!
YOU'RE NOT GOING TO TELL ANYONE THAT YOU WORK FOR EFFLUVIA, ARE YOU?
GEE, I HADN'T EVEN CONSIDERED THAT! SURE...DEB AND I COULD BOTH WEAR OUR EFFLUVIA T-SHIRTS! YOU NEVER KNOW WHO THAT MIGHT SCORE POINTS WITH!
DON'T DO THIS TO ME, WENDEL!...
SAY, I'VE GOT AN IDEA—WHY DON'T YOU COME MARCH WITH US?
ME?!... I'M NOT GAY!!

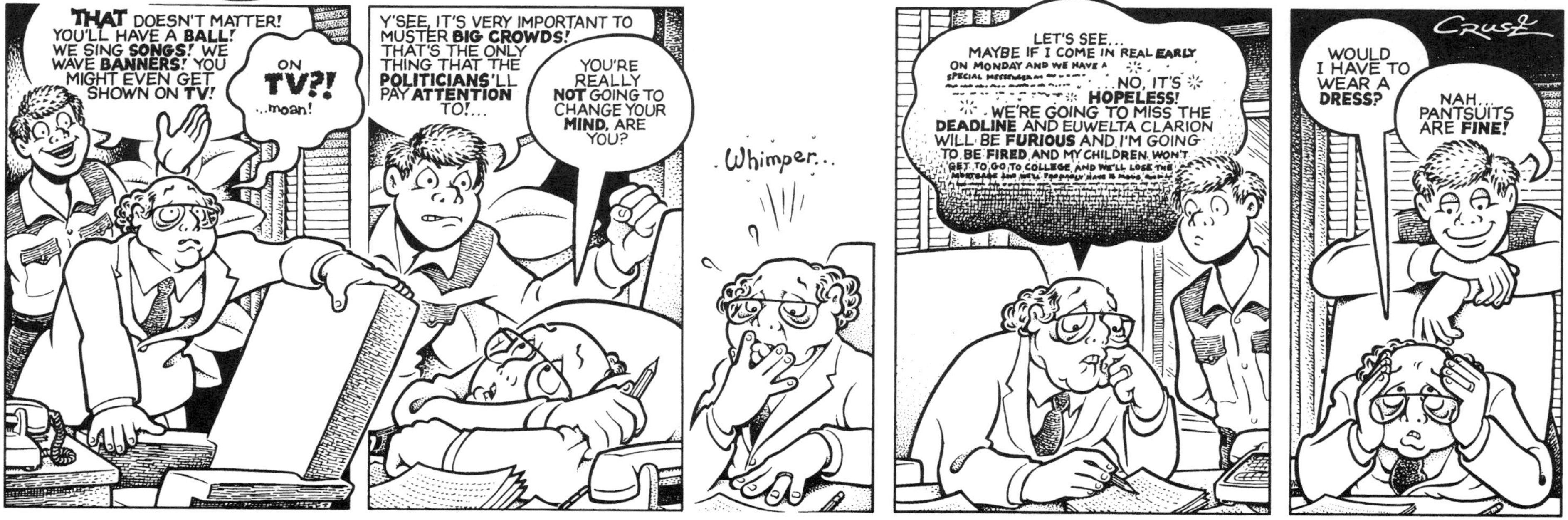
THAT DOESN'T MATTER! YOU'LL HAVE A BALL! WE SING SONGS! WE WAVE BANNERS! YOU MIGHT EVEN GET SHOWN ON TV!
ON TV?! ...moan!
Y'SEE, IT'S VERY IMPORTANT TO MUSTER BIG CROWDS! THAT'S THE ONLY THING THAT THE POLITICIANS'LL PAY ATTENTION TO!...
YOU'RE REALLY NOT GOING TO CHANGE YOUR MIND, ARE YOU?
Whimper...
LET'S SEE... MAYBE IF I COME IN REAL EARLY ON MONDAY AND WE HAVE A
NO, IT'S HOPELESS! WE'RE GOING TO MISS THE DEADLINE AND EUWELTA CLARION WILL BE FURIOUS AND I'M GOING TO BE FIRED AND MY CHILDREN WON'T GET TO GO TO COLLEGE AND WE'LL LOSE THE
CRUSE
WOULD I HAVE TO WEAR A DRESS?
NAH... PANTSUITS ARE FINE!

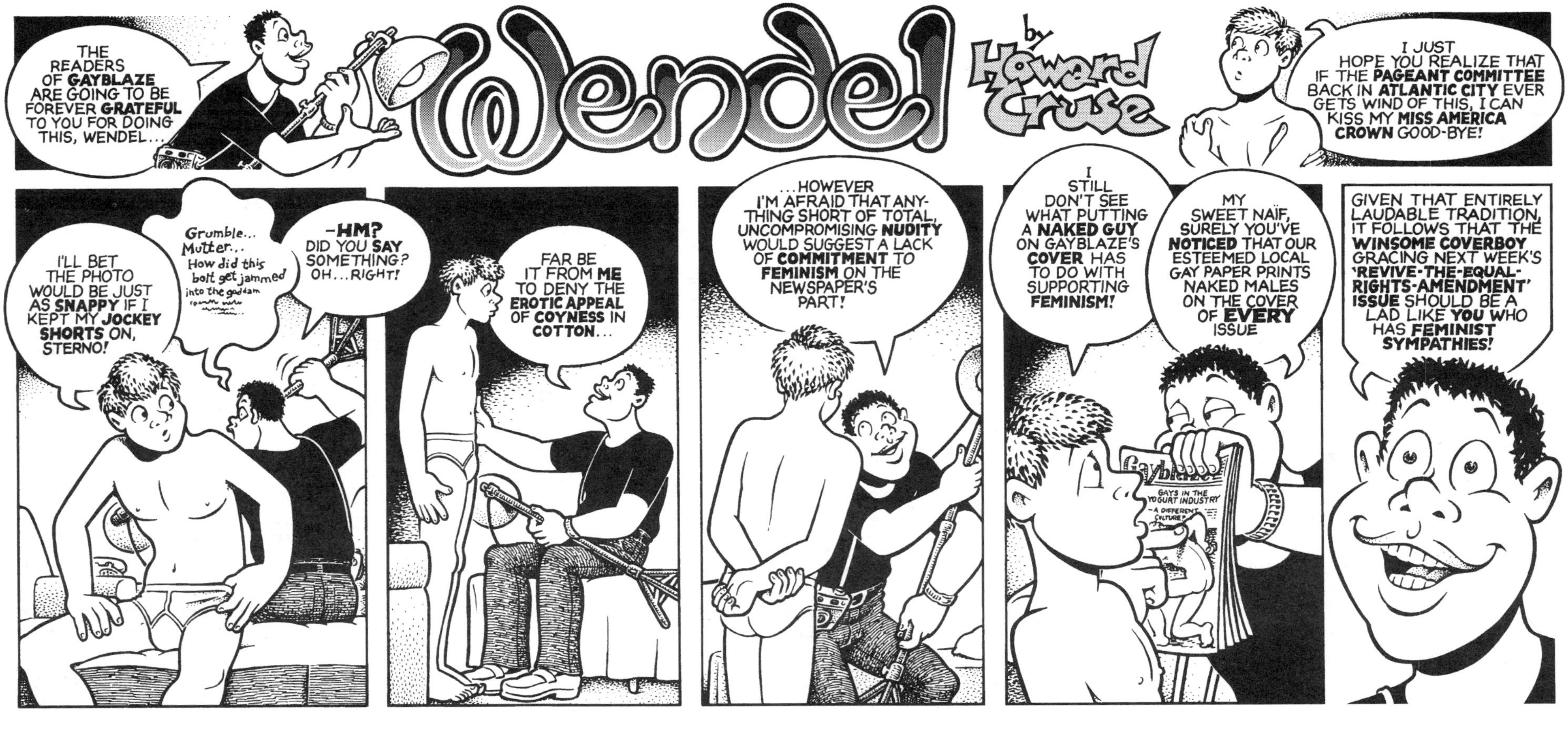
Wendel
by Howard Cruse
THE READERS OF GAYBLAZE ARE GOING TO BE FOREVER GRATEFUL TO YOU FOR DOING THIS, WENDEL...
I JUST HOPE YOU REALIZE THAT IF THE PAGEANT COMMITTEE BACK IN ATLANTIC CITY EVER GETS WIND OF THIS, I CAN KISS MY MISS AMERICA CROWN GOOD-BYE!
I'LL BET THE PHOTO WOULD BE JUST AS SNAPPY IF I KEPT MY JOCKEY SHORTS ON, STERNO!
Grumble... Mutter... How did this bolt get jammed into the goddam
-HM? DID YOU SAY SOMETHING? OH...RIGHT!
FAR BE IT FROM ME TO DENY THE EROTIC APPEAL OF COYNESS IN COTTON...
...HOWEVER I'M AFRAID THAT ANY-THING SHORT OF TOTAL, UNCOMPROMISING NUDITY WOULD SUGGEST A LACK OF COMMITMENT TO FEMINISM ON THE NEWSPAPER'S PART!
I STILL DON'T SEE WHAT PUTTING A NAKED GUY ON GAYBLAZE'S COVER HAS TO DO WITH SUPPORTING FEMINISM!
MY SWEET NAÏF, SURELY YOU'VE NOTICED THAT OUR ESTEEMED LOCAL GAY PAPER PRINTS NAKED MALES ON THE COVER OF EVERY ISSUE
Gayblaze
GAYS IN THE YOGURT INDUSTRY
GIVEN THAT ENTIRELY LAUDABLE TRADITION, IT FOLLOWS THAT THE WINSOME COVERBOY GRACING NEXT WEEK'S 'REVIVE-THE-EQUAL-RIGHTS-AMENDMENT' ISSUE SHOULD BE A LAD LIKE YOU WHO HAS FEMINIST SYMPATHIES!

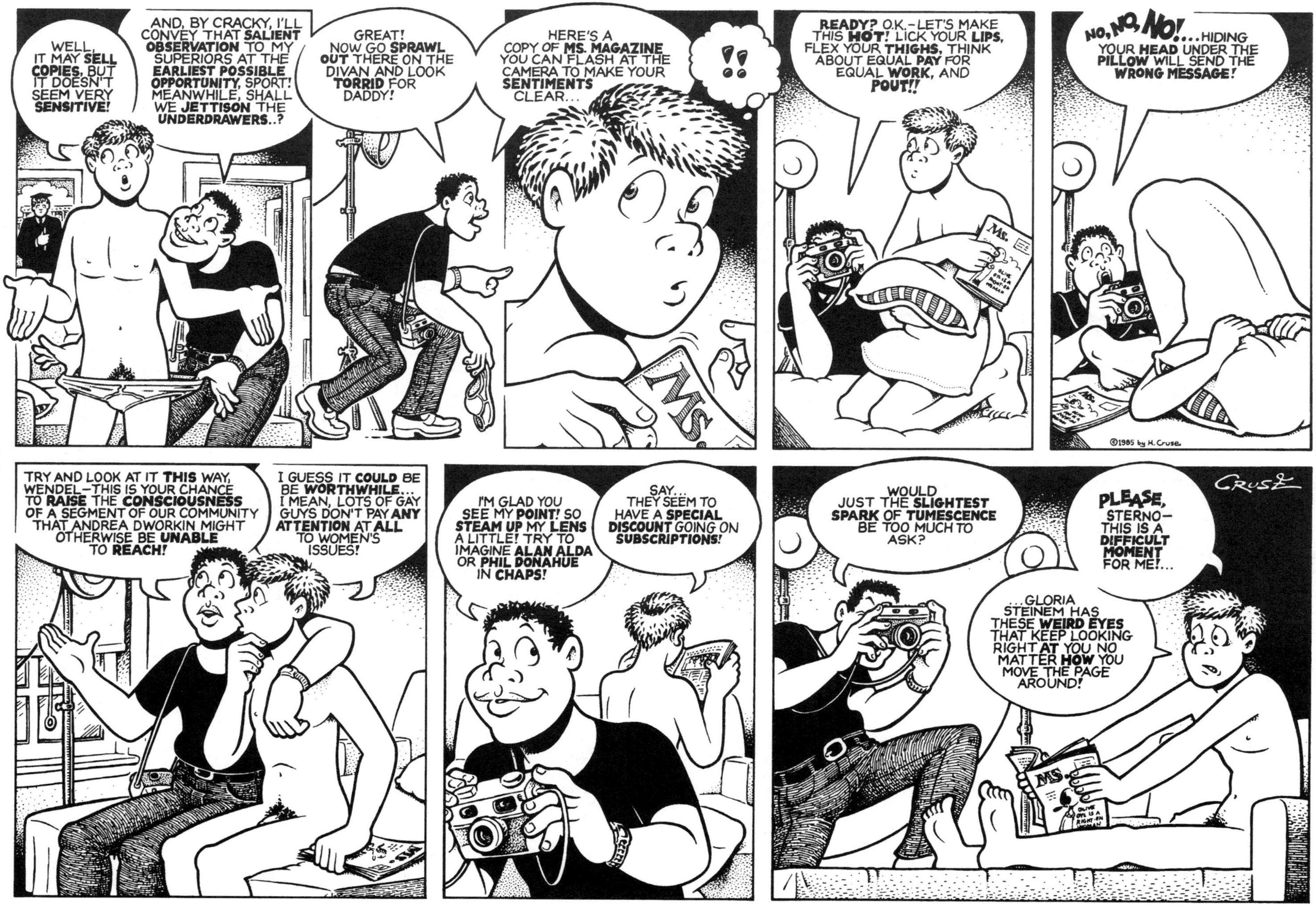
WELL, IT MAY **SELL COPIES**, BUT IT DOESN'T SEEM VERY **SENSITIVE!**
AND, BY CRACKY, I'LL CONVEY THAT **SALIENT OBSERVATION** TO MY SUPERIORS AT THE **EARLIEST POSSIBLE OPPORTUNITY**, SPORT! MEANWHILE, SHALL WE **JETTISON** THE **UNDERDRAWERS**..?
GREAT! NOW GO **SPRAWL OUT** THERE ON THE DIVAN AND LOOK **TORRID** FOR DADDY!
HERE'S A COPY OF **MS. MAGAZINE** YOU CAN FLASH AT THE CAMERA TO MAKE YOUR **SENTIMENTS** CLEAR...
!!
READY? O.K.–LET'S MAKE THIS **HOT!** LICK YOUR **LIPS**, FLEX YOUR **THIGHS**, THINK ABOUT EQUAL **PAY** FOR EQUAL **WORK**, AND **POUT!!**
NO, NO, NO!...HIDING YOUR **HEAD** UNDER THE **PILLOW** WILL SEND THE **WRONG MESSAGE!**
©1985 by H. Cruse
TRY AND LOOK AT IT **THIS** WAY, WENDEL–THIS IS YOUR CHANCE TO **RAISE** THE **CONSCIOUSNESS** OF A SEGMENT OF OUR COMMUNITY THAT ANDREA DWORKIN MIGHT OTHERWISE BE **UNABLE** TO **REACH!**
I GUESS IT **COULD** BE BE **WORTHWHILE**... I MEAN, LOTS OF GAY GUYS DON'T PAY **ANY ATTENTION** AT **ALL** TO WOMEN'S ISSUES!
I'M GLAD YOU SEE MY **POINT!** SO **STEAM UP** MY **LENS** A LITTLE! TRY TO IMAGINE **ALAN ALDA** OR **PHIL DONAHUE** IN **CHAPS!**
SAY... THEY SEEM TO HAVE A **SPECIAL DISCOUNT** GOING ON **SUBSCRIPTIONS!**
CRUSE
WOULD JUST THE **SLIGHTEST SPARK** OF **TUMESCENCE** BE TOO MUCH TO ASK?
PLEASE, STERNO– THIS IS A **DIFFICULT MOMENT** FOR ME!...
...GLORIA STEINEM HAS THESE **WEIRD EYES** THAT KEEP LOOKING RIGHT **AT** YOU NO MATTER **HOW** YOU MOVE THE PAGE AROUND!

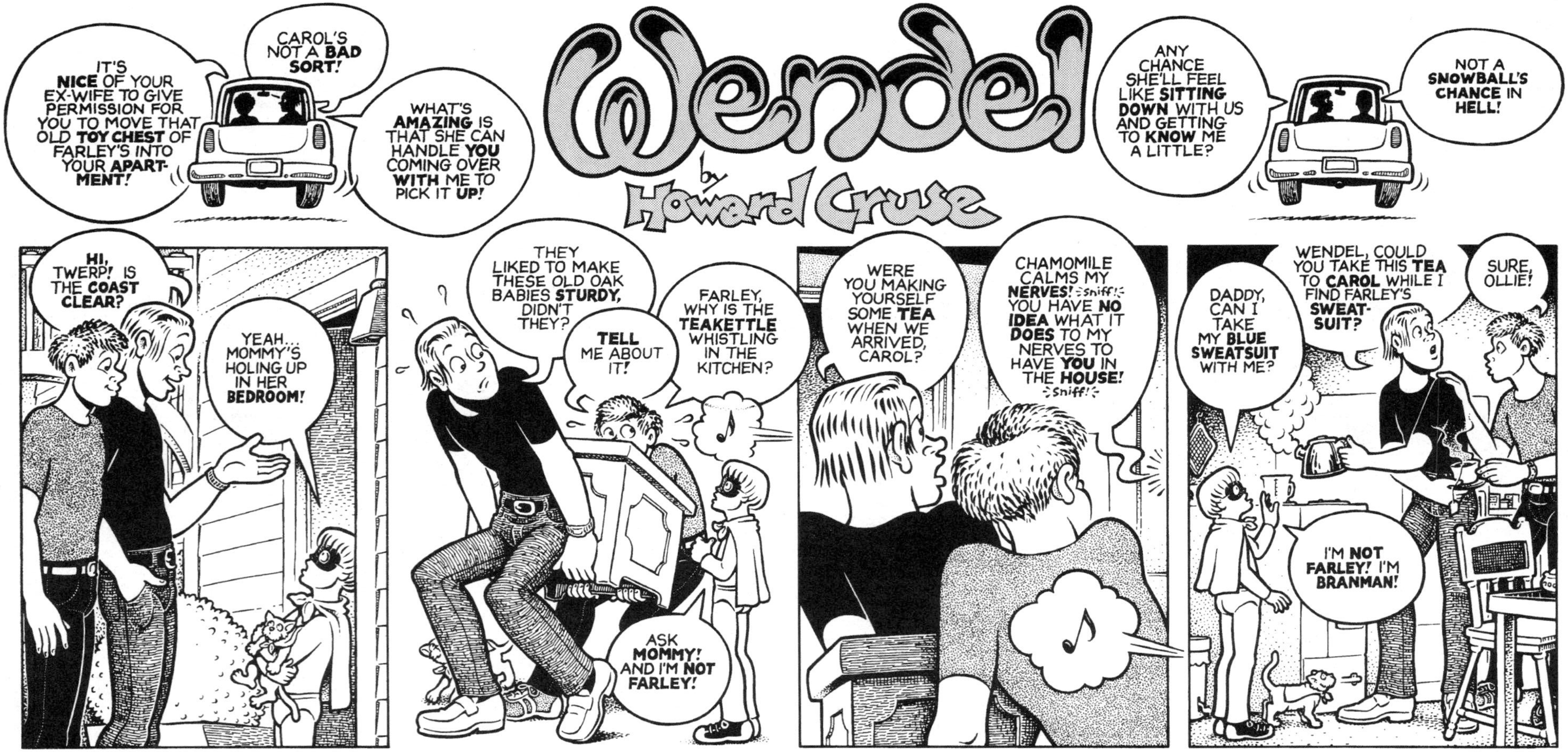
Wendel
by Howard Cruse
IT'S NICE OF YOUR EX-WIFE TO GIVE PERMISSION FOR YOU TO MOVE THAT OLD TOY CHEST OF FARLEY'S INTO YOUR APARTMENT!
CAROL'S NOT A BAD SORT!
WHAT'S AMAZING IS THAT SHE CAN HANDLE YOU COMING OVER WITH ME TO PICK IT UP!
ANY CHANCE SHE'LL FEEL LIKE SITTING DOWN WITH US AND GETTING TO KNOW ME A LITTLE?
NOT A SNOWBALL'S CHANCE IN HELL!
HI, TWERP! IS THE COAST CLEAR?
YEAH... MOMMY'S HOLING UP IN HER BEDROOM!
THEY LIKED TO MAKE THESE OLD OAK BABIES STURDY, DIDN'T THEY?
TELL ME ABOUT IT!
FARLEY, WHY IS THE TEAKETTLE WHISTLING IN THE KITCHEN?
ASK MOMMY! AND I'M NOT FARLEY!
WERE YOU MAKING YOURSELF SOME TEA WHEN WE ARRIVED, CAROL?
CHAMOMILE CALMS MY NERVES! :Sniff!: YOU HAVE NO IDEA WHAT IT DOES TO MY NERVES TO HAVE YOU IN THE HOUSE! :Sniff!:
WENDEL, COULD YOU TAKE THIS TEA TO CAROL WHILE I FIND FARLEY'S SWEATSUIT?
SURE, OLLIE!
DADDY, CAN I TAKE MY BLUE SWEATSUIT WITH ME?
I'M NOT FARLEY! I'M BRANMAN!

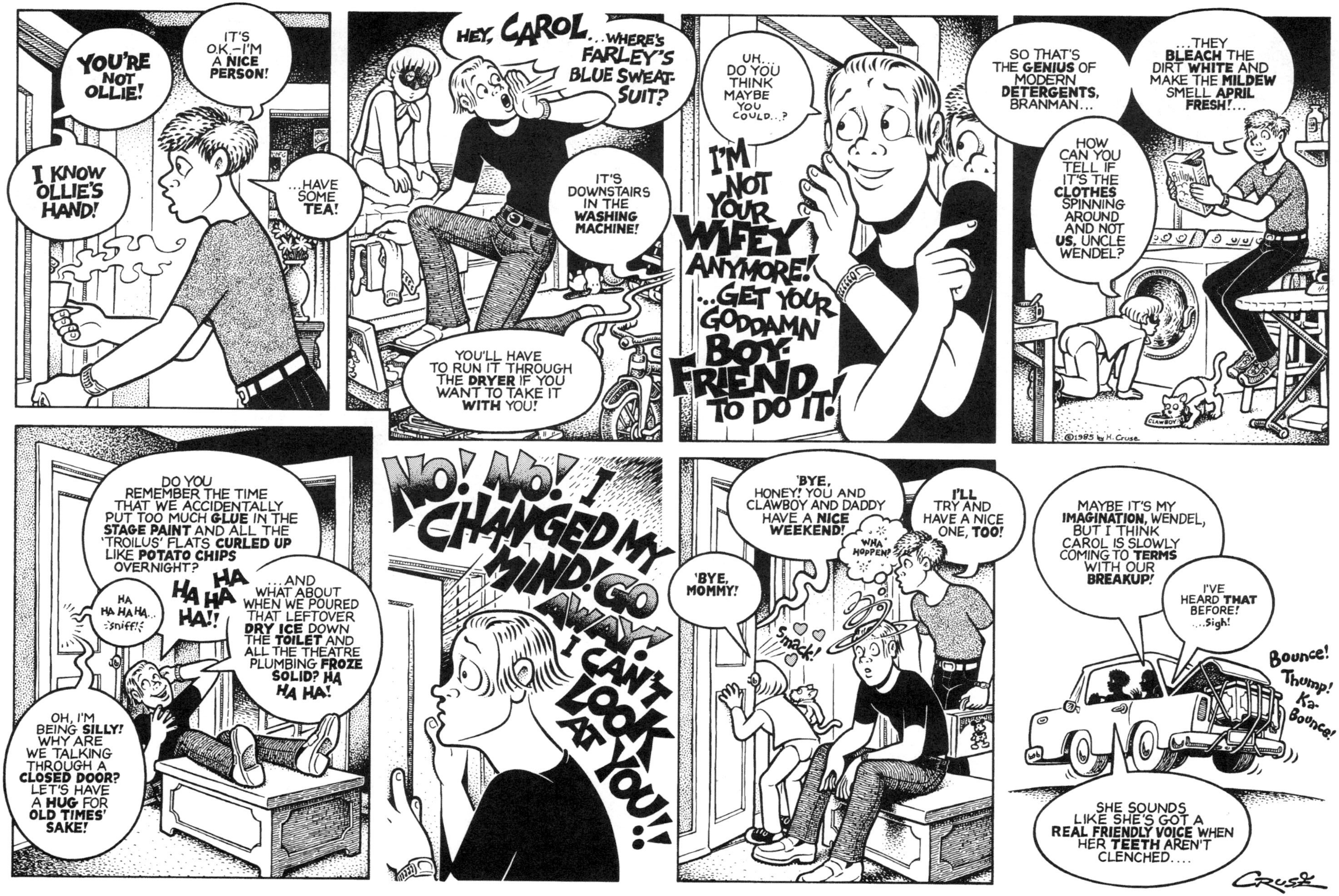

YOU'RE NOT OLLIE!
IT'S O.K.–I'M A NICE PERSON!
I KNOW OLLIE'S HAND!
...HAVE SOME TEA!
HEY, CAROL...WHERE'S FARLEY'S BLUE SWEAT-SUIT?
IT'S DOWNSTAIRS IN THE WASHING MACHINE!
YOU'LL HAVE TO RUN IT THROUGH THE DRYER IF YOU WANT TO TAKE IT WITH YOU!
UH... DO YOU THINK MAYBE YOU COULD...?
I'M NOT YOUR WIFEY ANYMORE! ...GET YOUR GODDAMN BOY-FRIEND TO DO IT!
SO THAT'S THE GENIUS OF MODERN DETERGENTS, BRANMAN...
...THEY BLEACH THE DIRT WHITE AND MAKE THE MILDEW SMELL APRIL FRESH!...
HOW CAN YOU TELL IF IT'S THE CLOTHES SPINNING AROUND AND NOT US, UNCLE WENDEL?
CLAWBOY
©1985 by H. Cruse
DO YOU REMEMBER THE TIME THAT WE ACCIDENTALLY PUT TOO MUCH GLUE IN THE STAGE PAINT AND ALL THE 'TROILUS' FLATS CURLED UP LIKE POTATO CHIPS OVERNIGHT?
HA HA HA HA!!
HA HA HA HA... sniff!
...AND WHAT ABOUT WHEN WE POURED THAT LEFTOVER DRY ICE DOWN THE TOILET AND ALL THE THEATRE PLUMBING FROZE SOLID? HA HA HA!
OH, I'M BEING SILLY! WHY ARE WE TALKING THROUGH A CLOSED DOOR? LET'S HAVE A HUG FOR OLD TIMES' SAKE!
NO! NO! I CHANGED MY MIND! GO AWAY! I CAN'T LOOK AT YOU!!
'BYE, HONEY! YOU AND CLAWBOY AND DADDY HAVE A NICE WEEKEND!
'BYE, MOMMY!
Smack!
WHA HOPPEN?
I'LL TRY AND HAVE A NICE ONE, TOO!
MAYBE IT'S MY IMAGINATION, WENDEL, BUT I THINK CAROL IS SLOWLY COMING TO TERMS WITH OUR BREAKUP!
I'VE HEARD THAT BEFORE! ...Sigh!
Bounce! Thump! Ka-Bounce!
SHE SOUNDS LIKE SHE'S GOT A REAL FRIENDLY VOICE WHEN HER TEETH AREN'T CLENCHED....
CRUSE

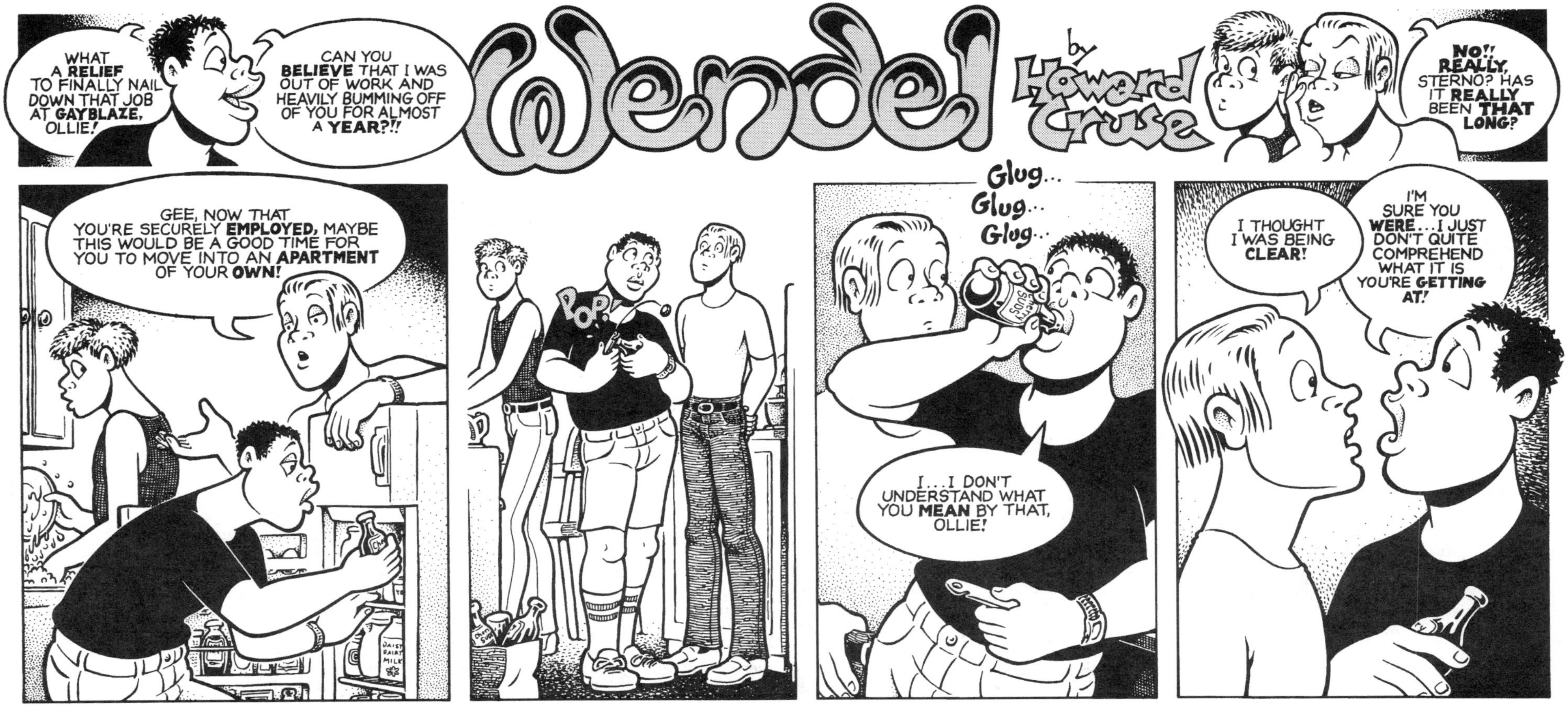
Wendel
by Howard Cruse
WHAT A RELIEF TO FINALLY NAIL DOWN THAT JOB AT GAYBLAZE, OLLIE!
CAN YOU BELIEVE THAT I WAS OUT OF WORK AND HEAVILY BUMMING OFF OF YOU FOR ALMOST A YEAR?!!
NO!! REALLY, STERNO? HAS IT REALLY BEEN THAT LONG?
GEE, NOW THAT YOU'RE SECURELY EMPLOYED, MAYBE THIS WOULD BE A GOOD TIME FOR YOU TO MOVE INTO AN APARTMENT OF YOUR OWN!
DAISY DAIRY MILK
POP!
Glug... Glug... Glug...
SUDS
I...I DON'T UNDERSTAND WHAT YOU MEAN BY THAT, OLLIE!
I THOUGHT I WAS BEING CLEAR!
I'M SURE YOU WERE...I JUST DON'T QUITE COMPREHEND WHAT IT IS YOU'RE GETTING AT!

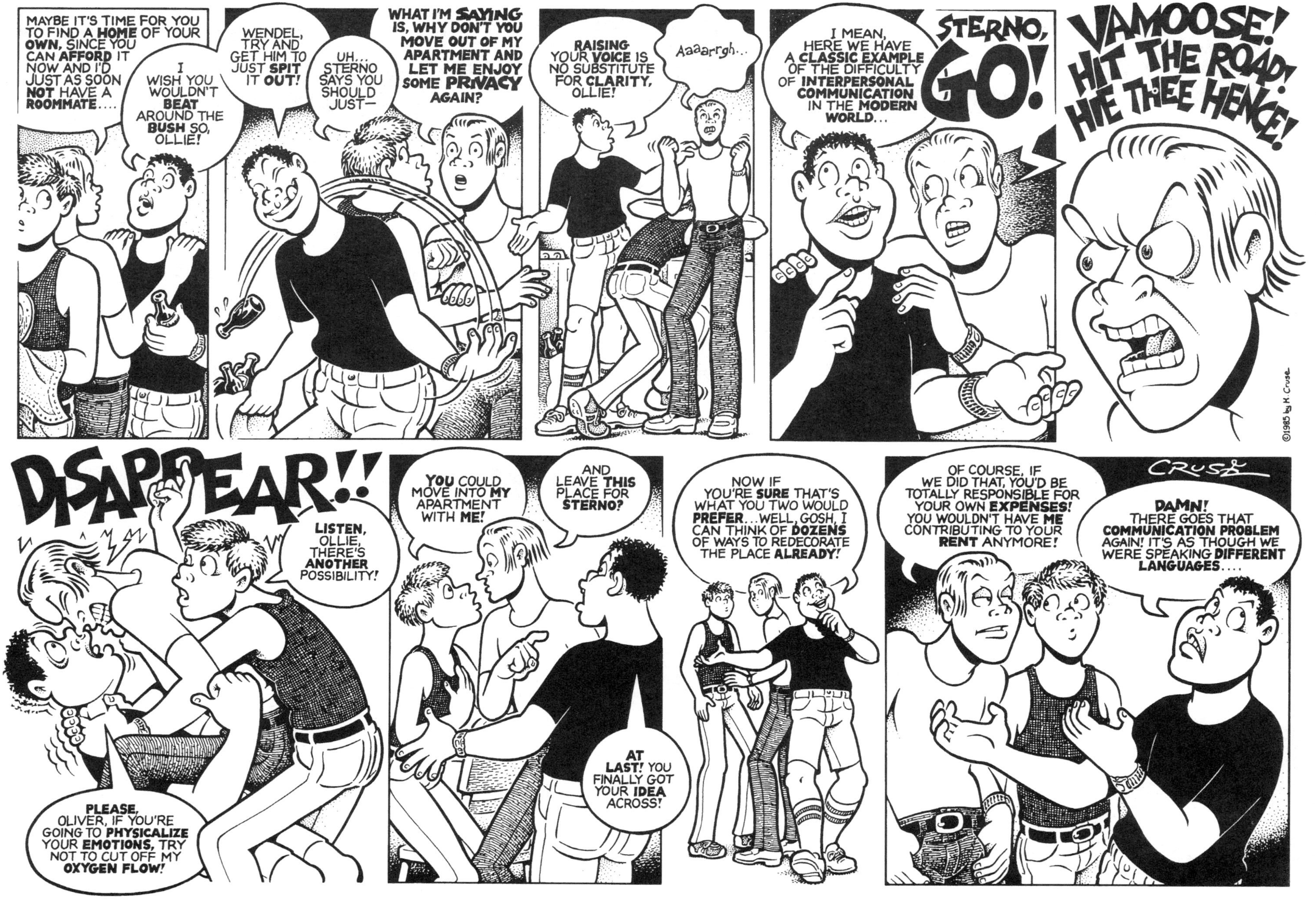
MAYBE IT'S TIME FOR YOU TO FIND A HOME OF YOUR OWN, SINCE YOU CAN AFFORD IT NOW AND I'D JUST AS SOON NOT HAVE A ROOMMATE....
I WISH YOU WOULDN'T BEAT AROUND THE BUSH SO, OLLIE!
WENDEL, TRY AND GET HIM TO JUST SPIT IT OUT!
UH... STERNO SAYS YOU SHOULD JUST—
WHAT I'M SAYING IS, WHY DON'T YOU MOVE OUT OF MY APARTMENT AND LET ME ENJOY SOME PRIVACY AGAIN?
RAISING YOUR VOICE IS NO SUBSTITUTE FOR CLARITY, OLLIE!
Aaaarrgh...
I MEAN, HERE WE HAVE A CLASSIC EXAMPLE OF THE DIFFICULTY OF INTERPERSONAL COMMUNICATION IN THE MODERN WORLD...
STERNO, GO!
VAMOOSE! HIT THE ROAD! HIE THEE HENCE!
©1985 by H. Cruse
DISAPPEAR!!
LISTEN, OLLIE, THERE'S ANOTHER POSSIBILITY!
PLEASE, OLIVER, IF YOU'RE GOING TO PHYSICALIZE YOUR EMOTIONS, TRY NOT TO CUT OFF MY OXYGEN FLOW!
YOU COULD MOVE INTO MY APARTMENT WITH ME!
AND LEAVE THIS PLACE FOR STERNO?
AT LAST! YOU FINALLY GOT YOUR IDEA ACROSS!
NOW IF YOU'RE SURE THAT'S WHAT YOU TWO WOULD PREFER...WELL, GOSH, I CAN THINK OF DOZENS OF WAYS TO REDECORATE THE PLACE ALREADY!
CRUSE
OF COURSE, IF WE DID THAT, YOU'D BE TOTALLY RESPONSIBLE FOR YOUR OWN EXPENSES! YOU WOULDN'T HAVE ME CONTRIBUTING TO YOUR RENT ANYMORE!
DAMN! THERE GOES THAT COMMUNICATION PROBLEM AGAIN! IT'S AS THOUGH WE WERE SPEAKING DIFFERENT LANGUAGES....

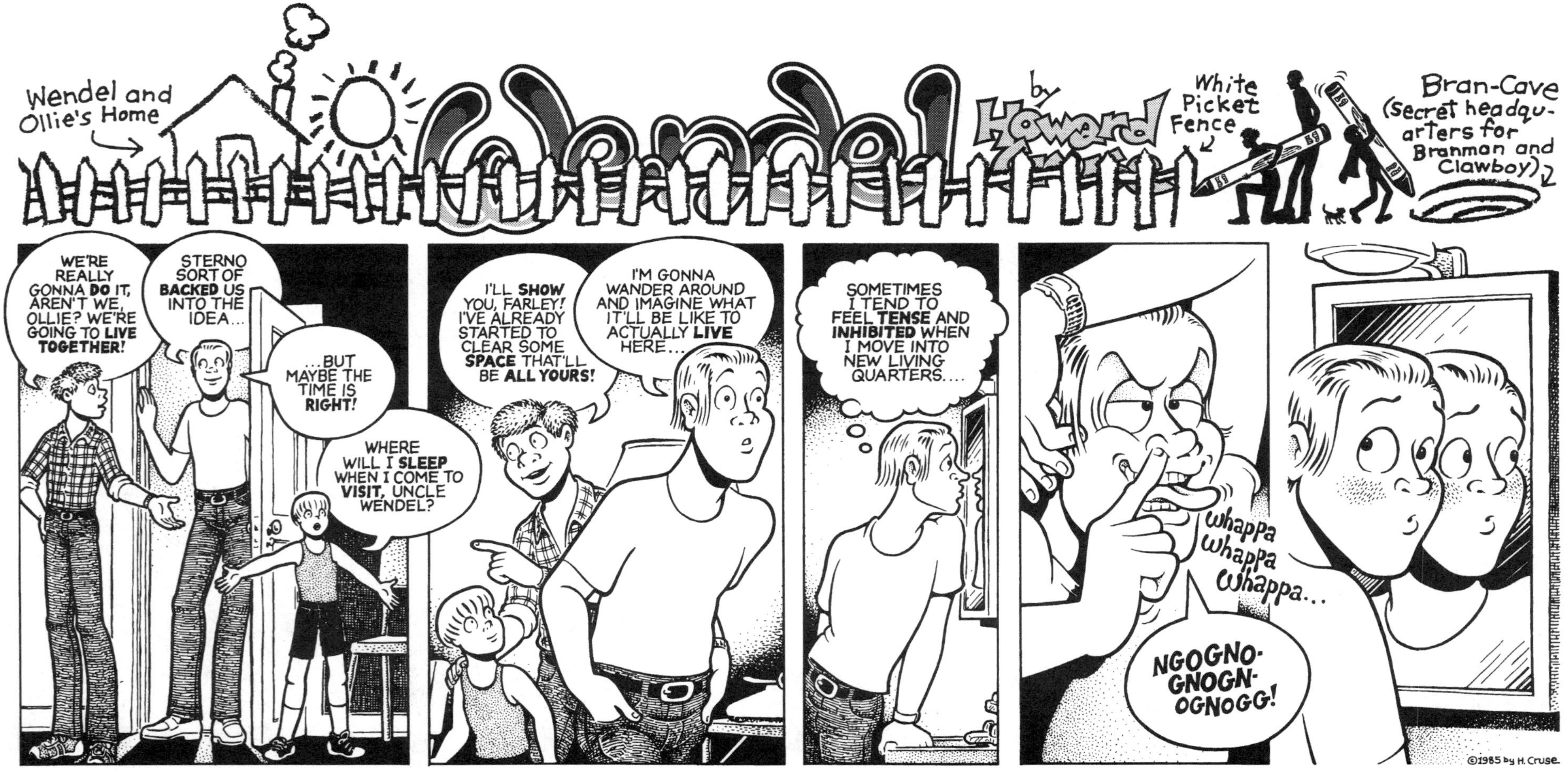
Wendel and Ollie's Home
Wendel
by Howard Cruse
White Picket Fence
Bran-Cave (Secret headquarters for Branman and Clawboy)
WE'RE REALLY GONNA DO IT, AREN'T WE, OLLIE? WE'RE GOING TO LIVE TOGETHER!
STERNO SORT OF BACKED US INTO THE IDEA...
...BUT MAYBE THE TIME IS RIGHT!
WHERE WILL I SLEEP WHEN I COME TO VISIT, UNCLE WENDEL?
I'LL SHOW YOU, FARLEY! I'VE ALREADY STARTED TO CLEAR SOME SPACE THAT'LL BE ALL YOURS!
I'M GONNA WANDER AROUND AND IMAGINE WHAT IT'LL BE LIKE TO ACTUALLY LIVE HERE...
SOMETIMES I TEND TO FEEL TENSE AND INHIBITED WHEN I MOVE INTO NEW LIVING QUARTERS....
Whappa Whappa Whappa...
NGOGNO-GNOGN-OGNOGG!
©1985 by H. Cruse

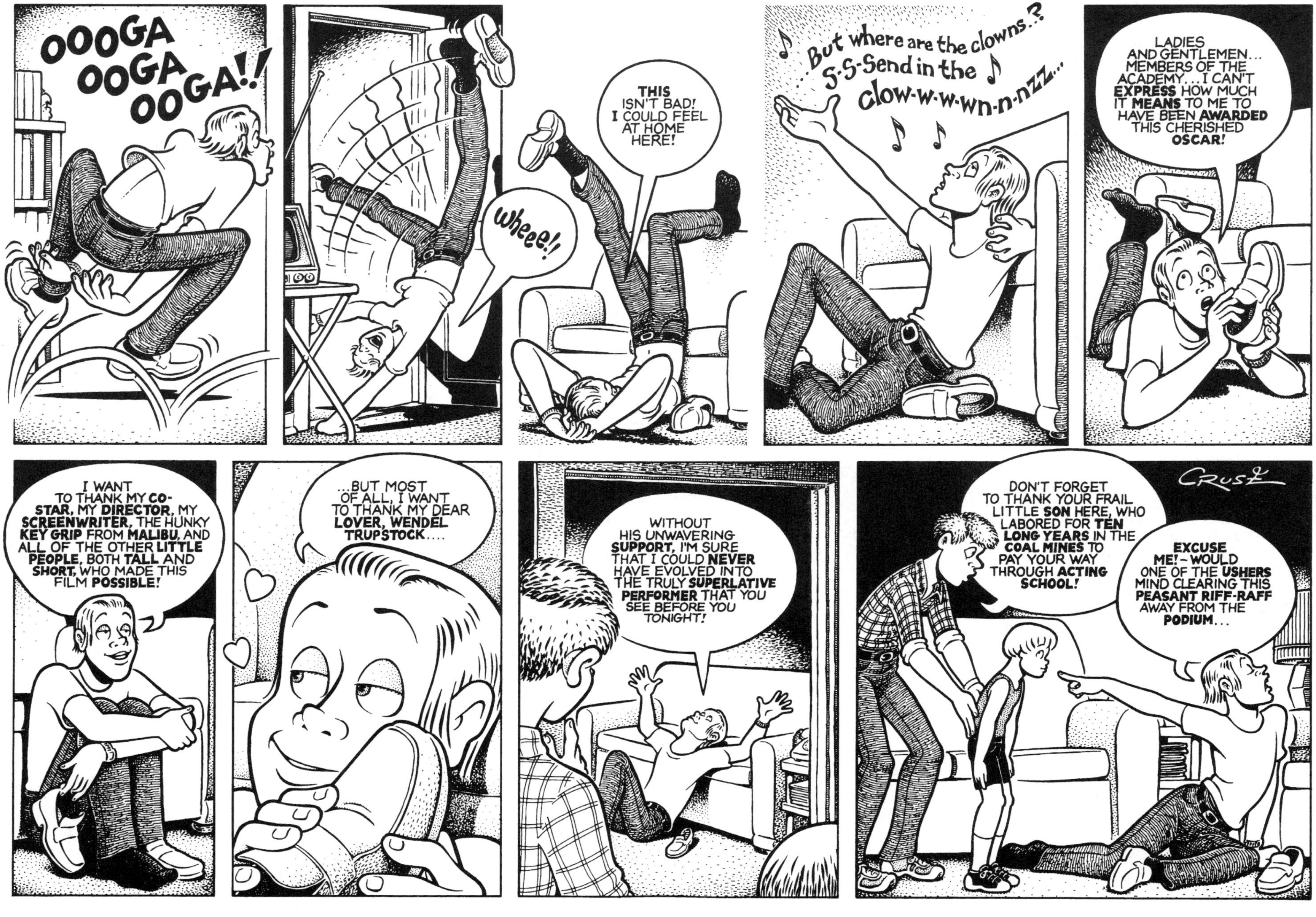
OOOGA OOGA OOGA!!
Wheee!!
THIS ISN'T BAD! I COULD FEEL AT HOME HERE!
But where are the clowns..? S-S-Send in the clow-w-w-wn-n-nzz...
LADIES AND GENTLEMEN... MEMBERS OF THE ACADEMY... I CAN'T EXPRESS HOW MUCH IT MEANS TO ME TO HAVE BEEN AWARDED THIS CHERISHED OSCAR!
I WANT TO THANK MY CO-STAR, MY DIRECTOR, MY SCREENWRITER, THE HUNKY KEY GRIP FROM MALIBU, AND ALL OF THE OTHER LITTLE PEOPLE, BOTH TALL AND SHORT, WHO MADE THIS FILM POSSIBLE!
...BUT MOST OF ALL, I WANT TO THANK MY DEAR LOVER, WENDEL TRUPSTOCK....
WITHOUT HIS UNWAVERING SUPPORT, I'M SURE THAT I COULD NEVER HAVE EVOLVED INTO THE TRULY SUPERLATIVE PERFORMER THAT YOU SEE BEFORE YOU TONIGHT!
CRUSE
DON'T FORGET TO THANK YOUR FRAIL LITTLE SON HERE, WHO LABORED FOR TEN LONG YEARS IN THE COAL MINES TO PAY YOUR WAY THROUGH ACTING SCHOOL!
EXCUSE ME! – WOULD ONE OF THE USHERS MIND CLEARING THIS PEASANT RIFF-RAFF AWAY FROM THE PODIUM...

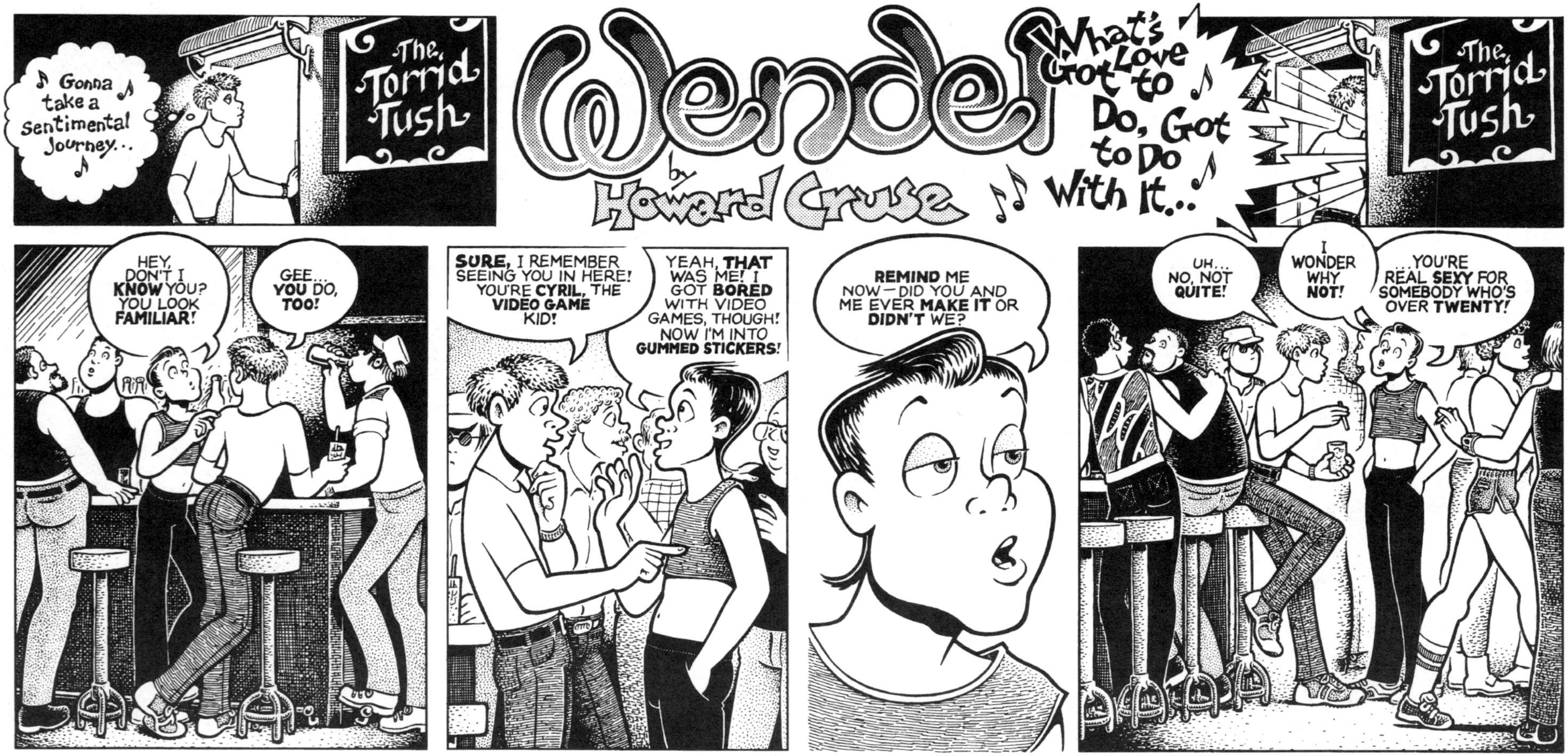
Wendel
by Howard Cruse
Gonna take a sentimental journey...
The Torrid Tush
What's Love Got to Do, Got to Do With It...
The Torrid Tush
HEY, DON'T I KNOW YOU? YOU LOOK FAMILIAR!
GEE... YOU DO, TOO!
SURE, I REMEMBER SEEING YOU IN HERE! YOU'RE CYRIL, THE VIDEO GAME KID!
YEAH, THAT WAS ME! I GOT BORED WITH VIDEO GAMES, THOUGH! NOW I'M INTO GUMMED STICKERS!
REMIND ME NOW—DID YOU AND ME EVER MAKE IT OR DIDN'T WE?
UH... NO, NOT QUITE!
I WONDER WHY NOT!
...YOU'RE REAL SEXY FOR SOMEBODY WHO'S OVER TWENTY!

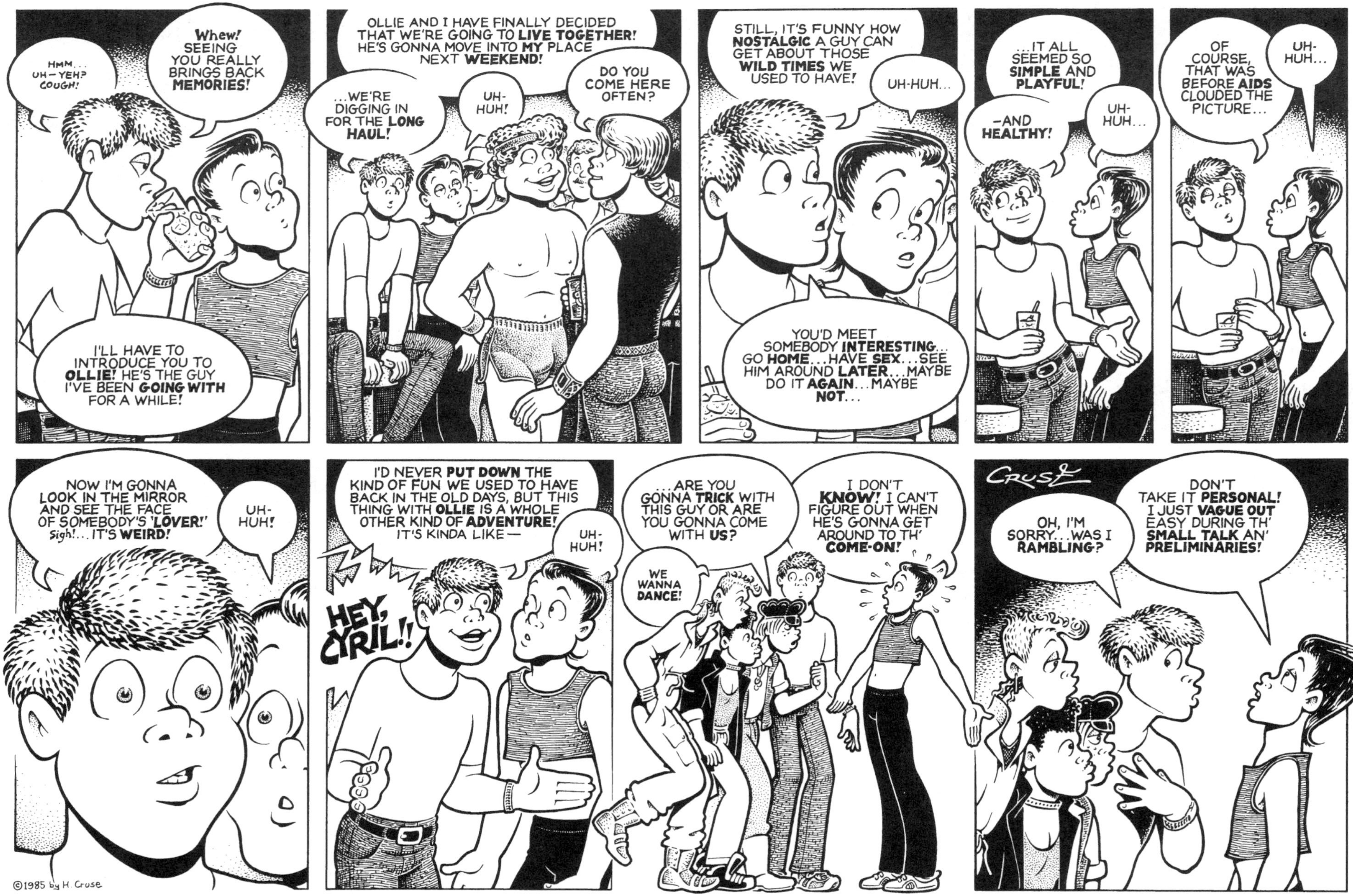
Whew! SEEING YOU REALLY BRINGS BACK MEMORIES!
HMM... UH—YEH? COUGH!
I'LL HAVE TO INTRODUCE YOU TO OLLIE! HE'S THE GUY I'VE BEEN GOING WITH FOR A WHILE!
OLLIE AND I HAVE FINALLY DECIDED THAT WE'RE GOING TO LIVE TOGETHER! HE'S GONNA MOVE INTO MY PLACE NEXT WEEKEND!
...WE'RE DIGGING IN FOR THE LONG HAUL!
UH-HUH!
DO YOU COME HERE OFTEN?
STILL, IT'S FUNNY HOW NOSTALGIC A GUY CAN GET ABOUT THOSE WILD TIMES WE USED TO HAVE!
UH-HUH...
YOU'D MEET SOMEBODY INTERESTING... GO HOME...HAVE SEX...SEE HIM AROUND LATER...MAYBE DO IT AGAIN...MAYBE NOT...
...IT ALL SEEMED SO SIMPLE AND PLAYFUL!
—AND HEALTHY!
UH-HUH...
OF COURSE, THAT WAS BEFORE AIDS CLOUDED THE PICTURE...
UH-HUH...
NOW I'M GONNA LOOK IN THE MIRROR AND SEE THE FACE OF SOMEBODY'S 'LOVER!' Sigh!...IT'S WEIRD!
UH-HUH!
I'D NEVER PUT DOWN THE KIND OF FUN WE USED TO HAVE BACK IN THE OLD DAYS, BUT THIS THING WITH OLLIE IS A WHOLE OTHER KIND OF ADVENTURE! IT'S KINDA LIKE—
UH-HUH!
HEY, CYRIL!!
...ARE YOU GONNA TRICK WITH THIS GUY OR ARE YOU GONNA COME WITH US?
WE WANNA DANCE!
I DON'T KNOW! I CAN'T FIGURE OUT WHEN HE'S GONNA GET AROUND TO TH' COME-ON!
CRUSE
OH, I'M SORRY...WAS I RAMBLING?
DON'T TAKE IT PERSONAL! I JUST VAGUE OUT EASY DURING TH' SMALL TALK AN' PRELIMINARIES!
©1985 by H. Cruse

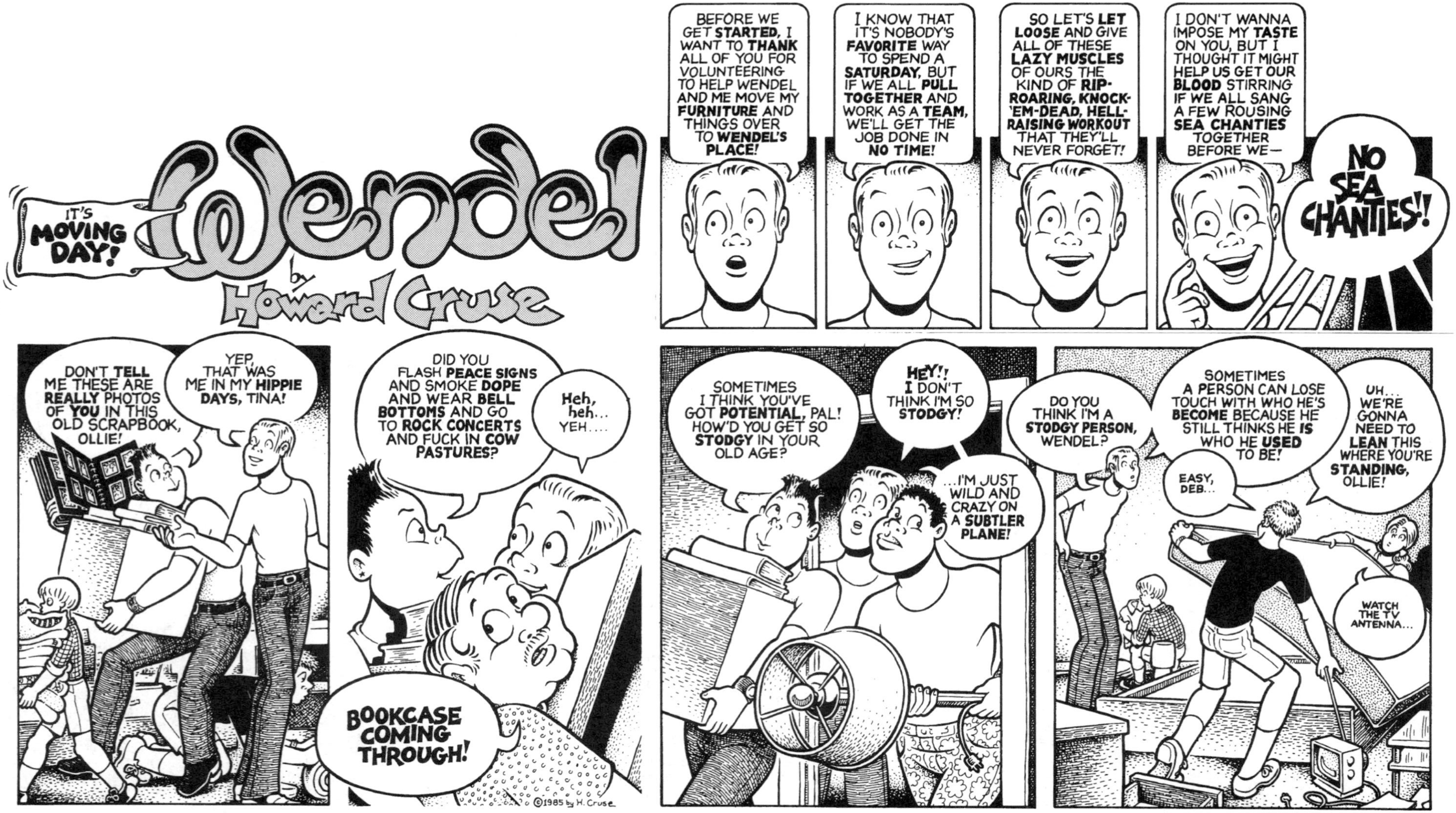
IT'S MOVING DAY!
Wendel
by Howard Cruse
BEFORE WE GET STARTED, I WANT TO THANK ALL OF YOU FOR VOLUNTEERING TO HELP WENDEL AND ME MOVE MY FURNITURE AND THINGS OVER TO WENDEL'S PLACE!
I KNOW THAT IT'S NOBODY'S FAVORITE WAY TO SPEND A SATURDAY, BUT IF WE ALL PULL TOGETHER AND WORK AS A TEAM, WE'LL GET THE JOB DONE IN NO TIME!
SO LET'S LET LOOSE AND GIVE ALL OF THESE LAZY MUSCLES OF OURS THE KIND OF RIP-ROARING, KNOCK-'EM-DEAD, HELL-RAISING WORKOUT THAT THEY'LL NEVER FORGET!
I DON'T WANNA IMPOSE MY TASTE ON YOU, BUT I THOUGHT IT MIGHT HELP US GET OUR BLOOD STIRRING IF WE ALL SANG A FEW ROUSING SEA CHANTIES TOGETHER BEFORE WE—
NO SEA CHANTIES!!
DON'T TELL ME THESE ARE REALLY PHOTOS OF YOU IN THIS OLD SCRAPBOOK, OLLIE!
YEP, THAT WAS ME IN MY HIPPIE DAYS, TINA!
DID YOU FLASH PEACE SIGNS AND SMOKE DOPE AND WEAR BELL BOTTOMS AND GO TO ROCK CONCERTS AND FUCK IN COW PASTURES?
Heh, heh... YEH....
BOOKCASE COMING THROUGH!
©1985 by H. Cruse
SOMETIMES I THINK YOU'VE GOT POTENTIAL, PAL! HOW'D YOU GET SO STODGY IN YOUR OLD AGE?
HEY!! I DON'T THINK I'M SO STODGY!
...I'M JUST WILD AND CRAZY ON A SUBTLER PLANE!
DO YOU THINK I'M A STODGY PERSON, WENDEL?
SOMETIMES A PERSON CAN LOSE TOUCH WITH WHO HE'S BECOME BECAUSE HE STILL THINKS HE IS WHO HE USED TO BE!
EASY, DEB...
UH... WE'RE GONNA NEED TO LEAN THIS WHERE YOU'RE STANDING, OLLIE!
WATCH THE TV ANTENNA...

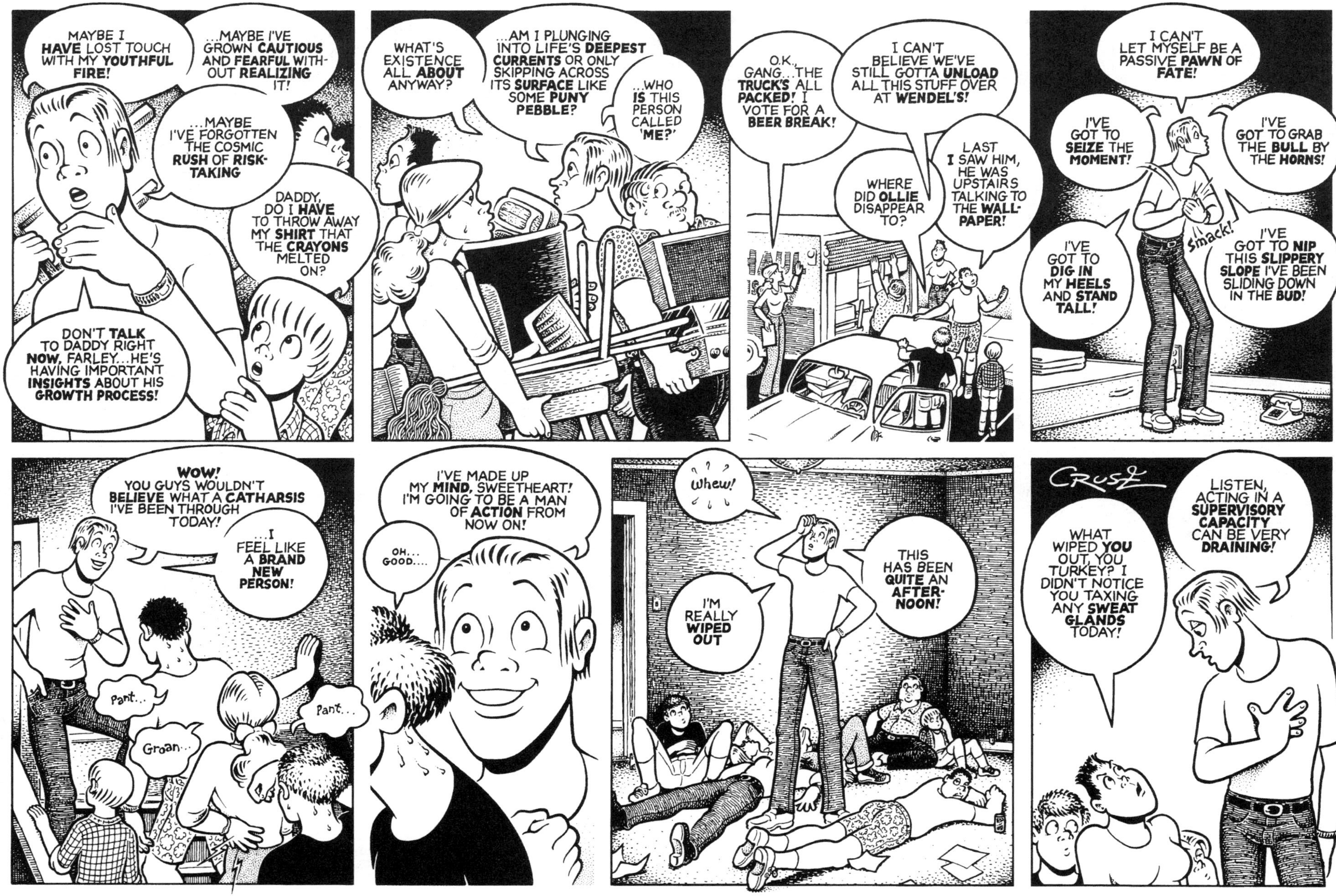
MAYBE I HAVE LOST TOUCH WITH MY YOUTHFUL FIRE!
...MAYBE I'VE GROWN CAUTIOUS AND FEARFUL WITHOUT REALIZING IT!
...MAYBE I'VE FORGOTTEN THE COSMIC RUSH OF RISK-TAKING
DADDY, DO I HAVE TO THROW AWAY MY SHIRT THAT THE CRAYONS MELTED ON?
DON'T TALK TO DADDY RIGHT NOW, FARLEY...HE'S HAVING IMPORTANT INSIGHTS ABOUT HIS GROWTH PROCESS!
WHAT'S EXISTENCE ALL ABOUT ANYWAY?
...AM I PLUNGING INTO LIFE'S DEEPEST CURRENTS OR ONLY SKIPPING ACROSS ITS SURFACE LIKE SOME PUNY PEBBLE?
...WHO IS THIS PERSON CALLED 'ME?'
O.K., GANG...THE TRUCK'S ALL PACKED! I VOTE FOR A BEER BREAK!
I CAN'T BELIEVE WE'VE STILL GOTTA UNLOAD ALL THIS STUFF OVER AT WENDEL'S!
WHERE DID OLLIE DISAPPEAR TO?
LAST I SAW HIM, HE WAS UPSTAIRS TALKING TO THE WALL-PAPER!
I CAN'T LET MYSELF BE A PASSIVE PAWN OF FATE!
I'VE GOT TO SEIZE THE MOMENT!
I'VE GOT TO GRAB THE BULL BY THE HORNS!
Smack!
I'VE GOT TO DIG IN MY HEELS AND STAND TALL!
I'VE GOT TO NIP THIS SLIPPERY SLOPE I'VE BEEN SLIDING DOWN IN THE BUD!
WOW! YOU GUYS WOULDN'T BELIEVE WHAT A CATHARSIS I'VE BEEN THROUGH TODAY!
...I FEEL LIKE A BRAND NEW PERSON!
Pant...
Groan...
Pant...
I'VE MADE UP MY MIND, SWEETHEART! I'M GOING TO BE A MAN OF ACTION FROM NOW ON!
OH... GOOD....
Whew!
I'M REALLY WIPED OUT
THIS HAS BEEN QUITE AN AFTER-NOON!
CRUSE
WHAT WIPED YOU OUT, YOU TURKEY? I DIDN'T NOTICE YOU TAXING ANY SWEAT GLANDS TODAY!
LISTEN, ACTING IN A SUPERVISORY CAPACITY CAN BE VERY DRAINING!

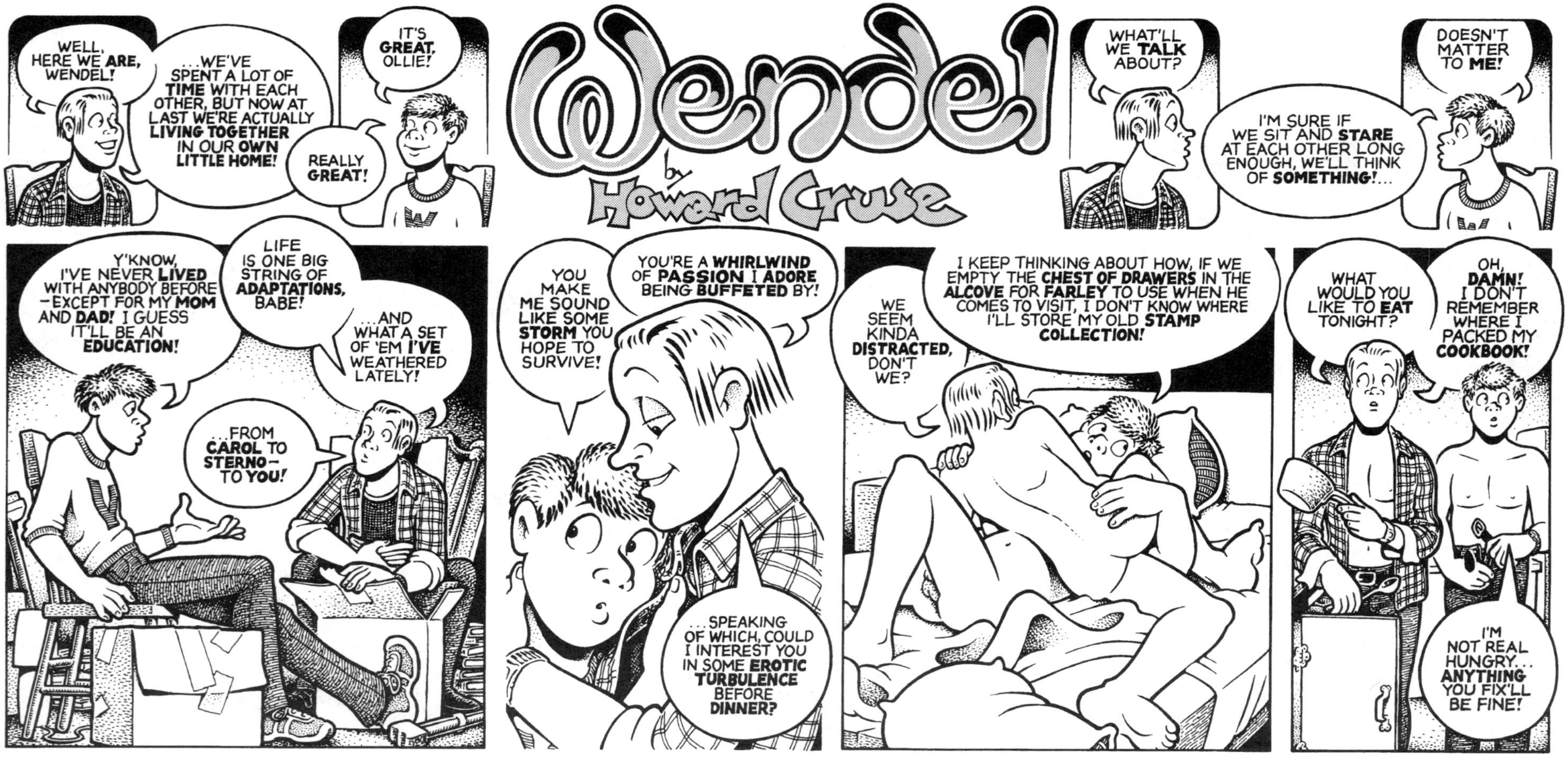
Wendel
by Howard Cruse
WELL, HERE WE ARE, WENDEL!
...WE'VE SPENT A LOT OF TIME WITH EACH OTHER, BUT NOW AT LAST WE'RE ACTUALLY LIVING TOGETHER IN OUR OWN LITTLE HOME!
IT'S GREAT, OLLIE!
REALLY GREAT!
WHAT'LL WE TALK ABOUT?
DOESN'T MATTER TO ME!
I'M SURE IF WE SIT AND STARE AT EACH OTHER LONG ENOUGH, WE'LL THINK OF SOMETHING!...
Y'KNOW, I'VE NEVER LIVED WITH ANYBODY BEFORE —EXCEPT FOR MY MOM AND DAD! I GUESS IT'LL BE AN EDUCATION!
LIFE IS ONE BIG STRING OF ADAPTATIONS, BABE!
...AND WHAT A SET OF 'EM I'VE WEATHERED LATELY!
...FROM CAROL TO STERNO— TO YOU!
YOU MAKE ME SOUND LIKE SOME STORM YOU HOPE TO SURVIVE!
YOU'RE A WHIRLWIND OF PASSION I ADORE BEING BUFFETED BY!
...SPEAKING OF WHICH, COULD I INTEREST YOU IN SOME EROTIC TURBULENCE BEFORE DINNER?
WE SEEM KINDA DISTRACTED, DON'T WE?
I KEEP THINKING ABOUT HOW, IF WE EMPTY THE CHEST OF DRAWERS IN THE ALCOVE FOR FARLEY TO USE WHEN HE COMES TO VISIT, I DON'T KNOW WHERE I'LL STORE MY OLD STAMP COLLECTION!
WHAT WOULD YOU LIKE TO EAT TONIGHT?
OH, DAMN! I DON'T REMEMBER WHERE I PACKED MY COOKBOOK!
I'M NOT REAL HUNGRY... ANYTHING YOU FIX'LL BE FINE!

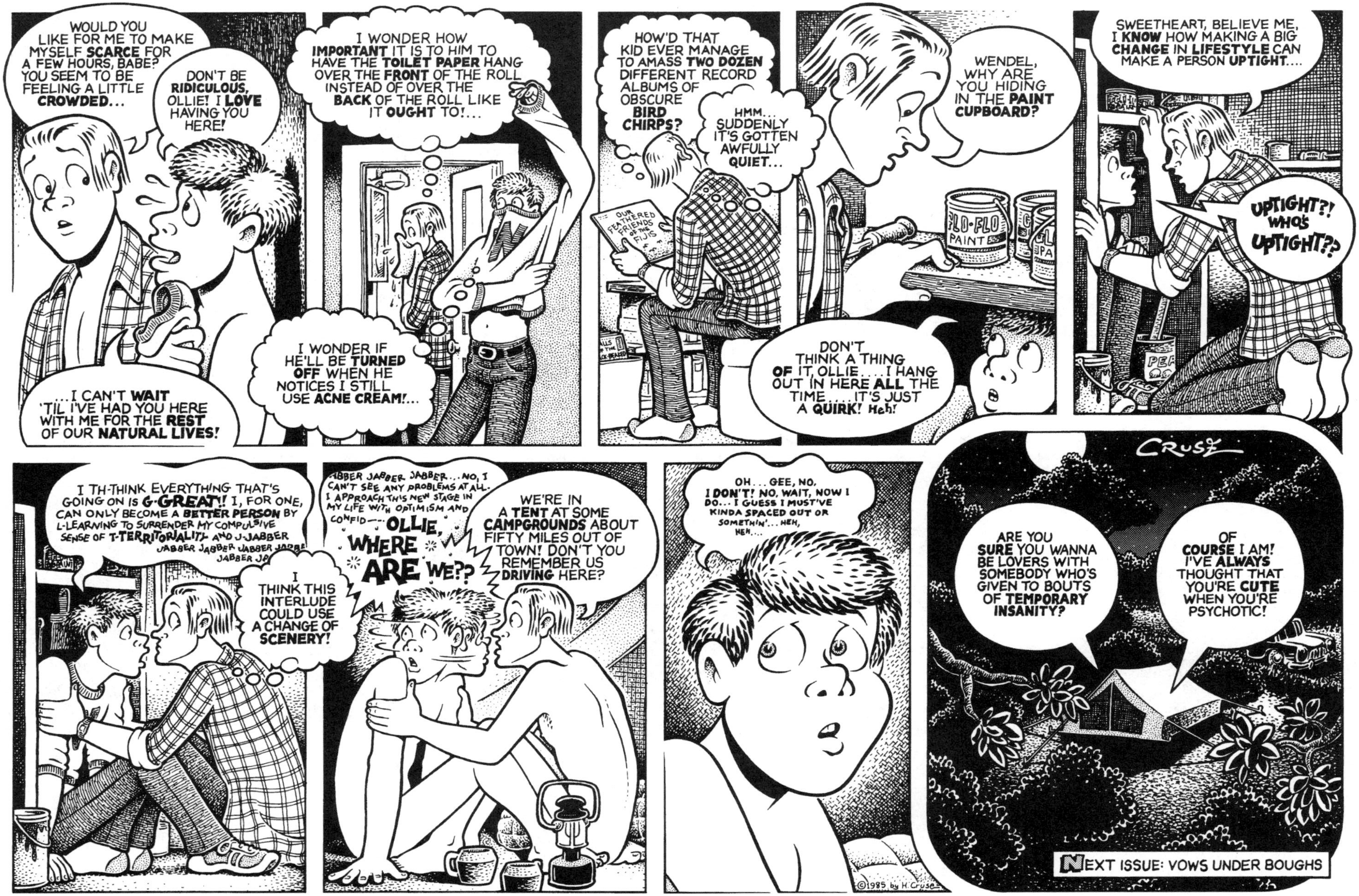
WOULD YOU LIKE FOR ME TO MAKE MYSELF SCARCE FOR A FEW HOURS, BABE? YOU SEEM TO BE FEELING A LITTLE CROWDED...
DON'T BE RIDICULOUS, OLLIE! I LOVE HAVING YOU HERE!
...I CAN'T WAIT 'TIL I'VE HAD YOU HERE WITH ME FOR THE REST OF OUR NATURAL LIVES!
I WONDER HOW IMPORTANT IT IS TO HIM TO HAVE THE TOILET PAPER HANG OVER THE FRONT OF THE ROLL INSTEAD OF OVER THE BACK OF THE ROLL LIKE IT OUGHT TO!...
I WONDER IF HE'LL BE TURNED OFF WHEN HE NOTICES I STILL USE ACNE CREAM!...
HOW'D THAT KID EVER MANAGE TO AMASS TWO DOZEN DIFFERENT RECORD ALBUMS OF OBSCURE BIRD CHIRPS?
OUR FEATHERED FRIENDS OF THE FIJIS
HMM... SUDDENLY IT'S GOTTEN AWFULLY QUIET...
WENDEL, WHY ARE YOU HIDING IN THE PAINT CUPBOARD?
FLO-FLO PAINT
DON'T THINK A THING OF IT, OLLIE.... I HANG OUT IN HERE ALL THE TIME.... IT'S JUST A QUIRK! Heh!
SWEETHEART, BELIEVE ME, I KNOW HOW MAKING A BIG CHANGE IN LIFESTYLE CAN MAKE A PERSON UPTIGHT....
UPTIGHT?! WHO'S UPTIGHT??
I TH-THINK EVERYTHING THAT'S GOING ON IS G-GREAT!! I, FOR ONE, CAN ONLY BECOME A BETTER PERSON BY L-LEARNING TO SURRENDER MY COMPULSIVE SENSE OF T-TERRITORIALITY AND J-JABBER JABBER JABBER JABBER JABBE JABBER JA
I THINK THIS INTERLUDE COULD USE A CHANGE OF SCENERY!
JABBER JABBER JABBER... NO, I CAN'T SEE ANY PROBLEMS AT ALL. I APPROACH THIS NEW STAGE IN MY LIFE WITH OPTIMISM AND CONFID— OLLIE, WHERE ARE WE??
WE'RE IN A TENT AT SOME CAMPGROUNDS ABOUT FIFTY MILES OUT OF TOWN! DON'T YOU REMEMBER US DRIVING HERE?
OH... GEE, NO. I DON'T! NO, WAIT, NOW I DO... I GUESS I MUST'VE KINDA SPACED OUT OR SOMETHIN'... HEH, HEH...
©1985 by H. Cruse
CRUSE
ARE YOU SURE YOU WANNA BE LOVERS WITH SOMEBODY WHO'S GIVEN TO BOUTS OF TEMPORARY INSANITY?
OF COURSE I AM! I'VE ALWAYS THOUGHT THAT YOU'RE CUTE WHEN YOU'RE PSYCHOTIC!
NEXT ISSUE: VOWS UNDER BOUGHS

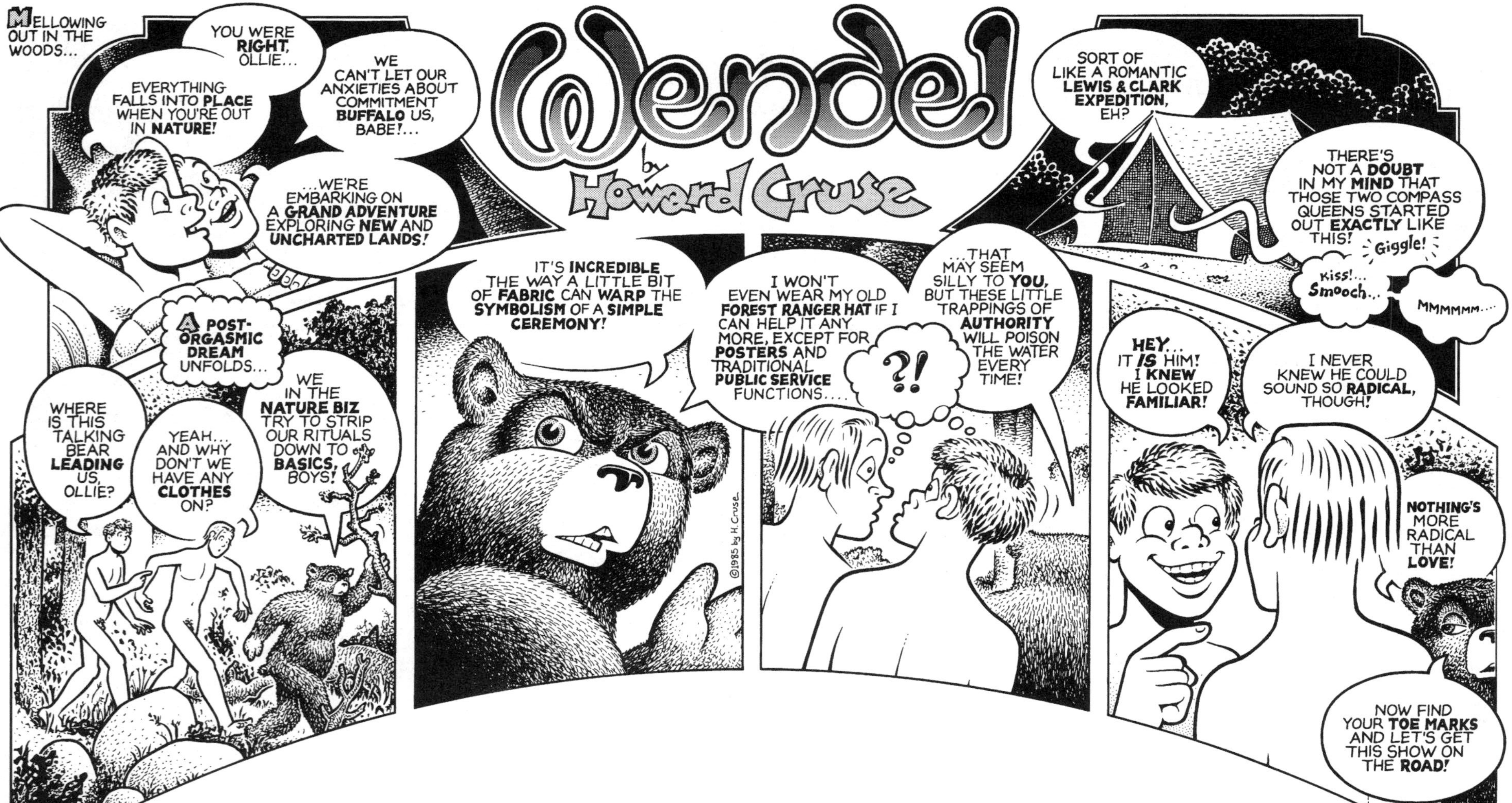
MELLOWING OUT IN THE WOODS...
YOU WERE RIGHT, OLLIE...
EVERYTHING FALLS INTO PLACE WHEN YOU'RE OUT IN NATURE!
WE CAN'T LET OUR ANXIETIES ABOUT COMMITMENT BUFFALO US, BABE!...
...WE'RE EMBARKING ON A GRAND ADVENTURE EXPLORING NEW AND UNCHARTED LANDS!
Wendel
by Howard Cruse
SORT OF LIKE A ROMANTIC LEWIS & CLARK EXPEDITION, EH?
THERE'S NOT A DOUBT IN MY MIND THAT THOSE TWO COMPASS QUEENS STARTED OUT EXACTLY LIKE THIS!
Giggle!
Kiss!... Smooch...
MMMMMM....
A POST-ORGASMIC DREAM UNFOLDS...
WHERE IS THIS TALKING BEAR LEADING US, OLLIE?
YEAH... AND WHY DON'T WE HAVE ANY CLOTHES ON?
WE IN THE NATURE BIZ TRY TO STRIP OUR RITUALS DOWN TO BASICS, BOYS!
IT'S INCREDIBLE THE WAY A LITTLE BIT OF FABRIC CAN WARP THE SYMBOLISM OF A SIMPLE CEREMONY!
©1985 by H. Cruse.
I WON'T EVEN WEAR MY OLD FOREST RANGER HAT IF I CAN HELP IT ANY MORE, EXCEPT FOR POSTERS AND TRADITIONAL PUBLIC SERVICE FUNCTIONS....
...THAT MAY SEEM SILLY TO YOU, BUT THESE LITTLE TRAPPINGS OF AUTHORITY WILL POISON THE WATER EVERY TIME!
?!
HEY... IT IS HIM! I KNEW HE LOOKED FAMILIAR!
I NEVER KNEW HE COULD SOUND SO RADICAL, THOUGH!
NOTHING'S MORE RADICAL THAN LOVE!
NOW FIND YOUR TOE MARKS AND LET'S GET THIS SHOW ON THE ROAD!

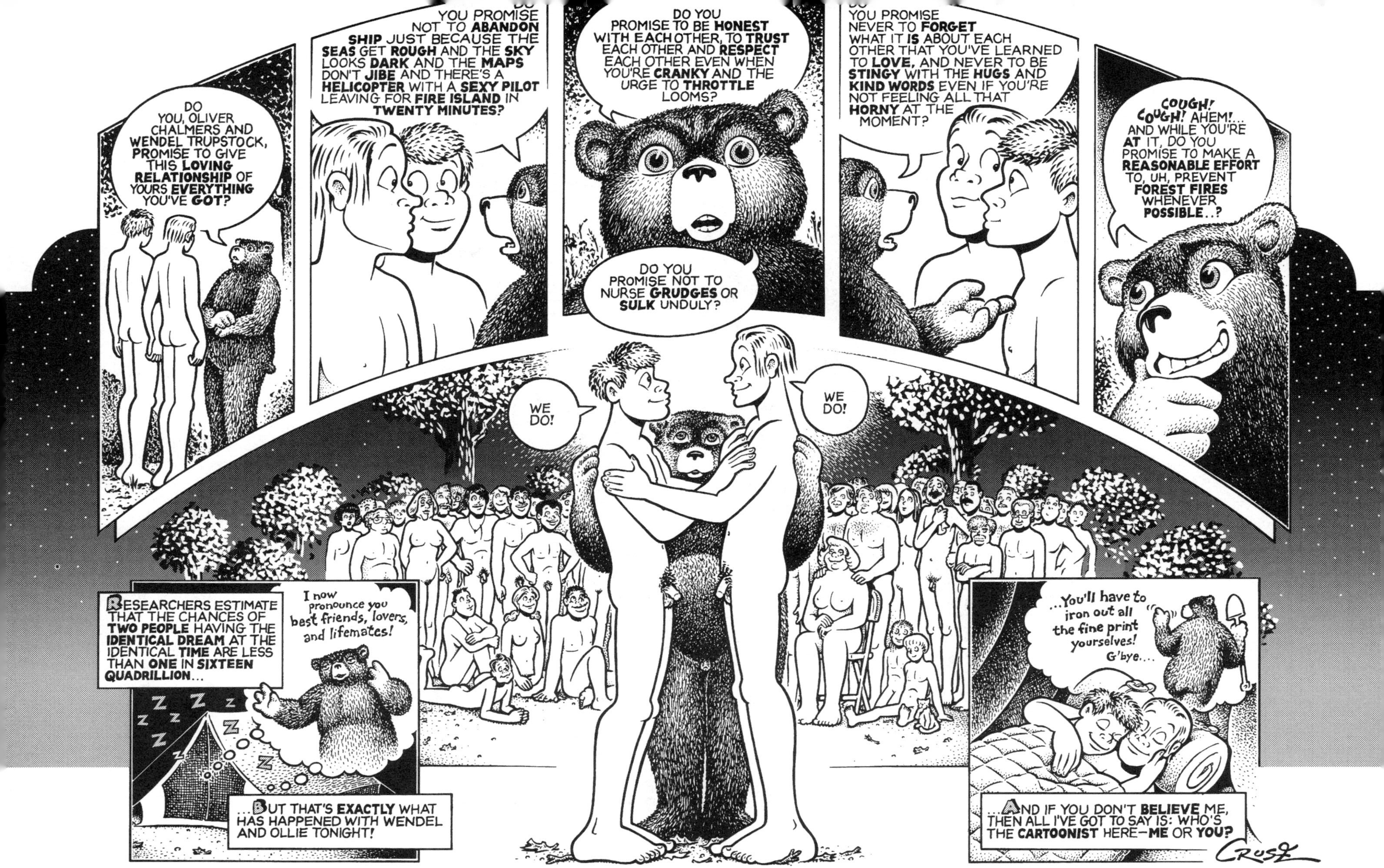
DO YOU, OLIVER CHALMERS AND WENDEL TRUPSTOCK, PROMISE TO GIVE THIS LOVING RELATIONSHIP OF YOURS EVERYTHING YOU'VE GOT?
DO YOU PROMISE NOT TO ABANDON SHIP JUST BECAUSE THE SEAS GET ROUGH AND THE SKY LOOKS DARK AND THE MAPS DON'T JIBE AND THERE'S A HELICOPTER WITH A SEXY PILOT LEAVING FOR FIRE ISLAND IN TWENTY MINUTES?
DO YOU PROMISE TO BE HONEST WITH EACH OTHER, TO TRUST EACH OTHER AND RESPECT EACH OTHER EVEN WHEN YOU'RE CRANKY AND THE URGE TO THROTTLE LOOMS?
DO YOU PROMISE NOT TO NURSE GRUDGES OR SULK UNDULY?
DO YOU PROMISE NEVER TO FORGET WHAT IT IS ABOUT EACH OTHER THAT YOU'VE LEARNED TO LOVE, AND NEVER TO BE STINGY WITH THE HUGS AND KIND WORDS EVEN IF YOU'RE NOT FEELING ALL THAT HORNY AT THE MOMENT?
COUGH! COUGH! AHEM!... AND WHILE YOU'RE AT IT, DO YOU PROMISE TO MAKE A REASONABLE EFFORT TO, UH, PREVENT FOREST FIRES WHENEVER POSSIBLE..?
WE DO!
WE DO!
RESEARCHERS ESTIMATE THAT THE CHANCES OF TWO PEOPLE HAVING THE IDENTICAL DREAM AT THE IDENTICAL TIME ARE LESS THAN ONE IN SIXTEEN QUADRILLION...
I now pronounce you best friends, lovers, and lifemates!
...BUT THAT'S EXACTLY WHAT HAS HAPPENED WITH WENDEL AND OLLIE TONIGHT!
...You'll have to iron out all the fine print yourselves! G'bye....
...AND IF YOU DON'T BELIEVE ME, THEN ALL I'VE GOT TO SAY IS: WHO'S THE CARTOONIST HERE—ME OR YOU?
CRUSE

My comic strip disappeared from ***The Advocate*** for a year after Wendel and Ollie merged households. The magazine's switch to a smaller format made preserving my feature's relaxed comedic structure impossible, since fewer square inches would have meant fewer panels, and racing through a strip in fewer panels would have forced me to place too much emphasis on quick set-ups and punchlines. So I closed out my story in the November 17, 1985 issue and turned to other ventures.

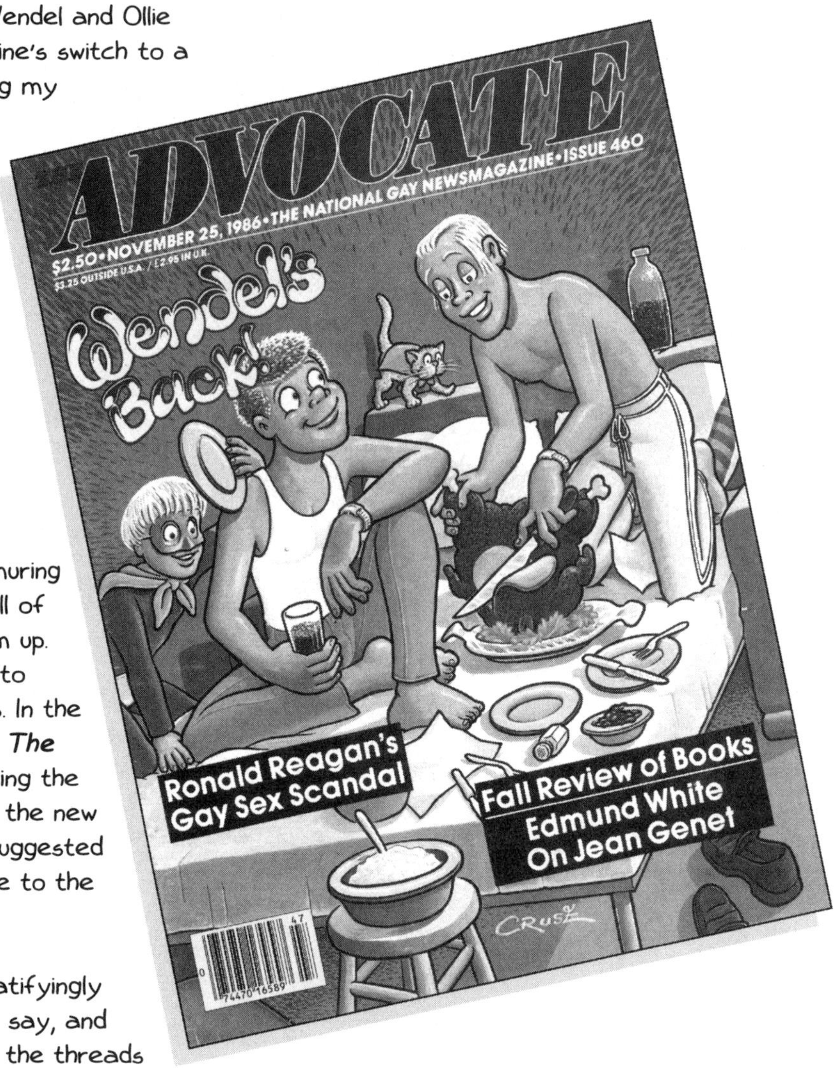

ADVOCATE
$2.50•NOVEMBER 25, 1986•THE NATIONAL GAY NEWSMAGAZINE•ISSUE 460
$3.25 OUTSIDE U.S.A. / £2.95 IN U.K.
Wendel's Back!
Ronald Reagan's Gay Sex Scandal
Fall Review of Books
Edmund White On Jean Genet
CRUSE

But the characters kept murmuring restlessly in my head despite all of my efforts to gently shut them up. Finally I bowed to their refusal to gracefully vacate the premises. In the summer of 1986 I proposed to ***The Advocate***'s editors that we bring the gang back. To compensate for the new format's reduced page size, I suggested we allot <u>two</u> pages in each issue to the comic strip instead of <u>one</u>.

The Strawhead received a gratifyingly hearty welcome, I'm pleased to say, and in November I happily picked up the threads of my character's lives. From my point of view, it was a treat to spend time with them again, and the fact that the second series debuted in the magazine's Thanksgiving issue couldn't have felt more appropriate.

THE SECOND SERIES

1986-89

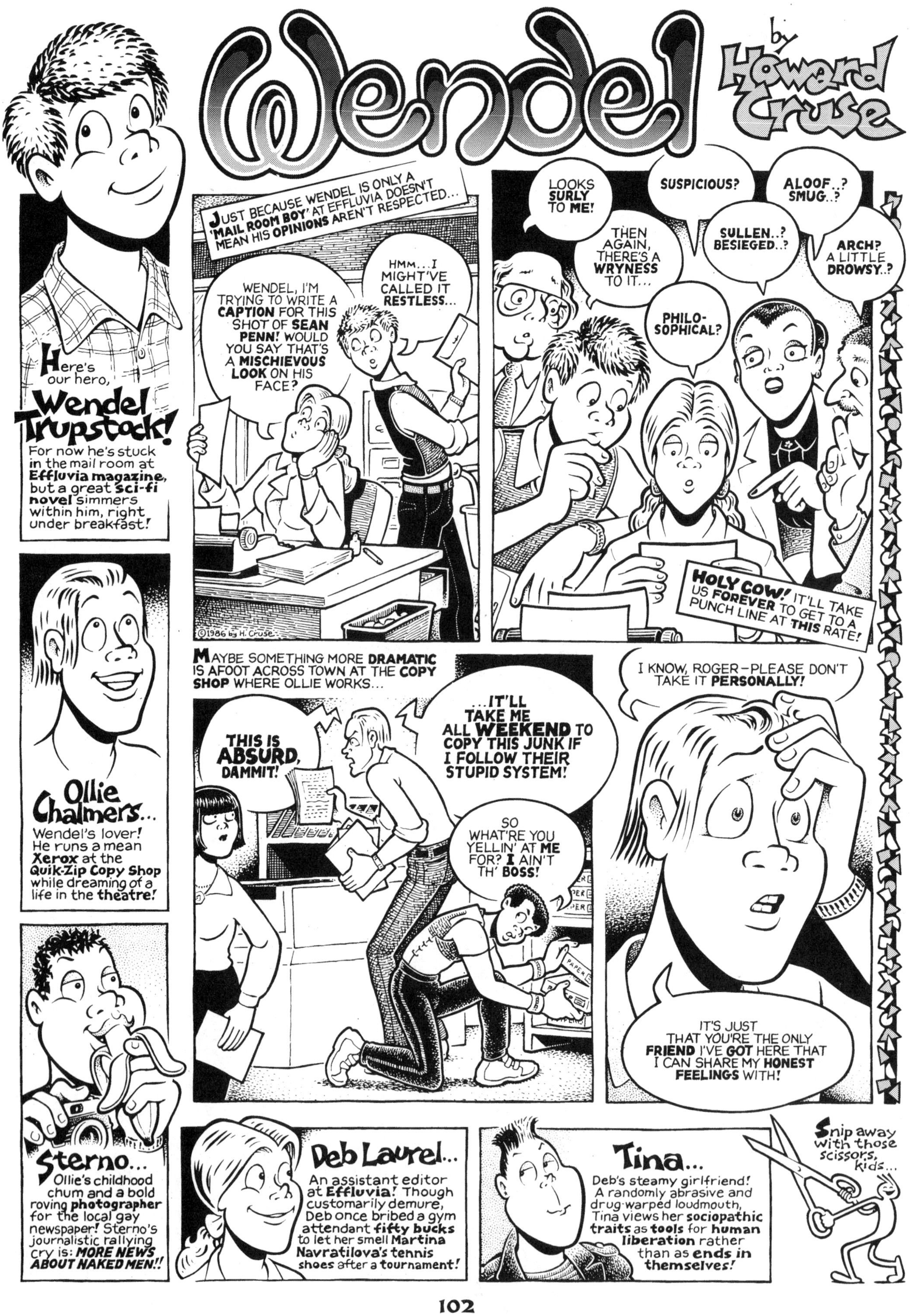

Wendel
by Howard Cruse
Here's our hero, Wendel Trupstock!
For now he's stuck in the mail room at Effluvia magazine, but a great sci-fi novel simmers within him, right under breakfast!
JUST BECAUSE WENDEL IS ONLY A 'MAIL ROOM BOY' AT EFFLUVIA DOESN'T MEAN HIS OPINIONS AREN'T RESPECTED...
WENDEL, I'M TRYING TO WRITE A CAPTION FOR THIS SHOT OF SEAN PENN! WOULD YOU SAY THAT'S A MISCHIEVOUS LOOK ON HIS FACE?
HMM...I MIGHT'VE CALLED IT RESTLESS...
©1986 by H. Cruse
LOOKS SURLY TO ME!
THEN AGAIN, THERE'S A WRYNESS TO IT...
SUSPICIOUS?
PHILO-SOPHICAL?
SULLEN..? BESIEGED..?
ALOOF..? SMUG..?
ARCH? A LITTLE DROWSY..?
HOLY COW! IT'LL TAKE US FOREVER TO GET TO A PUNCH LINE AT THIS RATE!
Ollie Chalmers...
Wendel's lover! He runs a mean Xerox at the Quik-Zip Copy Shop while dreaming of a life in the theatre!
MAYBE SOMETHING MORE DRAMATIC IS AFOOT ACROSS TOWN AT THE COPY SHOP WHERE OLLIE WORKS...
THIS IS ABSURD, DAMMIT!
...IT'LL TAKE ME ALL WEEKEND TO COPY THIS JUNK IF I FOLLOW THEIR STUPID SYSTEM!
SO WHAT'RE YOU YELLIN' AT ME FOR? I AIN'T TH' BOSS!
I KNOW, ROGER—PLEASE DON'T TAKE IT PERSONALLY!
IT'S JUST THAT YOU'RE THE ONLY FRIEND I'VE GOT HERE THAT I CAN SHARE MY HONEST FEELINGS WITH!
Sterno...
Ollie's childhood chum and a bold roving photographer for the local gay newspaper! Sterno's journalistic rallying cry is: MORE NEWS ABOUT NAKED MEN!!
Deb Laurel...
An assistant editor at Effluvia! Though customarily demure, Deb once bribed a gym attendant fifty bucks to let her smell Martina Navratilova's tennis shoes after a tournament!
Tina...
Deb's steamy girlfriend! A randomly abrasive and drug-warped loudmouth, Tina views her sociopathic traits as tools for human liberation rather than as ends in themselves!
Snip away with those scissors, kids...

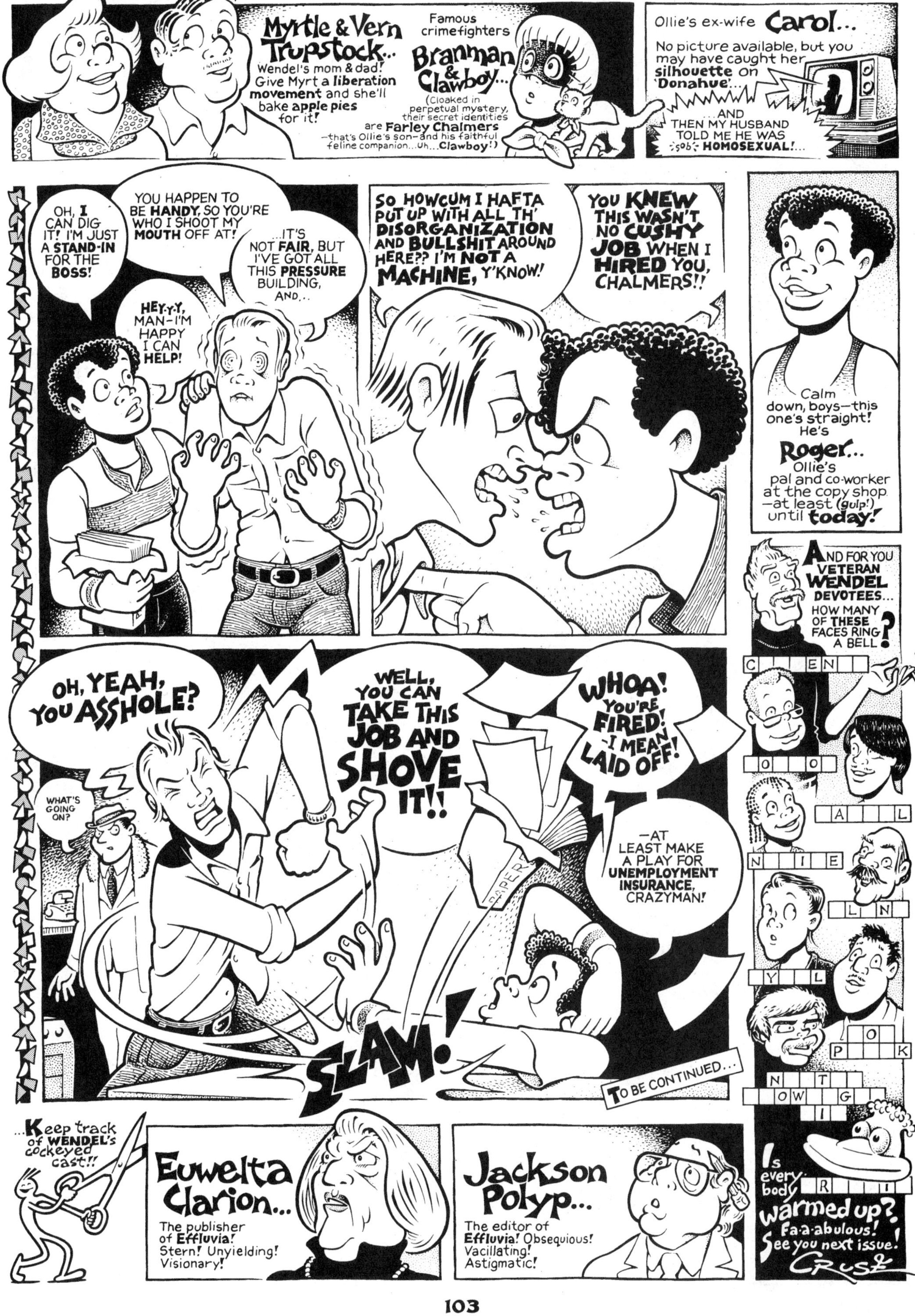

Myrtle & Vern Trupstock...
Wendel's mom & dad! Give Myrt a liberation movement and she'll bake apple pies for it!
Famous crimefighters
Branman & Clawboy...
(Cloaked in perpetual mystery, their secret identities are Farley Chalmers —that's Ollie's son—and his faithful feline companion...uh...Clawboy!)
Ollie's ex-wife Carol...
No picture available, but you may have caught her silhouette on 'Donahue'...
...AND THEN MY HUSBAND TOLD ME HE WAS sob HOMOSEXUAL!...
OH, I CAN DIG IT! I'M JUST A STAND-IN FOR THE BOSS!
YOU HAPPEN TO BE HANDY, SO YOU'RE WHO I SHOOT MY MOUTH OFF AT!
...IT'S NOT FAIR, BUT I'VE GOT ALL THIS PRESSURE BUILDING, AND...
HEY-Y-Y, MAN—I'M HAPPY I CAN HELP!
SO HOWCUM I HAFTA PUT UP WITH ALL TH' DISORGANIZATION AND BULLSHIT AROUND HERE?? I'M NOT A MACHINE, Y'KNOW!
YOU KNEW THIS WASN'T NO CUSHY JOB WHEN I HIRED YOU, CHALMERS!!
Calm down, boys—this one's straight! He's Roger... Ollie's pal and co-worker at the copy shop —at least (gulp!) until today!
AND FOR YOU VETERAN WENDEL DEVOTEES... HOW MANY OF THESE FACES RING A BELL?
OH, YEAH, YOU ASSHOLE?
WELL, YOU CAN TAKE THIS JOB AND SHOVE IT!!
WHOA! YOU'RE FIRED! -I MEAN LAID OFF!
WHAT'S GOING ON?
—AT LEAST MAKE A PLAY FOR UNEMPLOYMENT INSURANCE, CRAZYMAN!
PAPER
SLAM!
TO BE CONTINUED...
...Keep track of WENDEL's cockeyed cast!!
Euwelta Clarion...
The publisher of Effluvia! Stern! Unyielding! Visionary!
Jackson Polyp...
The editor of Effluvia! Obsequious! Vacillating! Astigmatic!
Is everybody warmed up? Fa-a-abulous! See you next issue!
CRUSE

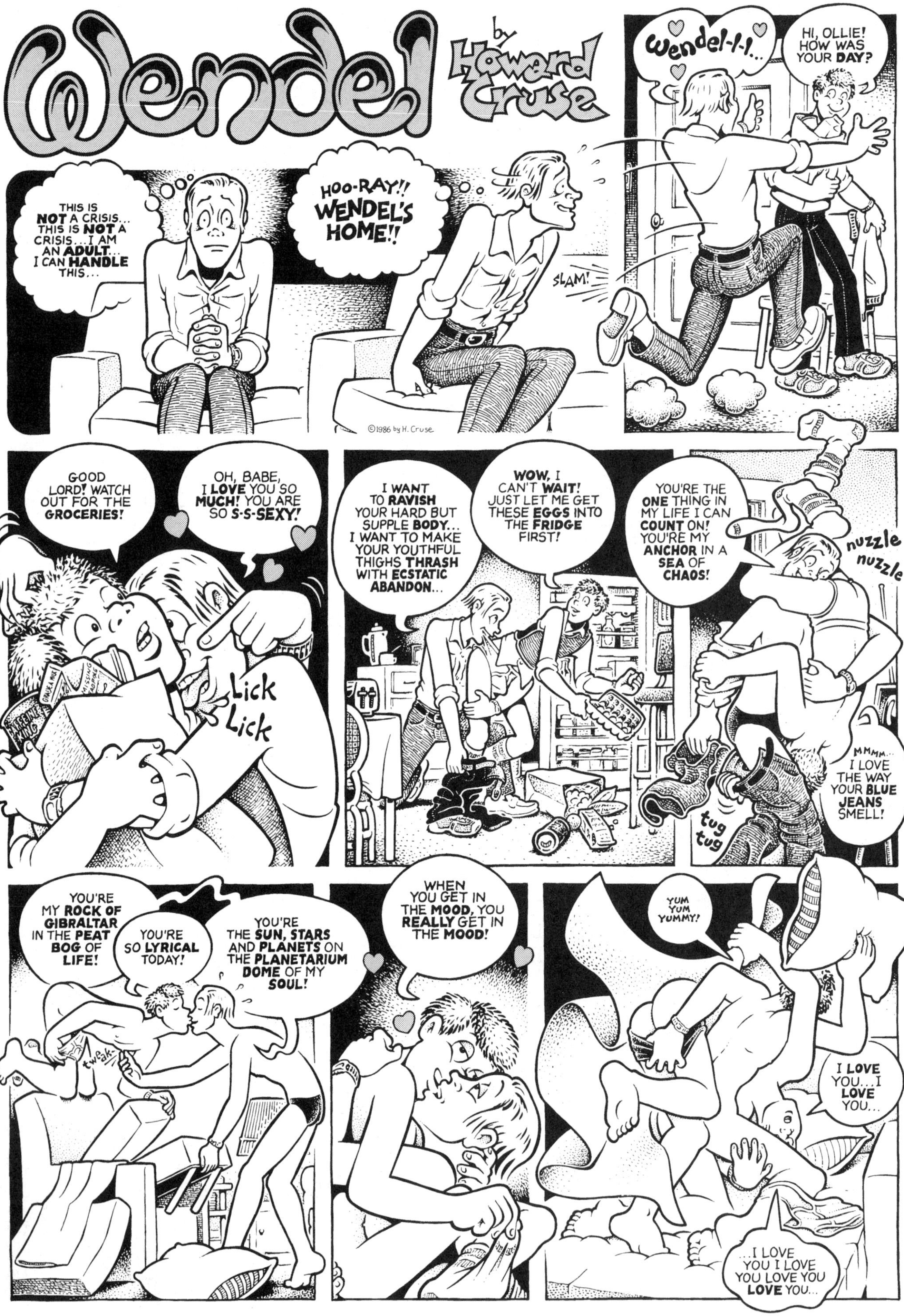
Wendel
by Howard Cruse
THIS IS NOT A CRISIS... THIS IS NOT A CRISIS... I AM AN ADULT... I CAN HANDLE THIS...
HOO-RAY!! WENDEL'S HOME!!
©1986 by H. Cruse
SLAM!
Wendel-l-l...
HI, OLLIE! HOW WAS YOUR DAY?
GOOD LORD! WATCH OUT FOR THE GROCERIES!
OH, BABE, I LOVE YOU SO MUCH! YOU ARE SO S-S-SEXY!
Lick Lick
I WANT TO RAVISH YOUR HARD BUT SUPPLE BODY... I WANT TO MAKE YOUR YOUTHFUL THIGHS THRASH WITH ECSTATIC ABANDON...
WOW, I CAN'T WAIT! JUST LET ME GET THESE EGGS INTO THE FRIDGE FIRST!
YOU'RE THE ONE THING IN MY LIFE I CAN COUNT ON! YOU'RE MY ANCHOR IN A SEA OF CHAOS!
nuzzle nuzzle
MMMM... I LOVE THE WAY YOUR BLUE JEANS SMELL!
tug tug
YOU'RE MY ROCK OF GIBRALTAR IN THE PEAT BOG OF LIFE!
YOU'RE SO LYRICAL TODAY!
YOU'RE THE SUN, STARS AND PLANETS ON THE PLANETARIUM DOME OF MY SOUL!
tweak
WHEN YOU GET IN THE MOOD, YOU REALLY GET IN THE MOOD!
YUM YUM YUMMY!
I LOVE YOU... I LOVE YOU...
...I LOVE YOU I LOVE YOU LOVE YOU LOVE YOU...

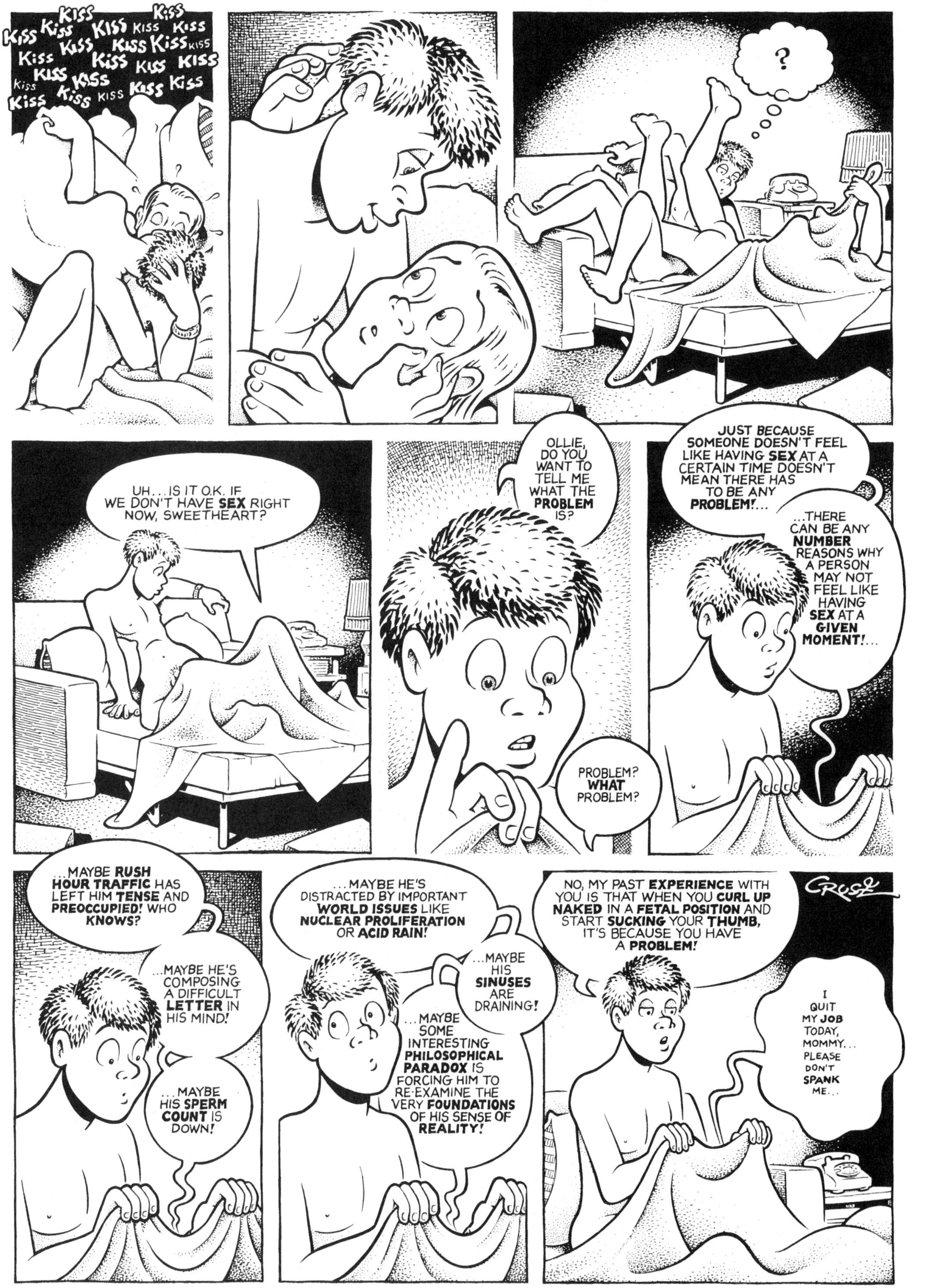
KISS KISS KISS KISS KISS KISS KISS KISS KISS KISS KISS KISS KISS KISS KISS KISS KISS KISS KISS KISS KISS KISS KISS
?
UH...IS IT O.K. IF WE DON'T HAVE **SEX** RIGHT NOW, SWEETHEART?
OLLIE, DO YOU WANT TO TELL ME WHAT THE **PROBLEM** IS?
PROBLEM? **WHAT** PROBLEM?
JUST BECAUSE SOMEONE DOESN'T FEEL LIKE HAVING **SEX** AT A CERTAIN TIME DOESN'T MEAN THERE HAS TO BE ANY **PROBLEM!**...
...THERE CAN BE ANY **NUMBER** REASONS WHY A PERSON MAY NOT FEEL LIKE HAVING **SEX** AT A **GIVEN MOMENT!**...
...MAYBE **RUSH HOUR TRAFFIC** HAS LEFT HIM **TENSE** AND **PREOCCUPIED!** WHO **KNOWS?**
...MAYBE HE'S COMPOSING A DIFFICULT **LETTER** IN HIS MIND!
...MAYBE HIS **SPERM COUNT** IS DOWN!
...MAYBE HE'S DISTRACTED BY IMPORTANT **WORLD ISSUES** LIKE **NUCLEAR PROLIFERATION** OR **ACID RAIN!**
...MAYBE HIS **SINUSES** ARE DRAINING!
...MAYBE SOME INTERESTING **PHILOSOPHICAL PARADOX** IS FORCING HIM TO RE-EXAMINE THE VERY **FOUNDATIONS** OF HIS SENSE OF **REALITY!**
NO, MY PAST **EXPERIENCE** WITH YOU IS THAT WHEN YOU **CURL UP NAKED** IN A **FETAL POSITION** AND START **SUCKING** YOUR **THUMB**, IT'S BECAUSE YOU HAVE A **PROBLEM!**
I QUIT MY **JOB** TODAY, MOMMY... PLEASE DON'T **SPANK** ME...
CRUSE

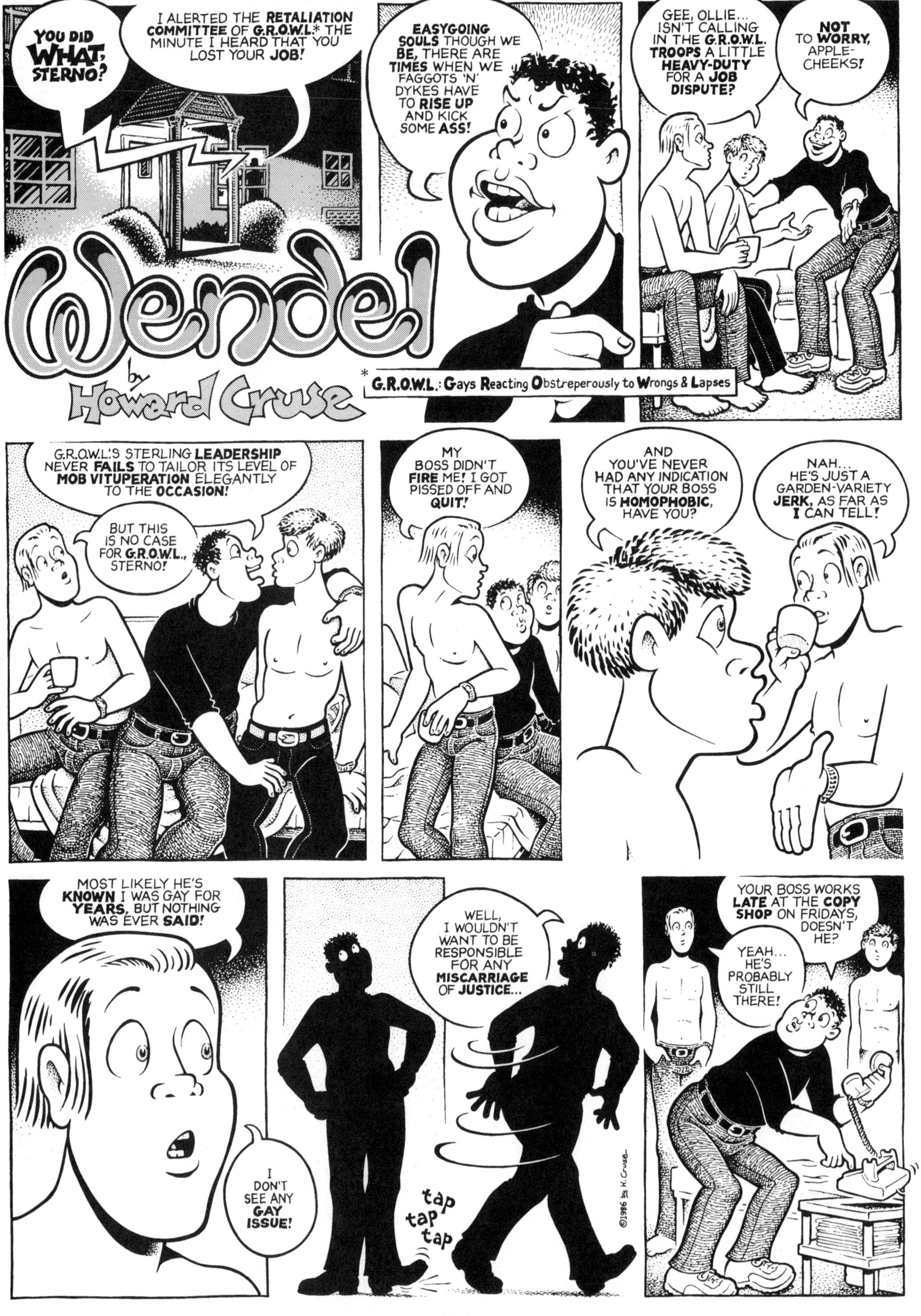
YOU DID WHAT, STERNO?
I ALERTED THE RETALIATION COMMITTEE OF G.R.O.W.L.* THE MINUTE I HEARD THAT YOU LOST YOUR JOB!
Wendel
by Howard Cruse
EASYGOING SOULS THOUGH WE BE, THERE ARE TIMES WHEN WE FAGGOTS 'N' DYKES HAVE TO RISE UP AND KICK SOME ASS!
*G.R.O.W.L.: Gays Reacting Obstreperously to Wrongs & Lapses
GEE, OLLIE... ISN'T CALLING IN THE G.R.O.W.L. TROOPS A LITTLE HEAVY-DUTY FOR A JOB DISPUTE?
NOT TO WORRY, APPLE-CHEEKS!
G.R.O.W.L.'S STERLING LEADERSHIP NEVER FAILS TO TAILOR ITS LEVEL OF MOB VITUPERATION ELEGANTLY TO THE OCCASION!
BUT THIS IS NO CASE FOR G.R.O.W.L., STERNO!
MY BOSS DIDN'T FIRE ME! I GOT PISSED OFF AND QUIT!
AND YOU'VE NEVER HAD ANY INDICATION THAT YOUR BOSS IS HOMOPHOBIC, HAVE YOU?
NAH... HE'S JUST A GARDEN-VARIETY JERK, AS FAR AS I CAN TELL!
MOST LIKELY HE'S KNOWN I WAS GAY FOR YEARS, BUT NOTHING WAS EVER SAID!
I DON'T SEE ANY GAY ISSUE!
WELL, I WOULDN'T WANT TO BE RESPONSIBLE FOR ANY MISCARRIAGE OF JUSTICE...
tap tap tap
©1986 by H. Cruse
YOUR BOSS WORKS LATE AT THE COPY SHOP ON FRIDAYS, DOESN'T HE?
YEAH... HE'S PROBABLY STILL THERE!

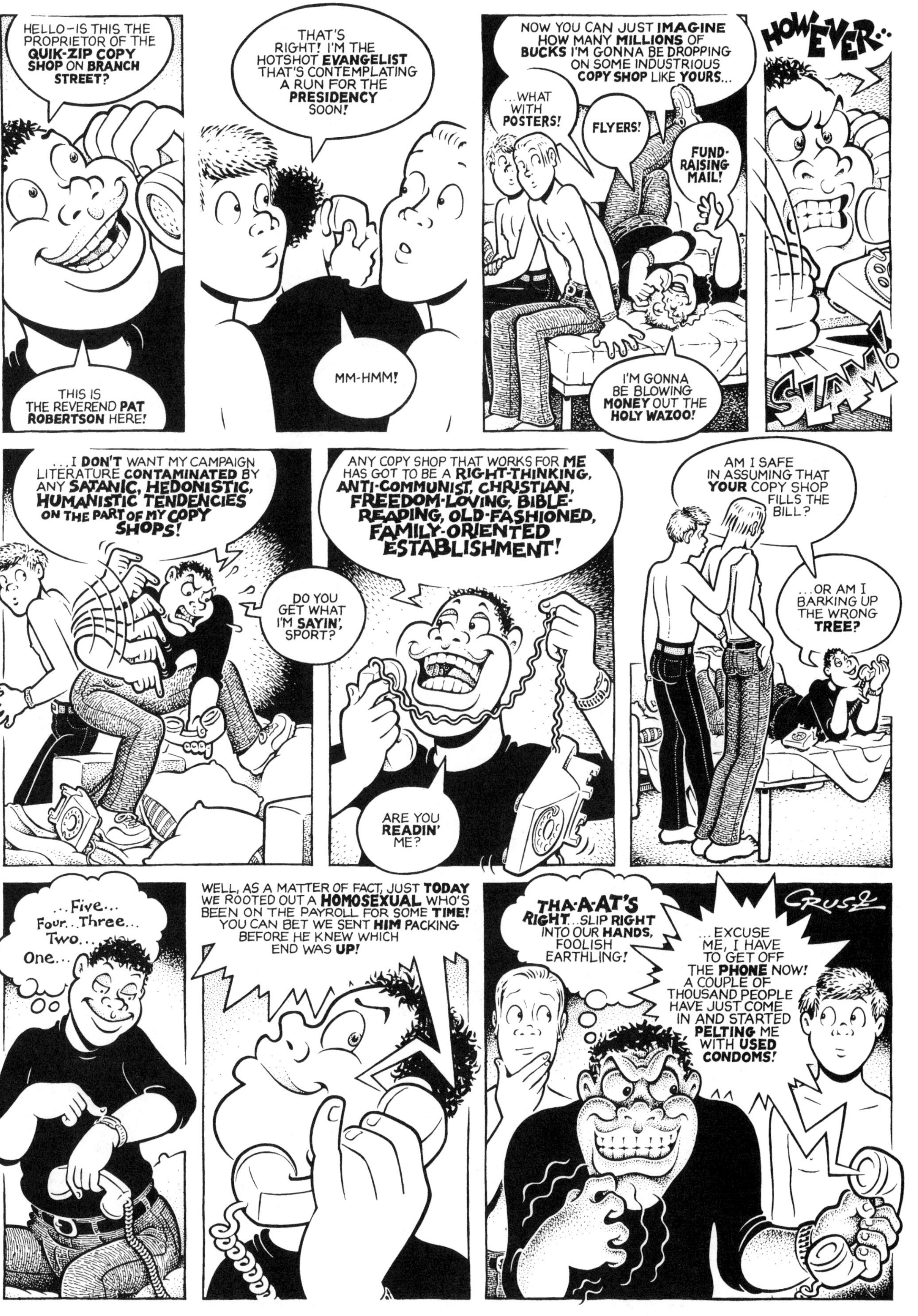
HELLO–IS THIS THE PROPRIETOR OF THE QUIK-ZIP COPY SHOP ON BRANCH STREET?
THIS IS THE REVEREND PAT ROBERTSON HERE!
THAT'S RIGHT! I'M THE HOTSHOT EVANGELIST THAT'S CONTEMPLATING A RUN FOR THE PRESIDENCY SOON!
MM-HMM!
NOW YOU CAN JUST IMAGINE HOW MANY MILLIONS OF BUCKS I'M GONNA BE DROPPING ON SOME INDUSTRIOUS COPY SHOP LIKE YOURS...
...WHAT WITH POSTERS!
FLYERS!
FUND-RAISING MAIL!
I'M GONNA BE BLOWING MONEY OUT THE HOLY WAZOO!
HOWEVER...
SLAM!
...I DON'T WANT MY CAMPAIGN LITERATURE CONTAMINATED BY ANY SATANIC, HEDONISTIC, HUMANISTIC TENDENCIES ON THE PART OF MY COPY SHOPS!
DO YOU GET WHAT I'M SAYIN', SPORT?
ANY COPY SHOP THAT WORKS FOR ME HAS GOT TO BE A RIGHT-THINKING, ANTI-COMMUNIST, CHRISTIAN, FREEDOM-LOVING, BIBLE-READING, OLD-FASHIONED, FAMILY-ORIENTED ESTABLISHMENT!
ARE YOU READIN' ME?
AM I SAFE IN ASSUMING THAT YOUR COPY SHOP FILLS THE BILL?
...OR AM I BARKING UP THE WRONG TREE?
...Five... Four...Three... Two... One...
WELL, AS A MATTER OF FACT, JUST TODAY WE ROOTED OUT A HOMOSEXUAL WHO'S BEEN ON THE PAYROLL FOR SOME TIME! YOU CAN BET WE SENT HIM PACKING BEFORE HE KNEW WHICH END WAS UP!
CRUSE
THA-A-AT'S RIGHT...SLIP RIGHT INTO OUR HANDS, FOOLISH EARTHLING!
...EXCUSE ME, I HAVE TO GET OFF THE PHONE NOW! A COUPLE OF THOUSAND PEOPLE HAVE JUST COME IN AND STARTED PELTING ME WITH USED CONDOMS!

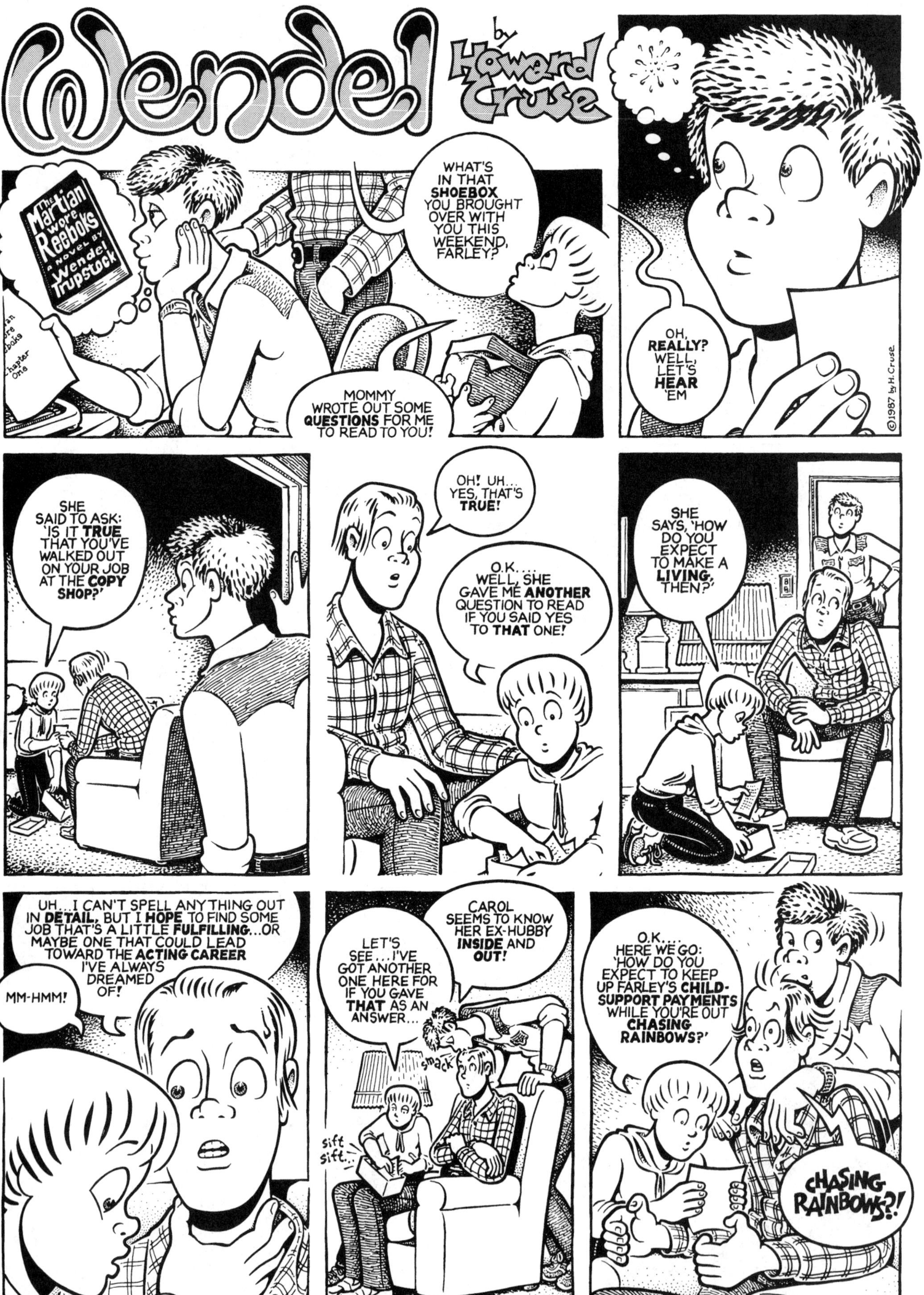
Wendel
by Howard Cruse
The Martian wore Reeboks a novel by Wendel Trupstock
WHAT'S IN THAT SHOEBOX YOU BROUGHT OVER WITH YOU THIS WEEKEND, FARLEY?
MOMMY WROTE OUT SOME QUESTIONS FOR ME TO READ TO YOU!
OH, REALLY? WELL, LET'S HEAR 'EM
©1987 by H. Cruse
SHE SAID TO ASK: 'IS IT TRUE THAT YOU'VE WALKED OUT ON YOUR JOB AT THE COPY SHOP?'
OH! UH... YES, THAT'S TRUE!
O.K.... WELL, SHE GAVE ME ANOTHER QUESTION TO READ IF YOU SAID YES TO THAT ONE!
SHE SAYS, 'HOW DO YOU EXPECT TO MAKE A LIVING, THEN?'
UH...I CAN'T SPELL ANYTHING OUT IN DETAIL, BUT I HOPE TO FIND SOME JOB THAT'S A LITTLE FULFILLING...OR MAYBE ONE THAT COULD LEAD TOWARD THE ACTING CAREER I'VE ALWAYS DREAMED OF!
MM-HMM!
CAROL SEEMS TO KNOW HER EX-HUBBY INSIDE AND OUT!
LET'S SEE...I'VE GOT ANOTHER ONE HERE FOR IF YOU GAVE THAT AS AN ANSWER...
SMACK
sift sift...
O.K.... HERE WE GO: 'HOW DO YOU EXPECT TO KEEP UP FARLEY'S CHILD-SUPPORT PAYMENTS WHILE YOU'RE OUT CHASING RAINBOWS?'
CHASING RAINBOWS?!

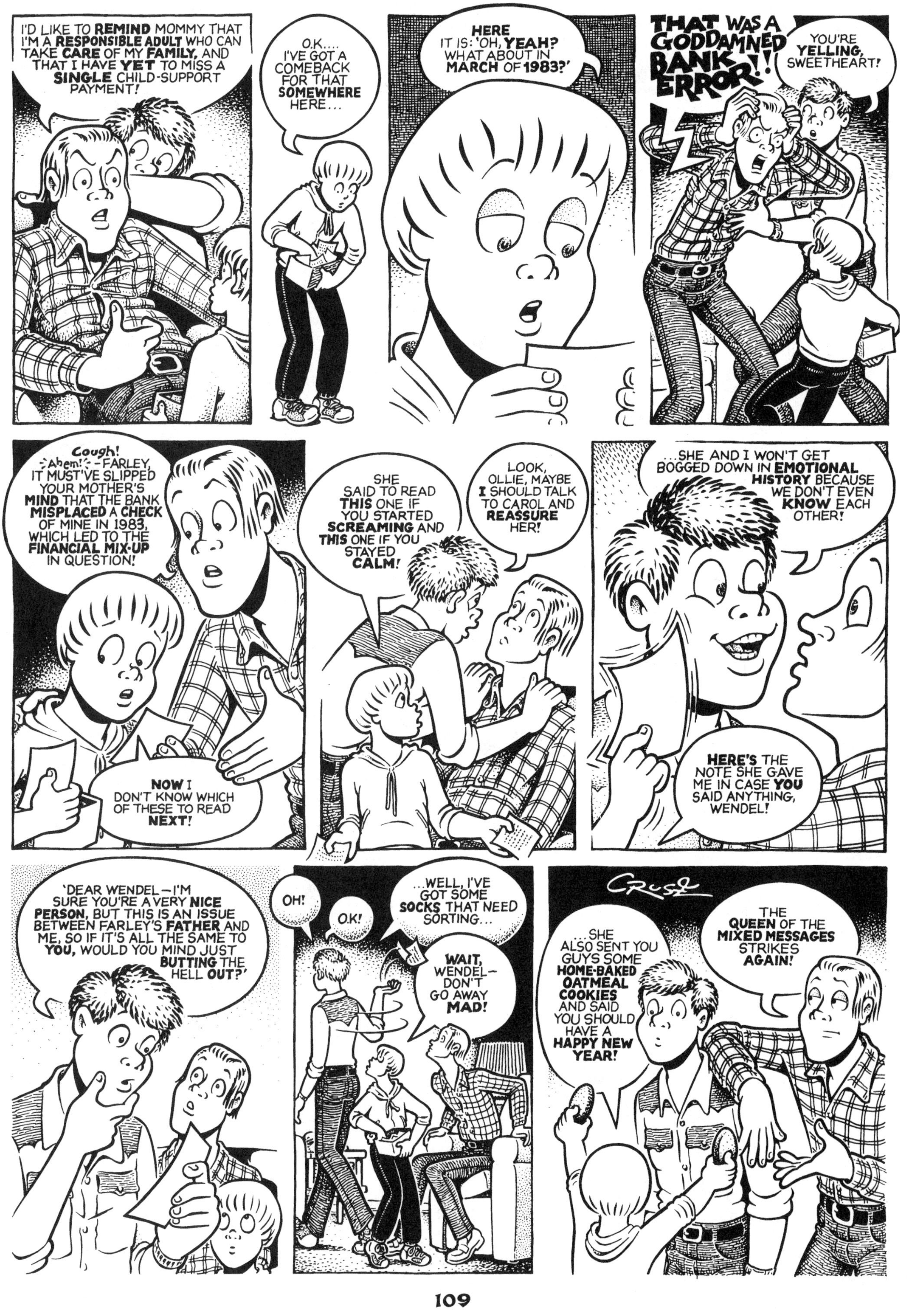
I'D LIKE TO REMIND MOMMY THAT I'M A RESPONSIBLE ADULT WHO CAN TAKE CARE OF MY FAMILY, AND THAT I HAVE YET TO MISS A SINGLE CHILD-SUPPORT PAYMENT!
O.K.... I'VE GOT A COMEBACK FOR THAT SOMEWHERE HERE...
HERE IT IS: 'OH, YEAH? WHAT ABOUT IN MARCH OF 1983?'
THAT WAS A GODDAMNED BANK ERROR!!
YOU'RE YELLING, SWEETHEART!
Cough! Ahem! — FARLEY, IT MUST'VE SLIPPED YOUR MOTHER'S MIND THAT THE BANK MISPLACED A CHECK OF MINE IN 1983, WHICH LED TO THE FINANCIAL MIX-UP IN QUESTION!
NOW I DON'T KNOW WHICH OF THESE TO READ NEXT!
SHE SAID TO READ THIS ONE IF YOU STARTED SCREAMING AND THIS ONE IF YOU STAYED CALM!
LOOK, OLLIE, MAYBE I SHOULD TALK TO CAROL AND REASSURE HER!
...SHE AND I WON'T GET BOGGED DOWN IN EMOTIONAL HISTORY BECAUSE WE DON'T EVEN KNOW EACH OTHER!
HERE'S THE NOTE SHE GAVE ME IN CASE YOU SAID ANYTHING, WENDEL!
'DEAR WENDEL — I'M SURE YOU'RE A VERY NICE PERSON, BUT THIS IS AN ISSUE BETWEEN FARLEY'S FATHER AND ME, SO IF IT'S ALL THE SAME TO YOU, WOULD YOU MIND JUST BUTTING THE HELL OUT?'
OH!
O.K!
...WELL, I'VE GOT SOME SOCKS THAT NEED SORTING...
WAIT, WENDEL— DON'T GO AWAY MAD!
CRUSE
...SHE ALSO SENT YOU GUYS SOME HOME-BAKED OATMEAL COOKIES AND SAID YOU SHOULD HAVE A HAPPY NEW YEAR!
THE QUEEN OF THE MIXED MESSAGES STRIKES AGAIN!

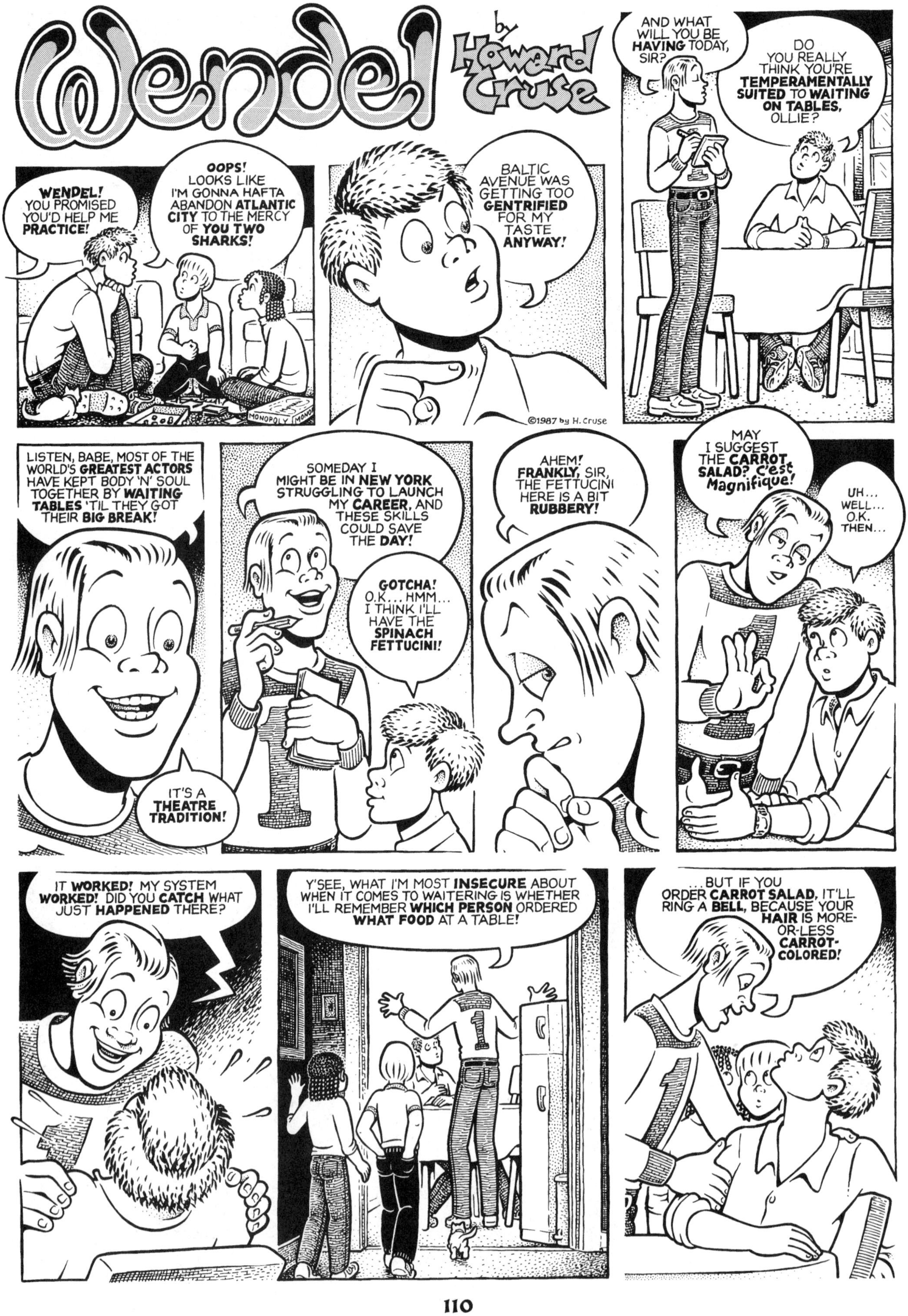
Wendel
by Howard Cruse
WENDEL! YOU PROMISED YOU'D HELP ME PRACTICE!
OOPS! LOOKS LIKE I'M GONNA HAFTA ABANDON ATLANTIC CITY TO THE MERCY OF YOU TWO SHARKS!
MONOPOLY
BALTIC AVENUE WAS GETTING TOO GENTRIFIED FOR MY TASTE ANYWAY!
©1987 by H. Cruse
AND WHAT WILL YOU BE HAVING TODAY, SIR?
DO YOU REALLY THINK YOU'RE TEMPERAMENTALLY SUITED TO WAITING ON TABLES, OLLIE?
LISTEN, BABE, MOST OF THE WORLD'S GREATEST ACTORS HAVE KEPT BODY 'N' SOUL TOGETHER BY WAITING TABLES 'TIL THEY GOT THEIR BIG BREAK!
IT'S A THEATRE TRADITION!
SOMEDAY I MIGHT BE IN NEW YORK STRUGGLING TO LAUNCH MY CAREER, AND THESE SKILLS COULD SAVE THE DAY!
GOTCHA! O.K... HMM... I THINK I'LL HAVE THE SPINACH FETTUCINI!
AHEM! FRANKLY, SIR, THE FETTUCINI HERE IS A BIT RUBBERY!
MAY I SUGGEST THE CARROT SALAD? C'est Magnifique!
UH... WELL... O.K. THEN...
IT WORKED! MY SYSTEM WORKED! DID YOU CATCH WHAT JUST HAPPENED THERE?
Y'SEE, WHAT I'M MOST INSECURE ABOUT WHEN IT COMES TO WAITERING IS WHETHER I'LL REMEMBER WHICH PERSON ORDERED WHAT FOOD AT A TABLE!
...BUT IF YOU ORDER CARROT SALAD, IT'LL RING A BELL, BECAUSE YOUR HAIR IS MORE-OR-LESS CARROT-COLORED!

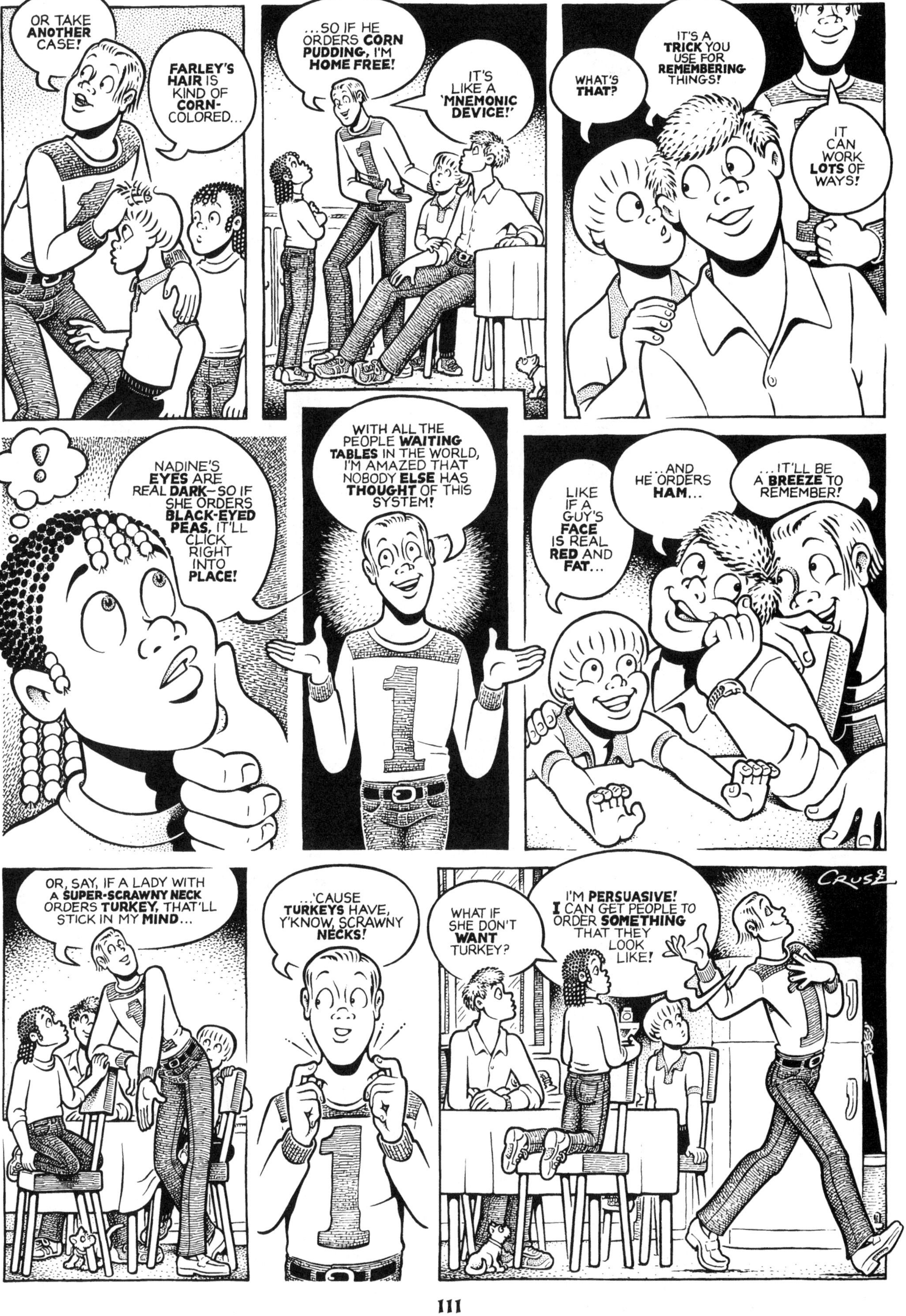
OR TAKE ANOTHER CASE!
FARLEY'S HAIR IS KIND OF CORN-COLORED...
...SO IF HE ORDERS CORN PUDDING, I'M HOME FREE!
IT'S LIKE A 'MNEMONIC DEVICE!'
WHAT'S THAT?
IT'S A TRICK YOU USE FOR REMEMBERING THINGS!
IT CAN WORK LOTS OF WAYS!
!
NADINE'S EYES ARE REAL DARK—SO IF SHE ORDERS BLACK-EYED PEAS, IT'LL CLICK RIGHT INTO PLACE!
WITH ALL THE PEOPLE WAITING TABLES IN THE WORLD, I'M AMAZED THAT NOBODY ELSE HAS THOUGHT OF THIS SYSTEM!
LIKE IF A GUY'S FACE IS REAL RED AND FAT...
...AND HE ORDERS HAM...
...IT'LL BE A BREEZE TO REMEMBER!
OR, SAY, IF A LADY WITH A SUPER-SCRAWNY NECK ORDERS TURKEY, THAT'LL STICK IN MY MIND...
...'CAUSE TURKEYS HAVE, Y'KNOW, SCRAWNY NECKS!
WHAT IF SHE DON'T WANT TURKEY?
I'M PERSUASIVE! I CAN GET PEOPLE TO ORDER SOMETHING THAT THEY LOOK LIKE!
CRUSE

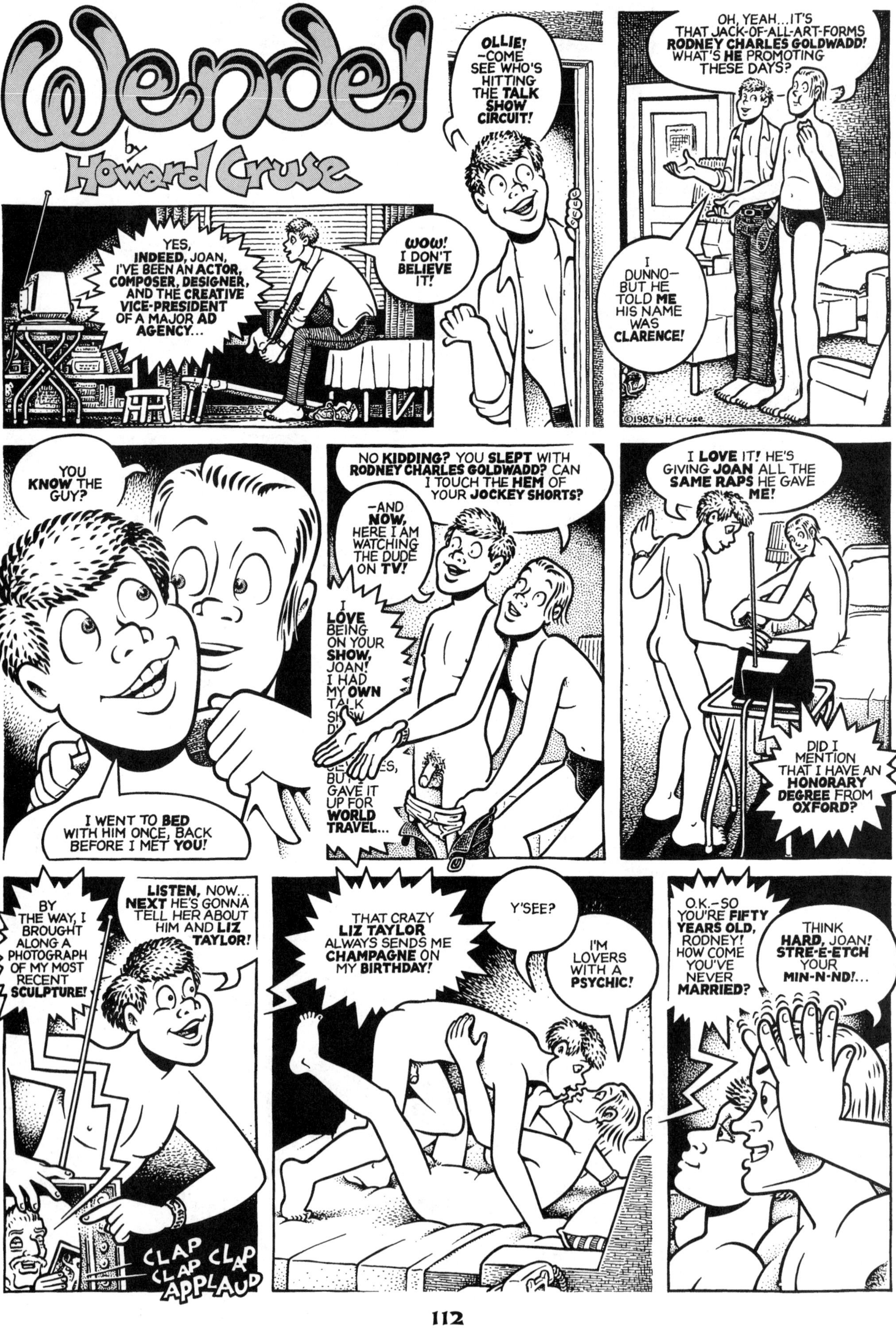
Wendel
by Howard Cruse
YES, INDEED, JOAN, I'VE BEEN AN ACTOR, COMPOSER, DESIGNER, AND THE CREATIVE VICE-PRESIDENT OF A MAJOR AD AGENCY...
WOW! I DON'T BELIEVE IT!
OLLIE! —COME SEE WHO'S HITTING THE TALK SHOW CIRCUIT!
OH, YEAH...IT'S THAT JACK-OF-ALL-ART-FORMS RODNEY CHARLES GOLDWADD! WHAT'S HE PROMOTING THESE DAYS?
I DUNNO— BUT HE TOLD ME HIS NAME WAS CLARENCE!
©1987 by H. Cruse
YOU KNOW THE GUY?
I WENT TO BED WITH HIM ONCE, BACK BEFORE I MET YOU!
NO KIDDING? YOU SLEPT WITH RODNEY CHARLES GOLDWADD? CAN I TOUCH THE HEM OF YOUR JOCKEY SHORTS?
—AND NOW, HERE I AM WATCHING THE DUDE ON TV!
I LOVE BEING ON YOUR SHOW, JOAN! I HAD MY OWN TALK
BUT GAVE IT UP FOR WORLD TRAVEL...
I LOVE IT! HE'S GIVING JOAN ALL THE SAME RAPS HE GAVE ME!
DID I MENTION THAT I HAVE AN HONORARY DEGREE FROM OXFORD?
BY THE WAY, I BROUGHT ALONG A PHOTOGRAPH OF MY MOST RECENT SCULPTURE!
LISTEN, NOW... NEXT HE'S GONNA TELL HER ABOUT HIM AND LIZ TAYLOR!
CLAP CLAP CLAP CLAP CLAP APPLAUD
THAT CRAZY LIZ TAYLOR ALWAYS SENDS ME CHAMPAGNE ON MY BIRTHDAY!
Y'SEE?
I'M LOVERS WITH A PSYCHIC!
O.K.—SO YOU'RE FIFTY YEARS OLD, RODNEY! HOW COME YOU'VE NEVER MARRIED?
THINK HARD, JOAN! STRE-E-ETCH YOUR MIN-N-ND!...

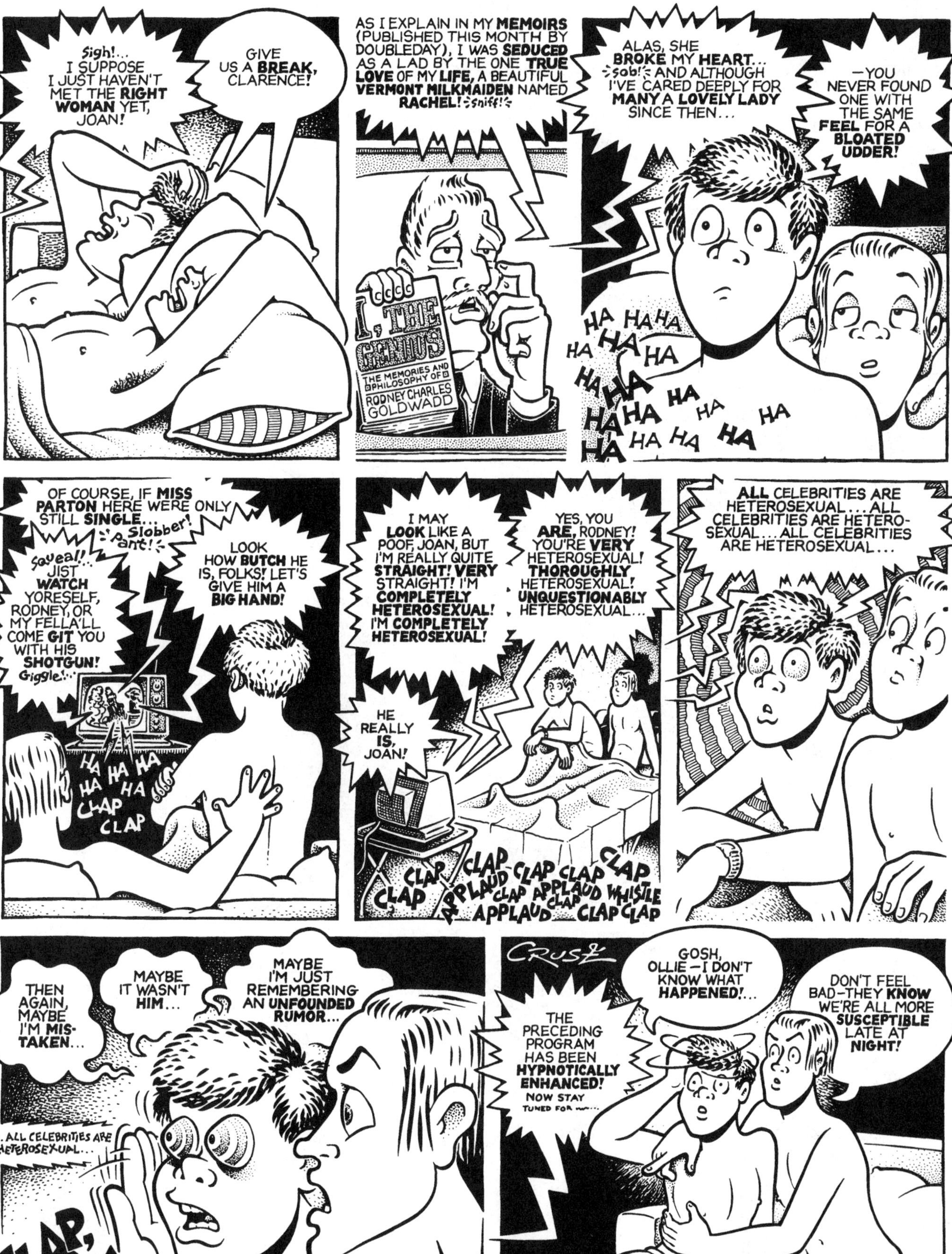

Sigh!... I SUPPOSE I JUST HAVEN'T MET THE RIGHT WOMAN YET, JOAN!
GIVE US A BREAK, CLARENCE!
AS I EXPLAIN IN MY MEMOIRS (PUBLISHED THIS MONTH BY DOUBLEDAY), I WAS SEDUCED AS A LAD BY THE ONE TRUE LOVE OF MY LIFE, A BEAUTIFUL VERMONT MILKMAIDEN NAMED RACHEL! sniff!
I, THE GENIUS
THE MEMORIES AND PHILOSOPHY OF RODNEY CHARLES GOLDWADD
ALAS, SHE BROKE MY HEART... sob! AND ALTHOUGH I'VE CARED DEEPLY FOR MANY A LOVELY LADY SINCE THEN...
—YOU NEVER FOUND ONE WITH THE SAME FEEL FOR A BLOATED UDDER!
HA HA HA HA HA HA HA HA HA HA HA HA HA HA HA HA HA HA HA
OF COURSE, IF MISS PARTON HERE WERE ONLY STILL SINGLE... Slobber! Pant!
Squeal!... JIST WATCH YORESELF, RODNEY, OR MY FELLA'LL COME GIT YOU WITH HIS SHOTGUN! Giggle!
LOOK HOW BUTCH HE IS, FOLKS! LET'S GIVE HIM A BIG HAND!
HA HA HA HA HA HA CLAP CLAP CLAP
I MAY LOOK LIKE A POOF, JOAN, BUT I'M REALLY QUITE STRAIGHT! VERY STRAIGHT! I'M COMPLETELY HETEROSEXUAL! I'M COMPLETELY HETEROSEXUAL!
YES, YOU ARE, RODNEY! YOU'RE VERY HETEROSEXUAL! THOROUGHLY HETEROSEXUAL! UNQUESTIONABLY HETEROSEXUAL...
HE REALLY IS, JOAN!
CLAP CLAP CLAP APPLAUD CLAP CLAP CLAP CLAP APPLAUD WHISTLE APPLAUD CLAP CLAP CLAP
ALL CELEBRITIES ARE HETEROSEXUAL... ALL CELEBRITIES ARE HETEROSEXUAL... ALL CELEBRITIES ARE HETEROSEXUAL...
THEN AGAIN, MAYBE I'M MISTAKEN...
MAYBE IT WASN'T HIM...
MAYBE I'M JUST REMEMBERING AN UNFOUNDED RUMOR...
...ALL CELEBRITIES ARE HETEROSEXUAL...
SLAP, SLAP!
WENDEL! SNAP OUT OF IT!
CRUSE
THE PRECEDING PROGRAM HAS BEEN HYPNOTICALLY ENHANCED! NOW STAY TUNED FOR
GOSH, OLLIE—I DON'T KNOW WHAT HAPPENED!...
DON'T FEEL BAD—THEY KNOW WE'RE ALL MORE SUSCEPTIBLE LATE AT NIGHT!

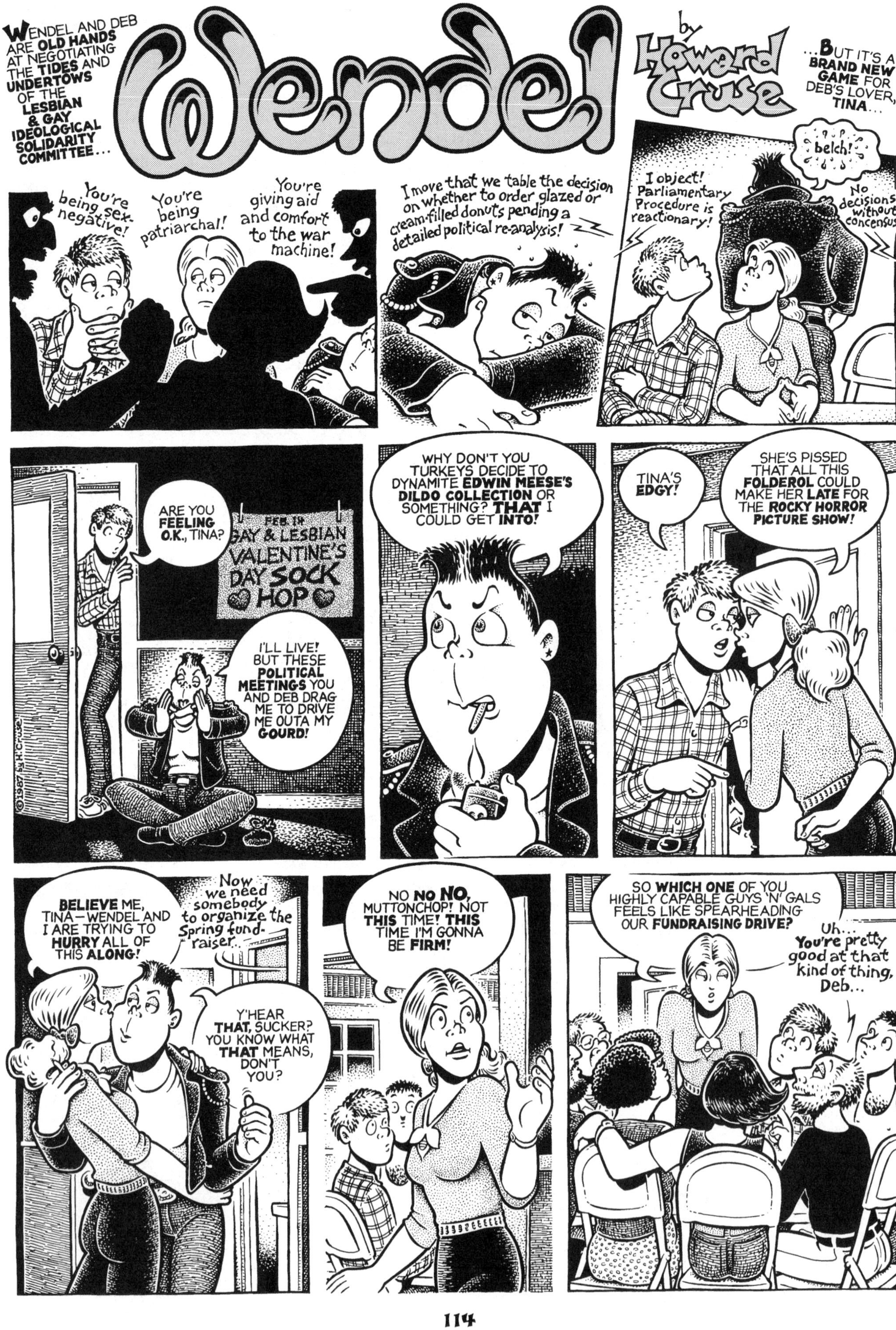
WENDEL AND DEB ARE OLD HANDS AT NEGOTIATING THE TIDES AND UNDERTOWS OF THE LESBIAN & GAY IDEOLOGICAL SOLIDARITY COMMITTEE...
Wendel
by Howard Cruse
...BUT IT'S A BRAND NEW GAME FOR DEB'S LOVER, TINA...
You're being sex-negative!
You're being patriarchal!
You're giving aid and comfort to the war machine!
I move that we table the decision on whether to order glazed or cream-filled donuts pending a detailed political re-analysis!
I object! Parliamentary Procedure is reactionary!
belch!
No decisions without concensus!
ARE YOU FEELING O.K., TINA?
FEB 14 GAY & LESBIAN VALENTINE'S DAY SOCK HOP
I'LL LIVE! BUT THESE POLITICAL MEETINGS YOU AND DEB DRAG ME TO DRIVE ME OUTA MY GOURD!
©1987 by H. Cruse
WHY DON'T YOU TURKEYS DECIDE TO DYNAMITE EDWIN MEESE'S DILDO COLLECTION OR SOMETHING? THAT I COULD GET INTO!
TINA'S EDGY!
SHE'S PISSED THAT ALL THIS FOLDEROL COULD MAKE HER LATE FOR THE ROCKY HORROR PICTURE SHOW!
BELIEVE ME, TINA—WENDEL AND I ARE TRYING TO HURRY ALL OF THIS ALONG!
Now we need somebody to organize the Spring fund-raiser...
Y'HEAR THAT, SUCKER? YOU KNOW WHAT THAT MEANS, DON'T YOU?
NO NO NO, MUTTONCHOP! NOT THIS TIME! THIS TIME I'M GONNA BE FIRM!
SO WHICH ONE OF YOU HIGHLY CAPABLE GUYS 'N' GALS FEELS LIKE SPEARHEADING OUR FUNDRAISING DRIVE?
Uh... You're pretty good at that kind of thing, Deb...

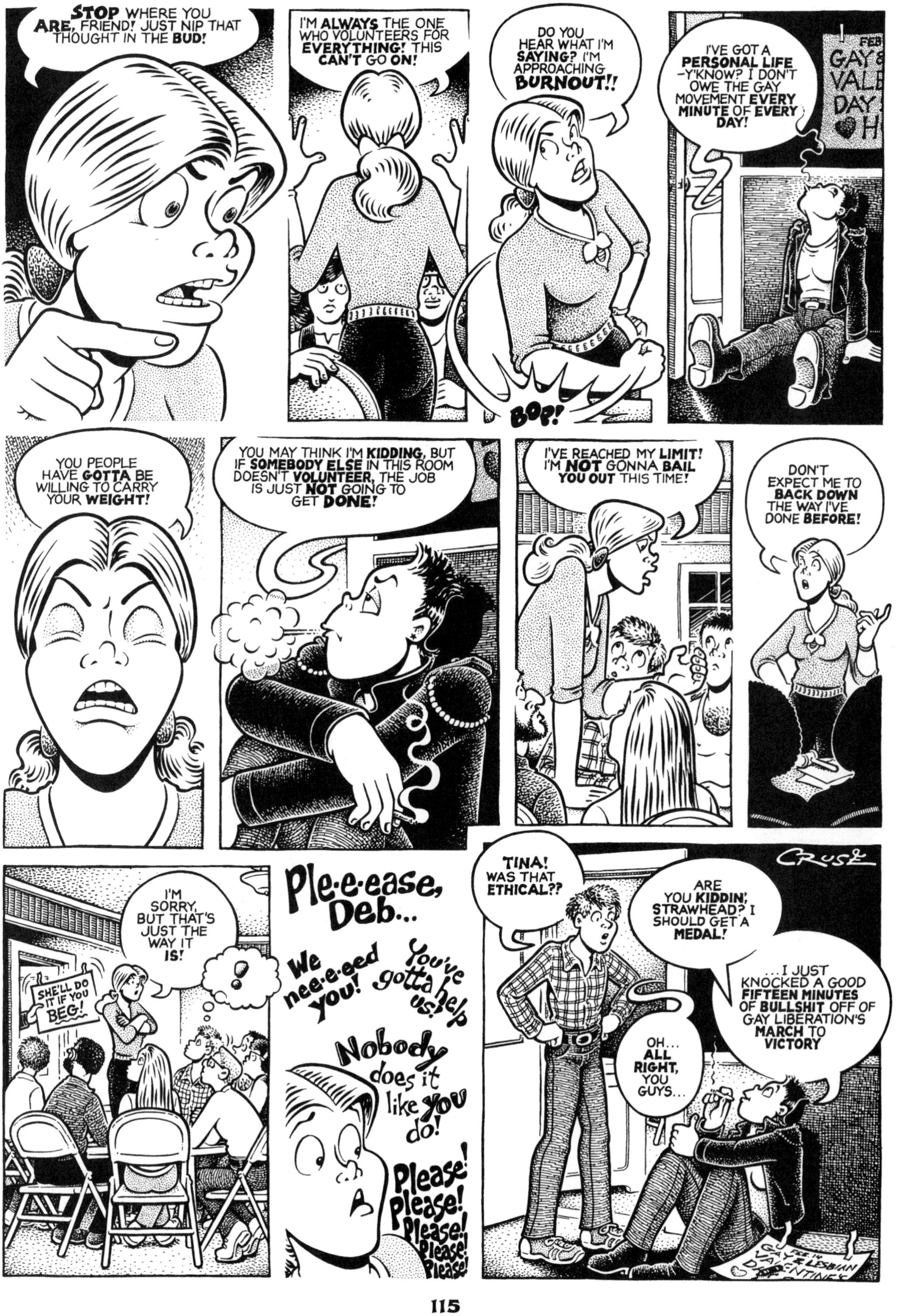
STOP WHERE YOU ARE, FRIEND! JUST NIP THAT THOUGHT IN THE BUD!
I'M ALWAYS THE ONE WHO VOLUNTEERS FOR EVERYTHING! THIS CAN'T GO ON!
DO YOU HEAR WHAT I'M SAYING? I'M APPROACHING BURNOUT!!
BOP!
I'VE GOT A PERSONAL LIFE —Y'KNOW? I DON'T OWE THE GAY MOVEMENT EVERY MINUTE OF EVERY DAY!
YOU PEOPLE HAVE GOTTA BE WILLING TO CARRY YOUR WEIGHT!
YOU MAY THINK I'M KIDDING, BUT IF SOMEBODY ELSE IN THIS ROOM DOESN'T VOLUNTEER, THE JOB IS JUST NOT GOING TO GET DONE!
I'VE REACHED MY LIMIT! I'M NOT GONNA BAIL YOU OUT THIS TIME!
DON'T EXPECT ME TO BACK DOWN THE WAY I'VE DONE BEFORE!
I'M SORRY, BUT THAT'S JUST THE WAY IT IS!
SHE'LL DO IT IF YOU BEG!
!
Ple-e-ease, Deb...
We nee-e-eed you!
You've gotta help us!
Nobody does it like you do!
Please! Please! Please! Please! Please!
CRUSE
TINA! WAS THAT ETHICAL??
ARE YOU KIDDIN', STRAWHEAD? I SHOULD GET A MEDAL!
...I JUST KNOCKED A GOOD FIFTEEN MINUTES OF BULLSHIT OFF OF GAY LIBERATION'S MARCH TO VICTORY
OH... ALL RIGHT, YOU GUYS...

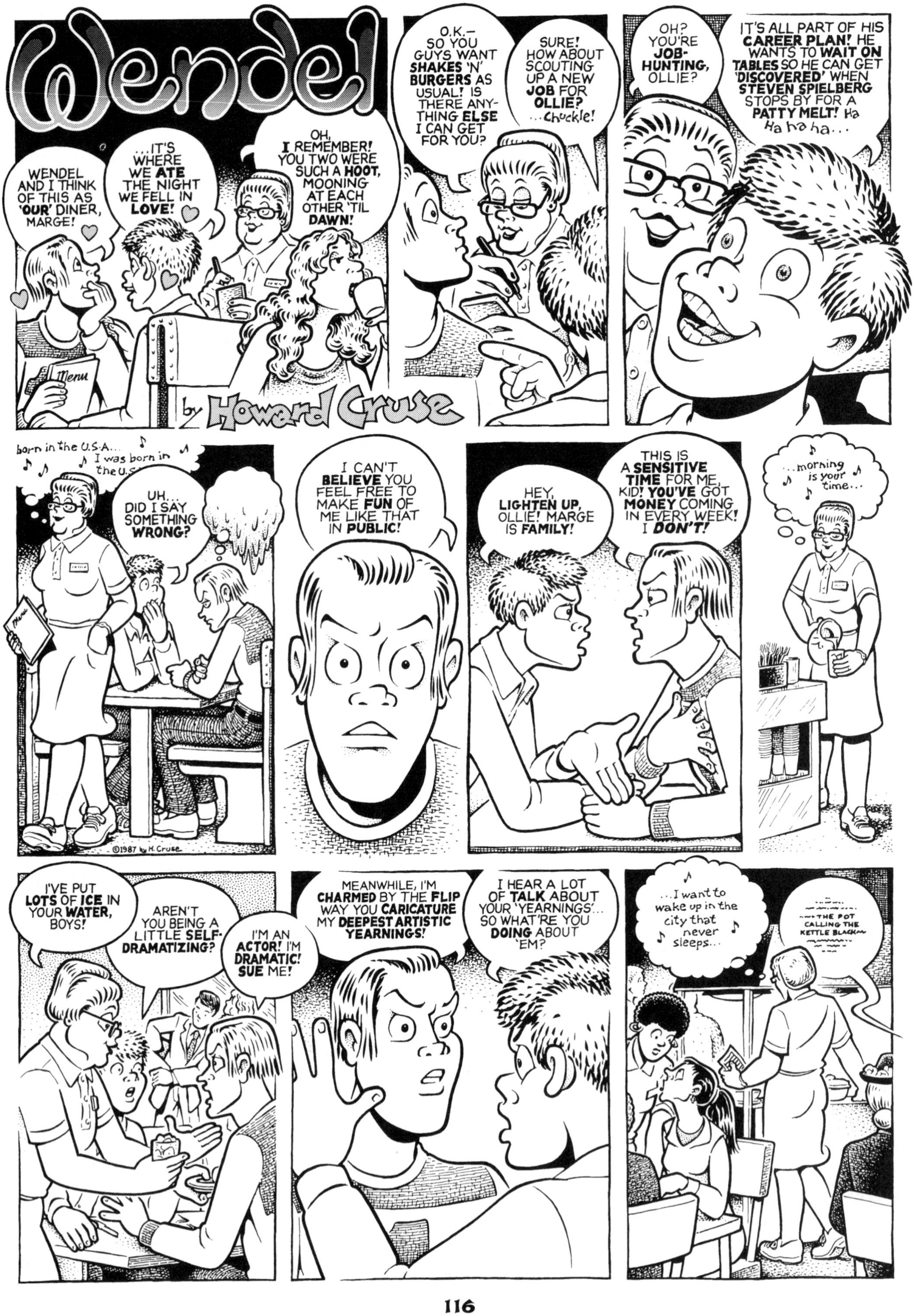
Wendel
by Howard Cruse
WENDEL AND I THINK OF THIS AS 'OUR' DINER, MARGE!
...IT'S WHERE WE ATE THE NIGHT WE FELL IN LOVE!
OH, I REMEMBER! YOU TWO WERE SUCH A HOOT, MOONING AT EACH OTHER 'TIL DAWN!
Menu
O.K.— SO YOU GUYS WANT SHAKES 'N' BURGERS AS USUAL! IS THERE ANYTHING ELSE I CAN GET FOR YOU?
SURE! HOW ABOUT SCOUTING UP A NEW JOB FOR OLLIE? ...Chuckle!
OH? YOU'RE JOB-HUNTING, OLLIE?
IT'S ALL PART OF HIS CAREER PLAN! HE WANTS TO WAIT ON TABLES SO HE CAN GET 'DISCOVERED' WHEN STEVEN SPIELBERG STOPS BY FOR A PATTY MELT! Ha Ha ha ha...
born in the U.S.A... I was born in the U.S.
UH... DID I SAY SOMETHING WRONG?
©1987 by H. Cruse
I CAN'T BELIEVE YOU FEEL FREE TO MAKE FUN OF ME LIKE THAT IN PUBLIC!
HEY, LIGHTEN UP, OLLIE! MARGE IS FAMILY!
THIS IS A SENSITIVE TIME FOR ME, KID! YOU'VE GOT MONEY COMING IN EVERY WEEK! I DON'T!
...morning is your time...
I'VE PUT LOTS OF ICE IN YOUR WATER, BOYS!
AREN'T YOU BEING A LITTLE SELF-DRAMATIZING?
I'M AN ACTOR! I'M DRAMATIC! SUE ME!
MEANWHILE, I'M CHARMED BY THE FLIP WAY YOU CARICATURE MY DEEPEST ARTISTIC YEARNINGS!
I HEAR A LOT OF TALK ABOUT YOUR 'YEARNINGS'... SO WHAT'RE YOU DOING ABOUT 'EM?
...I want to wake up in the city that never sleeps...
THE POT CALLING THE KETTLE BLACK

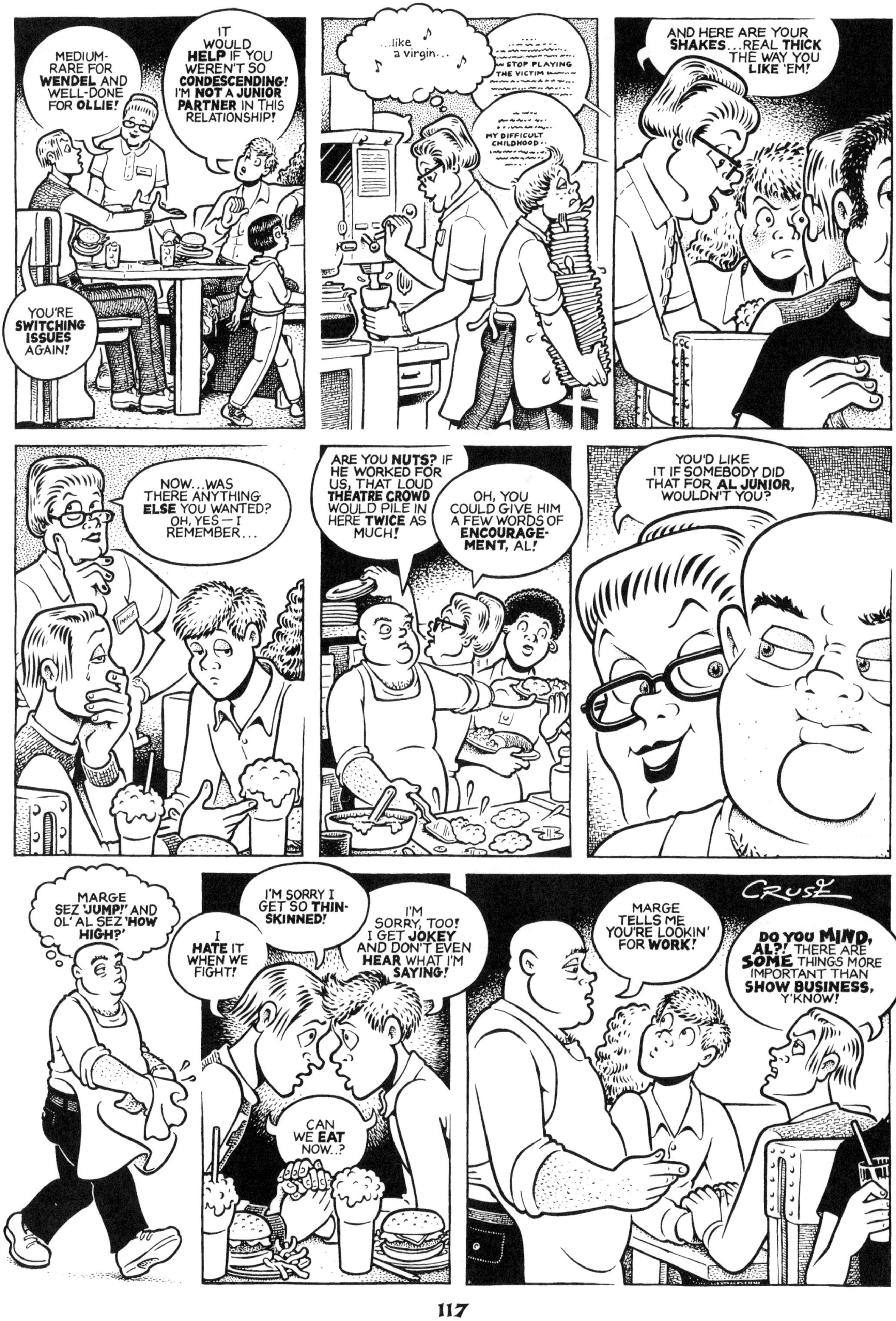

MEDIUM-RARE FOR WENDEL AND WELL-DONE FOR OLLIE!
IT WOULD HELP IF YOU WEREN'T SO CONDESCENDING! I'M NOT A JUNIOR PARTNER IN THIS RELATIONSHIP!
YOU'RE SWITCHING ISSUES AGAIN!
...like a virgin...
STOP PLAYING THE VICTIM
MY DIFFICULT CHILDHOOD
AND HERE ARE YOUR SHAKES...REAL THICK THE WAY YOU LIKE 'EM!
NOW...WAS THERE ANYTHING ELSE YOU WANTED? OH, YES—I REMEMBER...
ARE YOU NUTS? IF HE WORKED FOR US, THAT LOUD THEATRE CROWD WOULD PILE IN HERE TWICE AS MUCH!
OH, YOU COULD GIVE HIM A FEW WORDS OF ENCOURAGEMENT, AL!
YOU'D LIKE IT IF SOMEBODY DID THAT FOR AL JUNIOR, WOULDN'T YOU?
MARGE SEZ 'JUMP!' AND OL' AL SEZ 'HOW HIGH?'
I'M SORRY I GET SO THIN-SKINNED!
I HATE IT WHEN WE FIGHT!
I'M SORRY, TOO! I GET JOKEY AND DON'T EVEN HEAR WHAT I'M SAYING!
CAN WE EAT NOW..?
CRUSE
MARGE TELLS ME YOU'RE LOOKIN' FOR WORK!
DO YOU MIND, AL?! THERE ARE SOME THINGS MORE IMPORTANT THAN SHOW BUSINESS, Y'KNOW!

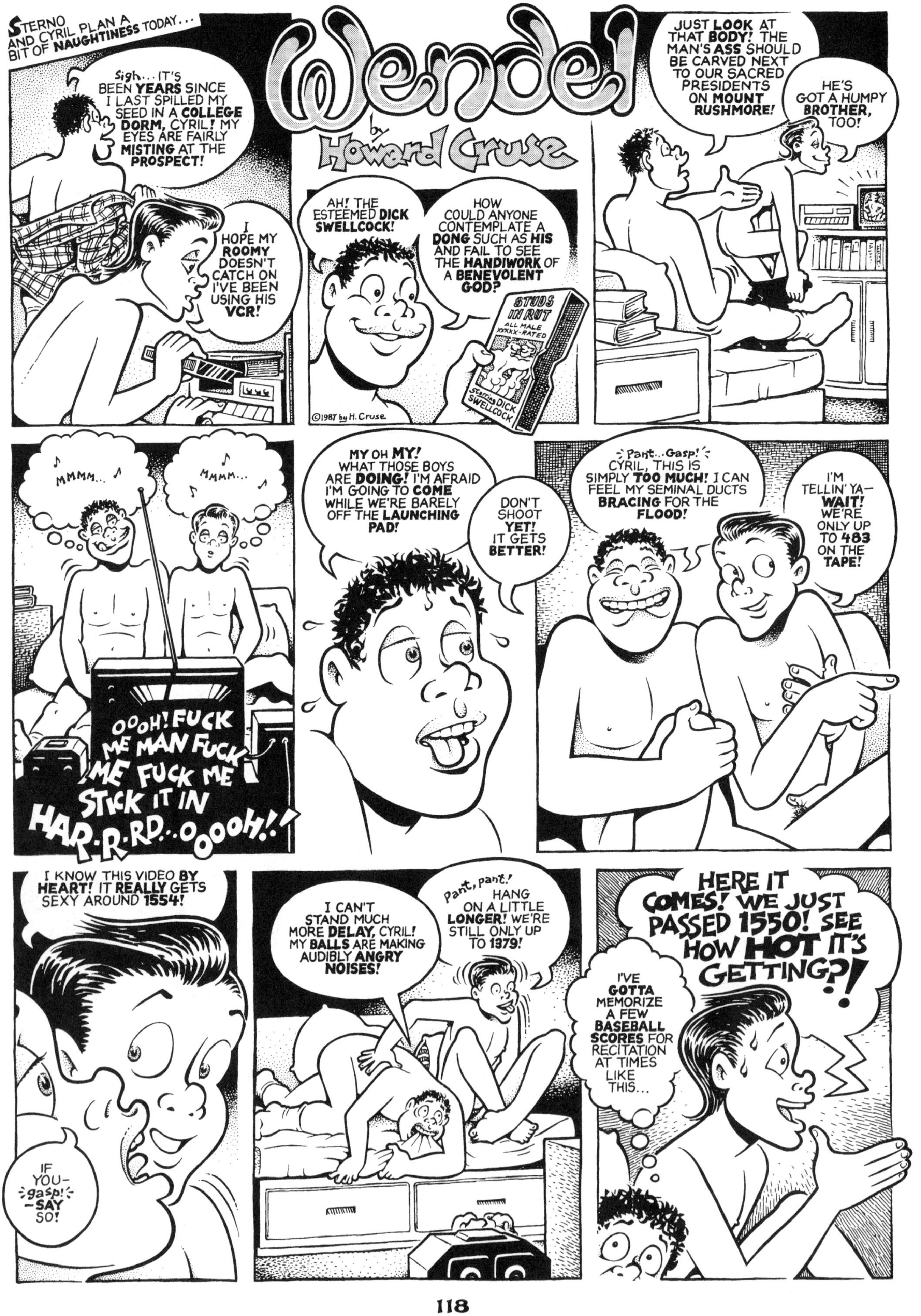
STERNO AND CYRIL PLAN A BIT OF NAUGHTINESS TODAY...
Wendel
by Howard Cruse
Sigh... IT'S BEEN YEARS SINCE I LAST SPILLED MY SEED IN A COLLEGE DORM, CYRIL! MY EYES ARE FAIRLY MISTING AT THE PROSPECT!
I HOPE MY ROOMY DOESN'T CATCH ON I'VE BEEN USING HIS VCR!
AH! THE ESTEEMED DICK SWELLCOCK!
HOW COULD ANYONE CONTEMPLATE A DONG SUCH AS HIS AND FAIL TO SEE THE HANDIWORK OF A BENEVOLENT GOD?
STUDS IN RUT
ALL MALE XXXXX-RATED
Starring DICK SWELLCOCK
©1987 by H. Cruse
JUST LOOK AT THAT BODY! THE MAN'S ASS SHOULD BE CARVED NEXT TO OUR SACRED PRESIDENTS ON MOUNT RUSHMORE!
HE'S GOT A HUMPY BROTHER, TOO!
MMMM...
MMMM...
OOOH! FUCK ME MAN FUCK ME FUCK ME STICK IT IN HAR-R-RD...OOOOH!!
MY OH MY! WHAT THOSE BOYS ARE DOING! I'M AFRAID I'M GOING TO COME WHILE WE'RE BARELY OFF THE LAUNCHING PAD!
DON'T SHOOT YET! IT GETS BETTER!
Pant... Gasp! CYRIL, THIS IS SIMPLY TOO MUCH! I CAN FEEL MY SEMINAL DUCTS BRACING FOR THE FLOOD!
I'M TELLIN' YA—WAIT! WE'RE ONLY UP TO 483 ON THE TAPE!
I KNOW THIS VIDEO BY HEART! IT REALLY GETS SEXY AROUND 1554!
IF YOU—gasp!—SAY SO!
I CAN'T STAND MUCH MORE DELAY, CYRIL! MY BALLS ARE MAKING AUDIBLY ANGRY NOISES!
Pant, pant! HANG ON A LITTLE LONGER! WE'RE STILL ONLY UP TO 1379!
HERE IT COMES! WE JUST PASSED 1550! SEE HOW HOT IT'S GETTING?!
I'VE GOTTA MEMORIZE A FEW BASEBALL SCORES FOR RECITATION AT TIMES LIKE THIS...

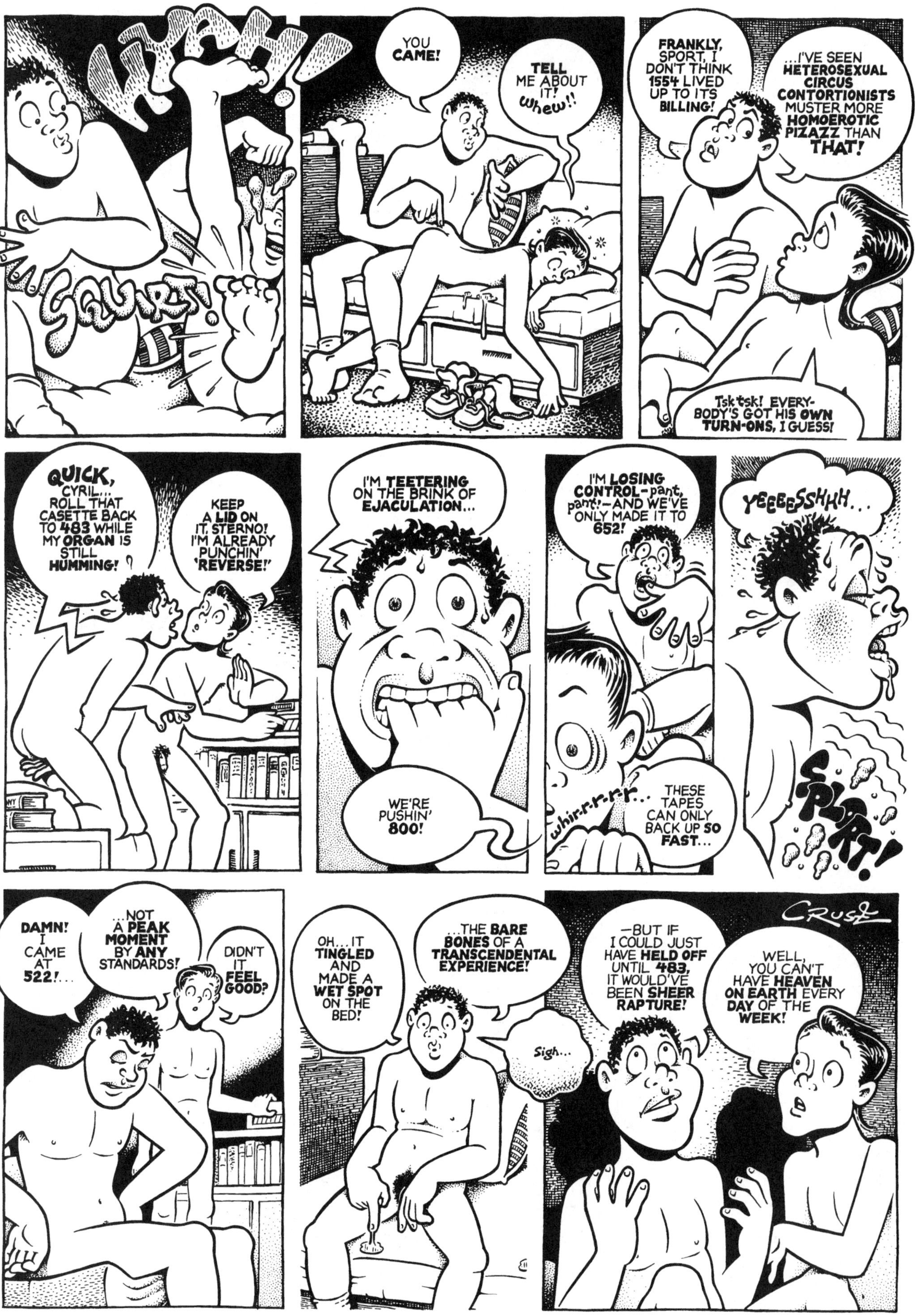

YYAH!
SQUIRT!
YOU CAME!
TELL ME ABOUT IT! Whew!!
FRANKLY, SPORT, I DON'T THINK 1554 LIVED UP TO ITS BILLING!
...I'VE SEEN HETEROSEXUAL CIRCUS CONTORTIONISTS MUSTER MORE HOMOEROTIC PIZAZZ THAN THAT!
Tsk tsk! EVERYBODY'S GOT HIS OWN TURN-ONS, I GUESS!
QUICK, CYRIL... ROLL THAT CASETTE BACK TO 483 WHILE MY ORGAN IS STILL HUMMING!
KEEP A LID ON IT, STERNO! I'M ALREADY PUNCHIN' 'REVERSE!'
I'M TEETERING ON THE BRINK OF EJACULATION...
WE'RE PUSHIN' 800!
I'M LOSING CONTROL-pant, pant!-AND WE'VE ONLY MADE IT TO 652!
whir-r-r-r-r...
THESE TAPES CAN ONLY BACK UP SO FAST...
YEEEESSHHH...
SPLORT!
DAMN! I CAME AT 522!...
...NOT A PEAK MOMENT BY ANY STANDARDS!
DIDN'T IT FEEL GOOD?
OH... IT TINGLED AND MADE A WET SPOT ON THE BED!
...THE BARE BONES OF A TRANSCENDENTAL EXPERIENCE!
Sigh...
—BUT IF I COULD JUST HAVE HELD OFF UNTIL 483, IT WOULD'VE BEEN SHEER RAPTURE!
WELL, YOU CAN'T HAVE HEAVEN ON EARTH EVERY DAY OF THE WEEK!
CRUSE

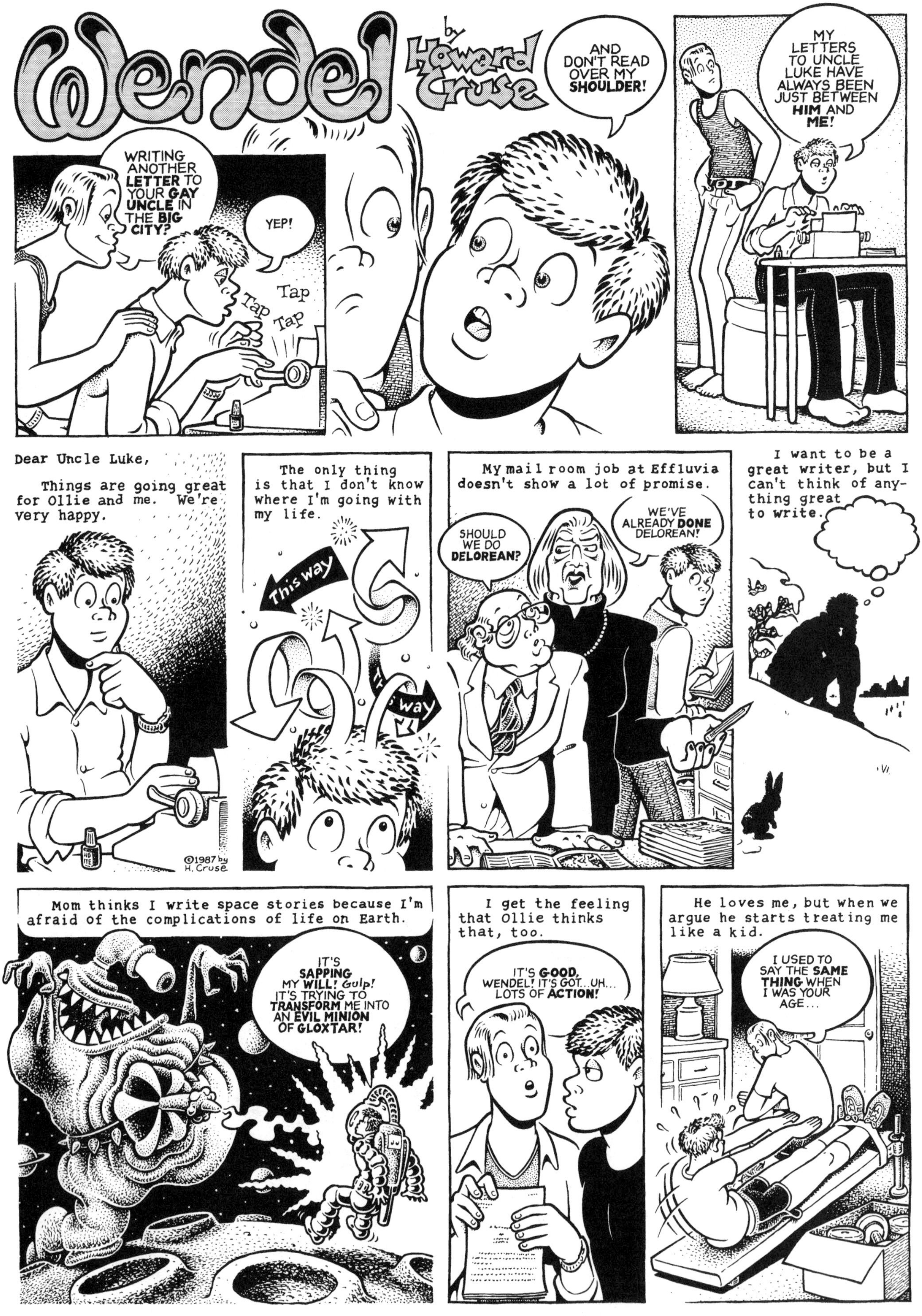
Wendel
by Howard Cruse
WRITING ANOTHER LETTER TO YOUR GAY UNCLE IN THE BIG CITY?
YEP!
Tap Tap Tap Tap
AND DON'T READ OVER MY SHOULDER!
MY LETTERS TO UNCLE LUKE HAVE ALWAYS BEEN JUST BETWEEN HIM AND ME!
Dear Uncle Luke,
Things are going great for Ollie and me. We're very happy.
©1987 by H. Cruse
The only thing is that I don't know where I'm going with my life.
This way
My mail room job at Effluvia doesn't show a lot of promise.
SHOULD WE DO DELOREAN?
WE'VE ALREADY DONE DELOREAN!
I want to be a great writer, but I can't think of anything great to write.
Mom thinks I write space stories because I'm afraid of the complications of life on Earth.
IT'S SAPPING MY WILL! Gulp! IT'S TRYING TO TRANSFORM ME INTO AN EVIL MINION OF GLOXTAR!
I get the feeling that Ollie thinks that, too.
IT'S GOOD, WENDEL! IT'S GOT...UH... LOTS OF ACTION!
He loves me, but when we argue he starts treating me like a kid.
I USED TO SAY THE SAME THING WHEN I WAS YOUR AGE...

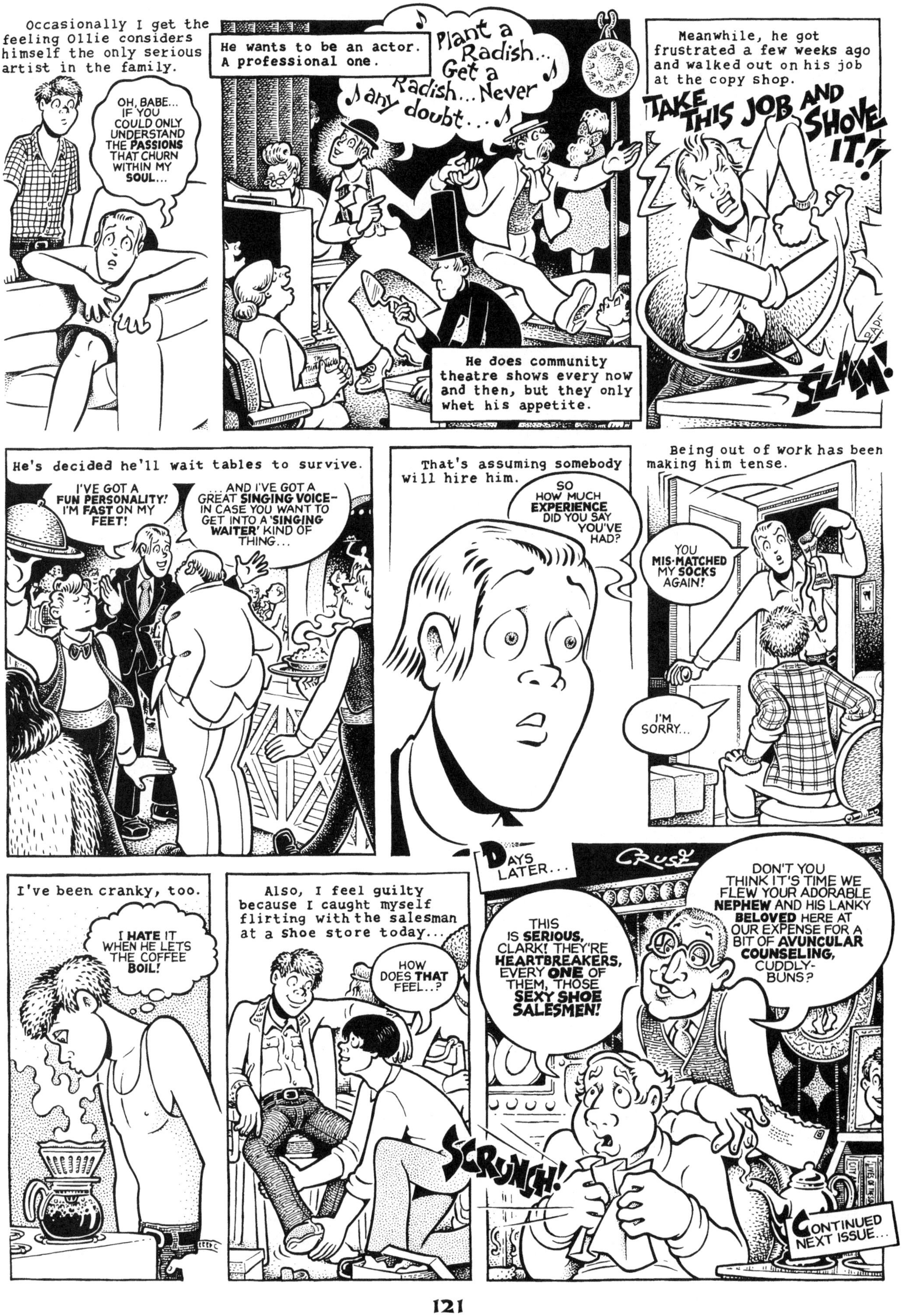

Occasionally I get the feeling Ollie considers himself the only serious artist in the family.
OH, BABE... IF YOU COULD ONLY UNDERSTAND THE PASSIONS THAT CHURN WITHIN MY SOUL...
He wants to be an actor. A professional one.
Plant a Radish... Get a Radish... Never any doubt...
He does community theatre shows every now and then, but they only whet his appetite.
Meanwhile, he got frustrated a few weeks ago and walked out on his job at the copy shop.
TAKE THIS JOB AND SHOVE IT!!
SLAM!
He's decided he'll wait tables to survive.
I'VE GOT A FUN PERSONALITY! I'M FAST ON MY FEET!
...AND I'VE GOT A GREAT SINGING VOICE— IN CASE YOU WANT TO GET INTO A 'SINGING WAITER' KIND OF THING...
That's assuming somebody will hire him.
SO HOW MUCH EXPERIENCE DID YOU SAY YOU'VE HAD?
Being out of work has been making him tense.
YOU MIS-MATCHED MY SOCKS AGAIN!
I'M SORRY...
I've been cranky, too.
I HATE IT WHEN HE LETS THE COFFEE BOIL!
Also, I feel guilty because I caught myself flirting with the salesman at a shoe store today...
HOW DOES THAT FEEL...?
DAYS LATER...
CRUSE
THIS IS SERIOUS, CLARK! THEY'RE HEARTBREAKERS, EVERY ONE OF THEM, THOSE SEXY SHOE SALESMEN!
DON'T YOU THINK IT'S TIME WE FLEW YOUR ADORABLE NEPHEW AND HIS LANKY BELOVED HERE AT OUR EXPENSE FOR A BIT OF AVUNCULAR COUNSELING, CUDDLY-BUNS?
SCRUNCH!
CONTINUED NEXT ISSUE...

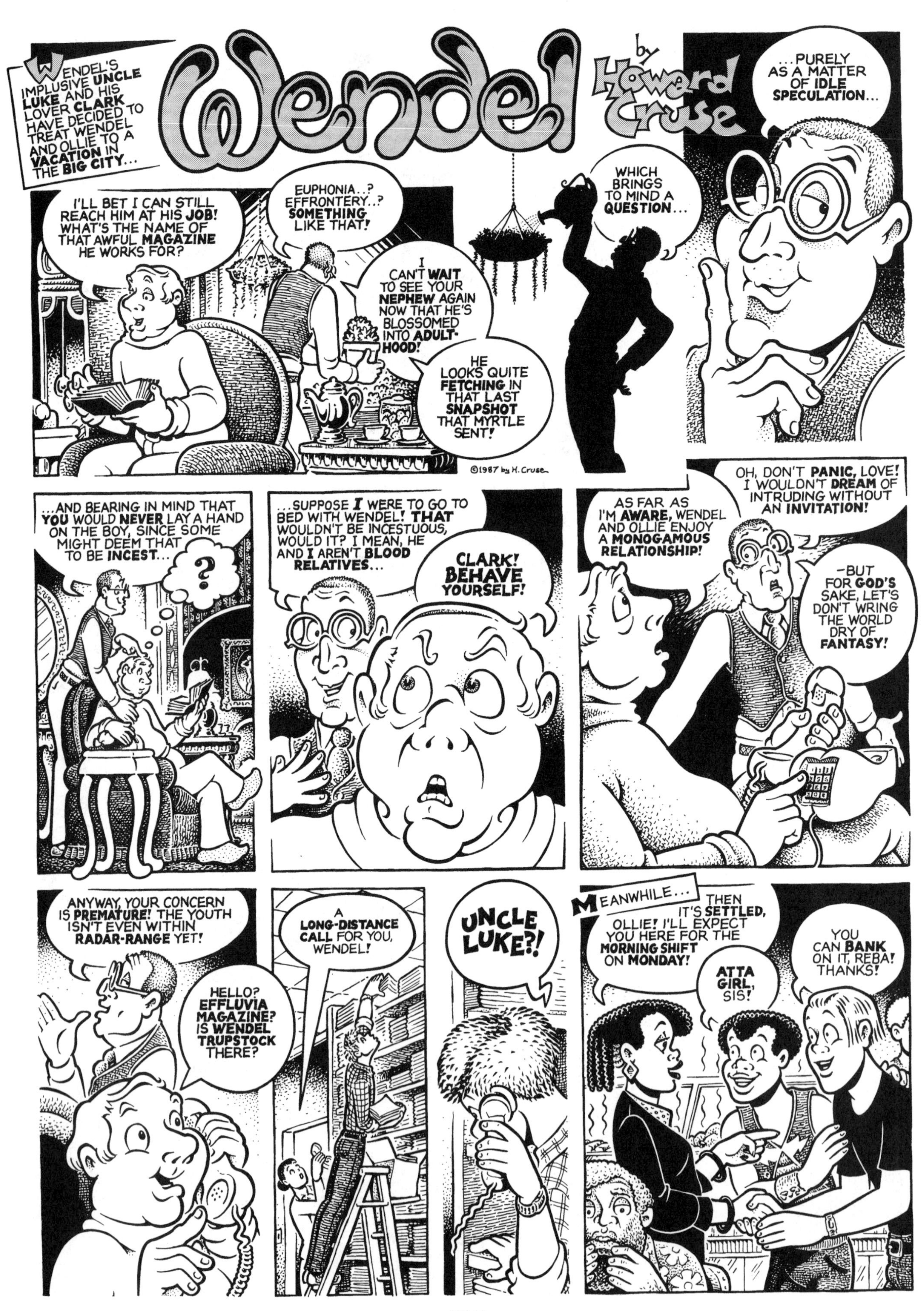

Wendel
by Howard Cruse
WENDEL'S IMPLUSIVE UNCLE LUKE AND HIS LOVER CLARK HAVE DECIDED TO TREAT WENDEL AND OLLIE TO A VACATION IN THE BIG CITY...
I'LL BET I CAN STILL REACH HIM AT HIS JOB! WHAT'S THE NAME OF THAT AWFUL MAGAZINE HE WORKS FOR?
EUPHONIA..? EFFRONTERY..? SOMETHING LIKE THAT!
I CAN'T WAIT TO SEE YOUR NEPHEW AGAIN NOW THAT HE'S BLOSSOMED INTO ADULT-HOOD!
HE LOOKS QUITE FETCHING IN THAT LAST SNAPSHOT THAT MYRTLE SENT!
WHICH BRINGS TO MIND A QUESTION...
...PURELY AS A MATTER OF IDLE SPECULATION...
©1987 by H. Cruse
...AND BEARING IN MIND THAT YOU WOULD NEVER LAY A HAND ON THE BOY, SINCE SOME MIGHT DEEM THAT TO BE INCEST...
?
...SUPPOSE I WERE TO GO TO BED WITH WENDEL! THAT WOULDN'T BE INCESTUOUS, WOULD IT? I MEAN, HE AND I AREN'T BLOOD RELATIVES...
CLARK! BEHAVE YOURSELF!
AS FAR AS I'M AWARE, WENDEL AND OLLIE ENJOY A MONOGAMOUS RELATIONSHIP!
OH, DON'T PANIC, LOVE! I WOULDN'T DREAM OF INTRUDING WITHOUT AN INVITATION!
-BUT FOR GOD'S SAKE, LET'S DON'T WRING THE WORLD DRY OF FANTASY!
ANYWAY, YOUR CONCERN IS PREMATURE! THE YOUTH ISN'T EVEN WITHIN RADAR-RANGE YET!
HELLO? EFFLUVIA MAGAZINE? IS WENDEL TRUPSTOCK THERE?
A LONG-DISTANCE CALL FOR YOU, WENDEL!
UNCLE LUKE?!
MEANWHILE...
THEN IT'S SETTLED, OLLIE! I'LL EXPECT YOU HERE FOR THE MORNING SHIFT ON MONDAY!
ATTA GIRL, SIS!
YOU CAN BANK ON IT, REBA! THANKS!

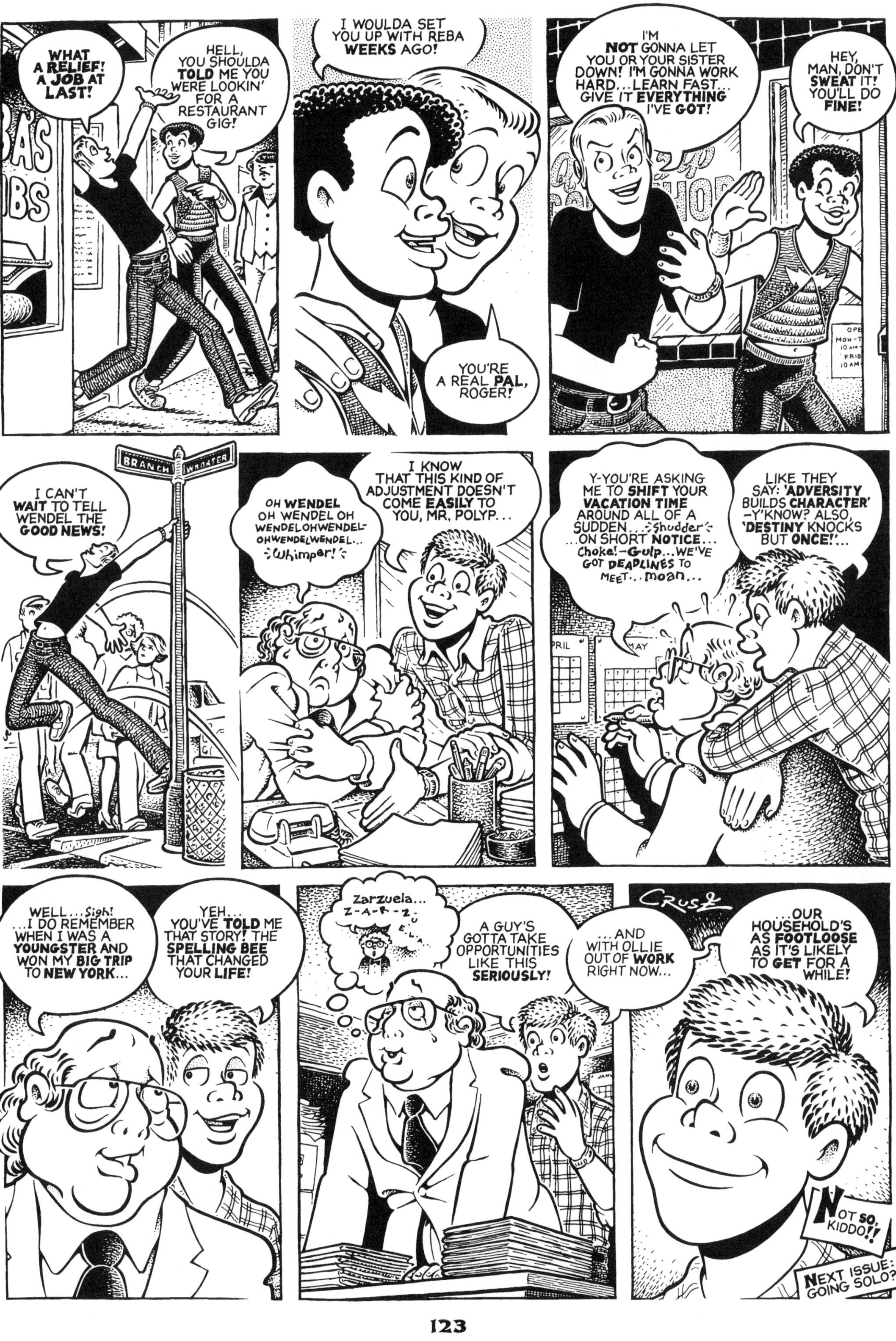

WHAT A RELIEF! A JOB AT LAST!
HELL, YOU SHOULDA TOLD ME YOU WERE LOOKIN' FOR A RESTAURANT GIG!
I WOULDA SET YOU UP WITH REBA WEEKS AGO!
YOU'RE A REAL PAL, ROGER!
I'M NOT GONNA LET YOU OR YOUR SISTER DOWN! I'M GONNA WORK HARD... LEARN FAST... GIVE IT EVERYTHING I'VE GOT!
HEY, MAN, DON'T SWEAT IT! YOU'LL DO FINE!
BRANCH
WHARTER
I CAN'T WAIT TO TELL WENDEL THE GOOD NEWS!
I KNOW THAT THIS KIND OF ADJUSTMENT DOESN'T COME EASILY TO YOU, MR. POLYP...
OH WENDEL OH WENDEL OH WENDELOHWENDEL-OHWENDELWENDEL... Whimper!
Y-YOU'RE ASKING ME TO SHIFT YOUR VACATION TIME AROUND ALL OF A SUDDEN... Shudder ...ON SHORT NOTICE... Choke!—Gulp... WE'VE GOT DEADLINES TO MEET... moan...
LIKE THEY SAY: 'ADVERSITY BUILDS CHARACTER' —Y'KNOW? ALSO, 'DESTINY KNOCKS BUT ONCE!'...
WELL... Sigh! ...I DO REMEMBER WHEN I WAS A YOUNGSTER AND WON MY BIG TRIP TO NEW YORK...
YEH... YOU'VE TOLD ME THAT STORY! THE SPELLING BEE THAT CHANGED YOUR LIFE!
Zarzuela... Z-A-R-Z-U-E-L-A
A GUY'S GOTTA TAKE OPPORTUNITIES LIKE THIS SERIOUSLY!
...AND WITH OLLIE OUT OF WORK RIGHT NOW...
CRUSE
...OUR HOUSEHOLD'S AS FOOTLOOSE AS IT'S LIKELY TO GET FOR A WHILE!
NOT SO, KIDDO!!
NEXT ISSUE: GOING SOLO?

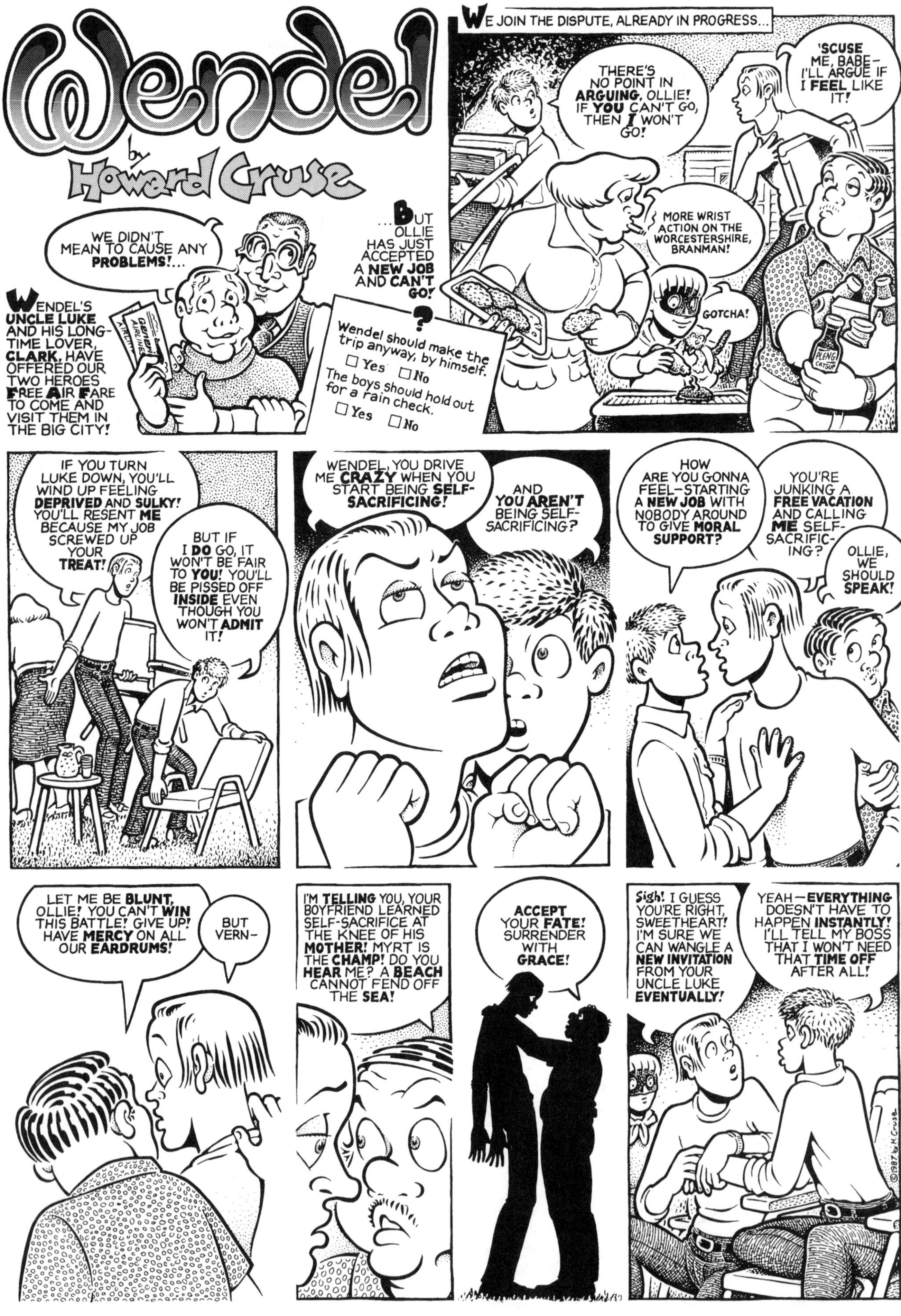

Wendel
by Howard Cruse
WENDEL'S UNCLE LUKE AND HIS LONG-TIME LOVER, CLARK, HAVE OFFERED OUR TWO HEROES FREE AIR FARE TO COME AND VISIT THEM IN THE BIG CITY!
WE DIDN'T MEAN TO CAUSE ANY PROBLEMS!...
...BUT OLLIE HAS JUST ACCEPTED A NEW JOB AND CAN'T GO!
?
Wendel should make the trip anyway, by himself.
☐ Yes ☐ No
The boys should hold out for a rain check.
☐ Yes ☐ No
WE JOIN THE DISPUTE, ALREADY IN PROGRESS...
THERE'S NO POINT IN ARGUING, OLLIE! IF YOU CAN'T GO, THEN I WON'T GO!
'SCUSE ME, BABE- I'LL ARGUE IF I FEEL LIKE IT!
MORE WRIST ACTION ON THE WORCESTERSHIRE, BRANMAN!
GOTCHA!
IF YOU TURN LUKE DOWN, YOU'LL WIND UP FEELING DEPRIVED AND SULKY! YOU'LL RESENT ME BECAUSE MY JOB SCREWED UP YOUR TREAT!
BUT IF I DO GO, IT WON'T BE FAIR TO YOU! YOU'LL BE PISSED OFF INSIDE EVEN THOUGH YOU WON'T ADMIT IT!
WENDEL, YOU DRIVE ME CRAZY WHEN YOU START BEING SELF-SACRIFICING!
AND YOU AREN'T BEING SELF-SACRIFICING?
HOW ARE YOU GONNA FEEL—STARTING A NEW JOB WITH NOBODY AROUND TO GIVE MORAL SUPPORT?
YOU'RE JUNKING A FREE VACATION AND CALLING ME SELF-SACRIFIC-ING?
OLLIE, WE SHOULD SPEAK!
LET ME BE BLUNT, OLLIE! YOU CAN'T WIN THIS BATTLE! GIVE UP! HAVE MERCY ON ALL OUR EARDRUMS!
BUT VERN-
I'M TELLING YOU, YOUR BOYFRIEND LEARNED SELF-SACRIFICE AT THE KNEE OF HIS MOTHER! MYRT IS THE CHAMP! DO YOU HEAR ME? A BEACH CANNOT FEND OFF THE SEA!
ACCEPT YOUR FATE! SURRENDER WITH GRACE!
Sigh! I GUESS YOU'RE RIGHT, SWEETHEART! I'M SURE WE CAN WANGLE A NEW INVITATION FROM YOUR UNCLE LUKE EVENTUALLY!
YEAH—EVERYTHING DOESN'T HAVE TO HAPPEN INSTANTLY! I'LL TELL MY BOSS THAT I WON'T NEED THAT TIME OFF AFTER ALL!
©1987 by H. Cruse

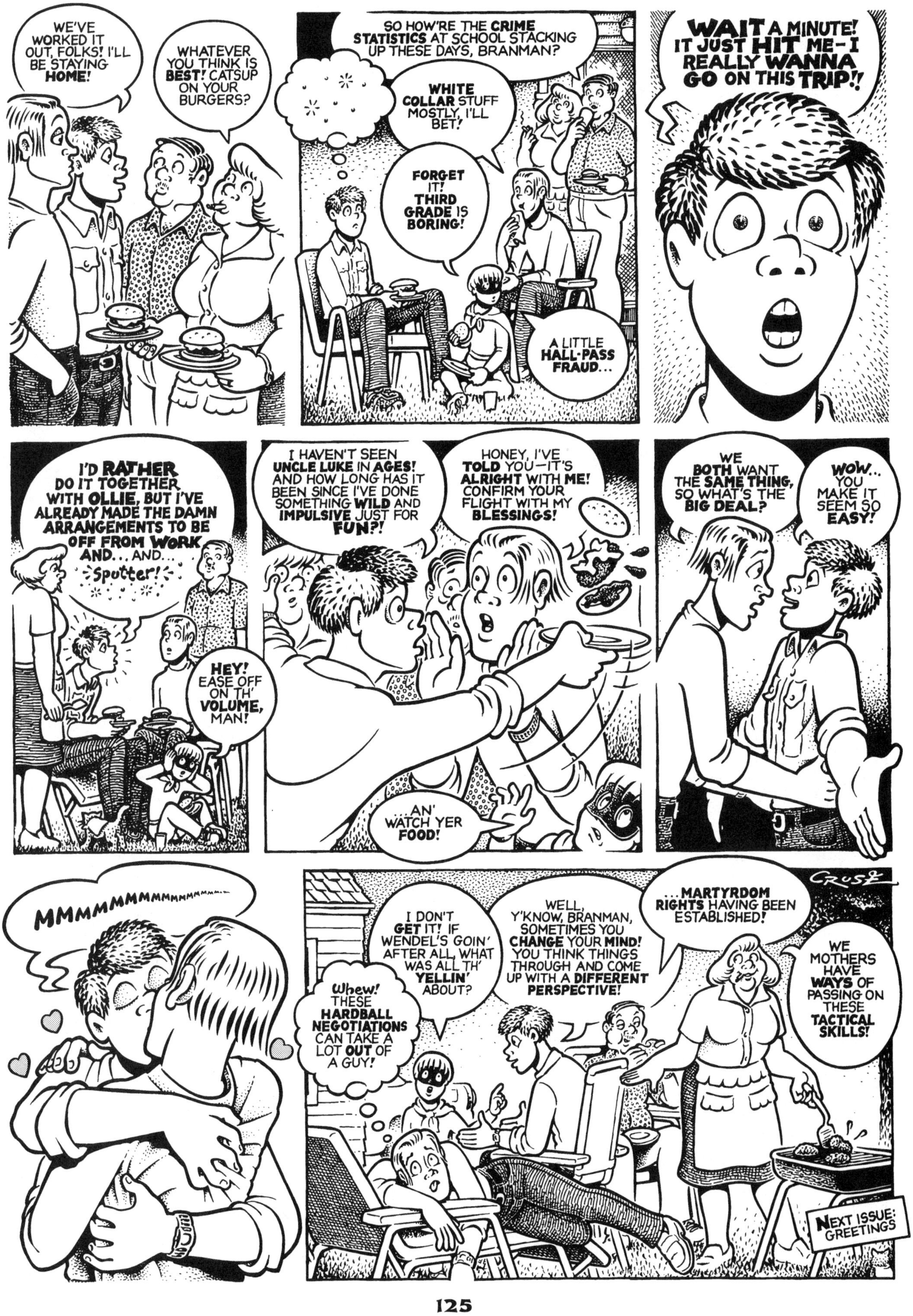
WE'VE WORKED IT OUT, FOLKS! I'LL BE STAYING HOME!
WHATEVER YOU THINK IS BEST! CATSUP ON YOUR BURGERS?
SO HOW'RE THE CRIME STATISTICS AT SCHOOL STACKING UP THESE DAYS, BRANMAN?
WHITE COLLAR STUFF MOSTLY, I'LL BET!
FORGET IT! THIRD GRADE IS BORING!
A LITTLE HALL-PASS FRAUD...
WAIT A MINUTE! IT JUST HIT ME-I REALLY WANNA GO ON THIS TRIP!!
I'D RATHER DO IT TOGETHER WITH OLLIE, BUT I'VE ALREADY MADE THE DAMN ARRANGEMENTS TO BE OFF FROM WORK AND... AND... Sputter!
HEY! EASE OFF ON TH' VOLUME, MAN!
I HAVEN'T SEEN UNCLE LUKE IN AGES! AND HOW LONG HAS IT BEEN SINCE I'VE DONE SOMETHING WILD AND IMPULSIVE JUST FOR FUN?!
HONEY, I'VE TOLD YOU—IT'S ALRIGHT WITH ME! CONFIRM YOUR FLIGHT WITH MY BLESSINGS!
...AN' WATCH YER FOOD!
WE BOTH WANT THE SAME THING, SO WHAT'S THE BIG DEAL?
WOW... YOU MAKE IT SEEM SO EASY!
MMMMMMMMMMMMMMMMM...
I DON'T GET IT! IF WENDEL'S GOIN' AFTER ALL, WHAT WAS ALL TH' YELLIN' ABOUT?
WELL, Y'KNOW, BRANMAN, SOMETIMES YOU CHANGE YOUR MIND! YOU THINK THINGS THROUGH AND COME UP WITH A DIFFERENT PERSPECTIVE!
...MARTYRDOM RIGHTS HAVING BEEN ESTABLISHED!
Whew! THESE HARDBALL NEGOTIATIONS CAN TAKE A LOT OUT OF A GUY!
WE MOTHERS HAVE WAYS OF PASSING ON THESE TACTICAL SKILLS!
CRUSE
NEXT ISSUE: GREETINGS

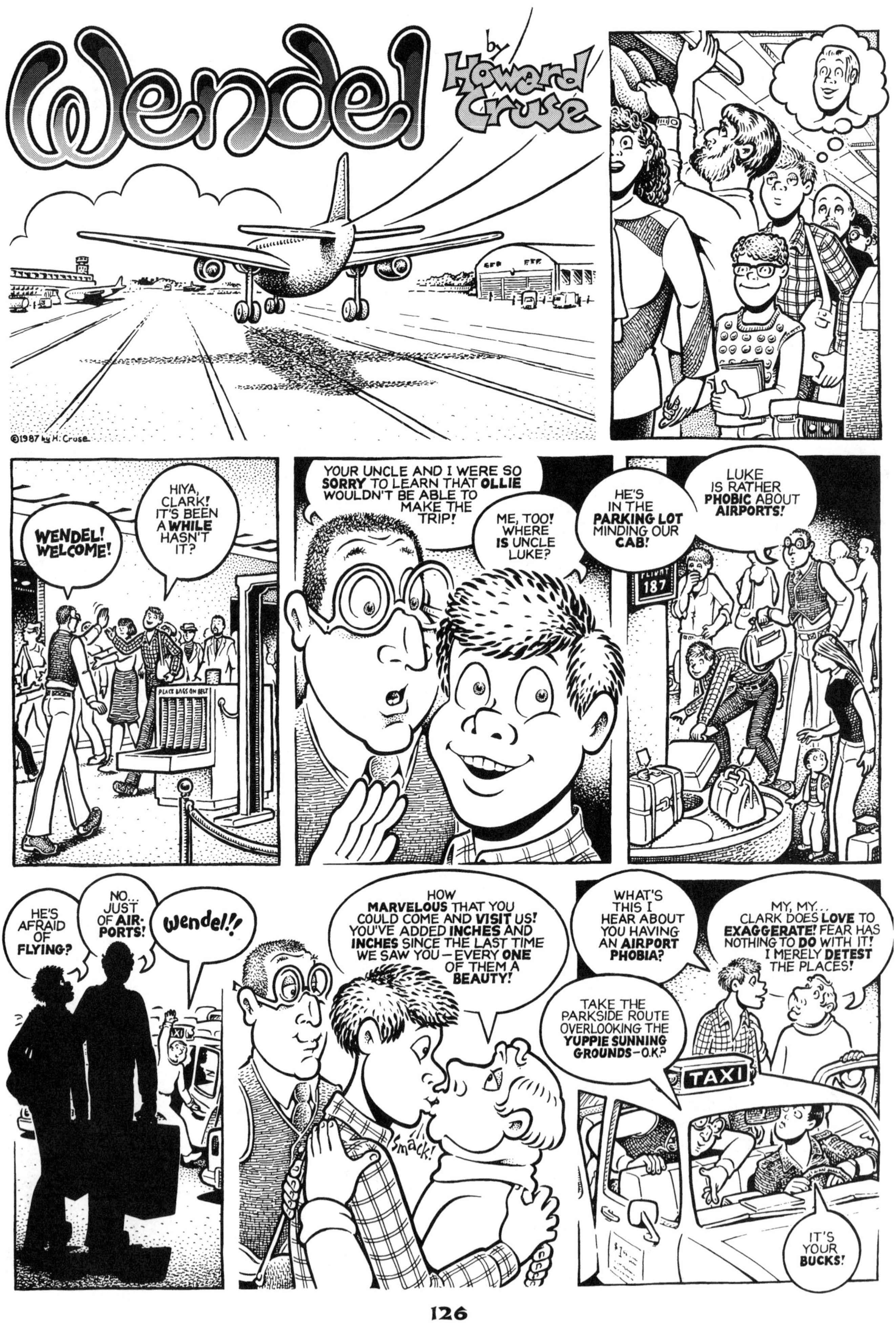
Wendel
by Howard Cruse
©1987 by H. Cruse
PLACE BAGS ON BELT
WENDEL! WELCOME!
HIYA, CLARK! IT'S BEEN A WHILE HASN'T IT?
YOUR UNCLE AND I WERE SO SORRY TO LEARN THAT OLLIE WOULDN'T BE ABLE TO MAKE THE TRIP!
ME, TOO! WHERE IS UNCLE LUKE?
HE'S IN THE PARKING LOT MINDING OUR CAB!
LUKE IS RATHER PHOBIC ABOUT AIRPORTS!
FLIGHT 187
HE'S AFRAID OF FLYING?
NO... JUST OF AIR-PORTS!
Wendel!!
HOW MARVELOUS THAT YOU COULD COME AND VISIT US! YOU'VE ADDED INCHES AND INCHES SINCE THE LAST TIME WE SAW YOU — EVERY ONE OF THEM A BEAUTY!
Smack!
WHAT'S THIS I HEAR ABOUT YOU HAVING AN AIRPORT PHOBIA?
MY, MY... CLARK DOES LOVE TO EXAGGERATE! FEAR HAS NOTHING TO DO WITH IT! I MERELY DETEST THE PLACES!
TAKE THE PARKSIDE ROUTE OVERLOOKING THE YUPPIE SUNNING GROUNDS — O.K.?
TAXI
IT'S YOUR BUCKS!

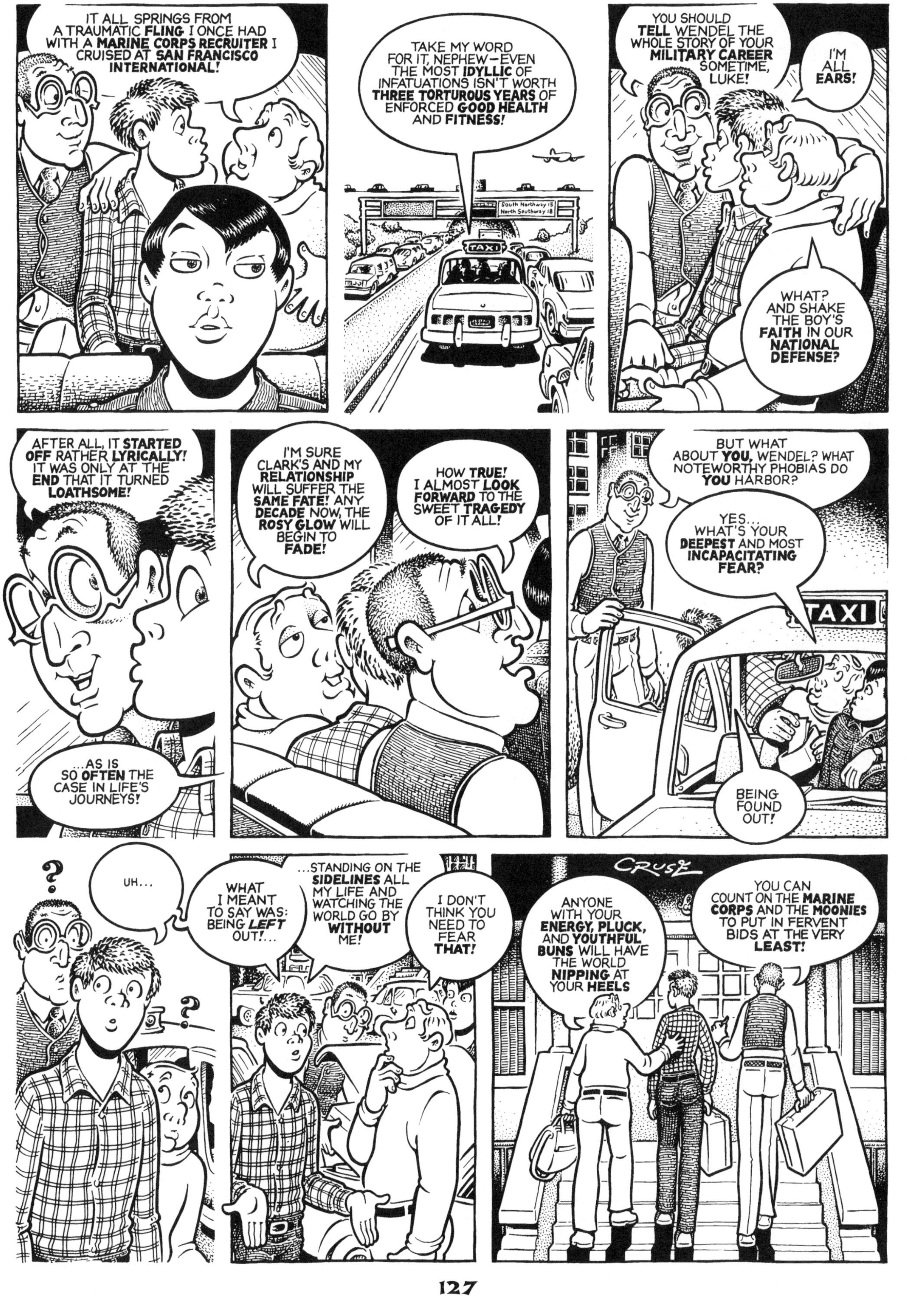
IT ALL SPRINGS FROM A TRAUMATIC FLING I ONCE HAD WITH A MARINE CORPS RECRUITER I CRUISED AT SAN FRANCISCO INTERNATIONAL!
TAKE MY WORD FOR IT, NEPHEW—EVEN THE MOST IDYLLIC OF INFATUATIONS ISN'T WORTH THREE TORTUROUS YEARS OF ENFORCED GOOD HEALTH AND FITNESS!
South Northway 15
North Southway 18
TAXI
YOU SHOULD TELL WENDEL THE WHOLE STORY OF YOUR MILITARY CAREER SOMETIME, LUKE!
I'M ALL EARS!
WHAT? AND SHAKE THE BOY'S FAITH IN OUR NATIONAL DEFENSE?
AFTER ALL, IT STARTED OFF RATHER LYRICALLY! IT WAS ONLY AT THE END THAT IT TURNED LOATHSOME!
...AS IS SO OFTEN THE CASE IN LIFE'S JOURNEYS!
I'M SURE CLARK'S AND MY RELATIONSHIP WILL SUFFER THE SAME FATE! ANY DECADE NOW, THE ROSY GLOW WILL BEGIN TO FADE!
HOW TRUE! I ALMOST LOOK FORWARD TO THE SWEET TRAGEDY OF IT ALL!
BUT WHAT ABOUT YOU, WENDEL? WHAT NOTEWORTHY PHOBIAS DO YOU HARBOR?
YES... WHAT'S YOUR DEEPEST AND MOST INCAPACITATING FEAR?
TAXI
BEING FOUND OUT!
?
UH...
?
WHAT I MEANT TO SAY WAS: BEING LEFT OUT!...
...STANDING ON THE SIDELINES ALL MY LIFE AND WATCHING THE WORLD GO BY WITHOUT ME!
I DON'T THINK YOU NEED TO FEAR THAT!
CRUSE
ANYONE WITH YOUR ENERGY, PLUCK, AND YOUTHFUL BUNS WILL HAVE THE WORLD NIPPING AT YOUR HEELS
YOU CAN COUNT ON THE MARINE CORPS AND THE MOONIES TO PUT IN FERVENT BIDS AT THE VERY LEAST!

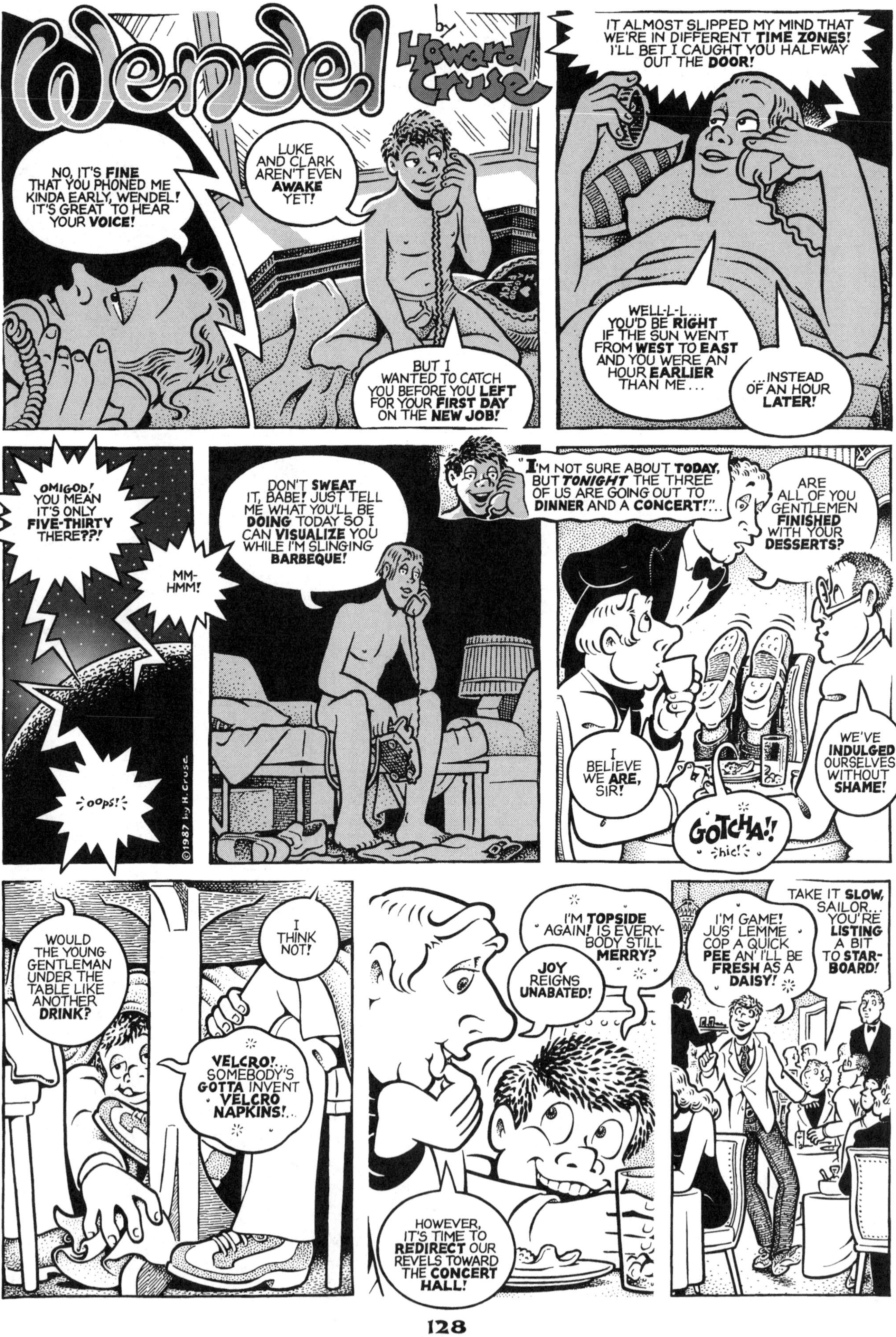
Wendel
by Howard Cruse
NO, IT'S FINE THAT YOU PHONED ME KINDA EARLY, WENDEL! IT'S GREAT TO HEAR YOUR VOICE!
LUKE AND CLARK AREN'T EVEN AWAKE YET!
BUT I WANTED TO CATCH YOU BEFORE YOU LEFT FOR YOUR FIRST DAY ON THE NEW JOB!
IT ALMOST SLIPPED MY MIND THAT WE'RE IN DIFFERENT TIME ZONES! I'LL BET I CAUGHT YOU HALFWAY OUT THE DOOR!
WELL-L-L... YOU'D BE RIGHT IF THE SUN WENT FROM WEST TO EAST AND YOU WERE AN HOUR EARLIER THAN ME...
...INSTEAD OF AN HOUR LATER!
OMIGOD! YOU MEAN IT'S ONLY FIVE-THIRTY THERE??!
MM-HMM!
OOPS!
©1987 by H. Cruse
DON'T SWEAT IT, BABE! JUST TELL ME WHAT YOU'LL BE DOING TODAY SO I CAN VISUALIZE YOU WHILE I'M SLINGING BARBEQUE!
"I'M NOT SURE ABOUT TODAY, BUT TONIGHT THE THREE OF US ARE GOING OUT TO DINNER AND A CONCERT!"...
ARE ALL OF YOU GENTLEMEN FINISHED WITH YOUR DESSERTS?
I BELIEVE WE ARE, SIR!
WE'VE INDULGED OURSELVES WITHOUT SHAME!
GOTCHA!!
hic!
WOULD THE YOUNG GENTLEMAN UNDER THE TABLE LIKE ANOTHER DRINK?
I THINK NOT!
VELCRO!... SOMEBODY'S GOTTA INVENT VELCRO NAPKINS!...
I'M TOPSIDE AGAIN! IS EVERYBODY STILL MERRY?
JOY REIGNS UNABATED!
HOWEVER, IT'S TIME TO REDIRECT OUR REVELS TOWARD THE CONCERT HALL!
I'M GAME! JUS' LEMME COP A QUICK PEE AN' I'LL BE FRESH AS A DAISY!
TAKE IT SLOW, SAILOR... YOU'RE LISTING A BIT TO STARBOARD!

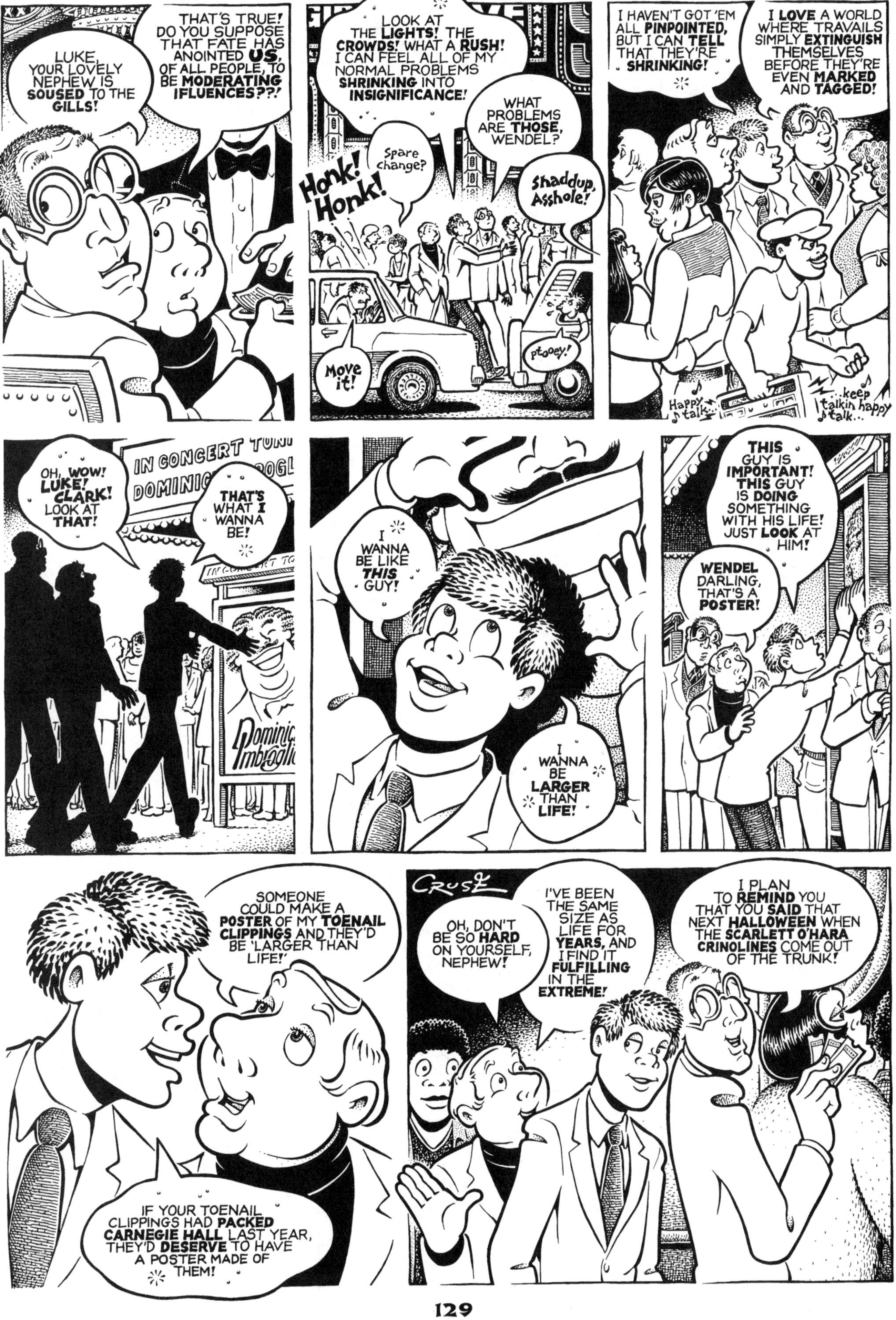
LUKE, YOUR LOVELY NEPHEW IS SOUSED TO THE GILLS!
THAT'S TRUE! DO YOU SUPPOSE THAT FATE HAS ANOINTED US, OF ALL PEOPLE, TO BE MODERATING IFLUENCES??!
LOOK AT THE LIGHTS! THE CROWDS! WHAT A RUSH! I CAN FEEL ALL OF MY NORMAL PROBLEMS SHRINKING INTO INSIGNIFICANCE!
Spare change?
Honk! Honk!
WHAT PROBLEMS ARE THOSE, WENDEL?
Shaddup, Asshole!
Move it!
ptooey!
I HAVEN'T GOT 'EM ALL PINPOINTED, BUT I CAN TELL THAT THEY'RE SHRINKING!
I LOVE A WORLD WHERE TRAVAILS SIMPLY EXTINGUISH THEMSELVES BEFORE THEY'RE EVEN MARKED AND TAGGED!
Happy talk... ...keep talkin happy talk...
IN CONCERT TONI
DOMINIC
OH, WOW! LUKE! CLARK! LOOK AT THAT!
THAT'S WHAT I WANNA BE!
Dominic Imbroglio
I WANNA BE LIKE THIS GUY!
I WANNA BE LARGER THAN LIFE!
THIS GUY IS IMPORTANT! THIS GUY IS DOING SOMETHING WITH HIS LIFE! JUST LOOK AT HIM!
WENDEL DARLING, THAT'S A POSTER!
SOMEONE COULD MAKE A POSTER OF MY TOENAIL CLIPPINGS AND THEY'D BE 'LARGER THAN LIFE!'
IF YOUR TOENAIL CLIPPINGS HAD PACKED CARNEGIE HALL LAST YEAR, THEY'D DESERVE TO HAVE A POSTER MADE OF THEM!
CRUSE
OH, DON'T BE SO HARD ON YOURSELF, NEPHEW!
I'VE BEEN THE SAME SIZE AS LIFE FOR YEARS, AND I FIND IT FULFILLING IN THE EXTREME!
I PLAN TO REMIND YOU THAT YOU SAID THAT NEXT HALLOWEEN WHEN THE SCARLETT O'HARA CRINOLINES COME OUT OF THE TRUNK!

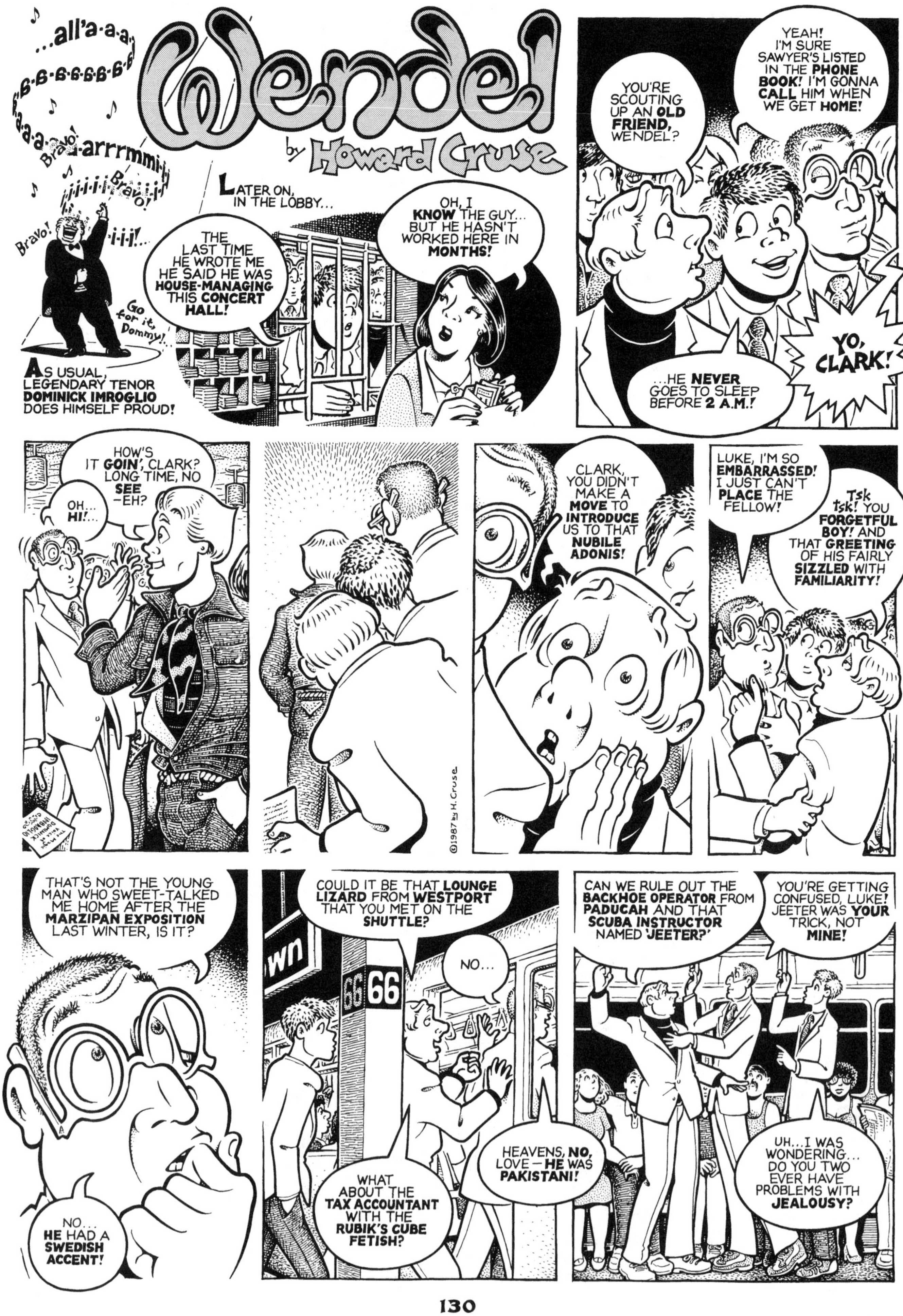
Wendel
by Howard Cruse
...all'a-a-a-B-B-B-B-B-B-B-B-B-a-a-a-arrrmmi-i-i-i-i-i-i-i-i-i-i!...
Bravo!
Bravo!
Bravo!
Go for it, Dommy!
AS USUAL, LEGENDARY TENOR DOMINICK IMROGLIO DOES HIMSELF PROUD!
LATER ON, IN THE LOBBY...
THE LAST TIME HE WROTE ME HE SAID HE WAS HOUSE-MANAGING THIS CONCERT HALL!
OH, I KNOW THE GUY... BUT HE HASN'T WORKED HERE IN MONTHS!
YOU'RE SCOUTING UP AN OLD FRIEND, WENDEL?
YEAH! I'M SURE SAWYER'S LISTED IN THE PHONE BOOK! I'M GONNA CALL HIM WHEN WE GET HOME!
...HE NEVER GOES TO SLEEP BEFORE 2 A.M.!
YO, CLARK!
HOW'S IT GOIN', CLARK? LONG TIME, NO SEE —EH?
OH... HI!...
©1987 by H. Cruse
CLARK, YOU DIDN'T MAKE A MOVE TO INTRODUCE US TO THAT NUBILE ADONIS!
LUKE, I'M SO EMBARRASSED! I JUST CAN'T PLACE THE FELLOW!
Tsk tsk! YOU FORGETFUL BOY! AND THAT GREETING OF HIS FAIRLY SIZZLED WITH FAMILIARITY!
THAT'S NOT THE YOUNG MAN WHO SWEET-TALKED ME HOME AFTER THE MARZIPAN EXPOSITION LAST WINTER, IS IT?
NO... HE HAD A SWEDISH ACCENT!
COULD IT BE THAT LOUNGE LIZARD FROM WESTPORT THAT YOU MET ON THE SHUTTLE?
NO...
WHAT ABOUT THE TAX ACCOUNTANT WITH THE RUBIK'S CUBE FETISH?
HEAVENS, NO, LOVE — HE WAS PAKISTANI!
66
66
CAN WE RULE OUT THE BACKHOE OPERATOR FROM PADUCAH AND THAT SCUBA INSTRUCTOR NAMED 'JEETER?'
YOU'RE GETTING CONFUSED, LUKE! JEETER WAS YOUR TRICK, NOT MINE!
UH...I WAS WONDERING... DO YOU TWO EVER HAVE PROBLEMS WITH JEALOUSY?

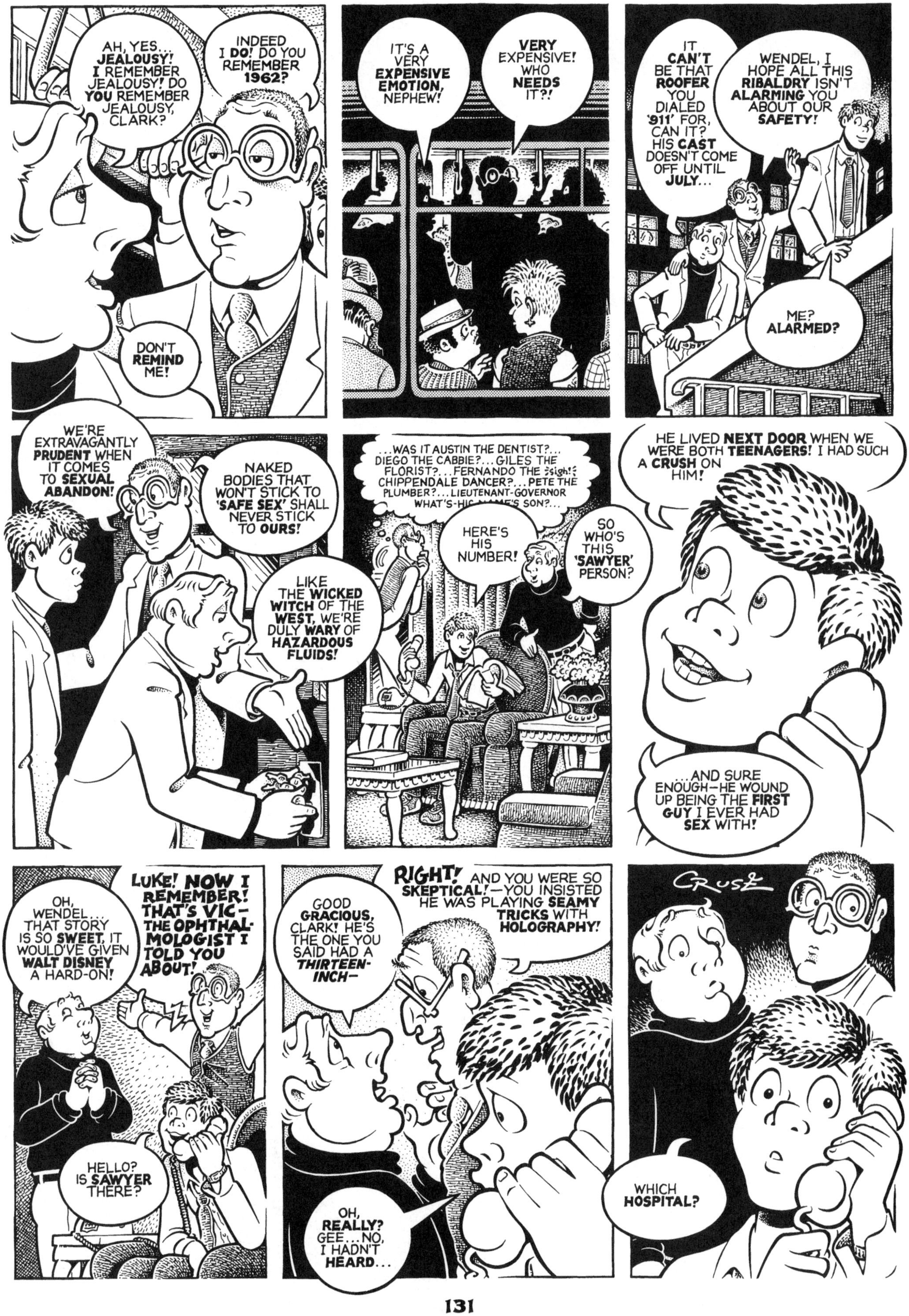
AH, YES... JEALOUSY! I REMEMBER JEALOUSY! DO YOU REMEMBER JEALOUSY, CLARK?
INDEED I DO! DO YOU REMEMBER 1962?
DON'T REMIND ME!
IT'S A VERY EXPENSIVE EMOTION, NEPHEW!
VERY EXPENSIVE! WHO NEEDS IT?!
IT CAN'T BE THAT ROOFER YOU DIALED '911' FOR, CAN IT? HIS CAST DOESN'T COME OFF UNTIL JULY...
WENDEL, I HOPE ALL THIS RIBALDRY ISN'T ALARMING YOU ABOUT OUR SAFETY!
ME? ALARMED?
WE'RE EXTRAVAGANTLY PRUDENT WHEN IT COMES TO SEXUAL ABANDON!
NAKED BODIES THAT WON'T STICK TO 'SAFE SEX' SHALL NEVER STICK TO OURS!
LIKE THE WICKED WITCH OF THE WEST, WE'RE DULY WARY OF HAZARDOUS FLUIDS!
...WAS IT AUSTIN THE DENTIST?... DIEGO THE CABBIE?... GILES THE FLORIST?... FERNANDO THE CHIPPENDALE DANCER?... PETE THE PLUMBER?... LIEUTENANT-GOVERNOR WHAT'S-HIS-NAME'S SON?...
sigh!
HERE'S HIS NUMBER!
SO WHO'S THIS 'SAWYER' PERSON?
HE LIVED NEXT DOOR WHEN WE WERE BOTH TEENAGERS! I HAD SUCH A CRUSH ON HIM!
...AND SURE ENOUGH—HE WOUND UP BEING THE FIRST GUY I EVER HAD SEX WITH!
OH, WENDEL... THAT STORY IS SO SWEET, IT WOULD'VE GIVEN WALT DISNEY A HARD-ON!
LUKE! NOW I REMEMBER! THAT'S VIC—THE OPHTHAL-MOLOGIST I TOLD YOU ABOUT!
HELLO? IS SAWYER THERE?
GOOD GRACIOUS, CLARK! HE'S THE ONE YOU SAID HAD A THIRTEEN-INCH—
RIGHT! AND YOU WERE SO SKEPTICAL!—YOU INSISTED HE WAS PLAYING SEAMY TRICKS WITH HOLOGRAPHY!
OH, REALLY? GEE... NO, I HADN'T HEARD...
CRUSE
WHICH HOSPITAL?

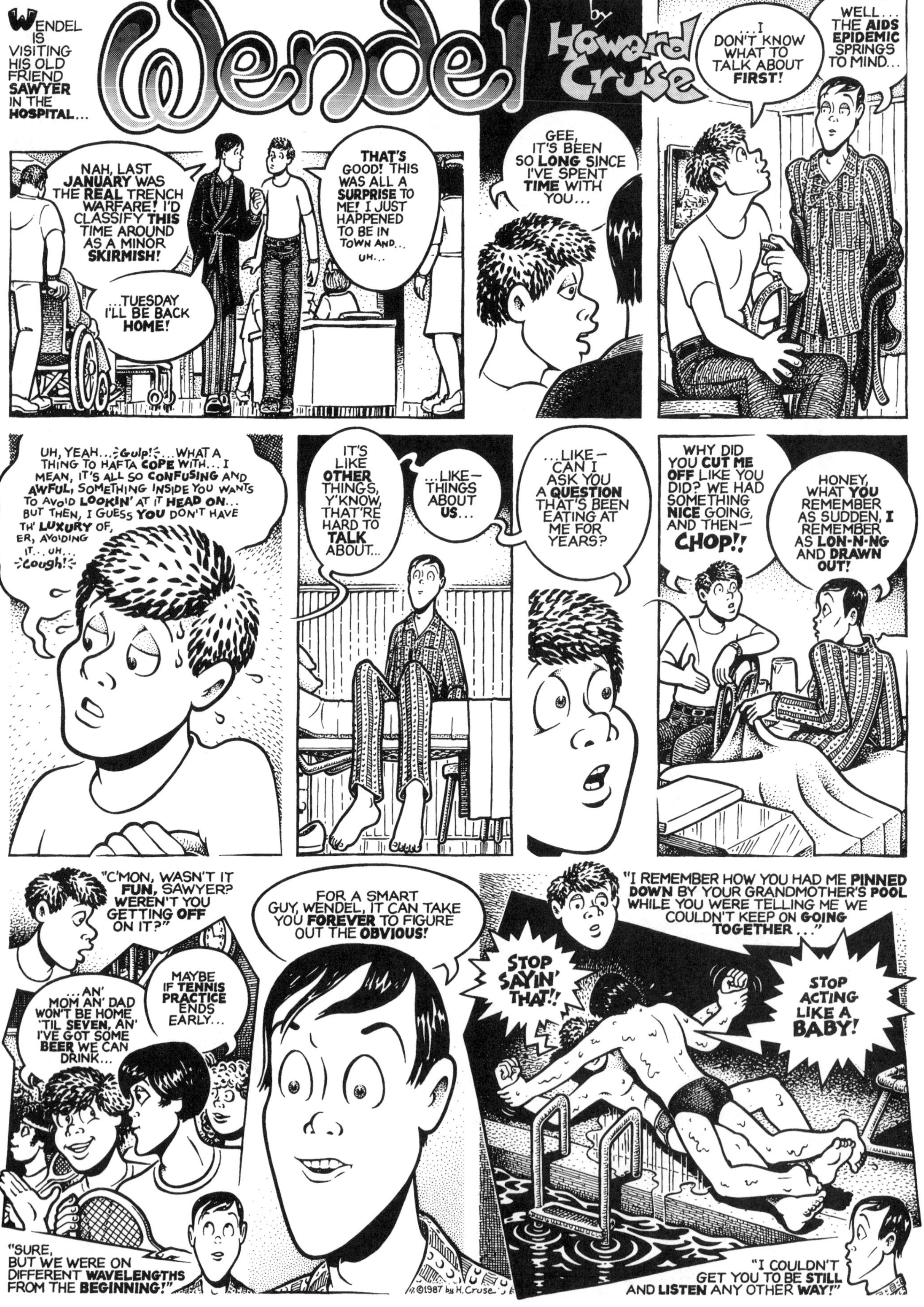

WENDEL IS VISITING HIS OLD FRIEND SAWYER IN THE HOSPITAL...
Wendel
by Howard Cruse
...I DON'T KNOW WHAT TO TALK ABOUT FIRST!
WELL... THE AIDS EPIDEMIC SPRINGS TO MIND...
NAH, LAST JANUARY WAS THE REAL TRENCH WARFARE! I'D CLASSIFY THIS TIME AROUND AS A MINOR SKIRMISH!
...TUESDAY I'LL BE BACK HOME!
THAT'S GOOD! THIS WAS ALL A SURPRISE TO ME! I JUST HAPPENED TO BE IN TOWN AND... UH...
GEE, IT'S BEEN SO LONG SINCE I'VE SPENT TIME WITH YOU...
UH, YEAH... ;Gulp!; ...WHAT A THING TO HAFTA COPE WITH... I MEAN, IT'S ALL SO CONFUSING AND AWFUL, SOMETHING INSIDE YOU WANTS TO AVOID LOOKIN' AT IT HEAD ON... BUT THEN, I GUESS YOU DON'T HAVE TH' LUXURY OF, ER, AVOIDING IT... UH... ;Cough!;
IT'S LIKE OTHER THINGS, Y'KNOW, THAT'RE HARD TO TALK ABOUT...
...LIKE— THINGS ABOUT US...
...LIKE— CAN I ASK YOU A QUESTION THAT'S BEEN EATING AT ME FOR YEARS?
WHY DID YOU CUT ME OFF LIKE YOU DID? WE HAD SOMETHING NICE GOING, AND THEN— CHOP!!
HONEY, WHAT YOU REMEMBER AS SUDDEN, I REMEMBER AS LON-N-NG AND DRAWN OUT!
"C'MON, WASN'T IT FUN, SAWYER? WEREN'T YOU GETTING OFF ON IT?"
...AN' MOM AN' DAD WON'T BE HOME 'TIL SEVEN, AN' I'VE GOT SOME BEER WE CAN DRINK...
MAYBE IF TENNIS PRACTICE ENDS EARLY...
"SURE, BUT WE WERE ON DIFFERENT WAVELENGTHS FROM THE BEGINNING!"
FOR A SMART GUY, WENDEL, IT CAN TAKE YOU FOREVER TO FIGURE OUT THE OBVIOUS!
"I REMEMBER HOW YOU HAD ME PINNED DOWN BY YOUR GRANDMOTHER'S POOL WHILE YOU WERE TELLING ME WE COULDN'T KEEP ON GOING TOGETHER..."
STOP SAYIN' THAT!!
STOP ACTING LIKE A BABY!
"I COULDN'T GET YOU TO BE STILL AND LISTEN ANY OTHER WAY!"
©1987 by H. Cruse

THAT'S THE ONLY **REJECTION** I EVER GOT THAT I CAN **MASTURBATE** TO THE **MEMORY** OF!

"JESUS! THINKIN' ABOUT THOSE DAYS... Y'KNOW, YOU'VE REALLY GOT A **CRUEL** STREAK, SAWYER!"

"HELL, I WAS **FIFTEEN!** YOU'RE **SUPPOSED** TO BE **IMMATURE** WHEN YOU'RE **FIFTEEN**..."

SO WHAT'RE WE **LEFT** WITH AFTER ALL THAT? I'M NOT **IN LOVE** WITH YOU ANYMORE!

I'M NOT 'IN LOVE' WITH **YOU** EITHER!

LINDA AND I ARE DRIVING TO **BALSA GROVE** ON **SATURDAY!** GET A **GIRL** AND LET'S **DOUBLE-DATE!**

Squeeze!

ASK **BETTY ANN** TO COME, **WENDEL!** SHE'S **CRAZY** ABOUT YOU!

...DON'T KNOW IF I EVER **WAS!**

I GUESS THAT **SIMPLIFIES** THINGS! I'VE GOT A **LOVER** NOW...

I DO **LOVE** YOU, THOUGH! Y'UNDERSTAND?

YEAH... WELL... ME... TOO!

ME, TOO! STICK AROUND AN HOUR AND YOU'LL **MEET** HIM!

WHEW! THAT REALLY **CLEARED** THE **AIR!** I'M SO **RELIEVED!**

WHAT'LL WE TALK ABOUT **NOW?**

OH, I DUNNO... THERE'S ALWAYS **LIFE- THREATENING ILLNESSES**...

OH, YEAH... THE BIG **TOPIC**...

I JUST DON'T KNOW WHAT TO **SAY,** SAWYER...UH...I MEAN, I HAVE ALL MY **OWN** FEARS ABOUT **MORTALITY** AND BEIN' **SCREWED** BY SOME STUPID HISTORICAL **ACCIDENT**... *-cough!*... UH... BUT WHAT RIGHT HAVE I GOT TO EVEN **TALK** ABOUT IT CONSIDERING THAT **I'M NOT** THE ONE WHO HAS TO **DEAL** WITH IT—EXCEPT THAT **NEXT** WEEK I **COULD** BE HAVIN' TO DEAL WITH IT... NOT MY, UH, FAVORITE **THOUGHT**... BUT OF COURSE, ME **FREAKIN'** OUT ISN'T BEIN' ANY HELP TO **YOU**... AS A FRIEND I OUGHTA... 'PORT YOU...

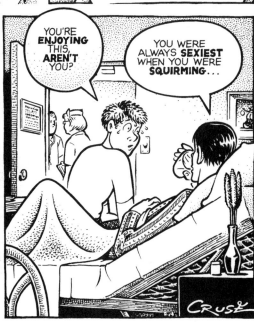

YOU'RE **ENJOYING** THIS, **AREN'T** YOU?

YOU WERE ALWAYS **SEXIEST** WHEN YOU WERE **SQUIRMING**...

CRUSE

133

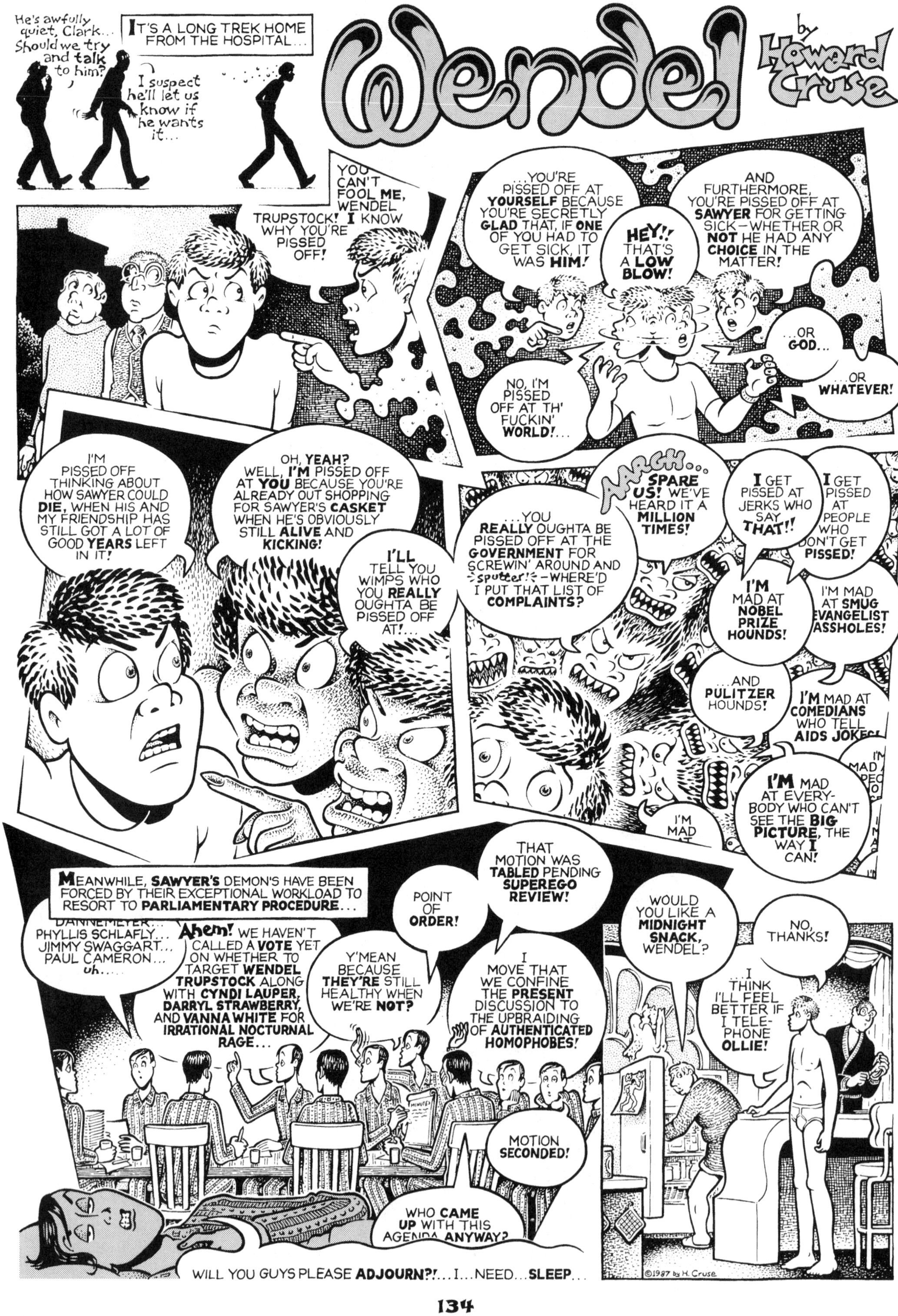
Wendel
by Howard Cruse
He's awfully quiet, Clark... Should we try and talk to him?
IT'S A LONG TREK HOME FROM THE HOSPITAL...
I suspect he'll let us know if he wants it...
YOU CAN'T FOOL ME, WENDEL TRUPSTOCK! I KNOW WHY YOU'RE PISSED OFF!
...YOU'RE PISSED OFF AT YOURSELF BECAUSE YOU'RE SECRETLY GLAD THAT, IF ONE OF YOU HAD TO GET SICK, IT WAS HIM!
HEY!! THAT'S A LOW BLOW!
AND FURTHERMORE, YOU'RE PISSED OFF AT SAWYER FOR GETTING SICK—WHETHER OR NOT HE HAD ANY CHOICE IN THE MATTER!
NO, I'M PISSED OFF AT TH' FUCKIN' WORLD!...
...OR GOD...
...OR WHATEVER!
I'M PISSED OFF THINKING ABOUT HOW SAWYER COULD DIE, WHEN HIS AND MY FRIENDSHIP HAS STILL GOT A LOT OF GOOD YEARS LEFT IN IT!
OH, YEAH? WELL, I'M PISSED OFF AT YOU BECAUSE YOU'RE ALREADY OUT SHOPPING FOR SAWYER'S CASKET WHEN HE'S OBVIOUSLY STILL ALIVE AND KICKING!
I'LL TELL YOU WIMPS WHO YOU REALLY OUGHTA BE PISSED OFF AT!...
...YOU REALLY OUGHTA BE PISSED OFF AT THE GOVERNMENT FOR SCREWIN' AROUND AND sputter!—WHERE'D I PUT THAT LIST OF COMPLAINTS?
AARGH... SPARE US! WE'VE HEARD IT A MILLION TIMES!
I GET PISSED AT JERKS WHO SAY THAT!!
I GET PISSED AT PEOPLE WHO DON'T GET PISSED!
I'M MAD AT NOBEL PRIZE HOUNDS!
I'M MAD AT SMUG EVANGELIST ASSHOLES!
...AND PULITZER HOUNDS!
I'M MAD AT COMEDIANS WHO TELL AIDS JOKES!
I'M MAD AT EVERYBODY WHO CAN'T SEE THE BIG PICTURE, THE WAY I CAN!
I'M MAD
MEANWHILE, SAWYER'S DEMON'S HAVE BEEN FORCED BY THEIR EXCEPTIONAL WORKLOAD TO RESORT TO PARLIAMENTARY PROCEDURE...
DANNEMEYER... PHYLLIS SCHLAFLY... JIMMY SWAGGART... PAUL CAMERON... uh....
Ahem! WE HAVEN'T CALLED A VOTE YET ON WHETHER TO TARGET WENDEL TRUPSTOCK ALONG WITH CYNDI LAUPER, DARRYL STRAWBERRY, AND VANNA WHITE FOR IRRATIONAL NOCTURNAL RAGE...
Y'MEAN BECAUSE THEY'RE STILL HEALTHY WHEN WE'RE NOT?
POINT OF ORDER!
THAT MOTION WAS TABLED PENDING SUPEREGO REVIEW!
I MOVE THAT WE CONFINE THE PRESENT DISCUSSION TO THE UPBRAIDING OF AUTHENTICATED HOMOPHOBES!
MOTION SECONDED!
MINUTES
WHO CAME UP WITH THIS AGENDA ANYWAY?
WILL YOU GUYS PLEASE ADJOURN?!... I... NEED... SLEEP...
WOULD YOU LIKE A MIDNIGHT SNACK, WENDEL?
NO, THANKS!
...I THINK I'LL FEEL BETTER IF I TELEPHONE OLLIE!
©1987 by H. Cruse

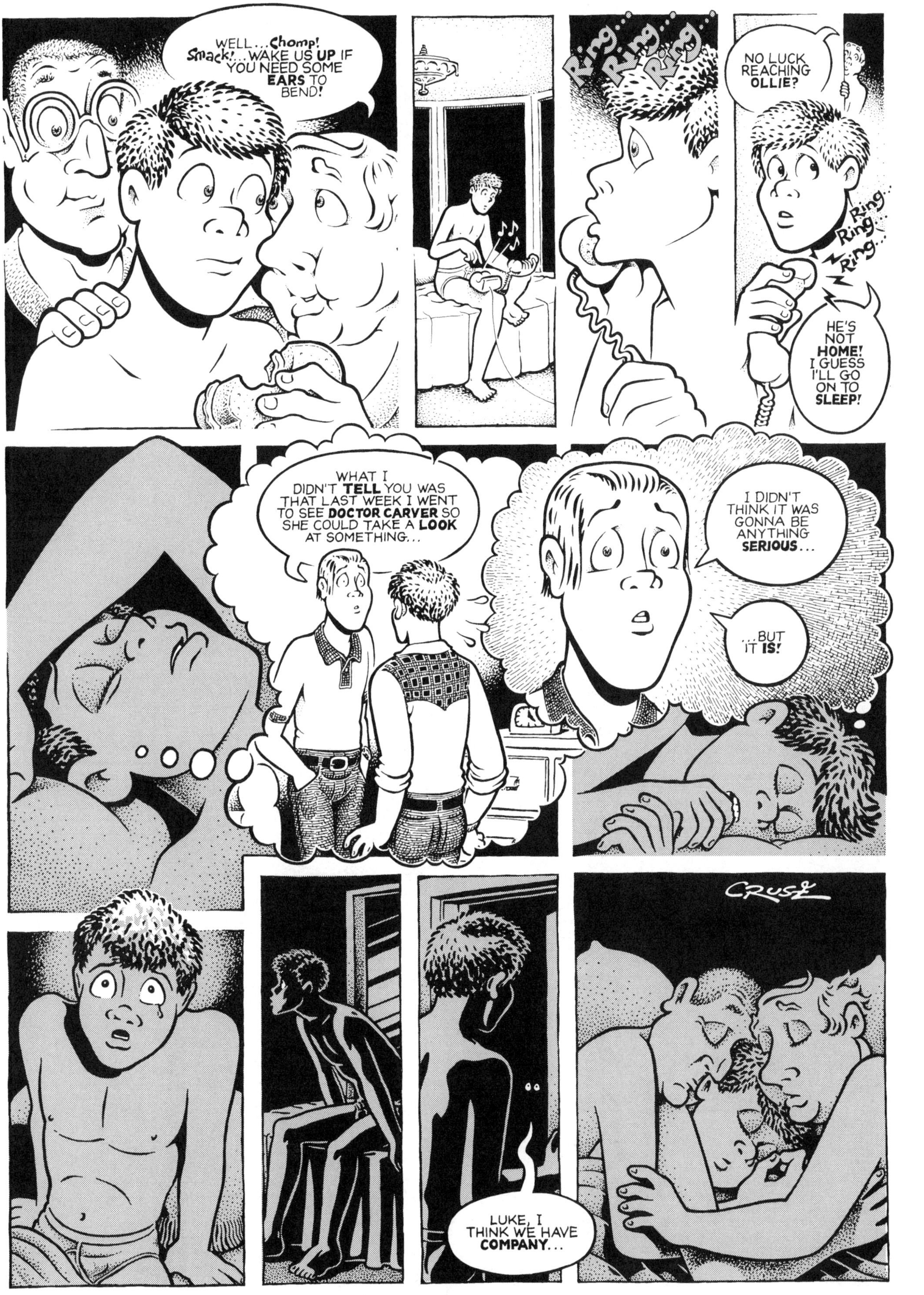
WELL... Chomp! Smack!... WAKE US UP IF YOU NEED SOME EARS TO BEND!
Ring... Ring... Ring...
NO LUCK REACHING OLLIE?
Ring... Ring... Ring...
HE'S NOT HOME! I GUESS I'LL GO ON TO SLEEP!
WHAT I DIDN'T TELL YOU WAS THAT LAST WEEK I WENT TO SEE DOCTOR CARVER SO SHE COULD TAKE A LOOK AT SOMETHING...
I DIDN'T THINK IT WAS GONNA BE ANYTHING SERIOUS...
...BUT IT IS!
CRUSE
LUKE, I THINK WE HAVE COMPANY...

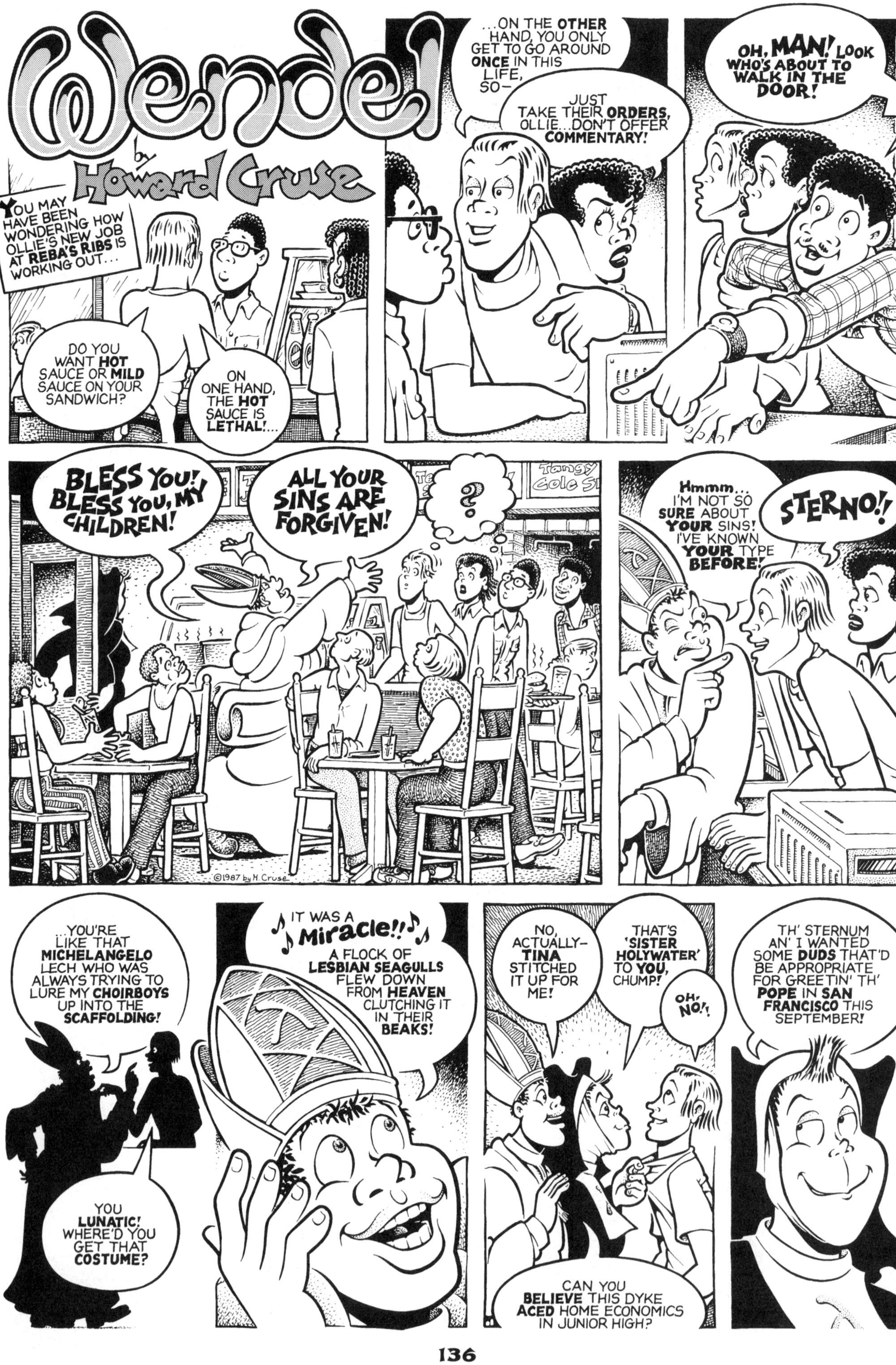
Wendel
by Howard Cruse
YOU MAY HAVE BEEN WONDERING HOW OLLIE'S NEW JOB AT REBA'S RIBS IS WORKING OUT...
DO YOU WANT HOT SAUCE OR MILD SAUCE ON YOUR SANDWICH?
ON ONE HAND, THE HOT SAUCE IS LETHAL!...
...ON THE OTHER HAND, YOU ONLY GET TO GO AROUND ONCE IN THIS LIFE, SO—
JUST TAKE THEIR ORDERS, OLLIE...DON'T OFFER COMMENTARY!
OH, MAN! LOOK WHO'S ABOUT TO WALK IN THE DOOR!
BLESS YOU! BLESS YOU, MY CHILDREN!
ALL YOUR SINS ARE FORGIVEN!
?
Tangy Cole Sl
©1987 by H. Cruse
Hmmm... I'M NOT SO SURE ABOUT YOUR SINS! I'VE KNOWN YOUR TYPE BEFORE!
STERNO!!
...YOU'RE LIKE THAT MICHELANGELO LECH WHO WAS ALWAYS TRYING TO LURE MY CHOIRBOYS UP INTO THE SCAFFOLDING!
YOU LUNATIC! WHERE'D YOU GET THAT COSTUME?
IT WAS A Miracle!!
A FLOCK OF LESBIAN SEAGULLS FLEW DOWN FROM HEAVEN CLUTCHING IT IN THEIR BEAKS!
NO, ACTUALLY— TINA STITCHED IT UP FOR ME!
THAT'S 'SISTER HOLYWATER' TO YOU, CHUMP!
OH, NO!!
CAN YOU BELIEVE THIS DYKE ACED HOME ECONOMICS IN JUNIOR HIGH?
TH' STERNUM AN' I WANTED SOME DUDS THAT'D BE APPROPRIATE FOR GREETIN' TH' POPE IN SAN FRANCISCO THIS SEPTEMBER!

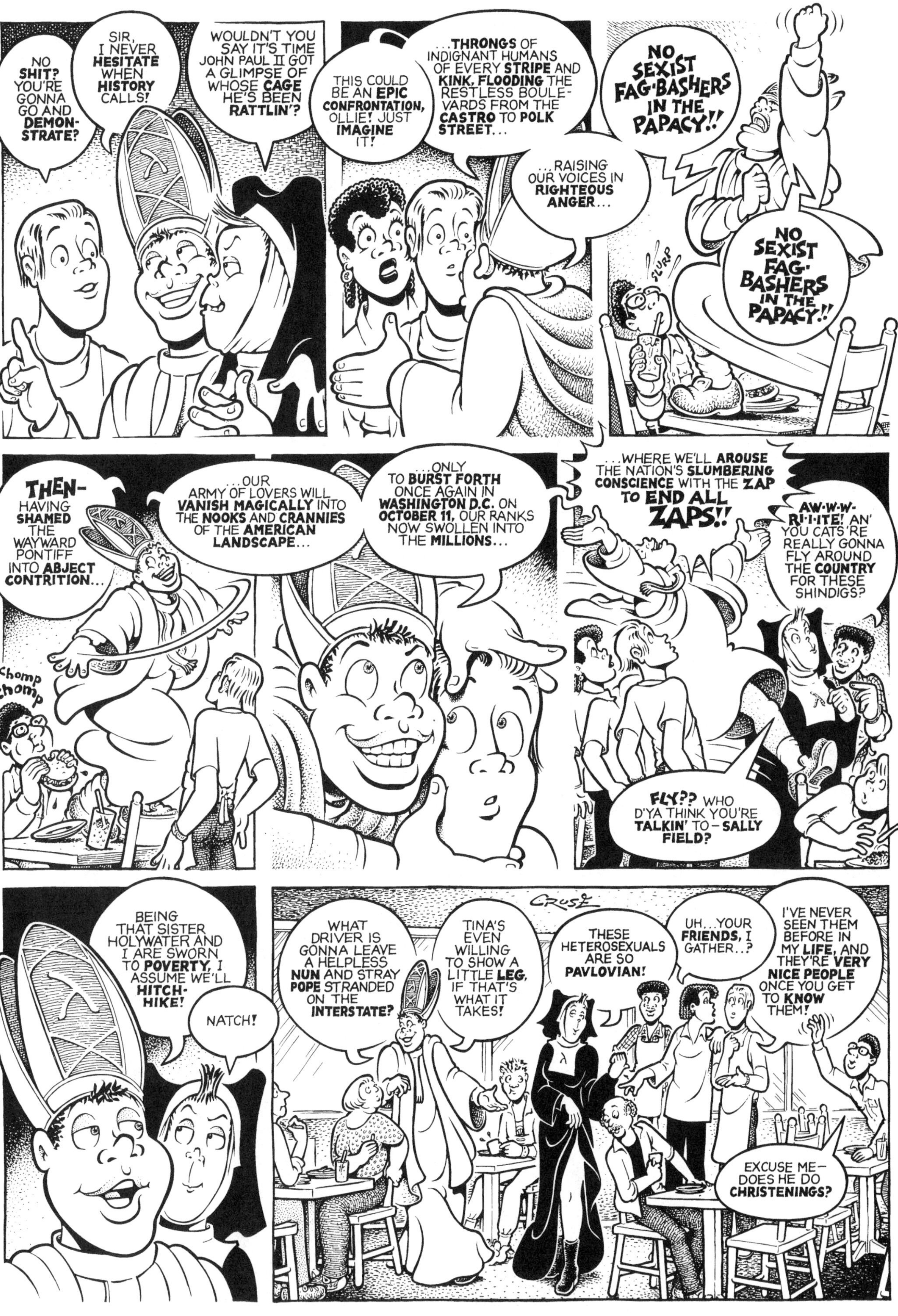
NO SHIT? YOU'RE GONNA GO AND DEMON-STRATE?
SIR, I NEVER HESITATE WHEN HISTORY CALLS!
WOULDN'T YOU SAY IT'S TIME JOHN PAUL II GOT A GLIMPSE OF WHOSE CAGE HE'S BEEN RATTLIN'?
THIS COULD BE AN EPIC CONFRONTATION, OLLIE! JUST IMAGINE IT!
...THRONGS OF INDIGNANT HUMANS OF EVERY STRIPE AND KINK, FLOODING THE RESTLESS BOULE-VARDS FROM THE CASTRO TO POLK STREET...
...RAISING OUR VOICES IN RIGHTEOUS ANGER...
NO SEXIST FAG-BASHERS IN THE PAPACY!!
SLURP
NO SEXIST FAG-BASHERS IN THE PAPACY!!
THEN— HAVING SHAMED THE WAYWARD PONTIFF INTO ABJECT CONTRITION...
...OUR ARMY OF LOVERS WILL VANISH MAGICALLY INTO THE NOOKS AND CRANNIES OF THE AMERICAN LANDSCAPE...
chomp chomp
...ONLY TO BURST FORTH ONCE AGAIN IN WASHINGTON D.C. ON OCTOBER 11, OUR RANKS NOW SWOLLEN INTO THE MILLIONS...
...WHERE WE'LL AROUSE THE NATION'S SLUMBERING CONSCIENCE WITH THE ZAP TO END ALL ZAPS!!
AW-W-W-RI-I-ITE! AN' YOU CATS'RE REALLY GONNA FLY AROUND THE COUNTRY FOR THESE SHINDIGS?
FLY?? WHO D'YA THINK YOU'RE TALKIN' TO—SALLY FIELD?
BEING THAT SISTER HOLYWATER AND I ARE SWORN TO POVERTY, I ASSUME WE'LL HITCH-HIKE!
NATCH!
CRUSE
WHAT DRIVER IS GONNA LEAVE A HELPLESS NUN AND STRAY POPE STRANDED ON THE INTERSTATE?
TINA'S EVEN WILLING TO SHOW A LITTLE LEG, IF THAT'S WHAT IT TAKES!
THESE HETEROSEXUALS ARE SO PAVLOVIAN!
UH...YOUR FRIENDS, I GATHER..?
I'VE NEVER SEEN THEM BEFORE IN MY LIFE, AND THEY'RE VERY NICE PEOPLE ONCE YOU GET TO KNOW THEM!
EXCUSE ME— DOES HE DO CHRISTENINGS?

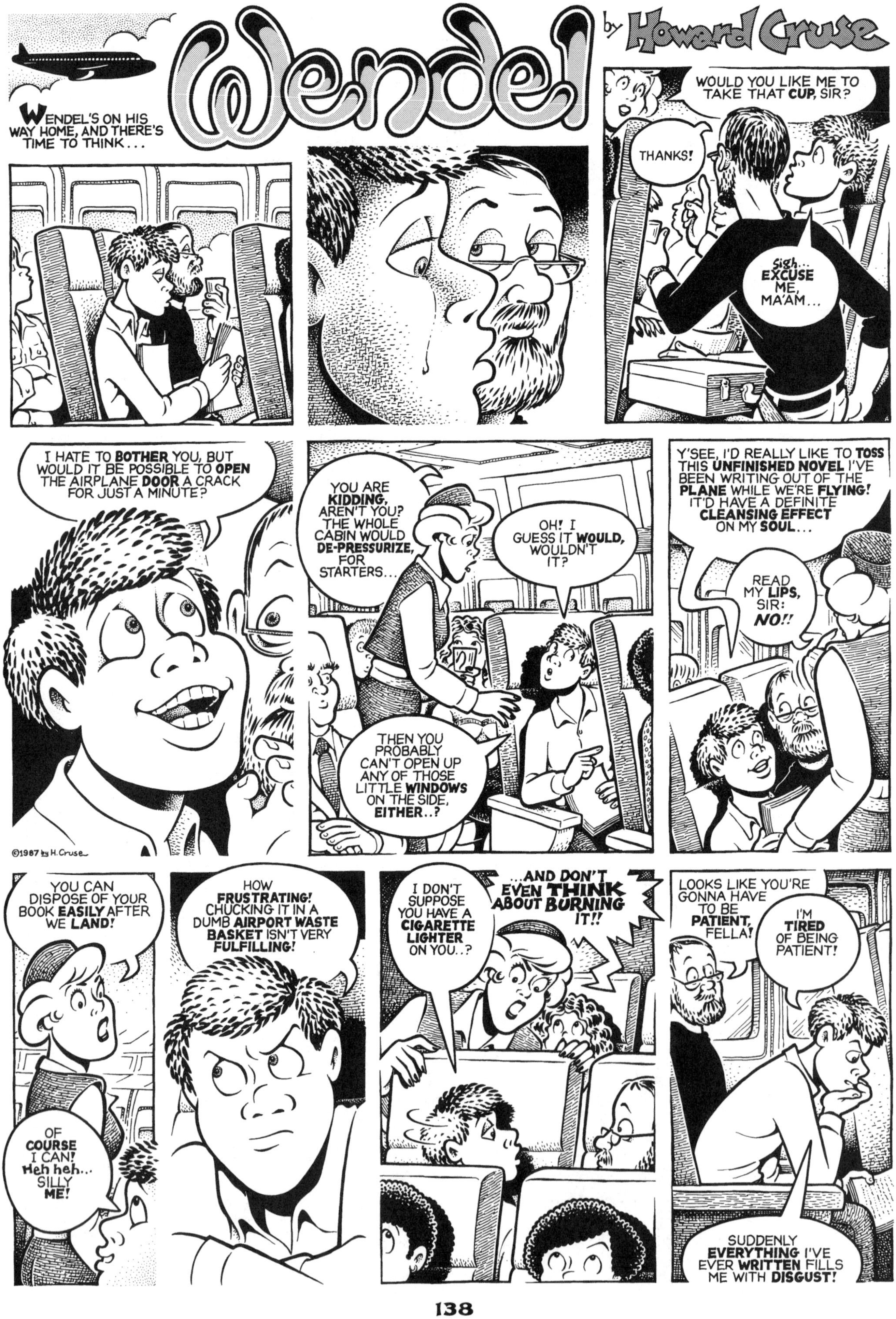
Wendel
by Howard Cruse
WENDEL'S ON HIS WAY HOME, AND THERE'S TIME TO THINK...
WOULD YOU LIKE ME TO TAKE THAT CUP, SIR?
THANKS!
Sigh... EXCUSE ME, MA'AM...
I HATE TO BOTHER YOU, BUT WOULD IT BE POSSIBLE TO OPEN THE AIRPLANE DOOR A CRACK FOR JUST A MINUTE?
©1987 by H. Cruse
YOU ARE KIDDING, AREN'T YOU? THE WHOLE CABIN WOULD DE-PRESSURIZE, FOR STARTERS...
OH! I GUESS IT WOULD, WOULDN'T IT?
THEN YOU PROBABLY CAN'T OPEN UP ANY OF THOSE LITTLE WINDOWS ON THE SIDE, EITHER..?
Y'SEE, I'D REALLY LIKE TO TOSS THIS UNFINISHED NOVEL I'VE BEEN WRITING OUT OF THE PLANE WHILE WE'RE FLYING! IT'D HAVE A DEFINITE CLEANSING EFFECT ON MY SOUL...
READ MY LIPS, SIR: NO!!
YOU CAN DISPOSE OF YOUR BOOK EASILY AFTER WE LAND!
OF COURSE I CAN! Heh heh... SILLY ME!
HOW FRUSTRATING! CHUCKING IT IN A DUMB AIRPORT WASTE BASKET ISN'T VERY FULFILLING!
I DON'T SUPPOSE YOU HAVE A CIGARETTE LIGHTER ON YOU..?
...AND DON'T EVEN THINK ABOUT BURNING IT!!
LOOKS LIKE YOU'RE GONNA HAVE TO BE PATIENT, FELLA!
I'M TIRED OF BEING PATIENT!
SUDDENLY EVERYTHING I'VE EVER WRITTEN FILLS ME WITH DISGUST!

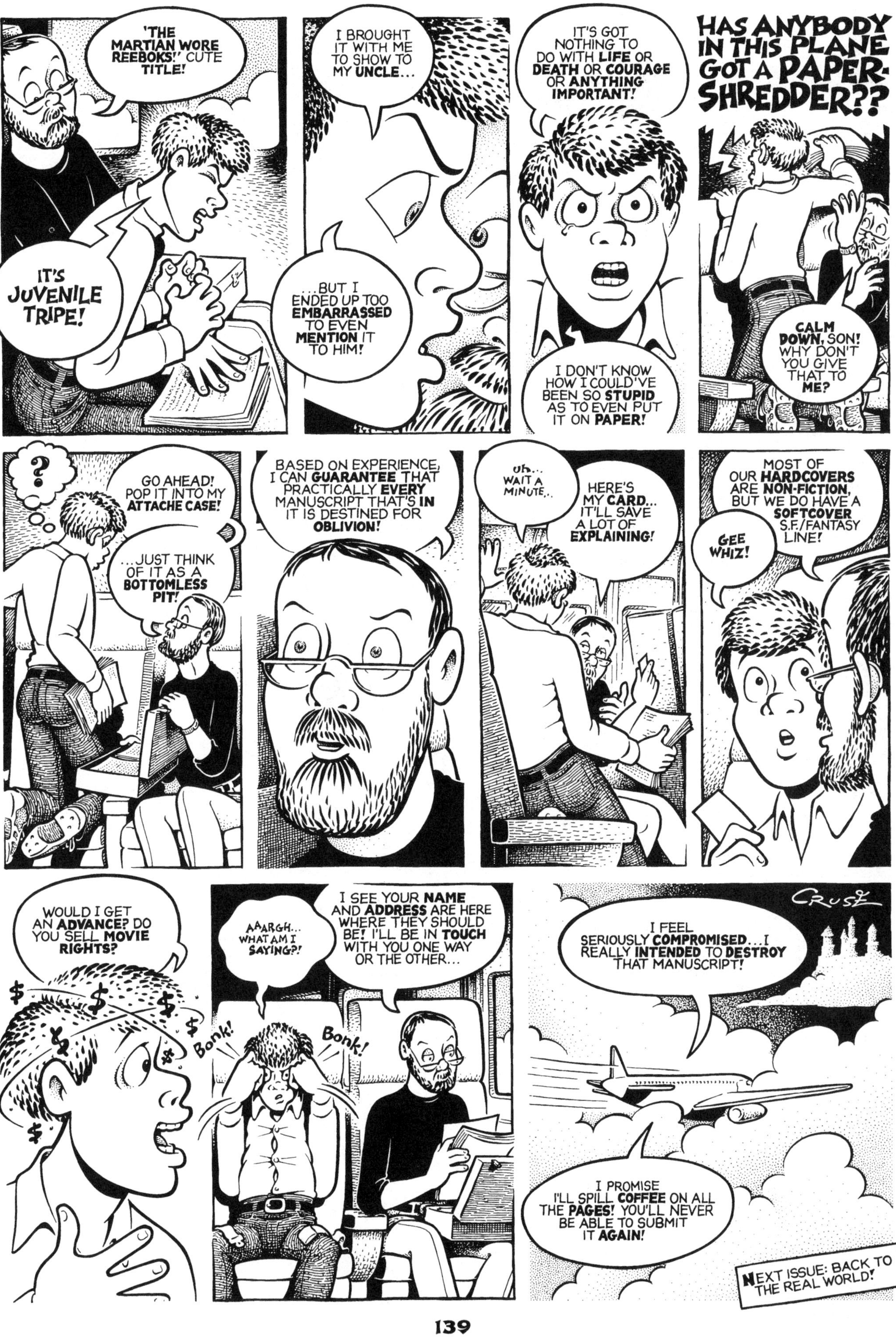
'THE MARTIAN WORE REEBOKS!' CUTE TITLE!
IT'S JUVENILE TRIPE!
I BROUGHT IT WITH ME TO SHOW TO MY UNCLE...
...BUT I ENDED UP TOO EMBARRASSED TO EVEN MENTION IT TO HIM!
IT'S GOT NOTHING TO DO WITH LIFE OR DEATH OR COURAGE OR ANYTHING IMPORTANT!
I DON'T KNOW HOW I COULD'VE BEEN SO STUPID AS TO EVEN PUT IT ON PAPER!
HAS ANYBODY IN THIS PLANE GOT A PAPER-SHREDDER??
CALM DOWN, SON! WHY DON'T YOU GIVE THAT TO ME?
?
GO AHEAD! POP IT INTO MY ATTACHE CASE!
...JUST THINK OF IT AS A BOTTOMLESS PIT!
BASED ON EXPERIENCE, I CAN GUARANTEE THAT PRACTICALLY EVERY MANUSCRIPT THAT'S IN IT IS DESTINED FOR OBLIVION!
uh... WAIT A MINUTE...
HERE'S MY CARD... IT'LL SAVE A LOT OF EXPLAINING!
MOST OF OUR HARDCOVERS ARE NON-FICTION, BUT WE DO HAVE A SOFTCOVER S.F./FANTASY LINE!
GEE WHIZ!
WOULD I GET AN ADVANCE? DO YOU SELL MOVIE RIGHTS?
AAARGH... WHAT AM I SAYING?!
I SEE YOUR NAME AND ADDRESS ARE HERE WHERE THEY SHOULD BE! I'LL BE IN TOUCH WITH YOU ONE WAY OR THE OTHER...
Bonk!
Bonk!
CRUSE
I FEEL SERIOUSLY COMPROMISED...I REALLY INTENDED TO DESTROY THAT MANUSCRIPT!
I PROMISE I'LL SPILL COFFEE ON ALL THE PAGES! YOU'LL NEVER BE ABLE TO SUBMIT IT AGAIN!
NEXT ISSUE: BACK TO THE REAL WORLD!

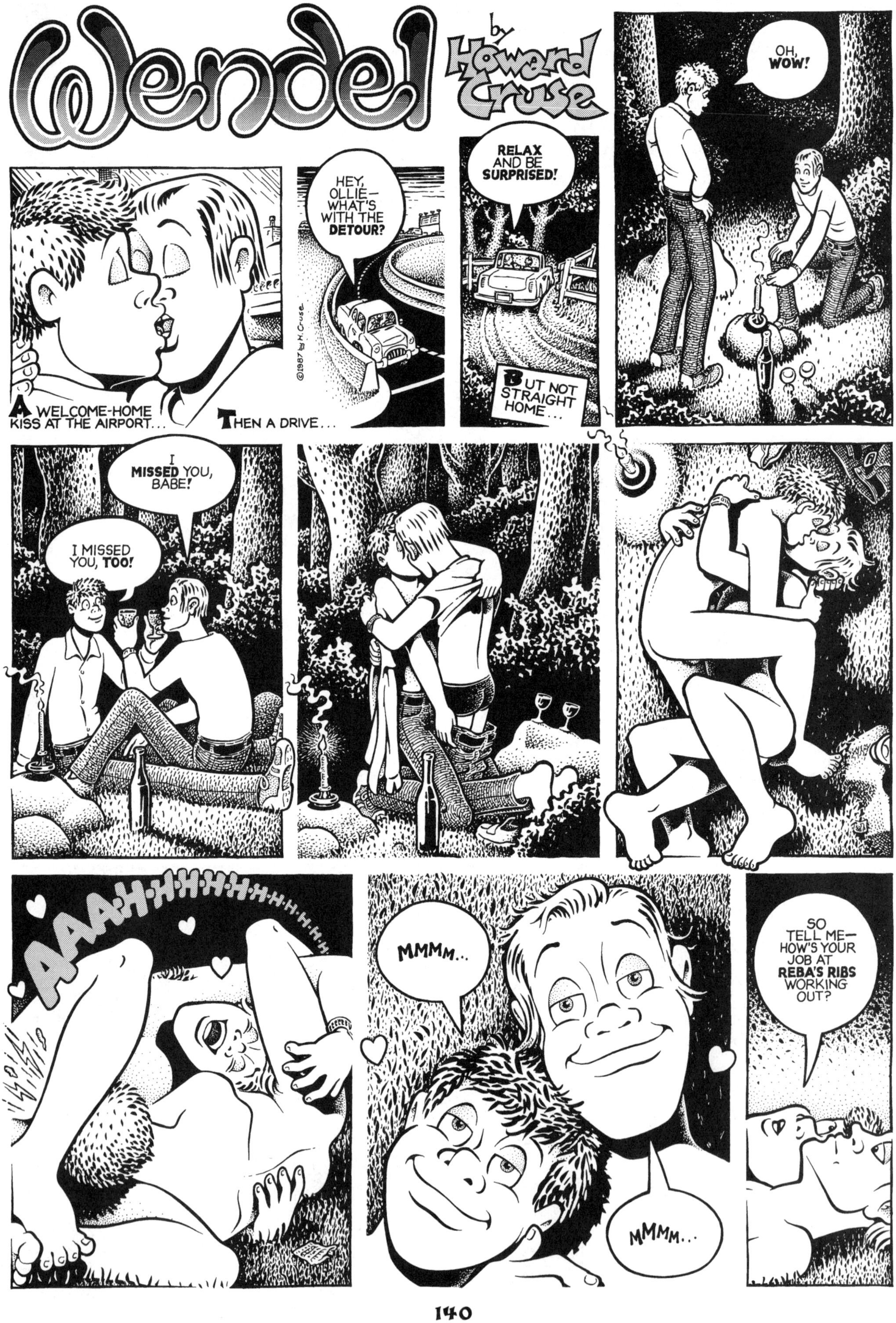
Wendel
by Howard Cruse
OH, WOW!
HEY, OLLIE— WHAT'S WITH THE DETOUR?
©1987 by H. Cruse
RELAX AND BE SURPRISED!
A WELCOME-HOME KISS AT THE AIRPORT...
THEN A DRIVE...
BUT NOT STRAIGHT HOME...
I MISSED YOU, BABE!
I MISSED YOU, TOO!
AAAH-H-H-H-H-H-H-H-H-H-H-H-H-H
MMMM...
MMMM...
SO TELL ME— HOW'S YOUR JOB AT REBA'S RIBS WORKING OUT?

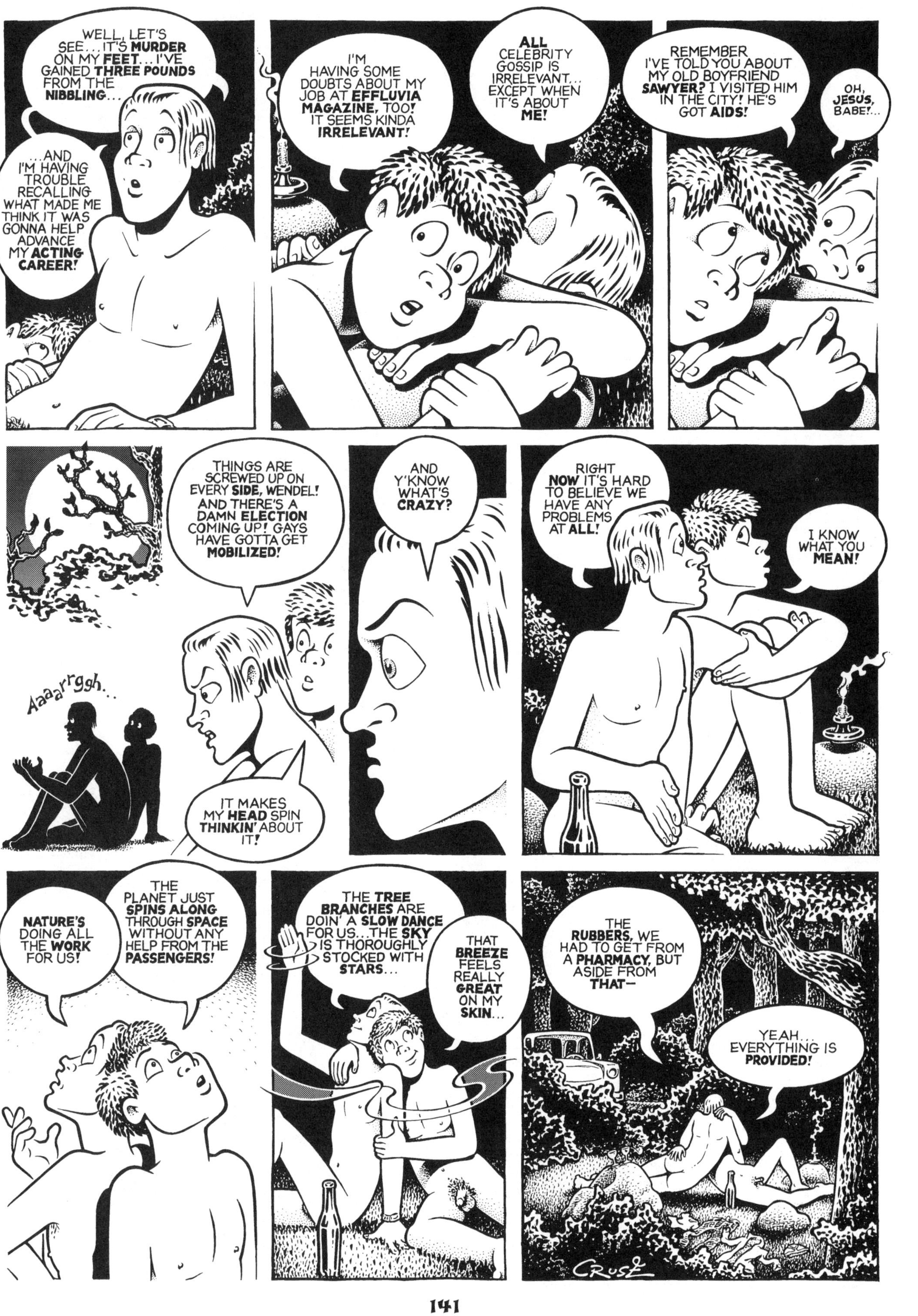
WELL, LET'S SEE... IT'S MURDER ON MY FEET... I'VE GAINED THREE POUNDS FROM THE NIBBLING...
...AND I'M HAVING TROUBLE RECALLING WHAT MADE ME THINK IT WAS GONNA HELP ADVANCE MY ACTING CAREER!
I'M HAVING SOME DOUBTS ABOUT MY JOB AT EFFLUVIA MAGAZINE, TOO! IT SEEMS KINDA IRRELEVANT!
ALL CELEBRITY GOSSIP IS IRRELEVANT... EXCEPT WHEN IT'S ABOUT ME!
REMEMBER I'VE TOLD YOU ABOUT MY OLD BOYFRIEND SAWYER? I VISITED HIM IN THE CITY! HE'S GOT AIDS!
OH, JESUS, BABE!...
Aaaarrggh...
THINGS ARE SCREWED UP ON EVERY SIDE, WENDEL! AND THERE'S A DAMN ELECTION COMING UP! GAYS HAVE GOTTA GET MOBILIZED!
IT MAKES MY HEAD SPIN THINKIN' ABOUT IT!
AND Y'KNOW WHAT'S CRAZY?
RIGHT NOW IT'S HARD TO BELIEVE WE HAVE ANY PROBLEMS AT ALL!
I KNOW WHAT YOU MEAN!
NATURE'S DOING ALL THE WORK FOR US!
THE PLANET JUST SPINS ALONG THROUGH SPACE WITHOUT ANY HELP FROM THE PASSENGERS!
THE TREE BRANCHES ARE DOIN' A SLOW DANCE FOR US... THE SKY IS THOROUGHLY STOCKED WITH STARS...
THAT BREEZE FEELS REALLY GREAT ON MY SKIN...
THE RUBBERS, WE HAD TO GET FROM A PHARMACY, BUT ASIDE FROM THAT–
YEAH... EVERYTHING IS PROVIDED!
CRUSE

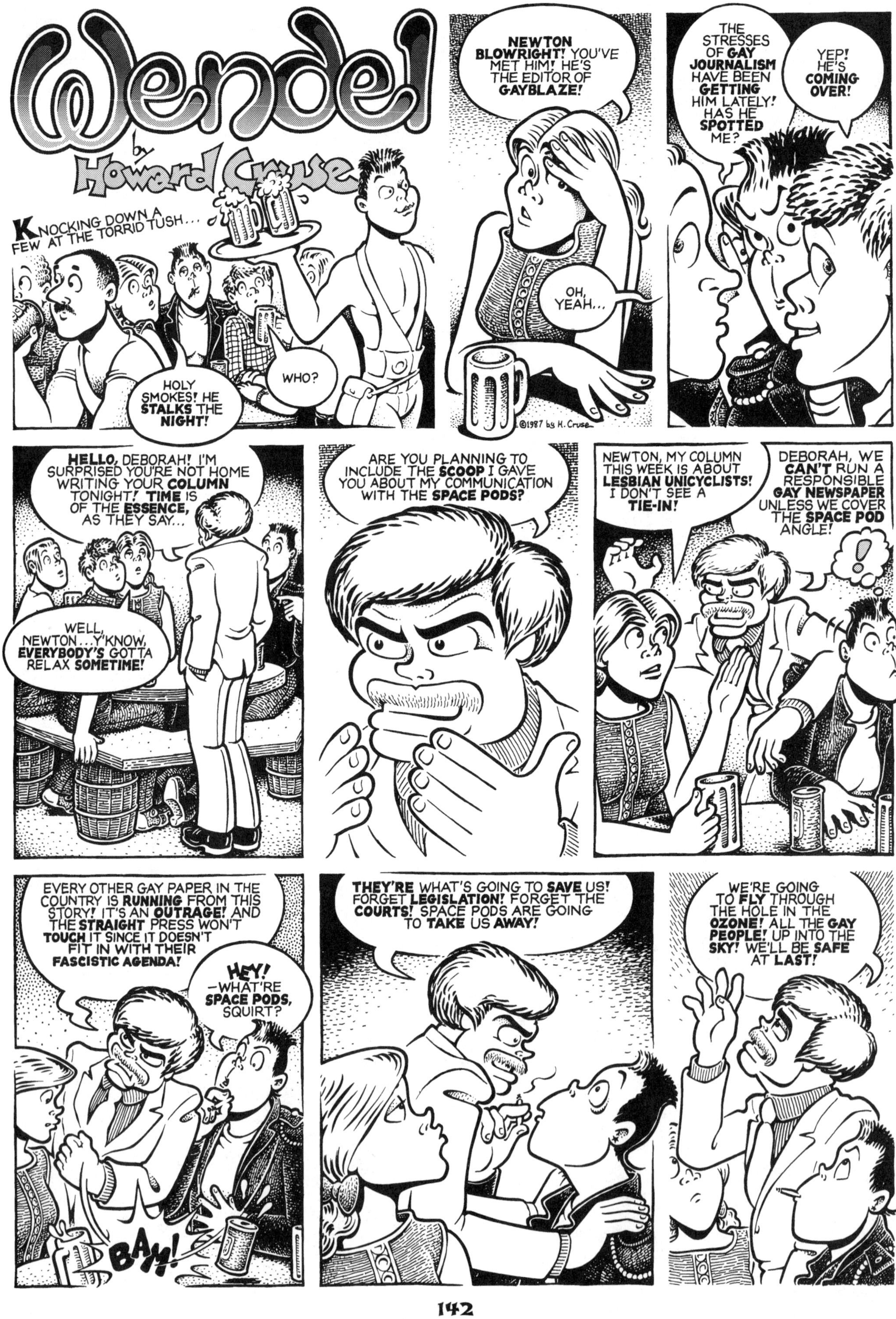

Wendel
by Howard Cruse
Knocking down a few at the Torrid Tush...
Holy smokes! He stalks the night!
Who?
©1987 by H. Cruse
Newton Blowright! You've met him! He's the editor of Gayblaze!
Oh, yeah...
The stresses of gay journalism have been getting him lately! Has he spotted me?
Yep! He's coming over!
Hello, Deborah! I'm surprised you're not home writing your column tonight! Time is of the essence, as they say...
Well, Newton... y'know, everybody's gotta relax sometime!
Are you planning to include the scoop I gave you about my communication with the space pods?
Newton, my column this week is about lesbian unicyclists! I don't see a tie-in!
Deborah, we can't run a responsible gay newspaper unless we cover the space pod angle!
!
Every other gay paper in the country is running from this story! It's an outrage! And the straight press won't touch it since it doesn't fit in with their fascistic agenda!
Hey! —What're space pods, squirt?
BAM!
They're what's going to save us! Forget legislation! Forget the courts! Space pods are going to take us away!
We're going to fly through the hole in the ozone! All the gay people! Up into the sky! We'll be safe at last!

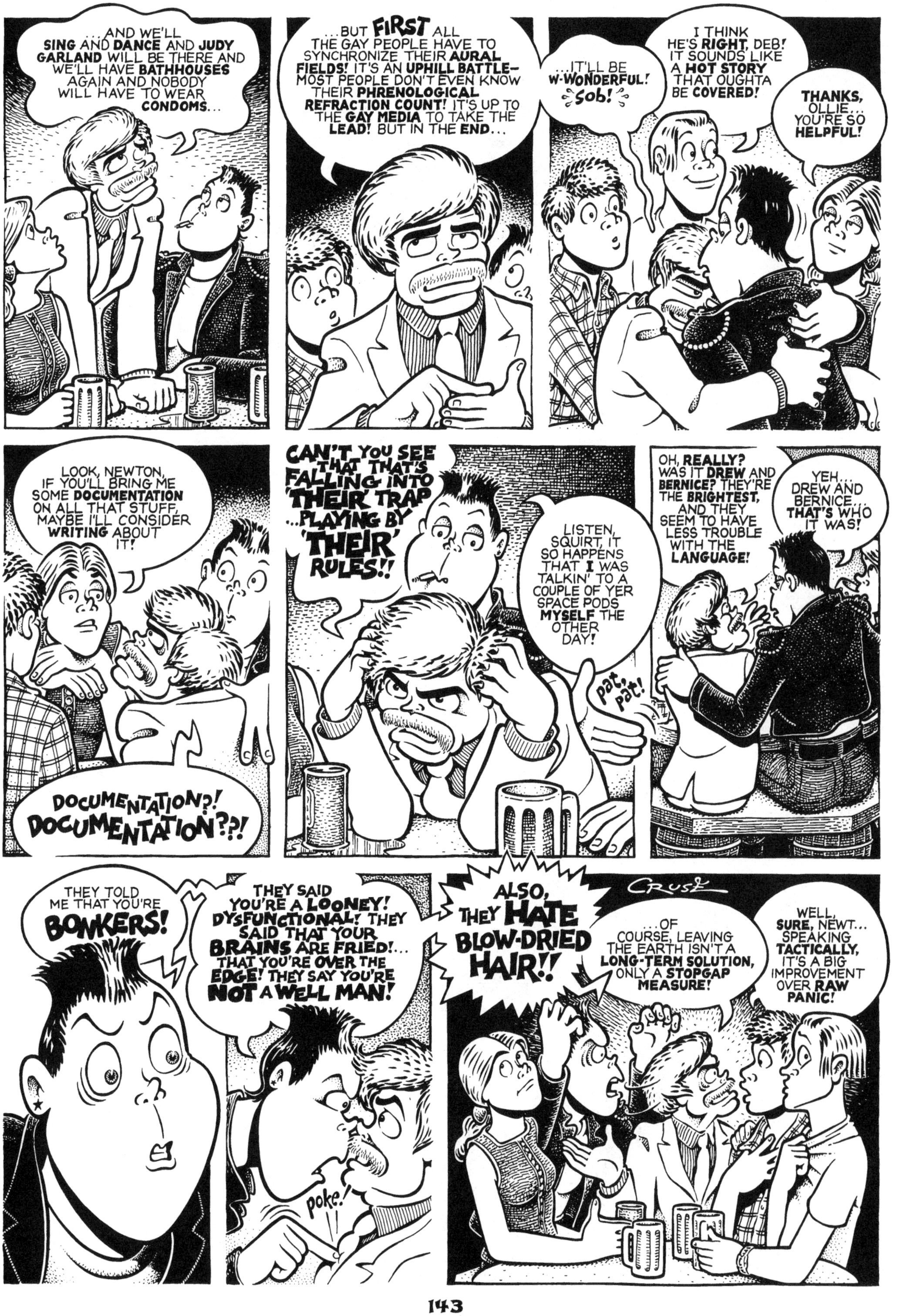

...AND WE'LL SING AND DANCE AND JUDY GARLAND WILL BE THERE AND WE'LL HAVE BATHHOUSES AGAIN AND NOBODY WILL HAVE TO WEAR CONDOMS...
...BUT FIRST ALL THE GAY PEOPLE HAVE TO SYNCHRONIZE THEIR AURAL FIELDS! IT'S AN UPHILL BATTLE— MOST PEOPLE DON'T EVEN KNOW THEIR PHRENOLOGICAL REFRACTION COUNT! IT'S UP TO THE GAY MEDIA TO TAKE THE LEAD! BUT IN THE END...
...IT'LL BE W-WONDERFUL! Sob!
I THINK HE'S RIGHT, DEB! IT SOUNDS LIKE A HOT STORY THAT OUGHTA BE COVERED!
THANKS, OLLIE... YOU'RE SO HELPFUL!
LOOK, NEWTON, IF YOU'LL BRING ME SOME DOCUMENTATION ON ALL THAT STUFF, MAYBE I'LL CONSIDER WRITING ABOUT IT!
DOCUMENTATION?! DOCUMENTATION?!?!
CAN'T YOU SEE THAT THAT'S FALLING INTO 'THEIR' TRAP ...PLAYING BY 'THEIR' RULES?!
LISTEN, SQUIRT, IT SO HAPPENS THAT I WAS TALKIN' TO A COUPLE OF YER SPACE PODS MYSELF THE OTHER DAY!
pat, pat!
OH, REALLY? WAS IT DREW AND BERNICE? THEY'RE THE BRIGHTEST, AND THEY SEEM TO HAVE LESS TROUBLE WITH THE LANGUAGE!
YEH... DREW AND BERNICE... THAT'S WHO IT WAS!
THEY TOLD ME THAT YOU'RE BONKERS!
THEY SAID YOU'RE A LOONEY! DYSFUNCTIONAL! THEY SAID THAT YOUR BRAINS ARE FRIED!... THAT YOU'RE OVER THE EDGE! THEY SAY YOU'RE NOT A WELL MAN!
poke!
ALSO, THEY HATE BLOW-DRIED HAIR!!
CRUSE
...OF COURSE, LEAVING THE EARTH ISN'T A LONG-TERM SOLUTION, ONLY A STOPGAP MEASURE!
WELL, SURE, NEWT... SPEAKING TACTICALLY, IT'S A BIG IMPROVEMENT OVER RAW PANIC!

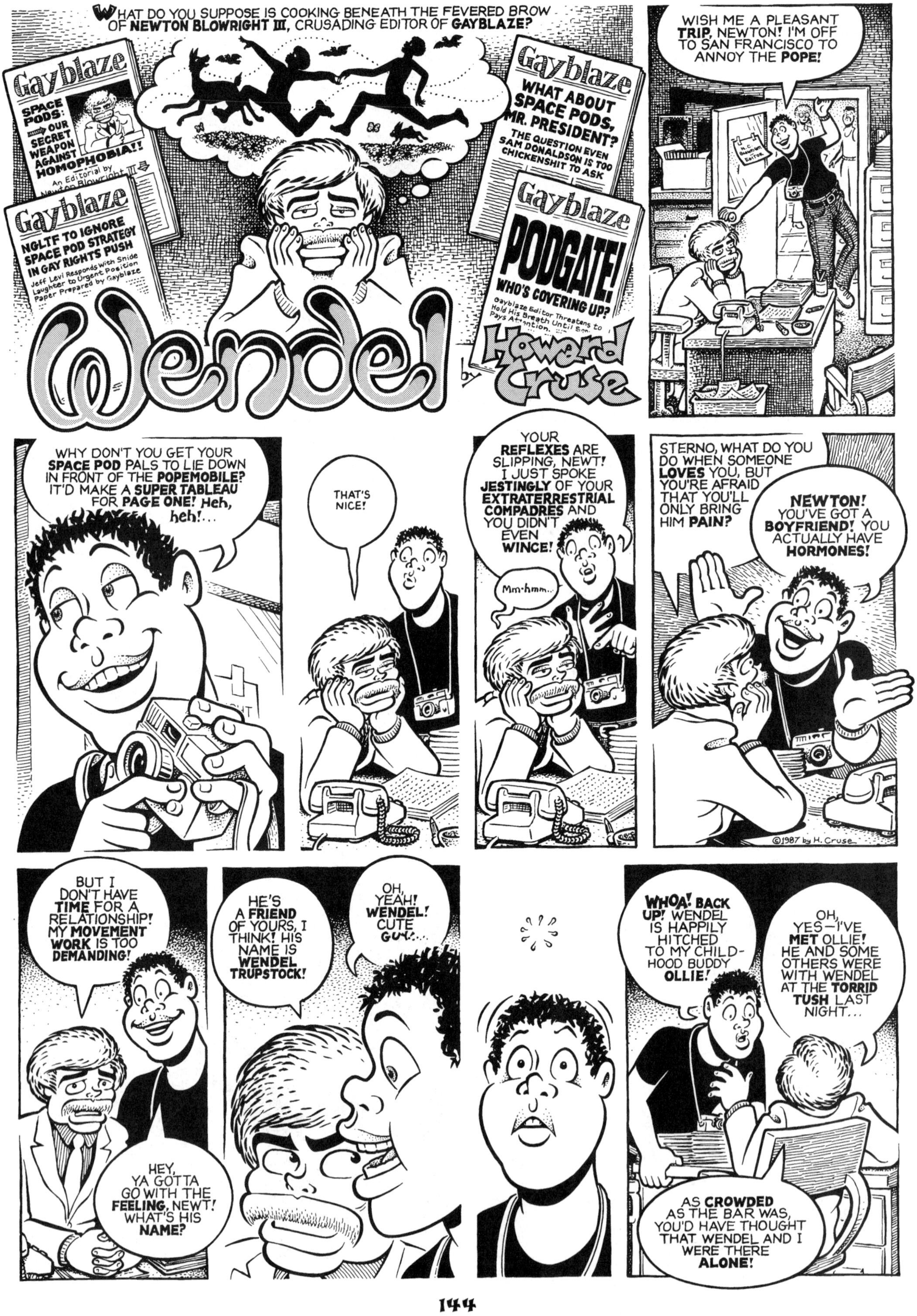
WHAT DO YOU SUPPOSE IS COOKING BENEATH THE FEVERED BROW OF NEWTON BLOWRIGHT III, CRUSADING EDITOR OF GAYBLAZE?
Gayblaze
SPACE PODS: OUR SECRET WEAPON AGAINST HOMOPHOBIA!!
An Editorial by
Gayblaze
NGLTF TO IGNORE SPACE POD STRATEGY IN GAY RIGHTS PUSH
Jeff Levi Responds With Snide Laughter to Urgent Position Paper Prepared by Gayblaze
Gayblaze
WHAT ABOUT SPACE PODS, MR. PRESIDENT?
THE QUESTION EVEN SAM DONALDSON IS TOO CHICKENSHIT TO ASK
Gayblaze
PODGATE!
WHO'S COVERING UP?
Gayblaze Editor Threatens to Hold His Breath Until
Wendel
by Howard Cruse
WISH ME A PLEASANT TRIP, NEWTON! I'M OFF TO SAN FRANCISCO TO ANNOY THE POPE!
WHY DON'T YOU GET YOUR SPACE POD PALS TO LIE DOWN IN FRONT OF THE POPEMOBILE? IT'D MAKE A SUPER TABLEAU FOR PAGE ONE! Heh, heh!...
THAT'S NICE!
YOUR REFLEXES ARE SLIPPING, NEWT! I JUST SPOKE JESTINGLY OF YOUR EXTRATERRESTRIAL COMPADRES AND YOU DIDN'T EVEN WINCE!
Mm-hmm...
STERNO, WHAT DO YOU DO WHEN SOMEONE LOVES YOU, BUT YOU'RE AFRAID THAT YOU'LL ONLY BRING HIM PAIN?
NEWTON! YOU'VE GOT A BOYFRIEND! YOU ACTUALLY HAVE HORMONES!
©1987 by H. Cruse
BUT I DON'T HAVE TIME FOR A RELATIONSHIP! MY MOVEMENT WORK IS TOO DEMANDING!
HEY, YA GOTTA GO WITH THE FEELING, NEWT! WHAT'S HIS NAME?
HE'S A FRIEND OF YOURS, I THINK! HIS NAME IS WENDEL TRUPSTOCK!
OH, YEAH! WENDEL! CUTE GUY!...
WHOA! BACK UP! WENDEL IS HAPPILY HITCHED TO MY CHILDHOOD BUDDY OLLIE!
OH, YES—I'VE MET OLLIE! HE AND SOME OTHERS WERE WITH WENDEL AT THE TORRID TUSH LAST NIGHT...
AS CROWDED AS THE BAR WAS, YOU'D HAVE THOUGHT THAT WENDEL AND I WERE THERE ALONE!

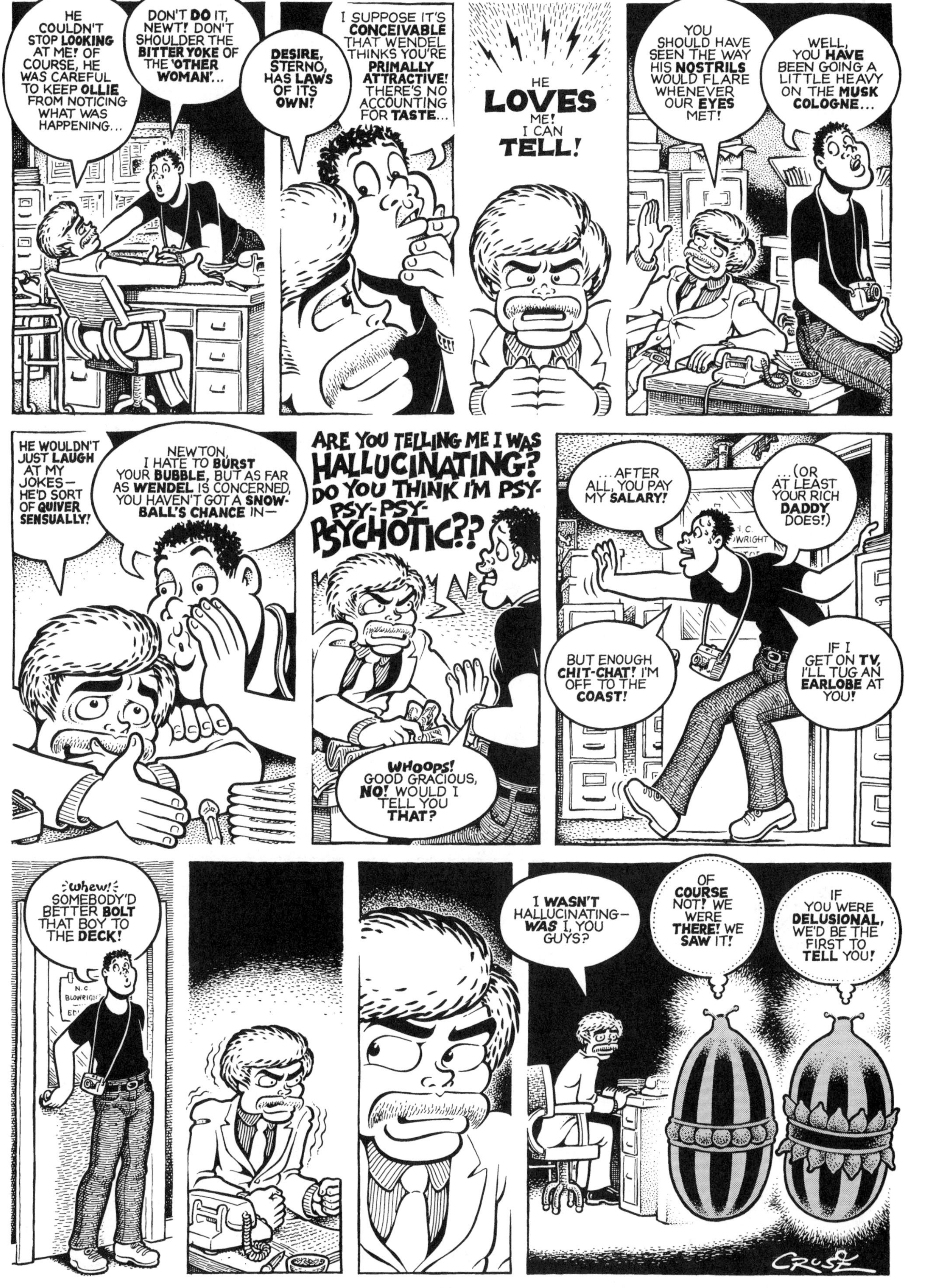

HE COULDN'T STOP LOOKING AT ME! OF COURSE, HE WAS CAREFUL TO KEEP OLLIE FROM NOTICING WHAT WAS HAPPENING...
DON'T DO IT, NEWT! DON'T SHOULDER THE BITTER YOKE OF THE 'OTHER WOMAN'...
DESIRE, STERNO, HAS LAWS OF ITS OWN!
I SUPPOSE IT'S CONCEIVABLE THAT WENDEL THINKS YOU'RE PRIMALLY ATTRACTIVE! THERE'S NO ACCOUNTING FOR TASTE...
HE LOVES ME! I CAN TELL!
YOU SHOULD HAVE SEEN THE WAY HIS NOSTRILS WOULD FLARE WHENEVER OUR EYES MET!
WELL, YOU HAVE BEEN GOING A LITTLE HEAVY ON THE MUSK COLOGNE...
HE WOULDN'T JUST LAUGH AT MY JOKES— HE'D SORT OF QUIVER SENSUALLY!
NEWTON, I HATE TO BURST YOUR BUBBLE, BUT AS FAR AS WENDEL IS CONCERNED, YOU HAVEN'T GOT A SNOW-BALL'S CHANCE IN—
ARE YOU TELLING ME I WAS HALLUCINATING? DO YOU THINK I'M PSY-PSY-PSY-PSYCHOTIC??
WHOOPS! GOOD GRACIOUS, NO! WOULD I TELL YOU THAT?
...AFTER ALL, YOU PAY MY SALARY!
...(OR AT LEAST YOUR RICH DADDY DOES!)
BUT ENOUGH CHIT-CHAT! I'M OFF TO THE COAST!
IF I GET ON TV, I'LL TUG AN EARLOBE AT YOU!
whew! SOMEBODY'D BETTER BOLT THAT BOY TO THE DECK!
N.C. BLOWRIGHT
I WASN'T HALLUCINATING— WAS I, YOU GUYS?
OF COURSE NOT! WE WERE THERE! WE SAW IT!
IF YOU WERE DELUSIONAL, WE'D BE THE FIRST TO TELL YOU!
CRUSE

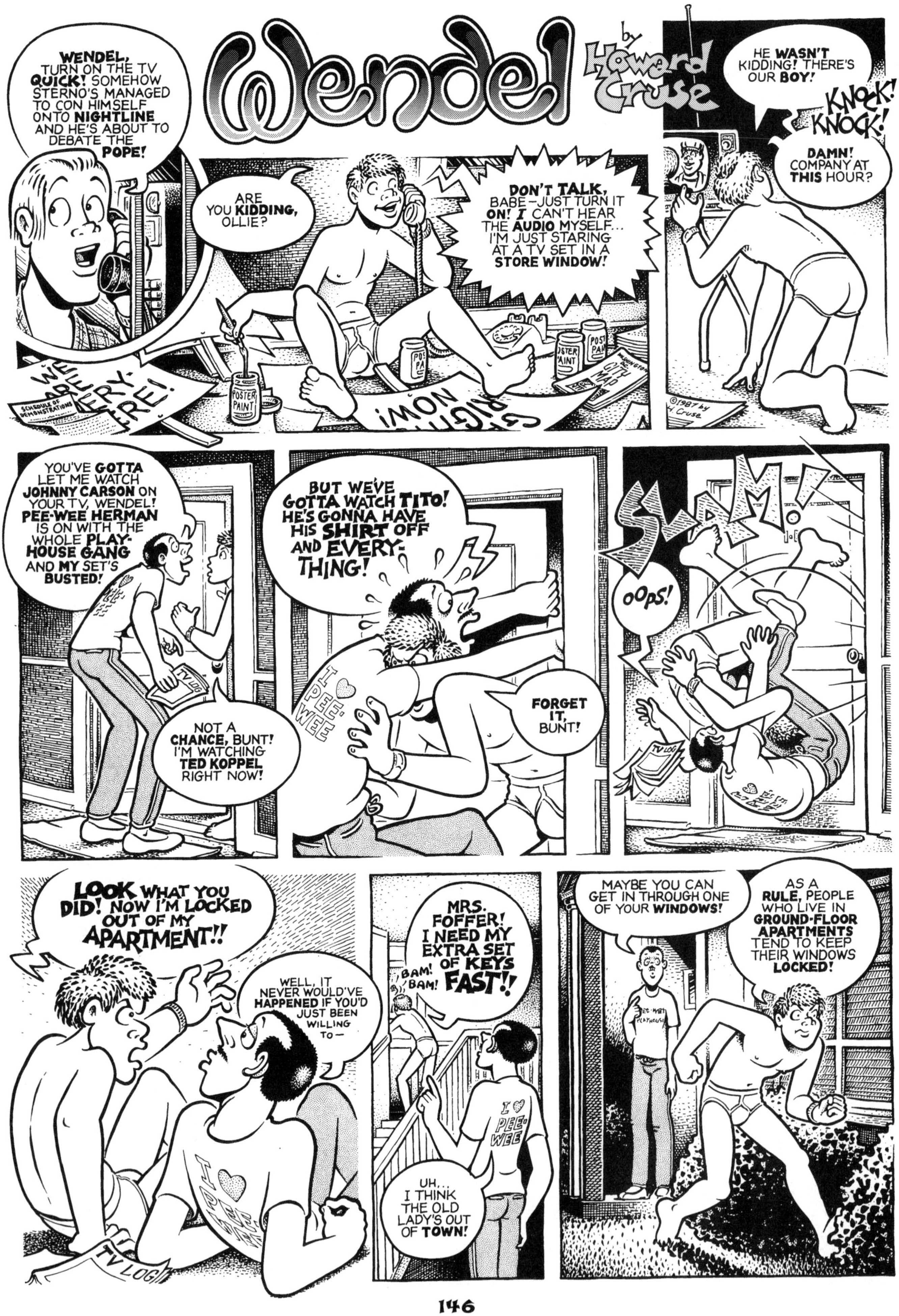

Wendel
by Howard Cruse
WENDEL, TURN ON THE TV QUICK! SOMEHOW STERNO'S MANAGED TO CON HIMSELF ONTO NIGHTLINE AND HE'S ABOUT TO DEBATE THE POPE!
ARE YOU KIDDING, OLLIE?
DON'T TALK, BABE—JUST TURN IT ON! I CAN'T HEAR THE AUDIO MYSELF... I'M JUST STARING AT A TV SET IN A STORE WINDOW!
POSTER PAINT
SCHEDULE OF DEMONSTRATIONS
CITY MAP
©1987 by H Cruse
HE WASN'T KIDDING! THERE'S OUR BOY!
KNOCK! KNOCK!
DAMN! COMPANY AT THIS HOUR?
YOU'VE GOTTA LET ME WATCH JOHNNY CARSON ON YOUR TV, WENDEL! PEE-WEE HERMAN IS ON WITH THE WHOLE PLAY-HOUSE GANG AND MY SET'S BUSTED!
TV LOG
NOT A CHANCE, BUNT! I'M WATCHING TED KOPPEL RIGHT NOW!
BUT WE'VE GOTTA WATCH TITO! HE'S GONNA HAVE HIS SHIRT OFF AND EVERY-THING!
I ♥ PEE-WEE
FORGET IT, BUNT!
SLAM!
OOPS!
LOOK WHAT YOU DID! NOW I'M LOCKED OUT OF MY APARTMENT!!
WELL, IT NEVER WOULD'VE HAPPENED IF YOU'D JUST BEEN WILLING TO—
TV LOG
BAM! BAM!
MRS. FOFFER! I NEED MY EXTRA SET OF KEYS FAST!!
UH... I THINK THE OLD LADY'S OUT OF TOWN!
MAYBE YOU CAN GET IN THROUGH ONE OF YOUR WINDOWS!
AS A RULE, PEOPLE WHO LIVE IN GROUND-FLOOR APARTMENTS TEND TO KEEP THEIR WINDOWS LOCKED!

IT'S **MADDENING!** I CAN **SEE** STERNO AND THE POPE ON THE **SCREEN** BUT I CAN'T HEAR WHAT THEY'RE **SAYING!**

THERE'S A WINDOW OVER **THERE** THAT OPENS UP A LITTLE BIT...

YEAH, BUT IT'S THE KIND WITH THESE STUPID **LOUVERS** THAT ONLY OPEN SO FAR...

Ahem!

IT'S **O.K.,** OFFICER— HE **LIVES** HERE...

?

PEE-WEE PLAYHO

YOU'D BETTER GET INSIDE AND PUT SOME **CLOTHES** ON, FELLA...

OFFICER, I'M GETTING INSIDE AS FAST AS I— **OH, SHIT!** NOW MY PHONE'S RINGING AGAIN!

PEE-WEE PLAYHO

RING!

RING!

STRICTLY SPEAKING, CITIZENS SHOULDN'T SAY 'SHIT' TO POLICE OFFICERS...

Grunt!

RING!!!

HELLO, WENDEL? THIS IS YOUR **MOTHER!** ARE YOU AND OLLIE WATCHING **NIGHTLINE?**

YOUR FRIEND **STERNO** IS DEBATING THE **POPE** ABOUT **GAY RIGHTS** AND HE'S GOT HIS HOLINESS RUNNING AROUND IN **CIRCLES!**

JUST NOW THE POPE CONCEDED THAT OF **COURSE** GOD WOULDN'T WANT ANYBODY **PUT DOWN** JUST BECAUSE THEY DON'T FIT SOME **RIGID STANDARD** FOR WHAT A MAN OR WOMAN IS **SUPPOSED** TO BE!

...AND HE SAYS IT'S **ALL RIGHT** FOR BOYS TO WEAR **LIPSTICK** AND **ROUGE** IF IT MAKES THEM **FEEL GOOD!**

POLICE

NOW **WAIT** A MINUTE, MOM...

...THAT CAN'T BE THE **POPE** TALKING— THAT'S **PEE-WEE HERMAN!**

OH... YOU'RE **RIGHT,** DEAR! YOUR FATHER SWITCHED **CHANNELS** WHEN I WASN'T **LOOKING!**

WELL, THERE'S ONLY **SO MUCH** OF THAT VATICAN LINE I CAN **TAKE!**

Next issue: ON THE ROAD TO WASHINGTON

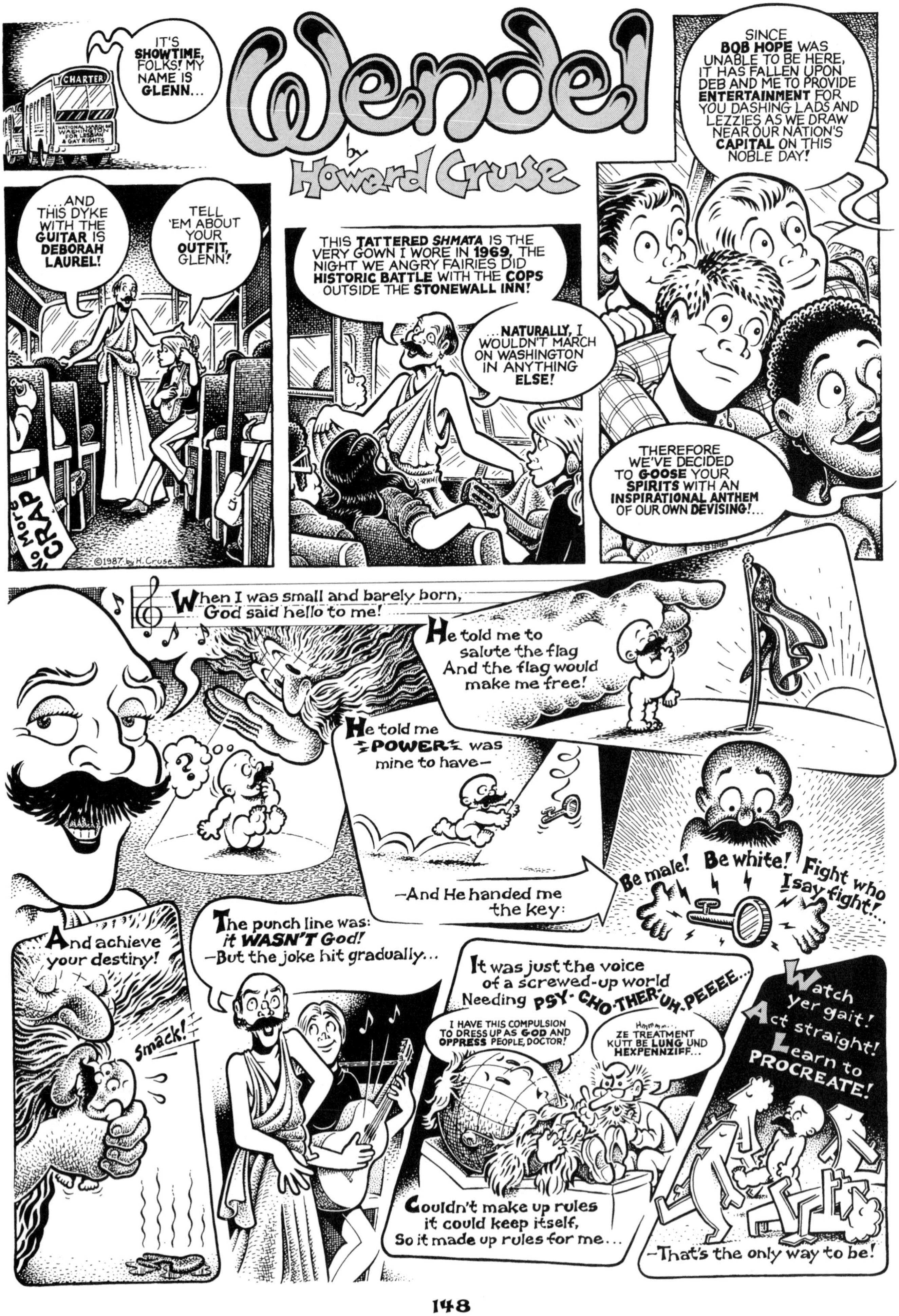
CHARTER
NATIONAL MARCH ON WASHINGTON FOR LESBIAN & GAY RIGHTS
IT'S SHOWTIME, FOLKS! MY NAME IS GLENN...
Wendel
by Howard Cruse
SINCE BOB HOPE WAS UNABLE TO BE HERE, IT HAS FALLEN UPON DEB AND ME TO PROVIDE ENTERTAINMENT FOR YOU DASHING LADS AND LEZZIES AS WE DRAW NEAR OUR NATION'S CAPITAL ON THIS NOBLE DAY!
...AND THIS DYKE WITH THE GUITAR IS DEBORAH LAUREL!
TELL 'EM ABOUT YOUR OUTFIT, GLENN!
No More CRAP
©1987 by H. Cruse
THIS TATTERED SHMATA IS THE VERY GOWN I WORE IN 1969, THE NIGHT WE ANGRY FAIRIES DID HISTORIC BATTLE WITH THE COPS OUTSIDE THE STONEWALL INN!
...NATURALLY, I WOULDN'T MARCH ON WASHINGTON IN ANYTHING ELSE!
THEREFORE WE'VE DECIDED TO GOOSE YOUR SPIRITS WITH AN INSPIRATIONAL ANTHEM OF OUR OWN DEVISING!...
When I was small and barely born, God said hello to me!
He told me to salute the flag And the flag would make me free!
He told me POWER was mine to have—
—And He handed me the key:
Be male! Be white! Fight who I say fight!...
And achieve your destiny!
Smack!
The punch line was: it WASN'T God! —But the joke hit gradually...
It was just the voice of a screwed-up world Needing PSY-CHO-THER-UH-PEEEE...
I HAVE THIS COMPULSION TO DRESS UP AS GOD AND OPPRESS PEOPLE, DOCTOR!
Hmmm... ZE TREATMENT KUTT BE LUNG UND HEXPENNZIFF...
Couldn't make up rules it could keep itself, So it made up rules for me...
Watch yer gait! Act straight! Learn to PROCREATE!
—That's the only way to be!

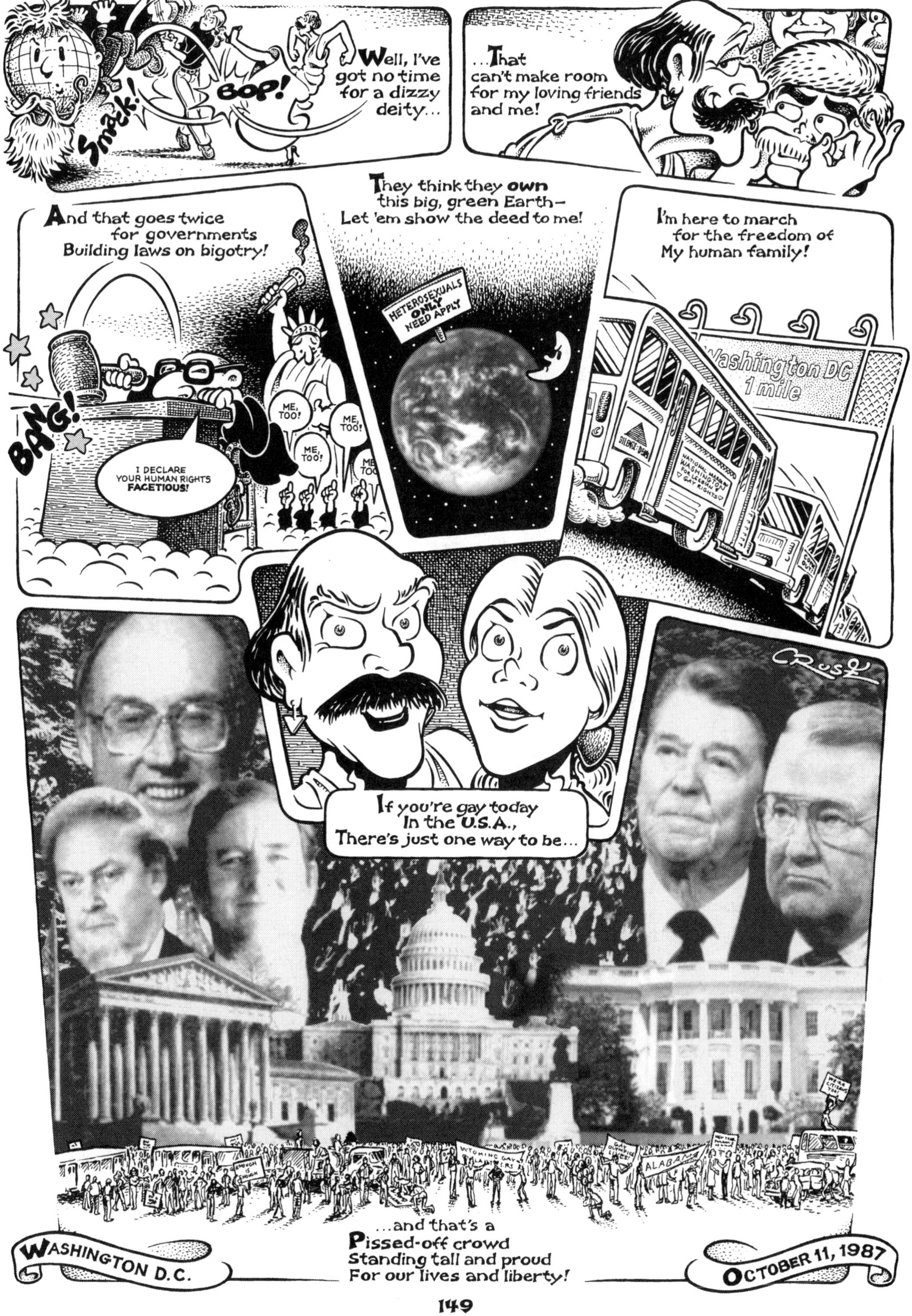
SMACK!
BOP!
Well, I've got no time for a dizzy deity...
...That can't make room for my loving friends and me!
And that goes twice for governments Building laws on bigotry!
BANG!
I DECLARE YOUR HUMAN RIGHTS FACETIOUS!
ME, TOO!
ME, TOO!
ME, TOO!
They think they own this big, green Earth– Let 'em show the deed to me!
HETEROSEXUALS ONLY NEED APPLY
I'm here to march for the freedom of My human family!
Washington DC 1 mile
SILENCE=DEATH
NATIONAL MARCH ON WASHINGTON FOR LESBIAN ♡ GAY RIGHTS ♡
CRUSE
If you're gay today In the U.S.A., There's just one way to be...
WYOMING GAYS
ALABAMA
...and that's a Pissed-off crowd Standing tall and proud For our lives and liberty!
WASHINGTON D.C.
OCTOBER 11, 1987

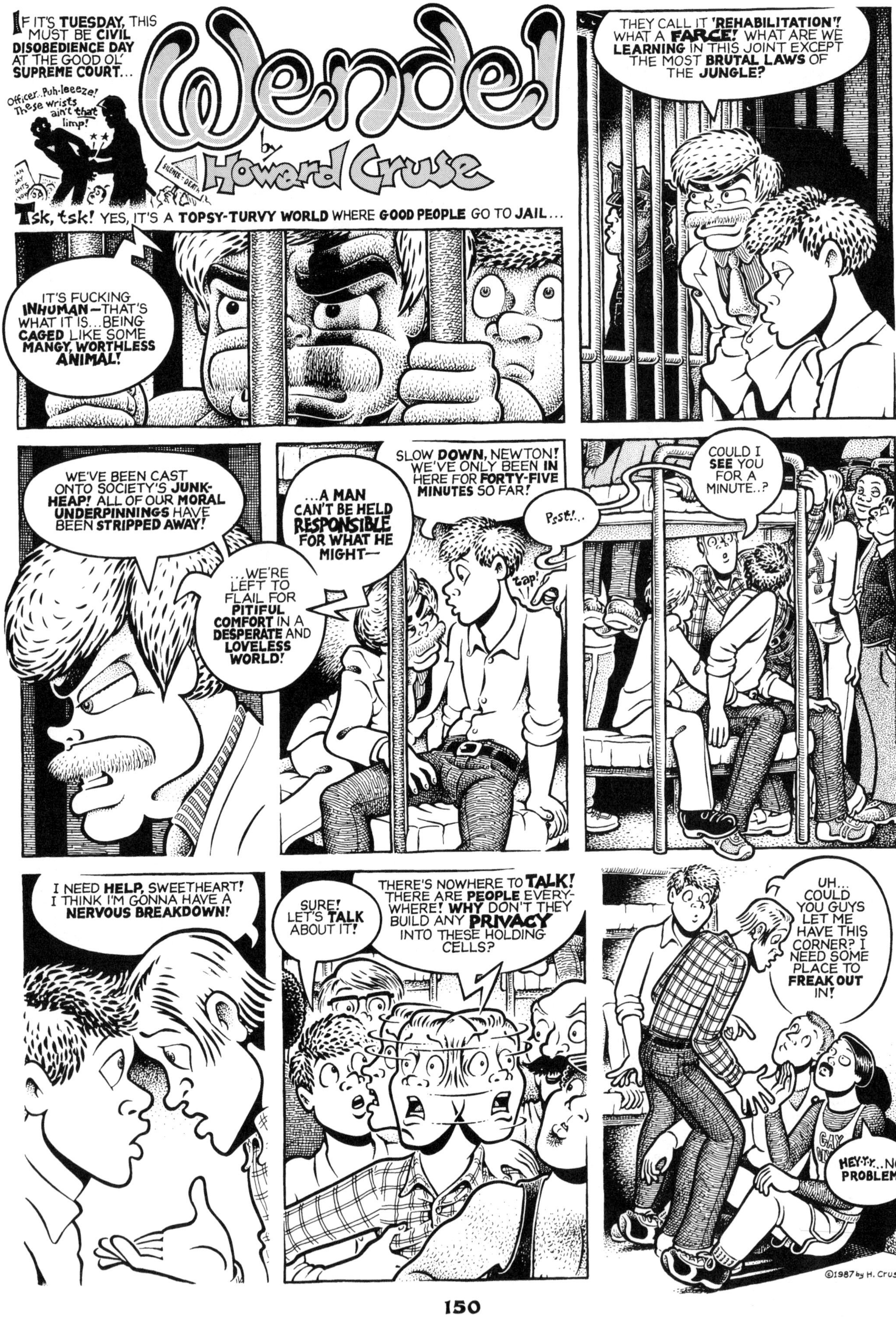

IF IT'S TUESDAY, THIS MUST BE CIVIL DISOBEDIENCE DAY AT THE GOOD OL' SUPREME COURT...
Wendel
by Howard Cruse
Officer..Puh-leeeze! These wrists ain't that limp!
Tsk, tsk! YES, IT'S A TOPSY-TURVY WORLD WHERE GOOD PEOPLE GO TO JAIL...
IT'S FUCKING INHUMAN—THAT'S WHAT IT IS...BEING CAGED LIKE SOME MANGY, WORTHLESS ANIMAL!
THEY CALL IT 'REHABILITATION'! WHAT A FARCE! WHAT ARE WE LEARNING IN THIS JOINT EXCEPT THE MOST BRUTAL LAWS OF THE JUNGLE?
WE'VE BEEN CAST ONTO SOCIETY'S JUNK-HEAP! ALL OF OUR MORAL UNDERPINNINGS HAVE BEEN STRIPPED AWAY!
...WE'RE LEFT TO FLAIL FOR PITIFUL COMFORT IN A DESPERATE AND LOVELESS WORLD!
...A MAN CAN'T BE HELD RESPONSIBLE FOR WHAT HE MIGHT—
SLOW DOWN, NEWTON! WE'VE ONLY BEEN IN HERE FOR FORTY-FIVE MINUTES SO FAR!
Psst!..
tap!
COULD I SEE YOU FOR A MINUTE..?
I NEED HELP, SWEETHEART! I THINK I'M GONNA HAVE A NERVOUS BREAKDOWN!
SURE! LET'S TALK ABOUT IT!
THERE'S NOWHERE TO TALK! THERE ARE PEOPLE EVERYWHERE! WHY DON'T THEY BUILD ANY PRIVACY INTO THESE HOLDING CELLS?
UH...COULD YOU GUYS LET ME HAVE THIS CORNER? I NEED SOME PLACE TO FREAK OUT IN!
HEY-Y-Y...NO PROBLEM!
©1987 by H. Cruse

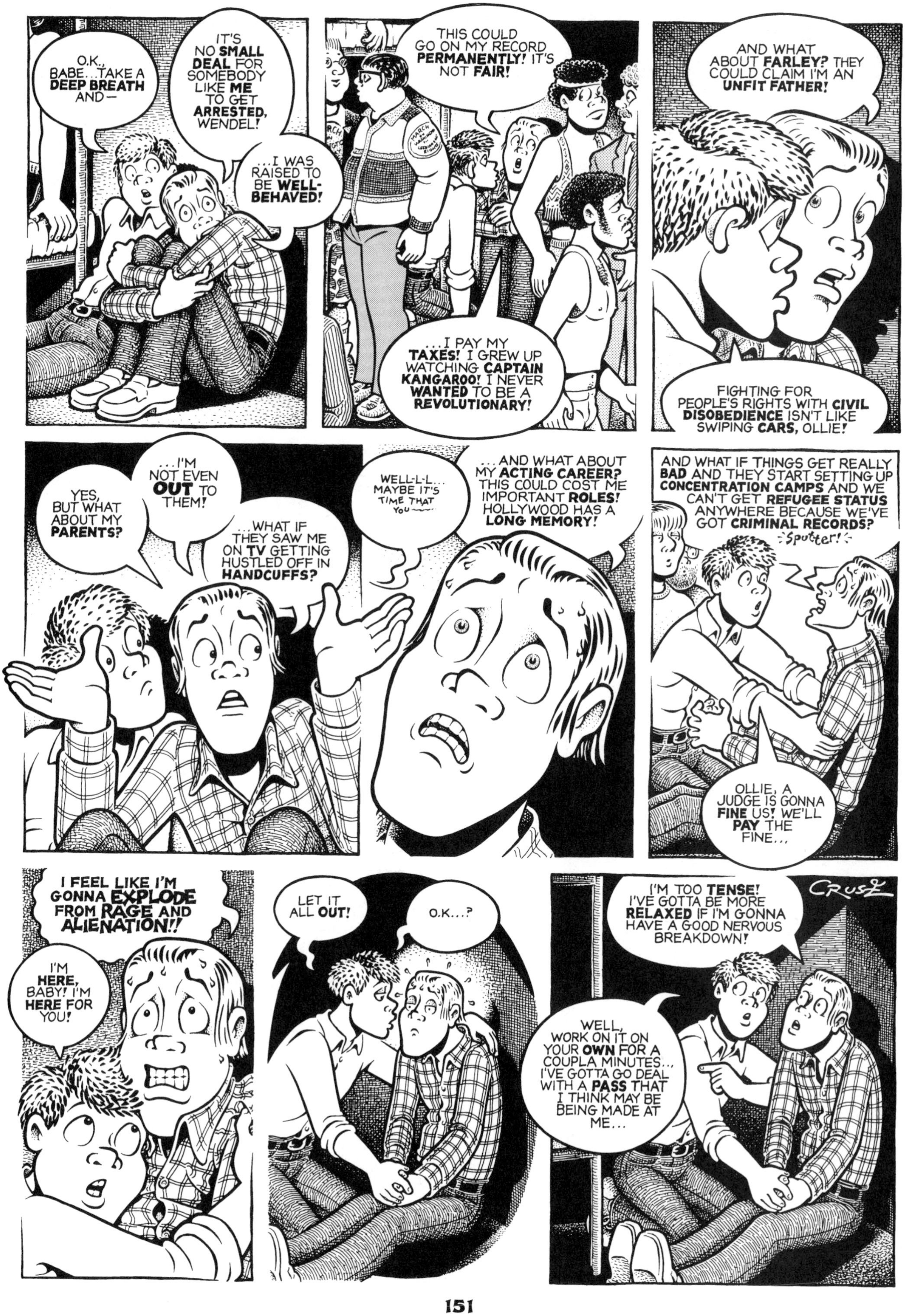
O.K., BABE...TAKE A DEEP BREATH AND—
IT'S NO SMALL DEAL FOR SOMEBODY LIKE ME TO GET ARRESTED, WENDEL!
...I WAS RAISED TO BE WELL-BEHAVED!
THIS COULD GO ON MY RECORD PERMANENTLY! IT'S NOT FAIR!
...I PAY MY TAXES! I GREW UP WATCHING CAPTAIN KANGAROO! I NEVER WANTED TO BE A REVOLUTIONARY!
AND WHAT ABOUT FARLEY? THEY COULD CLAIM I'M AN UNFIT FATHER!
FIGHTING FOR PEOPLE'S RIGHTS WITH CIVIL DISOBEDIENCE ISN'T LIKE SWIPING CARS, OLLIE!
YES, BUT WHAT ABOUT MY PARENTS?
...I'M NOT EVEN OUT TO THEM!
...WHAT IF THEY SAW ME ON TV GETTING HUSTLED OFF IN HANDCUFFS?
WELL-L-L... MAYBE IT'S TIME THAT YOU—
...AND WHAT ABOUT MY ACTING CAREER? THIS COULD COST ME IMPORTANT ROLES! HOLLYWOOD HAS A LONG MEMORY!
AND WHAT IF THINGS GET REALLY BAD AND THEY START SETTING UP CONCENTRATION CAMPS AND WE CAN'T GET REFUGEE STATUS ANYWHERE BECAUSE WE'VE GOT CRIMINAL RECORDS?
Sputter!
OLLIE, A JUDGE IS GONNA FINE US! WE'LL PAY THE FINE...
I FEEL LIKE I'M GONNA EXPLODE FROM RAGE AND ALIENATION!!
I'M HERE, BABY! I'M HERE FOR YOU!
LET IT ALL OUT!
O.K...?
CRUSE
I'M TOO TENSE! I'VE GOTTA BE MORE RELAXED IF I'M GONNA HAVE A GOOD NERVOUS BREAKDOWN!
WELL, WORK ON IT ON YOUR OWN FOR A COUPLA MINUTES... I'VE GOTTA GO DEAL WITH A PASS THAT I THINK MAY BE BEING MADE AT ME...

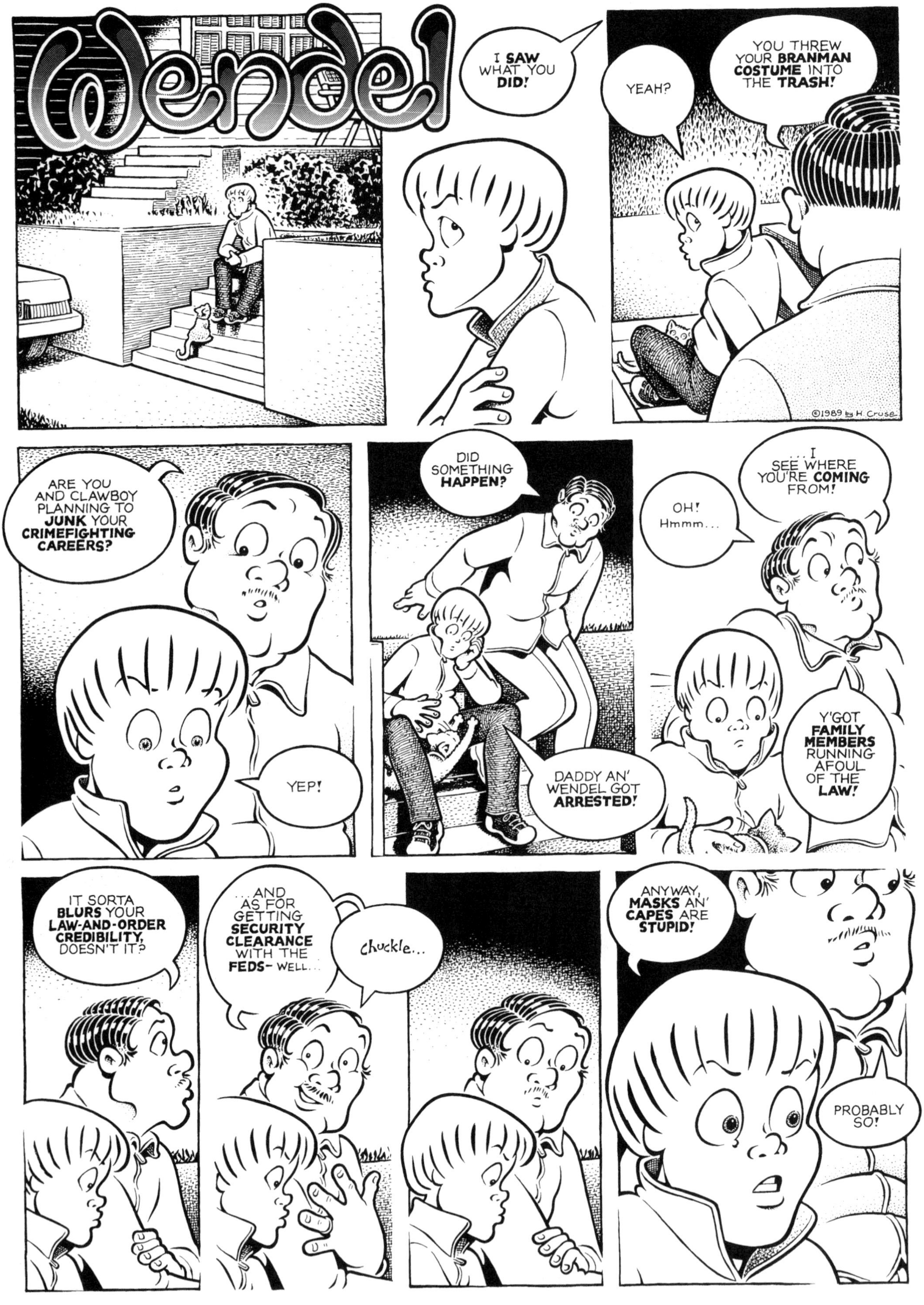
Wendel
I SAW WHAT YOU DID!
YEAH?
YOU THREW YOUR BRANMAN COSTUME INTO THE TRASH!
©1989 by H. Cruse
ARE YOU AND CLAWBOY PLANNING TO JUNK YOUR CRIMEFIGHTING CAREERS?
YEP!
DID SOMETHING HAPPEN?
DADDY AN' WENDEL GOT ARRESTED!
OH! Hmmm...
...I SEE WHERE YOU'RE COMING FROM!
Y'GOT FAMILY MEMBERS RUNNING AFOUL OF THE LAW!
IT SORTA BLURS YOUR LAW-AND-ORDER CREDIBILITY, DOESN'T IT?
...AND AS FOR GETTING SECURITY CLEARANCE WITH THE FEDS- WELL...
chuckle...
ANYWAY, MASKS AN' CAPES ARE STUPID!
PROBABLY SO!

WENDEL AND OLLIE WERE ARRESTED FOR A NOBLE **CAUSE**, FARLEY!

...WHICH, DID YOU KNOW THAT **MYRTLE** AND **I** HAVE BEEN IN THE CLINK, **TOO**?

OUR CROWD WAS A **FEISTY** ONE! WE WERE **ALWAYS** OUT IN THE STREETS **SINGING** AND **RAISING HELL** FOR NOBLE CAUSES...

WE WERE A REAL **INTERESTING** BUNCH OF **LAWBREAKERS**, KIDDO! YOU SHOULD'VE **SEEN** THE WAY WE **PACKED** THE SLAMMERS! IT WAS QUITE A **TIME**!

PICKETING... INTEGRATING **DIME** STORES... TRYING TO GET THE BIG **BOMB** BANNED...

BACK IN THOSE DAYS, THE IDEA OF **BANDING TOGETHER** TO TRY AND MAKE THE WORLD **BETTER** DIDN'T SEEM SO **WEIRD**!

WEIRD'S NOT THE WORD... **CORNY**'S THE WORD!

CORNY?

EVERY-THING'S SO **SCREWED UP**... IT ALL **STINKS**! WHAT'S THE **POINT**?

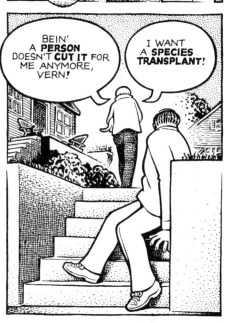

BEIN' A **PERSON** DOESN'T **CUT IT** FOR ME ANYMORE, VERN!

I WANT A **SPECIES** TRANSPLANT!

MYRT, DID YOU KNOW THAT, WHEN WE THOUGHT WE WERE **RADICALS**, WE WERE NOTHING BUT **CORNBALLS**?

HUH? DID THE JUDGMENT OF **HISTORY** GET RENDERED WHILE I HAD THE **RADIO** OFF?

HEY... **BUCK UP**, HONEY! THE **BEST** IS YET TO **COME**!

JUST **THINK**—THIS WEEK WE WATCHED THE COPS LEAD OUR ONLY **SON** AWAY IN HANDCUFFS!

Sigh... YOU'RE RIGHT! THE **TORCH** GETS PASSED **ONWARD**!

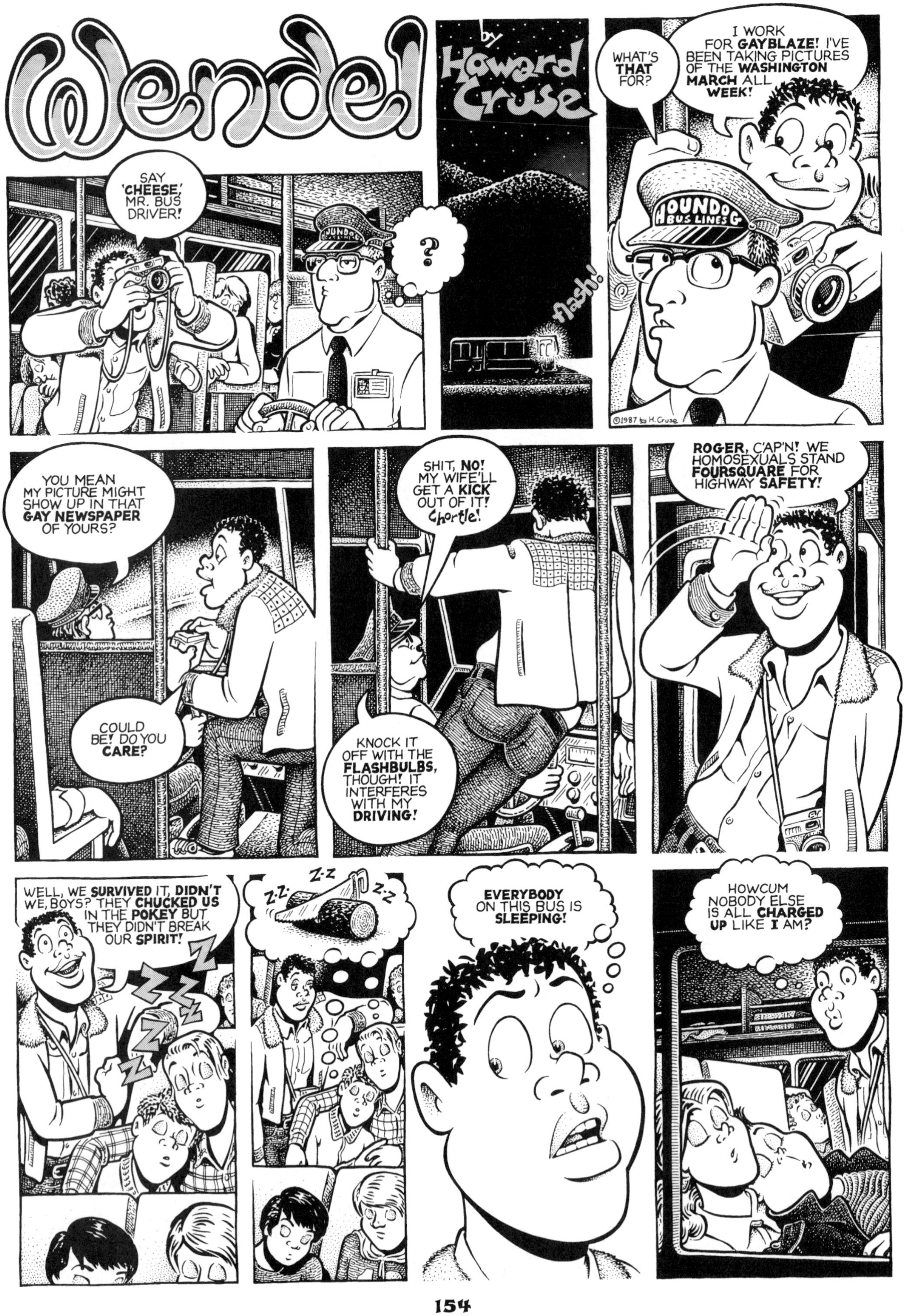

Wendel
by Howard Cruse
SAY 'CHEESE,' MR. BUS DRIVER!
?
flash!
WHAT'S THAT FOR?
I WORK FOR GAYBLAZE! I'VE BEEN TAKING PICTURES OF THE WASHINGTON MARCH ALL WEEK!
HOUNDOG BUS LINES
©1987 by H. Cruse
YOU MEAN MY PICTURE MIGHT SHOW UP IN THAT GAY NEWSPAPER OF YOURS?
COULD BE! DO YOU CARE?
SHIT, NO! MY WIFE'LL GET A KICK OUT OF IT! Chortle!
KNOCK IT OFF WITH THE FLASHBULBS, THOUGH! IT INTERFERES WITH MY DRIVING!
ROGER, C'AP'N! WE HOMOSEXUALS STAND FOURSQUARE FOR HIGHWAY SAFETY!
WELL, WE SURVIVED IT, DIDN'T WE, BOYS? THEY CHUCKED US IN THE POKEY BUT THEY DIDN'T BREAK OUR SPIRIT!
Z Z Z Z
Z-Z Z-Z Z-Z
EVERYBODY ON THIS BUS IS SLEEPING!
HOWCUM NOBODY ELSE IS ALL CHARGED UP LIKE I AM?

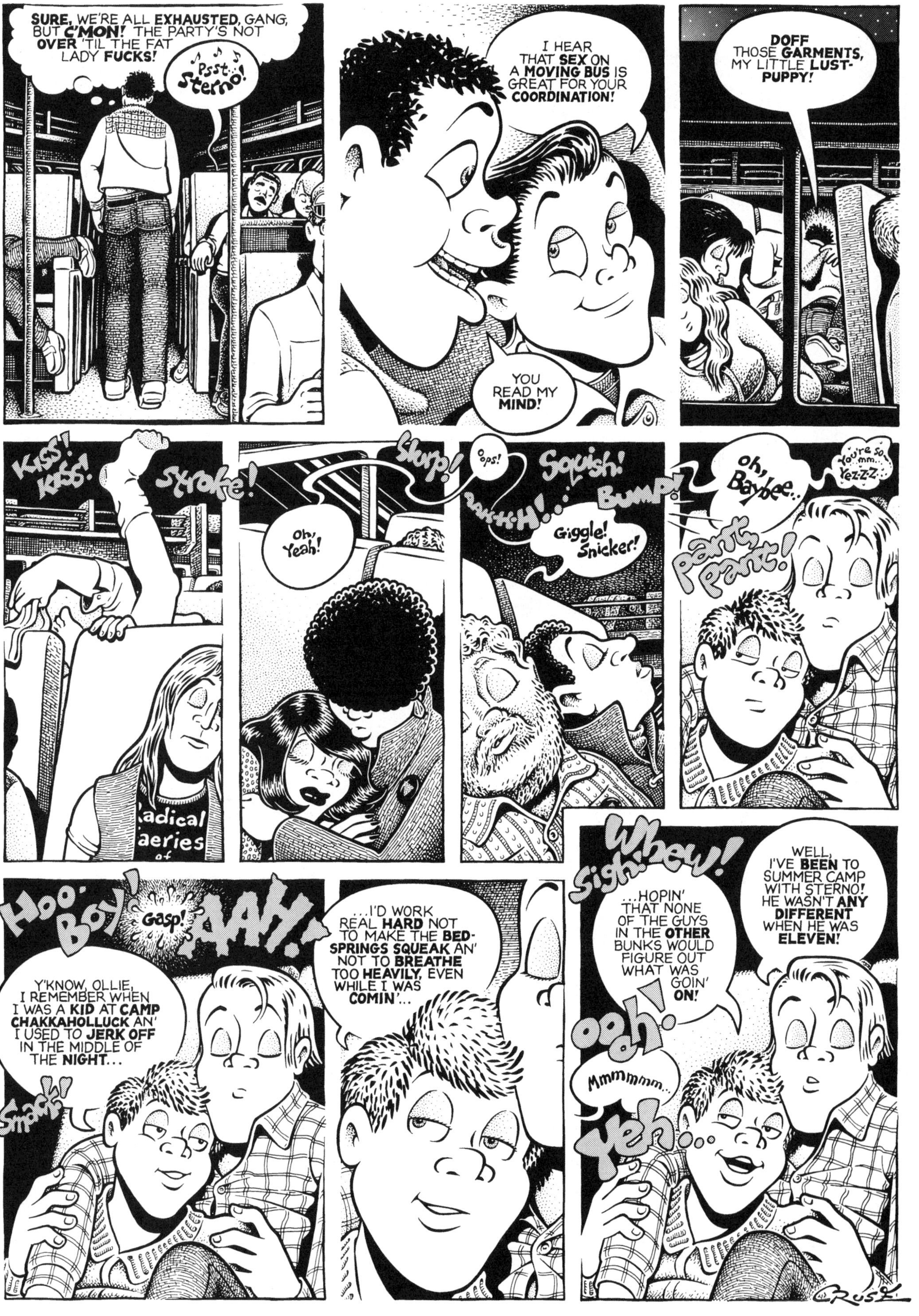
SURE, WE'RE ALL EXHAUSTED, GANG, BUT C'MON! THE PARTY'S NOT OVER 'TIL THE FAT LADY FUCKS!
Psst.. Sterno!
I HEAR THAT SEX ON A MOVING BUS IS GREAT FOR YOUR COORDINATION!
YOU READ MY MIND!
DOFF THOSE GARMENTS, MY LITTLE LUST-PUPPY!
KISS! KISS!
STROKE!
Slurp!
Oops!
Oh, Yeah!
Squish!
AHHH!..
BUMP!
Giggle! Snicker!
Oh, Baybee..
You're so.. mm.. Yez-z-z..
pant, pant!
Radical Faeries of
Whew!
Sigh..
HOO-BOY!
Gasp!
AAH!
Y'KNOW, OLLIE, I REMEMBER WHEN I WAS A KID AT CAMP CHAKKAHOLLUCK AN' I USED TO JERK OFF IN THE MIDDLE OF THE NIGHT...
Smack!
...I'D WORK REAL HARD NOT TO MAKE THE BED-SPRINGS SQUEAK AN' NOT TO BREATHE TOO HEAVILY, EVEN WHILE I WAS COMIN'...
...HOPIN' THAT NONE OF THE GUYS IN THE OTHER BUNKS WOULD FIGURE OUT WHAT WAS GOIN' ON!
WELL, I'VE BEEN TO SUMMER CAMP WITH STERNO! HE WASN'T ANY DIFFERENT WHEN HE WAS ELEVEN!
Oooh!
Mmmmmm..
Yeh!...
CRUSE

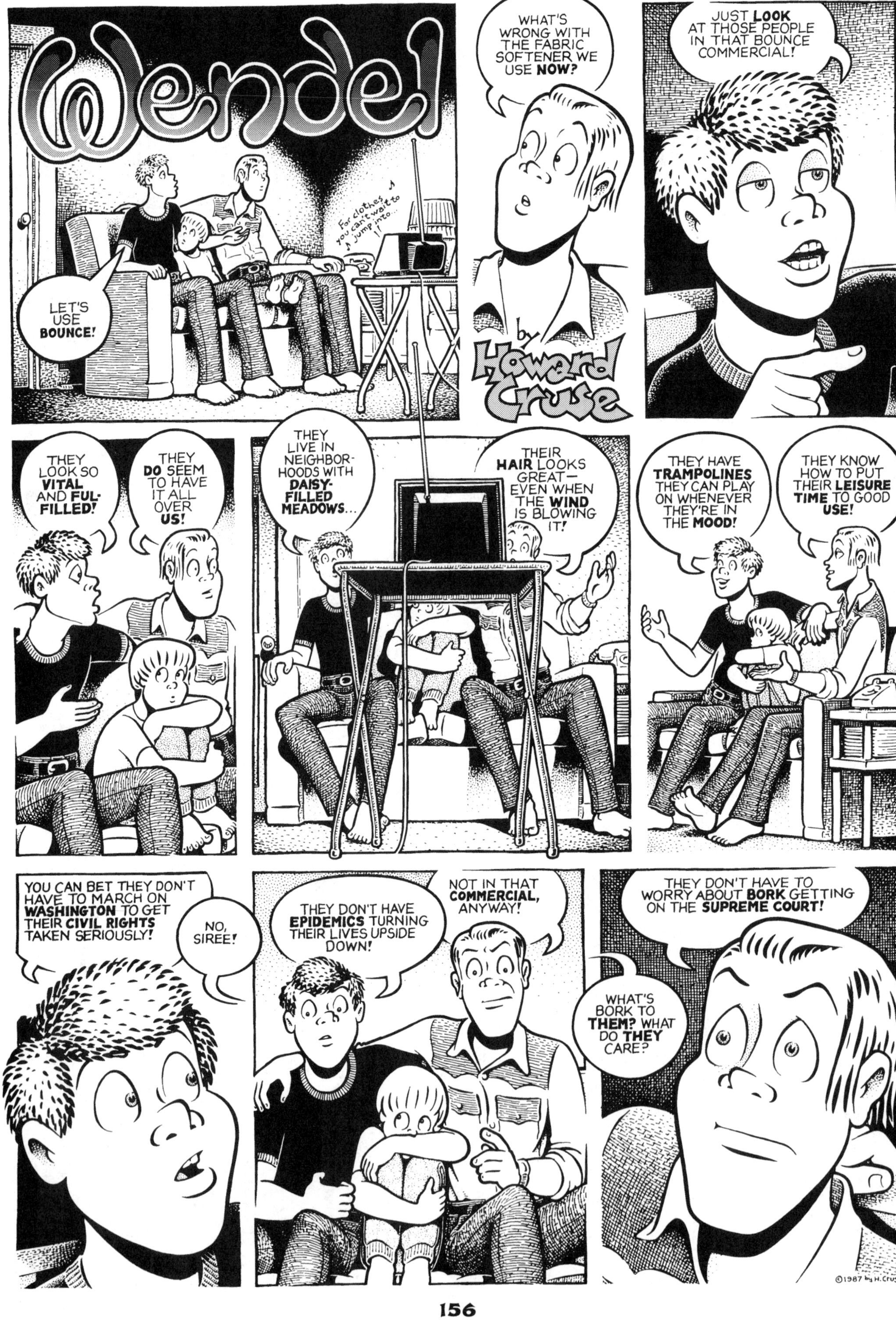
Wendel
LET'S USE BOUNCE!
For clothes you can't wait to jump into...!!
WHAT'S WRONG WITH THE FABRIC SOFTENER WE USE NOW?
by Howard Cruse
JUST LOOK AT THOSE PEOPLE IN THAT BOUNCE COMMERCIAL!
THEY LOOK SO VITAL AND FUL-FILLED!
THEY DO SEEM TO HAVE IT ALL OVER US!
THEY LIVE IN NEIGHBOR-HOODS WITH DAISY-FILLED MEADOWS...
THEIR HAIR LOOKS GREAT— EVEN WHEN THE WIND IS BLOWING IT!
THEY HAVE TRAMPOLINES THEY CAN PLAY ON WHENEVER THEY'RE IN THE MOOD!
THEY KNOW HOW TO PUT THEIR LEISURE TIME TO GOOD USE!
YOU CAN BET THEY DON'T HAVE TO MARCH ON WASHINGTON TO GET THEIR CIVIL RIGHTS TAKEN SERIOUSLY!
NO, SIREE!
THEY DON'T HAVE EPIDEMICS TURNING THEIR LIVES UPSIDE DOWN!
NOT IN THAT COMMERCIAL, ANYWAY!
THEY DON'T HAVE TO WORRY ABOUT BORK GETTING ON THE SUPREME COURT!
WHAT'S BORK TO THEM? WHAT DO THEY CARE?
©1987 by H. Cruse

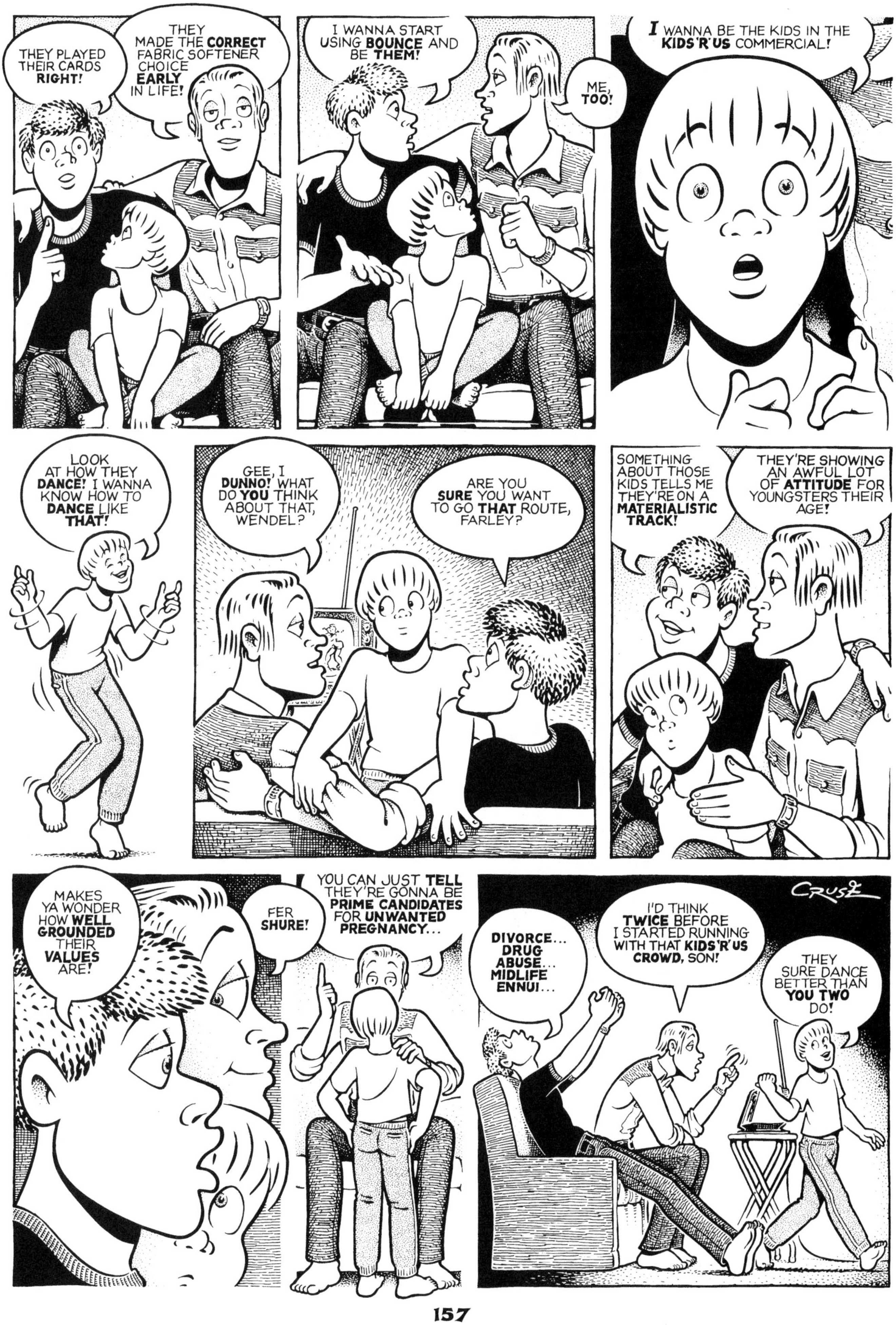

THEY PLAYED THEIR CARDS **RIGHT**!
THEY MADE THE **CORRECT** FABRIC SOFTENER CHOICE **EARLY** IN LIFE!
I WANNA START USING **BOUNCE** AND BE **THEM**!
ME, **TOO**!
I WANNA BE THE KIDS IN THE **KIDS 'R' US** COMMERCIAL!
LOOK AT HOW THEY **DANCE**! I WANNA KNOW HOW TO **DANCE** LIKE **THAT**!
GEE, I **DUNNO**! WHAT DO **YOU** THINK ABOUT THAT, WENDEL?
ARE YOU **SURE** YOU WANT TO GO **THAT** ROUTE, FARLEY?
SOMETHING ABOUT THOSE KIDS TELLS ME THEY'RE ON A **MATERIALISTIC TRACK**!
THEY'RE SHOWING AN AWFUL LOT OF **ATTITUDE** FOR YOUNGSTERS THEIR AGE!
MAKES YA WONDER HOW **WELL GROUNDED** THEIR **VALUES** ARE!
FER **SHURE**!
YOU CAN JUST **TELL** THEY'RE GONNA BE **PRIME CANDIDATES** FOR **UNWANTED PREGNANCY**...
CRUSE
DIVORCE... **DRUG ABUSE**... **MIDLIFE ENNUI**...
I'D THINK **TWICE** BEFORE I STARTED RUNNING WITH THAT **KIDS 'R' US CROWD**, SON!
THEY SURE DANCE BETTER THAN **YOU TWO** DO!

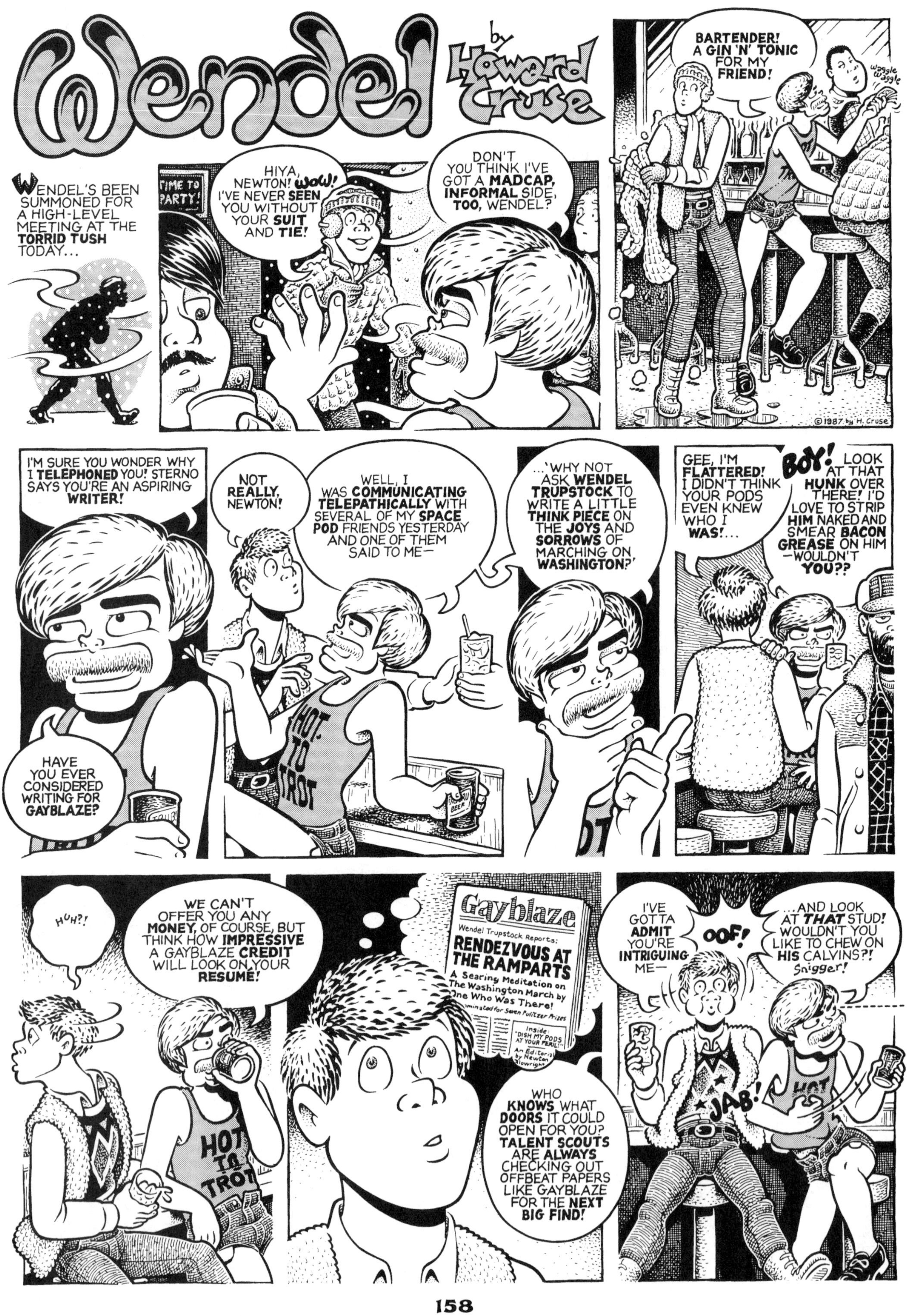

Wendel
by Howard Cruse
WENDEL'S BEEN SUMMONED FOR A HIGH-LEVEL MEETING AT THE TORRID TUSH TODAY...
TIME TO PARTY!
HIYA, NEWTON! WOW! I'VE NEVER SEEN YOU WITHOUT YOUR SUIT AND TIE!
DON'T YOU THINK I'VE GOT A MADCAP, INFORMAL SIDE, TOO, WENDEL?
BARTENDER! A GIN 'N' TONIC FOR MY FRIEND!
waggle waggle
©1987 by H. Cruse
I'M SURE YOU WONDER WHY I TELEPHONED YOU! STERNO SAYS YOU'RE AN ASPIRING WRITER!
HAVE YOU EVER CONSIDERED WRITING FOR GAYBLAZE?
NOT REALLY, NEWTON!
WELL, I WAS COMMUNICATING TELEPATHICALLY WITH SEVERAL OF MY SPACE POD FRIENDS YESTERDAY AND ONE OF THEM SAID TO ME—
HOT TO TROT
...'WHY NOT ASK WENDEL TRUPSTOCK TO WRITE A LITTLE THINK PIECE ON THE JOYS AND SORROWS OF MARCHING ON WASHINGTON?'
GEE, I'M FLATTERED! I DIDN'T THINK YOUR PODS EVEN KNEW WHO I WAS!...
BOY! LOOK AT THAT HUNK OVER THERE! I'D LOVE TO STRIP HIM NAKED AND SMEAR BACON GREASE ON HIM —WOULDN'T YOU??
HUH?!
WE CAN'T OFFER YOU ANY MONEY, OF COURSE, BUT THINK HOW IMPRESSIVE A GAYBLAZE CREDIT WILL LOOK ON YOUR RESUMÉ!
HOT TO TROT
Gayblaze
Wendel Trupstock Reports:
RENDEZVOUS AT THE RAMPARTS
A Searing Meditation on The Washington March by One Who Was There!
Inside: "DISH MY PODS AT YOUR PERIL!"
An Editorial by Newton
WHO KNOWS WHAT DOORS IT COULD OPEN FOR YOU? TALENT SCOUTS ARE ALWAYS CHECKING OUT OFFBEAT PAPERS LIKE GAYBLAZE FOR THE NEXT BIG FIND!
I'VE GOTTA ADMIT YOU'RE INTRIGUING ME—
OOF!
...AND LOOK AT THAT STUD! WOULDN'T YOU LIKE TO CHEW ON HIS CALVINS?! Snigger!
JAB!
HOT

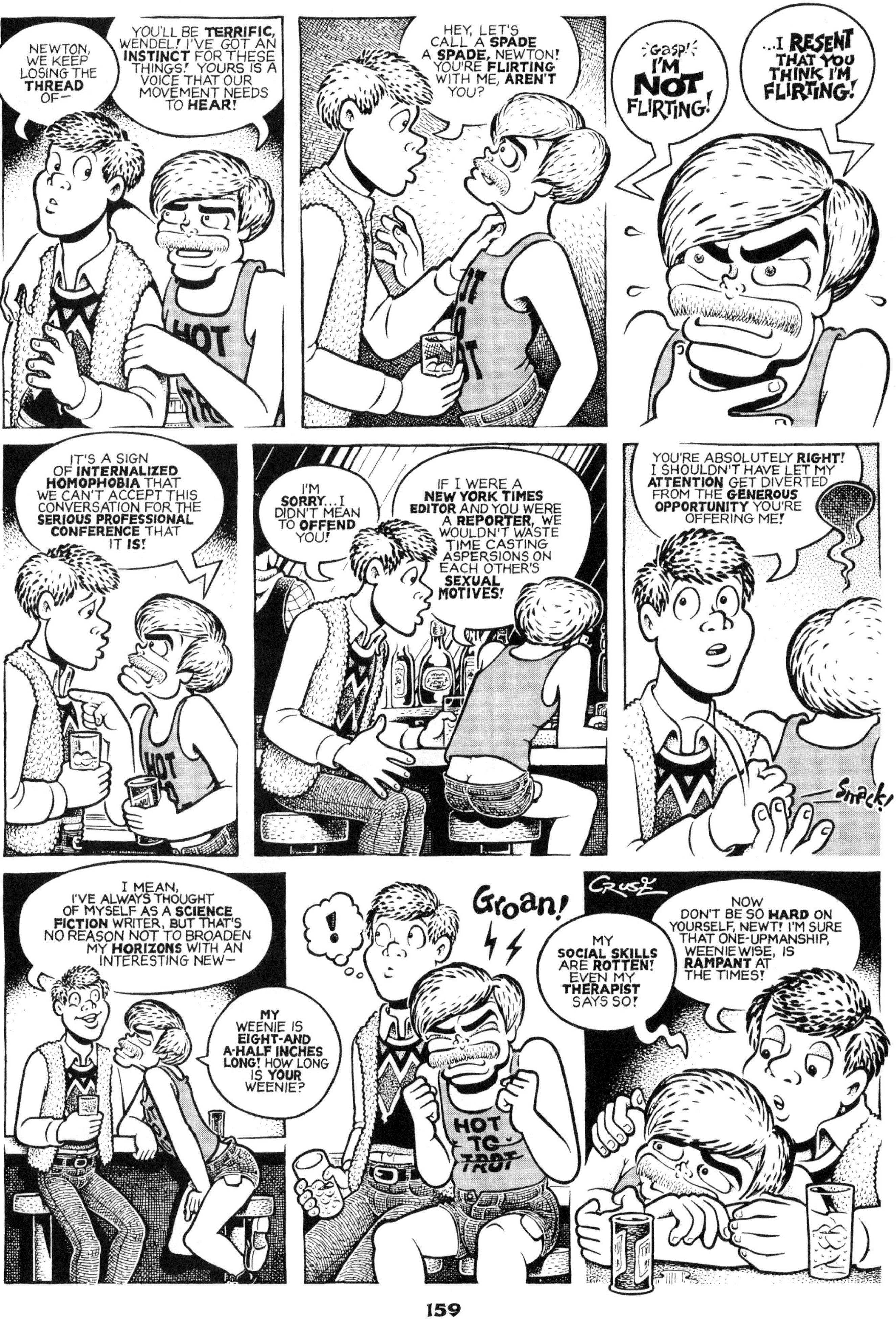

NEWTON, WE KEEP LOSING THE THREAD OF—
YOU'LL BE TERRIFIC, WENDEL! I'VE GOT AN INSTINCT FOR THESE THINGS! YOURS IS A VOICE THAT OUR MOVEMENT NEEDS TO HEAR!
HOT TO TROT
HEY, LET'S CALL A SPADE A SPADE, NEWTON! YOU'RE FLIRTING WITH ME, AREN'T YOU?
Gasp! I'M NOT FLIRTING!
...I RESENT THAT YOU THINK I'M FLIRTING!
IT'S A SIGN OF INTERNALIZED HOMOPHOBIA THAT WE CAN'T ACCEPT THIS CONVERSATION FOR THE SERIOUS PROFESSIONAL CONFERENCE THAT IT IS!
I'M SORRY... I DIDN'T MEAN TO OFFEND YOU!
IF I WERE A NEW YORK TIMES EDITOR AND YOU WERE A REPORTER, WE WOULDN'T WASTE TIME CASTING ASPERSIONS ON EACH OTHER'S SEXUAL MOTIVES!
YOU'RE ABSOLUTELY RIGHT! I SHOULDN'T HAVE LET MY ATTENTION GET DIVERTED FROM THE GENEROUS OPPORTUNITY YOU'RE OFFERING ME!
SMACK!
I MEAN, I'VE ALWAYS THOUGHT OF MYSELF AS A SCIENCE FICTION WRITER, BUT THAT'S NO REASON NOT TO BROADEN MY HORIZONS WITH AN INTERESTING NEW—
MY WEENIE IS EIGHT-AND A-HALF INCHES LONG! HOW LONG IS YOUR WEENIE?
!
Groan!
HOT TO TROT
CRUSE
MY SOCIAL SKILLS ARE ROTTEN! EVEN MY THERAPIST SAYS SO!
NOW DON'T BE SO HARD ON YOURSELF, NEWT! I'M SURE THAT ONE-UPMANSHIP, WEENIEWISE, IS RAMPANT AT THE TIMES!

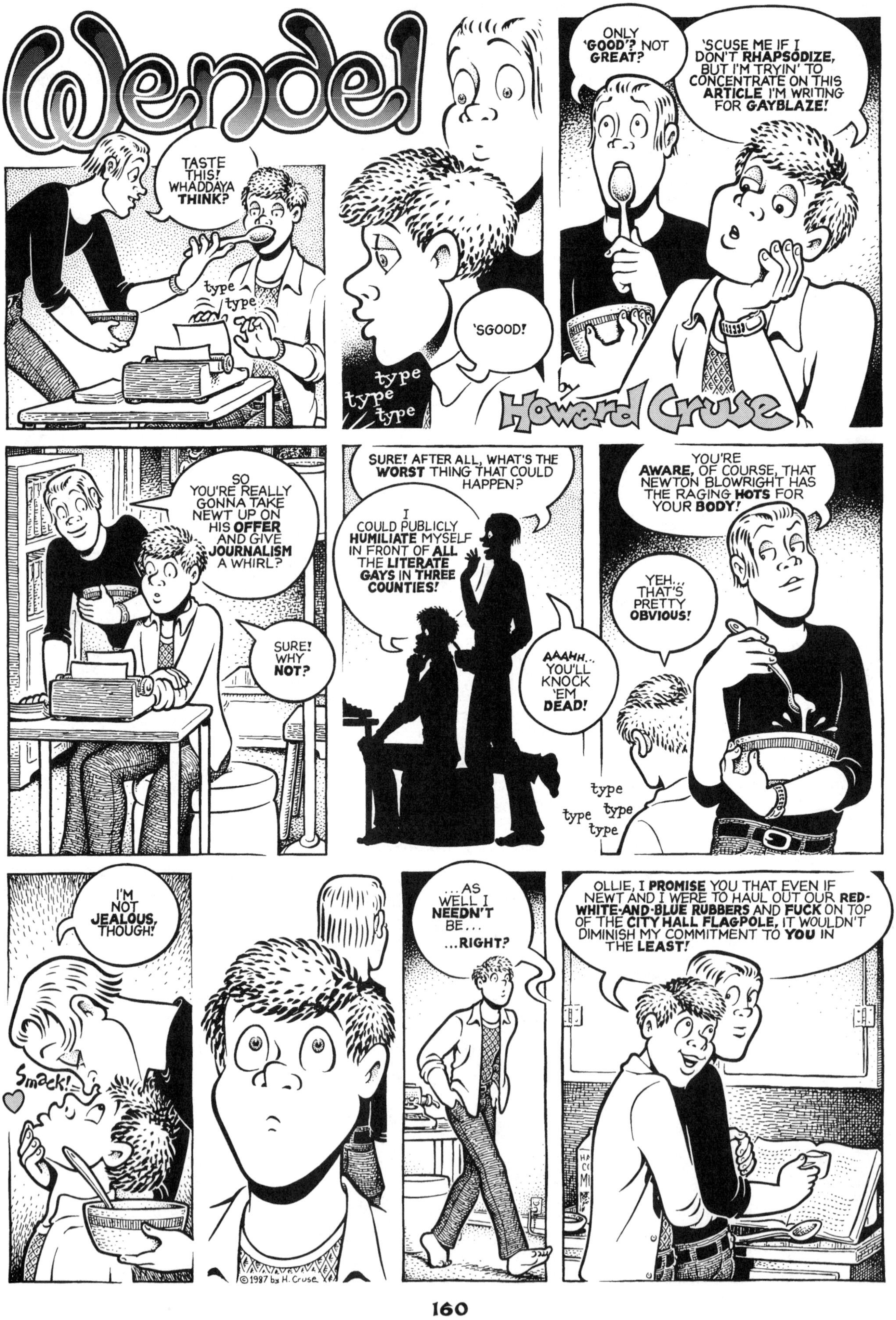
Wendel
TASTE THIS! WHADDAYA THINK?
type type
'SGOOD!
type type type
ONLY 'GOOD'? NOT GREAT?
'SCUSE ME IF I DON'T RHAPSODIZE, BUT I'M TRYIN' TO CONCENTRATE ON THIS ARTICLE I'M WRITING FOR GAYBLAZE!
by Howard Cruse
SO YOU'RE REALLY GONNA TAKE NEWT UP ON HIS OFFER AND GIVE JOURNALISM A WHIRL?
SURE! WHY NOT?
SURE! AFTER ALL, WHAT'S THE WORST THING THAT COULD HAPPEN?
I COULD PUBLICLY HUMILIATE MYSELF IN FRONT OF ALL THE LITERATE GAYS IN THREE COUNTIES!
AAAHH... YOU'LL KNOCK 'EM DEAD!
YOU'RE AWARE, OF COURSE, THAT NEWTON BLOWRIGHT HAS THE RAGING HOTS FOR YOUR BODY!
YEH... THAT'S PRETTY OBVIOUS!
type type type type
I'M NOT JEALOUS, THOUGH!
Smack!
...AS WELL I NEEDN'T BE...
...RIGHT?
OLLIE, I PROMISE YOU THAT EVEN IF NEWT AND I WERE TO HAUL OUT OUR RED-WHITE-AND-BLUE RUBBERS AND FUCK ON TOP OF THE CITY HALL FLAGPOLE, IT WOULDN'T DIMINISH MY COMMITMENT TO YOU IN THE LEAST!
©1987 by H. Cruse

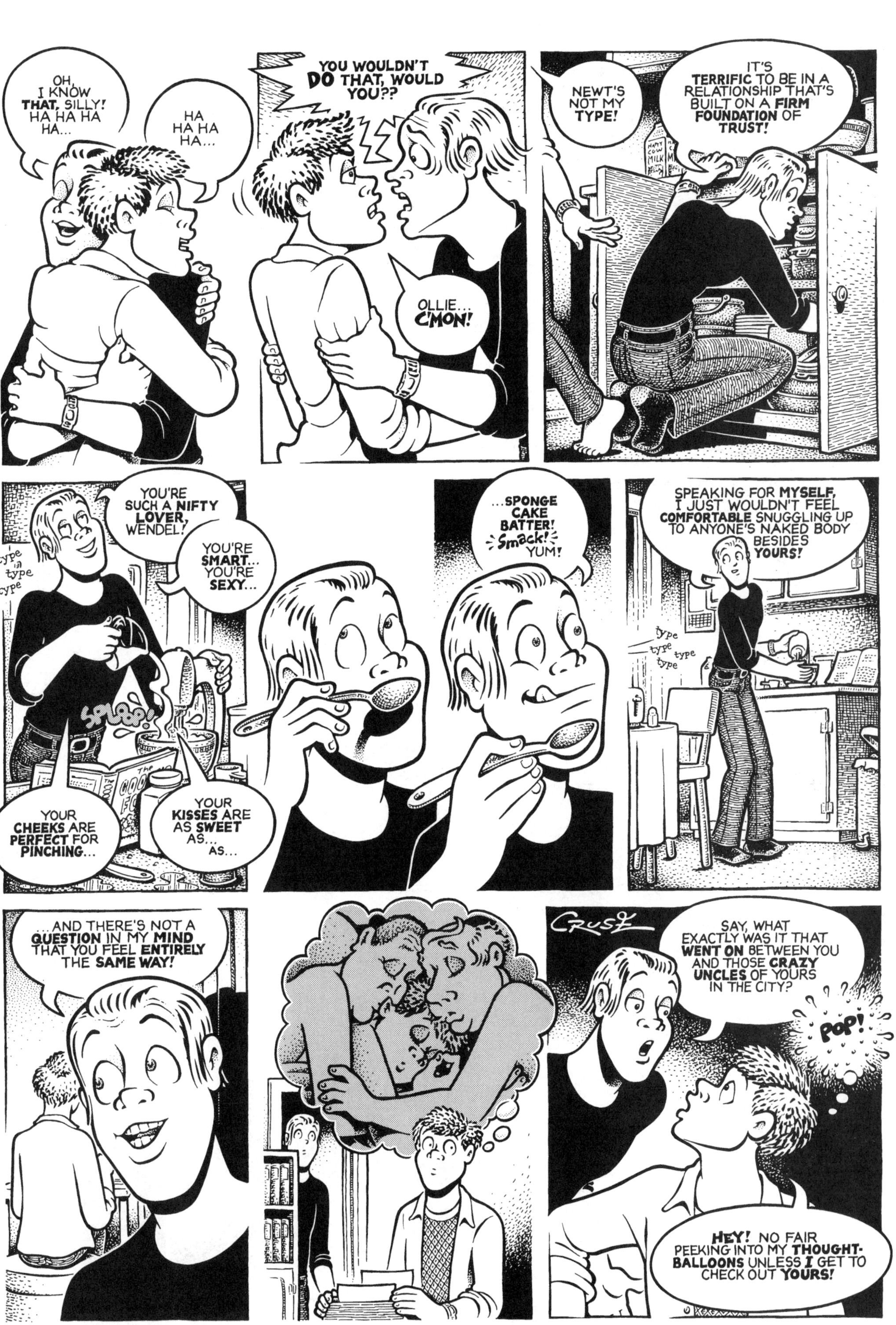
OH, I KNOW THAT, SILLY! HA HA HA HA...
HA HA HA HA...
YOU WOULDN'T DO THAT, WOULD YOU??
OLLIE... C'MON!
NEWT'S NOT MY TYPE!
IT'S TERRIFIC TO BE IN A RELATIONSHIP THAT'S BUILT ON A FIRM FOUNDATION OF TRUST!
YOU'RE SUCH A NIFTY LOVER, WENDEL!
YOU'RE SMART... YOU'RE SEXY...
type type type type
SPLOOP!
YOUR CHEEKS ARE PERFECT FOR PINCHING...
YOUR KISSES ARE AS SWEET AS... AS...
...SPONGE CAKE BATTER! Smack! YUM!
SPEAKING FOR MYSELF, I JUST WOULDN'T FEEL COMFORTABLE SNUGGLING UP TO ANYONE'S NAKED BODY BESIDES YOURS!
type type type type
...AND THERE'S NOT A QUESTION IN MY MIND THAT YOU FEEL ENTIRELY THE SAME WAY!
CRUSE
SAY, WHAT EXACTLY WAS IT THAT WENT ON BETWEEN YOU AND THOSE CRAZY UNCLES OF YOURS IN THE CITY?
POP!
HEY! NO FAIR PEEKING INTO MY THOUGHT-BALLOONS UNLESS I GET TO CHECK OUT YOURS!

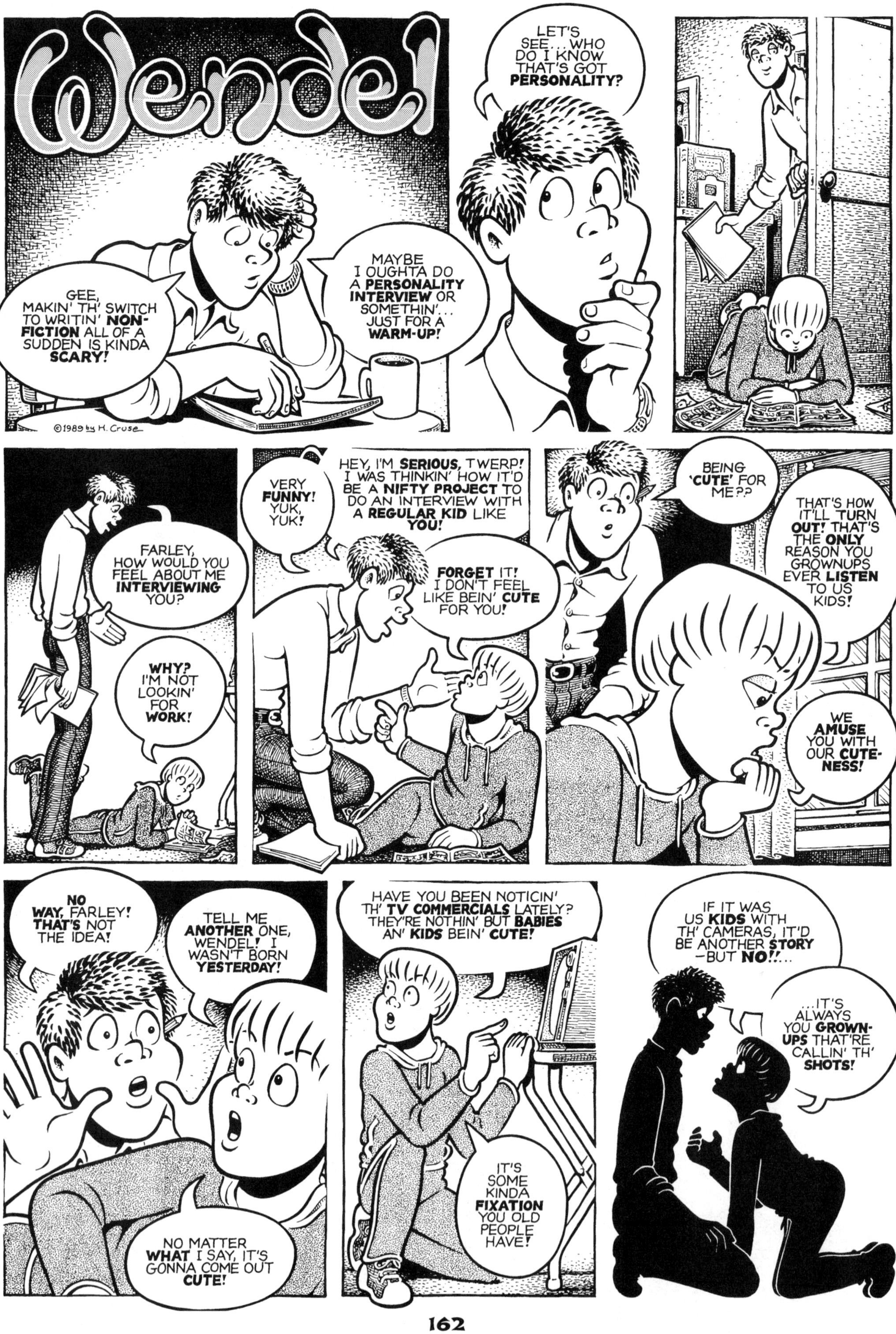
Wendel
GEE, MAKIN' TH' SWITCH TO WRITIN' NON-FICTION ALL OF A SUDDEN IS KINDA SCARY!
MAYBE I OUGHTA DO A PERSONALITY INTERVIEW OR SOMETHIN'... JUST FOR A WARM-UP!
©1989 by H. Cruse
LET'S SEE... WHO DO I KNOW THAT'S GOT PERSONALITY?
FARLEY, HOW WOULD YOU FEEL ABOUT ME INTERVIEWING YOU?
WHY? I'M NOT LOOKIN' FOR WORK!
VERY FUNNY! YUK, YUK!
HEY, I'M SERIOUS, TWERP! I WAS THINKIN' HOW IT'D BE A NIFTY PROJECT TO DO AN INTERVIEW WITH A REGULAR KID LIKE YOU!
FORGET IT! I DON'T FEEL LIKE BEIN' CUTE FOR YOU!
BEING 'CUTE' FOR ME??
THAT'S HOW IT'LL TURN OUT! THAT'S THE ONLY REASON YOU GROWNUPS EVER LISTEN TO US KIDS!
WE AMUSE YOU WITH OUR CUTE-NESS!
NO WAY, FARLEY! THAT'S NOT THE IDEA!
TELL ME ANOTHER ONE, WENDEL! I WASN'T BORN YESTERDAY!
NO MATTER WHAT I SAY, IT'S GONNA COME OUT CUTE!
HAVE YOU BEEN NOTICIN' TH' TV COMMERCIALS LATELY? THEY'RE NOTHIN' BUT BABIES AN' KIDS BEIN' CUTE!
IT'S SOME KINDA FIXATION YOU OLD PEOPLE HAVE!
IF IT WAS US KIDS WITH TH' CAMERAS, IT'D BE ANOTHER STORY —BUT NO!!...
...IT'S ALWAYS YOU GROWN-UPS THAT'RE CALLIN' TH' SHOTS!

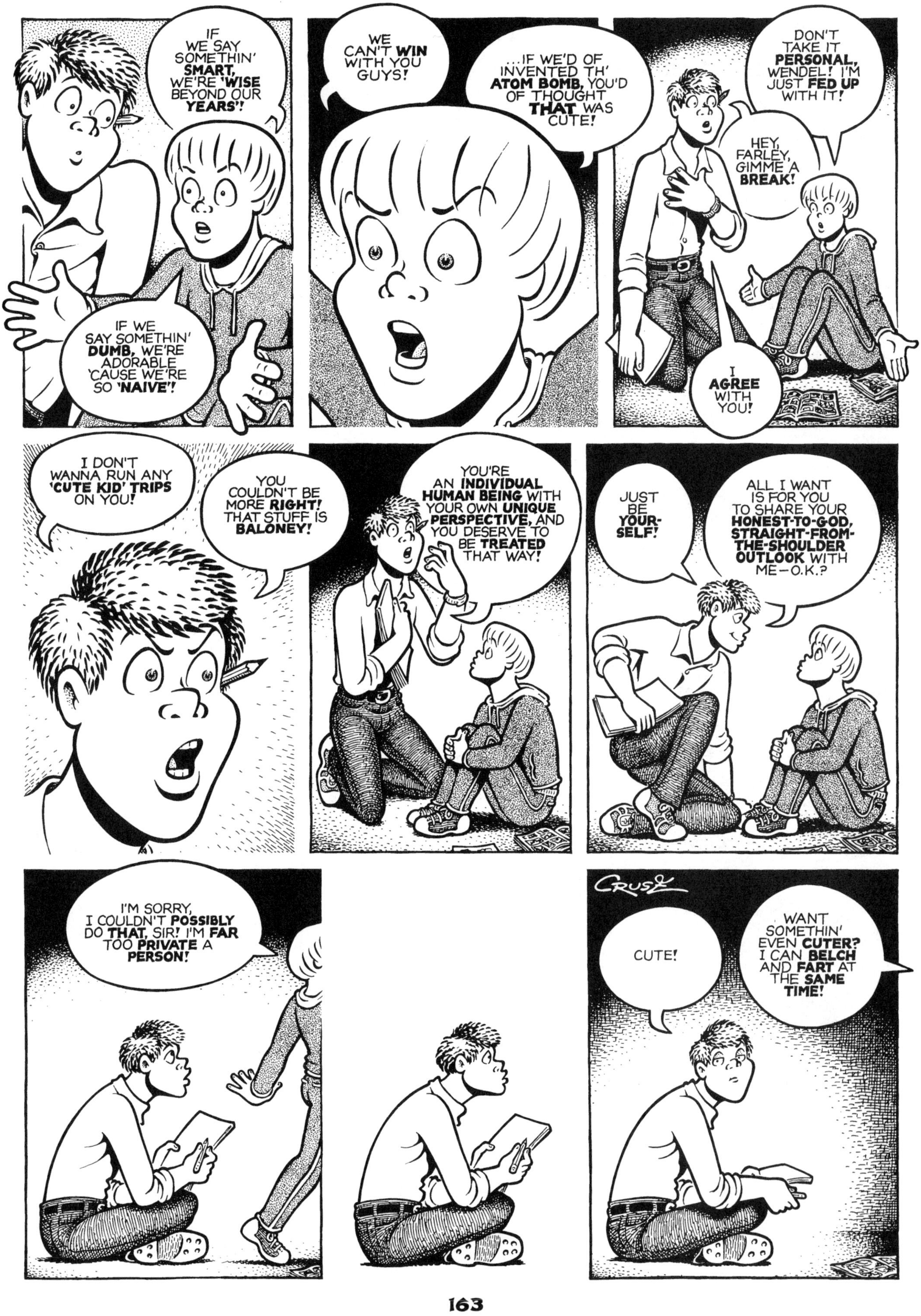
IF WE SAY SOMETHIN' SMART, WE'RE 'WISE BEYOND OUR YEARS'!
IF WE SAY SOMETHIN' DUMB, WE'RE ADORABLE 'CAUSE WE'RE SO 'NAIVE'!
WE CAN'T WIN WITH YOU GUYS!
...IF WE'D OF INVENTED TH' ATOM BOMB, YOU'D OF THOUGHT THAT WAS CUTE!
DON'T TAKE IT PERSONAL, WENDEL! I'M JUST FED UP WITH IT!
HEY, FARLEY, GIMME A BREAK!
I AGREE WITH YOU!
I DON'T WANNA RUN ANY 'CUTE KID' TRIPS ON YOU!
YOU COULDN'T BE MORE RIGHT! THAT STUFF IS BALONEY!
YOU'RE AN INDIVIDUAL HUMAN BEING WITH YOUR OWN UNIQUE PERSPECTIVE, AND YOU DESERVE TO BE TREATED THAT WAY!
JUST BE YOURSELF!
ALL I WANT IS FOR YOU TO SHARE YOUR HONEST-TO-GOD, STRAIGHT-FROM-THE-SHOULDER OUTLOOK WITH ME—O.K.?
I'M SORRY, I COULDN'T POSSIBLY DO THAT, SIR! I'M FAR TOO PRIVATE A PERSON!
CRUSE
CUTE!
WANT SOMETHIN' EVEN CUTER? I CAN BELCH AND FART AT THE SAME TIME!

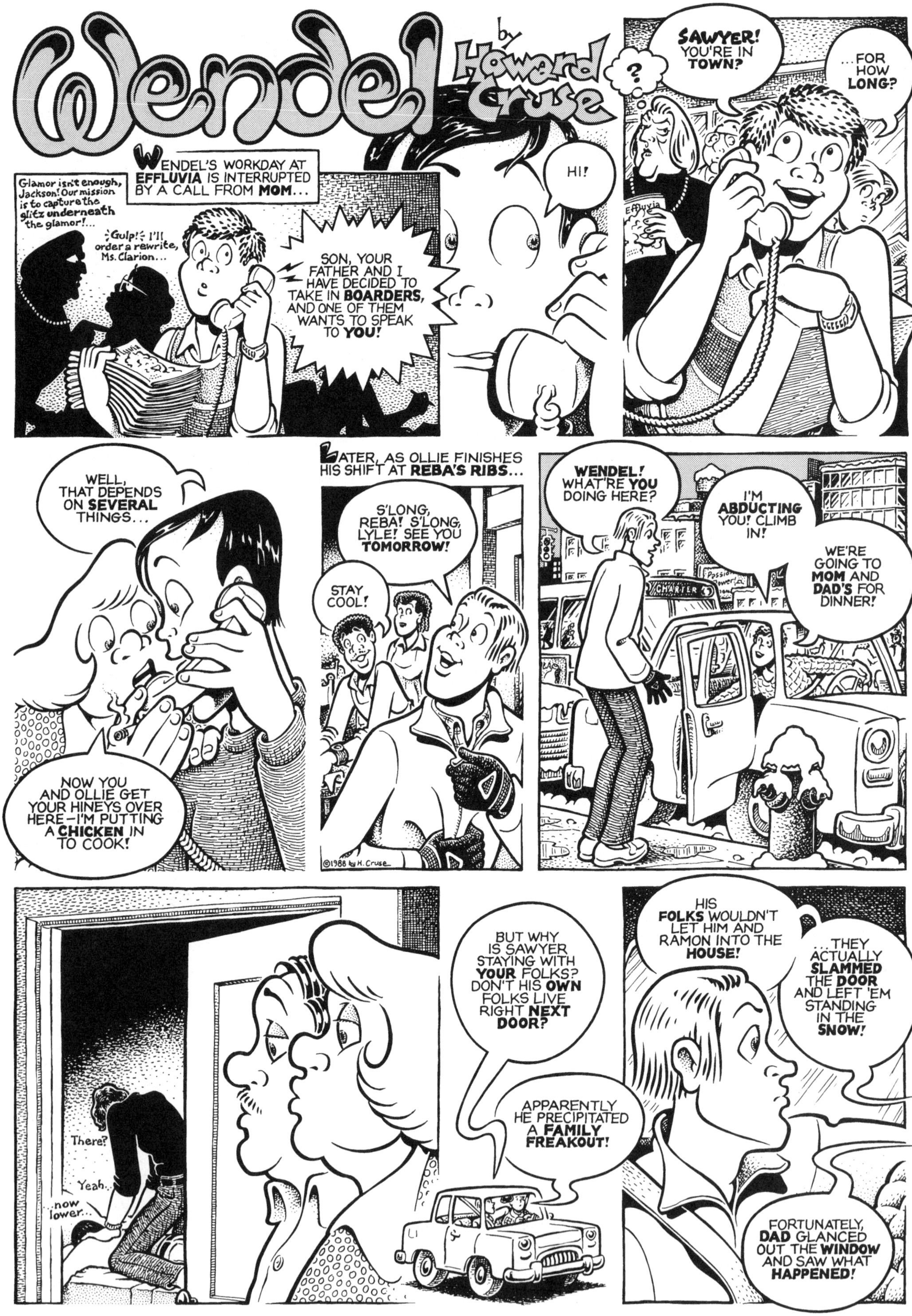

Wendel
by Howard Cruse
WENDEL'S WORKDAY AT EFFLUVIA IS INTERRUPTED BY A CALL FROM MOM...
Glamor isn't enough, Jackson! Our mission is to capture the glitz underneath the glamor!...
Gulp! I'll order a rewrite, Ms. Clarion...
SON, YOUR FATHER AND I HAVE DECIDED TO TAKE IN BOARDERS, AND ONE OF THEM WANTS TO SPEAK TO YOU!
HI!
?
SAWYER! YOU'RE IN TOWN?
...FOR HOW LONG?
Effluvia
WELL, THAT DEPENDS ON SEVERAL THINGS...
NOW YOU AND OLLIE GET YOUR HINEYS OVER HERE—I'M PUTTING A CHICKEN IN TO COOK!
LATER, AS OLLIE FINISHES HIS SHIFT AT REBA'S RIBS...
S'LONG, REBA! S'LONG, LYLE! SEE YOU TOMORROW!
STAY COOL!
©1988 by H. Cruse
WENDEL! WHAT'RE YOU DOING HERE?
I'M ABDUCTING YOU! CLIMB IN!
WE'RE GOING TO MOM AND DAD'S FOR DINNER!
CHARTER
There?
Yeah..
..now lower...
BUT WHY IS SAWYER STAYING WITH YOUR FOLKS? DON'T HIS OWN FOLKS LIVE RIGHT NEXT DOOR?
APPARENTLY HE PRECIPITATED A FAMILY FREAKOUT!
HIS FOLKS WOULDN'T LET HIM AND RAMON INTO THE HOUSE!
...THEY ACTUALLY SLAMMED THE DOOR AND LEFT 'EM STANDING IN THE SNOW!
FORTUNATELY, DAD GLANCED OUT THE WINDOW AND SAW WHAT HAPPENED!

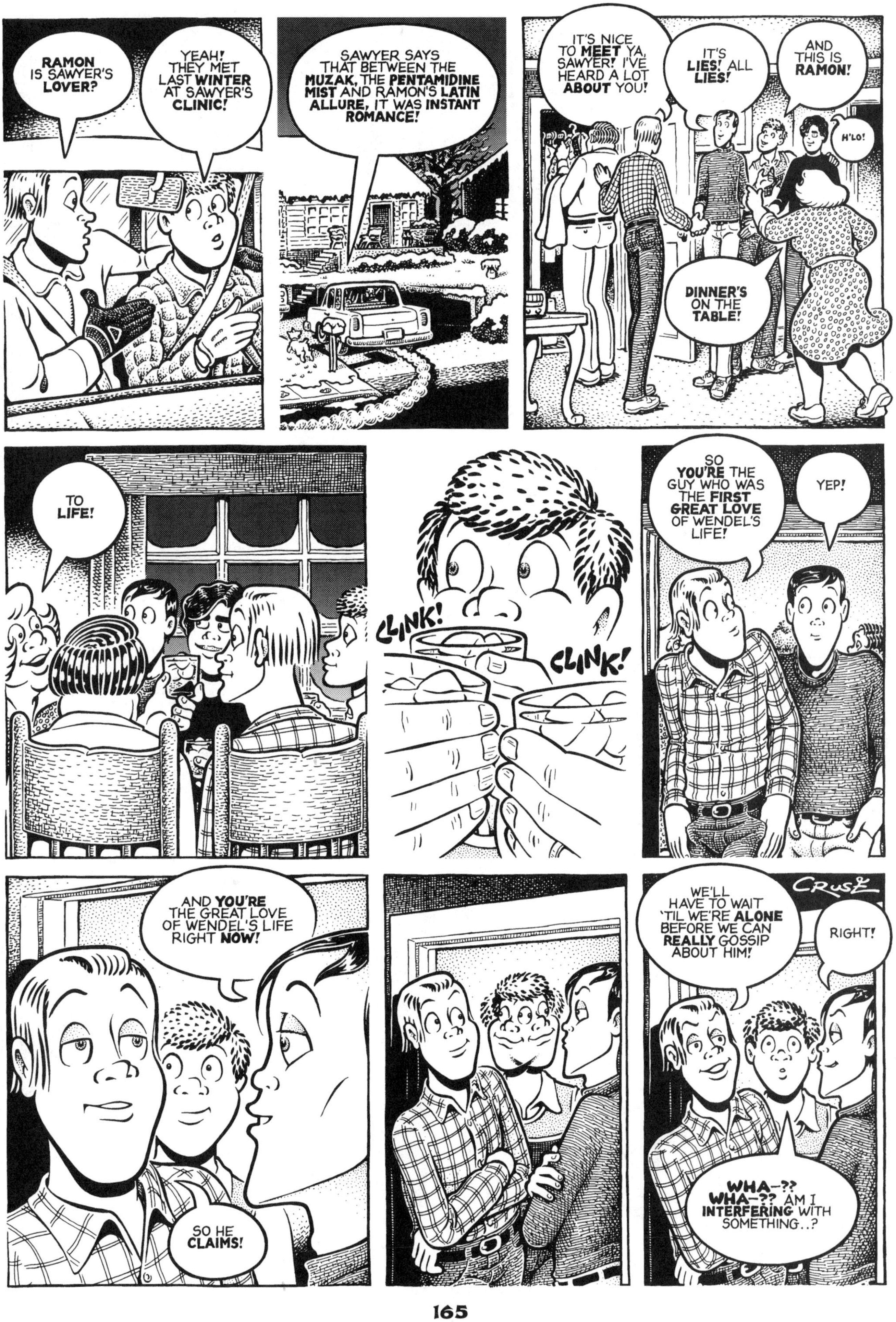
RAMON IS SAWYER'S LOVER?
YEAH! THEY MET LAST WINTER AT SAWYER'S CLINIC!
SAWYER SAYS THAT BETWEEN THE MUZAK, THE PENTAMIDINE MIST AND RAMON'S LATIN ALLURE, IT WAS INSTANT ROMANCE!
IT'S NICE TO MEET YA, SAWYER! I'VE HEARD A LOT ABOUT YOU!
IT'S LIES! ALL LIES!
AND THIS IS RAMON!
H'LO!
DINNER'S ON THE TABLE!
TO LIFE!
CLINK!
CLINK!
SO YOU'RE THE GUY WHO WAS THE FIRST GREAT LOVE OF WENDEL'S LIFE!
YEP!
AND YOU'RE THE GREAT LOVE OF WENDEL'S LIFE RIGHT NOW!
SO HE CLAIMS!
CRUSE
WE'LL HAVE TO WAIT 'TIL WE'RE ALONE BEFORE WE CAN REALLY GOSSIP ABOUT HIM!
RIGHT!
WHA-?? WHA-?? AM I INTERFERING WITH SOMETHING..?

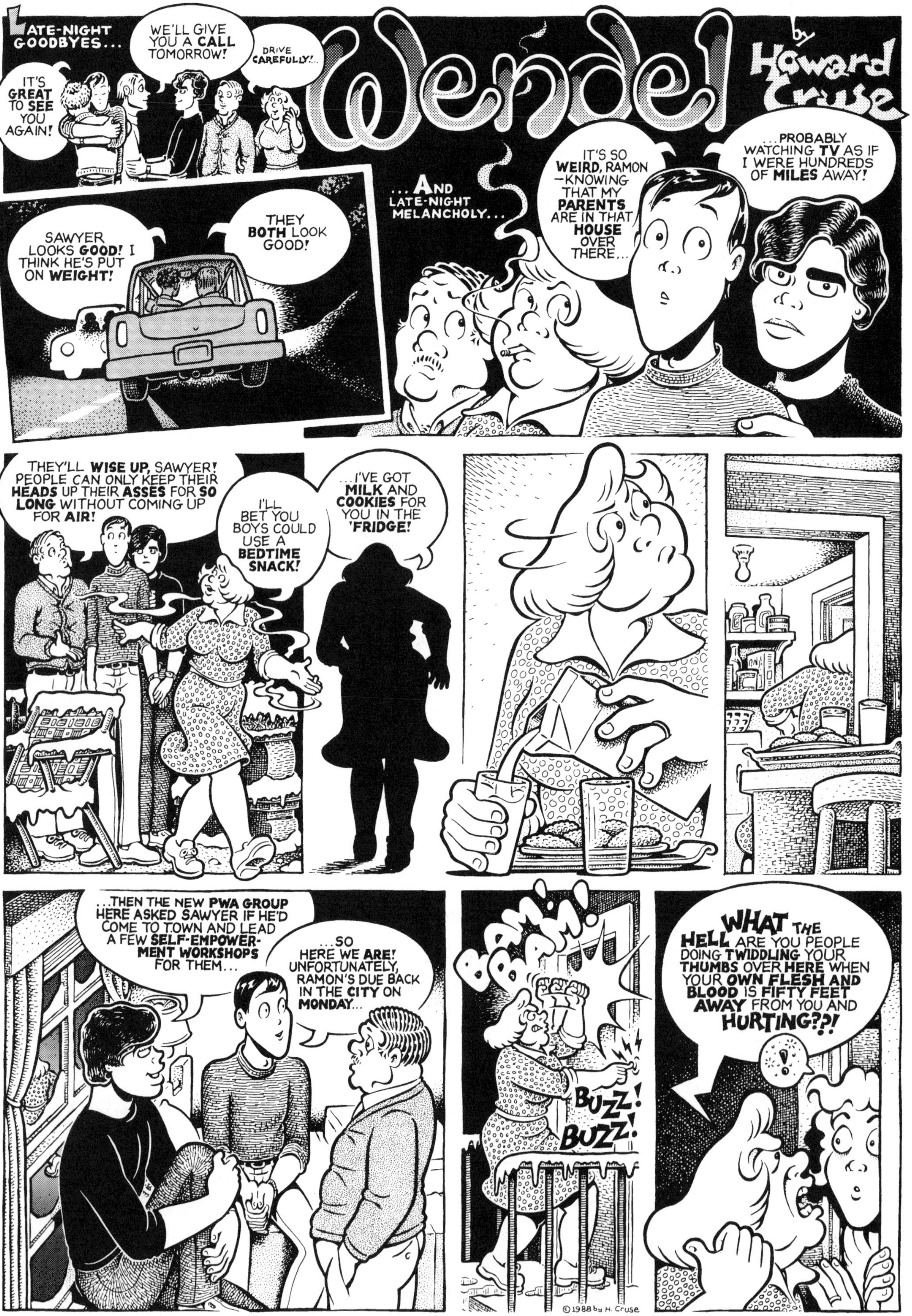

Wendel
by Howard Cruse
Late-night goodbyes...
It's great to see you again!
We'll give you a call tomorrow!
Drive carefully!..
Sawyer looks good! I think he's put on weight!
They both look good!
...And late-night melancholy...
It's so weird, Ramon —knowing that my parents are in that house over there...
...probably watching TV as if I were hundreds of miles away!
They'll wise up, Sawyer! People can only keep their heads up their asses for so long without coming up for air!
I'll bet you boys could use a bedtime snack!
...I've got milk and cookies for you in the 'fridge!
..Then the new PWA group here asked Sawyer if he'd come to town and lead a few self-empowerment workshops for them...
...So here we are! Unfortunately, Ramon's due back in the city on Monday...
Bam! Bam!
Buzz! Buzz!
What the hell are you people doing twiddling your thumbs over here when your own flesh and blood is fifty feet away from you and hurting??!
!
© 1988 by H. Cruse

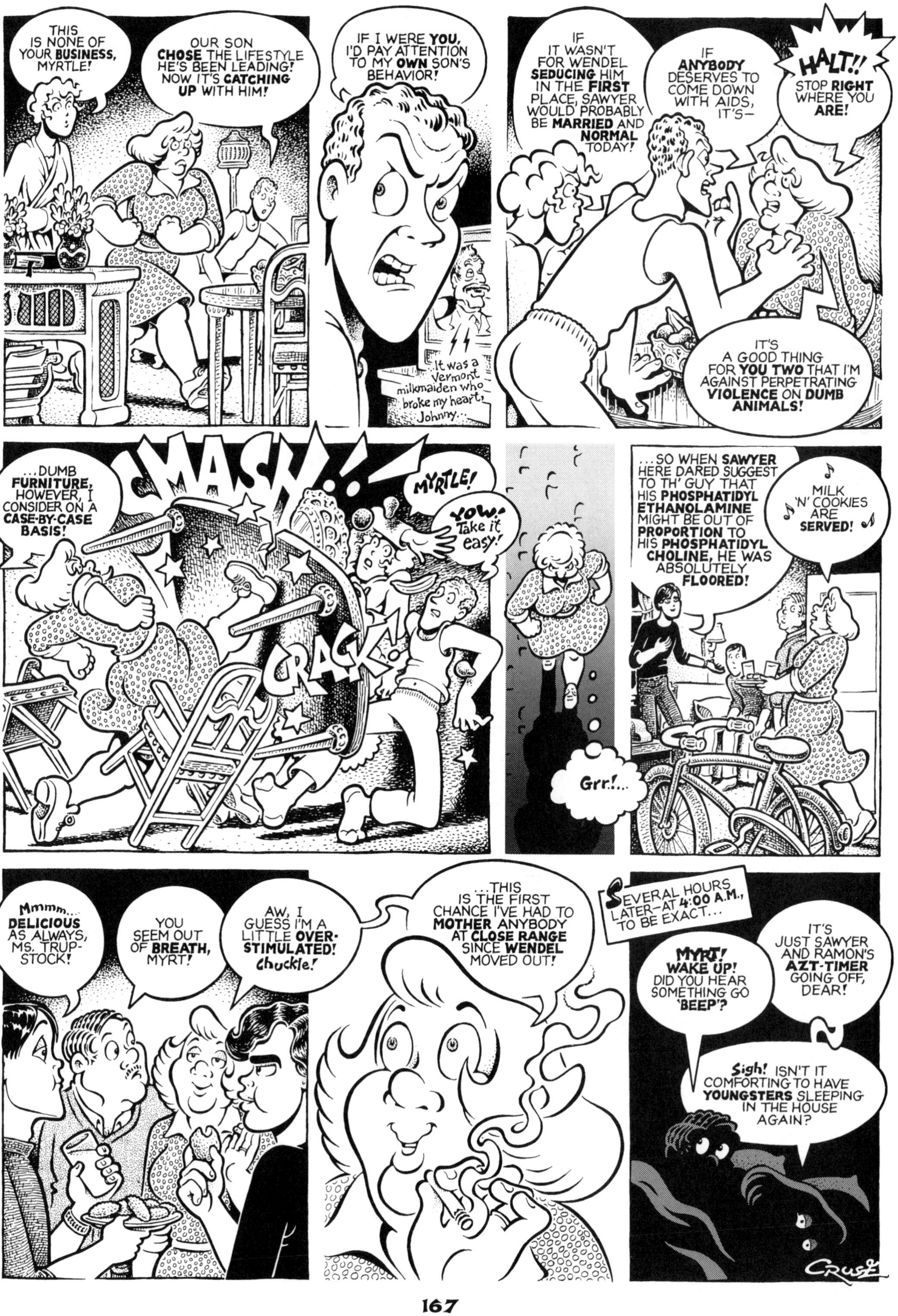
THIS IS NONE OF YOUR BUSINESS, MYRTLE!
OUR SON CHOSE THE LIFESTYLE HE'S BEEN LEADING! NOW IT'S CATCHING UP WITH HIM!
IF I WERE YOU, I'D PAY ATTENTION TO MY OWN SON'S BEHAVIOR!
...It was a Vermont milkmaiden who broke my heart, Johnny...
IF IT WASN'T FOR WENDEL SEDUCING HIM IN THE FIRST PLACE, SAWYER WOULD PROBABLY BE MARRIED AND NORMAL TODAY!
IF ANYBODY DESERVES TO COME DOWN WITH AIDS, IT'S—
HALT!! STOP RIGHT WHERE YOU ARE!
IT'S A GOOD THING FOR YOU TWO THAT I'M AGAINST PERPETRATING VIOLENCE ON DUMB ANIMALS!
...DUMB FURNITURE, HOWEVER, I CONSIDER ON A CASE-BY-CASE BASIS!
SMASH!!
MYRTLE!
YOW! Take it easy!
CRACK!
Grr!...
...SO WHEN SAWYER HERE DARED SUGGEST TO TH' GUY THAT HIS PHOSPHATIDYL ETHANOLAMINE MIGHT BE OUT OF PROPORTION TO HIS PHOSPHATIDYL CHOLINE, HE WAS ABSOLUTELY FLOORED!
MILK 'N' COOKIES ARE SERVED!
Mmmm... DELICIOUS AS ALWAYS, MS. TRUPSTOCK!
YOU SEEM OUT OF BREATH, MYRT!
AW, I GUESS I'M A LITTLE OVER-STIMULATED! Chuckle!
...THIS IS THE FIRST CHANCE I'VE HAD TO MOTHER ANYBODY AT CLOSE RANGE SINCE WENDEL MOVED OUT!
SEVERAL HOURS LATER—AT 4:00 A.M., TO BE EXACT...
MYRT! WAKE UP! DID YOU HEAR SOMETHING GO 'BEEP'?
IT'S JUST SAWYER AND RAMON'S AZT-TIMER GOING OFF, DEAR!
Sigh! ISN'T IT COMFORTING TO HAVE YOUNGSTERS SLEEPING IN THE HOUSE AGAIN?
CRUSE

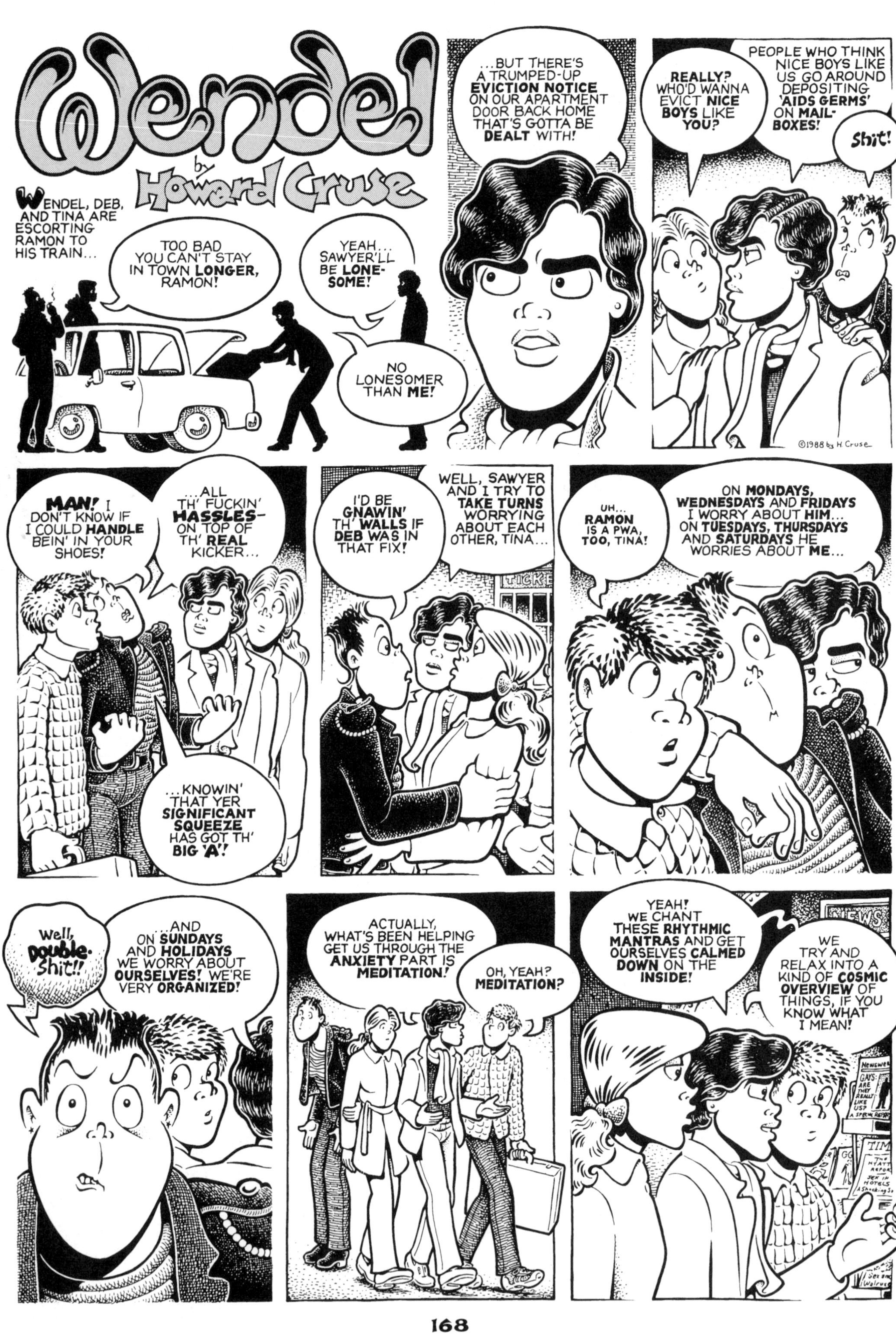
Wendel
by Howard Cruse
WENDEL, DEB, AND TINA ARE ESCORTING RAMON TO HIS TRAIN...
TOO BAD YOU CAN'T STAY IN TOWN LONGER, RAMON!
YEAH... SAWYER'LL BE LONESOME!
NO LONESOMER THAN ME!
...BUT THERE'S A TRUMPED-UP EVICTION NOTICE ON OUR APARTMENT DOOR BACK HOME THAT'S GOTTA BE DEALT WITH!
REALLY? WHO'D WANNA EVICT NICE BOYS LIKE YOU?
PEOPLE WHO THINK NICE BOYS LIKE US GO AROUND DEPOSITING 'AIDS GERMS' ON MAIL-BOXES!
Shit!
©1988 by H. Cruse
MAN! I DON'T KNOW IF I COULD HANDLE BEIN' IN YOUR SHOES!
...ALL TH' FUCKIN' HASSLES— ON TOP OF TH' REAL KICKER...
...KNOWIN' THAT YER SIGNIFICANT SQUEEZE HAS GOT TH' BIG 'A'!
I'D BE GNAWIN' TH' WALLS IF DEB WAS IN THAT FIX!
WELL, SAWYER AND I TRY TO TAKE TURNS WORRYING ABOUT EACH OTHER, TINA...
UH... RAMON IS A PWA, TOO, TINA!
ON MONDAYS, WEDNESDAYS AND FRIDAYS I WORRY ABOUT HIM... ON TUESDAYS, THURSDAYS AND SATURDAYS HE WORRIES ABOUT ME...
Well, Double-Shit!!
...AND ON SUNDAYS AND HOLIDAYS WE WORRY ABOUT OURSELVES! WE'RE VERY ORGANIZED!
ACTUALLY, WHAT'S BEEN HELPING GET US THROUGH THE ANXIETY PART IS MEDITATION!
OH, YEAH? MEDITATION?
YEAH! WE CHANT THESE RHYTHMIC MANTRAS AND GET OURSELVES CALMED DOWN ON THE INSIDE!
WE TRY AND RELAX INTO A KIND OF COSMIC OVERVIEW OF THINGS, IF YOU KNOW WHAT I MEAN!
NEWS
GAYS: ARE THEY REALLY LIKE US?

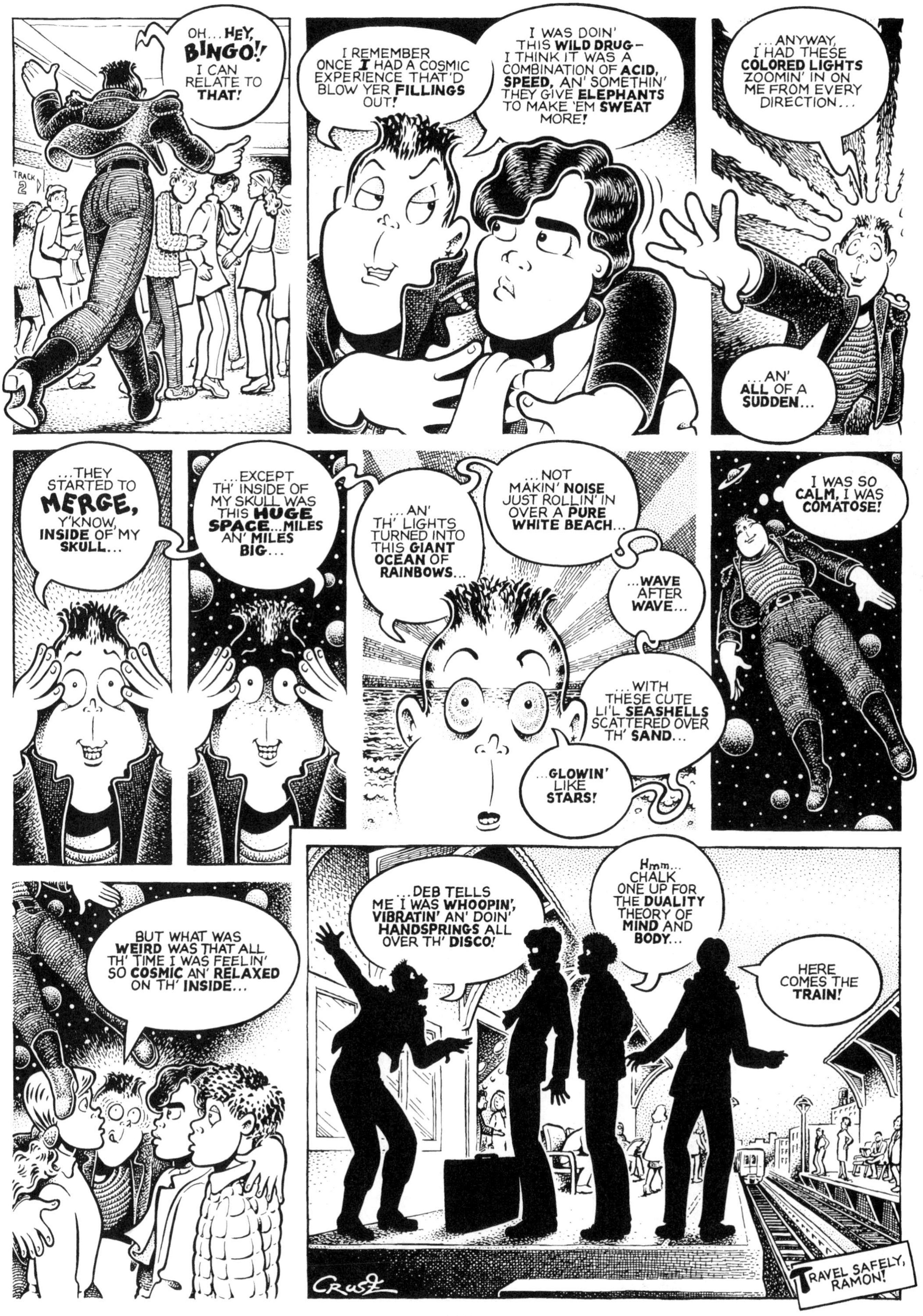

OH... HEY, BINGO!! I CAN RELATE TO THAT!
I REMEMBER ONCE I HAD A COSMIC EXPERIENCE THAT'D BLOW YER FILLINGS OUT!
I WAS DOIN' THIS WILD DRUG— I THINK IT WAS A COMBINATION OF ACID, SPEED, AN' SOMETHIN' THEY GIVE ELEPHANTS TO MAKE 'EM SWEAT MORE!
...ANYWAY, I HAD THESE COLORED LIGHTS ZOOMIN' IN ON ME FROM EVERY DIRECTION...
...AN' ALL OF A SUDDEN...
...THEY STARTED TO MERGE, Y'KNOW, INSIDE OF MY SKULL...
...EXCEPT TH' INSIDE OF MY SKULL WAS THIS HUGE SPACE...MILES AN' MILES BIG...
...AN' TH' LIGHTS TURNED INTO THIS GIANT OCEAN OF RAINBOWS...
...NOT MAKIN' NOISE JUST ROLLIN' IN OVER A PURE WHITE BEACH...
...WAVE AFTER WAVE...
...WITH THESE CUTE LI'L SEASHELLS SCATTERED OVER TH' SAND...
...GLOWIN' LIKE STARS!
I WAS SO CALM, I WAS COMATOSE!
BUT WHAT WAS WEIRD WAS THAT ALL TH' TIME I WAS FEELIN' SO COSMIC AN' RELAXED ON TH' INSIDE...
...DEB TELLS ME I WAS WHOOPIN', VIBRATIN' AN' DOIN' HANDSPRINGS ALL OVER TH' DISCO!
Hmm... CHALK ONE UP FOR THE DUALITY THEORY OF MIND AND BODY...
HERE COMES THE TRAIN!
TRAVEL SAFELY, RAMON!
CRUSE

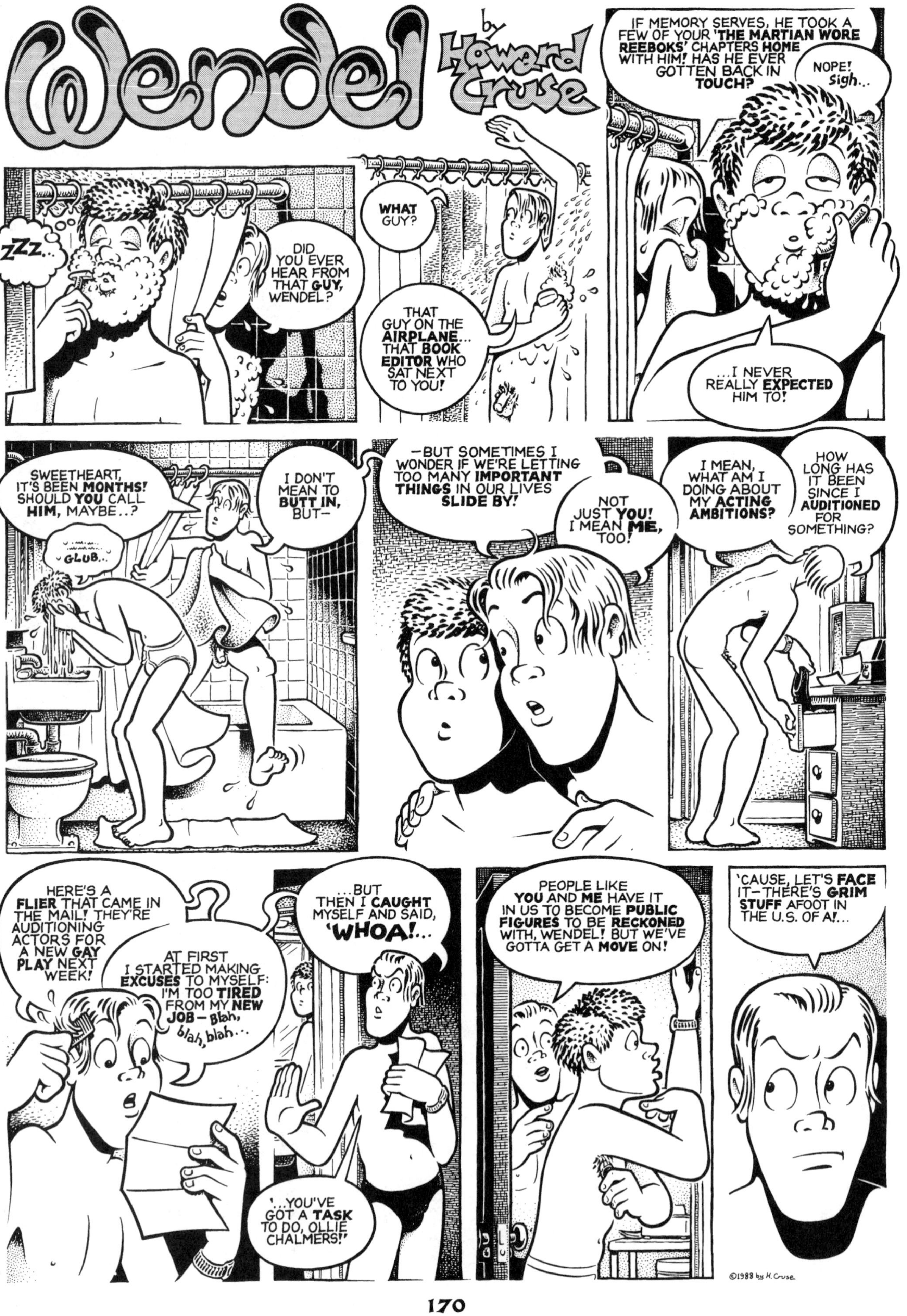
Wendel
by Howard Cruse
ZZZ...
DID YOU EVER HEAR FROM THAT GUY, WENDEL?
WHAT GUY?
THAT GUY ON THE AIRPLANE... THAT BOOK EDITOR WHO SAT NEXT TO YOU!
IF MEMORY SERVES, HE TOOK A FEW OF YOUR 'THE MARTIAN WORE REEBOKS' CHAPTERS HOME WITH HIM! HAS HE EVER GOTTEN BACK IN TOUCH?
NOPE! Sigh...
...I NEVER REALLY EXPECTED HIM TO!
SWEETHEART, IT'S BEEN MONTHS! SHOULD YOU CALL HIM, MAYBE..?
GLUB..
I DON'T MEAN TO BUTT IN, BUT—
—BUT SOMETIMES I WONDER IF WE'RE LETTING TOO MANY IMPORTANT THINGS IN OUR LIVES SLIDE BY!
NOT JUST YOU! I MEAN ME, TOO!
I MEAN, WHAT AM I DOING ABOUT MY ACTING AMBITIONS?
HOW LONG HAS IT BEEN SINCE I AUDITIONED FOR SOMETHING?
HERE'S A FLIER THAT CAME IN THE MAIL! THEY'RE AUDITIONING ACTORS FOR A NEW GAY PLAY NEXT WEEK!
AT FIRST I STARTED MAKING EXCUSES TO MYSELF: I'M TOO TIRED FROM MY NEW JOB — Blah, blah, blah...
...BUT THEN I CAUGHT MYSELF AND SAID, 'WHOA!...
'...YOU'VE GOT A TASK TO DO, OLLIE CHALMERS!'
PEOPLE LIKE YOU AND ME HAVE IT IN US TO BECOME PUBLIC FIGURES TO BE RECKONED WITH, WENDEL! BUT WE'VE GOTTA GET A MOVE ON!
'CAUSE, LET'S FACE IT—THERE'S GRIM STUFF AFOOT IN THE U.S. OF A!...
©1988 by H. Cruse

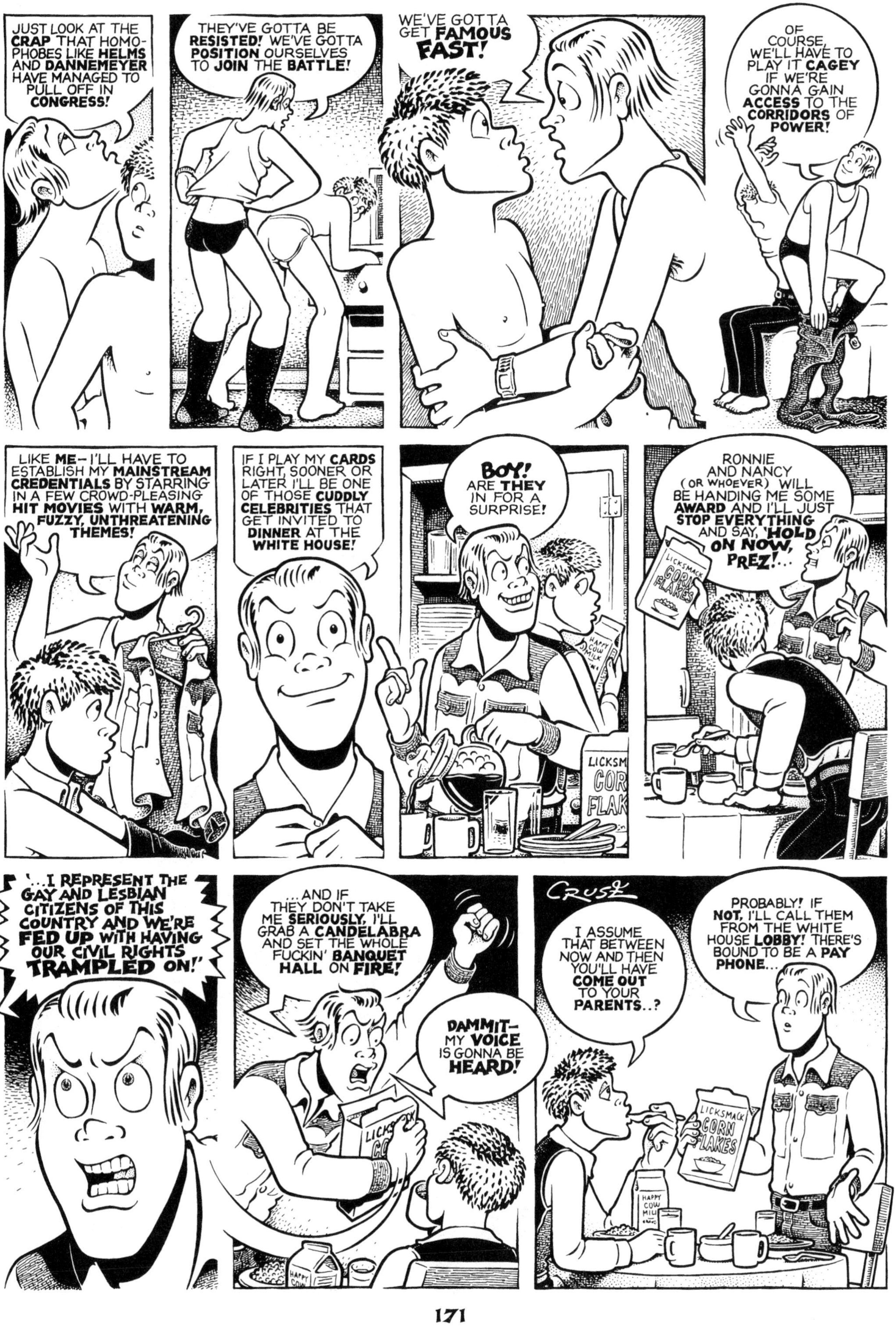
JUST LOOK AT THE CRAP THAT HOMO-PHOBES LIKE HELMS AND DANNEMEYER HAVE MANAGED TO PULL OFF IN CONGRESS!
THEY'VE GOTTA BE RESISTED! WE'VE GOTTA POSITION OURSELVES TO JOIN THE BATTLE!
WE'VE GOTTA GET FAMOUS FAST!
OF COURSE, WE'LL HAVE TO PLAY IT CAGEY IF WE'RE GONNA GAIN ACCESS TO THE CORRIDORS OF POWER!
LIKE ME– I'LL HAVE TO ESTABLISH MY MAINSTREAM CREDENTIALS BY STARRING IN A FEW CROWD-PLEASING HIT MOVIES WITH WARM, FUZZY, UNTHREATENING THEMES!
IF I PLAY MY CARDS RIGHT, SOONER OR LATER I'LL BE ONE OF THOSE CUDDLY CELEBRITIES THAT GET INVITED TO DINNER AT THE WHITE HOUSE!
BOY! ARE THEY IN FOR A SURPRISE!
RONNIE AND NANCY (OR WHOEVER) WILL BE HANDING ME SOME AWARD AND I'LL JUST STOP EVERYTHING AND SAY, 'HOLD ON NOW, PREZ!...
LICKSMACK CORN FLAKES
'...I REPRESENT THE GAY AND LESBIAN CITIZENS OF THIS COUNTRY AND WE'RE FED UP WITH HAVING OUR CIVIL RIGHTS TRAMPLED ON!'
...AND IF THEY DON'T TAKE ME SERIOUSLY, I'LL GRAB A CANDELABRA AND SET THE WHOLE FUCKIN' BANQUET HALL ON FIRE!
DAMMIT– MY VOICE IS GONNA BE HEARD!
CRUSE
I ASSUME THAT BETWEEN NOW AND THEN YOU'LL HAVE COME OUT TO YOUR PARENTS..?
PROBABLY! IF NOT, I'LL CALL THEM FROM THE WHITE HOUSE LOBBY! THERE'S BOUND TO BE A PAY PHONE...
LICKSMACK CORN FLAKES

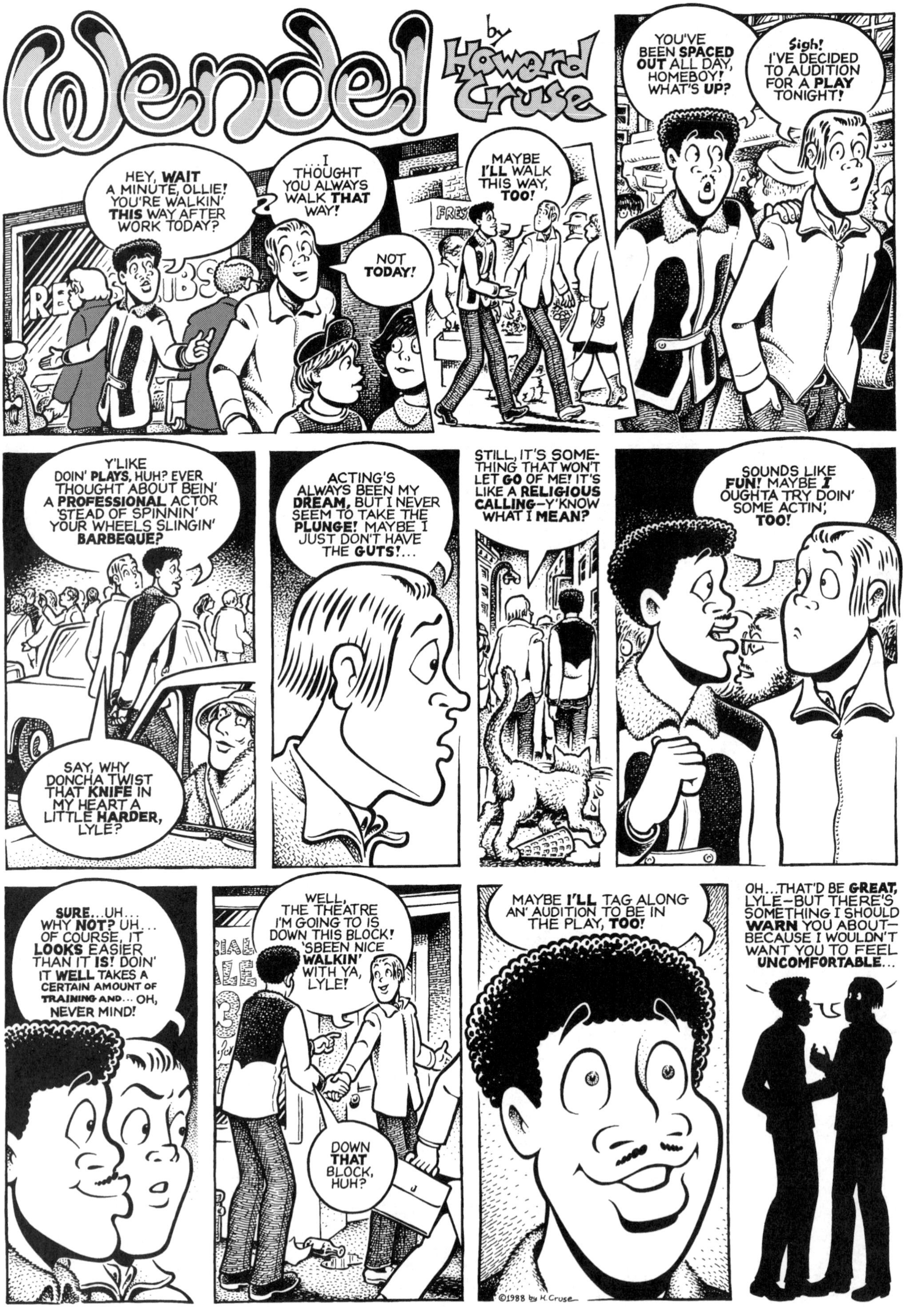
Wendel
by Howard Cruse
HEY, WAIT A MINUTE, OLLIE! YOU'RE WALKIN' THIS WAY AFTER WORK TODAY?
...I THOUGHT YOU ALWAYS WALK THAT WAY!
NOT TODAY!
MAYBE I'LL WALK THIS WAY, TOO!
YOU'VE BEEN SPACED OUT ALL DAY, HOMEBOY! WHAT'S UP?
Sigh! I'VE DECIDED TO AUDITION FOR A PLAY TONIGHT!
Y'LIKE DOIN' PLAYS, HUH? EVER THOUGHT ABOUT BEIN' A PROFESSIONAL ACTOR 'STEAD OF SPINNIN' YOUR WHEELS SLINGIN' BARBEQUE?
SAY, WHY DONCHA TWIST THAT KNIFE IN MY HEART A LITTLE HARDER, LYLE?
ACTING'S ALWAYS BEEN MY DREAM, BUT I NEVER SEEM TO TAKE THE PLUNGE! MAYBE I JUST DON'T HAVE THE GUTS!...
STILL, IT'S SOMETHING THAT WON'T LET GO OF ME! IT'S LIKE A RELIGIOUS CALLING—Y'KNOW WHAT I MEAN?
SOUNDS LIKE FUN! MAYBE I OUGHTA TRY DOIN' SOME ACTIN', TOO!
SURE...UH... WHY NOT? UH... OF COURSE, IT LOOKS EASIER THAN IT IS! DOIN' IT WELL TAKES A CERTAIN AMOUNT OF TRAINING AND... OH, NEVER MIND!
WELL, THE THEATRE I'M GOING TO IS DOWN THIS BLOCK! 'SBEEN NICE WALKIN' WITH YA, LYLE!
DOWN THAT BLOCK, HUH?
MAYBE I'LL TAG ALONG AN' AUDITION TO BE IN THE PLAY, TOO!
©1988 by H. Cruse
OH...THAT'D BE GREAT, LYLE—BUT THERE'S SOMETHING I SHOULD WARN YOU ABOUT—BECAUSE I WOULDN'T WANT YOU TO FEEL UNCOMFORTABLE...

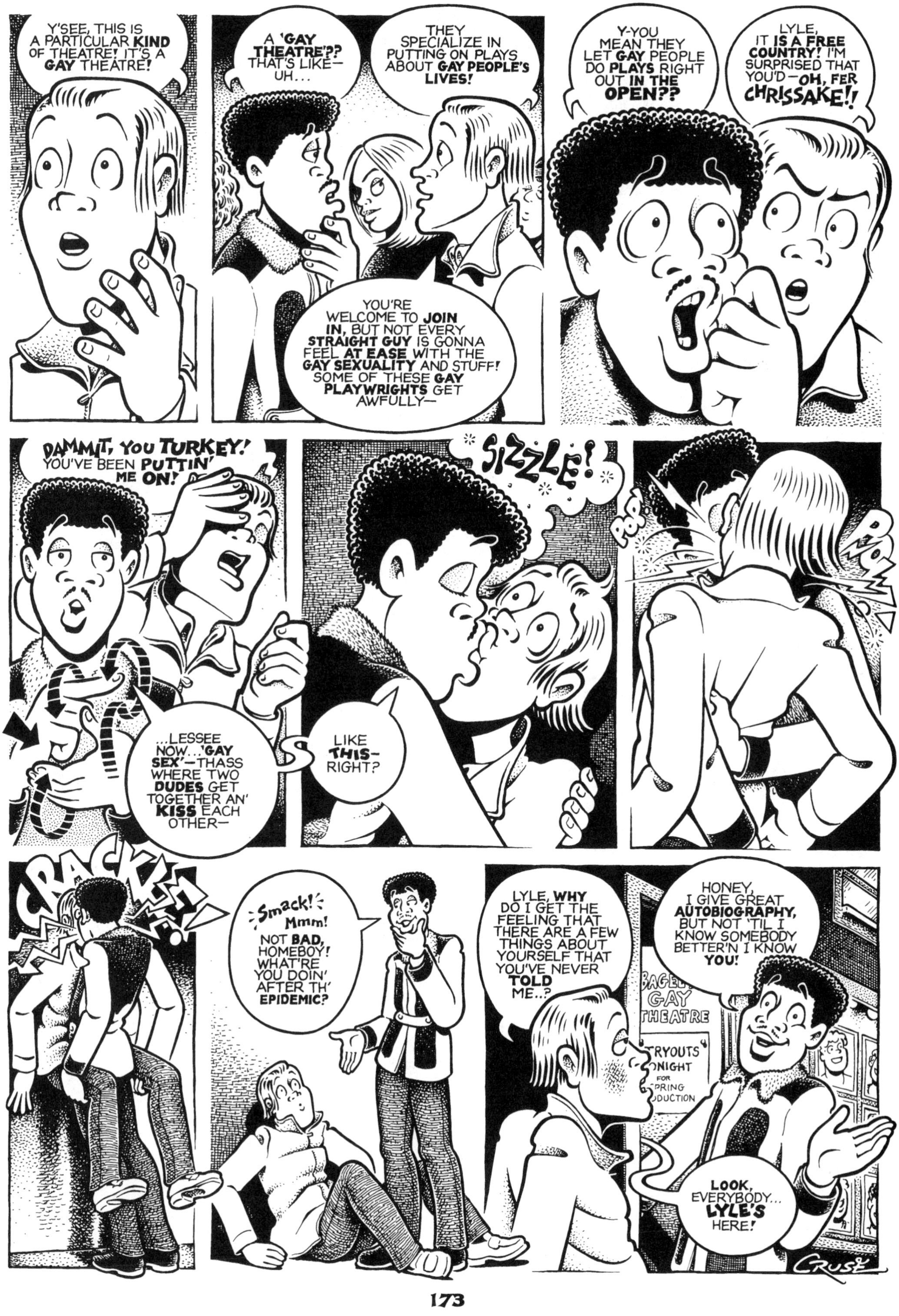
Y'SEE, THIS IS A PARTICULAR KIND OF THEATRE! IT'S A GAY THEATRE!
A 'GAY THEATRE'?? THAT'S LIKE— UH...
THEY SPECIALIZE IN PUTTING ON PLAYS ABOUT GAY PEOPLE'S LIVES!
YOU'RE WELCOME TO JOIN IN, BUT NOT EVERY STRAIGHT GUY IS GONNA FEEL AT EASE WITH THE GAY SEXUALITY AND STUFF! SOME OF THESE GAY PLAYWRIGHTS GET AWFULLY—
Y-YOU MEAN THEY LET GAY PEOPLE DO PLAYS RIGHT OUT IN THE OPEN??
LYLE, IT IS A FREE COUNTRY! I'M SURPRISED THAT YOU'D —OH, FER CHRISSAKE!!
DAMMIT, YOU TURKEY! YOU'VE BEEN PUTTIN' ME ON!
...LESSEE NOW...'GAY SEX'—THASS WHERE TWO DUDES GET TOGETHER AN' KISS EACH OTHER—
LIKE THIS—RIGHT?
SIZZLE!
POP!
POW!
CRACK!
Smack! Mmm! NOT BAD, HOMEBOY! WHAT'RE YOU DOIN' AFTER TH' EPIDEMIC?
LYLE, WHY DO I GET THE FEELING THAT THERE ARE A FEW THINGS ABOUT YOURSELF THAT YOU'VE NEVER TOLD ME..?
HONEY, I GIVE GREAT AUTOBIOGRAPHY, BUT NOT 'TIL I KNOW SOMEBODY BETTER'N I KNOW YOU!
BAGEL GAY THEATRE
TRYOUTS ONIGHT FOR PRING ODUCTION
LOOK, EVERYBODY... LYLE'S HERE!
CRUSE

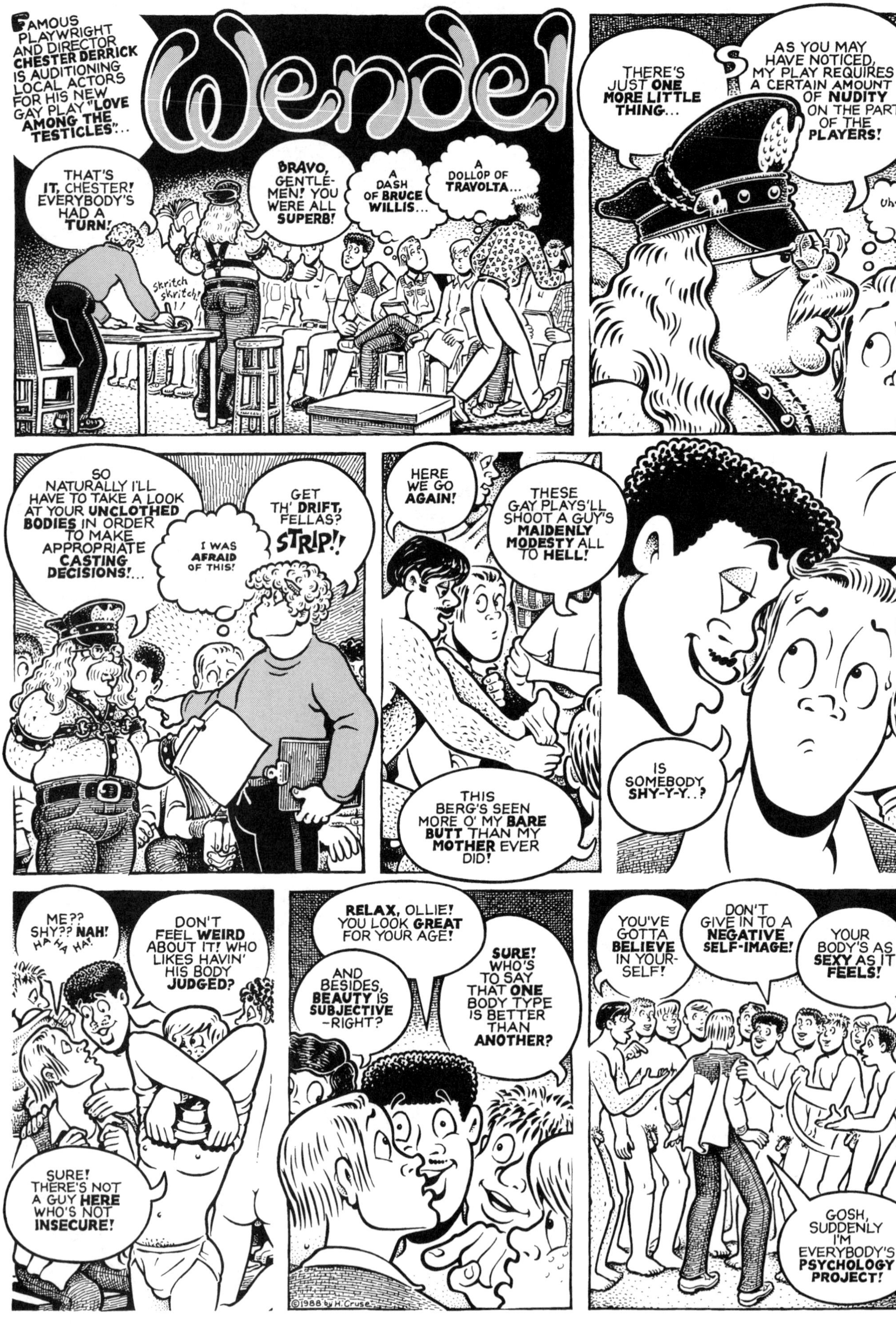
Wendel
FAMOUS PLAYWRIGHT AND DIRECTOR CHESTER DERRICK IS AUDITIONING LOCAL ACTORS FOR HIS NEW GAY PLAY "LOVE AMONG THE TESTICLES"...
THAT'S IT, CHESTER! EVERYBODY'S HAD A TURN!
skritch skritch!
BRAVO, GENTLE-MEN! YOU WERE ALL SUPERB!
A DASH OF BRUCE WILLIS...
A DOLLOP OF TRAVOLTA...
THERE'S JUST ONE MORE LITTLE THING...
AS YOU MAY HAVE NOTICED, MY PLAY REQUIRES A CERTAIN AMOUNT OF NUDITY ON THE PART OF THE PLAYERS!
Uh-oh...
SO NATURALLY I'LL HAVE TO TAKE A LOOK AT YOUR UNCLOTHED BODIES IN ORDER TO MAKE APPROPRIATE CASTING DECISIONS!...
I WAS AFRAID OF THIS!
GET TH' DRIFT, FELLAS? STRIP!!
HERE WE GO AGAIN!
THESE GAY PLAYS'LL SHOOT A GUY'S MAIDENLY MODESTY ALL TO HELL!
THIS BERG'S SEEN MORE O' MY BARE BUTT THAN MY MOTHER EVER DID!
IS SOMEBODY SHY-Y-Y..?
ME?? SHY?? NAH! HA HA HA!
DON'T FEEL WEIRD ABOUT IT! WHO LIKES HAVIN' HIS BODY JUDGED?
SURE! THERE'S NOT A GUY HERE WHO'S NOT INSECURE!
RELAX, OLLIE! YOU LOOK GREAT FOR YOUR AGE!
AND BESIDES, BEAUTY IS SUBJECTIVE -RIGHT?
SURE! WHO'S TO SAY THAT ONE BODY TYPE IS BETTER THAN ANOTHER?
©1988 by H. Cruse
YOU'VE GOTTA BELIEVE IN YOUR-SELF!
DON'T GIVE IN TO A NEGATIVE SELF-IMAGE!
YOUR BODY'S AS SEXY AS IT FEELS!
GOSH, SUDDENLY I'M EVERYBODY'S PSYCHOLOGY PROJECT!

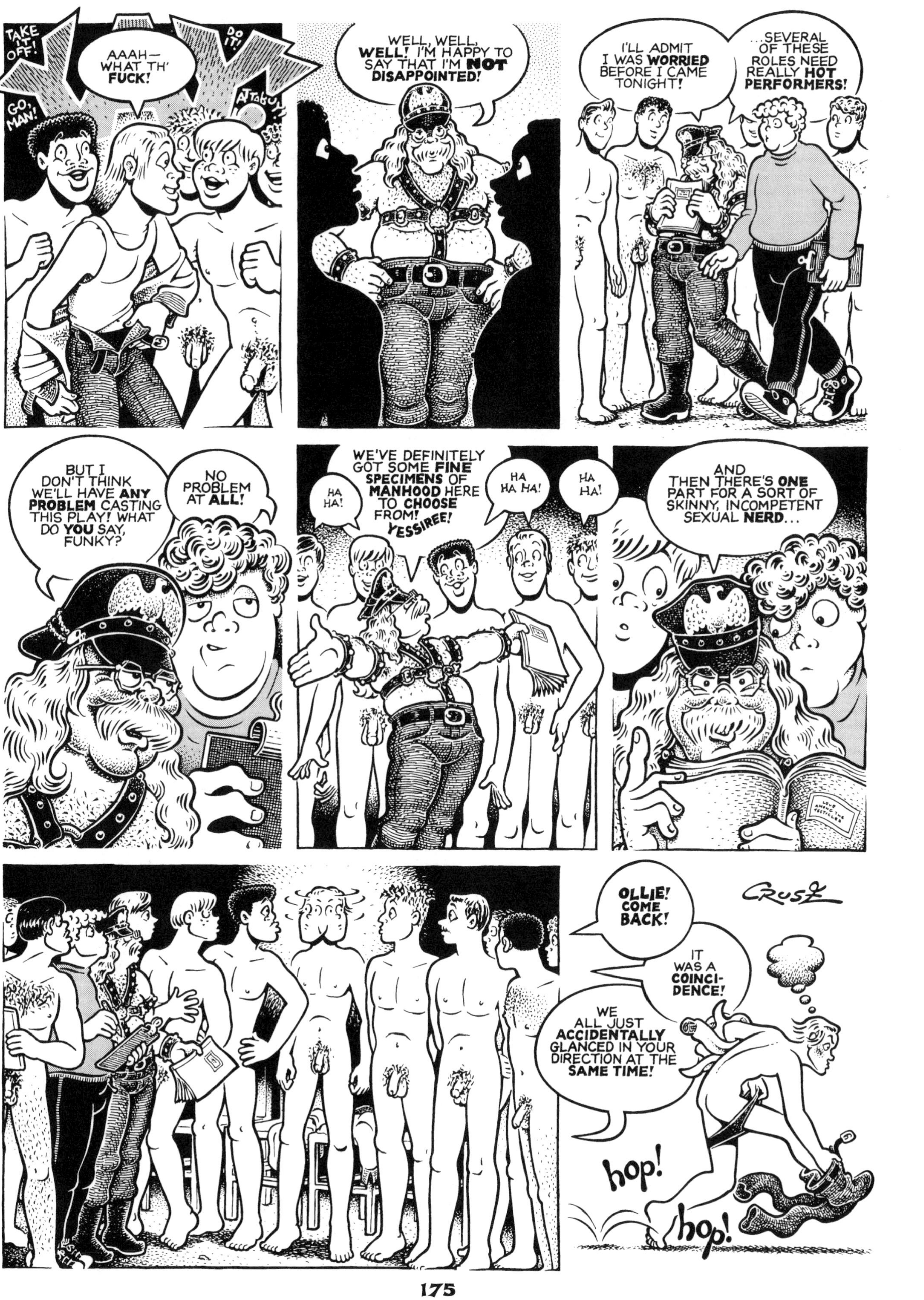
TAKE IT OFF!
DO IT!
AAAH— WHAT TH' FUCK!
GO, MAN!
ATTABOY!
WELL, WELL, WELL! I'M HAPPY TO SAY THAT I'M NOT DISAPPOINTED!
I'LL ADMIT I WAS WORRIED BEFORE I CAME TONIGHT!
...SEVERAL OF THESE ROLES NEED REALLY HOT PERFORMERS!
BUT I DON'T THINK WE'LL HAVE ANY PROBLEM CASTING THIS PLAY! WHAT DO YOU SAY, FUNKY?
NO PROBLEM AT ALL!
HA HA!
WE'VE DEFINITELY GOT SOME FINE SPECIMENS OF MANHOOD HERE TO CHOOSE FROM! YESSIREE!
HA HA HA!
HA HA!
AND THEN THERE'S ONE PART FOR A SORT OF SKINNY, INCOMPETENT SEXUAL NERD...
CRUSE
OLLIE! COME BACK!
IT WAS A COINCIDENCE!
WE ALL JUST ACCIDENTALLY GLANCED IN YOUR DIRECTION AT THE SAME TIME!
hop!
hop!

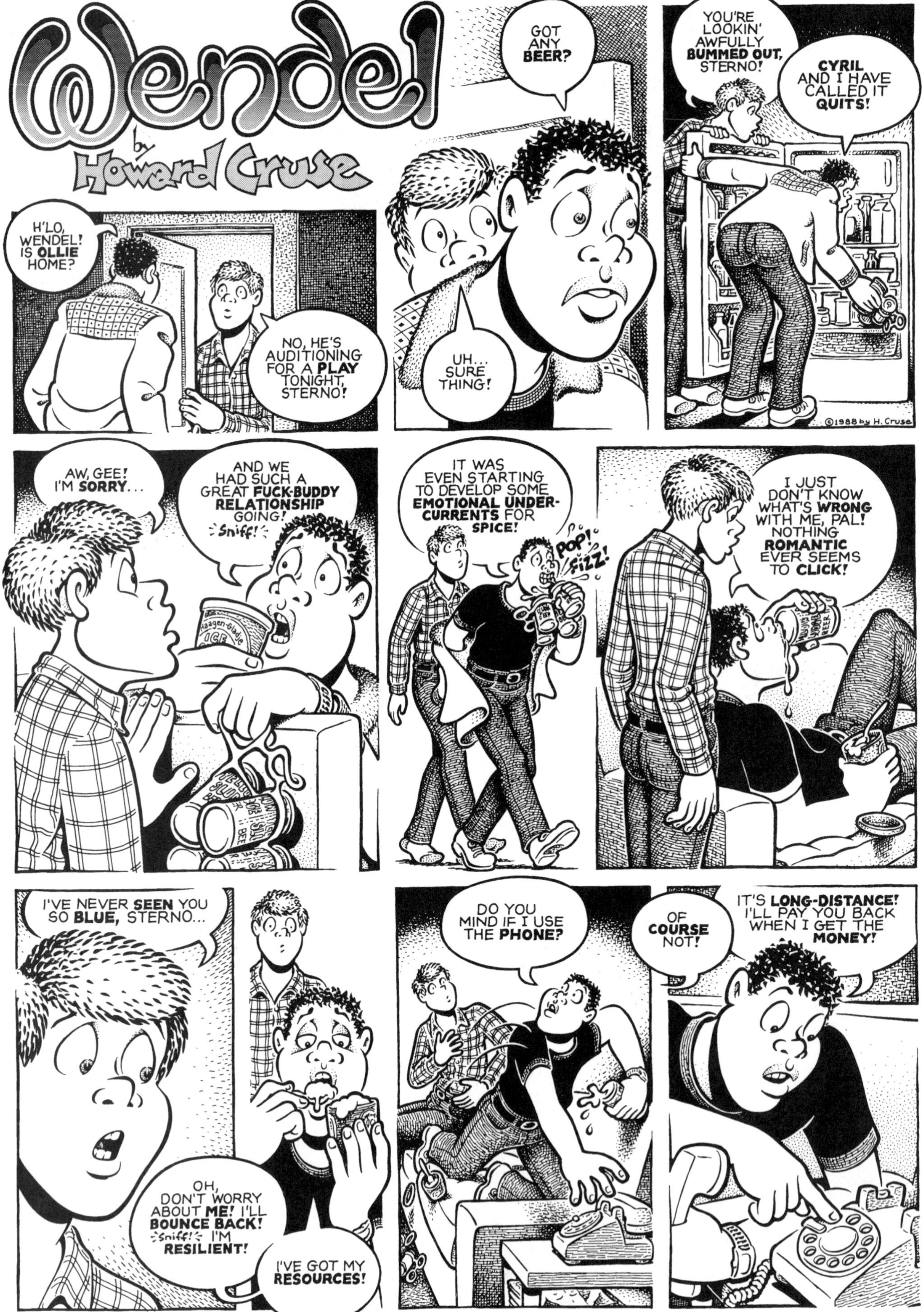
Wendel
by Howard Cruse
H'LO, WENDEL! IS OLLIE HOME?
NO, HE'S AUDITIONING FOR A PLAY TONIGHT, STERNO!
GOT ANY BEER?
UH... SURE THING!
YOU'RE LOOKIN' AWFULLY BUMMED OUT, STERNO!
CYRIL AND I HAVE CALLED IT QUITS!
©1988 by H. Cruse
AW, GEE! I'M SORRY...
AND WE HAD SUCH A GREAT FUCK-BUDDY RELATIONSHIP GOING! Sniff!
IT WAS EVEN STARTING TO DEVELOP SOME EMOTIONAL UNDER-CURRENTS FOR SPICE!
POP! FIZZ!
I JUST DON'T KNOW WHAT'S WRONG WITH ME, PAL! NOTHING ROMANTIC EVER SEEMS TO CLICK!
I'VE NEVER SEEN YOU SO BLUE, STERNO...
OH, DON'T WORRY ABOUT ME! I'LL BOUNCE BACK! Sniff! I'M RESILIENT!
I'VE GOT MY RESOURCES!
DO YOU MIND IF I USE THE PHONE?
OF COURSE NOT!
IT'S LONG-DISTANCE! I'LL PAY YOU BACK WHEN I GET THE MONEY!

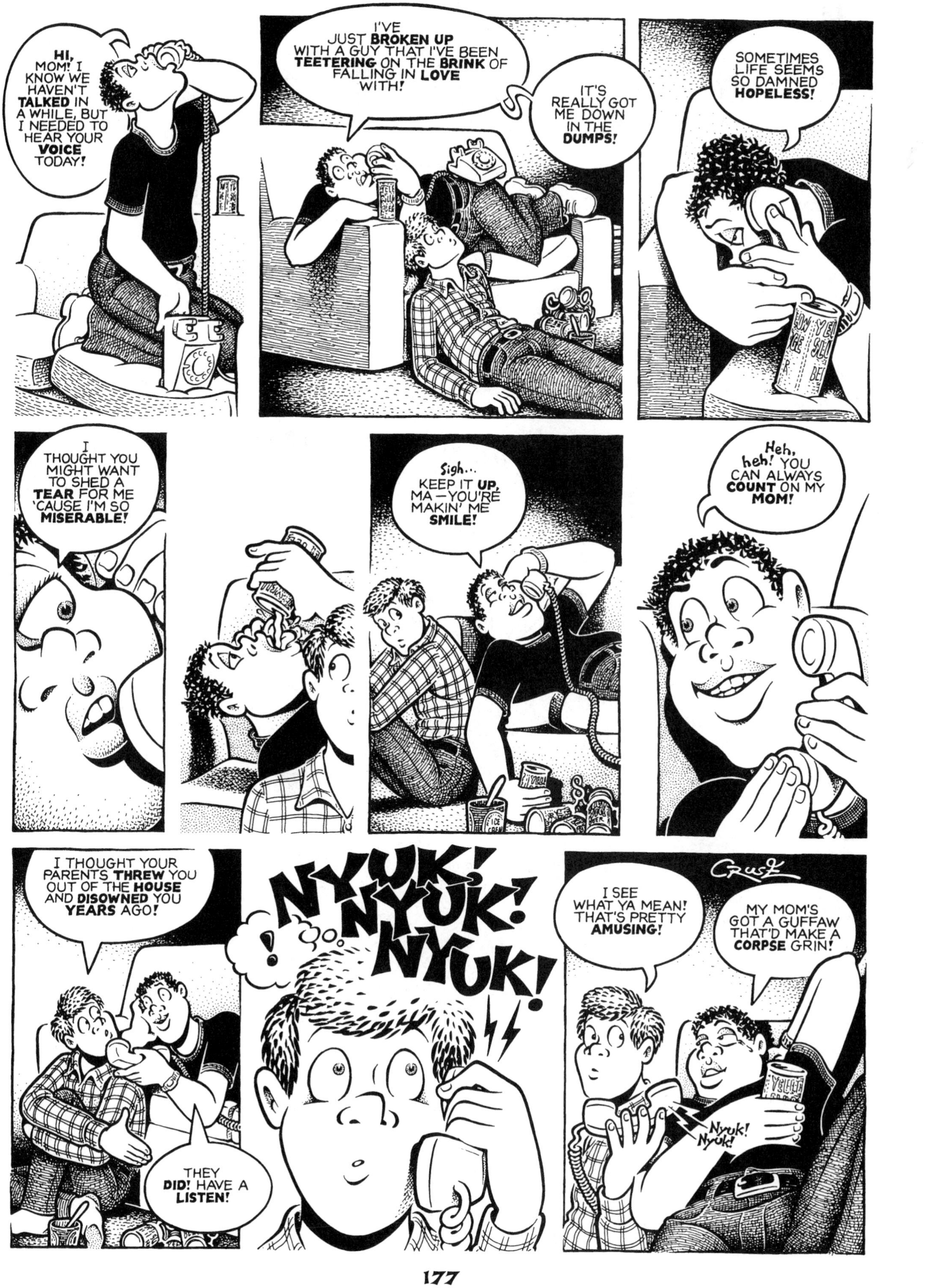
HI, MOM! I KNOW WE HAVEN'T TALKED IN A WHILE, BUT I NEEDED TO HEAR YOUR VOICE TODAY!
I'VE JUST BROKEN UP WITH A GUY THAT I'VE BEEN TEETERING ON THE BRINK OF FALLING IN LOVE WITH!
IT'S REALLY GOT ME DOWN IN THE DUMPS!
SOMETIMES LIFE SEEMS SO DAMNED HOPELESS!
I THOUGHT YOU MIGHT WANT TO SHED A TEAR FOR ME 'CAUSE I'M SO MISERABLE!
Sigh... KEEP IT UP, MA — YOU'RE MAKIN' ME SMILE!
Heh, heh! YOU CAN ALWAYS COUNT ON MY MOM!
I THOUGHT YOUR PARENTS THREW YOU OUT OF THE HOUSE AND DISOWNED YOU YEARS AGO!
THEY DID! HAVE A LISTEN!
NYUK! NYUK! NYUK!
!
CRUSE
I SEE WHAT YA MEAN! THAT'S PRETTY AMUSING!
MY MOM'S GOT A GUFFAW THAT'D MAKE A CORPSE GRIN!
Nyuk! Nyuk!

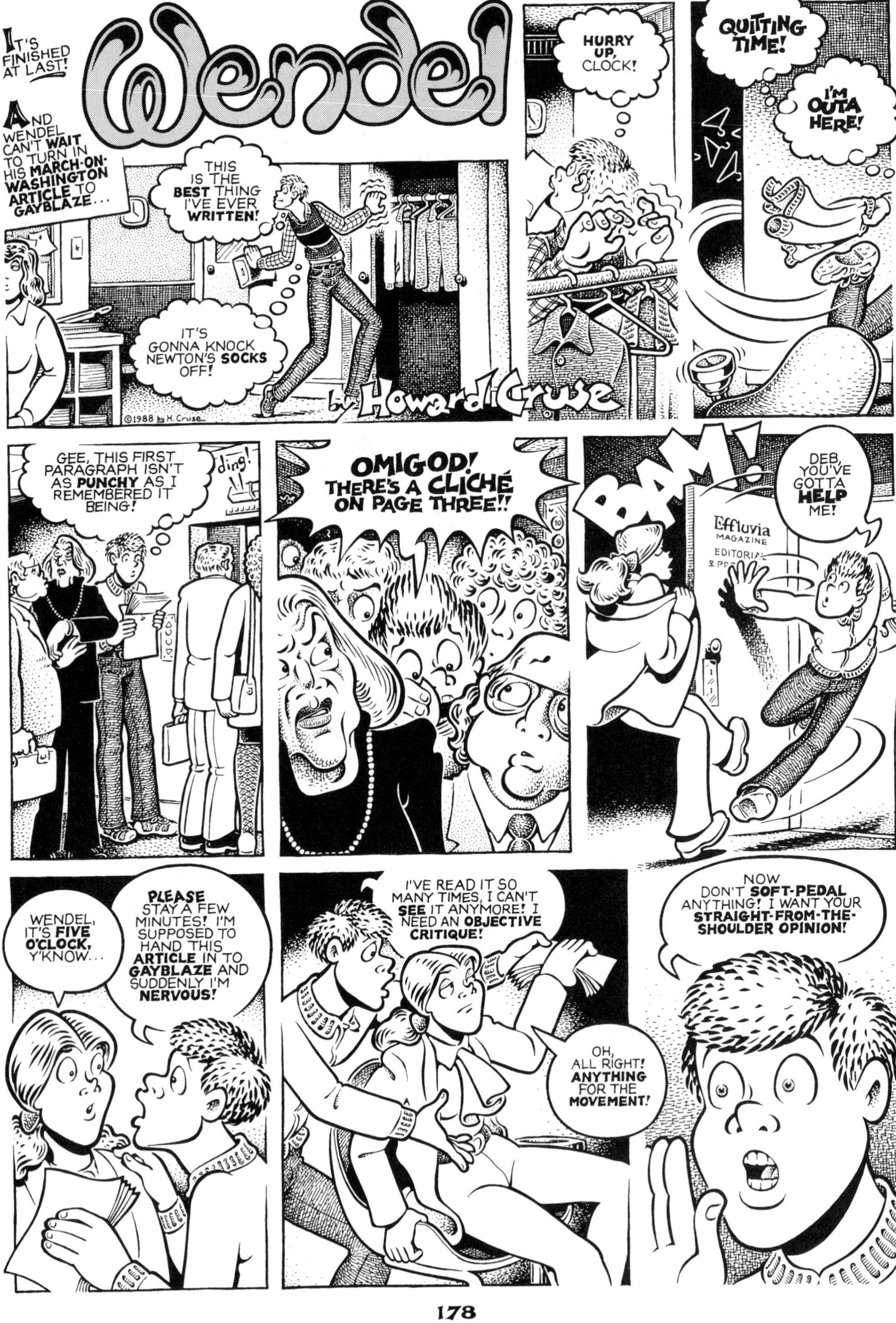
Wendel
It's finished at last!
And Wendel can't wait to turn in his March-on-Washington article to Gayblaze...
THIS IS THE BEST THING I'VE EVER WRITTEN!
IT'S GONNA KNOCK NEWTON'S SOCKS OFF!
by Howard Cruse
©1988 by H. Cruse
HURRY UP, CLOCK!
QUITTING TIME!
I'M OUTA HERE!
GEE, THIS FIRST PARAGRAPH ISN'T AS PUNCHY AS I REMEMBERED IT BEING!
ding!
OMIGOD! THERE'S A CLICHÉ ON PAGE THREE!!
BAM!
DEB, YOU'VE GOTTA HELP ME!
Effluvia MAGAZINE EDITORIAL
WENDEL, IT'S FIVE O'CLOCK, Y'KNOW...
PLEASE STAY A FEW MINUTES! I'M SUPPOSED TO HAND THIS ARTICLE IN TO GAYBLAZE AND SUDDENLY I'M NERVOUS!
I'VE READ IT SO MANY TIMES, I CAN'T SEE IT ANYMORE! I NEED AN OBJECTIVE CRITIQUE!
OH, ALL RIGHT! ANYTHING FOR THE MOVEMENT!
NOW DON'T SOFT-PEDAL ANYTHING! I WANT YOUR STRAIGHT-FROM-THE-SHOULDER OPINION!

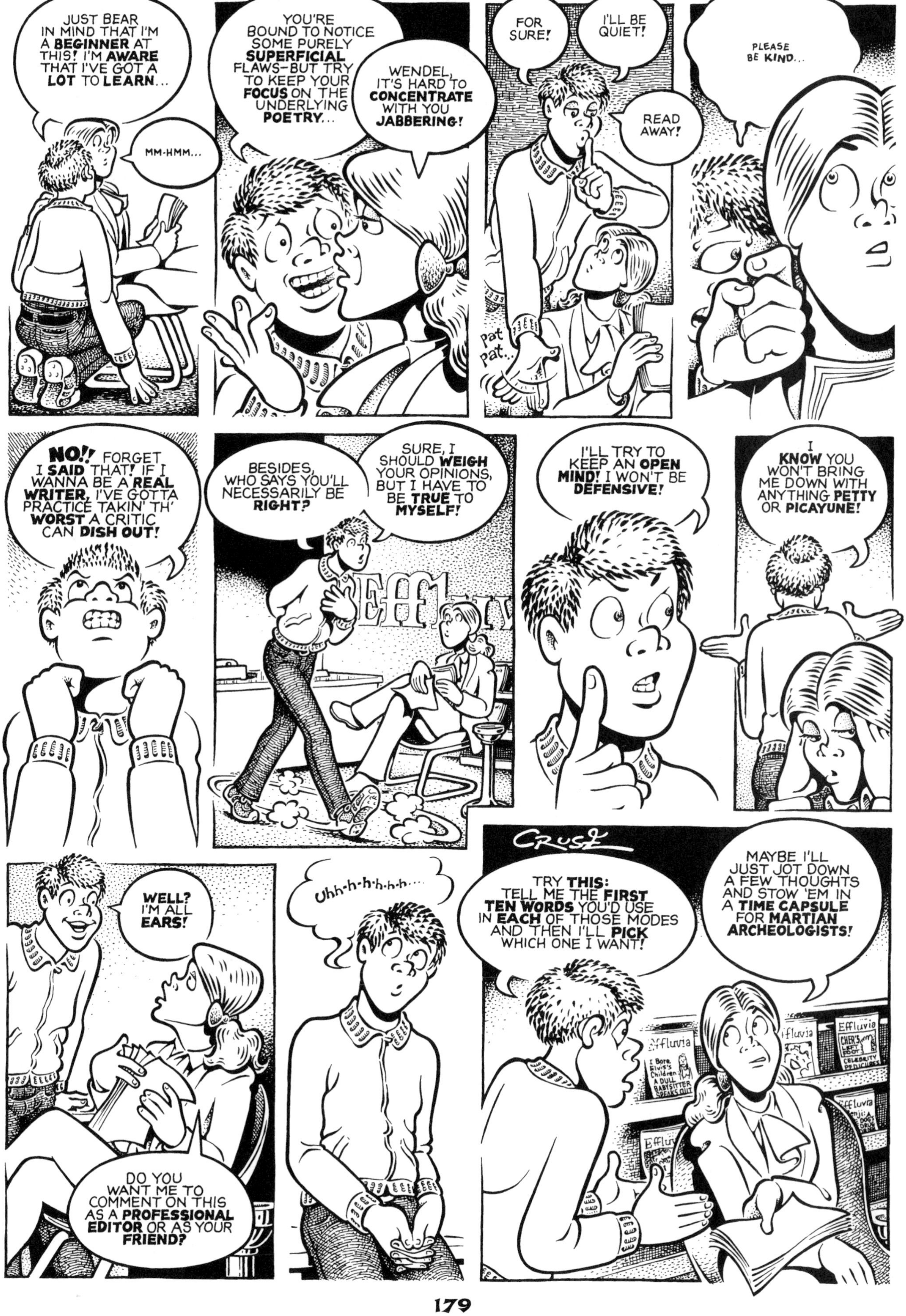
JUST BEAR IN MIND THAT I'M A BEGINNER AT THIS! I'M AWARE THAT I'VE GOT A LOT TO LEARN...
MM-HMM...
YOU'RE BOUND TO NOTICE SOME PURELY SUPERFICIAL FLAWS–BUT TRY TO KEEP YOUR FOCUS ON THE UNDERLYING POETRY...
WENDEL, IT'S HARD TO CONCENTRATE WITH YOU JABBERING!
FOR SURE!
I'LL BE QUIET!
READ AWAY!
Pat pat..
PLEASE BE KIND...
NO!! FORGET I SAID THAT! IF I WANNA BE A REAL WRITER, I'VE GOTTA PRACTICE TAKIN' TH' WORST A CRITIC CAN DISH OUT!
BESIDES, WHO SAYS YOU'LL NECESSARILY BE RIGHT?
SURE, I SHOULD WEIGH YOUR OPINIONS, BUT I HAVE TO BE TRUE TO MYSELF!
I'LL TRY TO KEEP AN OPEN MIND! I WON'T BE DEFENSIVE!
I KNOW YOU WON'T BRING ME DOWN WITH ANYTHING PETTY OR PICAYUNE!
WELL? I'M ALL EARS!
DO YOU WANT ME TO COMMENT ON THIS AS A PROFESSIONAL EDITOR OR AS YOUR FRIEND?
Uhh-h-h-h-h-h...
CRUSE
TRY THIS: TELL ME THE FIRST TEN WORDS YOU'D USE IN EACH OF THOSE MODES AND THEN I'LL PICK WHICH ONE I WANT!
MAYBE I'LL JUST JOT DOWN A FEW THOUGHTS AND STOW 'EM IN A TIME CAPSULE FOR MARTIAN ARCHEOLOGISTS!

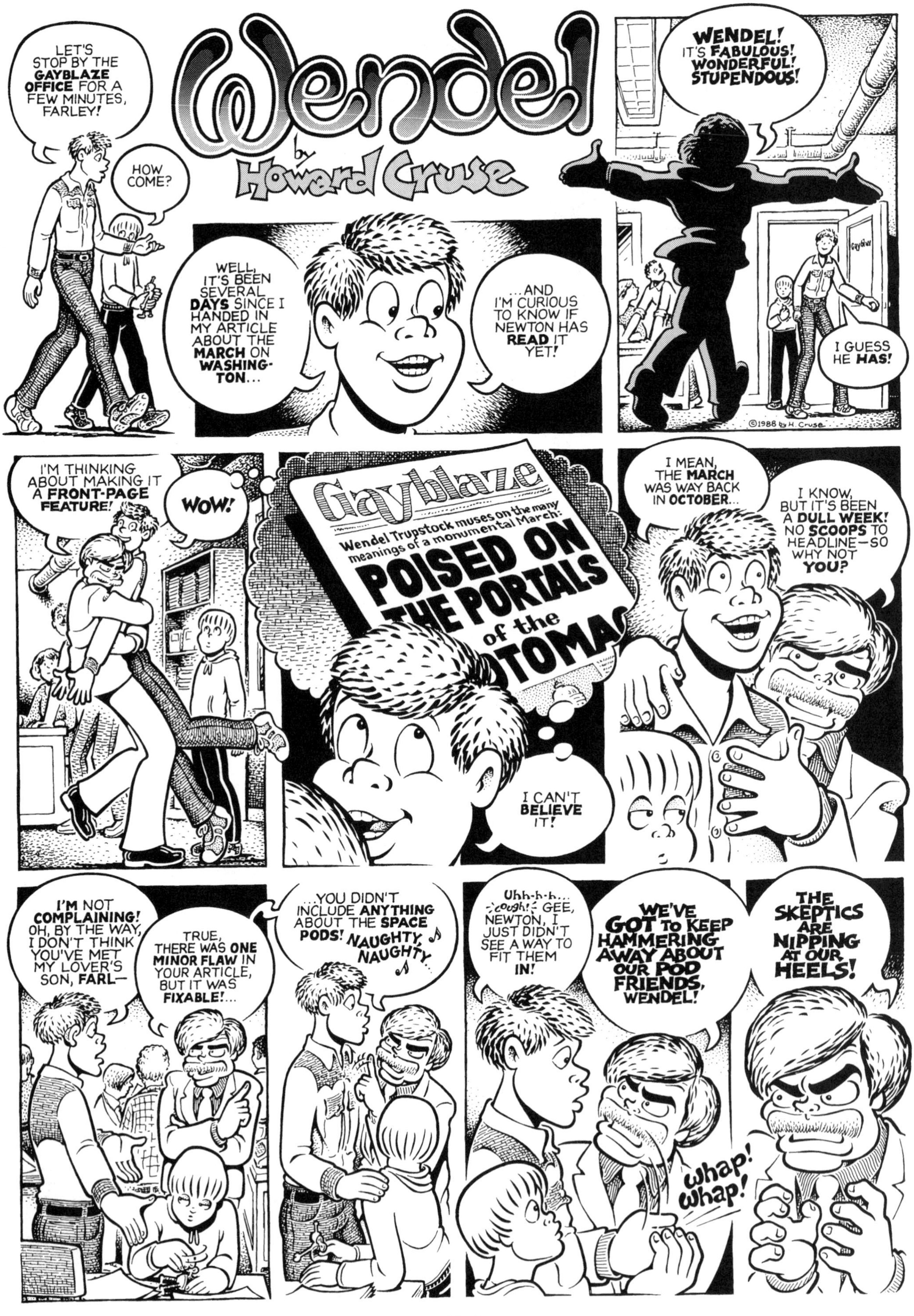

Wendel
by Howard Cruse
LET'S STOP BY THE GAYBLAZE OFFICE FOR A FEW MINUTES, FARLEY!
HOW COME?
WELL, IT'S BEEN SEVERAL DAYS SINCE I HANDED IN MY ARTICLE ABOUT THE MARCH ON WASHINGTON...
...AND I'M CURIOUS TO KNOW IF NEWTON HAS READ IT YET!
WENDEL! IT'S FABULOUS! WONDERFUL! STUPENDOUS!
GAYBLAZE
I GUESS HE HAS!
©1988 by H. Cruse
I'M THINKING ABOUT MAKING IT A FRONT-PAGE FEATURE!
WOW!
Gayblaze
Wendel Trupstock muses on the many meanings of a monumental March:
POISED ON THE PORTALS of the POTOMAC
I CAN'T BELIEVE IT!
I MEAN, THE MARCH WAS WAY BACK IN OCTOBER...
I KNOW, BUT IT'S BEEN A DULL WEEK! NO SCOOPS TO HEADLINE—SO WHY NOT YOU?
I'M NOT COMPLAINING! OH, BY THE WAY, I DON'T THINK YOU'VE MET MY LOVER'S SON, FARL—
TRUE, THERE WAS ONE MINOR FLAW IN YOUR ARTICLE, BUT IT WAS FIXABLE!...
...YOU DIDN'T INCLUDE ANYTHING ABOUT THE SPACE PODS! NAUGHTY, NAUGHTY...
Uhh-h-h... -cough!- GEE, NEWTON, I JUST DIDN'T SEE A WAY TO FIT THEM IN!
WE'VE GOT TO KEEP HAMMERING AWAY ABOUT OUR POD FRIENDS, WENDEL!
whap! whap!
THE SKEPTICS ARE NIPPING AT OUR HEELS!

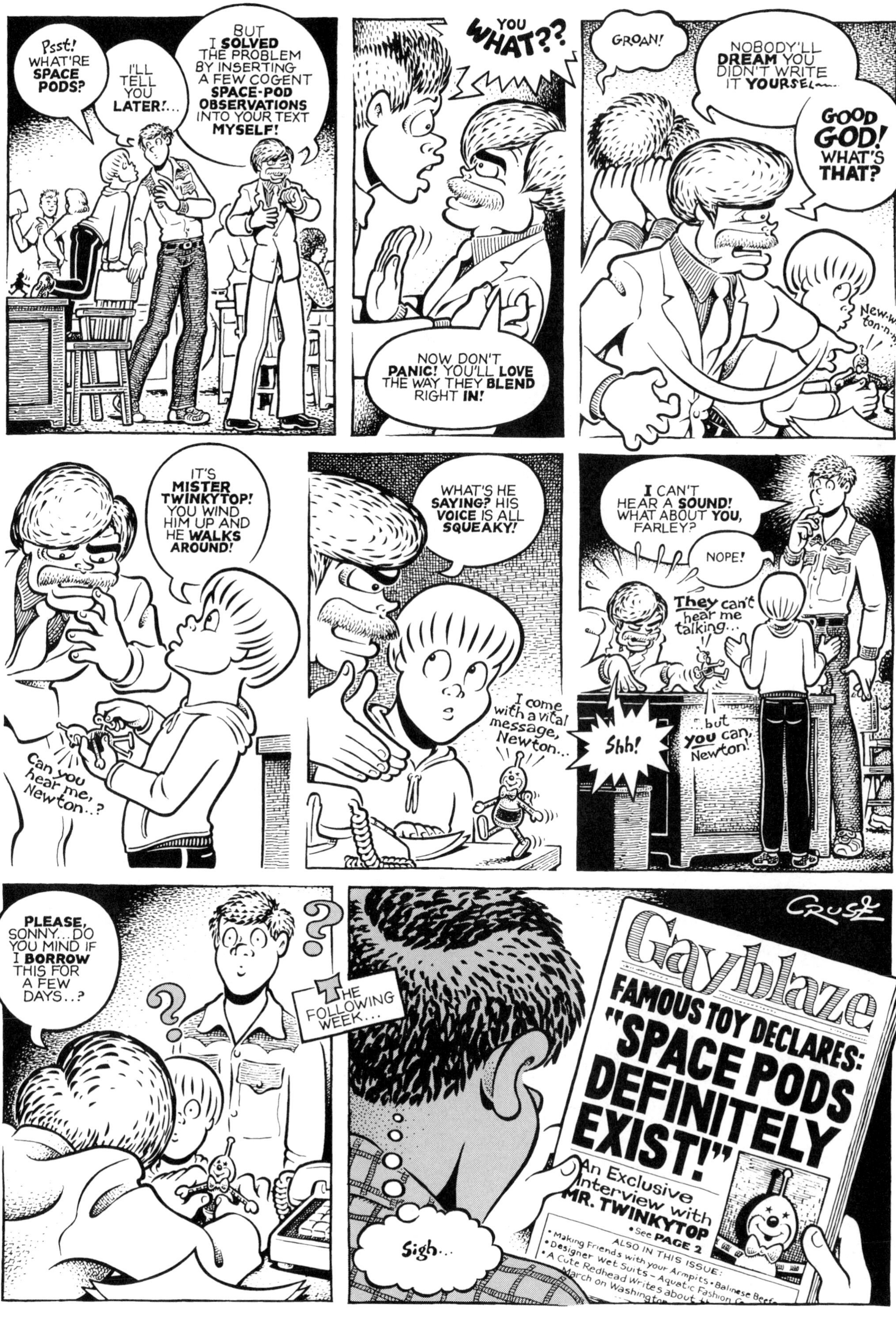
Psst! WHAT'RE SPACE PODS?
I'LL TELL YOU LATER!...
BUT I SOLVED THE PROBLEM BY INSERTING A FEW COGENT SPACE-POD OBSERVATIONS INTO YOUR TEXT MYSELF!
YOU WHAT??
NOW DON'T PANIC! YOU'LL LOVE THE WAY THEY BLEND RIGHT IN!
GROAN!
NOBODY'LL DREAM YOU DIDN'T WRITE IT YOURSEL—
GOOD GOD! WHAT'S THAT?
New-w-w-ton-n-n!
IT'S MISTER TWINKYTOP! YOU WIND HIM UP AND HE WALKS AROUND!
Can you hear me, Newton..?
WHAT'S HE SAYING? HIS VOICE IS ALL SQUEAKY!
I come with a vital message, Newton...
I CAN'T HEAR A SOUND! WHAT ABOUT YOU, FARLEY?
NOPE!
They can't hear me talking...
Shh!
...but you can, Newton!
PLEASE, SONNY... DO YOU MIND IF I BORROW THIS FOR A FEW DAYS..?
THE FOLLOWING WEEK...
CRUSE
Gayblaze
FAMOUS TOY DECLARES: "SPACE PODS DEFINITELY EXIST!"
An Exclusive Interview with MR. TWINKYTOP
• See PAGE 2
ALSO IN THIS ISSUE:
• Making Friends with your Armpits • Balinese Beef
• Designer Wet Suits – Aquatic Fashion
• A Cute Redhead Writes about
March on Washington
Sigh...

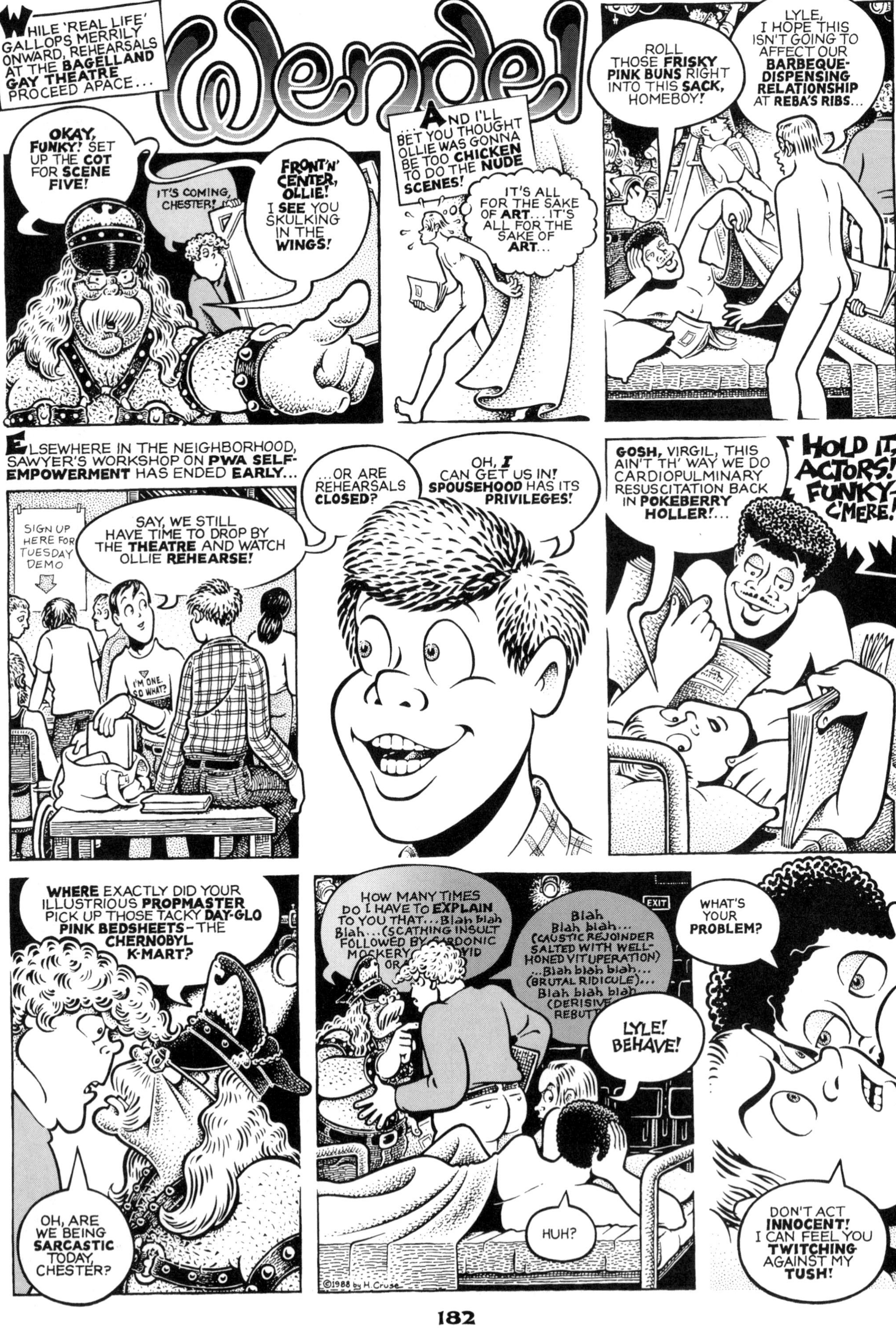
Wendel
While 'real life' gallops merrily onward, rehearsals at the Bagelland Gay Theatre proceed apace...
Okay, Funky! Set up the cot for scene five!
It's coming, Chester!
Front'n' center, Ollie! I see you skulking in the wings!
...And I'll bet you thought Ollie was gonna be too chicken to do the nude scenes!
It's all for the sake of art... It's all for the sake of art...
Roll those frisky pink buns right into this sack, homeboy!
Lyle, I hope this isn't going to affect our barbeque-dispensing relationship at Reba's Ribs...
Elsewhere in the neighborhood, Sawyer's workshop on PWA self-empowerment has ended early...
Sign up here for Tuesday demo
Say, we still have time to drop by the theatre and watch Ollie rehearse!
I'm one. So what?
...Or are rehearsals closed?
Oh, I can get us in! Spousehood has its privileges!
Gosh, Virgil, this ain't th' way we do cardiopulminary resuscitation back in Pokeberry Holler!...
Hold it, actors! Funky- c'mere!
Where exactly did your illustrious propmaster pick up those tacky Day-Glo pink bedsheets — the Chernobyl K-Mart?
Oh, are we being sarcastic today, Chester?
How many times do I have to explain to you that... Blah blah blah...(scathing insult followed by sardonic mockery...
Blah blah blah... (caustic rejoinder salted with well-honed vituperation) ...Blah blah blah... (brutal ridicule)... Blah blah blah
EXIT
Lyle! Behave!
Huh?
©1988 by H. Cruse
What's your problem?
Don't act innocent! I can feel you twitching against my tush!

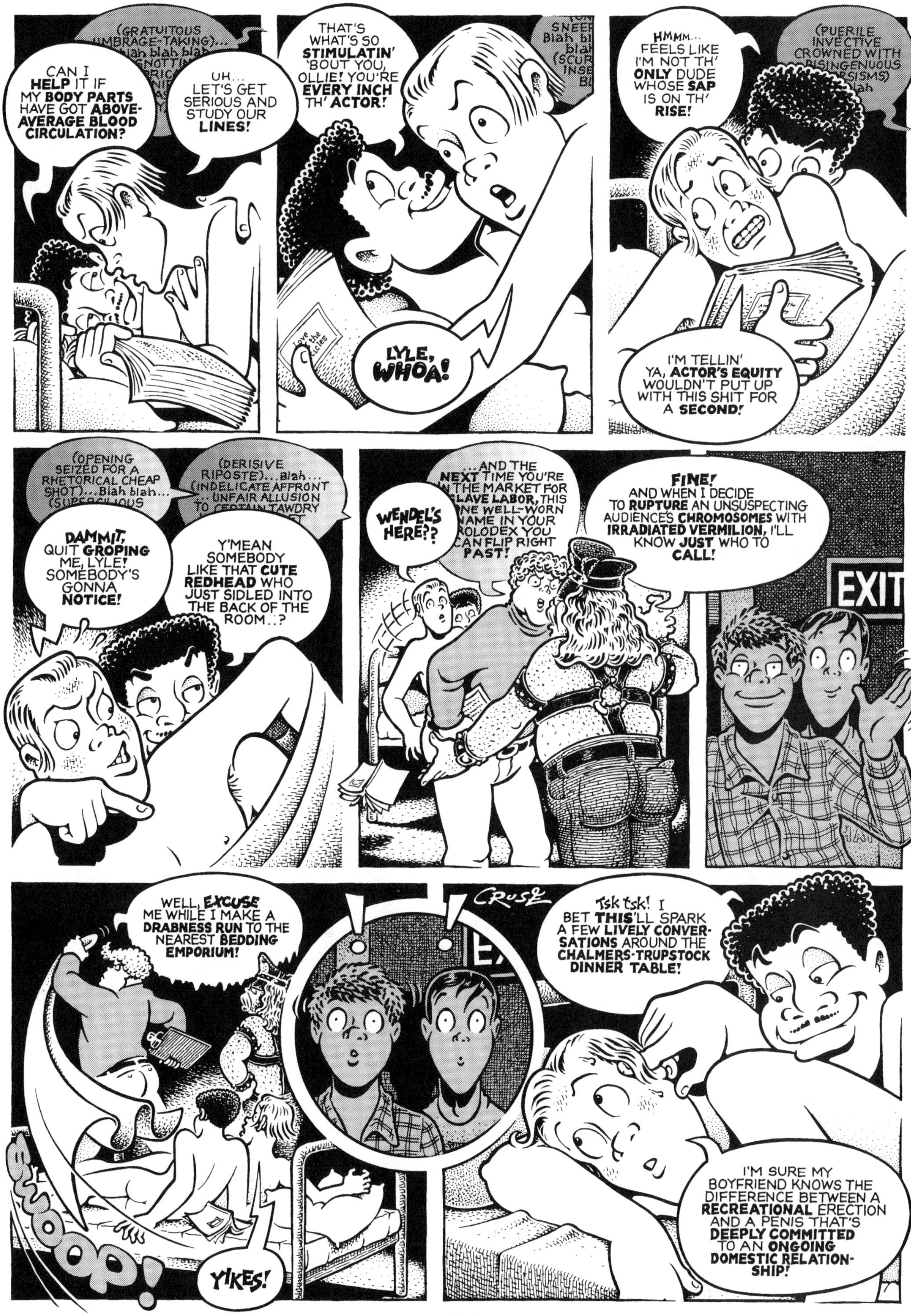
(GRATUITOUS UMBRAGE-TAKING)...
CAN I HELP IT IF MY BODY PARTS HAVE GOT ABOVE-AVERAGE BLOOD CIRCULATION?
UH... LET'S GET SERIOUS AND STUDY OUR LINES!
THAT'S WHAT'S SO STIMULATIN' 'BOUT YOU, OLLIE! YOU'RE EVERY INCH TH' ACTOR!
LYLE, WHOA!
HMMM... FEELS LIKE I'M NOT TH' ONLY DUDE WHOSE SAP IS ON TH' RISE!
(PUERILE INVECTIVE CROWNED WITH
I'M TELLIN' YA, ACTOR'S EQUITY WOULDN'T PUT UP WITH THIS SHIT FOR A SECOND!
(OPENING SEIZED FOR A RHETORICAL CHEAP SHOT)... Blah blah...
(DERISIVE RIPOSTE)... Blah...
DAMMIT, QUIT GROPING ME, LYLE! SOMEBODY'S GONNA NOTICE!
Y'MEAN SOMEBODY LIKE THAT CUTE REDHEAD WHO JUST SIDLED INTO THE BACK OF THE ROOM..?
WENDEL'S HERE??
...AND THE NEXT TIME YOU'RE IN THE MARKET FOR SLAVE LABOR, THIS ONE WELL-WORN NAME IN YOUR ROLODEX YOU CAN FLIP RIGHT PAST!
FINE! AND WHEN I DECIDE TO RUPTURE AN UNSUSPECTING AUDIENCE'S CHROMOSOMES WITH IRRADIATED VERMILION, I'LL KNOW JUST WHO TO CALL!
EXIT
WELL, EXCUSE ME WHILE I MAKE A DRABNESS RUN TO THE NEAREST BEDDING EMPORIUM!
SWOOP!
YIKES!
CRUSE
Tsk tsk! I BET THIS'LL SPARK A FEW LIVELY CONVERSATIONS AROUND THE CHALMERS-TRUPSTOCK DINNER TABLE!
I'M SURE MY BOYFRIEND KNOWS THE DIFFERENCE BETWEEN A RECREATIONAL ERECTION AND A PENIS THAT'S DEEPLY COMMITTED TO AN ONGOING DOMESTIC RELATIONSHIP!

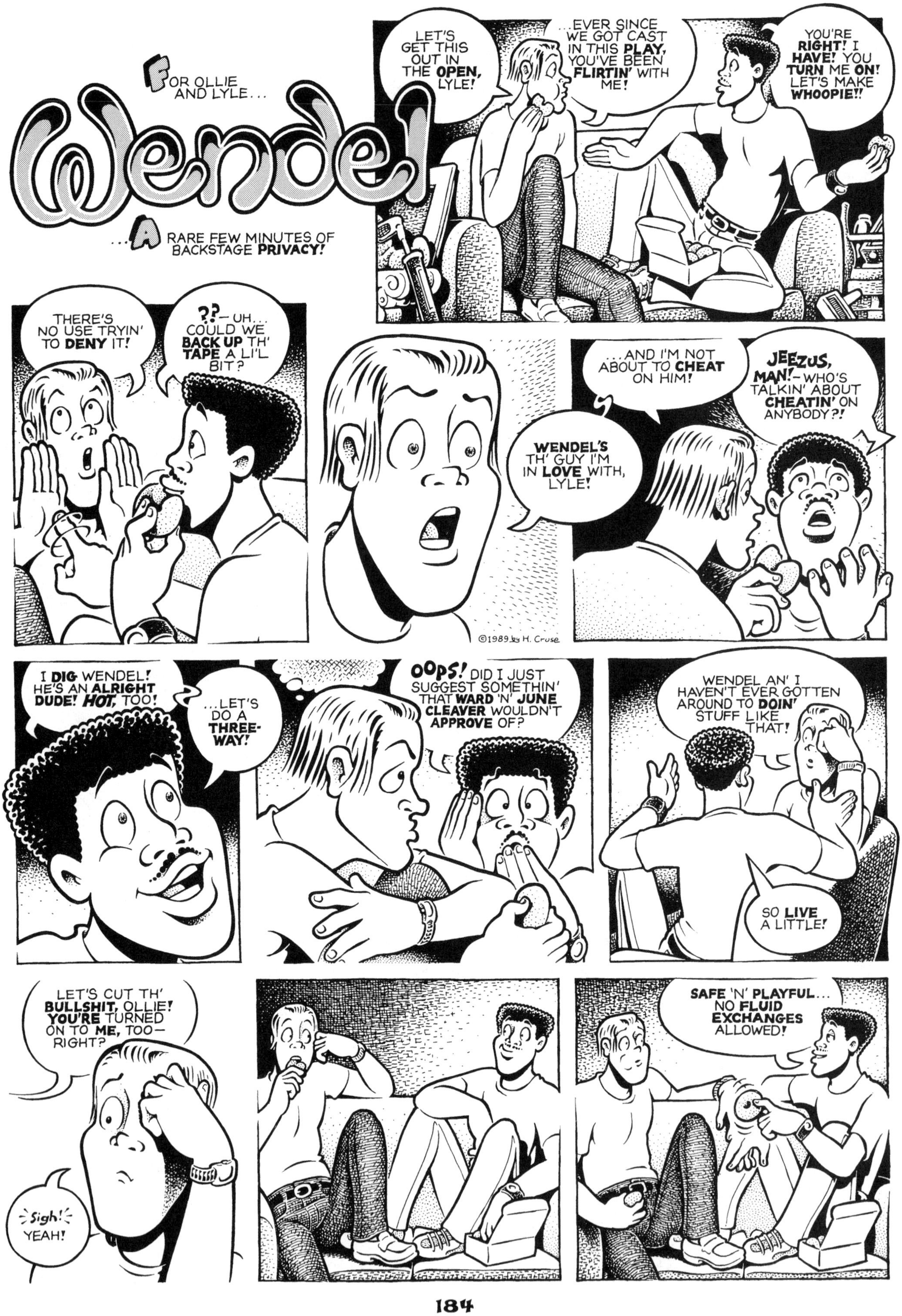
FOR OLLIE AND LYLE...
Wendel
...A RARE FEW MINUTES OF BACKSTAGE PRIVACY!
LET'S GET THIS OUT IN THE OPEN, LYLE!
...EVER SINCE WE GOT CAST IN THIS PLAY, YOU'VE BEEN FLIRTIN' WITH ME!
YOU'RE RIGHT! I HAVE! YOU TURN ME ON! LET'S MAKE WHOOPIE!!
THERE'S NO USE TRYIN' TO DENY IT!
??–UH... COULD WE BACK UP TH' TAPE A LI'L BIT?
WENDEL'S TH' GUY I'M IN LOVE WITH, LYLE!
...AND I'M NOT ABOUT TO CHEAT ON HIM!
JEEZUS, MAN!–WHO'S TALKIN' ABOUT CHEATIN' ON ANYBODY?!
©1989 by H. Cruse
I DIG WENDEL! HE'S AN ALRIGHT DUDE! HOT, TOO!
...LET'S DO A THREE-WAY!
OOPS! DID I JUST SUGGEST SOMETHIN' THAT WARD 'N' JUNE CLEAVER WOULDN'T APPROVE OF?
WENDEL AN' I HAVEN'T EVER GOTTEN AROUND TO DOIN' STUFF LIKE THAT!
SO LIVE A LITTLE!
LET'S CUT TH' BULLSHIT, OLLIE! YOU'RE TURNED ON TO ME, TOO–RIGHT?
Sigh! YEAH!
SAFE 'N' PLAYFUL... NO FLUID EXCHANGES ALLOWED!

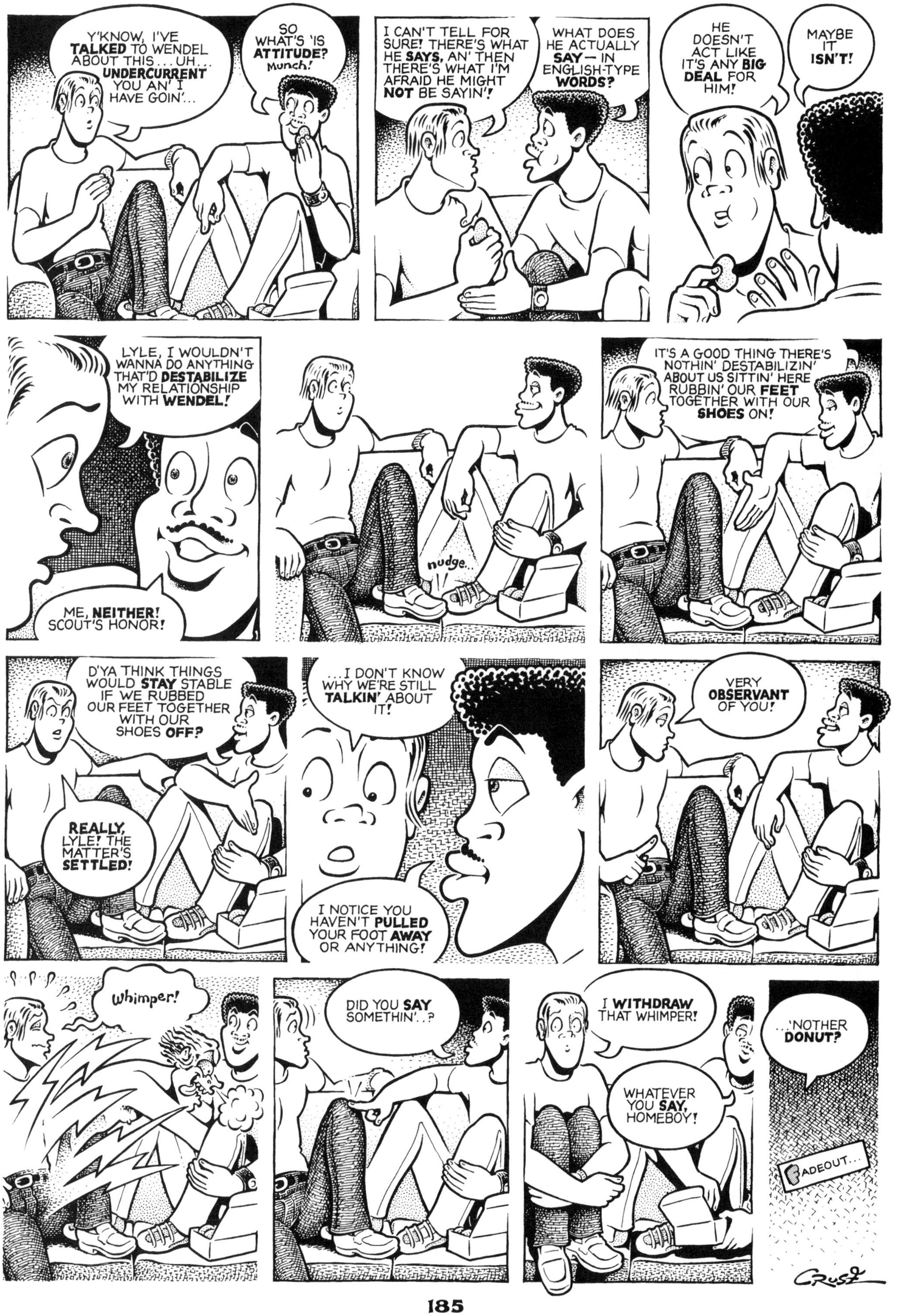

Y'KNOW, I'VE TALKED TO WENDEL ABOUT THIS... UH... UNDERCURRENT YOU AN' I HAVE GOIN'...
SO WHAT'S 'IS ATTITUDE? Munch!
I CAN'T TELL FOR SURE! THERE'S WHAT HE SAYS, AN' THEN THERE'S WHAT I'M AFRAID HE MIGHT NOT BE SAYIN'!
WHAT DOES HE ACTUALLY SAY — IN ENGLISH-TYPE WORDS?
HE DOESN'T ACT LIKE IT'S ANY BIG DEAL FOR HIM!
MAYBE IT ISN'T!
LYLE, I WOULDN'T WANNA DO ANYTHING THAT'D DESTABILIZE MY RELATIONSHIP WITH WENDEL!
ME, NEITHER! SCOUT'S HONOR!
nudge..
IT'S A GOOD THING THERE'S NOTHIN' DESTABILIZIN' ABOUT US SITTIN' HERE RUBBIN' OUR FEET TOGETHER WITH OUR SHOES ON!
D'YA THINK THINGS WOULD STAY STABLE IF WE RUBBED OUR FEET TOGETHER WITH OUR SHOES OFF?
REALLY, LYLE! THE MATTER'S SETTLED!
...I DON'T KNOW WHY WE'RE STILL TALKIN' ABOUT IT!
I NOTICE YOU HAVEN'T PULLED YOUR FOOT AWAY OR ANYTHING!
VERY OBSERVANT OF YOU!
Whimper!
DID YOU SAY SOMETHIN'..?
I WITHDRAW THAT WHIMPER!
WHATEVER YOU SAY, HOMEBOY!
...'NOTHER DONUT?
FADEOUT...
CRUSE

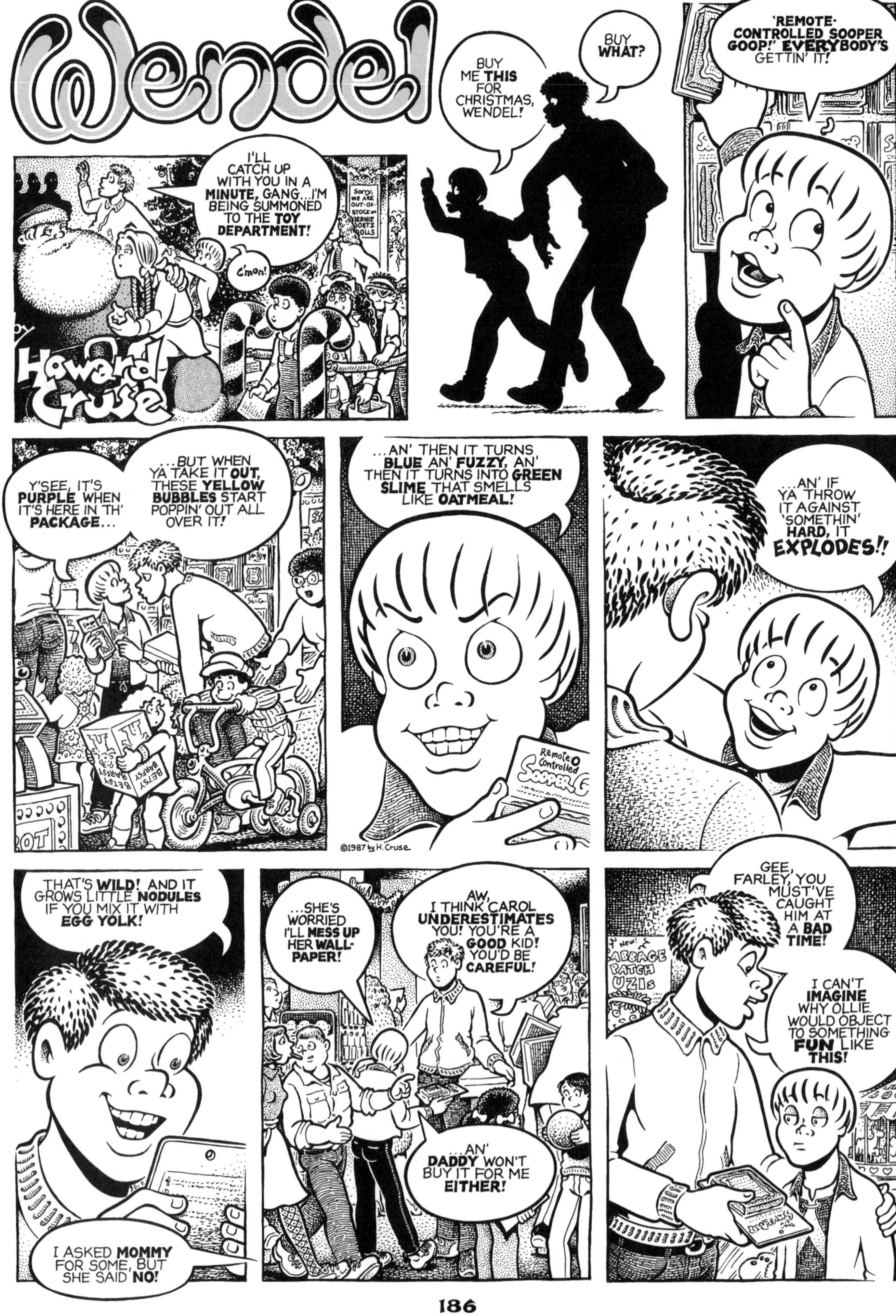

Wendel
by Howard Cruse
I'LL CATCH UP WITH YOU IN A MINUTE, GANG...I'M BEING SUMMONED TO THE TOY DEPARTMENT!
Sorry, WE ARE OUT-OF-STOCK on BERNIE GOETZ DOLLS
C'mon!
BUY ME THIS FOR CHRISTMAS, WENDEL!
BUY WHAT?
'REMOTE-CONTROLLED SOOPER GOOP!' EVERYBODY'S GETTIN' IT!
Y'SEE, IT'S PURPLE WHEN IT'S HERE IN TH' PACKAGE...
...BUT WHEN YA TAKE IT OUT, THESE YELLOW BUBBLES START POPPIN' OUT ALL OVER IT!
...AN' THEN IT TURNS BLUE AN' FUZZY, AN' THEN IT TURNS INTO GREEN SLIME THAT SMELLS LIKE OATMEAL!
Remote-O Controlled
©1987 by H. Cruse
...AN' IF YA THROW IT AGAINST 'SOMETHIN' HARD, IT EXPLODES!!
THAT'S WILD! AND IT GROWS LITTLE NODULES IF YOU MIX IT WITH EGG YOLK!
I ASKED MOMMY FOR SOME, BUT SHE SAID NO!
...SHE'S WORRIED I'LL MESS UP HER WALL-PAPER!
AW, I THINK CAROL UNDERESTIMATES YOU! YOU'RE A GOOD KID! YOU'D BE CAREFUL!
...AN' DADDY WON'T BUY IT FOR ME EITHER!
GEE, FARLEY, YOU MUST'VE CAUGHT HIM AT A BAD TIME!
I CAN'T IMAGINE WHY OLLIE WOULD OBJECT TO SOMETHING FUN LIKE THIS!

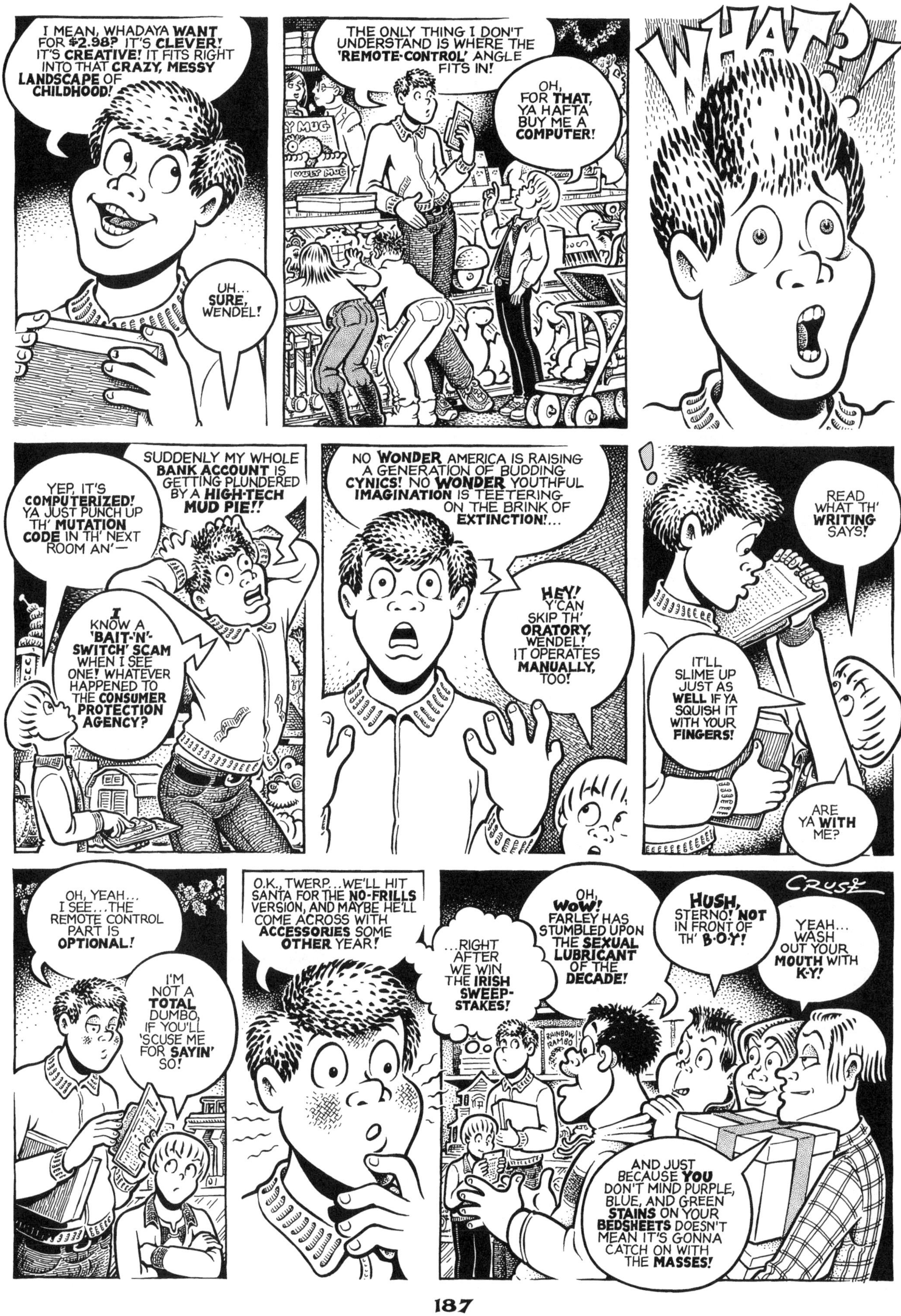
I MEAN, WHADAYA WANT FOR $2.98? IT'S CLEVER! IT'S CREATIVE! IT FITS RIGHT INTO THAT CRAZY, MESSY LANDSCAPE OF CHILDHOOD!
UH... SURE, WENDEL!
THE ONLY THING I DON'T UNDERSTAND IS WHERE THE 'REMOTE-CONTROL' ANGLE FITS IN!
OH, FOR THAT, YA HAFTA BUY ME A COMPUTER!
UGLY MUG
WHAT?!
YEP, IT'S COMPUTERIZED! YA JUST PUNCH UP TH' MUTATION CODE IN TH' NEXT ROOM AN'—
SUDDENLY MY WHOLE BANK ACCOUNT IS GETTING PLUNDERED BY A HIGH-TECH MUD PIE!!
I KNOW A 'BAIT-'N'-SWITCH' SCAM WHEN I SEE ONE! WHATEVER HAPPENED TO THE CONSUMER PROTECTION AGENCY?
NO WONDER AMERICA IS RAISING A GENERATION OF BUDDING CYNICS! NO WONDER YOUTHFUL IMAGINATION IS TEETERING ON THE BRINK OF EXTINCTION!...
HEY! Y'CAN SKIP TH' ORATORY, WENDEL! IT OPERATES MANUALLY, TOO!
!
READ WHAT TH' WRITING SAYS!
IT'LL SLIME UP JUST AS WELL IF YA SQUISH IT WITH YOUR FINGERS!
ARE YA WITH ME?
OH, YEAH... I SEE... THE REMOTE CONTROL PART IS OPTIONAL!
I'M NOT A TOTAL DUMBO, IF YOU'LL 'SCUSE ME FOR SAYIN' SO!
O.K., TWERP... WE'LL HIT SANTA FOR THE NO-FRILLS VERSION, AND MAYBE HE'LL COME ACROSS WITH ACCESSORIES SOME OTHER YEAR!
...RIGHT AFTER WE WIN THE IRISH SWEEP-STAKES!
CRUSE
OH, WOW! FARLEY HAS STUMBLED UPON THE SEXUAL LUBRICANT OF THE DECADE!
HUSH, STERNO! NOT IN FRONT OF TH' B-O-Y!
YEAH... WASH OUT YOUR MOUTH WITH K-Y!
RAINBOW RAMBO
AND JUST BECAUSE YOU DON'T MIND PURPLE, BLUE, AND GREEN STAINS ON YOUR BEDSHEETS DOESN'T MEAN IT'S GONNA CATCH ON WITH THE MASSES!

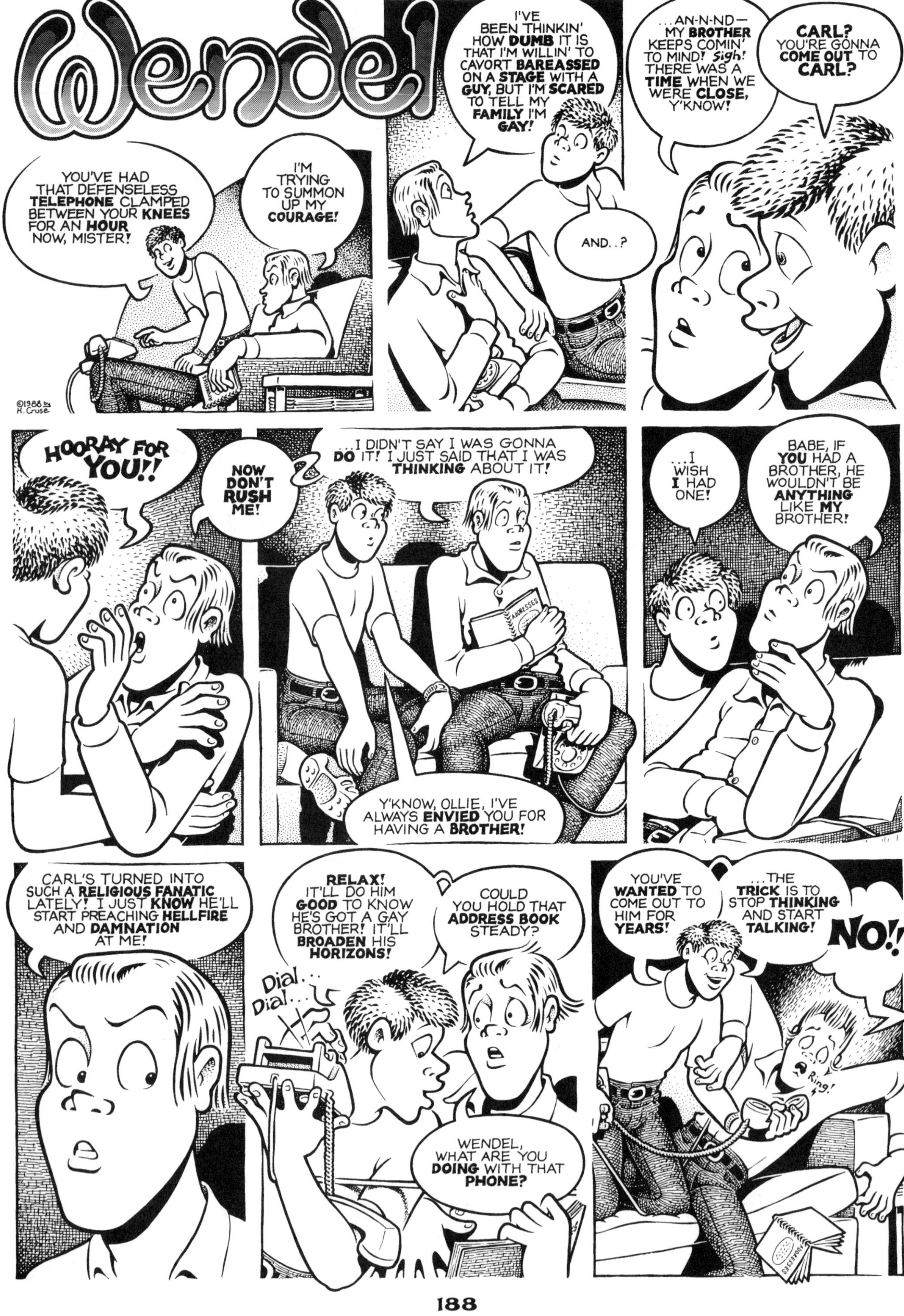
Wendel
YOU'VE HAD THAT DEFENSELESS TELEPHONE CLAMPED BETWEEN YOUR KNEES FOR AN HOUR NOW, MISTER!
I'M TRYING TO SUMMON UP MY COURAGE!
©1988 by H. Cruse
I'VE BEEN THINKIN' HOW DUMB IT IS THAT I'M WILLIN' TO CAVORT BAREASSED ON A STAGE WITH A GUY, BUT I'M SCARED TO TELL MY FAMILY I'M GAY!
AND..?
...AN-N-ND— MY BROTHER KEEPS COMIN' TO MIND! Sigh! THERE WAS A TIME WHEN WE WERE CLOSE, Y'KNOW!
CARL? YOU'RE GONNA COME OUT TO CARL?
HOORAY FOR YOU!!
NOW DON'T RUSH ME!
...I DIDN'T SAY I WAS GONNA DO IT! I JUST SAID THAT I WAS THINKING ABOUT IT!
ADDRESSES
Y'KNOW, OLLIE, I'VE ALWAYS ENVIED YOU FOR HAVING A BROTHER!
...I WISH I HAD ONE!
BABE, IF YOU HAD A BROTHER, HE WOULDN'T BE ANYTHING LIKE MY BROTHER!
CARL'S TURNED INTO SUCH A RELIGIOUS FANATIC LATELY! I JUST KNOW HE'LL START PREACHING HELLFIRE AND DAMNATION AT ME!
RELAX! IT'LL DO HIM GOOD TO KNOW HE'S GOT A GAY BROTHER! IT'LL BROADEN HIS HORIZONS!
COULD YOU HOLD THAT ADDRESS BOOK STEADY?
Dial... Dial...
WENDEL, WHAT ARE YOU DOING WITH THAT PHONE?
YOU'VE WANTED TO COME OUT TO HIM FOR YEARS!
...THE TRICK IS TO STOP THINKING AND START TALKING!
NO!!
Ring!
ADDRESSES

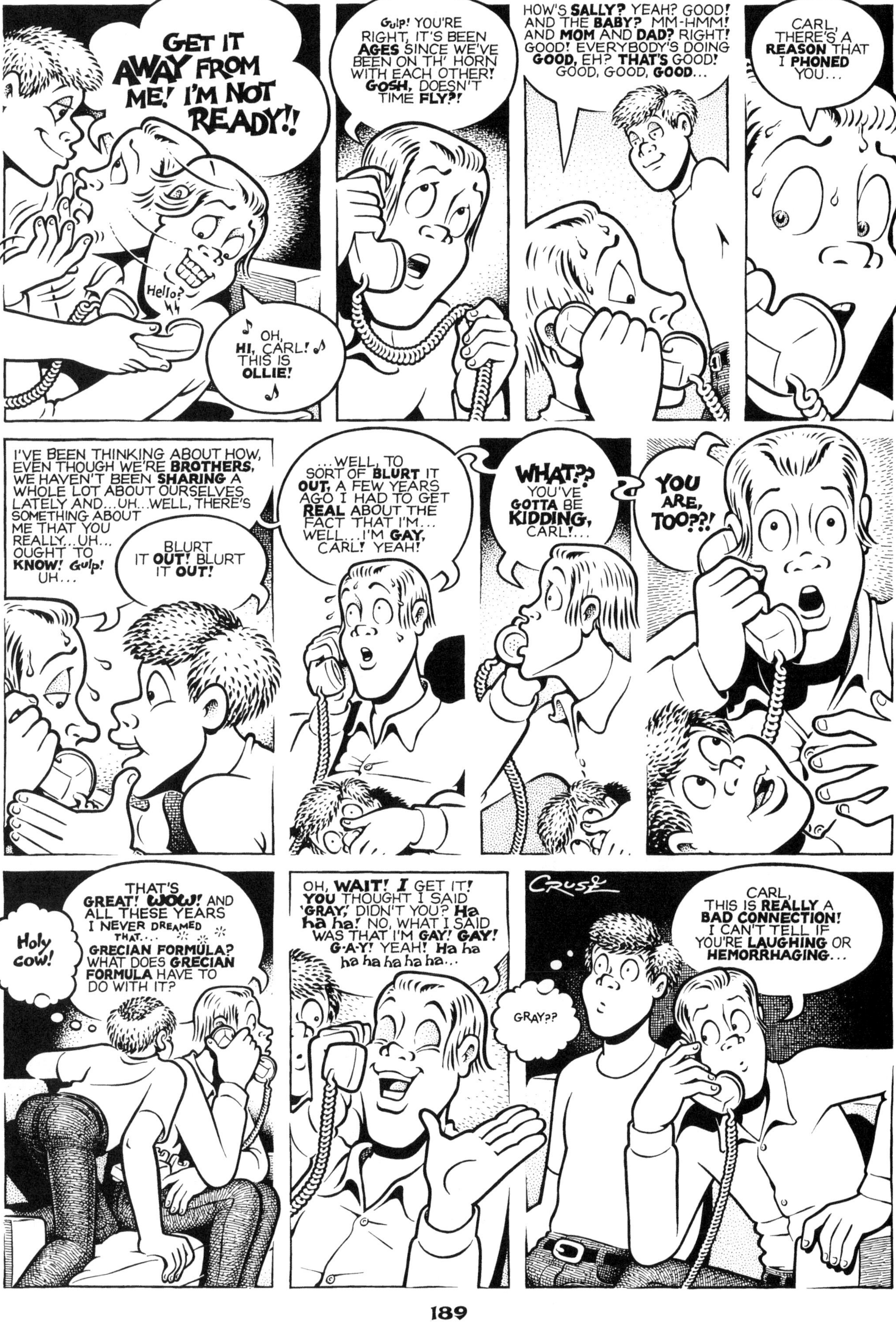
GET IT AWAY FROM ME! I'M NOT READY!!
Hello?
OH, HI, CARL! THIS IS OLLIE!
Gulp! YOU'RE RIGHT, IT'S BEEN AGES SINCE WE'VE BEEN ON TH' HORN WITH EACH OTHER! GOSH, DOESN'T TIME FLY?!
HOW'S SALLY? YEAH? GOOD! AND THE BABY? MM-HMM! AND MOM AND DAD? RIGHT! GOOD! EVERYBODY'S DOING GOOD, EH? THAT'S GOOD! GOOD, GOOD, GOOD...
CARL, THERE'S A REASON THAT I PHONED YOU...
I'VE BEEN THINKING ABOUT HOW, EVEN THOUGH WE'RE BROTHERS, WE HAVEN'T BEEN SHARING A WHOLE LOT ABOUT OURSELVES LATELY AND...UH...WELL, THERE'S SOMETHING ABOUT ME THAT YOU REALLY...UH... OUGHT TO KNOW! Gulp! UH...
BLURT IT OUT! BLURT IT OUT!
...WELL, TO SORT OF BLURT IT OUT, A FEW YEARS AGO I HAD TO GET REAL ABOUT THE FACT THAT I'M... WELL...I'M GAY, CARL! YEAH!
WHAT?? YOU'VE GOTTA BE KIDDING, CARL!...
YOU ARE, TOO??!
Holy cow!
THAT'S GREAT! WOW! AND ALL THESE YEARS I NEVER DREAMED THAT...
GRECIAN FORMULA? WHAT DOES GRECIAN FORMULA HAVE TO DO WITH IT?
OH, WAIT! I GET IT! YOU THOUGHT I SAID 'GRAY,' DIDN'T YOU? Ha ha ha! NO, WHAT I SAID WAS THAT I'M GAY! GAY! G-A-Y! YEAH! Ha ha ha ha ha ha ha...
CRUSE
GRAY??
CARL, THIS IS REALLY A BAD CONNECTION! I CAN'T TELL IF YOU'RE LAUGHING OR HEMORRHAGING...

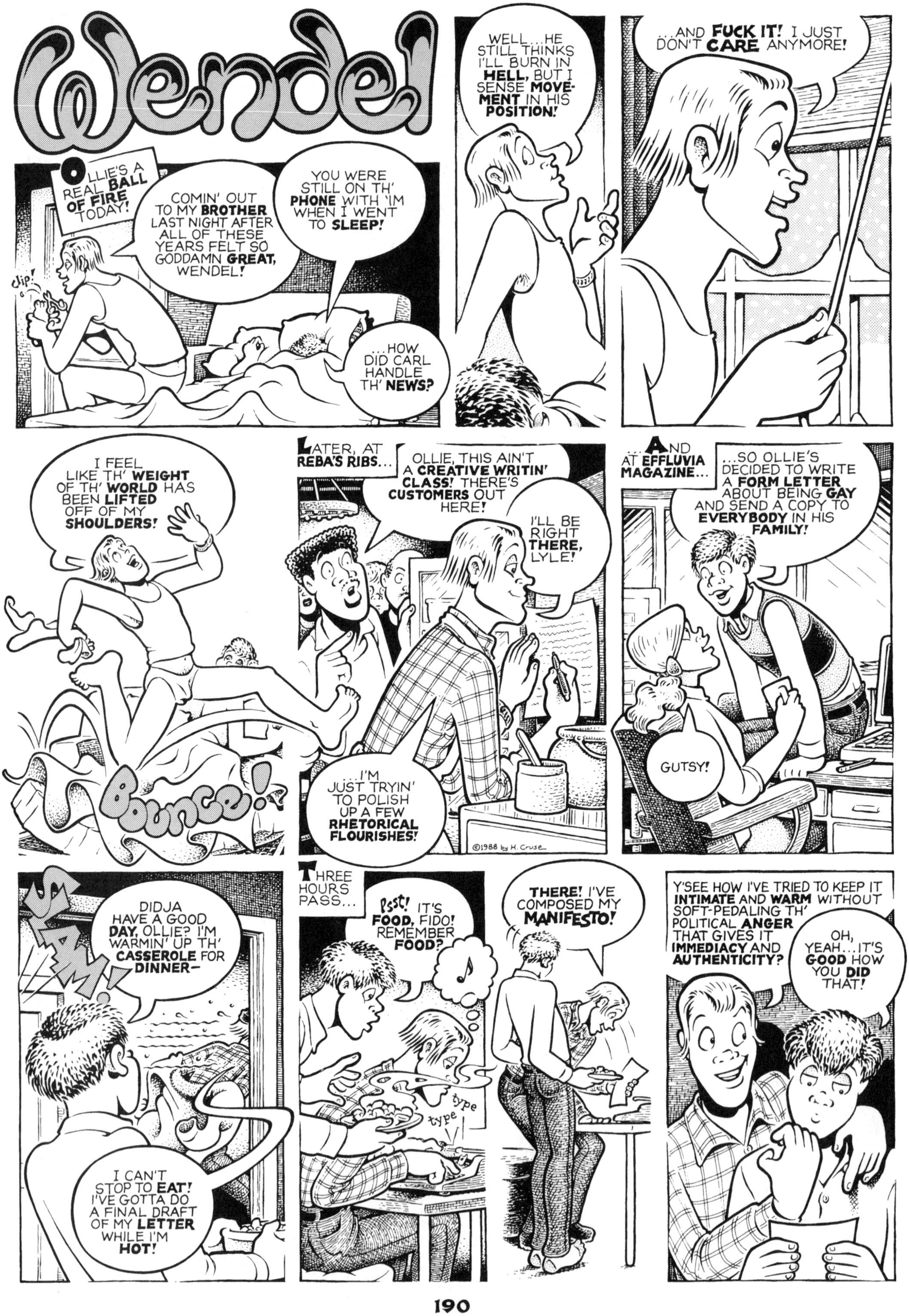
Wendel
OLLIE'S A REAL BALL OF FIRE TODAY!
Clip!
COMIN' OUT TO MY BROTHER LAST NIGHT AFTER ALL OF THESE YEARS FELT SO GODDAMN GREAT, WENDEL!
YOU WERE STILL ON TH' PHONE WITH 'IM WHEN I WENT TO SLEEP!
...HOW DID CARL HANDLE TH' NEWS?
WELL...HE STILL THINKS I'LL BURN IN HELL, BUT I SENSE MOVEMENT IN HIS POSITION!
...AND FUCK IT! I JUST DON'T CARE ANYMORE!
I FEEL LIKE TH' WEIGHT OF TH' WORLD HAS BEEN LIFTED OFF OF MY SHOULDERS!
BOUNCE!
LATER, AT REBA'S RIBS...
OLLIE, THIS AIN'T A CREATIVE WRITIN' CLASS! THERE'S CUSTOMERS OUT HERE!
I'LL BE RIGHT THERE, LYLE!
...I'M JUST TRYIN' TO POLISH UP A FEW RHETORICAL FLOURISHES!
©1988 by H. Cruse
...AND AT EFFLUVIA MAGAZINE...
...SO OLLIE'S DECIDED TO WRITE A FORM LETTER ABOUT BEING GAY AND SEND A COPY TO EVERYBODY IN HIS FAMILY!
GUTSY!
SLAM!
DIDJA HAVE A GOOD DAY, OLLIE? I'M WARMIN' UP TH' CASSEROLE FOR DINNER–
I CAN'T STOP TO EAT! I'VE GOTTA DO A FINAL DRAFT OF MY LETTER WHILE I'M HOT!
THREE HOURS PASS...
Psst! IT'S FOOD, FIDO! REMEMBER FOOD?
type
type
THERE! I'VE COMPOSED MY MANIFESTO!
Y'SEE HOW I'VE TRIED TO KEEP IT INTIMATE AND WARM WITHOUT SOFT-PEDALING TH' POLITICAL ANGER THAT GIVES IT IMMEDIACY AND AUTHENTICITY?
OH, YEAH...IT'S GOOD HOW YOU DID THAT!

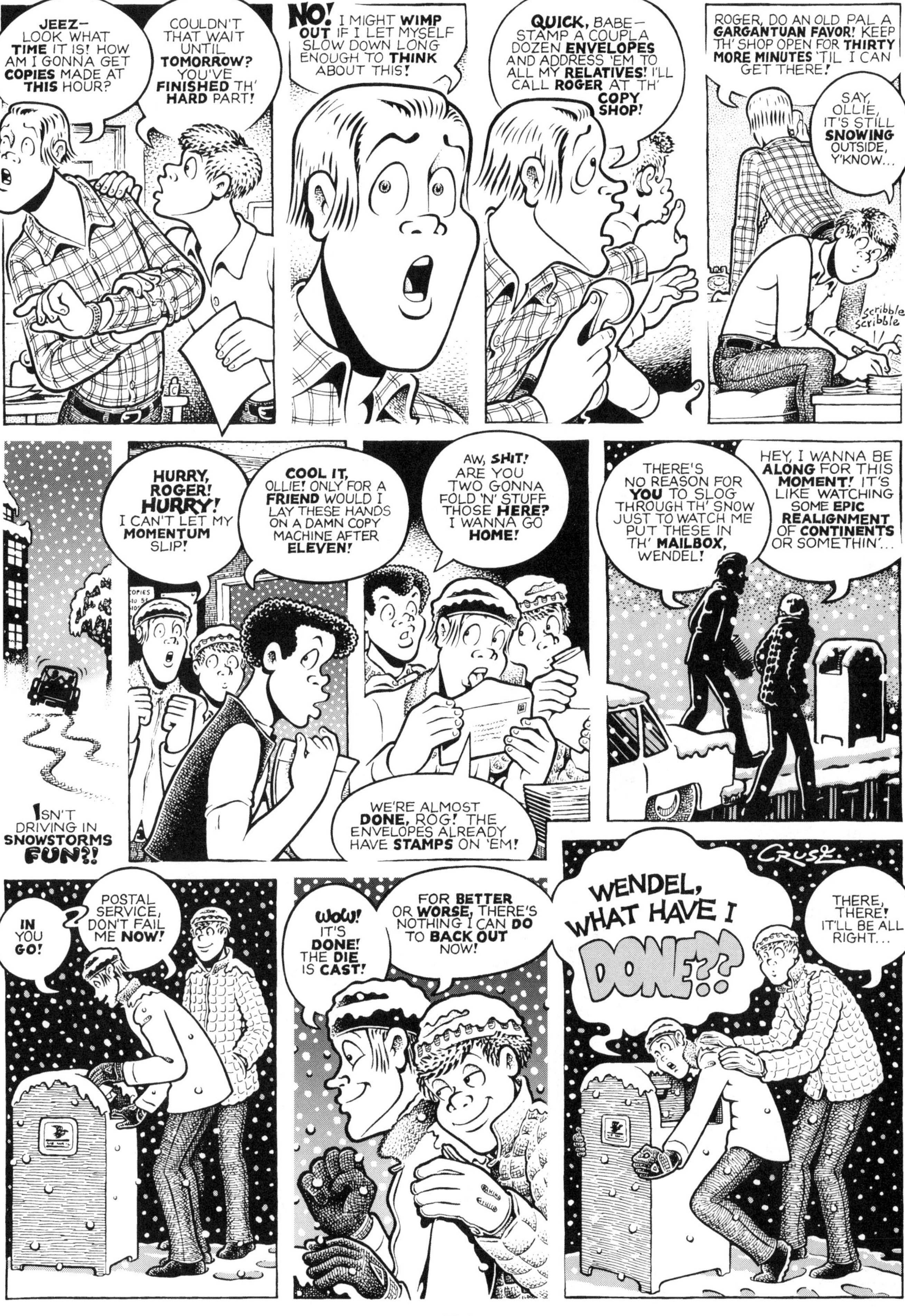
JEEZ— LOOK WHAT TIME IT IS! HOW AM I GONNA GET COPIES MADE AT THIS HOUR?
COULDN'T THAT WAIT UNTIL TOMORROW? YOU'VE FINISHED TH' HARD PART!
NO! I MIGHT WIMP OUT IF I LET MYSELF SLOW DOWN LONG ENOUGH TO THINK ABOUT THIS!
QUICK, BABE— STAMP A COUPLA DOZEN ENVELOPES AND ADDRESS 'EM TO ALL MY RELATIVES! I'LL CALL ROGER AT TH' COPY SHOP!
ROGER, DO AN OLD PAL A GARGANTUAN FAVOR! KEEP TH' SHOP OPEN FOR THIRTY MORE MINUTES 'TIL I CAN GET THERE!
SAY, OLLIE, IT'S STILL SNOWING OUTSIDE, Y'KNOW...
scribble scribble
ISN'T DRIVING IN SNOWSTORMS FUN?!
HURRY, ROGER! HURRY! I CAN'T LET MY MOMENTUM SLIP!
COOL IT, OLLIE! ONLY FOR A FRIEND WOULD I LAY THESE HANDS ON A DAMN COPY MACHINE AFTER ELEVEN!
AW, SHIT! ARE YOU TWO GONNA FOLD 'N' STUFF THOSE HERE? I WANNA GO HOME!
WE'RE ALMOST DONE, ROG! THE ENVELOPES ALREADY HAVE STAMPS ON 'EM!
THERE'S NO REASON FOR YOU TO SLOG THROUGH TH' SNOW JUST TO WATCH ME PUT THESE IN TH' MAILBOX, WENDEL!
HEY, I WANNA BE ALONG FOR THIS MOMENT! IT'S LIKE WATCHING SOME EPIC REALIGNMENT OF CONTINENTS OR SOMETHIN'...
POSTAL SERVICE, DON'T FAIL ME NOW!
IN YOU GO!
WOW! IT'S DONE! THE DIE IS CAST!
FOR BETTER OR WORSE, THERE'S NOTHING I CAN DO TO BACK OUT NOW!
WENDEL, WHAT HAVE I DONE?!?
THERE, THERE! IT'LL BE ALL RIGHT...
CRUSE

Wendel

YOUR **RELATIVES** MUST'VE ALL GOTTEN YOUR **FORM LETTER** BY NOW, OLLIE!

♪ Rudolph, the Red-Nosed Rein-deeeeer... ♪

...HAVE MOST OF THEM GOTTEN **BACK** TO YOU?

SOME **HAVE**... SOME **HAVEN'T**!

REACTIONS HAVE BEEN **VARIED**...

"MY SISTER **IRIS** WAS **COMPETITIVE**, AS USUAL..."

YOU JUST **HAD** TO HAVE SOME GRAND **CAUSE** THAT WE'RE ALL SUPPOSED TO **RALLY AROUND**, DIDN'T YOU!

"UNCLE LOUIE WAS **STOIC**..."

⸭Sigh!⸭ WELL, IF I LIVED THROUGH THE **GREAT DEPRESSION**, I GUESS I CAN LIVE THROUGH **THIS**!

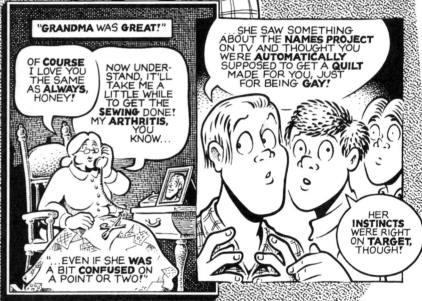

"GRANDMA WAS **GREAT**!"

OF **COURSE** I LOVE YOU THE SAME AS **ALWAYS**, HONEY!

NOW UNDER-STAND, IT'LL TAKE ME A LITTLE WHILE TO GET THE **SEWING** DONE! MY **ARTHRITIS**, YOU KNOW...

"...EVEN IF SHE **WAS** A BIT **CONFUSED** ON A POINT OR TWO!"

SHE SAW SOMETHING ABOUT THE **NAMES PROJECT** ON TV AND THOUGHT YOU WERE **AUTOMATICALLY** SUPPOSED TO GET A **QUILT** MADE FOR YOU, JUST FOR BEING **GAY**!

HER **INSTINCTS** WERE RIGHT ON **TARGET**, THOUGH!

"**AUNT IVY** WAS SCARED THAT THE **NEIGHBORS** WOULD FIND OUT..."

FOR THE SAKE OF YOUR **FAMILY**, YOU MUST **NEVER** USE THE WORD **'GAY'** IN **PUBLIC**, OLIVER!

...SUBSTITUTE THE WORD **'TURNIP'**! WE'LL KNOW WHAT YOU MEAN...

"MY BROTHER **CARL** JUST WANTED TO **HELP**..."

YOU CAN **PREVAIL** OVER DEMONIC FORCES, OLLIE! **SELF-FLAGELLATION** HAS WORKED FOR **ME** ANY **NUMBER** OF TIMES...

WE **LOVE** HAVING YOU HERE WITH **US**, OLLIE—BUT YOU'VE JUST GIVEN YOUR PARENTS A **JOLT**! DID YOU GIVE ANY THOUGHT TO SPENDING THE HOLIDAY WITH **THEM**?

©1988 by H. Cruse

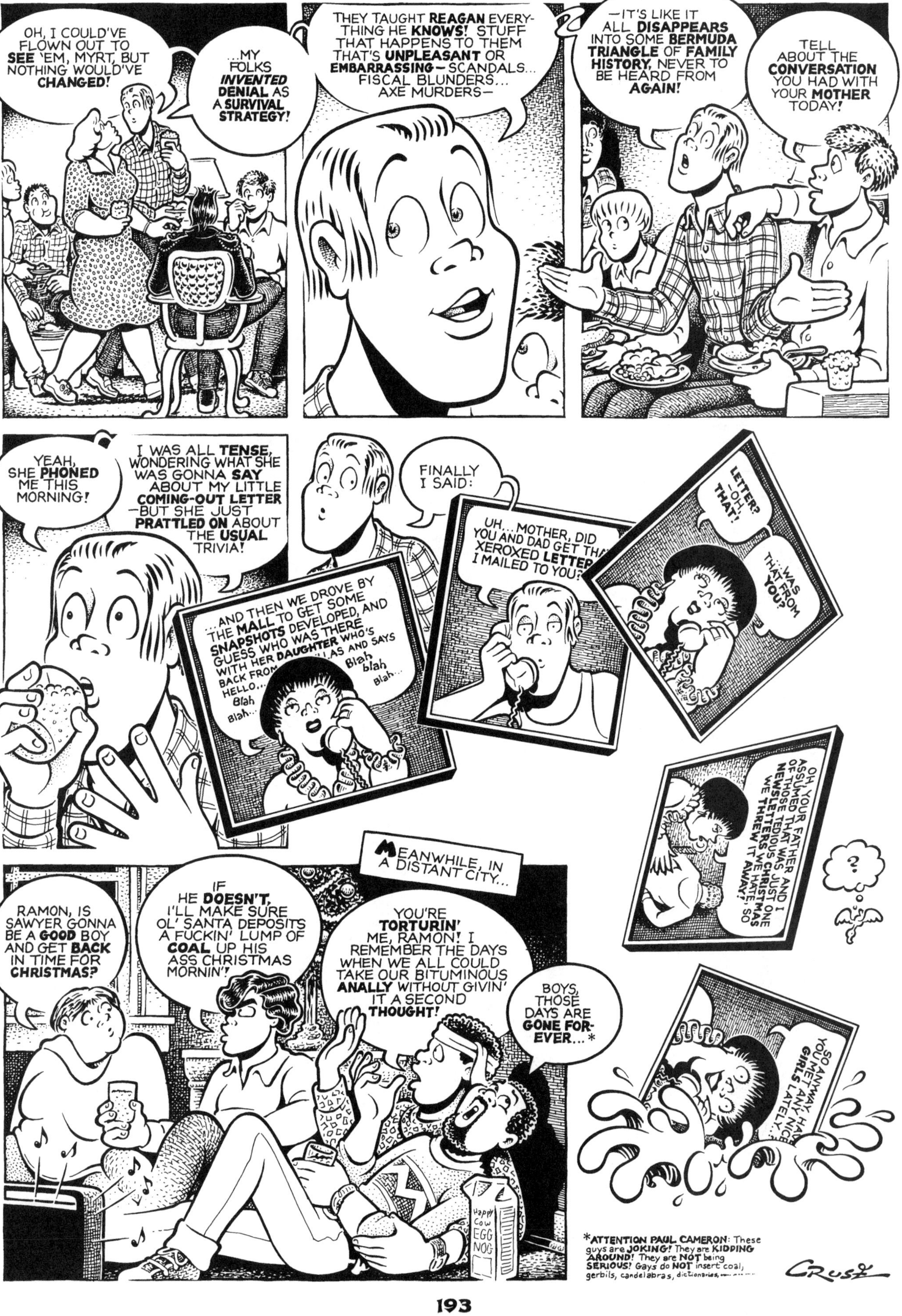
OH, I COULD'VE FLOWN OUT TO SEE 'EM, MYRT, BUT NOTHING WOULD'VE CHANGED!
...MY FOLKS INVENTED DENIAL AS A SURVIVAL STRATEGY!
THEY TAUGHT REAGAN EVERYTHING HE KNOWS! STUFF THAT HAPPENS TO THEM THAT'S UNPLEASANT OR EMBARRASSING—SCANDALS... FISCAL BLUNDERS... AXE MURDERS—
—IT'S LIKE IT ALL DISAPPEARS INTO SOME BERMUDA TRIANGLE OF FAMILY HISTORY, NEVER TO BE HEARD FROM AGAIN!
TELL ABOUT THE CONVERSATION YOU HAD WITH YOUR MOTHER TODAY!
YEAH, SHE PHONED ME THIS MORNING!
I WAS ALL TENSE, WONDERING WHAT SHE WAS GONNA SAY ABOUT MY LITTLE COMING-OUT LETTER —BUT SHE JUST PRATTLED ON ABOUT THE USUAL TRIVIA!
...AND THEN WE DROVE BY THE MALL TO GET SOME SNAPSHOTS DEVELOPED, AND GUESS WHO WAS THERE WITH HER DAUGHTER WHO'S BACK FROM ...LAS AND SAYS HELLO... Blah Blah... Blah blah Blah...
FINALLY I SAID:
UH... MOTHER, DID YOU AND DAD GET THAT XEROXED LETTER I MAILED TO YOU?
LETTER? —OH, THAT!
...WAS THAT FROM YOU?
OH, YOUR FATHER AND I ASSUMED THAT WAS JUST ONE OF THOSE TEDIOUS CHRISTMAS NEWSLETTERS WE HATE, SO WE THREW IT AWAY!
?
SO ANYWAY, HAVE YOU MET ANY NICE GIRLS LATELY...?
MEANWHILE, IN A DISTANT CITY...
RAMON, IS SAWYER GONNA BE A GOOD BOY AND GET BACK IN TIME FOR CHRISTMAS?
IF HE DOESN'T, I'LL MAKE SURE OL' SANTA DEPOSITS A FUCKIN' LUMP OF COAL UP HIS ASS CHRISTMAS MORNIN'!
YOU'RE TORTURIN' ME, RAMON! I REMEMBER THE DAYS WHEN WE ALL COULD TAKE OUR BITUMINOUS ANALLY WITHOUT GIVIN' IT A SECOND THOUGHT!
BOYS, THOSE DAYS ARE GONE FOREVER...*
Happy Cow EGG NOG
*ATTENTION PAUL CAMERON: These guys are JOKING! They are KIDDING AROUND! They are NOT being SERIOUS! Gays do NOT insert coal, gerbils, candelabras, dictionaries, ...
CRUSE

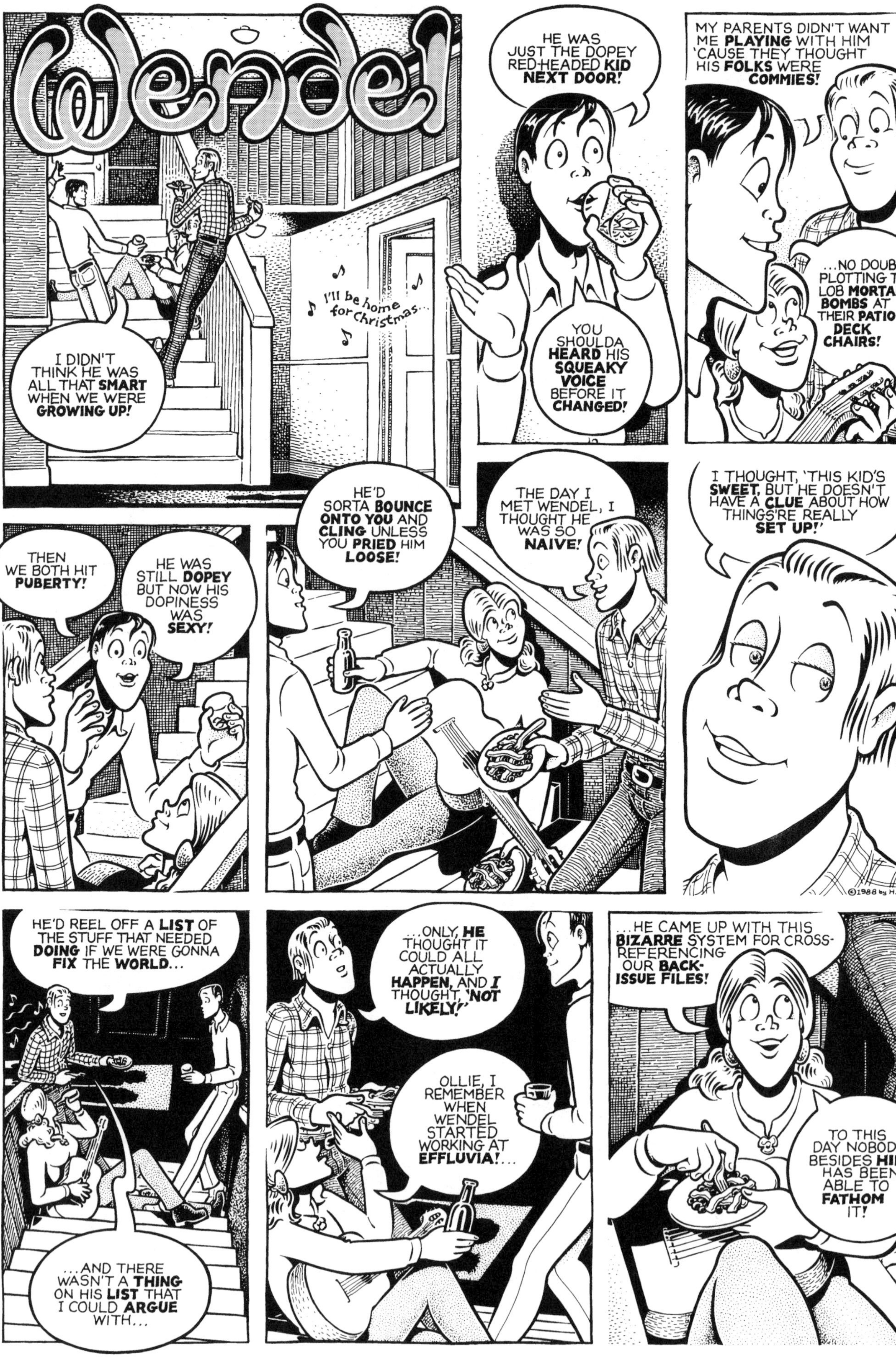
Wendel
I DIDN'T THINK HE WAS ALL THAT SMART WHEN WE WERE GROWING UP!
I'll be home for Christmas...
HE WAS JUST THE DOPEY RED-HEADED KID NEXT DOOR!
YOU SHOULDA HEARD HIS SQUEAKY VOICE BEFORE IT CHANGED!
MY PARENTS DIDN'T WANT ME PLAYING WITH HIM 'CAUSE THEY THOUGHT HIS FOLKS WERE COMMIES!
...NO DOUBT PLOTTING TO LOB MORTAR BOMBS AT THEIR PATIO DECK CHAIRS!
THEN WE BOTH HIT PUBERTY!
HE WAS STILL DOPEY BUT NOW HIS DOPINESS WAS SEXY!
HE'D SORTA BOUNCE ONTO YOU AND CLING UNLESS YOU PRIED HIM LOOSE!
THE DAY I MET WENDEL, I THOUGHT HE WAS SO NAIVE!
I THOUGHT, 'THIS KID'S SWEET, BUT HE DOESN'T HAVE A CLUE ABOUT HOW THINGS'RE REALLY SET UP!'
©1988 by H. Cruse
HE'D REEL OFF A LIST OF THE STUFF THAT NEEDED DOING IF WE WERE GONNA FIX THE WORLD...
...AND THERE WASN'T A THING ON HIS LIST THAT I COULD ARGUE WITH...
...ONLY, HE THOUGHT IT COULD ALL ACTUALLY HAPPEN, AND I THOUGHT, 'NOT LIKELY!'
OLLIE, I REMEMBER WHEN WENDEL STARTED WORKING AT EFFLUVIA!...
...HE CAME UP WITH THIS BIZARRE SYSTEM FOR CROSS-REFERENCING OUR BACK-ISSUE FILES!
TO THIS DAY NOBODY BESIDES HIM HAS BEEN ABLE TO FATHOM IT!

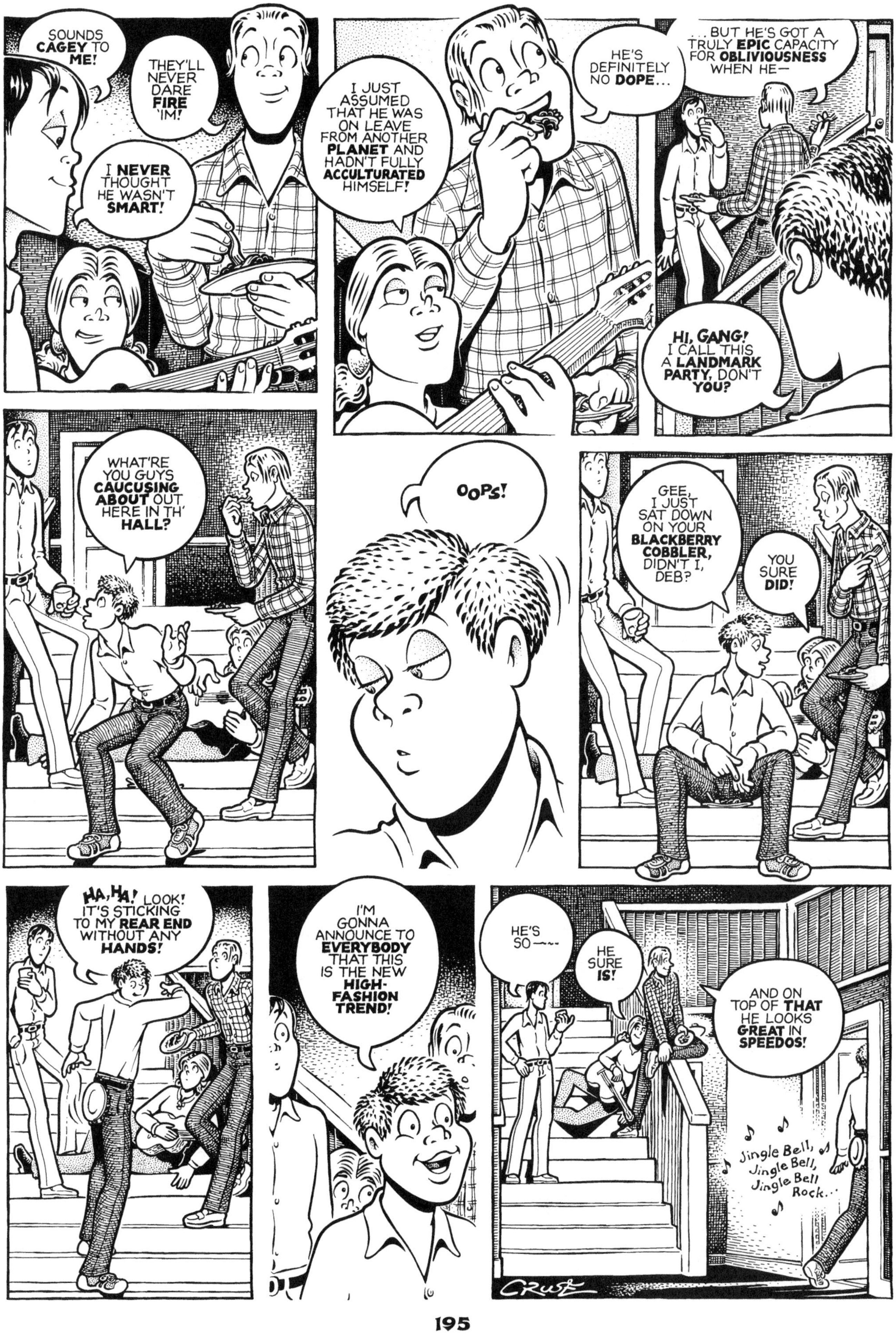
SOUNDS CAGEY TO ME!
THEY'LL NEVER DARE FIRE 'IM!
I NEVER THOUGHT HE WASN'T SMART!
I JUST ASSUMED THAT HE WAS ON LEAVE FROM ANOTHER PLANET AND HADN'T FULLY ACCULTURATED HIMSELF!
HE'S DEFINITELY NO DOPE...
...BUT HE'S GOT A TRULY EPIC CAPACITY FOR OBLIVIOUSNESS WHEN HE—
HI, GANG! I CALL THIS A LANDMARK PARTY, DON'T YOU?
WHAT'RE YOU GUYS CAUCUSING ABOUT OUT HERE IN TH' HALL?
OOPS!
GEE, I JUST SAT DOWN ON YOUR BLACKBERRY COBBLER, DIDN'T I, DEB?
YOU SURE DID!
HA, HA! LOOK! IT'S STICKING TO MY REAR END WITHOUT ANY HANDS!
I'M GONNA ANNOUNCE TO EVERYBODY THAT THIS IS THE NEW HIGH-FASHION TREND!
HE'S SO—
HE SURE IS!
AND ON TOP OF THAT HE LOOKS GREAT IN SPEEDOS!
Jingle Bell, Jingle Bell, Jingle Bell Rock...
CRUSE

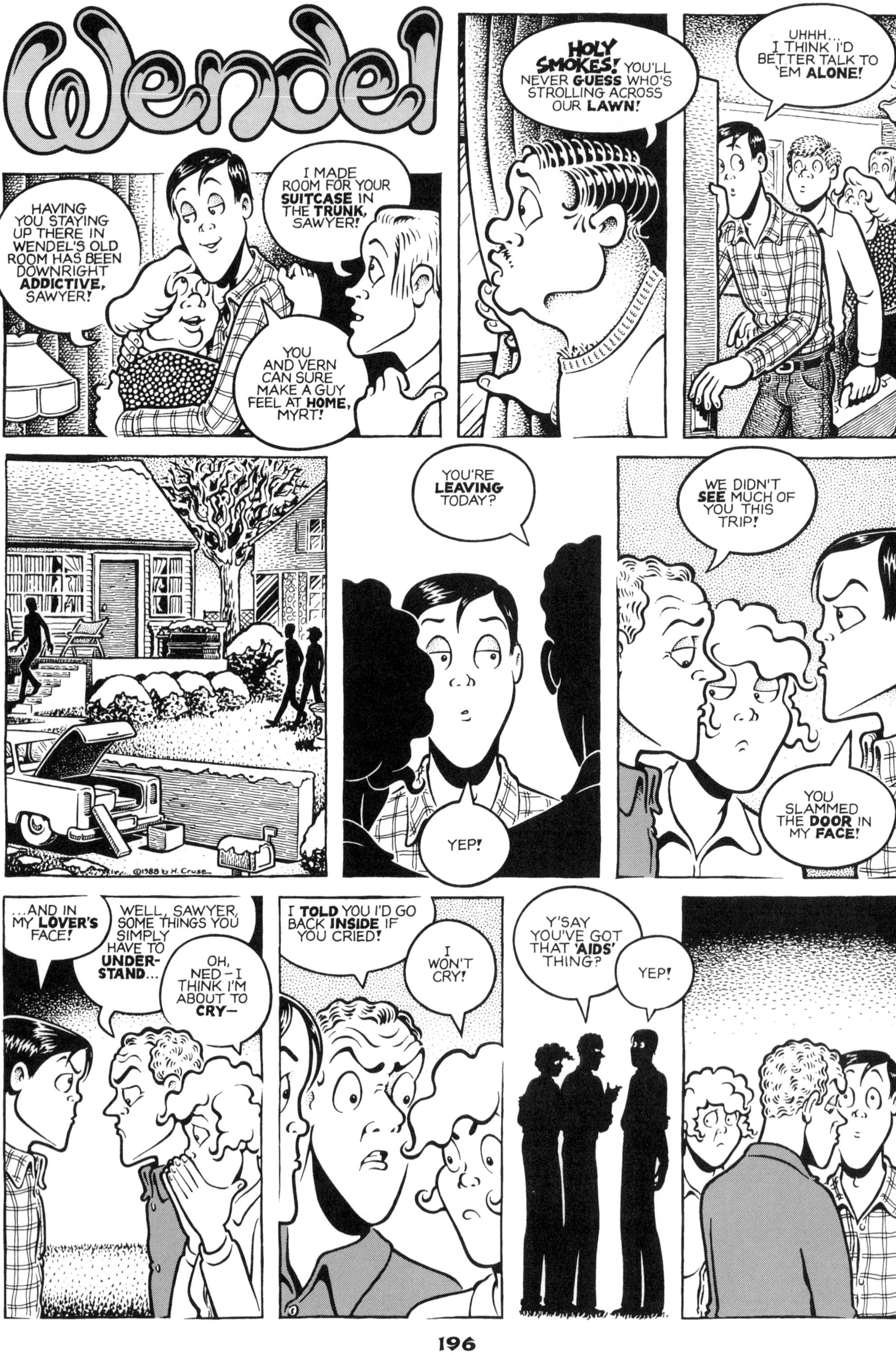
Wendel
HAVING YOU STAYING UP THERE IN WENDEL'S OLD ROOM HAS BEEN DOWNRIGHT ADDICTIVE, SAWYER!
I MADE ROOM FOR YOUR SUITCASE IN THE TRUNK, SAWYER!
YOU AND VERN CAN SURE MAKE A GUY FEEL AT HOME, MYRT!
HOLY SMOKES! YOU'LL NEVER GUESS WHO'S STROLLING ACROSS OUR LAWN!
UHHH... I THINK I'D BETTER TALK TO 'EM ALONE!
©1988 by H. Cruse
YOU'RE LEAVING TODAY?
YEP!
WE DIDN'T SEE MUCH OF YOU THIS TRIP!
YOU SLAMMED THE DOOR IN MY FACE!
...AND IN MY LOVER'S FACE!
WELL, SAWYER, SOME THINGS YOU SIMPLY HAVE TO UNDERSTAND...
OH, NED – I THINK I'M ABOUT TO CRY–
I TOLD YOU I'D GO BACK INSIDE IF YOU CRIED!
I WON'T CRY!
Y'SAY YOU'VE GOT THAT 'AIDS' THING?
YEP!

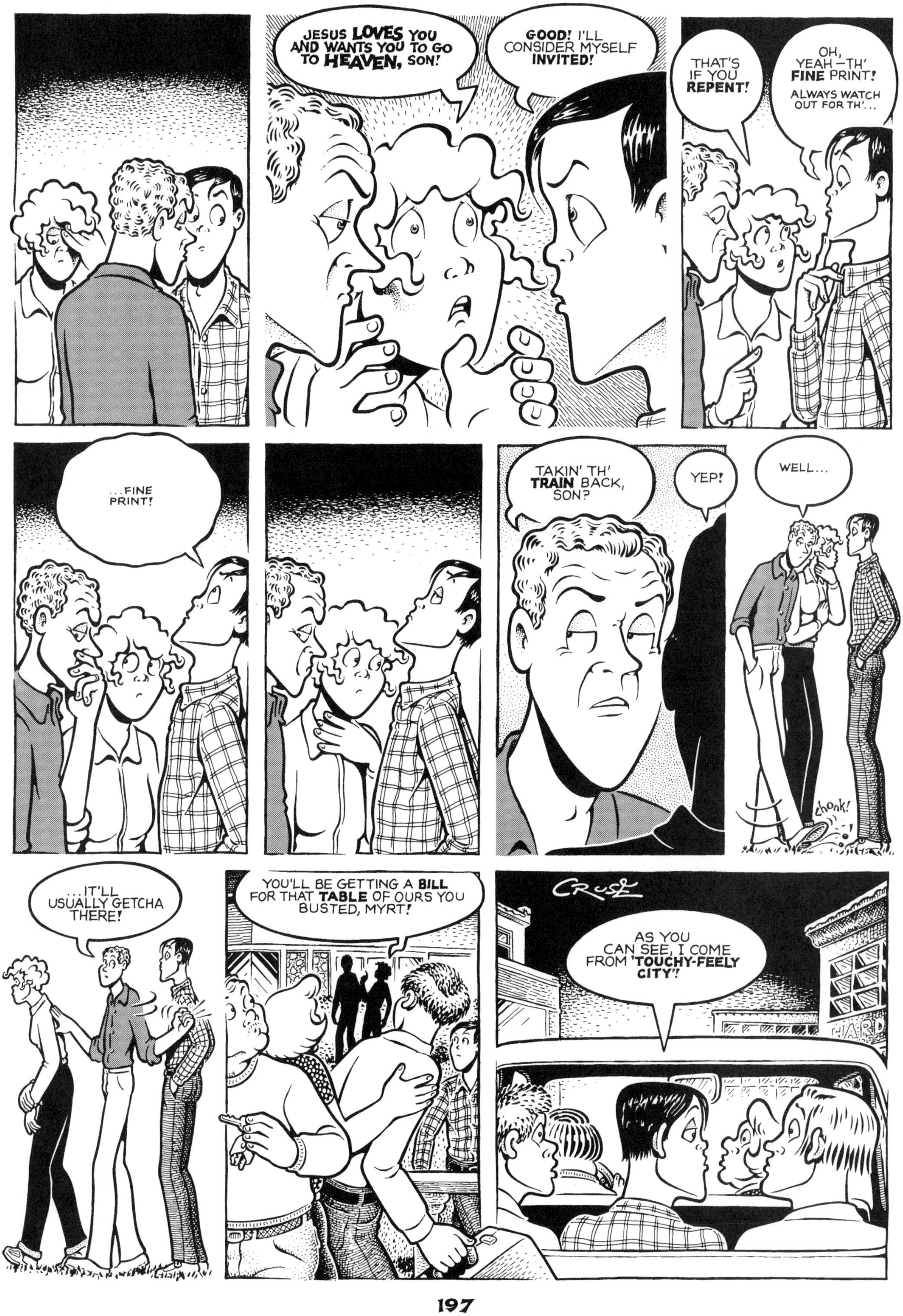

JESUS LOVES YOU AND WANTS YOU TO GO TO HEAVEN, SON!
GOOD! I'LL CONSIDER MYSELF INVITED!
THAT'S IF YOU REPENT!
OH, YEAH—TH' FINE PRINT! ALWAYS WATCH OUT FOR TH'...
...FINE PRINT!
TAKIN' TH' TRAIN BACK, SON?
YEP!
WELL...
chonk!
...IT'LL USUALLY GETCHA THERE!
YOU'LL BE GETTING A BILL FOR THAT TABLE OF OURS YOU BUSTED, MYRT!
CRUSE
AS YOU CAN SEE, I COME FROM 'TOUCHY-FEELY CITY'!
HARD

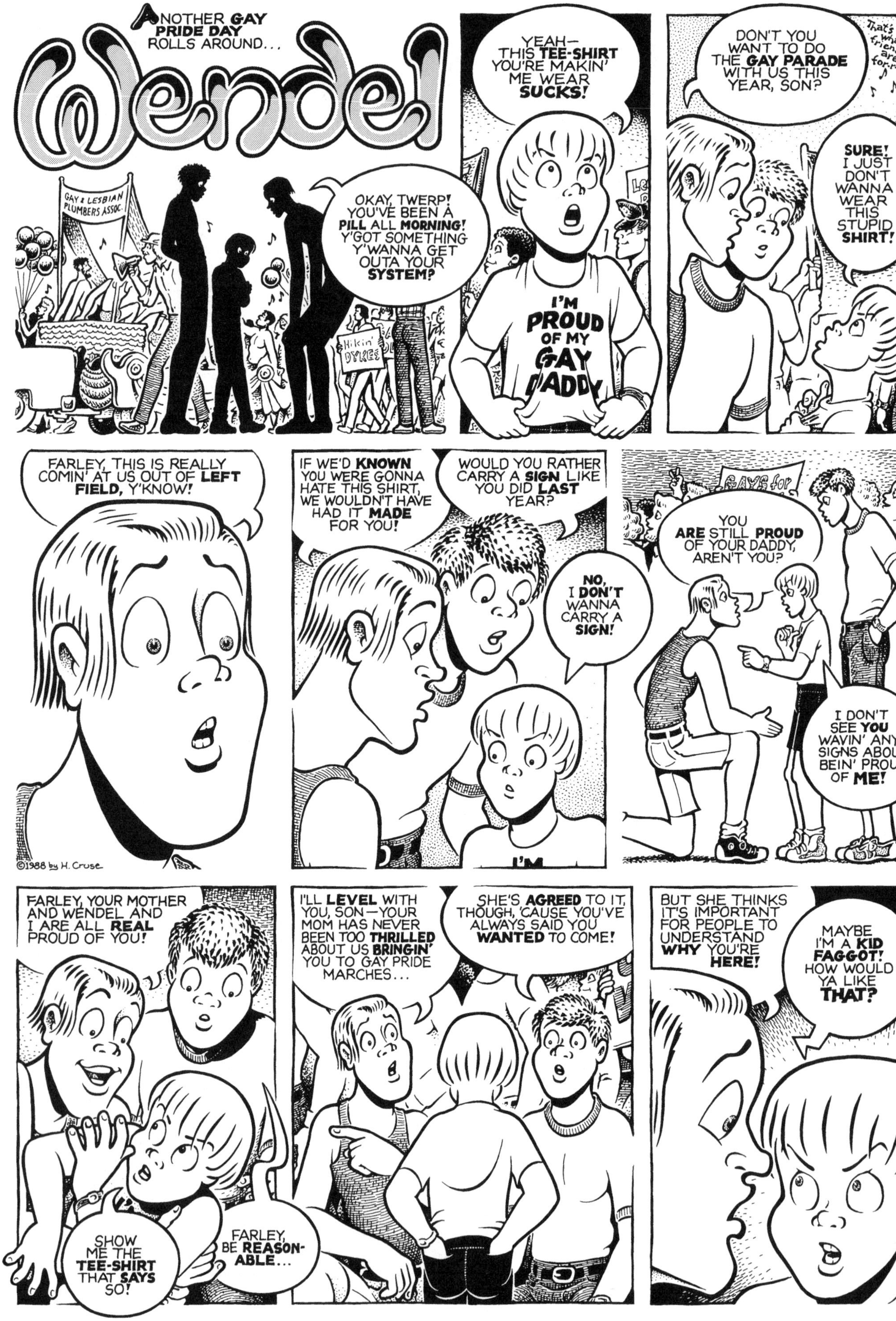

ANOTHER GAY PRIDE DAY ROLLS AROUND...
Wendel
GAY & LESBIAN PLUMBERS ASSOC.
OKAY, TWERP! YOU'VE BEEN A PILL ALL MORNING! Y'GOT SOMETHING Y'WANNA GET OUTA YOUR SYSTEM?
Hikin' DYKES
YEAH— THIS TEE-SHIRT YOU'RE MAKIN' ME WEAR SUCKS!
I'M PROUD OF MY GAY DADDY
DON'T YOU WANT TO DO THE GAY PARADE WITH US THIS YEAR, SON?
That's what friends are for-r-r.
SURE! I JUST DON'T WANNA WEAR THIS STUPID SHIRT!
FARLEY, THIS IS REALLY COMIN' AT US OUT OF LEFT FIELD, Y'KNOW!
©1988 by H. Cruse
IF WE'D KNOWN YOU WERE GONNA HATE THIS SHIRT, WE WOULDN'T HAVE HAD IT MADE FOR YOU!
WOULD YOU RATHER CARRY A SIGN LIKE YOU DID LAST YEAR?
NO, I DON'T WANNA CARRY A SIGN!
I'M
YOU ARE STILL PROUD OF YOUR DADDY, AREN'T YOU?
I DON'T SEE YOU WAVIN' ANY SIGNS ABOUT BEIN' PROUD OF ME!
FARLEY, YOUR MOTHER AND WENDEL AND I ARE ALL REAL PROUD OF YOU!
SHOW ME THE TEE-SHIRT THAT SAYS SO!
FARLEY, BE REASONABLE...
I'LL LEVEL WITH YOU, SON—YOUR MOM HAS NEVER BEEN TOO THRILLED ABOUT US BRINGIN' YOU TO GAY PRIDE MARCHES...
SHE'S AGREED TO IT, THOUGH, 'CAUSE YOU'VE ALWAYS SAID YOU WANTED TO COME!
BUT SHE THINKS IT'S IMPORTANT FOR PEOPLE TO UNDERSTAND WHY YOU'RE HERE!
MAYBE I'M A KID FAGGOT! HOW WOULD YA LIKE THAT?

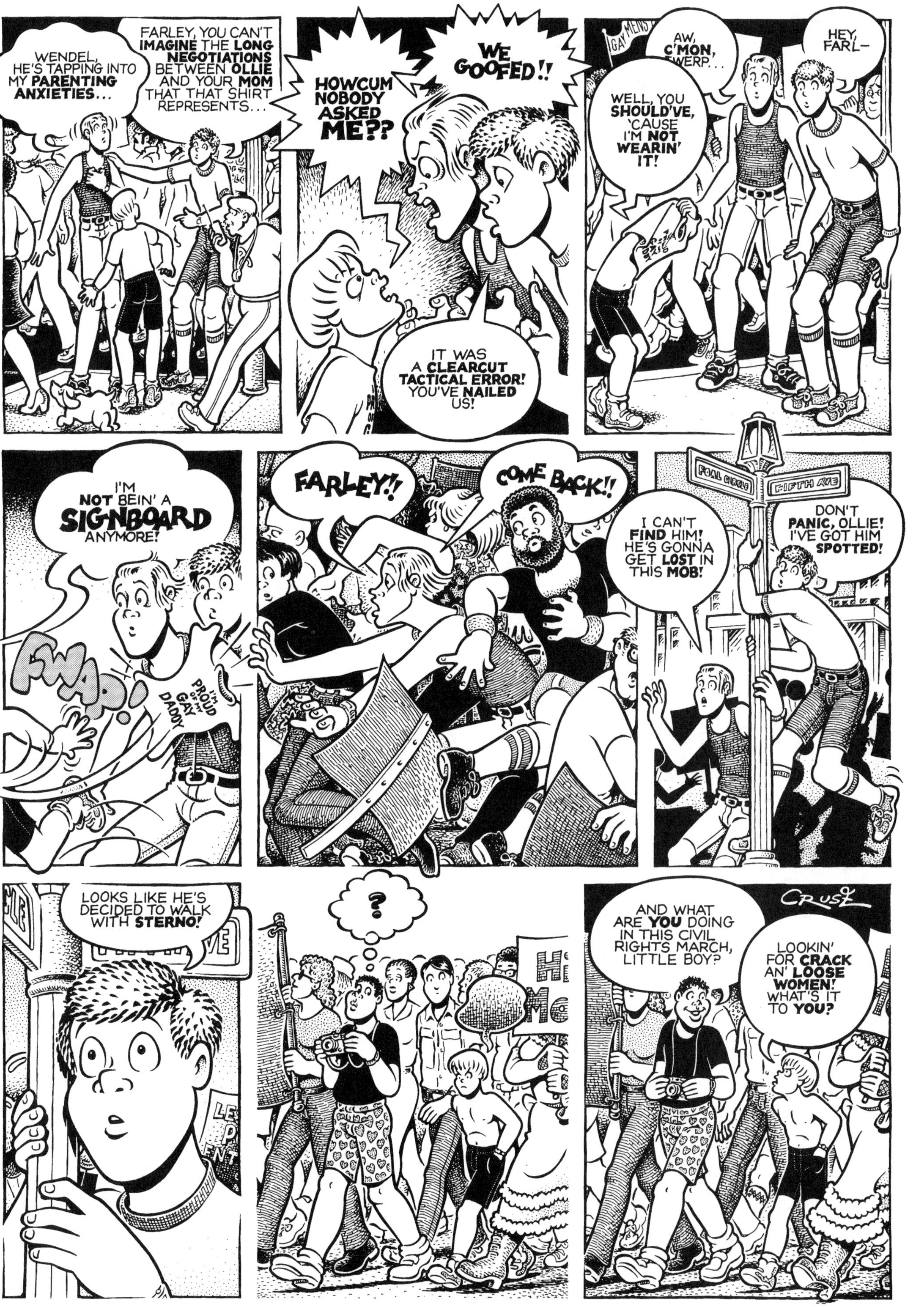

WENDEL, HE'S TAPPING INTO MY PARENTING ANXIETIES...
FARLEY, YOU CAN'T IMAGINE THE LONG NEGOTIATIONS BETWEEN OLLIE AND YOUR MOM THAT THAT SHIRT REPRESENTS...
HOWCUM NOBODY ASKED ME??
WE GOOFED!!
IT WAS A CLEARCUT TACTICAL ERROR! YOU'VE NAILED US!
GAY MEN'S
AW, C'MON, TWERP...
HEY, FARL—
WELL, YOU SHOULD'VE, 'CAUSE I'M NOT WEARIN' IT!
I'M NOT BEIN' A SIGNBOARD ANYMORE!
FWAP!
I'M PROUD OF MY GAY DADDY
FARLEY!!
COME BACK!!
POAL CIRCLE
FIFTH AVE
I CAN'T FIND HIM! HE'S GONNA GET LOST IN THIS MOB!
DON'T PANIC, OLLIE! I'VE GOT HIM SPOTTED!
LOOKS LIKE HE'S DECIDED TO WALK WITH STERNO!
?
AND WHAT ARE YOU DOING IN THIS CIVIL RIGHTS MARCH, LITTLE BOY?
LOOKIN' FOR CRACK AN' LOOSE WOMEN! WHAT'S IT TO YOU?
CRUSE

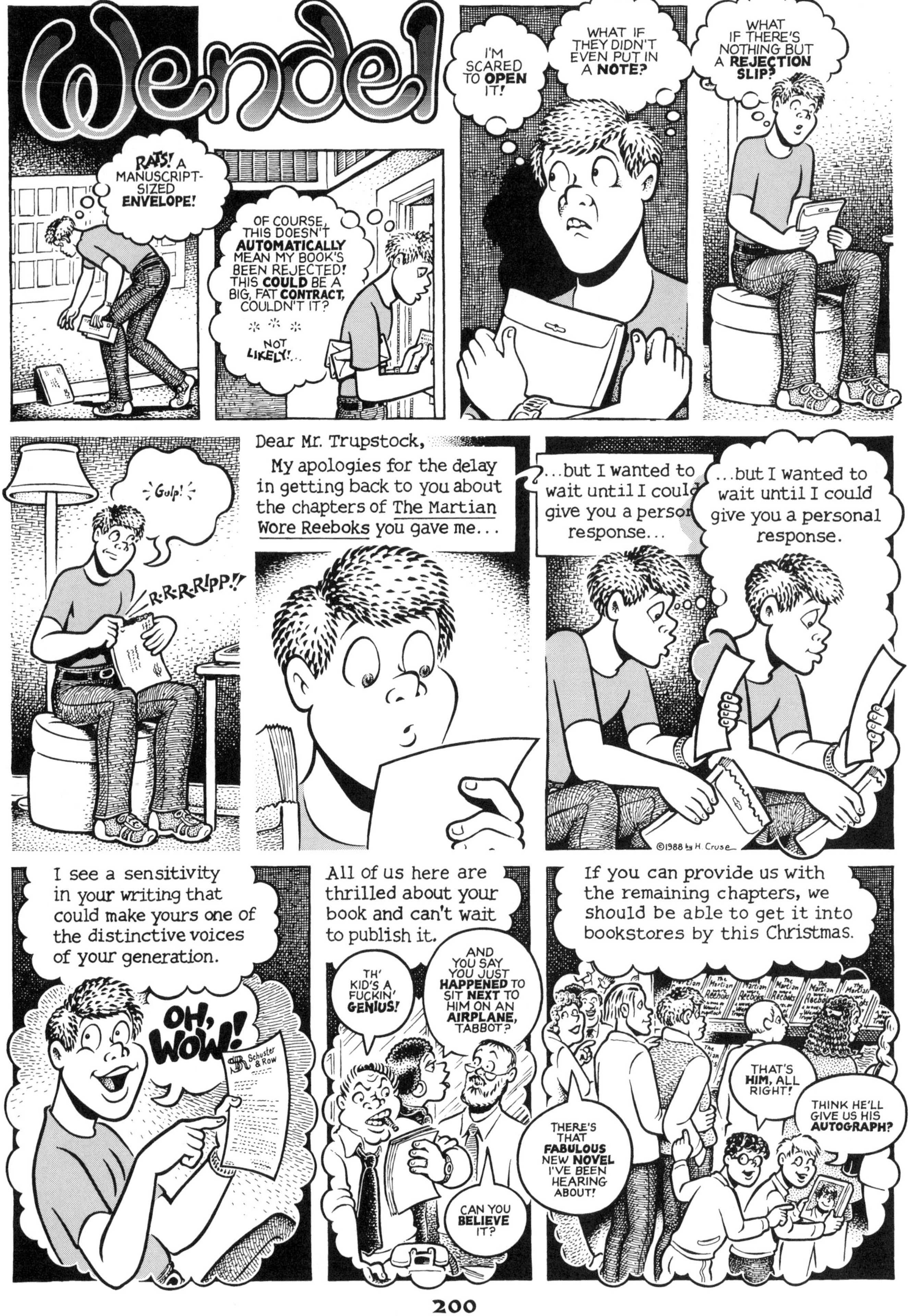
Wendel
RATS! A MANUSCRIPT-SIZED ENVELOPE!
OF COURSE, THIS DOESN'T AUTOMATICALLY MEAN MY BOOK'S BEEN REJECTED! THIS COULD BE A BIG, FAT CONTRACT, COULDN'T IT?
NOT LIKELY!...
I'M SCARED TO OPEN IT!
WHAT IF THEY DIDN'T EVEN PUT IN A NOTE?
WHAT IF THERE'S NOTHING BUT A REJECTION SLIP?
Gulp!
R-R-R-RIPP!!
Dear Mr. Trupstock,
My apologies for the delay in getting back to you about the chapters of The Martian Wore Reeboks you gave me...
...but I wanted to wait until I could give you a person response...
...but I wanted to wait until I could give you a personal response.
©1988 by H. Cruse
I see a sensitivity in your writing that could make yours one of the distinctive voices of your generation.
OH, WOW!
Schuster & Row
All of us here are thrilled about your book and can't wait to publish it.
TH' KID'S A FUCKIN' GENIUS!
AND YOU SAY YOU JUST HAPPENED TO SIT NEXT TO HIM ON AN AIRPLANE, TABBOT?
CAN YOU BELIEVE IT?
If you can provide us with the remaining chapters, we should be able to get it into bookstores by this Christmas.
THERE'S THAT FABULOUS NEW NOVEL I'VE BEEN HEARING ABOUT!
THAT'S HIM, ALL RIGHT!
THINK HE'LL GIVE US HIS AUTOGRAPH?

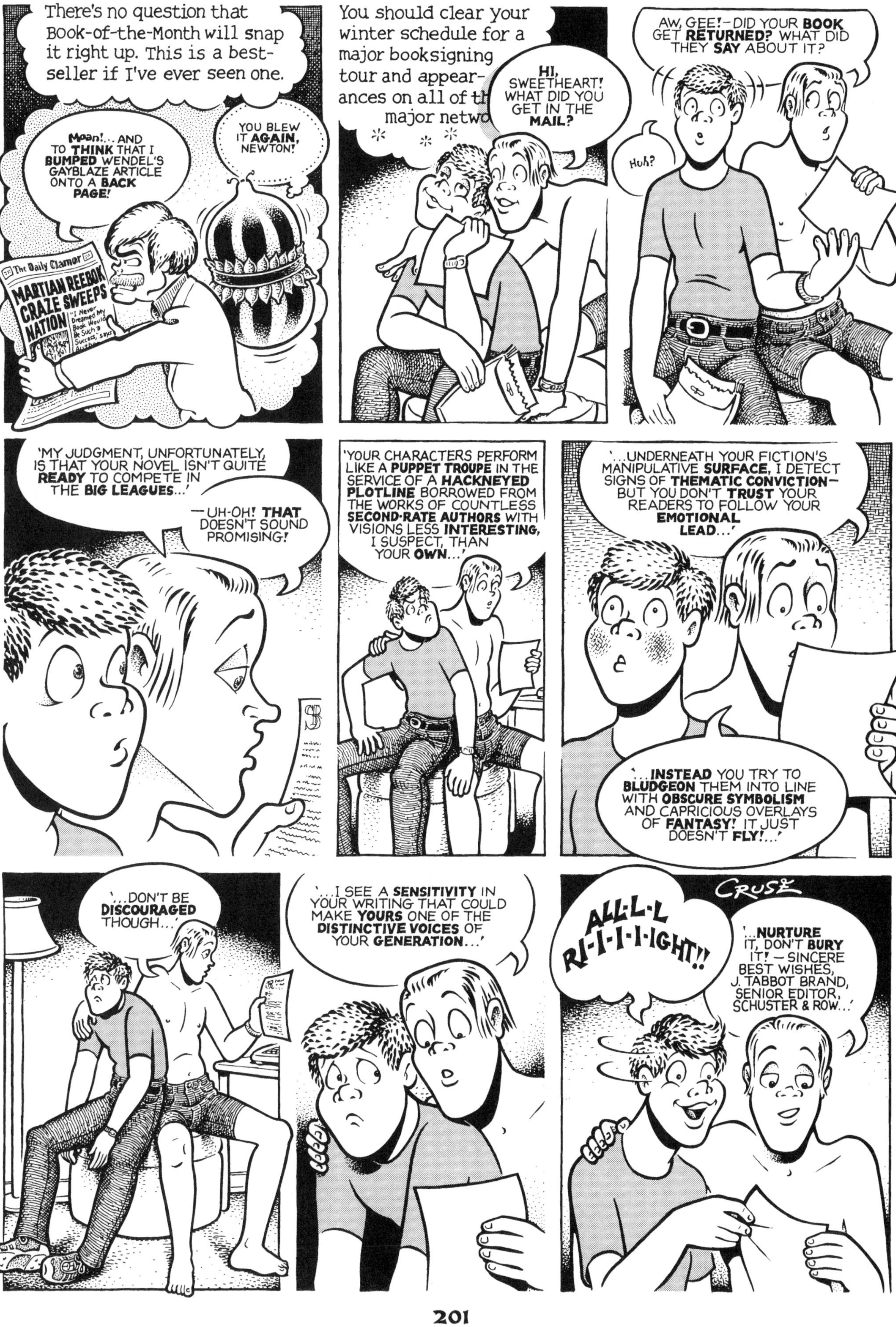

There's no question that Book-of-the-Month will snap it right up. This is a best-seller if I've ever seen one.
Moan!... AND TO THINK THAT I BUMPED WENDEL'S GAYBLAZE ARTICLE ONTO A BACK PAGE!
YOU BLEW IT AGAIN, NEWTON!
The Daily Clamor
MARTIAN REEBOK CRAZE SWEEPS NATION
"I Never Dreamed My Book Would Be Such a Success," says
You should clear your winter schedule for a major booksigning tour and appearances on all of th major netwo
HI, SWEETHEART! WHAT DID YOU GET IN THE MAIL?
AW, GEE!—DID YOUR BOOK GET RETURNED? WHAT DID THEY SAY ABOUT IT?
Huh?
'MY JUDGMENT, UNFORTUNATELY, IS THAT YOUR NOVEL ISN'T QUITE READY TO COMPETE IN THE BIG LEAGUES...'
—UH-OH! THAT DOESN'T SOUND PROMISING!
'YOUR CHARACTERS PERFORM LIKE A PUPPET TROUPE IN THE SERVICE OF A HACKNEYED PLOTLINE BORROWED FROM THE WORKS OF COUNTLESS SECOND-RATE AUTHORS WITH VISIONS LESS INTERESTING, I SUSPECT, THAN YOUR OWN...'
'...UNDERNEATH YOUR FICTION'S MANIPULATIVE SURFACE, I DETECT SIGNS OF THEMATIC CONVICTION—BUT YOU DON'T TRUST YOUR READERS TO FOLLOW YOUR EMOTIONAL LEAD...'
'...INSTEAD YOU TRY TO BLUDGEON THEM INTO LINE WITH OBSCURE SYMBOLISM AND CAPRICIOUS OVERLAYS OF FANTASY! IT JUST DOESN'T FLY!...'
'...DON'T BE DISCOURAGED THOUGH...'
'...I SEE A SENSITIVITY IN YOUR WRITING THAT COULD MAKE YOURS ONE OF THE DISTINCTIVE VOICES OF YOUR GENERATION...'
CRUSE
ALL-L-L RI-I-I-I-IGHT!!
'...NURTURE IT, DON'T BURY IT!—SINCERE BEST WISHES, J. TABBOT BRAND, SENIOR EDITOR, SCHUSTER & ROW...'

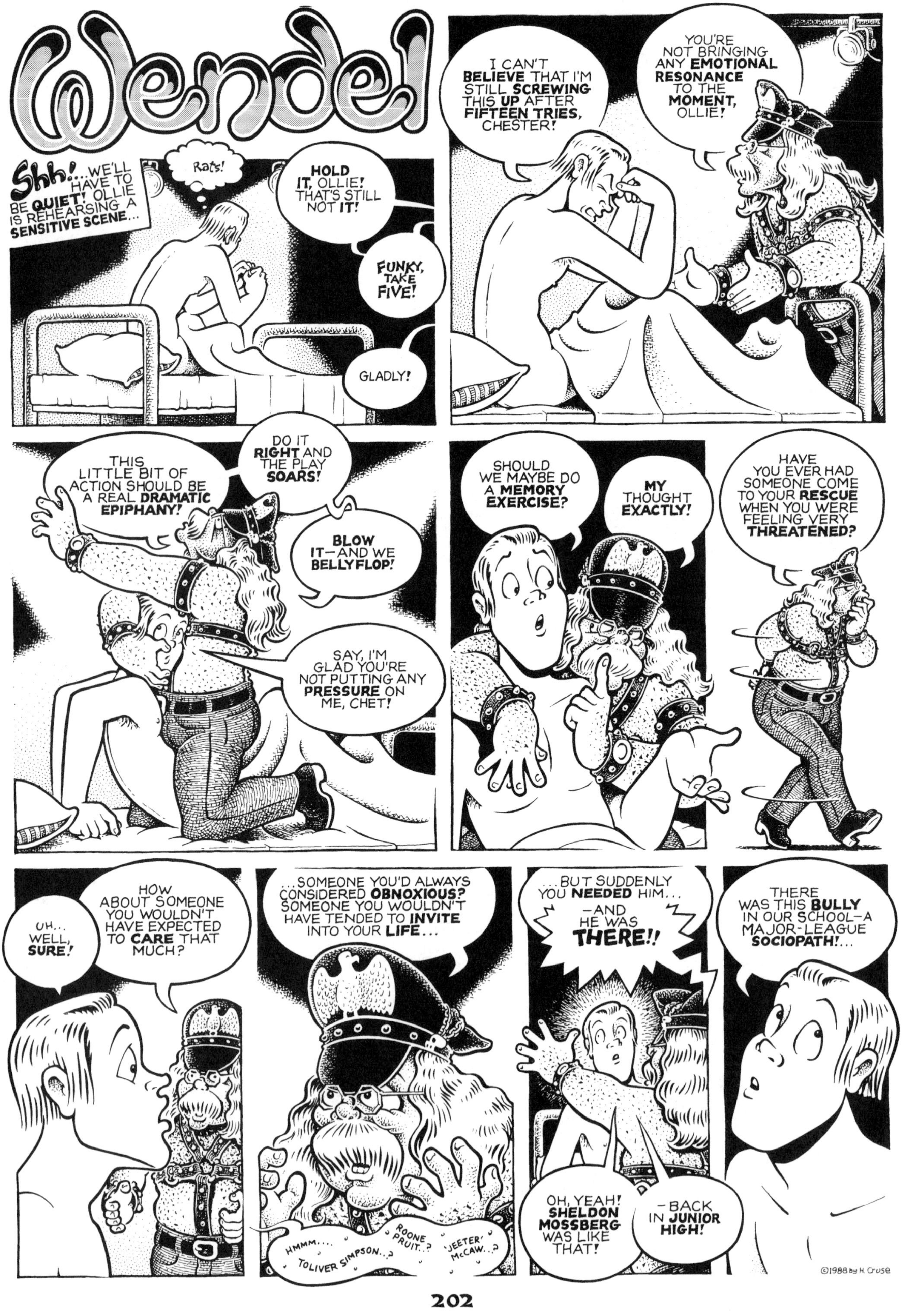
Wendel
Shh!... WE'LL HAVE TO BE QUIET! OLLIE IS REHEARSING A SENSITIVE SCENE...
Rats!
HOLD IT, OLLIE! THAT'S STILL NOT IT!
FUNKY, TAKE FIVE!
GLADLY!
I CAN'T BELIEVE THAT I'M STILL SCREWING THIS UP AFTER FIFTEEN TRIES, CHESTER!
YOU'RE NOT BRINGING ANY EMOTIONAL RESONANCE TO THE MOMENT, OLLIE!
THIS LITTLE BIT OF ACTION SHOULD BE A REAL DRAMATIC EPIPHANY!
DO IT RIGHT AND THE PLAY SOARS!
BLOW IT—AND WE BELLYFLOP!
SAY, I'M GLAD YOU'RE NOT PUTTING ANY PRESSURE ON ME, CHET!
SHOULD WE MAYBE DO A MEMORY EXERCISE?
MY THOUGHT EXACTLY!
HAVE YOU EVER HAD SOMEONE COME TO YOUR RESCUE WHEN YOU WERE FEELING VERY THREATENED?
UH... WELL, SURE!
HOW ABOUT SOMEONE YOU WOULDN'T HAVE EXPECTED TO CARE THAT MUCH?
...SOMEONE YOU'D ALWAYS CONSIDERED OBNOXIOUS? SOMEONE YOU WOULDN'T HAVE TENDED TO INVITE INTO YOUR LIFE...
HMMM.... TOLIVER SIMPSON..? ROONE PRUIT..? JEETER McCAW..?
...BUT SUDDENLY YOU NEEDED HIM...
—AND HE WAS THERE!!
OH, YEAH! SHELDON MOSSBERG WAS LIKE THAT!
—BACK IN JUNIOR HIGH!
THERE WAS THIS BULLY IN OUR SCHOOL—A MAJOR-LEAGUE SOCIOPATH!...
©1988 by H. Cruse

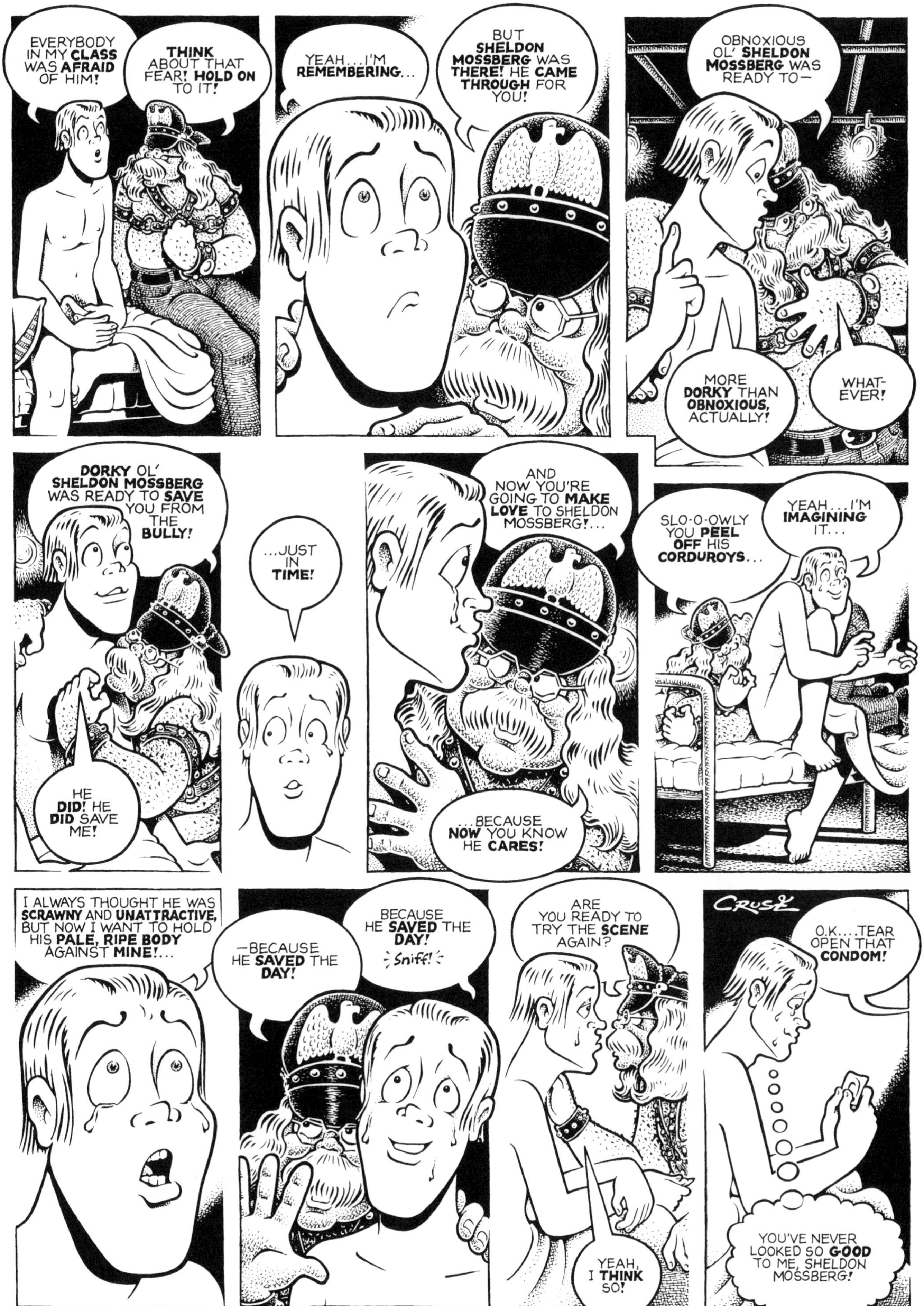

EVERYBODY IN MY **CLASS** WAS **AFRAID** OF HIM!
THINK ABOUT THAT FEAR! **HOLD ON** TO IT!
YEAH...I'M **REMEMBERING**...
BUT **SHELDON MOSSBERG** WAS **THERE!** HE **CAME THROUGH** FOR YOU!
OBNOXIOUS OL' **SHELDON MOSSBERG** WAS READY TO—
MORE **DORKY** THAN **OBNOXIOUS,** ACTUALLY!
WHAT-EVER!
DORKY OL' **SHELDON MOSSBERG** WAS READY TO **SAVE** YOU FROM THE **BULLY!**
HE **DID!** HE **DID** SAVE ME!
...JUST IN **TIME!**
AND NOW YOU'RE GOING TO **MAKE LOVE** TO SHELDON MOSSBERG!...
...BECAUSE **NOW** YOU KNOW HE **CARES!**
SLO-O-OWLY YOU **PEEL OFF** HIS **CORDUROYS**...
YEAH...I'M **IMAGINING** IT...
I ALWAYS THOUGHT HE WAS **SCRAWNY** AND **UNATTRACTIVE**, BUT NOW I WANT TO HOLD HIS **PALE, RIPE BODY** AGAINST **MINE!**...
—BECAUSE HE **SAVED** THE **DAY!**
BECAUSE HE **SAVED** THE **DAY!** *Sniff!*
ARE YOU READY TO TRY THE **SCENE** AGAIN?
YEAH, I **THINK** SO!
CRUSE
O.K....TEAR OPEN THAT **CONDOM!**
YOU'VE NEVER LOOKED SO **GOOD** TO ME, SHELDON MOSSBERG!

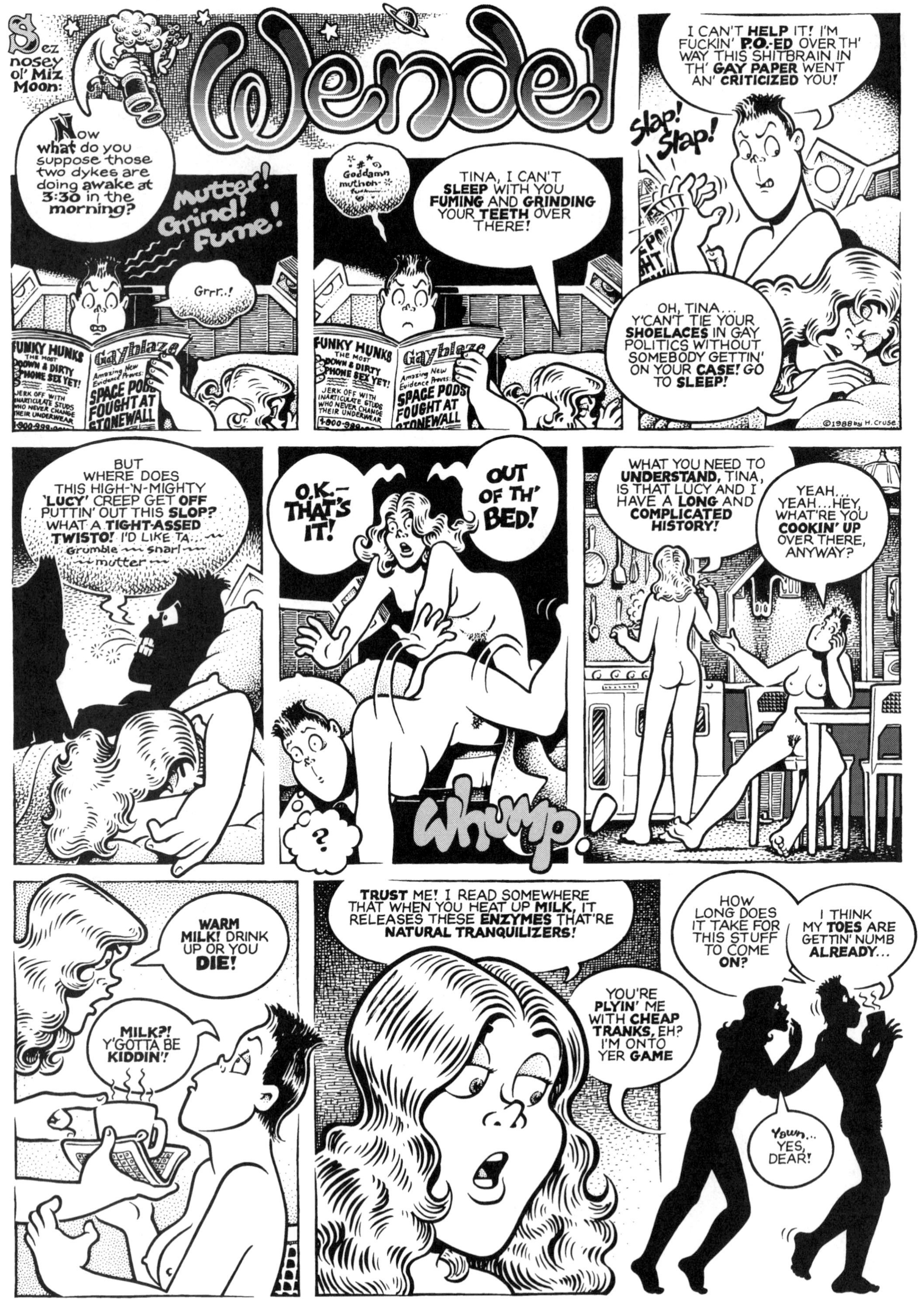
Sez nosey ol' Miz Moon:
Wendel
Now what do you suppose those two dykes are doing awake at 3:30 in the morning?
Mutter! Grind! Fume!
Grrr..!
FUNKY HUNKS THE MOST DOWN & DIRTY PHONE SEX YET! JERK OFF WITH INARTICULATE STUDS WHO NEVER CHANGE THEIR UNDERWEAR
Gayblaze
Amazing New Evidence Proves: SPACE PODS FOUGHT AT STONEWALL
Goddamn
TINA, I CAN'T SLEEP WITH YOU FUMING AND GRINDING YOUR TEETH OVER THERE!
I CAN'T HELP IT! I'M FUCKIN' P.O.-ED OVER TH' WAY THIS SHITBRAIN IN TH' GAY PAPER WENT AN' CRITICIZED YOU!
Slap! Slap!
OH, TINA... Y'CAN'T TIE YOUR SHOELACES IN GAY POLITICS WITHOUT SOMEBODY GETTIN' ON YOUR CASE! GO TO SLEEP!
©1988 by H. Cruse
BUT WHERE DOES THIS HIGH-'N-MIGHTY 'LUCY' CREEP GET OFF PUTTIN' OUT THIS SLOP? WHAT A TIGHT-ASSED TWISTO! I'D LIKE TA... Grumble snarl mutter
O.K.– THAT'S IT!
OUT OF TH' BED!
?
Whump!
WHAT YOU NEED TO UNDERSTAND, TINA, IS THAT LUCY AND I HAVE A LONG AND COMPLICATED HISTORY!
YEAH... YEAH... HEY, WHAT'RE YOU COOKIN' UP OVER THERE, ANYWAY?
WARM MILK! DRINK UP OR YOU DIE!
MILK?! Y'GOTTA BE KIDDIN'!
TRUST ME! I READ SOMEWHERE THAT WHEN YOU HEAT UP MILK, IT RELEASES THESE ENZYMES THAT'RE NATURAL TRANQUILIZERS!
YOU'RE PLYIN' ME WITH CHEAP TRANKS, EH? I'M ONTO YER GAME
HOW LONG DOES IT TAKE FOR THIS STUFF TO COME ON?
I THINK MY TOES ARE GETTIN' NUMB ALREADY...
Yawn... YES, DEAR!

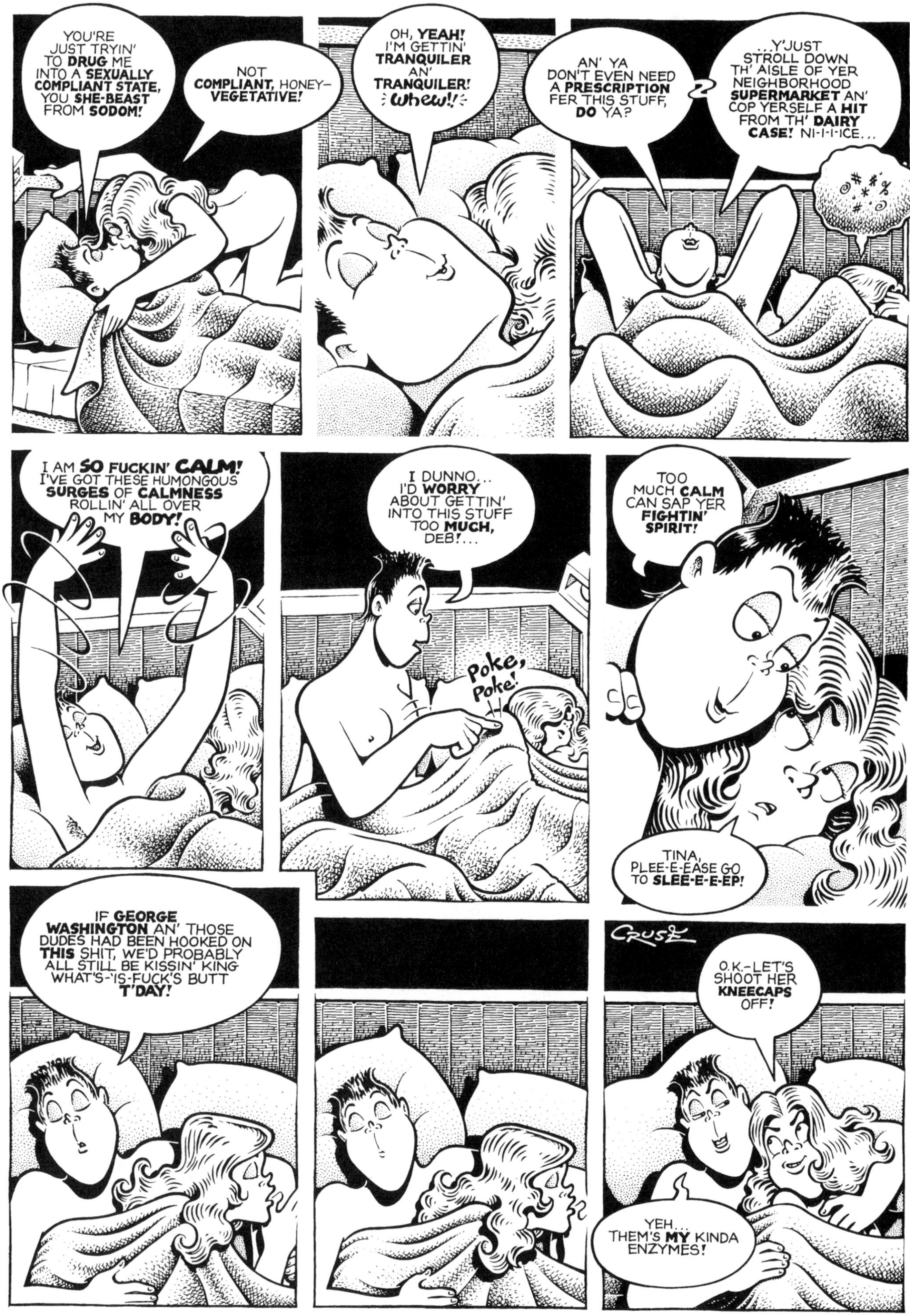
YOU'RE JUST TRYIN' TO DRUG ME INTO A SEXUALLY COMPLIANT STATE, YOU SHE-BEAST FROM SODOM!
NOT COMPLIANT, HONEY— VEGETATIVE!
OH, YEAH! I'M GETTIN' TRANQUILER AN' TRANQUILER! Whew!!
AN' YA DON'T EVEN NEED A PRESCRIPTION FER THIS STUFF, DO YA?
...Y'JUST STROLL DOWN TH' AISLE OF YER NEIGHBORHOOD SUPERMARKET AN' COP YERSELF A HIT FROM TH' DAIRY CASE! NI-I-I-ICE...
I AM SO FUCKIN' CALM! I'VE GOT THESE HUMONGOUS SURGES OF CALMNESS ROLLIN' ALL OVER MY BODY!
I DUNNO... I'D WORRY ABOUT GETTIN' INTO THIS STUFF TOO MUCH, DEB!...
Poke, Poke!
TOO MUCH CALM CAN SAP YER FIGHTIN' SPIRIT!
TINA, PLEE-E-EASE GO TO SLEE-E-E-EP!
IF GEORGE WASHINGTON AN' THOSE DUDES HAD BEEN HOOKED ON THIS SHIT, WE'D PROBABLY ALL STILL BE KISSIN' KING WHAT'S-'IS-FUCK'S BUTT T'DAY!
CRUSE
O.K.-LET'S SHOOT HER KNEECAPS OFF!
YEH... THEM'S MY KINDA ENZYMES!

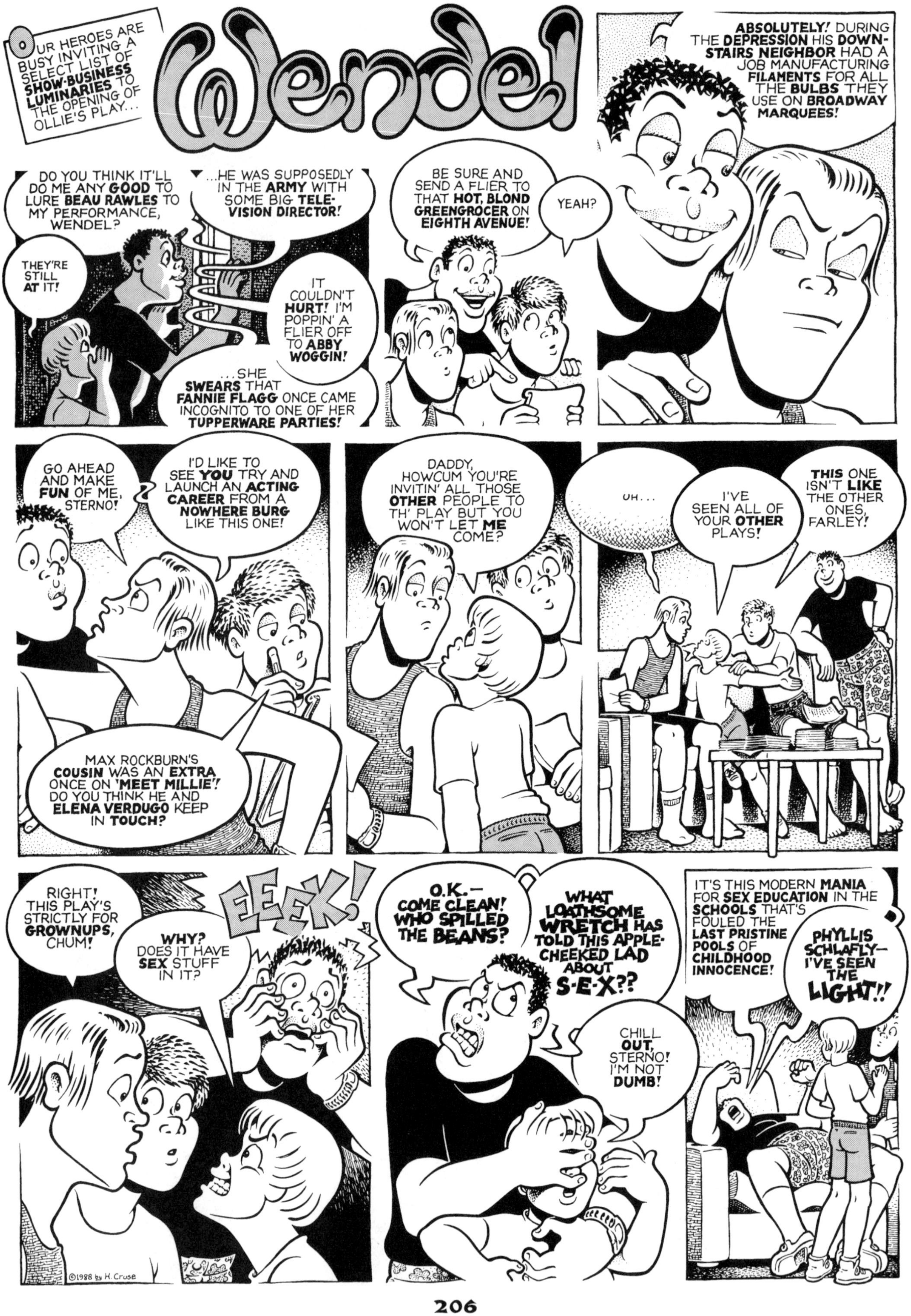

OUR HEROES ARE BUSY INVITING A SELECT LIST OF SHOW-BUSINESS LUMINARIES TO THE OPENING OF OLLIE'S PLAY...
Wendel
ABSOLUTELY! DURING THE DEPRESSION HIS DOWNSTAIRS NEIGHBOR HAD A JOB MANUFACTURING FILAMENTS FOR ALL THE BULBS THEY USE ON BROADWAY MARQUEES!
DO YOU THINK IT'LL DO ME ANY GOOD TO LURE BEAU RAWLES TO MY PERFORMANCE, WENDEL?
...HE WAS SUPPOSEDLY IN THE ARMY WITH SOME BIG TELEVISION DIRECTOR!
THEY'RE STILL AT IT!
IT COULDN'T HURT! I'M POPPIN' A FLIER OFF TO ABBY WOGGIN!
...SHE SWEARS THAT FANNIE FLAGG ONCE CAME INCOGNITO TO ONE OF HER TUPPERWARE PARTIES!
BE SURE AND SEND A FLIER TO THAT HOT, BLOND GREENGROCER ON EIGHTH AVENUE!
YEAH?
GO AHEAD AND MAKE FUN OF ME, STERNO!
I'D LIKE TO SEE YOU TRY AND LAUNCH AN ACTING CAREER FROM A NOWHERE BURG LIKE THIS ONE!
MAX ROCKBURN'S COUSIN WAS AN EXTRA ONCE ON 'MEET MILLIE'! DO YOU THINK HE AND ELENA VERDUGO KEEP IN TOUCH?
DADDY, HOWCUM YOU'RE INVITIN' ALL THOSE OTHER PEOPLE TO TH' PLAY BUT YOU WON'T LET ME COME?
UH...
I'VE SEEN ALL OF YOUR OTHER PLAYS!
THIS ONE ISN'T LIKE THE OTHER ONES, FARLEY!
RIGHT! THIS PLAY'S STRICTLY FOR GROWNUPS, CHUM!
WHY? DOES IT HAVE SEX STUFF IN IT?
EEEK!
O.K.— COME CLEAN! WHO SPILLED THE BEANS?
WHAT LOATHSOME WRETCH HAS TOLD THIS APPLE-CHEEKED LAD ABOUT S-E-X??
CHILL OUT, STERNO! I'M NOT DUMB!
IT'S THIS MODERN MANIA FOR SEX EDUCATION IN THE SCHOOLS THAT'S FOULED THE LAST PRISTINE POOLS OF CHILDHOOD INNOCENCE!
PHYLLIS SCHLAFLY— I'VE SEEN THE LIGHT!!
©1988 by H. Cruse

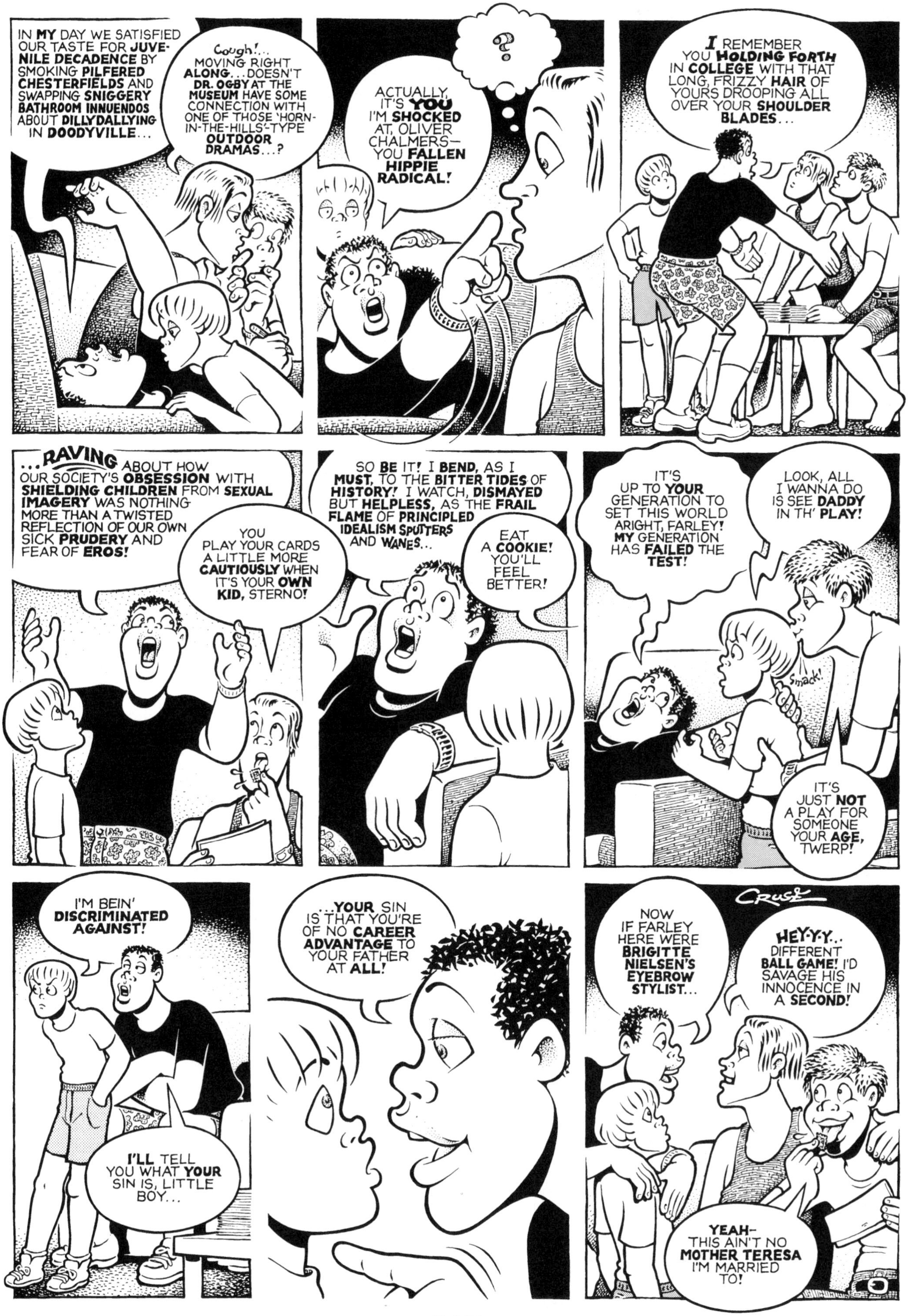
IN MY DAY WE SATISFIED OUR TASTE FOR JUVENILE DECADENCE BY SMOKING PILFERED CHESTERFIELDS AND SWAPPING SNIGGERY BATHROOM INNUENDOS ABOUT DILLYDALLYING IN DOODYVILLE...
Cough!... MOVING RIGHT ALONG...DOESN'T DR. OGBY AT THE MUSEUM HAVE SOME CONNECTION WITH ONE OF THOSE 'HORN-IN-THE-HILLS'-TYPE OUTDOOR DRAMAS...?
?
ACTUALLY, IT'S YOU I'M SHOCKED AT, OLIVER CHALMERS— YOU FALLEN HIPPIE RADICAL!
I REMEMBER YOU HOLDING FORTH IN COLLEGE WITH THAT LONG, FRIZZY HAIR OF YOURS DROOPING ALL OVER YOUR SHOULDER BLADES...
...RAVING ABOUT HOW OUR SOCIETY'S OBSESSION WITH SHIELDING CHILDREN FROM SEXUAL IMAGERY WAS NOTHING MORE THAN A TWISTED REFLECTION OF OUR OWN SICK PRUDERY AND FEAR OF EROS!
YOU PLAY YOUR CARDS A LITTLE MORE CAUTIOUSLY WHEN IT'S YOUR OWN KID, STERNO!
SO BE IT! I BEND, AS I MUST, TO THE BITTER TIDES OF HISTORY! I WATCH, DISMAYED BUT HELPLESS, AS THE FRAIL FLAME OF PRINCIPLED IDEALISM SPUTTERS AND WANES...
EAT A COOKIE! YOU'LL FEEL BETTER!
IT'S UP TO YOUR GENERATION TO SET THIS WORLD ARIGHT, FARLEY! MY GENERATION HAS FAILED THE TEST!
LOOK, ALL I WANNA DO IS SEE DADDY IN TH' PLAY!
Smack!
IT'S JUST NOT A PLAY FOR SOMEONE YOUR AGE, TWERP!
I'M BEIN' DISCRIMINATED AGAINST!
I'LL TELL YOU WHAT YOUR SIN IS, LITTLE BOY...
...YOUR SIN IS THAT YOU'RE OF NO CAREER ADVANTAGE TO YOUR FATHER AT ALL!
CRUSE
NOW IF FARLEY HERE WERE BRIGITTE NIELSEN'S EYEBROW STYLIST...
HEY-Y-Y... DIFFERENT BALL GAME! I'D SAVAGE HIS INNOCENCE IN A SECOND!
YEAH– THIS AIN'T NO MOTHER TERESA I'M MARRIED TO!

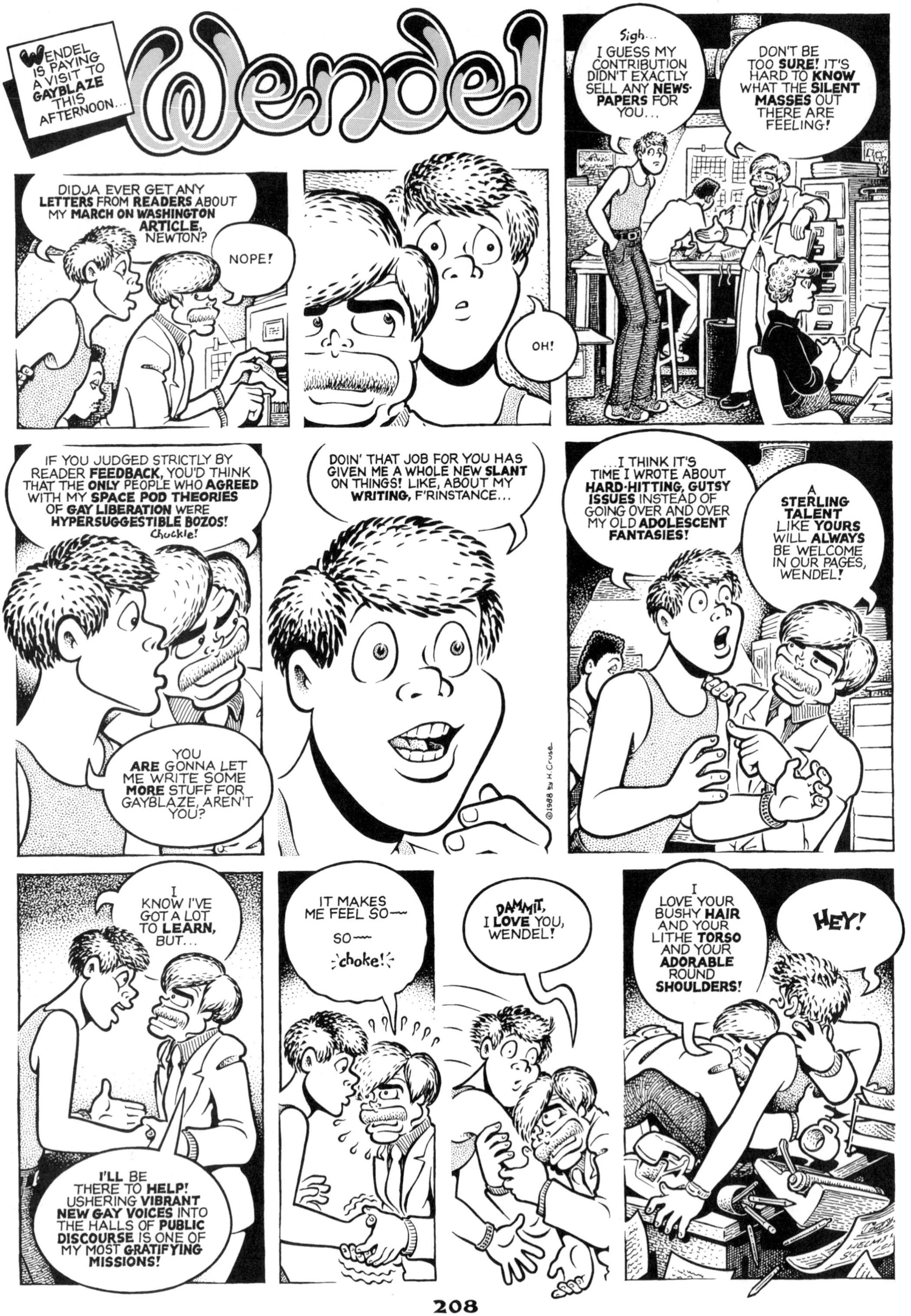

WENDEL IS PAYING A VISIT TO GAYBLAZE THIS AFTERNOON...
Wendel
DIDJA EVER GET ANY LETTERS FROM READERS ABOUT MY MARCH ON WASHINGTON ARTICLE, NEWTON?
NOPE!
OH!
Sigh... I GUESS MY CONTRIBUTION DIDN'T EXACTLY SELL ANY NEWS-PAPERS FOR YOU...
DON'T BE TOO SURE! IT'S HARD TO KNOW WHAT THE SILENT MASSES OUT THERE ARE FEELING!
IF YOU JUDGED STRICTLY BY READER FEEDBACK, YOU'D THINK THAT THE ONLY PEOPLE WHO AGREED WITH MY SPACE POD THEORIES OF GAY LIBERATION WERE HYPERSUGGESTIBLE BOZOS!
Chuckle!
YOU ARE GONNA LET ME WRITE SOME MORE STUFF FOR GAYBLAZE, AREN'T YOU?
DOIN' THAT JOB FOR YOU HAS GIVEN ME A WHOLE NEW SLANT ON THINGS! LIKE, ABOUT MY WRITING, F'RINSTANCE...
©1988 by H. Cruse
...I THINK IT'S TIME I WROTE ABOUT HARD-HITTING, GUTSY ISSUES INSTEAD OF GOING OVER AND OVER MY OLD ADOLESCENT FANTASIES!
A STERLING TALENT LIKE YOURS WILL ALWAYS BE WELCOME IN OUR PAGES, WENDEL!
I KNOW I'VE GOT A LOT TO LEARN, BUT...
I'LL BE THERE TO HELP! USHERING VIBRANT NEW GAY VOICES INTO THE HALLS OF PUBLIC DISCOURSE IS ONE OF MY MOST GRATIFYING MISSIONS!
IT MAKES ME FEEL SO— SO— choke!
DAMMIT, I LOVE YOU, WENDEL!
I LOVE YOUR BUSHY HAIR AND YOUR LITHE TORSO AND YOUR ADORABLE ROUND SHOULDERS!
HEY!

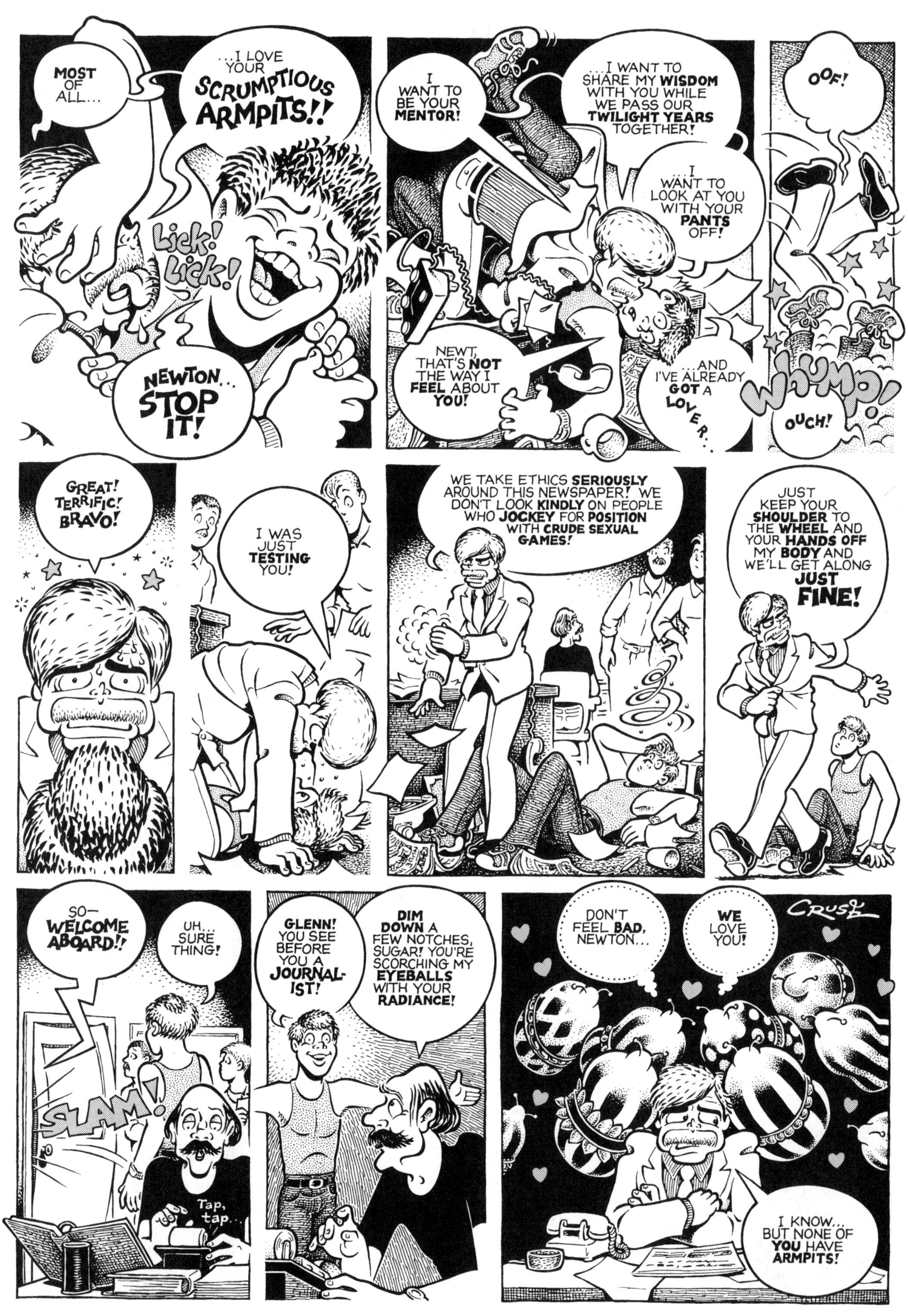
MOST OF ALL...
...I LOVE YOUR SCRUMPTIOUS ARMPITS!!
LICK! LICK!
NEWTON... STOP IT!
I WANT TO BE YOUR MENTOR!
...I WANT TO SHARE MY WISDOM WITH YOU WHILE WE PASS OUR TWILIGHT YEARS TOGETHER!
...I WANT TO LOOK AT YOU WITH YOUR PANTS OFF!
NEWT, THAT'S NOT THE WAY I FEEL ABOUT YOU!
...AND I'VE ALREADY GOT A LOVER...
OOF!
WHUMP!
OUCH!
GREAT! TERRIFIC! BRAVO!
I WAS JUST TESTING YOU!
WE TAKE ETHICS SERIOUSLY AROUND THIS NEWSPAPER! WE DON'T LOOK KINDLY ON PEOPLE WHO JOCKEY FOR POSITION WITH CRUDE SEXUAL GAMES!
JUST KEEP YOUR SHOULDER TO THE WHEEL AND YOUR HANDS OFF MY BODY AND WE'LL GET ALONG JUST FINE!
SO— WELCOME ABOARD!!
UH... SURE THING!
SLAM!
Tap, tap...
GLENN! YOU SEE BEFORE YOU A JOURNAL-IST!
DIM DOWN A FEW NOTCHES, SUGAR! YOU'RE SCORCHING MY EYEBALLS WITH YOUR RADIANCE!
CRUSE
DON'T FEEL BAD, NEWTON...
WE LOVE YOU!
I KNOW... BUT NONE OF YOU HAVE ARMPITS!

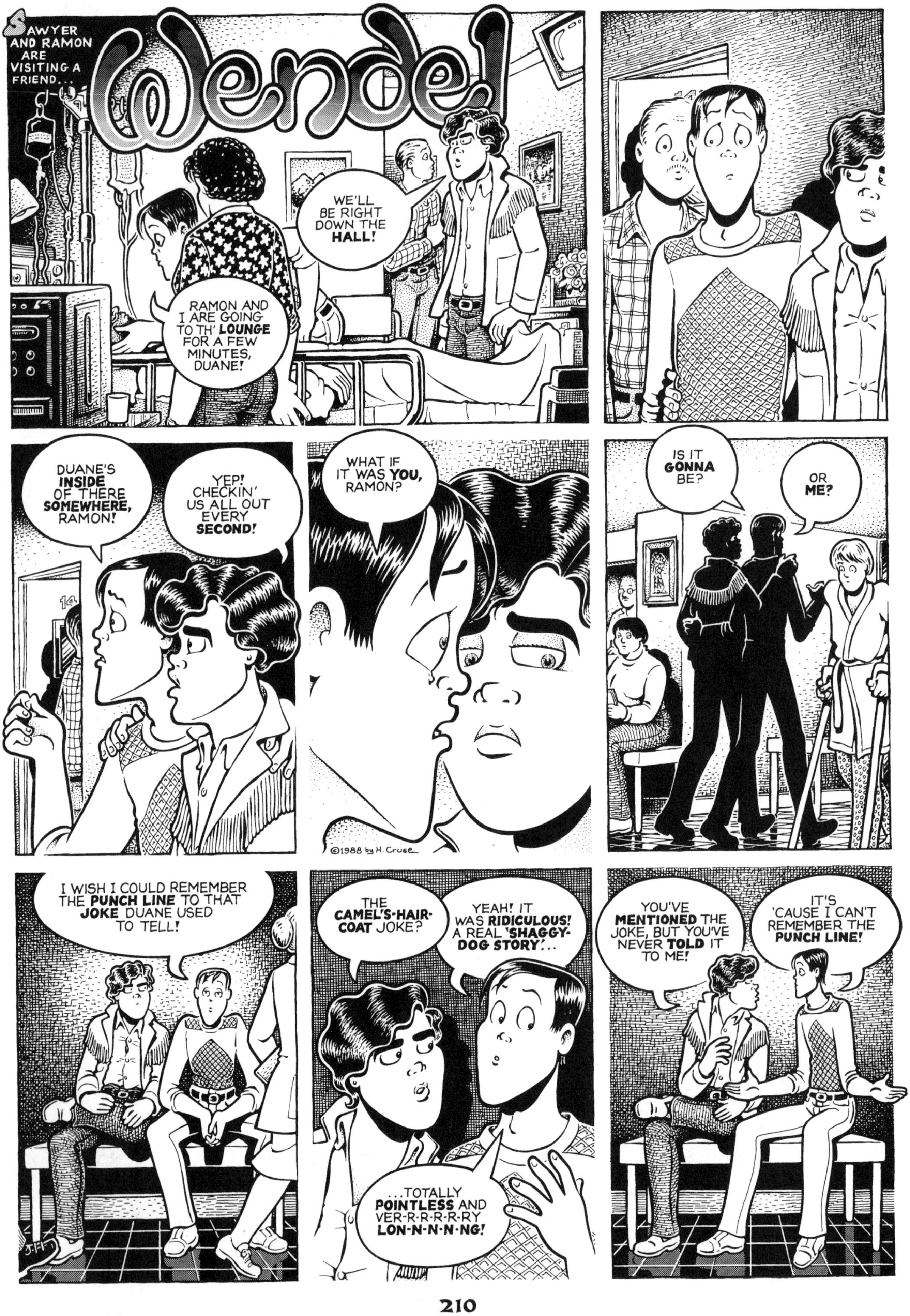
SAWYER AND RAMON ARE VISITING A FRIEND...
Wendel
RAMON AND I ARE GOING TO TH' LOUNGE FOR A FEW MINUTES, DUANE!
WE'LL BE RIGHT DOWN THE HALL!
14
DUANE'S INSIDE OF THERE SOMEWHERE, RAMON!
YEP! CHECKIN' US ALL OUT EVERY SECOND!
WHAT IF IT WAS YOU, RAMON?
©1988 by H. Cruse
IS IT GONNA BE?
OR ME?
I WISH I COULD REMEMBER THE PUNCH LINE TO THAT JOKE DUANE USED TO TELL!
THE CAMEL'S-HAIR-COAT JOKE?
YEAH! IT WAS RIDICULOUS! A REAL 'SHAGGY-DOG STORY'...
...TOTALLY POINTLESS AND VER-R-R-R-RY LON-N-N-N-NG!
YOU'VE MENTIONED THE JOKE, BUT YOU'VE NEVER TOLD IT TO ME!
IT'S 'CAUSE I CAN'T REMEMBER THE PUNCH LINE!

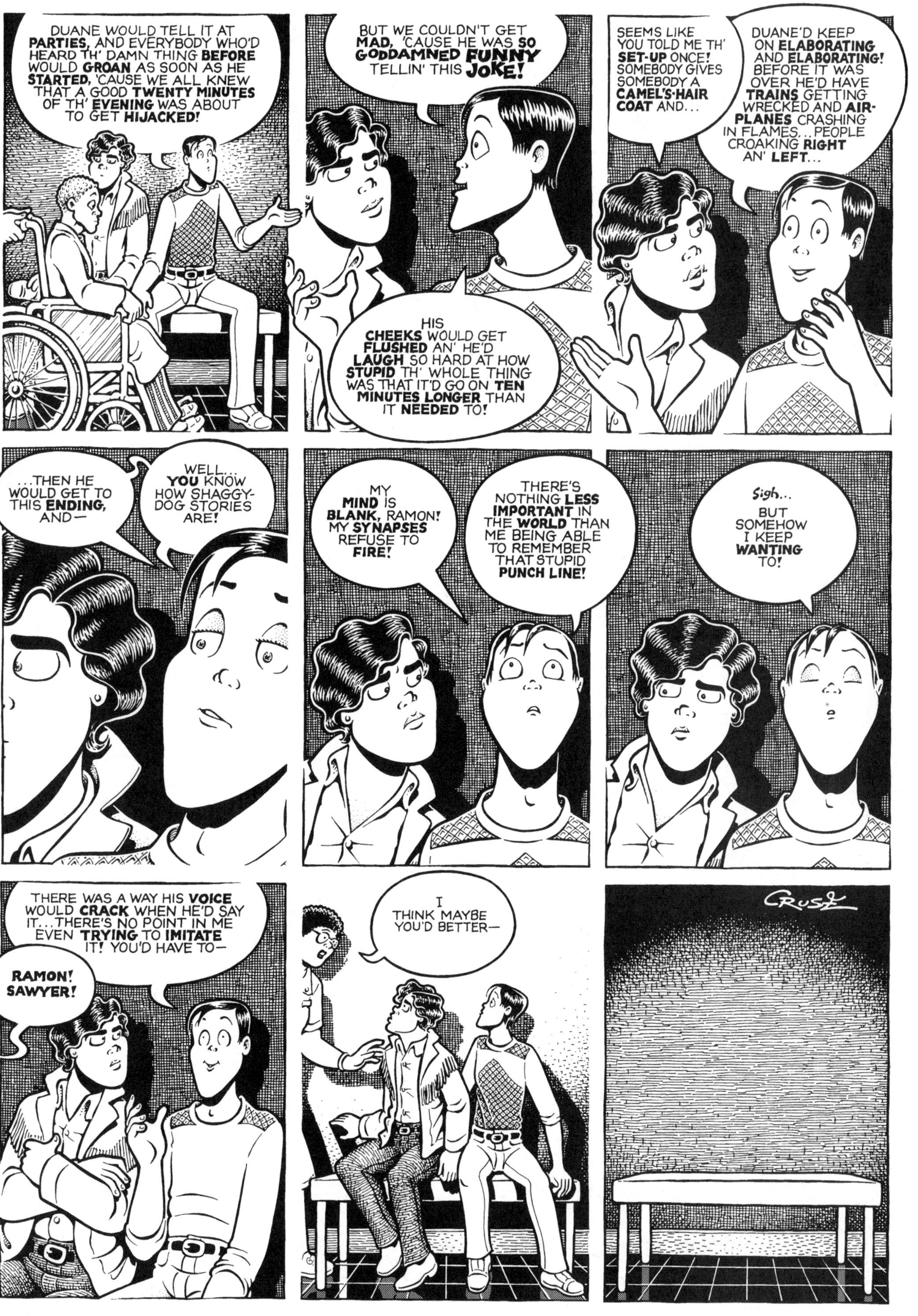
DUANE WOULD TELL IT AT PARTIES, AND EVERYBODY WHO'D HEARD TH' DAMN THING BEFORE WOULD GROAN AS SOON AS HE STARTED, 'CAUSE WE ALL KNEW THAT A GOOD TWENTY MINUTES OF TH' EVENING WAS ABOUT TO GET HIJACKED!
BUT WE COULDN'T GET MAD, 'CAUSE HE WAS SO GODDAMNED FUNNY TELLIN' THIS JOKE!
HIS CHEEKS WOULD GET FLUSHED AN' HE'D LAUGH SO HARD AT HOW STUPID TH' WHOLE THING WAS THAT IT'D GO ON TEN MINUTES LONGER THAN IT NEEDED TO!
SEEMS LIKE YOU TOLD ME TH' SET-UP ONCE! SOMEBODY GIVES SOMEBODY A CAMEL'S-HAIR COAT AND...
DUANE'D KEEP ON ELABORATING AND ELABORATING! BEFORE IT WAS OVER HE'D HAVE TRAINS GETTING WRECKED AND AIR-PLANES CRASHING IN FLAMES... PEOPLE CROAKING RIGHT AN' LEFT...
...THEN HE WOULD GET TO THIS ENDING, AND—
WELL... YOU KNOW HOW SHAGGY-DOG STORIES ARE!
MY MIND IS BLANK, RAMON! MY SYNAPSES REFUSE TO FIRE!
THERE'S NOTHING LESS IMPORTANT IN THE WORLD THAN ME BEING ABLE TO REMEMBER THAT STUPID PUNCH LINE!
Sigh...
BUT SOMEHOW I KEEP WANTING TO!
THERE WAS A WAY HIS VOICE WOULD CRACK WHEN HE'D SAY IT... THERE'S NO POINT IN ME EVEN TRYING TO IMITATE IT! YOU'D HAVE TO—
RAMON! SAWYER!
I THINK MAYBE YOU'D BETTER—
CRUSE

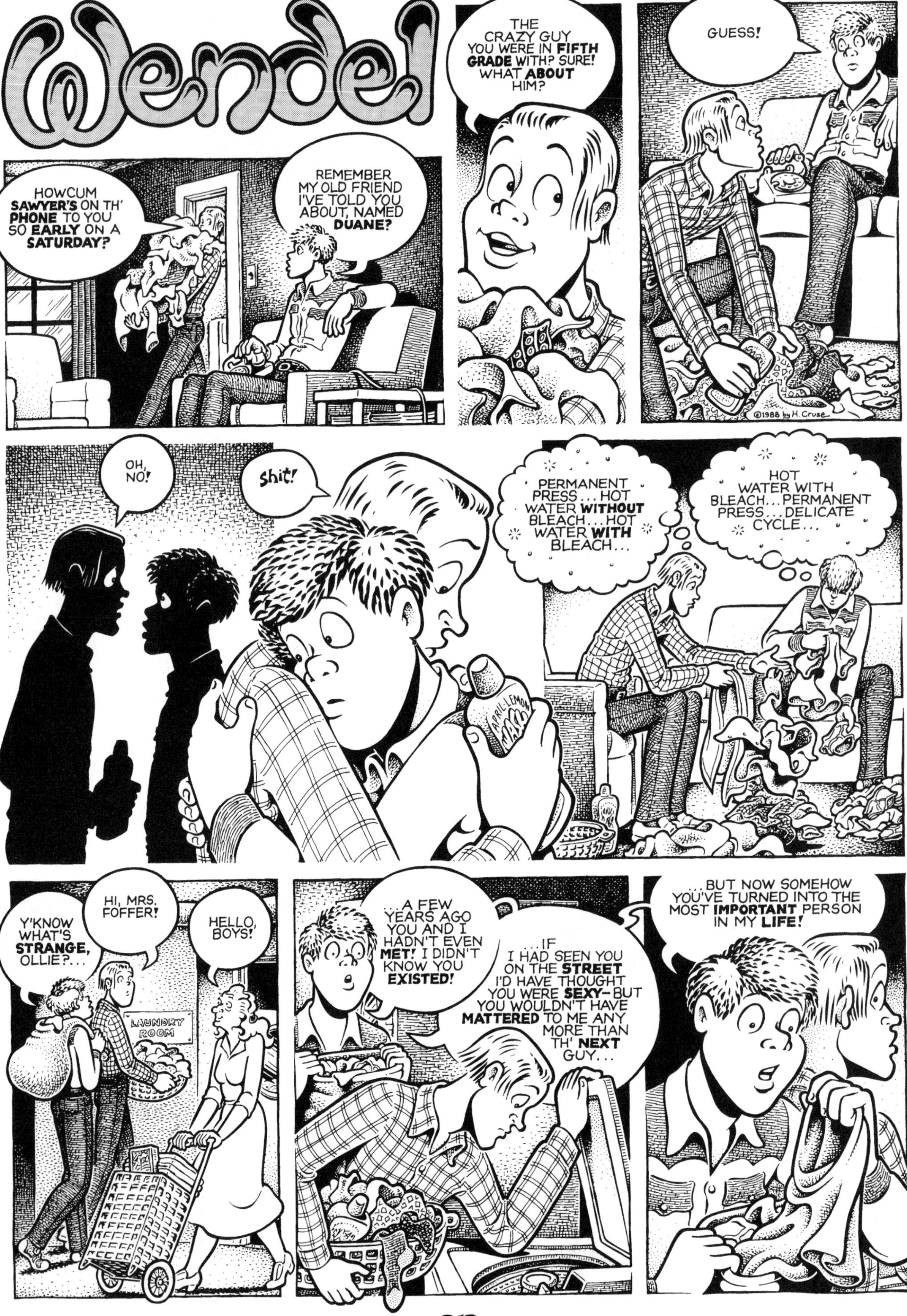
Wendel
HOWCUM SAWYER'S ON TH' PHONE TO YOU SO EARLY ON A SATURDAY?
REMEMBER MY OLD FRIEND I'VE TOLD YOU ABOUT, NAMED DUANE?
THE CRAZY GUY YOU WERE IN FIFTH GRADE WITH? SURE! WHAT ABOUT HIM?
GUESS!
©1988 by H. Cruse
OH, NO!
Shit!
APRIL LEMON
PERMANENT PRESS... HOT WATER WITHOUT BLEACH... HOT WATER WITH BLEACH...
HOT WATER WITH BLEACH... PERMANENT PRESS... DELICATE CYCLE...
Y'KNOW WHAT'S STRANGE, OLLIE?...
HI, MRS. FOFFER!
HELLO, BOYS!
LAUNDRY ROOM
...A FEW YEARS AGO YOU AND I HADN'T EVEN MET! I DIDN'T KNOW YOU EXISTED!
...IF I HAD SEEN YOU ON THE STREET I'D HAVE THOUGHT YOU WERE SEXY– BUT YOU WOULDN'T HAVE MATTERED TO ME ANY MORE THAN TH' NEXT GUY...
...BUT NOW SOMEHOW YOU'VE TURNED INTO THE MOST IMPORTANT PERSON IN MY LIFE!

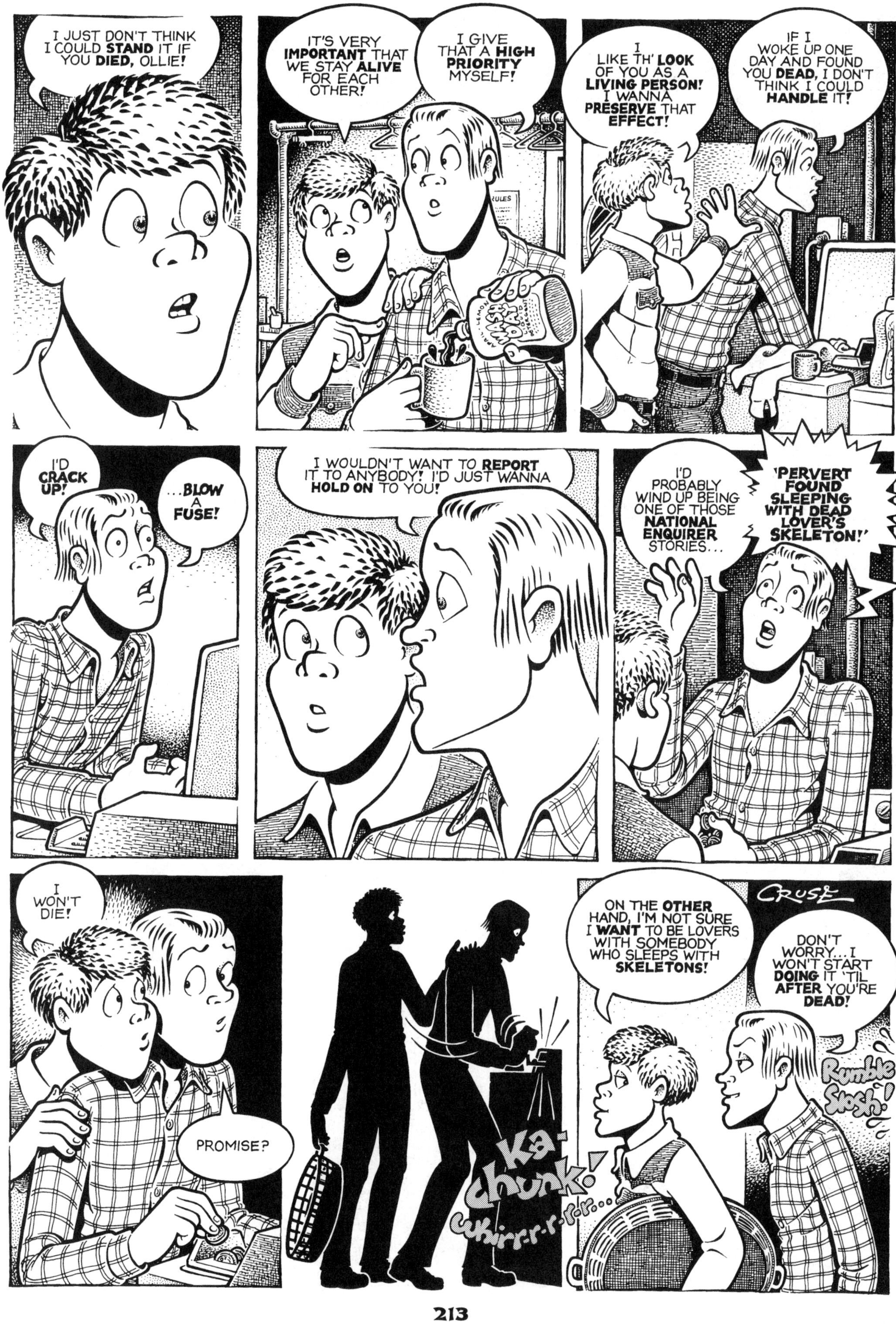
I JUST DON'T THINK I COULD STAND IT IF YOU DIED, OLLIE!
IT'S VERY IMPORTANT THAT WE STAY ALIVE FOR EACH OTHER!
I GIVE THAT A HIGH PRIORITY MYSELF!
I LIKE TH' LOOK OF YOU AS A LIVING PERSON! I WANNA PRESERVE THAT EFFECT!
IF I WOKE UP ONE DAY AND FOUND YOU DEAD, I DON'T THINK I COULD HANDLE IT!
I'D CRACK UP!
...BLOW A FUSE!
I WOULDN'T WANT TO REPORT IT TO ANYBODY! I'D JUST WANNA HOLD ON TO YOU!
I'D PROBABLY WIND UP BEING ONE OF THOSE NATIONAL ENQUIRER STORIES...
'PERVERT FOUND SLEEPING WITH DEAD LOVER'S SKELETON!'
I WON'T DIE!
PROMISE?
Ka-chunk!
Whirr-r-r-r-r...
CRUSE
ON THE OTHER HAND, I'M NOT SURE I WANT TO BE LOVERS WITH SOMEBODY WHO SLEEPS WITH SKELETONS!
DON'T WORRY... I WON'T START DOING IT 'TIL AFTER YOU'RE DEAD!
Rumble! Slosh!

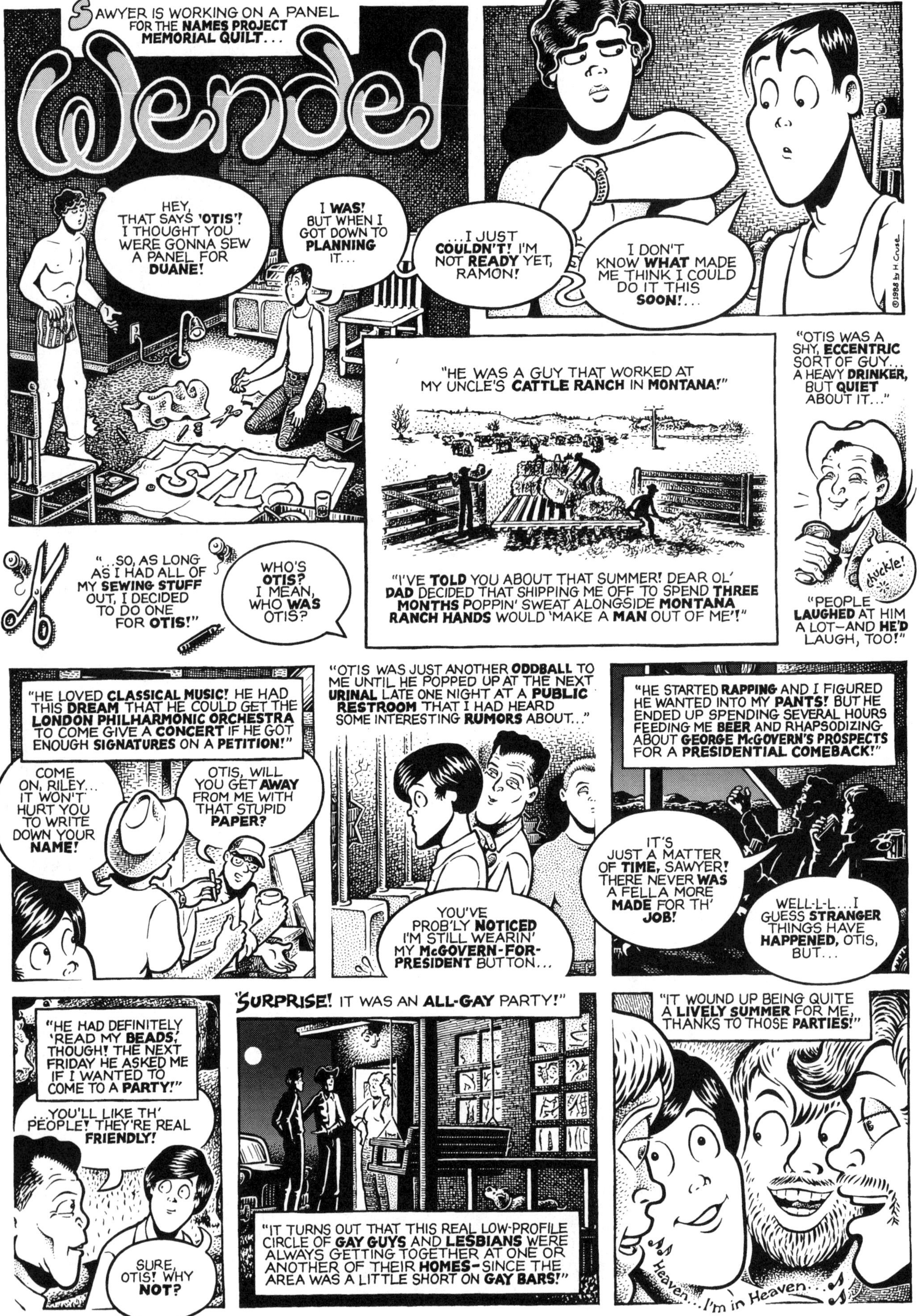
SAWYER IS WORKING ON A PANEL FOR THE NAMES PROJECT MEMORIAL QUILT...
Wendel
HEY, THAT SAYS 'OTIS'! I THOUGHT YOU WERE GONNA SEW A PANEL FOR DUANE!
I WAS! BUT WHEN I GOT DOWN TO PLANNING IT...
...I JUST COULDN'T! I'M NOT READY YET, RAMON!
I DON'T KNOW WHAT MADE ME THINK I COULD DO IT THIS SOON!...
©1988 by H. Cruse
"...SO, AS LONG AS I HAD ALL OF MY SEWING STUFF OUT, I DECIDED TO DO ONE FOR OTIS!"
WHO'S OTIS? I MEAN, WHO WAS OTIS?
"HE WAS A GUY THAT WORKED AT MY UNCLE'S CATTLE RANCH IN MONTANA!"
"I'VE TOLD YOU ABOUT THAT SUMMER! DEAR OL' DAD DECIDED THAT SHIPPING ME OFF TO SPEND THREE MONTHS POPPIN' SWEAT ALONGSIDE MONTANA RANCH HANDS WOULD 'MAKE A MAN OUT OF ME'!"
"OTIS WAS A SHY, ECCENTRIC SORT OF GUY... A HEAVY DRINKER, BUT QUIET ABOUT IT..."
chuckle!
"PEOPLE LAUGHED AT HIM A LOT—AND HE'D LAUGH, TOO!"
"HE LOVED CLASSICAL MUSIC! HE HAD THIS DREAM THAT HE COULD GET THE LONDON PHILHARMONIC ORCHESTRA TO COME GIVE A CONCERT IF HE GOT ENOUGH SIGNATURES ON A PETITION!"
COME ON, RILEY... IT WON'T HURT YOU TO WRITE DOWN YOUR NAME!
OTIS, WILL YOU GET AWAY FROM ME WITH THAT STUPID PAPER?
"OTIS WAS JUST ANOTHER ODDBALL TO ME UNTIL HE POPPED UP AT THE NEXT URINAL LATE ONE NIGHT AT A PUBLIC RESTROOM THAT I HAD HEARD SOME INTERESTING RUMORS ABOUT..."
YOU'VE PROB'LY NOTICED I'M STILL WEARIN' MY McGOVERN-FOR-PRESIDENT BUTTON...
"HE STARTED RAPPING AND I FIGURED HE WANTED INTO MY PANTS! BUT HE ENDED UP SPENDING SEVERAL HOURS FEEDING ME BEER AND RHAPSODIZING ABOUT GEORGE McGOVERN'S PROSPECTS FOR A PRESIDENTIAL COMEBACK!"
IT'S JUST A MATTER OF TIME, SAWYER! THERE NEVER WAS A FELLA MORE MADE FOR TH' JOB!
WELL-L-L...I GUESS STRANGER THINGS HAVE HAPPENED, OTIS, BUT...
"HE HAD DEFINITELY 'READ MY BEADS,' THOUGH! THE NEXT FRIDAY HE ASKED ME IF I WANTED TO COME TO A PARTY!"
...YOU'LL LIKE TH' PEOPLE! THEY'RE REAL FRIENDLY!
SURE, OTIS! WHY NOT?
"SURPRISE! IT WAS AN ALL-GAY PARTY!"
"IT TURNS OUT THAT THIS REAL LOW-PROFILE CIRCLE OF GAY GUYS AND LESBIANS WERE ALWAYS GETTING TOGETHER AT ONE OR ANOTHER OF THEIR HOMES—SINCE THE AREA WAS A LITTLE SHORT ON GAY BARS!"
"IT WOUND UP BEING QUITE A LIVELY SUMMER FOR ME, THANKS TO THOSE PARTIES!"
Heaven... I'm in Heaven...

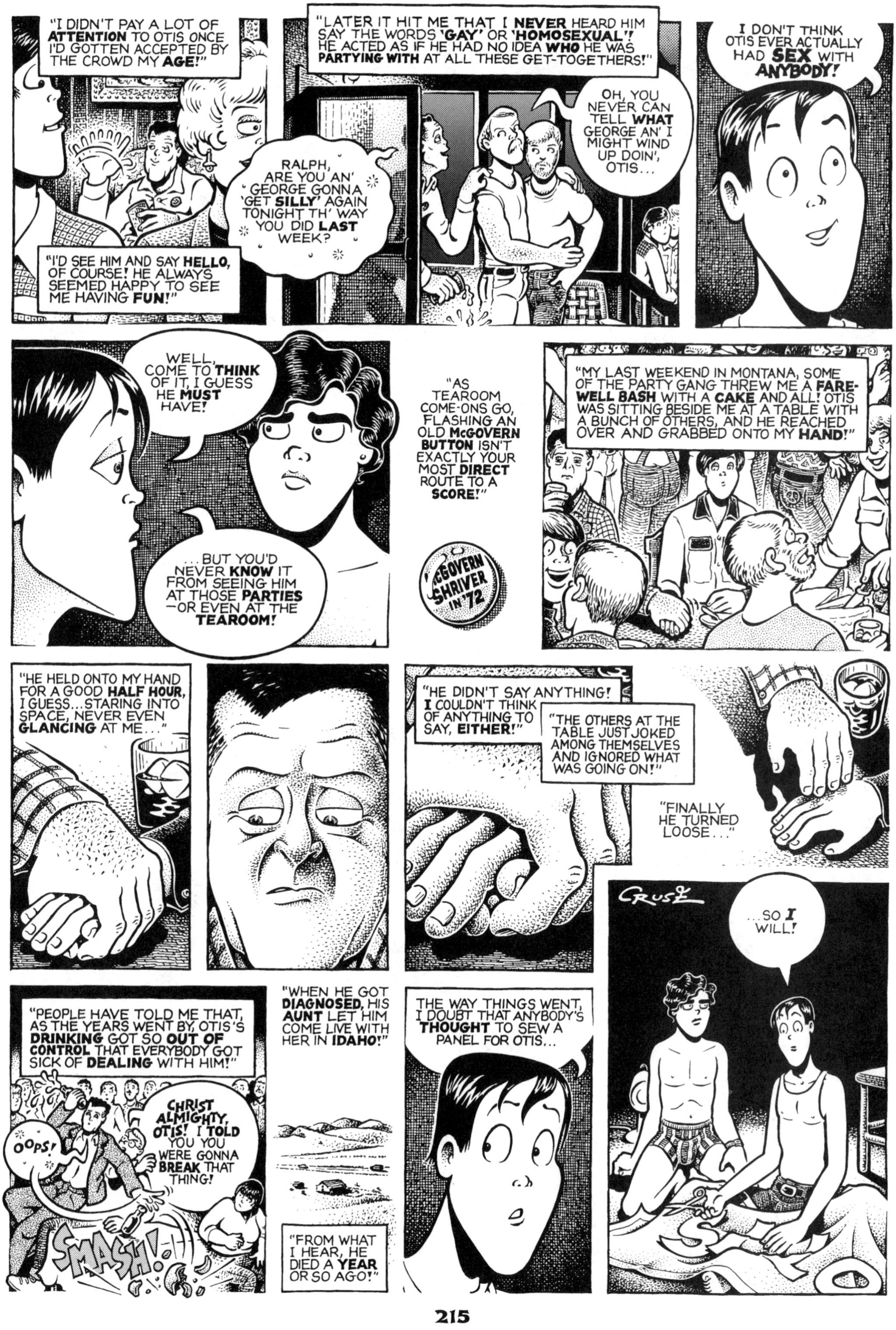
"I DIDN'T PAY A LOT OF ATTENTION TO OTIS ONCE I'D GOTTEN ACCEPTED BY THE CROWD MY AGE!"
"I'D SEE HIM AND SAY HELLO, OF COURSE! HE ALWAYS SEEMED HAPPY TO SEE ME HAVING FUN!"
"LATER IT HIT ME THAT I NEVER HEARD HIM SAY THE WORDS 'GAY' OR 'HOMOSEXUAL'! HE ACTED AS IF HE HAD NO IDEA WHO HE WAS PARTYING WITH AT ALL THESE GET-TOGETHERS!"
RALPH, ARE YOU AN' GEORGE GONNA 'GET SILLY' AGAIN TONIGHT TH' WAY YOU DID LAST WEEK?
OH, YOU NEVER CAN TELL WHAT GEORGE AN' I MIGHT WIND UP DOIN', OTIS...
I DON'T THINK OTIS EVER ACTUALLY HAD SEX WITH ANYBODY!
WELL, COME TO THINK OF IT, I GUESS HE MUST HAVE!
...BUT YOU'D NEVER KNOW IT FROM SEEING HIM AT THOSE PARTIES —OR EVEN AT THE TEAROOM!
"AS TEAROOM COME-ONS GO, FLASHING AN OLD McGOVERN BUTTON ISN'T EXACTLY YOUR MOST DIRECT ROUTE TO A SCORE!"
McGOVERN SHRIVER IN '72
"MY LAST WEEKEND IN MONTANA, SOME OF THE PARTY GANG THREW ME A FAREWELL BASH WITH A CAKE AND ALL! OTIS WAS SITTING BESIDE ME AT A TABLE WITH A BUNCH OF OTHERS, AND HE REACHED OVER AND GRABBED ONTO MY HAND!"
"HE HELD ONTO MY HAND FOR A GOOD HALF HOUR, I GUESS...STARING INTO SPACE, NEVER EVEN GLANCING AT ME..."
"HE DIDN'T SAY ANYTHING! I COULDN'T THINK OF ANYTHING TO SAY, EITHER!"
"THE OTHERS AT THE TABLE JUST JOKED AMONG THEMSELVES AND IGNORED WHAT WAS GOING ON!"
"FINALLY HE TURNED LOOSE..."
"PEOPLE HAVE TOLD ME THAT, AS THE YEARS WENT BY, OTIS'S DRINKING GOT SO OUT OF CONTROL THAT EVERYBODY GOT SICK OF DEALING WITH HIM!"
OOPS!
CHRIST ALMIGHTY, OTIS! I TOLD YOU YOU WERE GONNA BREAK THAT THING!
SMASH!
"WHEN HE GOT DIAGNOSED, HIS AUNT LET HIM COME LIVE WITH HER IN IDAHO!"
"FROM WHAT I HEAR, HE DIED A YEAR OR SO AGO!"
THE WAY THINGS WENT, I DOUBT THAT ANYBODY'S THOUGHT TO SEW A PANEL FOR OTIS...
CRUSE
...SO I WILL!

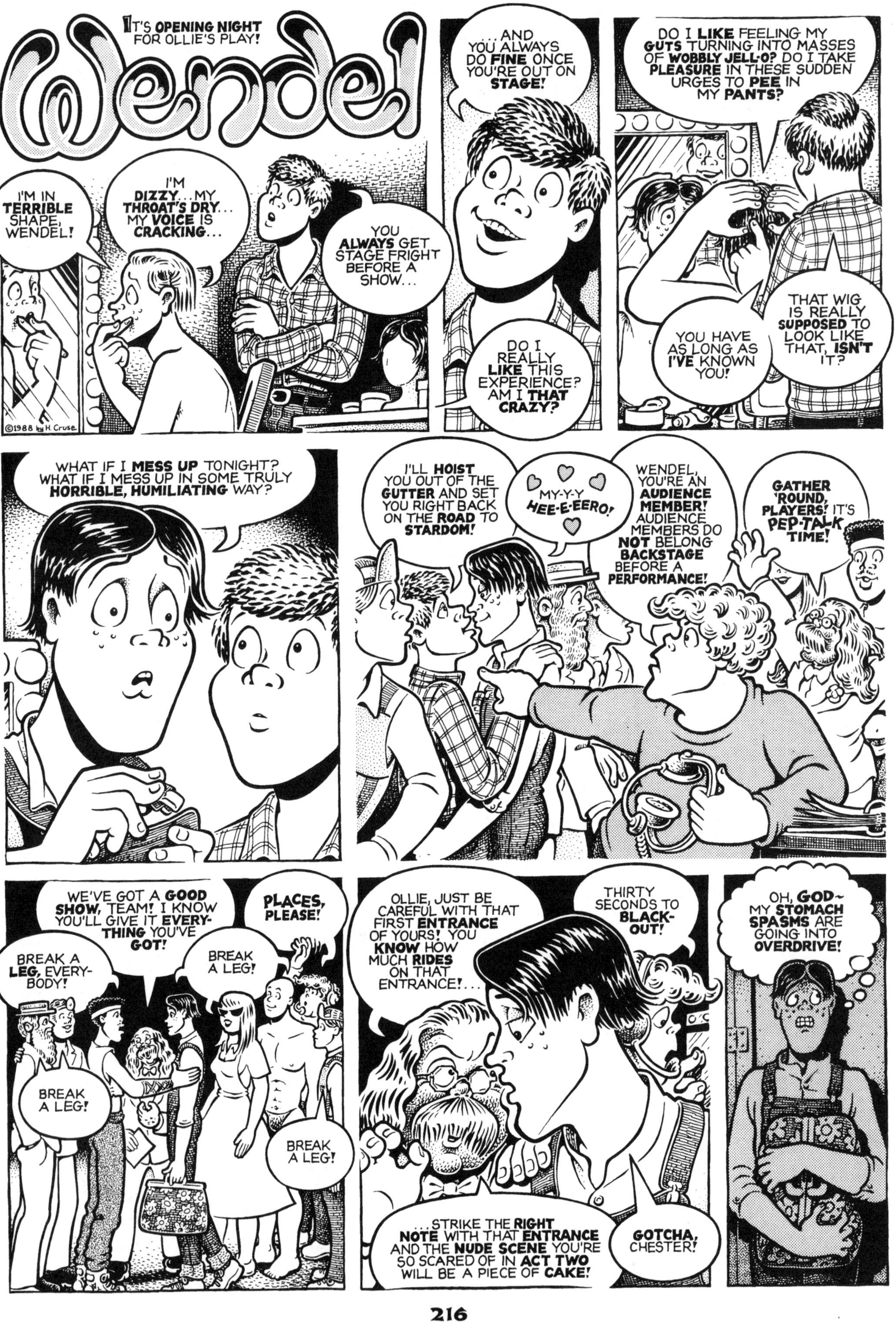
Wendel
IT'S OPENING NIGHT FOR OLLIE'S PLAY!
I'M IN TERRIBLE SHAPE, WENDEL!
I'M DIZZY... MY THROAT'S DRY... MY VOICE IS CRACKING...
YOU ALWAYS GET STAGE FRIGHT BEFORE A SHOW...
©1988 by H. Cruse
...AND YOU ALWAYS DO FINE ONCE YOU'RE OUT ON STAGE!
DO I REALLY LIKE THIS EXPERIENCE? AM I THAT CRAZY?
DO I LIKE FEELING MY GUTS TURNING INTO MASSES OF WOBBLY JELL-O? DO I TAKE PLEASURE IN THESE SUDDEN URGES TO PEE IN MY PANTS?
YOU HAVE AS LONG AS I'VE KNOWN YOU!
THAT WIG IS REALLY SUPPOSED TO LOOK LIKE THAT, ISN'T IT?
WHAT IF I MESS UP TONIGHT? WHAT IF I MESS UP IN SOME TRULY HORRIBLE, HUMILIATING WAY?
I'LL HOIST YOU OUT OF THE GUTTER AND SET YOU RIGHT BACK ON THE ROAD TO STARDOM!
MY-Y-Y HEE-E-EERO!
WENDEL, YOU'RE AN AUDIENCE MEMBER! AUDIENCE MEMBERS DO NOT BELONG BACKSTAGE BEFORE A PERFORMANCE!
GATHER 'ROUND, PLAYERS! IT'S PEP-TALK TIME!
WE'VE GOT A GOOD SHOW, TEAM! I KNOW YOU'LL GIVE IT EVERYTHING YOU'VE GOT!
PLACES, PLEASE!
BREAK A LEG, EVERYBODY!
BREAK A LEG!
BREAK A LEG!
BREAK A LEG!
OLLIE, JUST BE CAREFUL WITH THAT FIRST ENTRANCE OF YOURS! YOU KNOW HOW MUCH RIDES ON THAT ENTRANCE!...
THIRTY SECONDS TO BLACKOUT!
...STRIKE THE RIGHT NOTE WITH THAT ENTRANCE AND THE NUDE SCENE YOU'RE SO SCARED OF IN ACT TWO WILL BE A PIECE OF CAKE!
GOTCHA, CHESTER!
OH, GOD~ MY STOMACH SPASMS ARE GOING INTO OVERDRIVE!

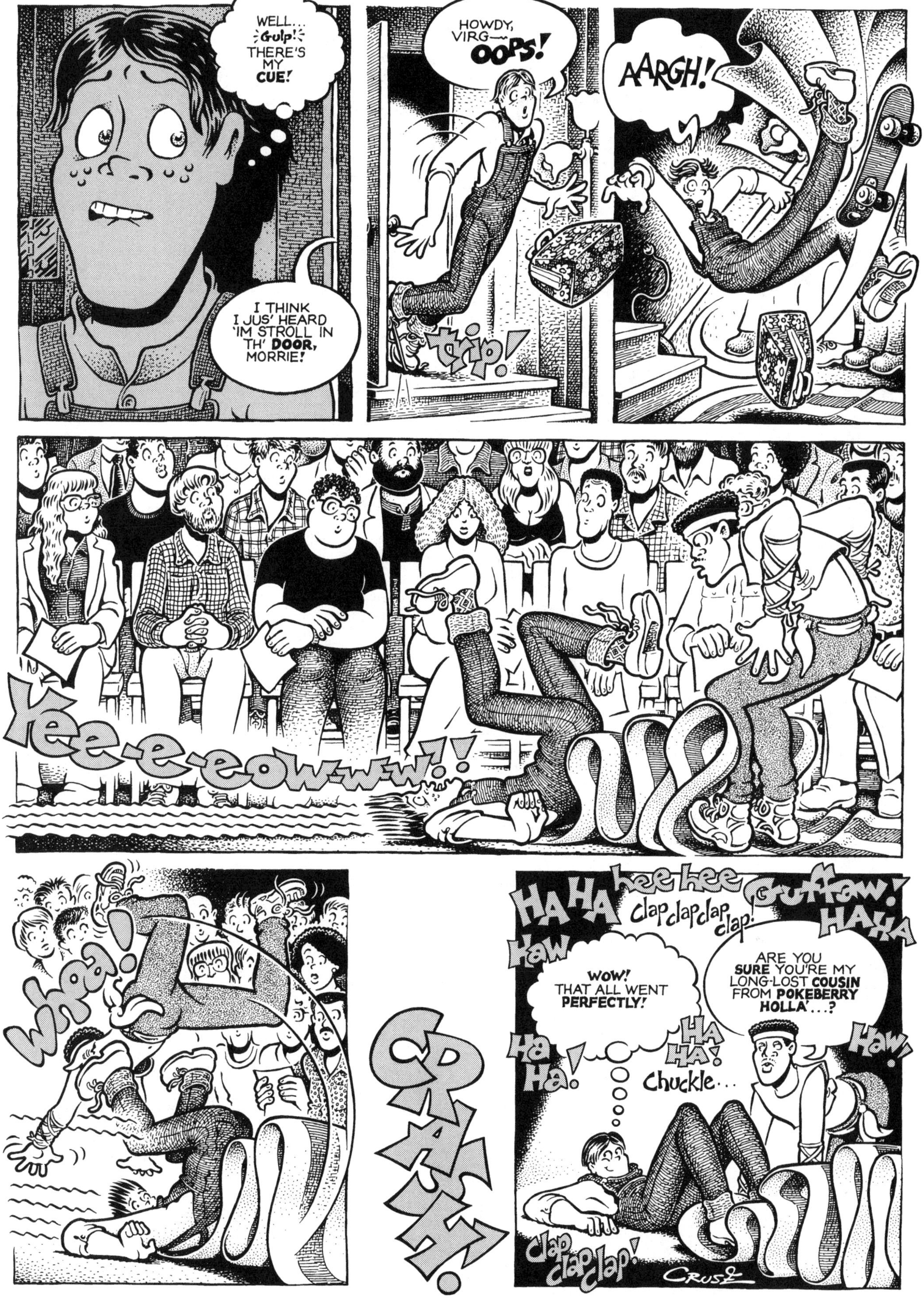
WELL... Gulp! THERE'S MY CUE!
I THINK I JUS' HEARD 'IM STROLL IN TH' DOOR, MORRIE!
HOWDY, VIRG— OOPS!
trip!
AARGH!
Yee-e-eow-ww!!
whoa!
CRASH!
HA HA hee hee Guffaw! HAHA
Clap clap clap clap!
Haw
WOW! THAT ALL WENT PERFECTLY!
ARE YOU SURE YOU'RE MY LONG-LOST COUSIN FROM POKEBERRY HOLLA'...?
Ha Ha!
HA HA!
Chuckle...
Haw!
clap clap clap!
CRUSE

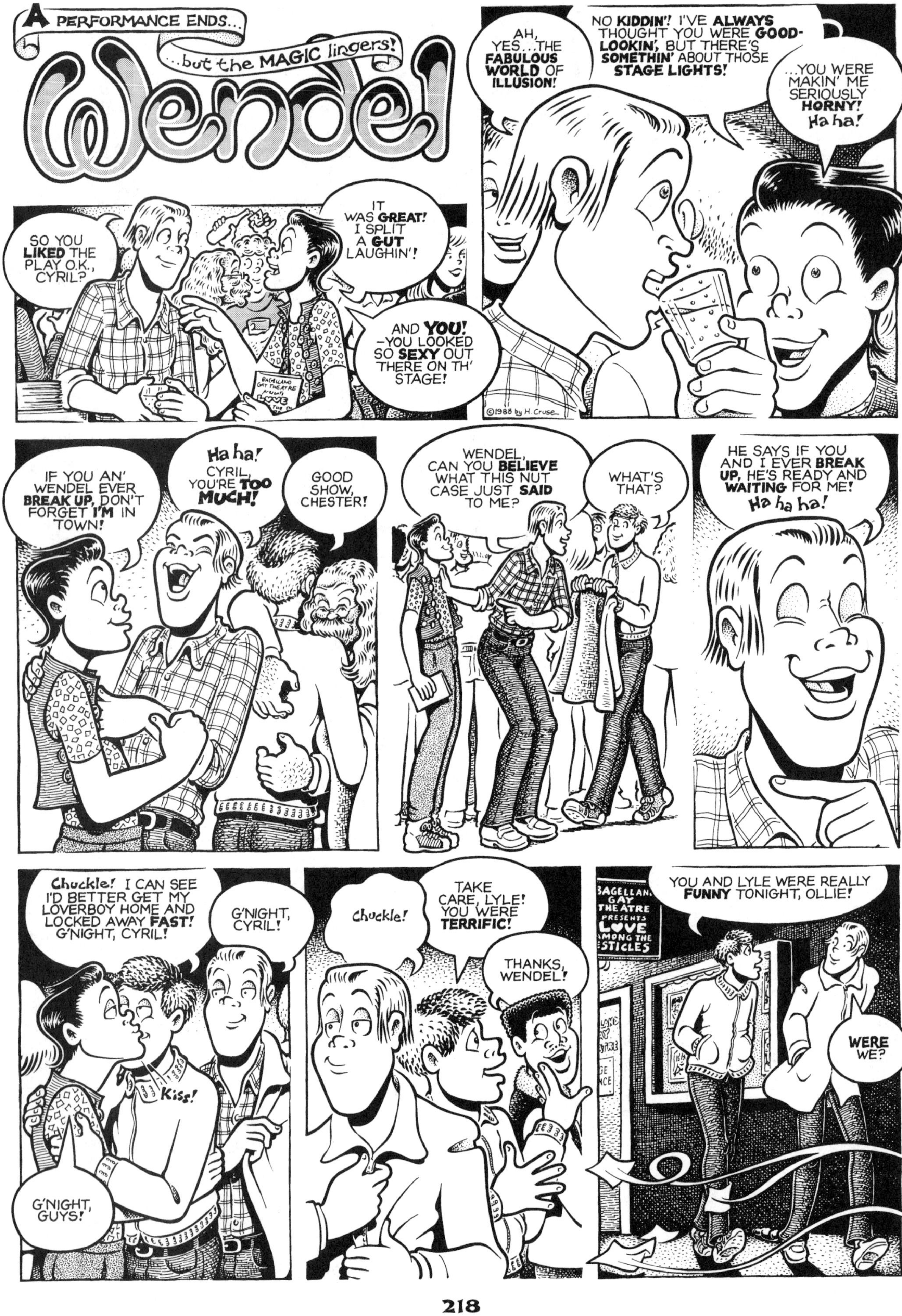
A PERFORMANCE ENDS...
...but the MAGIC lingers!
Wendel
SO YOU LIKED THE PLAY O.K., CYRIL?
IT WAS GREAT! I SPLIT A GUT LAUGHIN'!
AND YOU! –YOU LOOKED SO SEXY OUT THERE ON TH' STAGE!
AH, YES...THE FABULOUS WORLD OF ILLUSION!
NO KIDDIN'! I'VE ALWAYS THOUGHT YOU WERE GOOD-LOOKIN', BUT THERE'S SOMETHIN' ABOUT THOSE STAGE LIGHTS!
...YOU WERE MAKIN' ME SERIOUSLY HORNY! Ha ha!
©1988 by H. Cruse
IF YOU AN' WENDEL EVER BREAK UP, DON'T FORGET I'M IN TOWN!
Ha ha! CYRIL, YOU'RE TOO MUCH!
GOOD SHOW, CHESTER!
WENDEL, CAN YOU BELIEVE WHAT THIS NUT CASE JUST SAID TO ME?
WHAT'S THAT?
HE SAYS IF YOU AND I EVER BREAK UP, HE'S READY AND WAITING FOR ME! Ha ha ha!
Chuckle! I CAN SEE I'D BETTER GET MY LOVERBOY HOME AND LOCKED AWAY FAST! G'NIGHT, CYRIL!
G'NIGHT, CYRIL!
Kiss!
G'NIGHT, GUYS!
Chuckle!
TAKE CARE, LYLE! YOU WERE TERRIFIC!
THANKS, WENDEL!
YOU AND LYLE WERE REALLY FUNNY TONIGHT, OLLIE!
WERE WE?

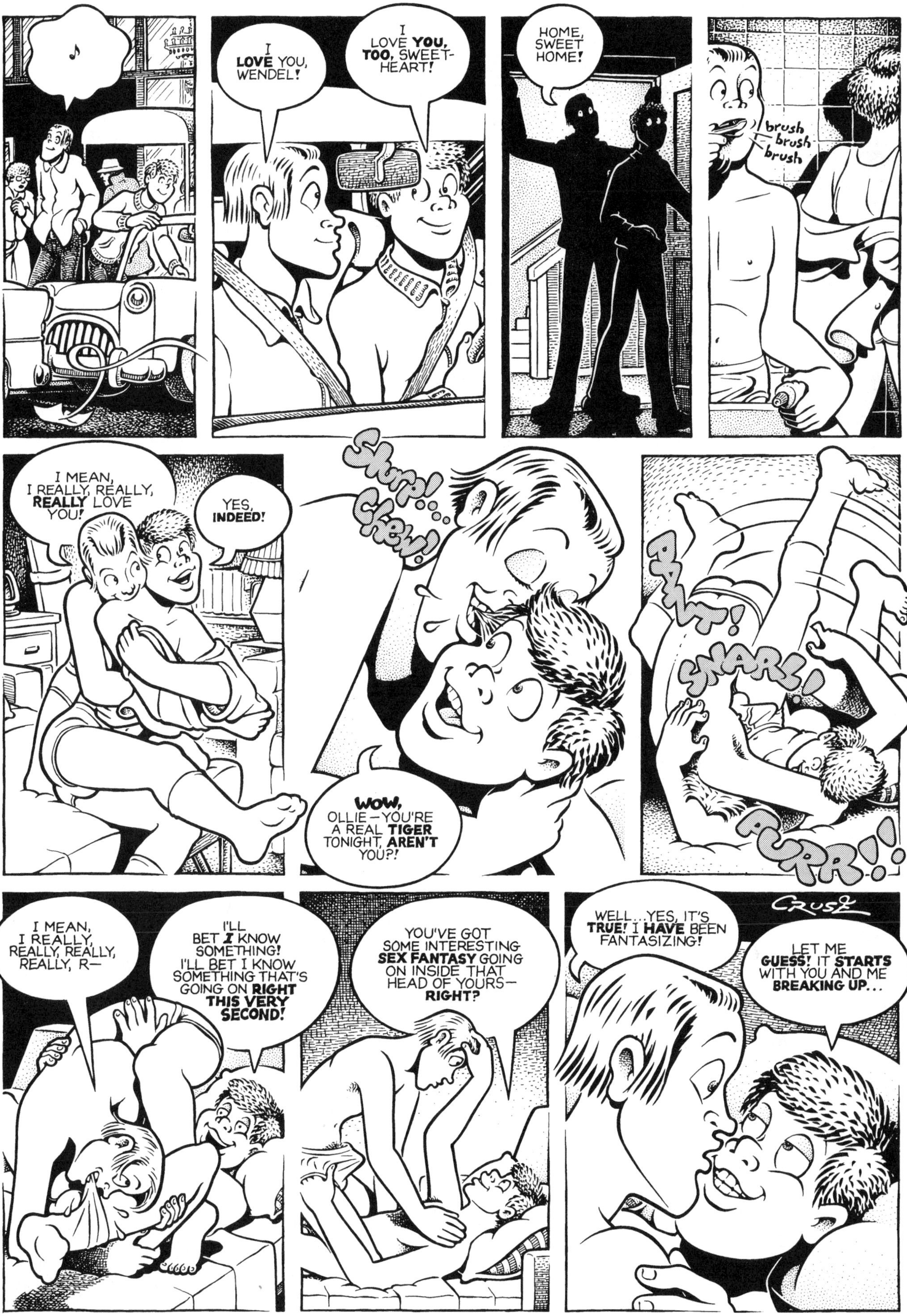
♪
I LOVE YOU, WENDEL!
I LOVE YOU, TOO, SWEET-HEART!
HOME, SWEET HOME!
brush brush brush
I MEAN, I REALLY, REALLY, REALLY LOVE YOU!
YES, INDEED!
SLURP!... CHEW!
WOW, OLLIE—YOU'RE A REAL TIGER TONIGHT, AREN'T YOU?!
PANT!
SNARL!
PURR!!
I MEAN, I REALLY, REALLY, REALLY, REALLY, R—
I'LL BET I KNOW SOMETHING! I'LL BET I KNOW SOMETHING THAT'S GOING ON RIGHT THIS VERY SECOND!
YOU'VE GOT SOME INTERESTING SEX FANTASY GOING ON INSIDE THAT HEAD OF YOURS—RIGHT?
WELL...YES, IT'S TRUE! I HAVE BEEN FANTASIZING!
LET ME GUESS! IT STARTS WITH YOU AND ME BREAKING UP...
CRUSE

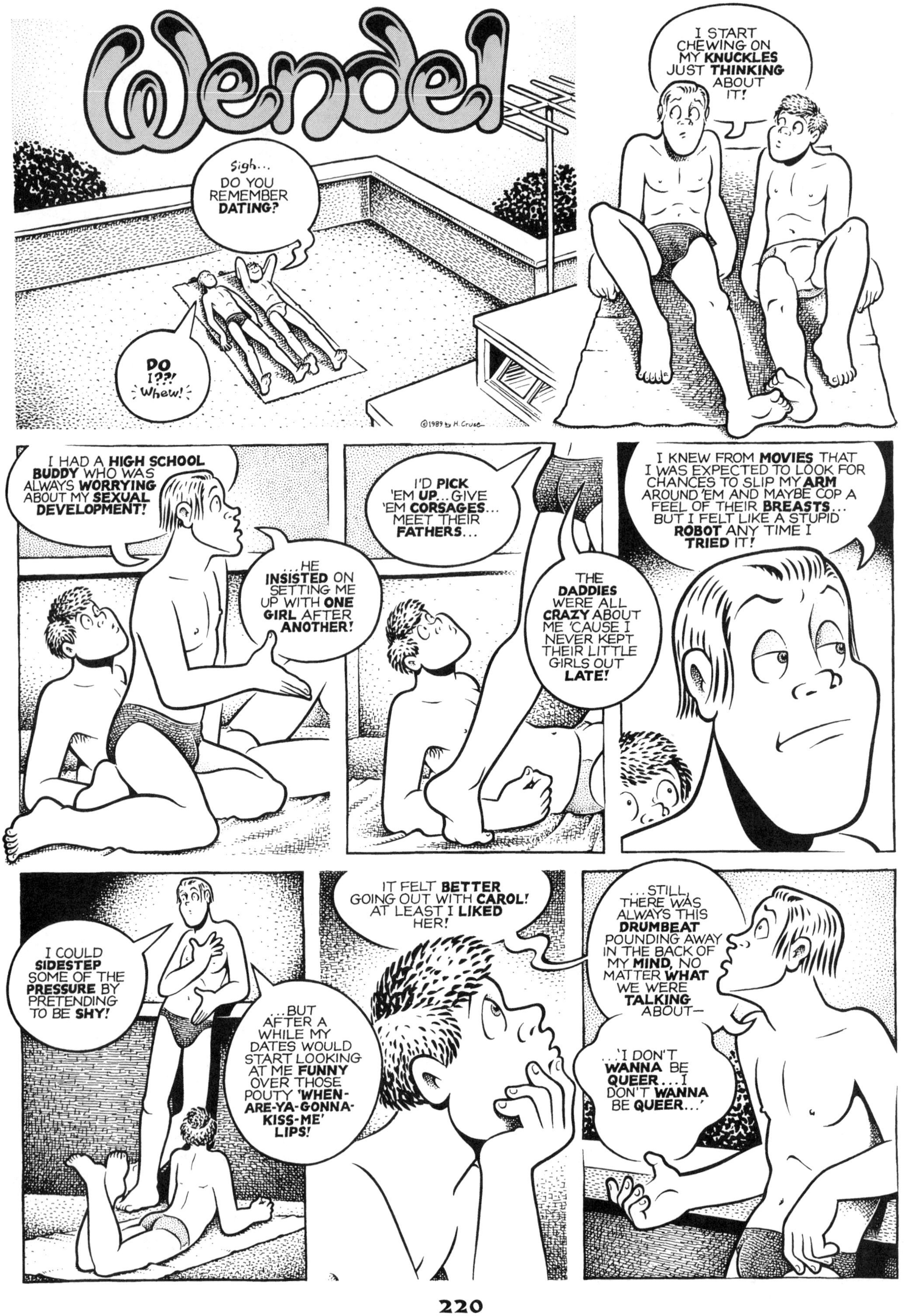

Wendel
Sigh... DO YOU REMEMBER DATING?
DO I??! Whew!
©1989 by H. Cruse
I START CHEWING ON MY KNUCKLES JUST THINKING ABOUT IT!
I HAD A HIGH SCHOOL BUDDY WHO WAS ALWAYS WORRYING ABOUT MY SEXUAL DEVELOPMENT!
...HE INSISTED ON SETTING ME UP WITH ONE GIRL AFTER ANOTHER!
I'D PICK 'EM UP...GIVE 'EM CORSAGES... MEET THEIR FATHERS...
THE DADDIES WERE ALL CRAZY ABOUT ME 'CAUSE I NEVER KEPT THEIR LITTLE GIRLS OUT LATE!
I KNEW FROM MOVIES THAT I WAS EXPECTED TO LOOK FOR CHANCES TO SLIP MY ARM AROUND 'EM AND MAYBE COP A FEEL OF THEIR BREASTS... BUT I FELT LIKE A STUPID ROBOT ANY TIME I TRIED IT!
I COULD SIDESTEP SOME OF THE PRESSURE BY PRETENDING TO BE SHY!
...BUT AFTER A WHILE MY DATES WOULD START LOOKING AT ME FUNNY OVER THOSE POUTY 'WHEN-ARE-YA-GONNA-KISS-ME' LIPS!
IT FELT BETTER GOING OUT WITH CAROL! AT LEAST I LIKED HER!
...STILL, THERE WAS ALWAYS THIS DRUMBEAT POUNDING AWAY IN THE BACK OF MY MIND, NO MATTER WHAT WE WERE TALKING ABOUT—
...'I DON'T WANNA BE QUEER... I DON'T WANNA BE QUEER...'

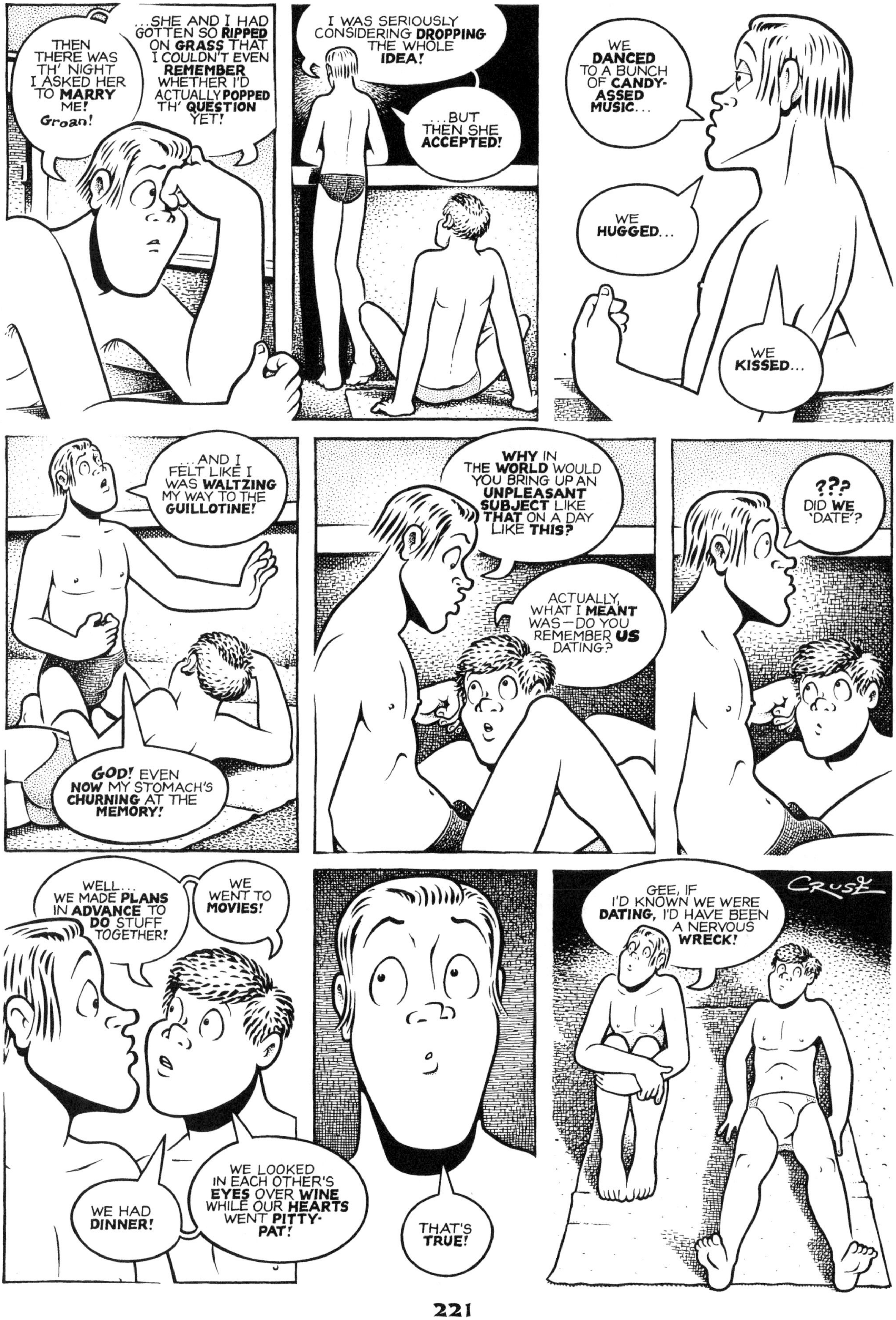
THEN THERE WAS TH' NIGHT I ASKED HER TO MARRY ME! Groan!
...SHE AND I HAD GOTTEN SO RIPPED ON GRASS THAT I COULDN'T EVEN REMEMBER WHETHER I'D ACTUALLY POPPED TH' QUESTION YET!
I WAS SERIOUSLY CONSIDERING DROPPING THE WHOLE IDEA!
...BUT THEN SHE ACCEPTED!
WE DANCED TO A BUNCH OF CANDY-ASSED MUSIC...
WE HUGGED...
WE KISSED...
...AND I FELT LIKE I WAS WALTZING MY WAY TO THE GUILLOTINE!
GOD! EVEN NOW MY STOMACH'S CHURNING AT THE MEMORY!
WHY IN THE WORLD WOULD YOU BRING UP AN UNPLEASANT SUBJECT LIKE THAT ON A DAY LIKE THIS?
ACTUALLY, WHAT I MEANT WAS—DO YOU REMEMBER US DATING?
??? DID WE 'DATE'?
WELL... WE MADE PLANS IN ADVANCE TO DO STUFF TOGETHER!
WE WENT TO MOVIES!
WE HAD DINNER!
WE LOOKED IN EACH OTHER'S EYES OVER WINE WHILE OUR HEARTS WENT PITTY-PAT!
THAT'S TRUE!
CRUSE
GEE, IF I'D KNOWN WE WERE DATING, I'D HAVE BEEN A NERVOUS WRECK!

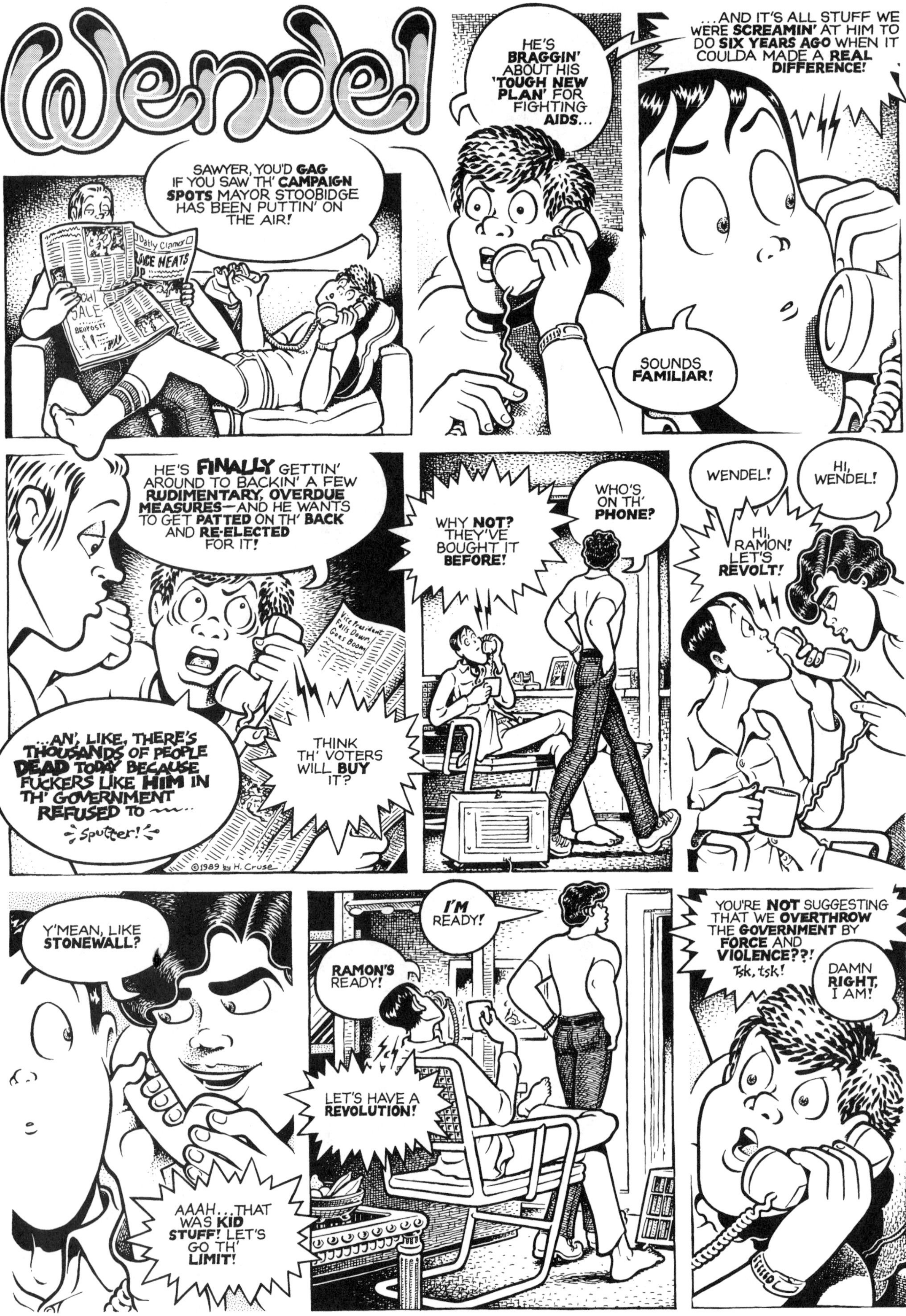
Wendel
SAWYER, YOU'D GAG IF YOU SAW TH' CAMPAIGN SPOTS MAYOR STOOBIDGE HAS BEEN PUTTIN' ON THE AIR!
Daily Clamor
RACE HEATS UP
HE'S BRAGGIN' ABOUT HIS 'TOUGH NEW PLAN' FOR FIGHTING AIDS...
...AND IT'S ALL STUFF WE WERE SCREAMIN' AT HIM TO DO SIX YEARS AGO WHEN IT COULDA MADE A REAL DIFFERENCE!
SOUNDS FAMILIAR!
HE'S FINALLY GETTIN' AROUND TO BACKIN' A FEW RUDIMENTARY, OVERDUE MEASURES—AND HE WANTS TO GET PATTED ON TH' BACK AND RE-ELECTED FOR IT!
Vice President Falls Down, Goes Boom
...AN', LIKE, THERE'S THOUSANDS OF PEOPLE DEAD TODAY BECAUSE FUCKERS LIKE HIM IN TH' GOVERNMENT REFUSED TO ~~...
Sputter!
THINK TH' VOTERS WILL BUY IT?
©1989 by H. Cruse
WHY NOT? THEY'VE BOUGHT IT BEFORE!
WHO'S ON TH' PHONE?
WENDEL!
HI, WENDEL!
HI, RAMON! LET'S REVOLT!
Y'MEAN, LIKE STONEWALL?
AAAH...THAT WAS KID STUFF! LET'S GO TH' LIMIT!
I'M READY!
RAMON'S READY!
LET'S HAVE A REVOLUTION!
YOU'RE NOT SUGGESTING THAT WE OVERTHROW THE GOVERNMENT BY FORCE AND VIOLENCE??!
Tsk, tsk!
DAMN RIGHT, I AM!

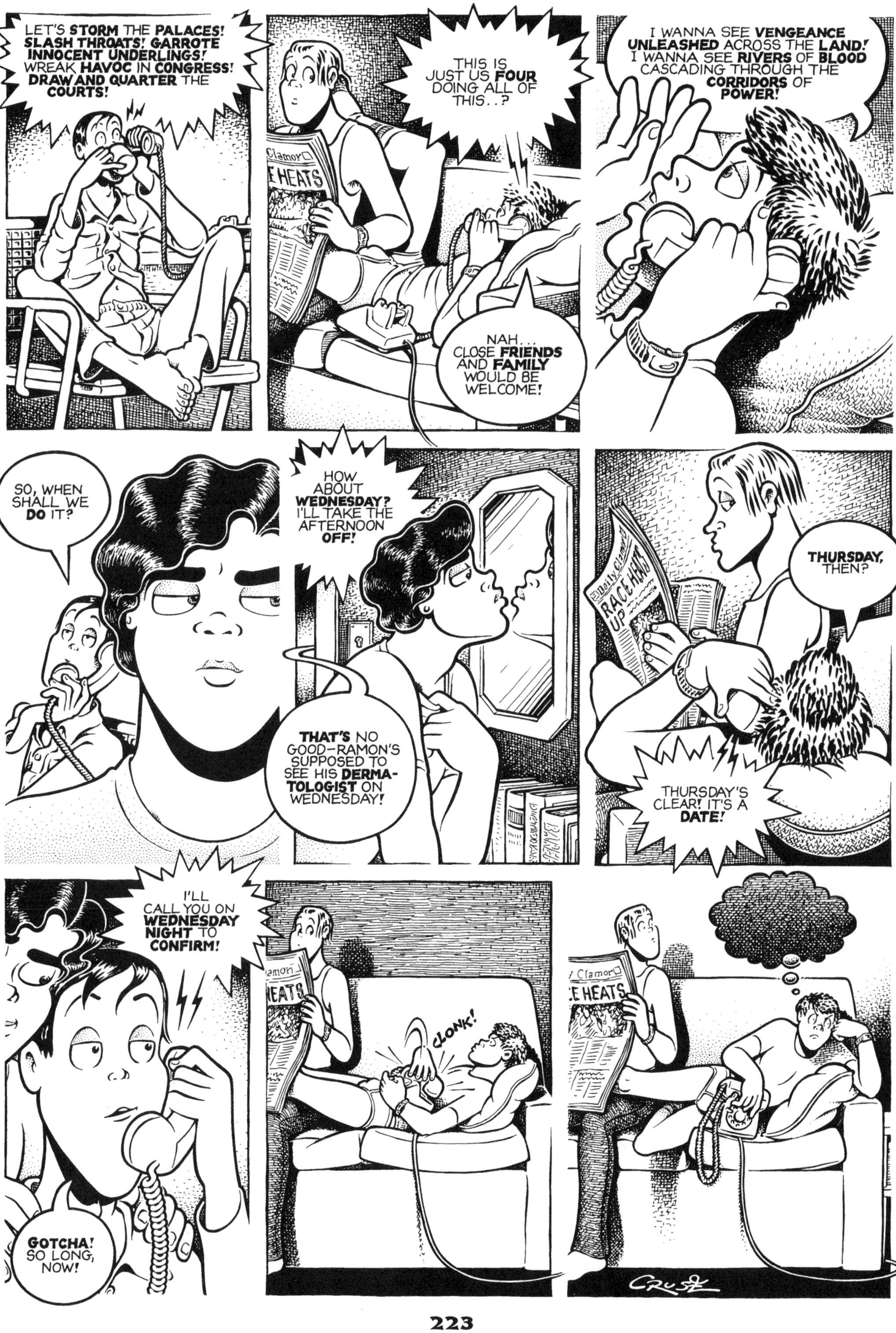
LET'S STORM THE PALACES! SLASH THROATS! GARROTE INNOCENT UNDERLINGS! WREAK HAVOC IN CONGRESS! DRAW AND QUARTER THE COURTS!
THIS IS JUST US FOUR DOING ALL OF THIS..?
Clamor
E HEATS
NAH... CLOSE FRIENDS AND FAMILY WOULD BE WELCOME!
I WANNA SEE VENGEANCE UNLEASHED ACROSS THE LAND! I WANNA SEE RIVERS OF BLOOD CASCADING THROUGH THE CORRIDORS OF POWER!
SO, WHEN SHALL WE DO IT?
HOW ABOUT WEDNESDAY? I'LL TAKE THE AFTERNOON OFF!
THAT'S NO GOOD–RAMON'S SUPPOSED TO SEE HIS DERMATOLOGIST ON WEDNESDAY!
RACE HEATS UP
THURSDAY, THEN?
THURSDAY'S CLEAR! IT'S A DATE!
I'LL CALL YOU ON WEDNESDAY NIGHT TO CONFIRM!
GOTCHA! SO LONG, NOW!
CLONK!
E HEATS
CRUSE

A Splash Page Break!

The sequence that follows represents an experimental departure for me. Instead of weaving my strip's narrative fabric out of several plot threads simultaneously as I

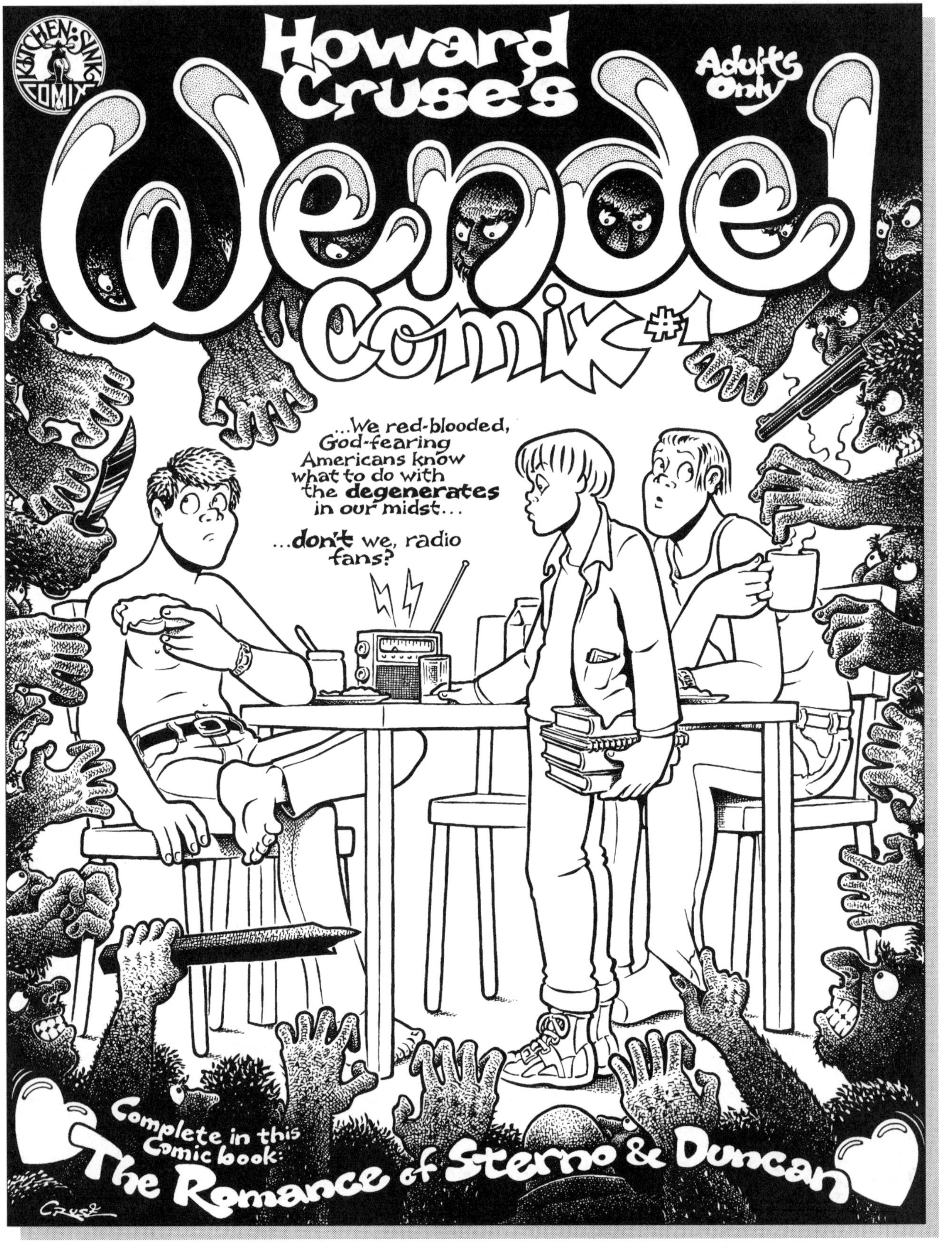

Kitchen Sink Comix
Howard Cruse's
Adults Only
Wendel Comix #1
...We red-blooded, God-fearing Americans know what to do with the **degenerates** in our midst...
...**don't** we, radio fans?
Complete in this comic book:
The Romance of Sterno & Duncan
Cruse

had done before, I devoted twelve episodes without interruption to the single story of Sterno's troublesome infatuation with the gym god Duncan.

The tale served as the centerpiece for ***Wendel Comix***, a one-shot comic book that Kitchen Sink published in 1990, for which I drew the splash panel below.

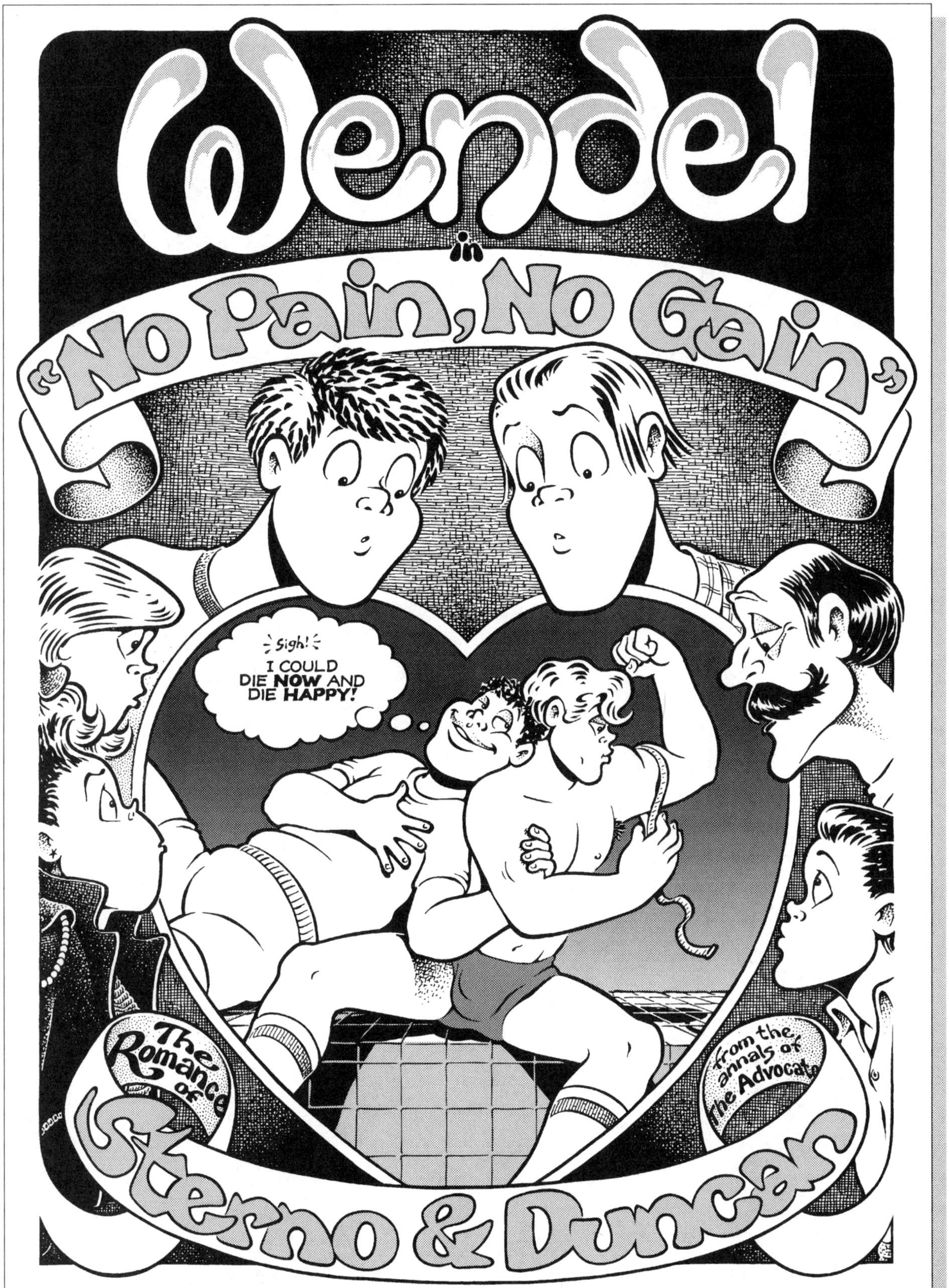
Wendel
in
"No Pain, No Gain"
Sigh!
I COULD DIE NOW AND DIE HAPPY!
The Romance of
from the annals of The Advocate
Sterno & Duncan

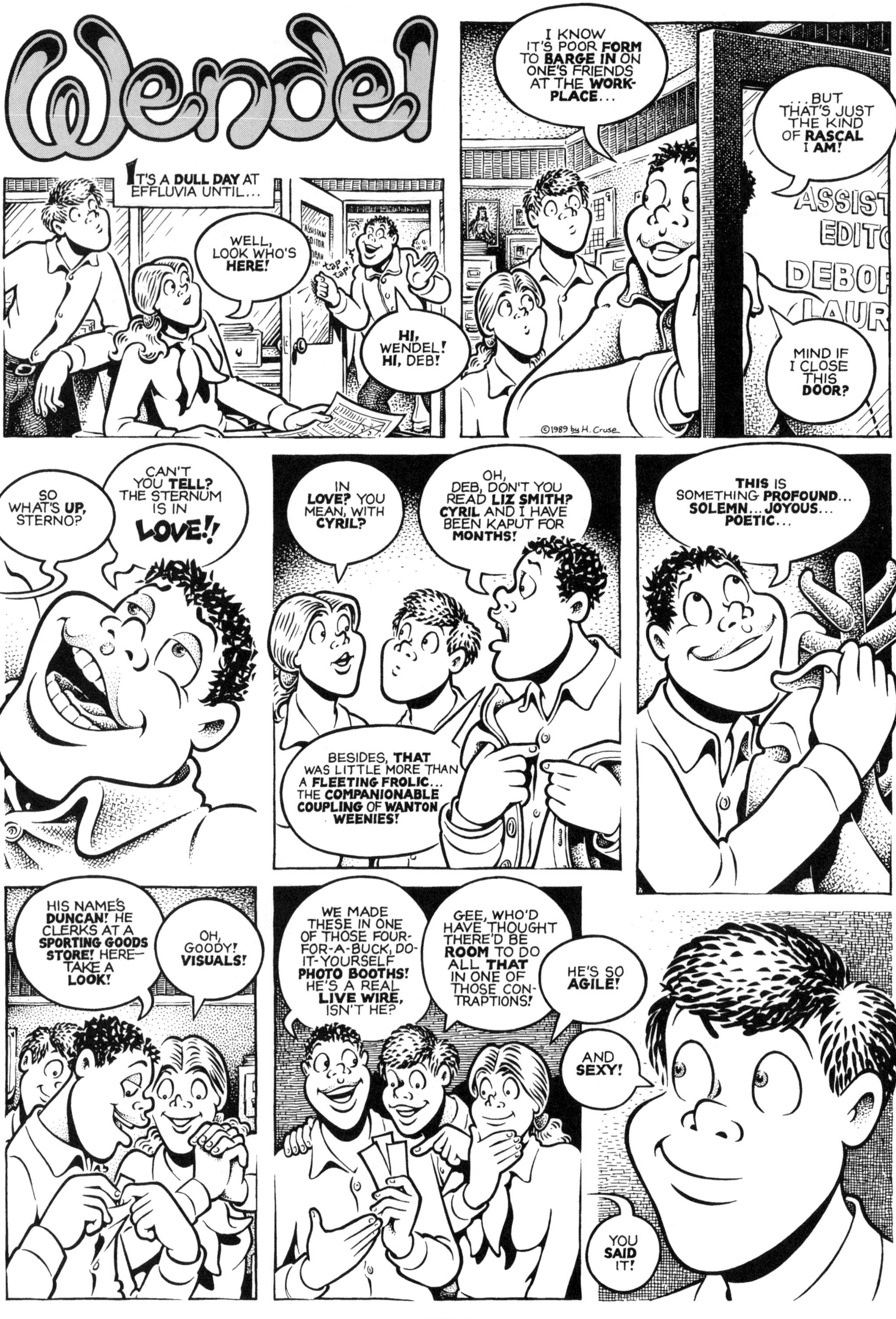
Wendel
IT'S A DULL DAY AT EFFLUVIA UNTIL...
WELL, LOOK WHO'S HERE!
tap tap!
HI, WENDEL! HI, DEB!
I KNOW IT'S POOR FORM TO BARGE IN ON ONE'S FRIENDS AT THE WORK-PLACE...
...BUT THAT'S JUST THE KIND OF RASCAL I AM!
ASSIST EDITO DEBOR LAUR
MIND IF I CLOSE THIS DOOR?
©1989 by H. Cruse
SO WHAT'S UP, STERNO?
CAN'T YOU TELL? THE STERNUM IS IN LOVE!!
IN LOVE? YOU MEAN, WITH CYRIL?
OH, DEB, DON'T YOU READ LIZ SMITH? CYRIL AND I HAVE BEEN KAPUT FOR MONTHS!
BESIDES, THAT WAS LITTLE MORE THAN A FLEETING FROLIC... THE COMPANIONABLE COUPLING OF WANTON WEENIES!
THIS IS SOMETHING PROFOUND... SOLEMN... JOYOUS... POETIC...
HIS NAME'S DUNCAN! HE CLERKS AT A SPORTING GOODS STORE! HERE-TAKE A LOOK!
OH, GOODY! VISUALS!
WE MADE THESE IN ONE OF THOSE FOUR-FOR-A-BUCK, DO-IT-YOURSELF PHOTO BOOTHS! HE'S A REAL LIVE WIRE, ISN'T HE?
GEE, WHO'D HAVE THOUGHT THERE'D BE ROOM TO DO ALL THAT IN ONE OF THOSE CON-TRAPTIONS!
HE'S SO AGILE!
AND SEXY!
YOU SAID IT!

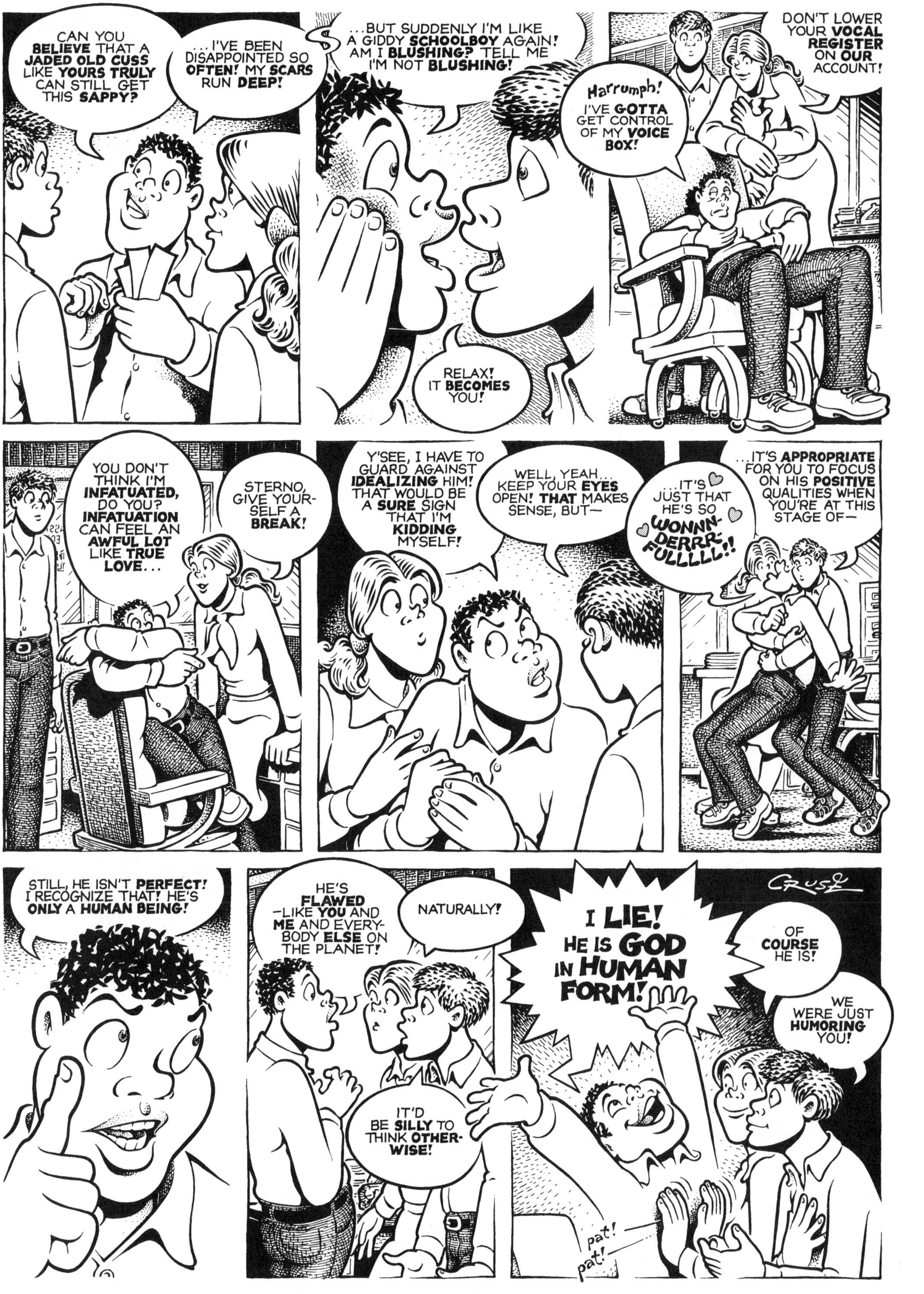
CAN YOU BELIEVE THAT A JADED OLD CUSS LIKE YOURS TRULY CAN STILL GET THIS SAPPY?
...I'VE BEEN DISAPPOINTED SO OFTEN! MY SCARS RUN DEEP!
...BUT SUDDENLY I'M LIKE A GIDDY SCHOOLBOY AGAIN! AM I BLUSHING? TELL ME I'M NOT BLUSHING!
RELAX! IT BECOMES YOU!
Harrumph! I'VE GOTTA GET CONTROL OF MY VOICE BOX!
DON'T LOWER YOUR VOCAL REGISTER ON OUR ACCOUNT!
YOU DON'T THINK I'M INFATUATED, DO YOU? INFATUATION CAN FEEL AN AWFUL LOT LIKE TRUE LOVE...
STERNO, GIVE YOURSELF A BREAK!
Y'SEE, I HAVE TO GUARD AGAINST IDEALIZING HIM! THAT WOULD BE A SURE SIGN THAT I'M KIDDING MYSELF!
WELL, YEAH... KEEP YOUR EYES OPEN! THAT MAKES SENSE, BUT—
...IT'S JUST THAT HE'S SO WONNN-DERRR-FULLLLL!!
...IT'S APPROPRIATE FOR YOU TO FOCUS ON HIS POSITIVE QUALITIES WHEN YOU'RE AT THIS STAGE OF—
STILL, HE ISN'T PERFECT! I RECOGNIZE THAT! HE'S ONLY A HUMAN BEING!
HE'S FLAWED —LIKE YOU AND ME AND EVERYBODY ELSE ON THE PLANET!
NATURALLY!
IT'D BE SILLY TO THINK OTHERWISE!
CRUSE
I LIE! HE IS GOD IN HUMAN FORM!
OF COURSE HE IS!
WE WERE JUST HUMORING YOU!
pat!
pat!

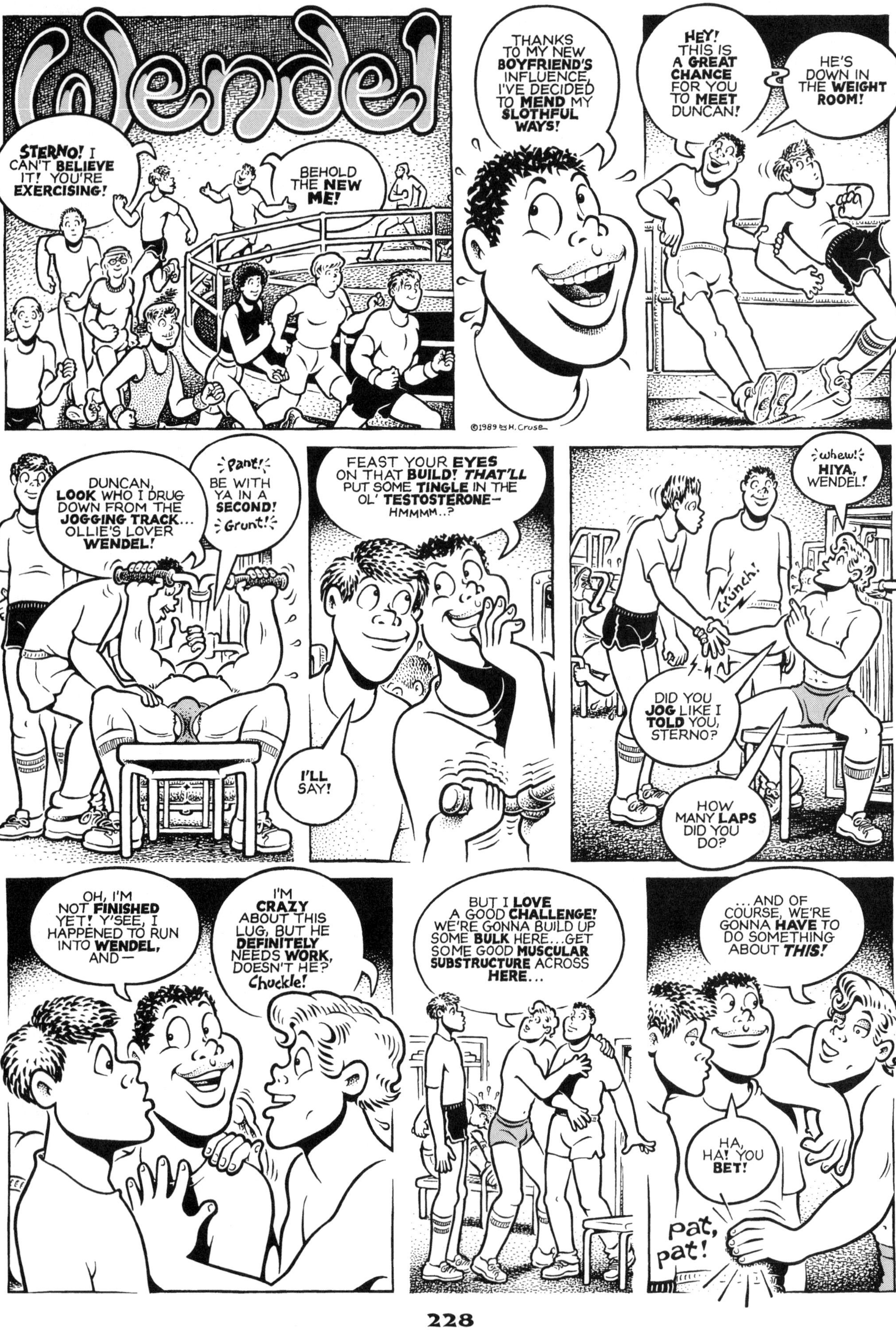
Wendel
STERNO! I CAN'T BELIEVE IT! YOU'RE EXERCISING!
BEHOLD THE NEW ME!
©1989 by H. Cruse
THANKS TO MY NEW BOYFRIEND'S INFLUENCE, I'VE DECIDED TO MEND MY SLOTHFUL WAYS!
HEY! THIS IS A GREAT CHANCE FOR YOU TO MEET DUNCAN!
HE'S DOWN IN THE WEIGHT ROOM!
DUNCAN, LOOK WHO I DRUG DOWN FROM THE JOGGING TRACK... OLLIE'S LOVER WENDEL!
Pant! BE WITH YA IN A SECOND! Grunt!
FEAST YOUR EYES ON THAT BUILD! THAT'LL PUT SOME TINGLE IN THE OL' TESTOSTERONE— HMMMM..?
I'LL SAY!
whew! HIYA, WENDEL!
Crunch!
DID YOU JOG LIKE I TOLD YOU, STERNO?
HOW MANY LAPS DID YOU DO?
OH, I'M NOT FINISHED YET! Y'SEE, I HAPPENED TO RUN INTO WENDEL, AND—
I'M CRAZY ABOUT THIS LUG, BUT HE DEFINITELY NEEDS WORK, DOESN'T HE? Chuckle!
BUT I LOVE A GOOD CHALLENGE! WE'RE GONNA BUILD UP SOME BULK HERE... GET SOME GOOD MUSCULAR SUBSTRUCTURE ACROSS HERE...
...AND OF COURSE, WE'RE GONNA HAVE TO DO SOMETHING ABOUT THIS!
HA, HA! YOU BET!
pat, pat!

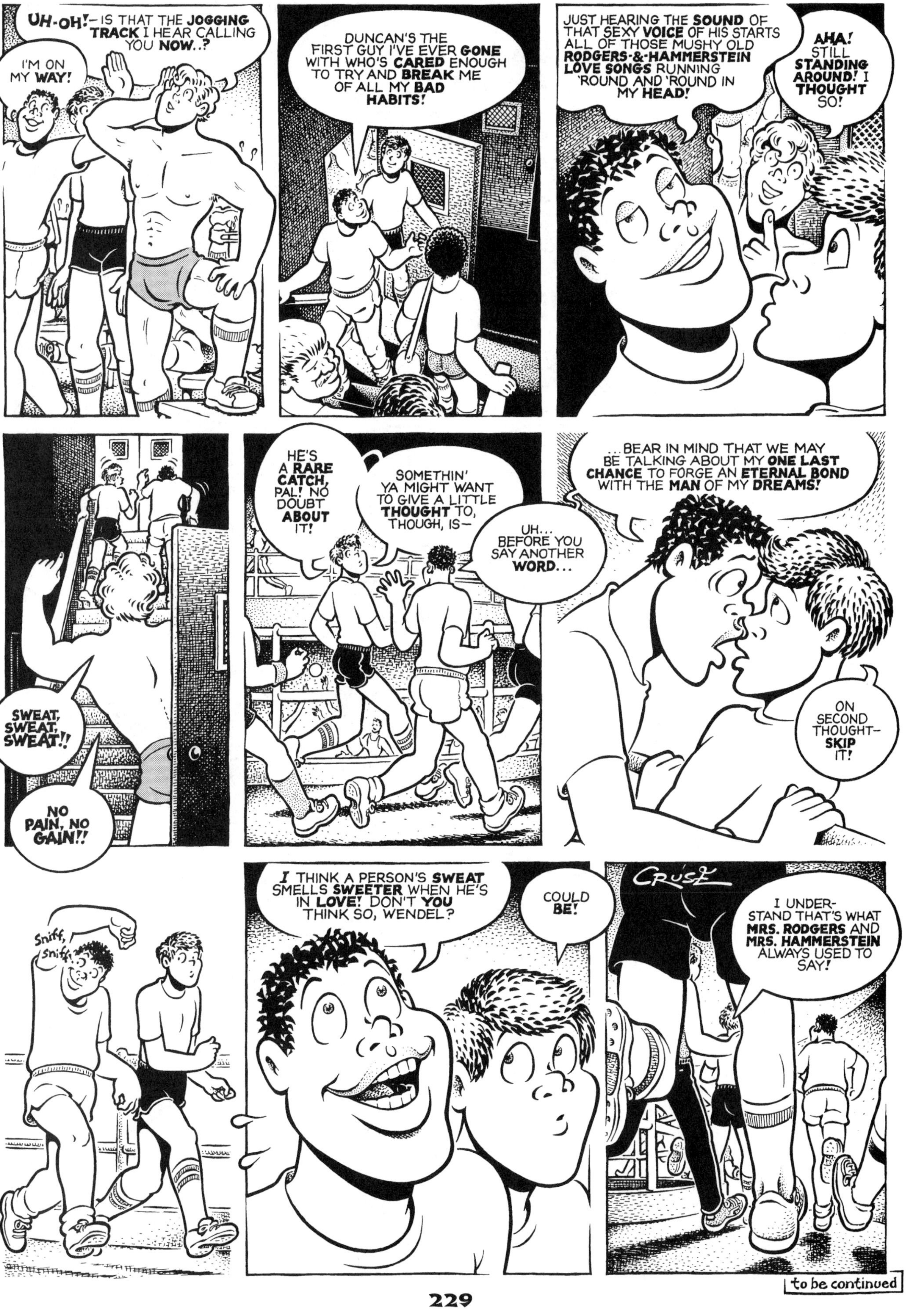
UH-OH!— IS THAT THE JOGGING TRACK I HEAR CALLING YOU NOW..?
I'M ON MY WAY!
DUNCAN'S THE FIRST GUY I'VE EVER GONE WITH WHO'S CARED ENOUGH TO TRY AND BREAK ME OF ALL MY BAD HABITS!
JUST HEARING THE SOUND OF THAT SEXY VOICE OF HIS STARTS ALL OF THOSE MUSHY OLD RODGERS-&-HAMMERSTEIN LOVE SONGS RUNNING 'ROUND AND 'ROUND IN MY HEAD!
AHA! STILL STANDING AROUND! I THOUGHT SO!
SWEAT, SWEAT, SWEAT!!
NO PAIN, NO GAIN!!
HE'S A RARE CATCH, PAL! NO DOUBT ABOUT IT!
SOMETHIN' YA MIGHT WANT TO GIVE A LITTLE THOUGHT TO, THOUGH, IS—
UH... BEFORE YOU SAY ANOTHER WORD...
...BEAR IN MIND THAT WE MAY BE TALKING ABOUT MY ONE LAST CHANCE TO FORGE AN ETERNAL BOND WITH THE MAN OF MY DREAMS!
ON SECOND THOUGHT— SKIP IT!
Sniff, Sniff!
I THINK A PERSON'S SWEAT SMELLS SWEETER WHEN HE'S IN LOVE! DON'T YOU THINK SO, WENDEL?
COULD BE!
CRUSE
I UNDER-STAND THAT'S WHAT MRS. RODGERS AND MRS. HAMMERSTEIN ALWAYS USED TO SAY!
to be continued

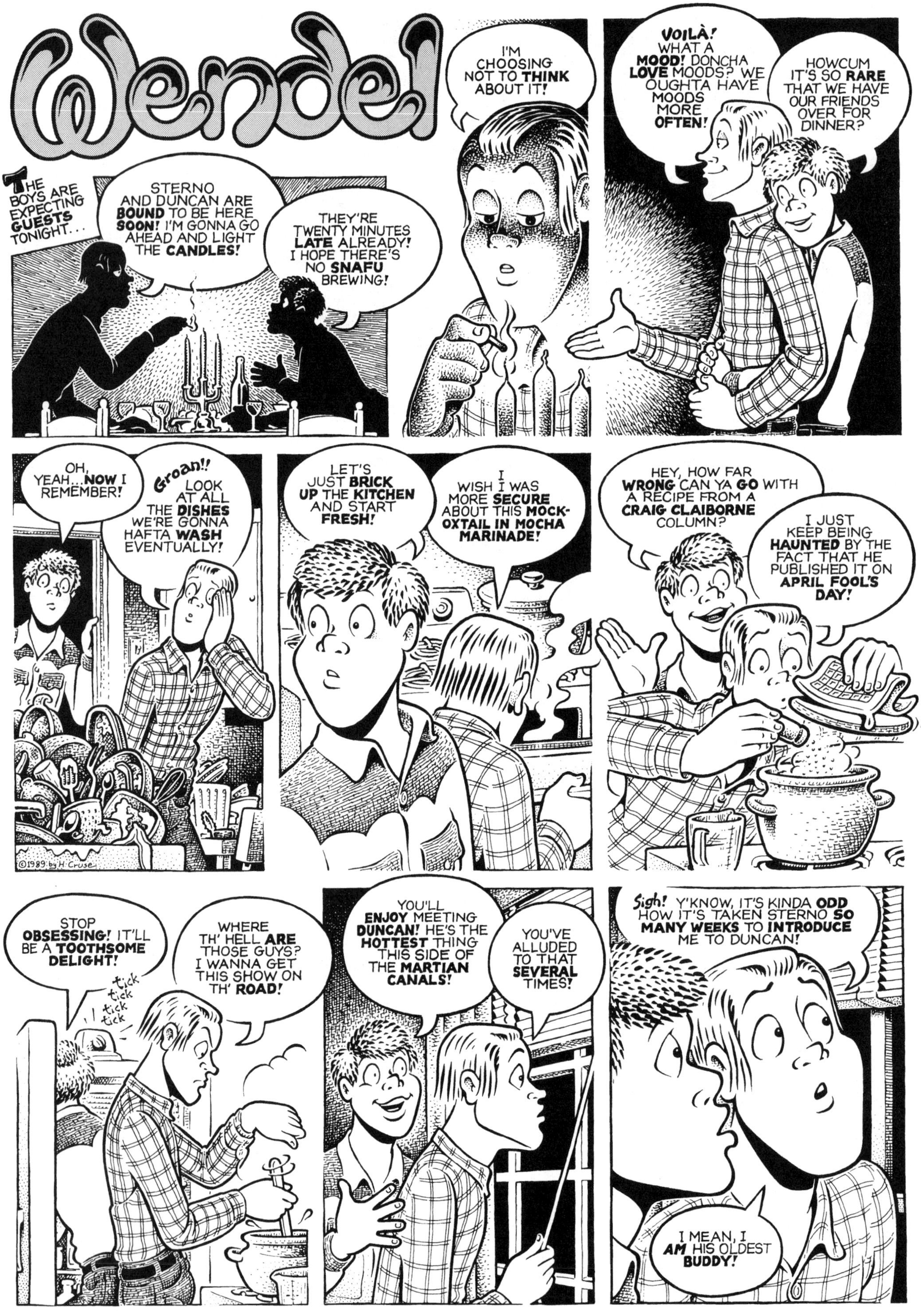
Wendel
THE BOYS ARE EXPECTING GUESTS TONIGHT...
STERNO AND DUNCAN ARE BOUND TO BE HERE SOON! I'M GONNA GO AHEAD AND LIGHT THE CANDLES!
THEY'RE TWENTY MINUTES LATE ALREADY! I HOPE THERE'S NO SNAFU BREWING!
I'M CHOOSING NOT TO THINK ABOUT IT!
VOILÀ! WHAT A MOOD! DONCHA LOVE MOODS? WE OUGHTA HAVE MOODS MORE OFTEN!
HOWCUM IT'S SO RARE THAT WE HAVE OUR FRIENDS OVER FOR DINNER?
OH, YEAH...NOW I REMEMBER!
Groan!! LOOK AT ALL THE DISHES WE'RE GONNA HAFTA WASH EVENTUALLY!
©1989 by H. Cruse
LET'S JUST BRICK UP THE KITCHEN AND START FRESH!
I WISH I WAS MORE SECURE ABOUT THIS MOCK-OXTAIL IN MOCHA MARINADE!
HEY, HOW FAR WRONG CAN YA GO WITH A RECIPE FROM A CRAIG CLAIBORNE COLUMN?
I JUST KEEP BEING HAUNTED BY THE FACT THAT HE PUBLISHED IT ON APRIL FOOL'S DAY!
STOP OBSESSING! IT'LL BE A TOOTHSOME DELIGHT!
tick tick tick
WHERE TH' HELL ARE THOSE GUYS? I WANNA GET THIS SHOW ON TH' ROAD!
YOU'LL ENJOY MEETING DUNCAN! HE'S THE HOTTEST THING THIS SIDE OF THE MARTIAN CANALS!
YOU'VE ALLUDED TO THAT SEVERAL TIMES!
Sigh! Y'KNOW, IT'S KINDA ODD HOW IT'S TAKEN STERNO SO MANY WEEKS TO INTRODUCE ME TO DUNCAN!
I MEAN, I AM HIS OLDEST BUDDY!

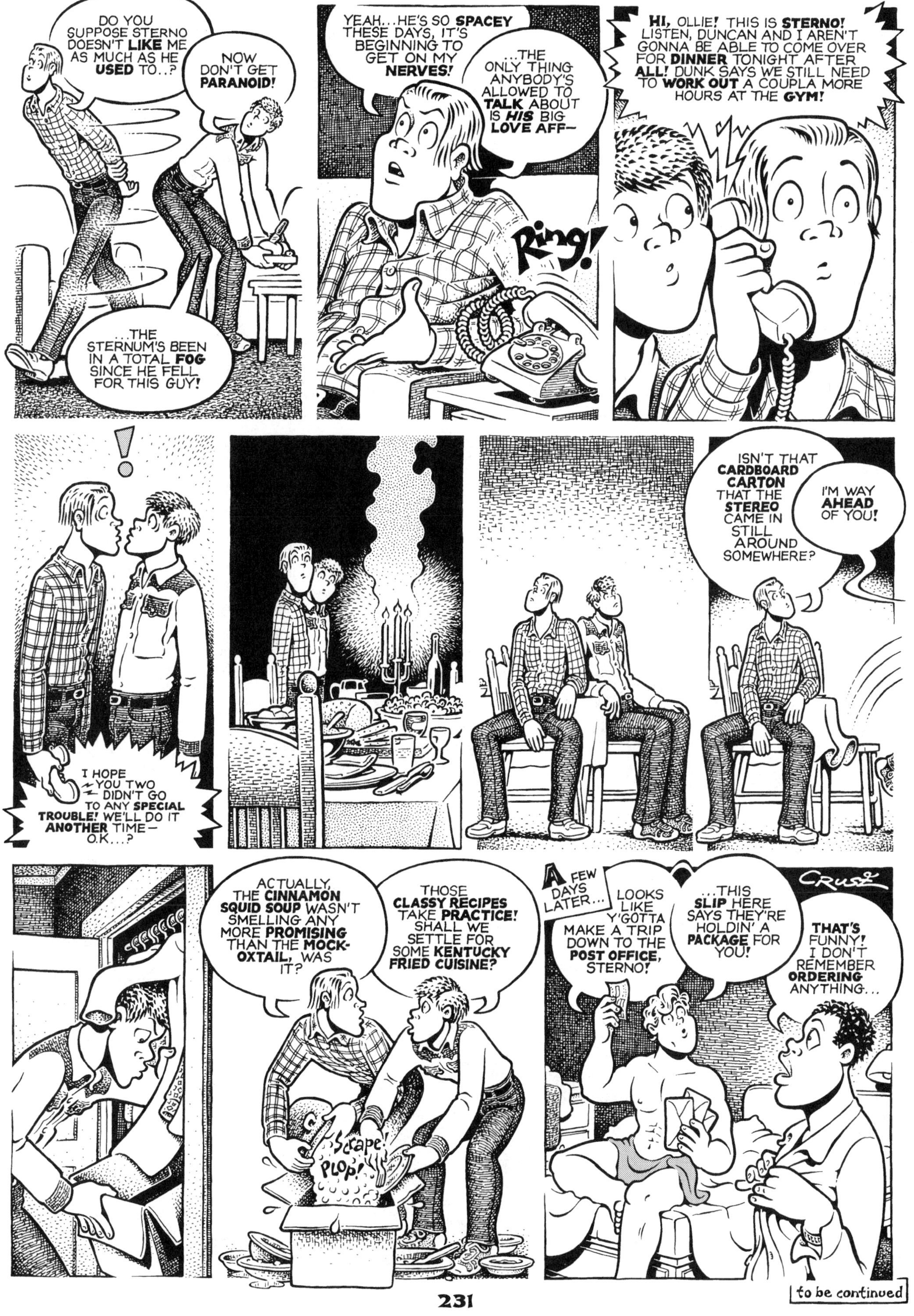

DO YOU SUPPOSE STERNO DOESN'T LIKE ME AS MUCH AS HE USED TO..?
NOW DON'T GET PARANOID!
...THE STERNUM'S BEEN IN A TOTAL FOG SINCE HE FELL FOR THIS GUY!
YEAH...HE'S SO SPACEY THESE DAYS, IT'S BEGINNING TO GET ON MY NERVES!
...THE ONLY THING ANYBODY'S ALLOWED TO TALK ABOUT IS HIS BIG LOVE AFF—
RING!
HI, OLLIE! THIS IS STERNO! LISTEN, DUNCAN AND I AREN'T GONNA BE ABLE TO COME OVER FOR DINNER TONIGHT AFTER ALL! DUNK SAYS WE STILL NEED TO WORK OUT A COUPLA MORE HOURS AT THE GYM!
!
I HOPE YOU TWO DIDN'T GO TO ANY SPECIAL TROUBLE! WE'LL DO IT ANOTHER TIME—O.K...?
ISN'T THAT CARDBOARD CARTON THAT THE STEREO CAME IN STILL AROUND SOMEWHERE?
I'M WAY AHEAD OF YOU!
ACTUALLY, THE CINNAMON SQUID SOUP WASN'T SMELLING ANY MORE PROMISING THAN THE MOCK-OXTAIL, WAS IT?
THOSE CLASSY RECIPES TAKE PRACTICE! SHALL WE SETTLE FOR SOME KENTUCKY FRIED CUISINE?
SCRAPE! PLOP!
A FEW DAYS LATER...
LOOKS LIKE Y'GOTTA MAKE A TRIP DOWN TO THE POST OFFICE, STERNO!
...THIS SLIP HERE SAYS THEY'RE HOLDIN' A PACKAGE FOR YOU!
THAT'S FUNNY! I DON'T REMEMBER ORDERING ANYTHING...
CRUSE
to be continued

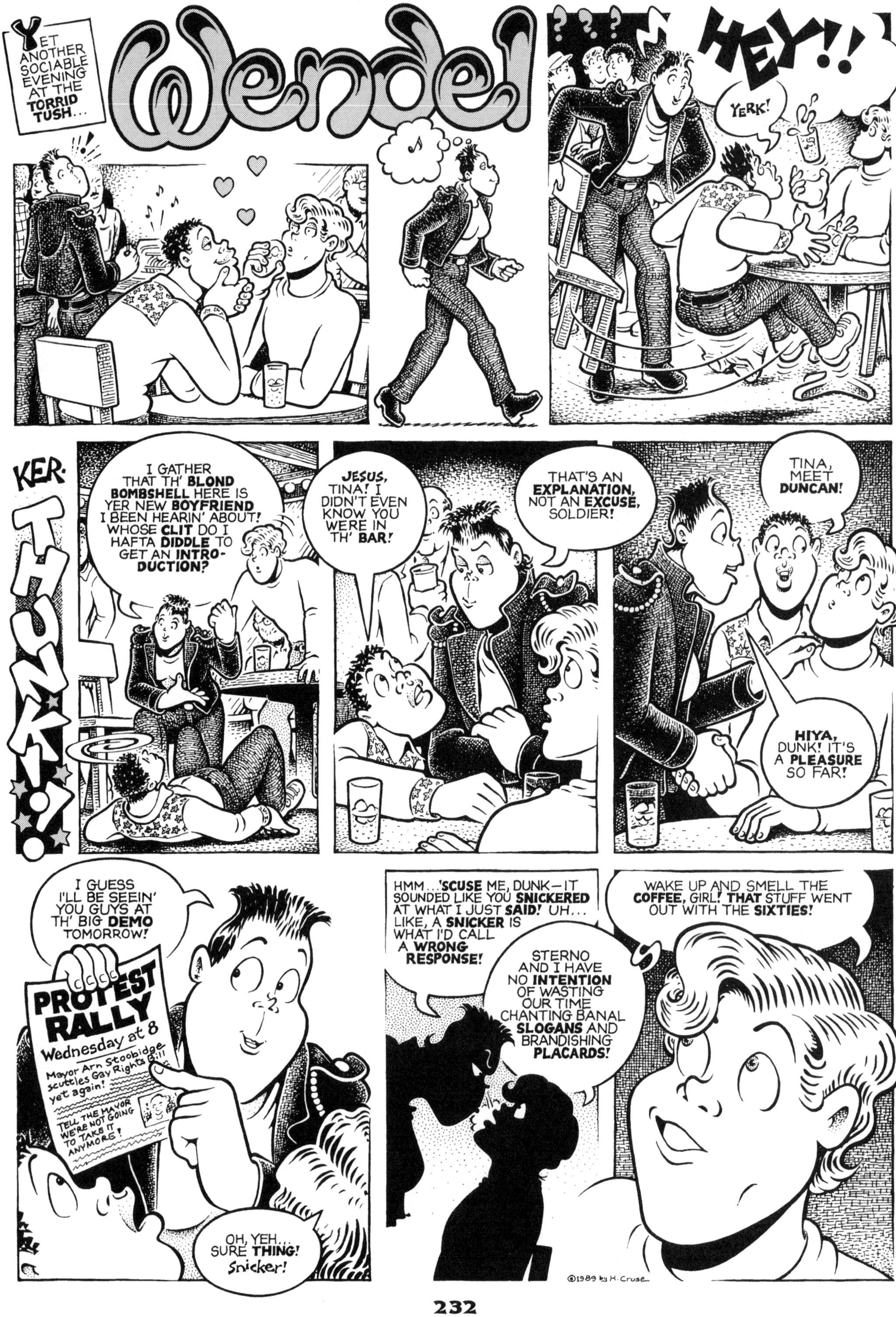
Yet another sociable evening at the Torrid Tush...
Wendel
!!!
HEY!!!
YERK!
KER-THUNK!!
I GATHER THAT TH' BLOND BOMBSHELL HERE IS YER NEW BOYFRIEND I BEEN HEARIN' ABOUT! WHOSE CLIT DO I HAFTA DIDDLE TO GET AN INTRODUCTION?
JESUS, TINA! I DIDN'T EVEN KNOW YOU WERE IN TH' BAR!
THAT'S AN EXPLANATION, NOT AN EXCUSE, SOLDIER!
TINA, MEET DUNCAN!
HIYA, DUNK! IT'S A PLEASURE SO FAR!
I GUESS I'LL BE SEEIN' YOU GUYS AT TH' BIG DEMO TOMORROW!
PROTEST RALLY
Wednesday at 8
Mayor Arn Stoobidge scuttles Gay Rights Bill yet again!
TELL THE MAYOR WE'RE NOT GOING TO TAKE IT ANYMORE!
OH, YEH... SURE THING! Snicker!
HMM...'SCUSE ME, DUNK—IT SOUNDED LIKE YOU SNICKERED AT WHAT I JUST SAID! UH... LIKE, A SNICKER IS WHAT I'D CALL A WRONG RESPONSE!
STERNO AND I HAVE NO INTENTION OF WASTING OUR TIME CHANTING BANAL SLOGANS AND BRANDISHING PLACARDS!
WAKE UP AND SMELL THE COFFEE, GIRL! THAT STUFF WENT OUT WITH THE SIXTIES!
©1989 by H. Cruse

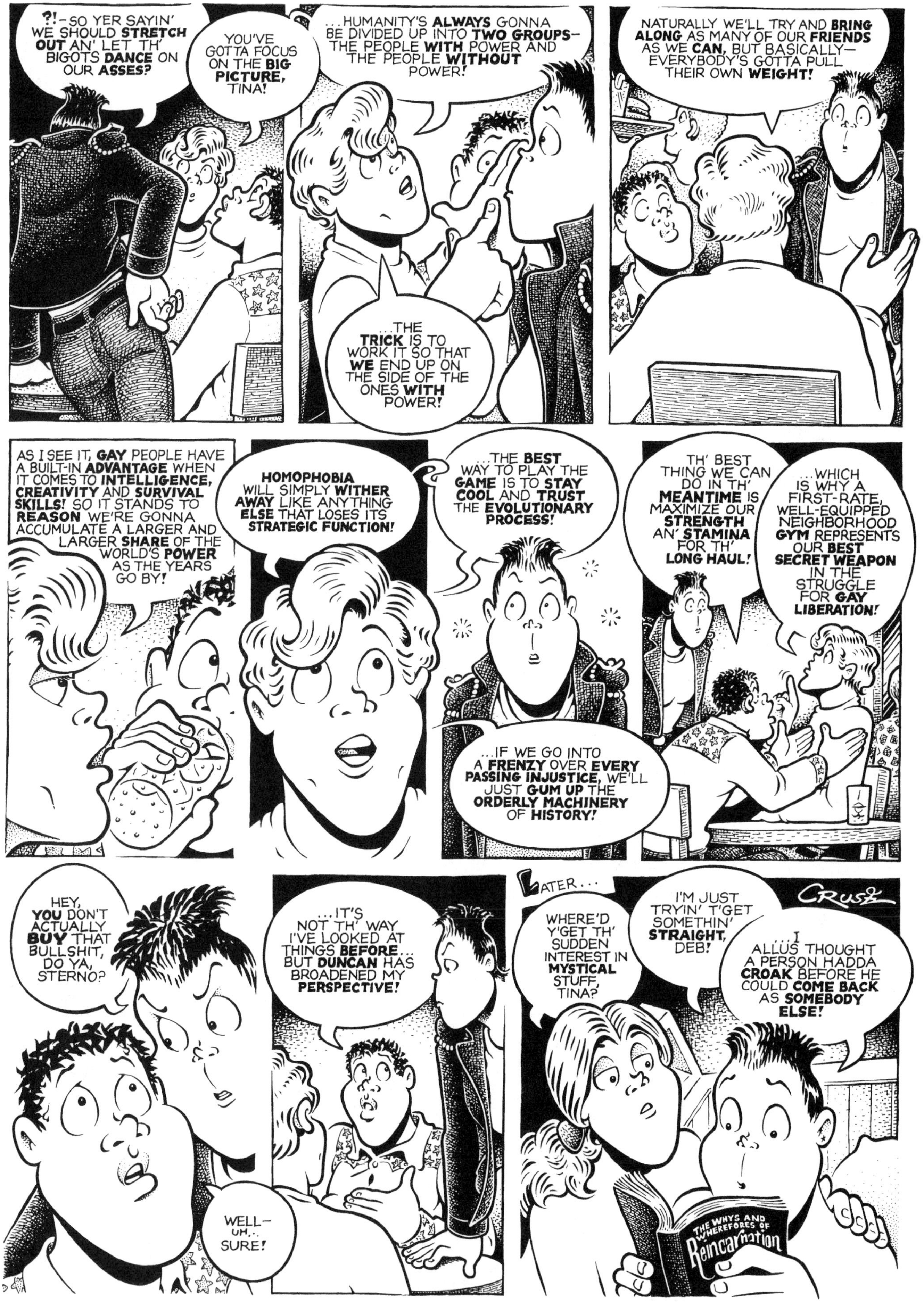
?!–SO YER SAYIN' WE SHOULD STRETCH OUT AN' LET TH' BIGOTS DANCE ON OUR ASSES?
YOU'VE GOTTA FOCUS ON THE BIG PICTURE, TINA!
...HUMANITY'S ALWAYS GONNA BE DIVIDED UP INTO TWO GROUPS– THE PEOPLE WITH POWER AND THE PEOPLE WITHOUT POWER!
...THE TRICK IS TO WORK IT SO THAT WE END UP ON THE SIDE OF THE ONES WITH POWER!
NATURALLY WE'LL TRY AND BRING ALONG AS MANY OF OUR FRIENDS AS WE CAN, BUT BASICALLY– EVERYBODY'S GOTTA PULL THEIR OWN WEIGHT!
AS I SEE IT, GAY PEOPLE HAVE A BUILT-IN ADVANTAGE WHEN IT COMES TO INTELLIGENCE, CREATIVITY AND SURVIVAL SKILLS! SO IT STANDS TO REASON WE'RE GONNA ACCUMULATE A LARGER AND LARGER SHARE OF THE WORLD'S POWER AS THE YEARS GO BY!
HOMOPHOBIA WILL SIMPLY WITHER AWAY LIKE ANYTHING ELSE THAT LOSES ITS STRATEGIC FUNCTION!
...THE BEST WAY TO PLAY THE GAME IS TO STAY COOL AND TRUST THE EVOLUTIONARY PROCESS!
...IF WE GO INTO A FRENZY OVER EVERY PASSING INJUSTICE, WE'LL JUST GUM UP THE ORDERLY MACHINERY OF HISTORY!
TH' BEST THING WE CAN DO IN TH' MEANTIME IS MAXIMIZE OUR STRENGTH AN' STAMINA FOR TH' LONG HAUL!
...WHICH IS WHY A FIRST-RATE, WELL-EQUIPPED NEIGHBORHOOD GYM REPRESENTS OUR BEST SECRET WEAPON IN THE STRUGGLE FOR GAY LIBERATION!
HEY, YOU DON'T ACTUALLY BUY THAT BULLSHIT, DO YA, STERNO?
WELL– UH,.. SURE!
...IT'S NOT TH' WAY I'VE LOOKED AT THINGS BEFORE... BUT DUNCAN HAS BROADENED MY PERSPECTIVE!
LATER...
CRUSE
WHERE'D Y'GET TH' SUDDEN INTEREST IN MYSTICAL STUFF, TINA?
I'M JUST TRYIN' T'GET SOMETHIN' STRAIGHT, DEB!
...I ALLUS THOUGHT A PERSON HADDA CROAK BEFORE HE COULD COME BACK AS SOMEBODY ELSE!
THE WHYS AND WHEREFORES OF Reincarnation

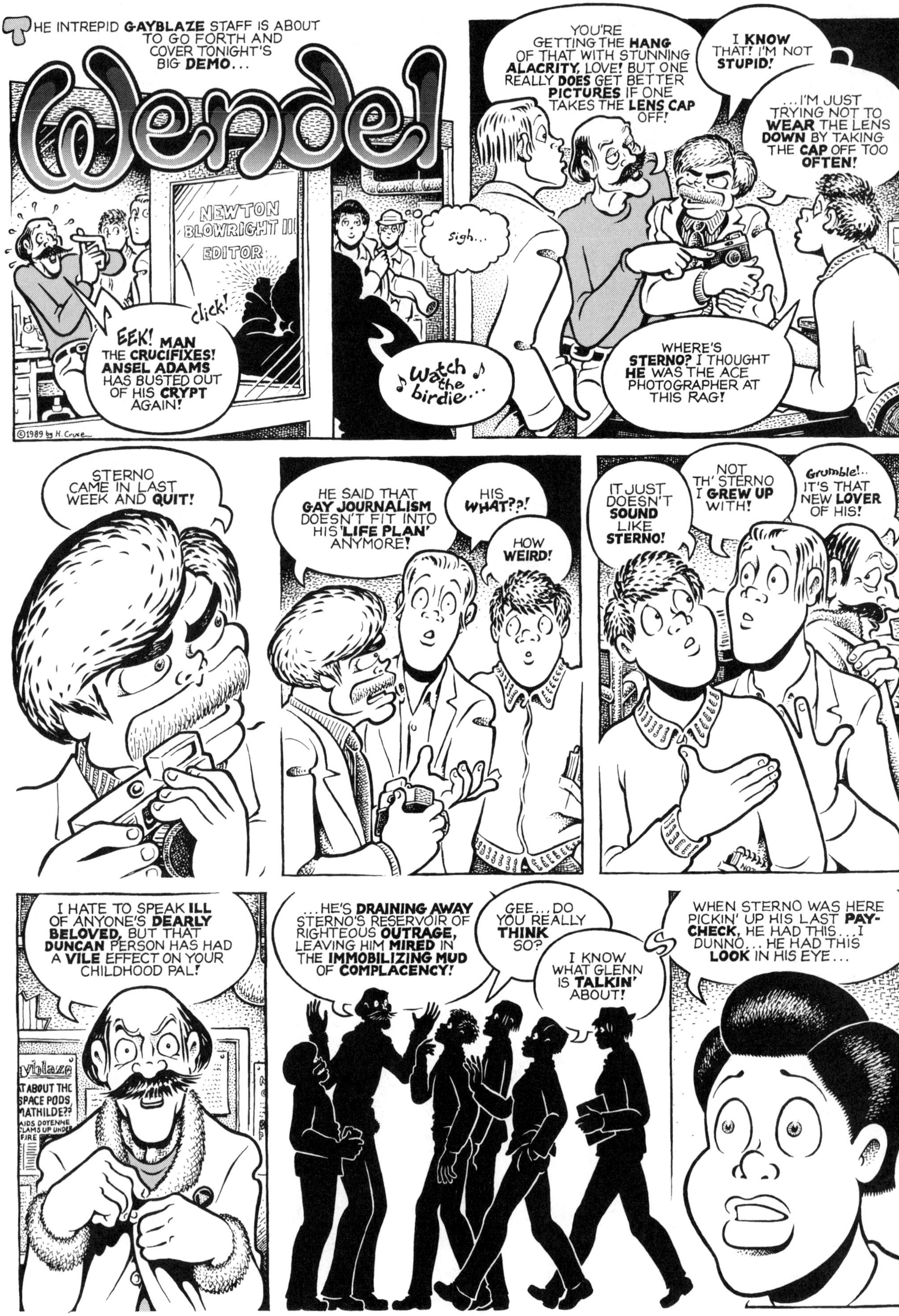
THE INTREPID GAYBLAZE STAFF IS ABOUT TO GO FORTH AND COVER TONIGHT'S BIG DEMO...
Wendel
NEWTON BLOWRIGHT III EDITOR
EEK! MAN THE CRUCIFIXES! ANSEL ADAMS HAS BUSTED OUT OF HIS CRYPT AGAIN!
click!
©1989 by H. Cruse
YOU'RE GETTING THE HANG OF THAT WITH STUNNING ALACRITY, LOVE! BUT ONE REALLY DOES GET BETTER PICTURES IF ONE TAKES THE LENS CAP OFF!
I KNOW THAT! I'M NOT STUPID!
...I'M JUST TRYING NOT TO WEAR THE LENS DOWN BY TAKING THE CAP OFF TOO OFTEN!
sigh...
Watch the birdie...
WHERE'S STERNO? I THOUGHT HE WAS THE ACE PHOTOGRAPHER AT THIS RAG!
STERNO CAME IN LAST WEEK AND QUIT!
HE SAID THAT GAY JOURNALISM DOESN'T FIT INTO HIS 'LIFE PLAN' ANYMORE!
HIS WHAT??!
HOW WEIRD!
IT JUST DOESN'T SOUND LIKE STERNO!
NOT TH' STERNO I GREW UP WITH!
Grumble!.. IT'S THAT NEW LOVER OF HIS!
I HATE TO SPEAK ILL OF ANYONE'S DEARLY BELOVED, BUT THAT DUNCAN PERSON HAS HAD A VILE EFFECT ON YOUR CHILDHOOD PAL!
...HE'S DRAINING AWAY STERNO'S RESERVOIR OF RIGHTEOUS OUTRAGE, LEAVING HIM MIRED IN THE IMMOBILIZING MUD OF COMPLACENCY!
GEE... DO YOU REALLY THINK SO?
I KNOW WHAT GLENN IS TALKIN' ABOUT!
WHEN STERNO WAS HERE PICKIN' UP HIS LAST PAY-CHECK, HE HAD THIS... I DUNNO... HE HAD THIS LOOK IN HIS EYE...

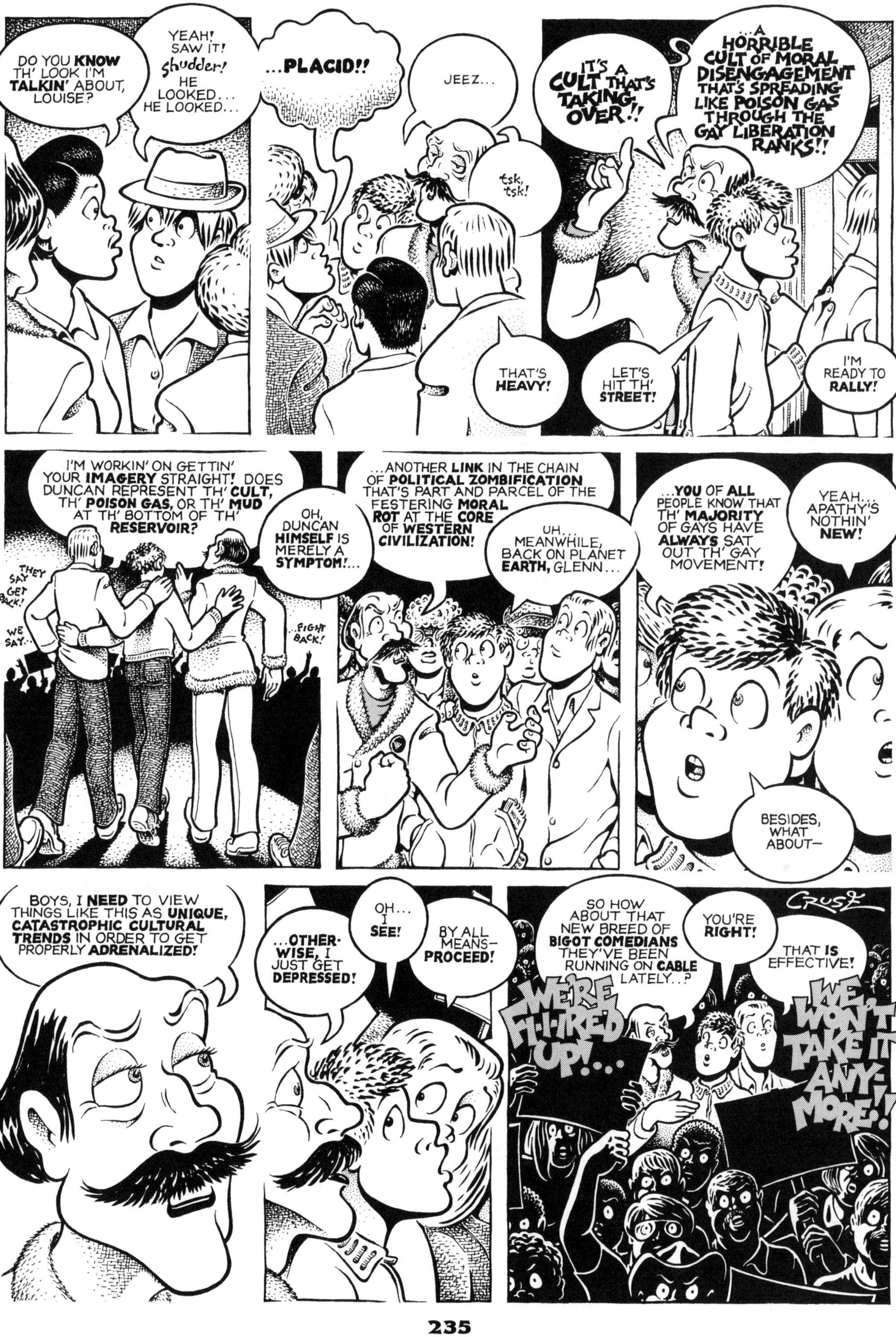
DO YOU KNOW TH' LOOK I'M TALKIN' ABOUT, LOUISE?
YEAH! SAW IT! shudder! HE LOOKED... HE LOOKED...
...PLACID!!
JEEZ...
tsk, tsk!
THAT'S HEAVY!
IT'S A CULT THAT'S TAKING OVER!!
...A HORRIBLE CULT OF MORAL DISENGAGEMENT THAT'S SPREADING LIKE POISON GAS THROUGH THE GAY LIBERATION RANKS!!
LET'S HIT TH' STREET!
I'M READY TO RALLY!
I'M WORKIN' ON GETTIN' YOUR IMAGERY STRAIGHT! DOES DUNCAN REPRESENT TH' CULT, TH' POISON GAS, OR TH' MUD AT TH' BOTTOM OF TH' RESERVOIR?
THEY SAY GET BACK!
WE SAY...
...FIGHT BACK!
OH, DUNCAN HIMSELF IS MERELY A SYMPTOM!...
...ANOTHER LINK IN THE CHAIN OF POLITICAL ZOMBIFICATION THAT'S PART AND PARCEL OF THE FESTERING MORAL ROT AT THE CORE OF WESTERN CIVILIZATION!
UH... MEANWHILE, BACK ON PLANET EARTH, GLENN...
...YOU OF ALL PEOPLE KNOW THAT TH' MAJORITY OF GAYS HAVE ALWAYS SAT OUT TH' GAY MOVEMENT!
YEAH... APATHY'S NOTHIN' NEW!
BESIDES, WHAT ABOUT—
BOYS, I NEED TO VIEW THINGS LIKE THIS AS UNIQUE, CATASTROPHIC CULTURAL TRENDS IN ORDER TO GET PROPERLY ADRENALIZED!
...OTHER-WISE, I JUST GET DEPRESSED!
OH... I SEE!
BY ALL MEANS— PROCEED!
SO HOW ABOUT THAT NEW BREED OF BIGOT COMEDIANS THEY'VE BEEN RUNNING ON CABLE LATELY...?
YOU'RE RIGHT!
THAT IS EFFECTIVE!
WE'RE FI-I-IRED UP!...
WE WON'T TAKE IT ANY-MORE!!
CRUSE

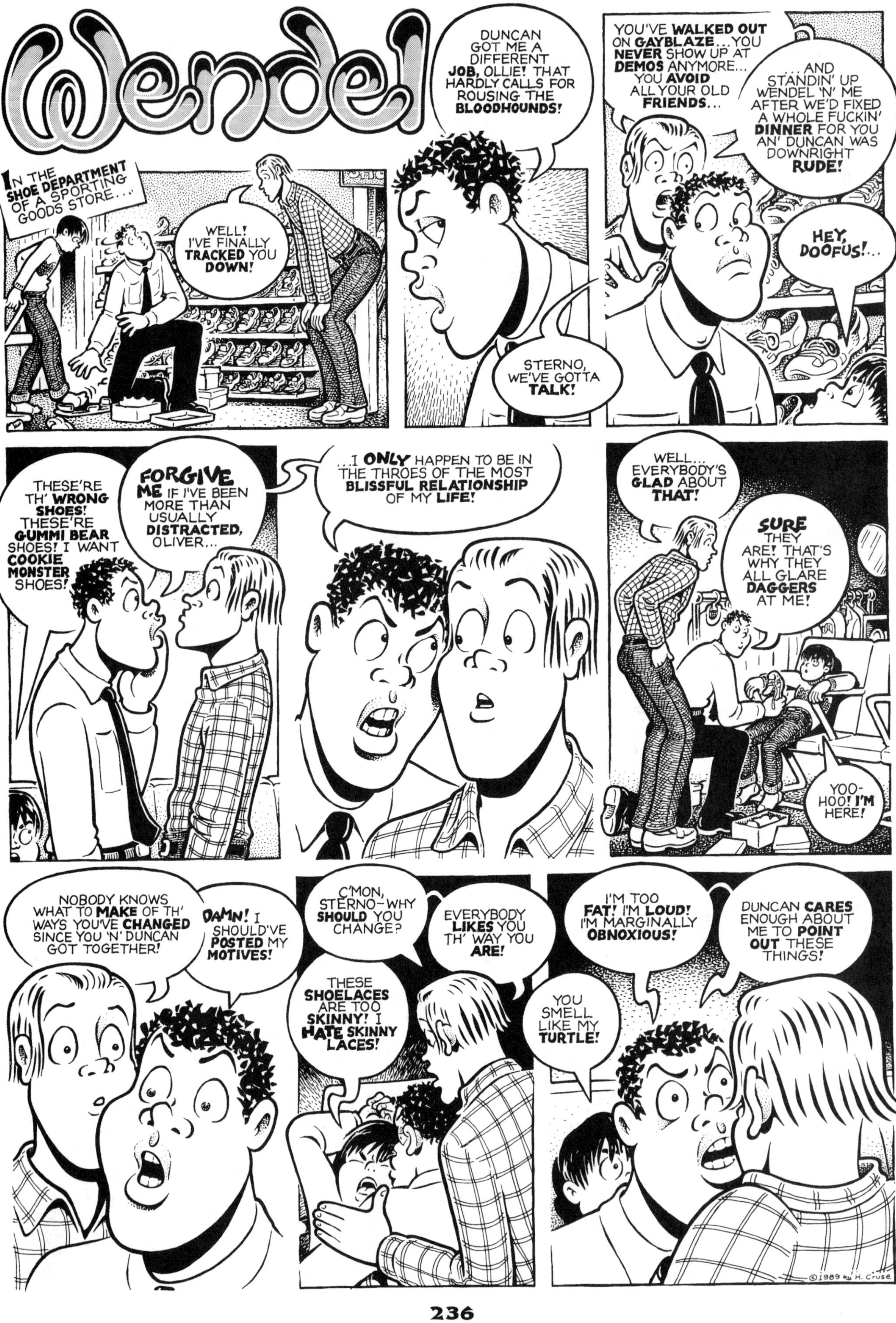
Wendel
IN THE SHOE DEPARTMENT OF A SPORTING GOODS STORE...
WELL! I'VE FINALLY TRACKED YOU DOWN!
DUNCAN GOT ME A DIFFERENT JOB, OLLIE! THAT HARDLY CALLS FOR ROUSING THE BLOODHOUNDS!
STERNO, WE'VE GOTTA TALK!
YOU'VE WALKED OUT ON GAYBLAZE... YOU NEVER SHOW UP AT DEMOS ANYMORE... YOU AVOID ALL YOUR OLD FRIENDS...
...AND STANDIN' UP WENDEL 'N' ME AFTER WE'D FIXED A WHOLE FUCKIN' DINNER FOR YOU AN' DUNCAN WAS DOWNRIGHT RUDE!
HEY, DOOFUS!...
THESE'RE TH' WRONG SHOES! THESE'RE GUMMI BEAR SHOES! I WANT COOKIE MONSTER SHOES!
FORGIVE ME IF I'VE BEEN MORE THAN USUALLY DISTRACTED, OLIVER...
...I ONLY HAPPEN TO BE IN THE THROES OF THE MOST BLISSFUL RELATIONSHIP OF MY LIFE!
WELL... EVERYBODY'S GLAD ABOUT THAT!
SURE THEY ARE! THAT'S WHY THEY ALL GLARE DAGGERS AT ME!
YOO-HOO! I'M HERE!
NOBODY KNOWS WHAT TO MAKE OF TH' WAYS YOU'VE CHANGED SINCE YOU 'N' DUNCAN GOT TOGETHER!
DAMN! I SHOULD'VE POSTED MY MOTIVES!
C'MON, STERNO—WHY SHOULD YOU CHANGE?
EVERYBODY LIKES YOU TH' WAY YOU ARE!
THESE SHOELACES ARE TOO SKINNY! I HATE SKINNY LACES!
I'M TOO FAT! I'M LOUD! I'M MARGINALLY OBNOXIOUS!
DUNCAN CARES ENOUGH ABOUT ME TO POINT OUT THESE THINGS!
YOU SMELL LIKE MY TURTLE!
©1989 by H. Cruse

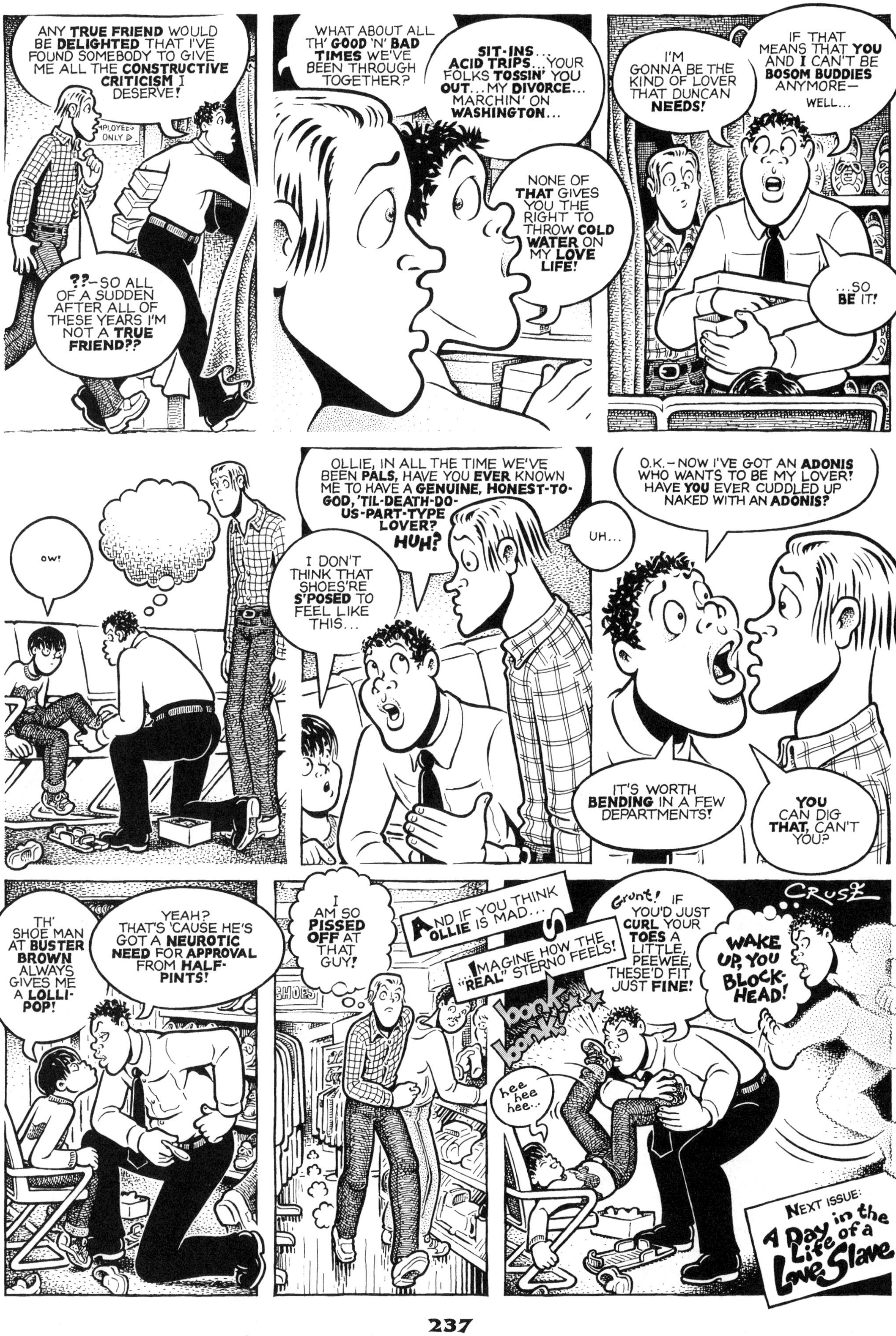
ANY TRUE FRIEND WOULD BE DELIGHTED THAT I'VE FOUND SOMEBODY TO GIVE ME ALL THE CONSTRUCTIVE CRITICISM I DESERVE!
EMPLOYEES ONLY
??–SO ALL OF A SUDDEN AFTER ALL OF THESE YEARS I'M NOT A TRUE FRIEND??
WHAT ABOUT ALL TH' GOOD 'N' BAD TIMES WE'VE BEEN THROUGH TOGETHER?
SIT-INS... ACID TRIPS... YOUR FOLKS TOSSIN' YOU OUT... MY DIVORCE... MARCHIN' ON WASHINGTON...
NONE OF THAT GIVES YOU THE RIGHT TO THROW COLD WATER ON MY LOVE LIFE!
I'M GONNA BE THE KIND OF LOVER THAT DUNCAN NEEDS!
IF THAT MEANS THAT YOU AND I CAN'T BE BOSOM BUDDIES ANYMORE— WELL...
...SO BE IT!
OW!
I DON'T THINK THAT SHOES'RE S'POSED TO FEEL LIKE THIS...
OLLIE, IN ALL THE TIME WE'VE BEEN PALS, HAVE YOU EVER KNOWN ME TO HAVE A GENUINE, HONEST-TO-GOD, 'TIL-DEATH-DO-US-PART-TYPE LOVER? HUH?
UH...
O.K.–NOW I'VE GOT AN ADONIS WHO WANTS TO BE MY LOVER! HAVE YOU EVER CUDDLED UP NAKED WITH AN ADONIS?
IT'S WORTH BENDING IN A FEW DEPARTMENTS!
YOU CAN DIG THAT, CAN'T YOU?
TH' SHOE MAN AT BUSTER BROWN ALWAYS GIVES ME A LOLLIPOP!
YEAH? THAT'S 'CAUSE HE'S GOT A NEUROTIC NEED FOR APPROVAL FROM HALF-PINTS!
I AM SO PISSED OFF AT THAT GUY!
SHOES
AND IF YOU THINK OLLIE IS MAD...
...IMAGINE HOW THE "REAL" STERNO FEELS!
CRUSE
Grunt! IF YOU'D JUST CURL YOUR TOES A LITTLE, PEEWEE, THESE'D FIT JUST FINE!
WAKE UP, YOU BLOCK-HEAD!
bonk bonk!
hee hee hee...
NEXT ISSUE: A Day in the Life of a Love Slave

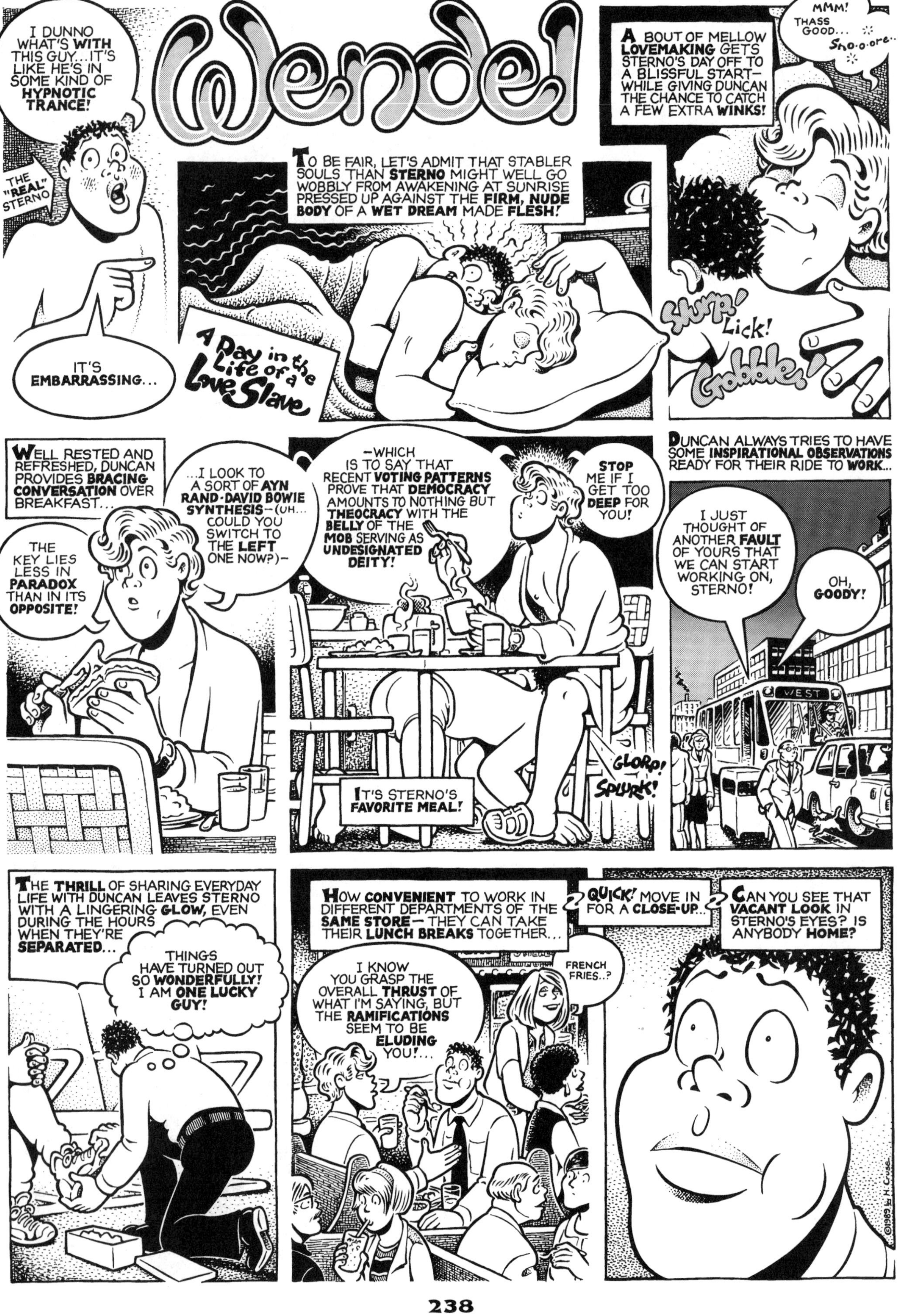
I DUNNO WHAT'S WITH THIS GUY... IT'S LIKE HE'S IN SOME KIND OF HYPNOTIC TRANCE!
Wendel
THE "REAL" STERNO
IT'S EMBARRASSING...
TO BE FAIR, LET'S ADMIT THAT STABLER SOULS THAN STERNO MIGHT WELL GO WOBBLY FROM AWAKENING AT SUNRISE PRESSED UP AGAINST THE FIRM, NUDE BODY OF A WET DREAM MADE FLESH!
A Day in the Life of a Love Slave
A BOUT OF MELLOW LOVEMAKING GETS STERNO'S DAY OFF TO A BLISSFUL START— WHILE GIVING DUNCAN THE CHANCE TO CATCH A FEW EXTRA WINKS!
MMM! THASS GOOD... Sno-o-ore...
Slurp! Lick! Gobble!
WELL RESTED AND REFRESHED, DUNCAN PROVIDES BRACING CONVERSATION OVER BREAKFAST...
THE KEY LIES LESS IN PARADOX THAN IN ITS OPPOSITE!
...I LOOK TO A SORT OF AYN RAND-DAVID BOWIE SYNTHESIS—(UH... COULD YOU SWITCH TO THE LEFT ONE NOW?)—
—WHICH IS TO SAY THAT RECENT VOTING PATTERNS PROVE THAT DEMOCRACY AMOUNTS TO NOTHING BUT THEOCRACY WITH THE BELLY OF THE MOB SERVING AS UNDESIGNATED DEITY!
STOP ME IF I GET TOO DEEP FOR YOU!
GLORP! SPLURK!
IT'S STERNO'S FAVORITE MEAL!
DUNCAN ALWAYS TRIES TO HAVE SOME INSPIRATIONAL OBSERVATIONS READY FOR THEIR RIDE TO WORK...
I JUST THOUGHT OF ANOTHER FAULT OF YOURS THAT WE CAN START WORKING ON, STERNO!
OH, GOODY!
WEST
THE THRILL OF SHARING EVERYDAY LIFE WITH DUNCAN LEAVES STERNO WITH A LINGERING GLOW, EVEN DURING THE HOURS WHEN THEY'RE SEPARATED...
THINGS HAVE TURNED OUT SO WONDERFULLY! I AM ONE LUCKY GUY!
HOW CONVENIENT TO WORK IN DIFFERENT DEPARTMENTS OF THE SAME STORE — THEY CAN TAKE THEIR LUNCH BREAKS TOGETHER...
FRENCH FRIES..?
I KNOW YOU GRASP THE OVERALL THRUST OF WHAT I'M SAYING, BUT THE RAMIFICATIONS SEEM TO BE ELUDING YOU!...
QUICK! MOVE IN FOR A CLOSE-UP...
CAN YOU SEE THAT VACANT LOOK IN STERNO'S EYES? IS ANYBODY HOME?
©1989 by H. Cruse

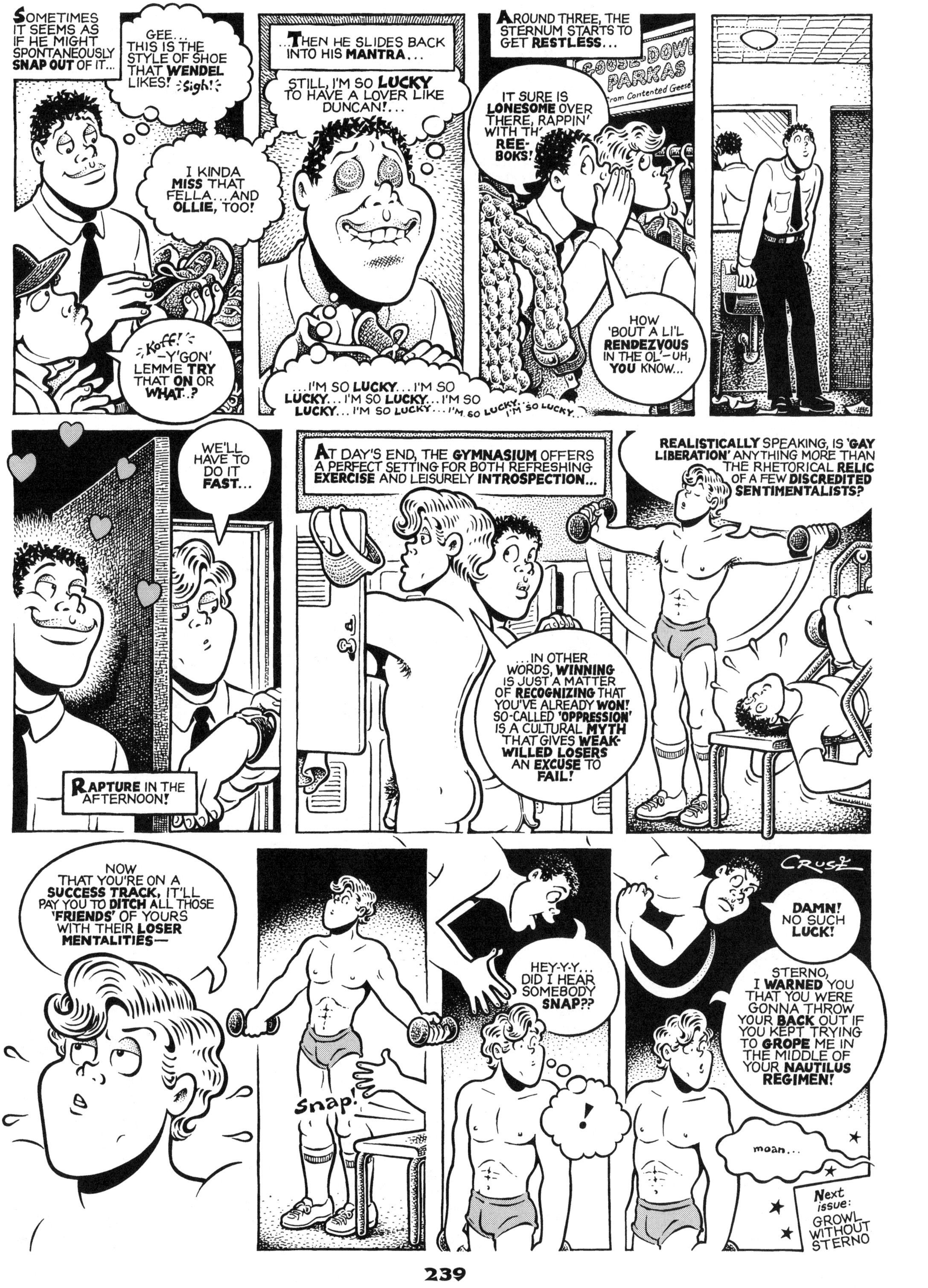
SOMETIMES IT SEEMS AS IF HE MIGHT SPONTANEOUSLY SNAP OUT OF IT...
GEE... THIS IS THE STYLE OF SHOE THAT WENDEL LIKES! Sigh!
I KINDA MISS THAT FELLA... AND OLLIE, TOO!
Koff! —Y'GON' LEMME TRY THAT ON OR WHAT..?
...THEN HE SLIDES BACK INTO HIS MANTRA...
STILL, I'M SO LUCKY TO HAVE A LOVER LIKE DUNCAN!...
...I'M SO LUCKY... I'M SO LUCKY... I'M SO LUCKY... I'M SO LUCKY... I'M SO LUCKY... I'M SO LUCKY, I'M SO LUCKY...
AROUND THREE, THE STERNUM STARTS TO GET RESTLESS...
GOOSE-DOWN PARKAS
From Contented Geese
IT SURE IS LONESOME OVER THERE, RAPPIN' WITH TH' REE-BOKS!
HOW 'BOUT A LI'L RENDEZVOUS IN THE OL'—UH, YOU KNOW...
WE'LL HAVE TO DO IT FAST...
RAPTURE IN THE AFTERNOON!
AT DAY'S END, THE GYMNASIUM OFFERS A PERFECT SETTING FOR BOTH REFRESHING EXERCISE AND LEISURELY INTROSPECTION...
...IN OTHER WORDS, WINNING IS JUST A MATTER OF RECOGNIZING THAT YOU'VE ALREADY WON! SO-CALLED 'OPPRESSION' IS A CULTURAL MYTH THAT GIVES WEAK-WILLED LOSERS AN EXCUSE TO FAIL!
REALISTICALLY SPEAKING, IS 'GAY LIBERATION' ANYTHING MORE THAN THE RHETORICAL RELIC OF A FEW DISCREDITED SENTIMENTALISTS?
NOW THAT YOU'RE ON A SUCCESS TRACK, IT'LL PAY YOU TO DITCH ALL THOSE 'FRIENDS' OF YOURS WITH THEIR LOSER MENTALITIES—
Snap!
HEY-Y-Y... DID I HEAR SOMEBODY SNAP??
!
CRUSE
DAMN! NO SUCH LUCK!
STERNO, I WARNED YOU THAT YOU WERE GONNA THROW YOUR BACK OUT IF YOU KEPT TRYING TO GROPE ME IN THE MIDDLE OF YOUR NAUTILUS REGIMEN!
moan...
Next issue: GROWL WITHOUT STERNO

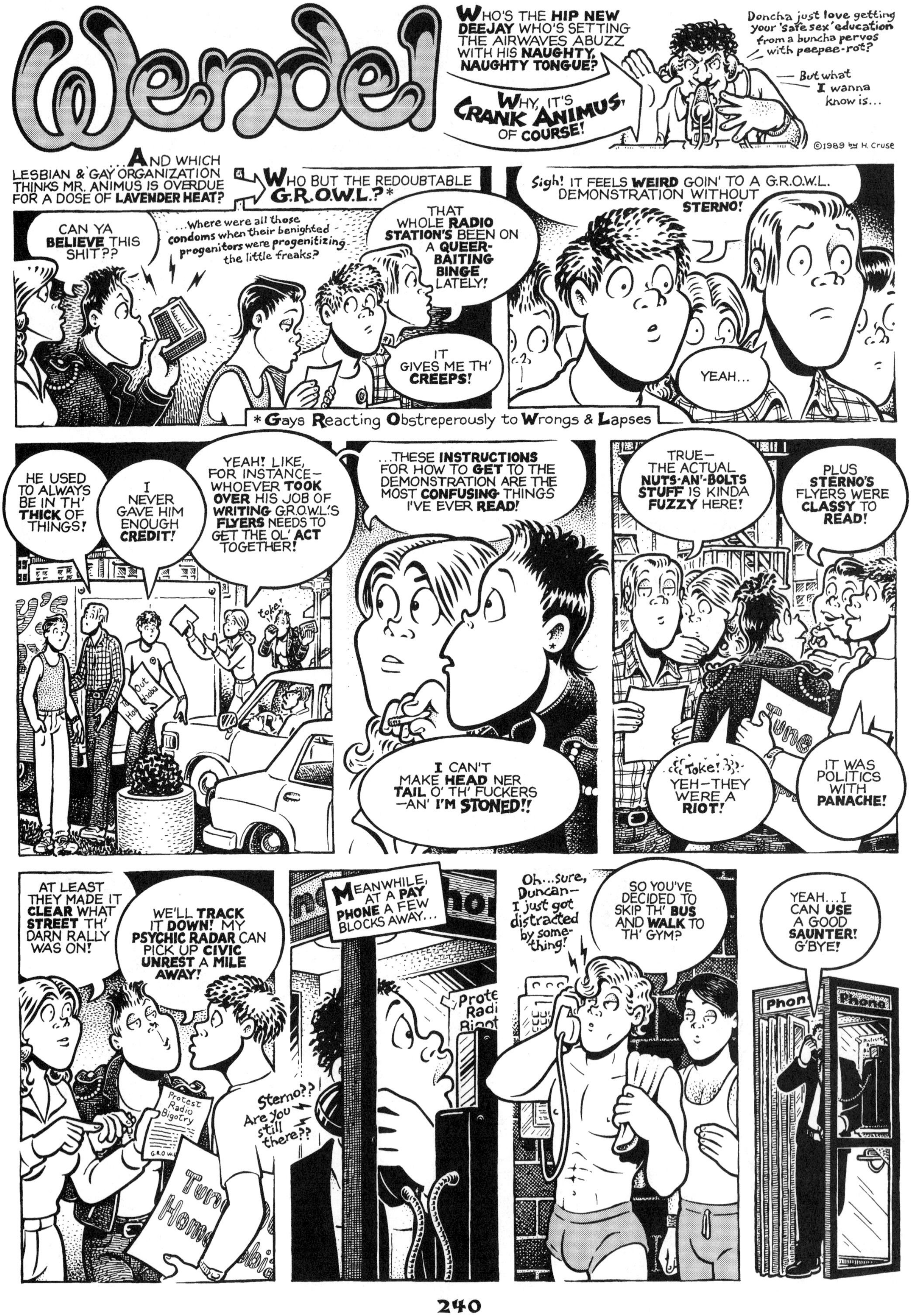
Wendel
WHO'S THE HIP NEW DEEJAY WHO'S SETTING THE AIRWAVES ABUZZ WITH HIS NAUGHTY, NAUGHTY TONGUE?
WHY, IT'S CRANK ANIMUS, OF COURSE!
Doncha just love getting your 'safe sex' education from a buncha pervos with peepee-rot?
But what I wanna know is...
©1989 by H. Cruse
...AND WHICH LESBIAN & GAY ORGANIZATION THINKS MR. ANIMUS IS OVERDUE FOR A DOSE OF LAVENDER HEAT?
WHO BUT THE REDOUBTABLE G.R.O.W.L.?*
CAN YA BELIEVE THIS SHIT??
...Where were all those condoms when their benighted progenitors were progenitizing the little freaks?
THAT WHOLE RADIO STATION'S BEEN ON A QUEER-BAITING BINGE LATELY!
IT GIVES ME TH' CREEPS!
Sigh! IT FEELS WEIRD GOIN' TO A G.R.O.W.L. DEMONSTRATION WITHOUT STERNO!
YEAH...
*Gays Reacting Obstreperously to Wrongs & Lapses
HE USED TO ALWAYS BE IN TH' THICK OF THINGS!
I NEVER GAVE HIM ENOUGH CREDIT!
YEAH! LIKE, FOR INSTANCE— WHOEVER TOOK OVER HIS JOB OF WRITING G.R.O.W.L.'S FLYERS NEEDS TO GET THE OL' ACT TOGETHER!
toke!
...THESE INSTRUCTIONS FOR HOW TO GET TO THE DEMONSTRATION ARE THE MOST CONFUSING THINGS I'VE EVER READ!
I CAN'T MAKE HEAD NER TAIL O' TH' FUCKERS —AN' I'M STONED!!
TRUE— THE ACTUAL NUTS-AN'-BOLTS STUFF IS KINDA FUZZY HERE!
PLUS STERNO'S FLYERS WERE CLASSY TO READ!
Toke! YEH—THEY WERE A RIOT!
IT WAS POLITICS WITH PANACHE!
AT LEAST THEY MADE IT CLEAR WHAT STREET TH' DARN RALLY WAS ON!
WE'LL TRACK IT DOWN! MY PSYCHIC RADAR CAN PICK UP CIVIC UNREST A MILE AWAY!
Protest Radio Bigotry
MEANWHILE, AT A PAY PHONE A FEW BLOCKS AWAY...
Sterno?? Are you still there??
Oh...sure, Duncan— I just got distracted by something!
SO YOU'VE DECIDED TO SKIP TH' BUS AND WALK TO TH' GYM?
YEAH...I CAN USE A GOOD SAUNTER! G'BYE!
Phone

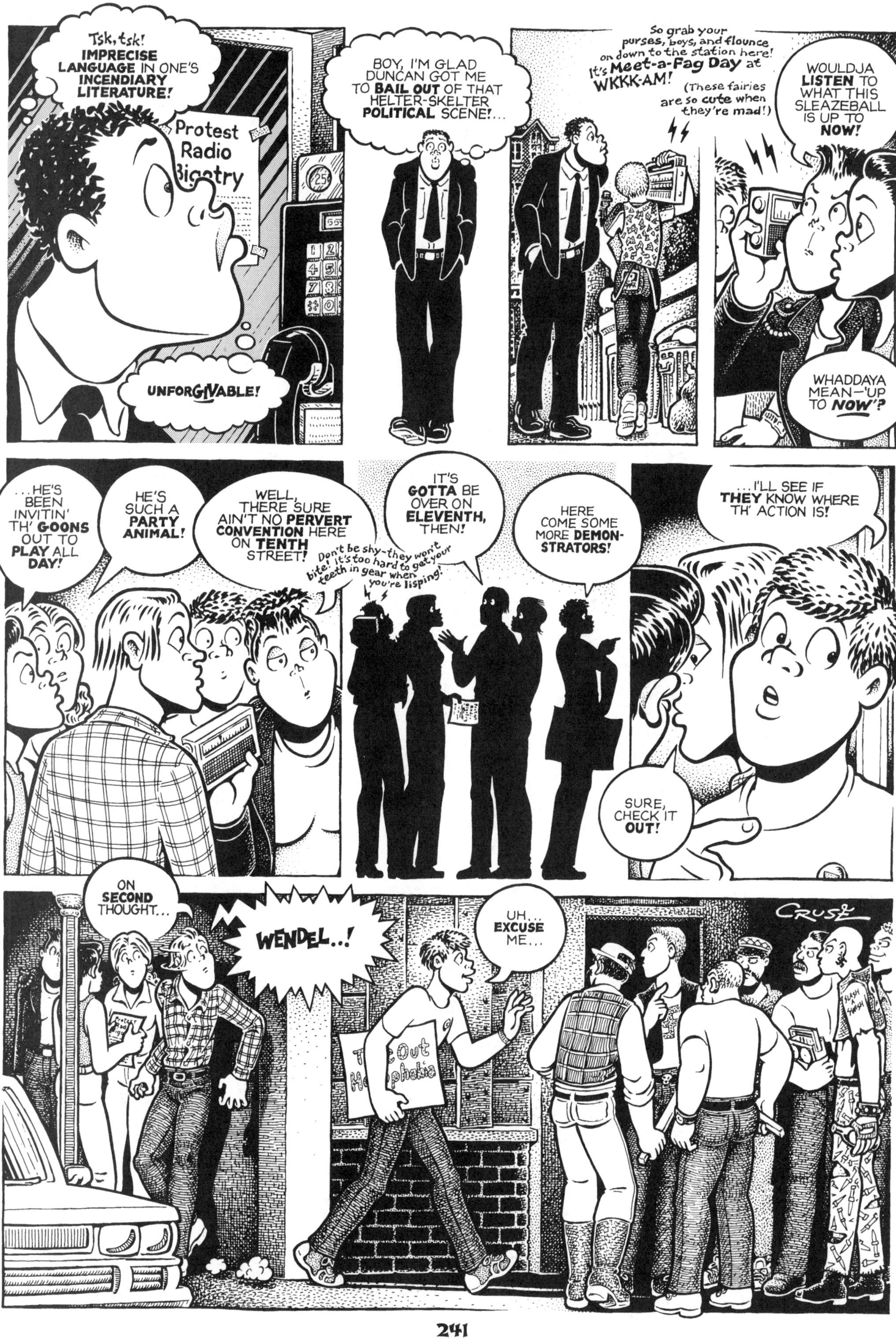

Tsk, tsk! IMPRECISE LANGUAGE IN ONE'S INCENDIARY LITERATURE!
Protest Radio Bigotry
UNFORGIVABLE!
BOY, I'M GLAD DUNCAN GOT ME TO BAIL OUT OF THAT HELTER-SKELTER POLITICAL SCENE!...
So grab your purses, boys, and flounce on down to the station here! It's Meet-a-Fag Day at WKKK-AM!
(These fairies are so cute when they're mad!)
WOULDJA LISTEN TO WHAT THIS SLEAZEBALL IS UP TO NOW!
WHADDAYA MEAN—'UP TO NOW'?
...HE'S BEEN INVITIN' TH' GOONS OUT TO PLAY ALL DAY!
HE'S SUCH A PARTY ANIMAL!
WELL, THERE SURE AIN'T NO PERVERT CONVENTION HERE ON TENTH STREET!
Don't be shy—they won't bite! It's too hard to get your teeth in gear when you're lisping!
IT'S GOTTA BE OVER ON ELEVENTH, THEN!
HERE COME SOME MORE DEMON-STRATORS!
...I'LL SEE IF THEY KNOW WHERE TH' ACTION IS!
SURE, CHECK IT OUT!
ON SECOND THOUGHT...
WENDEL..!
UH... EXCUSE ME...
CRUSE

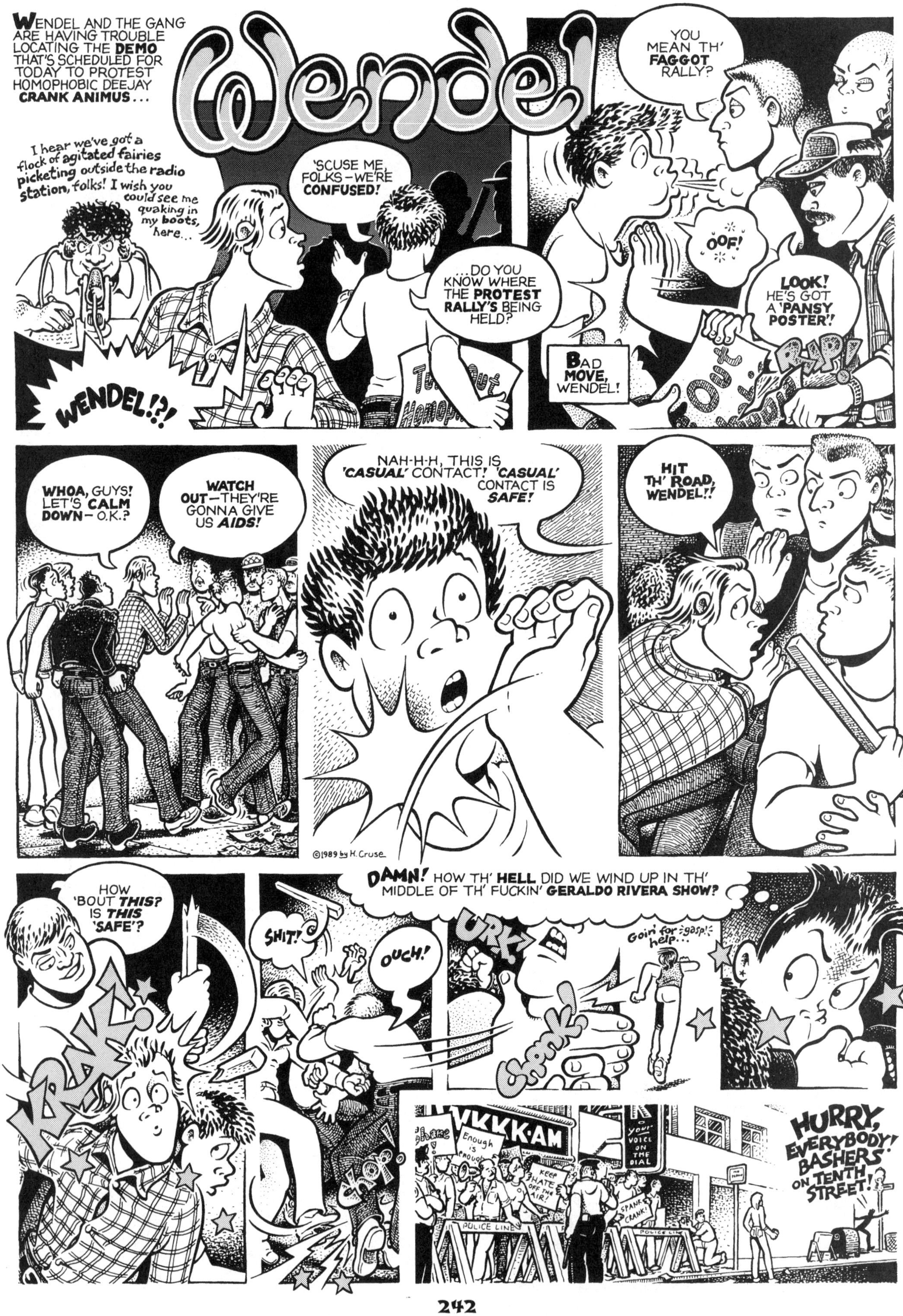

WENDEL AND THE GANG ARE HAVING TROUBLE LOCATING THE DEMO THAT'S SCHEDULED FOR TODAY TO PROTEST HOMOPHOBIC DEEJAY CRANK ANIMUS...
Wendel
I hear we've got a flock of agitated fairies picketing outside the radio station, folks! I wish you could see me quaking in my boots, here...
'SCUSE ME, FOLKS—WE'RE CONFUSED!
...DO YOU KNOW WHERE THE PROTEST RALLY'S BEING HELD?
WENDEL!?!
YOU MEAN TH' FAGGOT RALLY?
OOF!
LOOK! HE'S GOT A 'PANSY POSTER'!
BAD MOVE, WENDEL!
WHOA, GUYS! LET'S CALM DOWN—O.K.?
WATCH OUT—THEY'RE GONNA GIVE US AIDS!
NAH-H-H, THIS IS 'CASUAL' CONTACT! 'CASUAL' CONTACT IS SAFE!
HIT TH' ROAD, WENDEL!!
©1989 by H. Cruse
HOW 'BOUT THIS? IS THIS 'SAFE'?
KRAK!
SHIT!
OUCH!
DAMN! HOW TH' HELL DID WE WIND UP IN TH' MIDDLE OF TH' FUCKIN' GERALDO RIVERA SHOW?
URK!
Goin' for gasp! help...
WKKK-AM
Enough is enough
YOUR VOICE ON THE DIAL
KEEP HATE OFF THE AIR!
SPANK CRANK!
POLICE LINE
HURRY, EVERYBODY! BASHERS ON TENTH STREET!

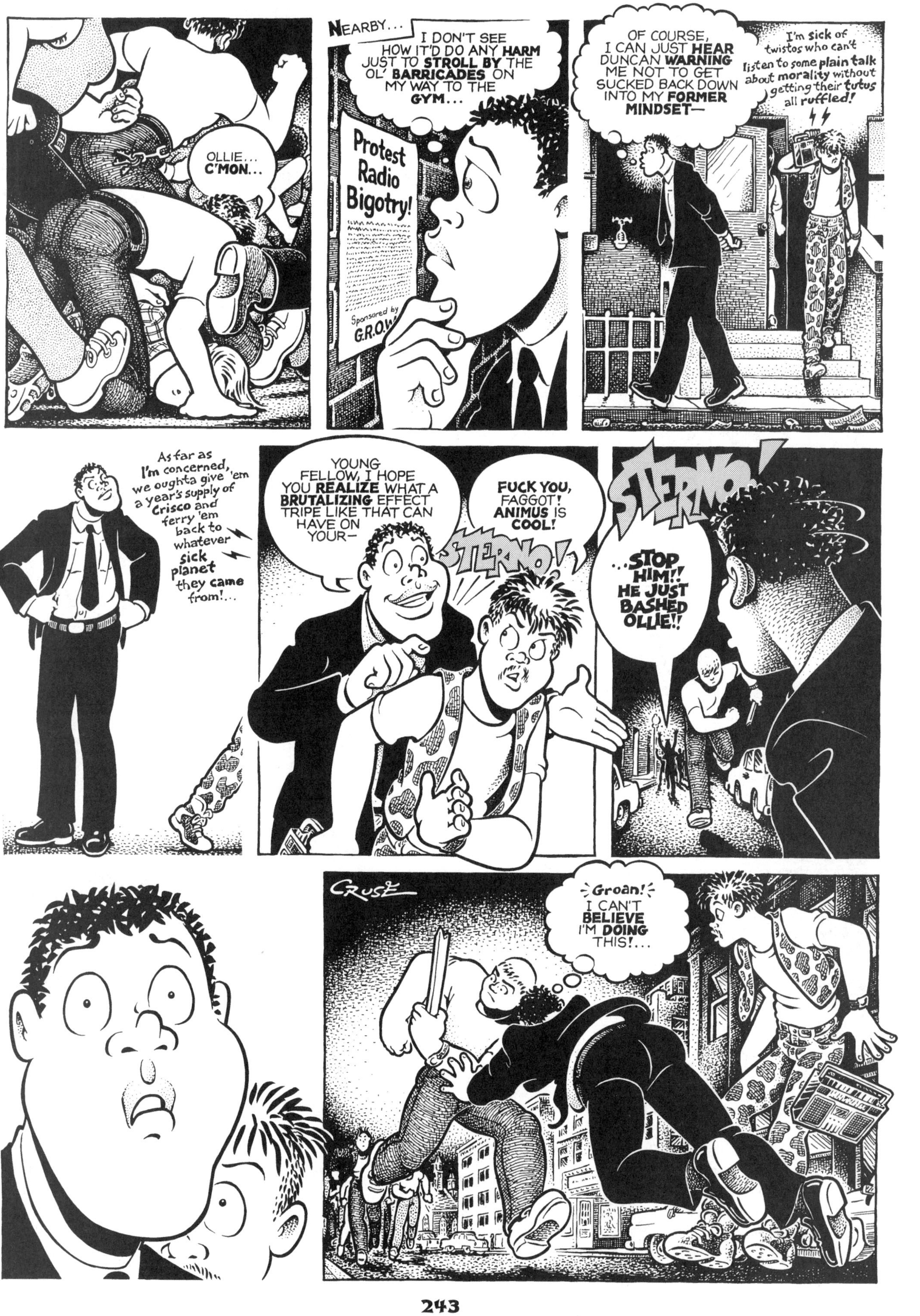
OLLIE... C'MON...
NEARBY...
I DON'T SEE HOW IT'D DO ANY HARM JUST TO STROLL BY THE OL' BARRICADES ON MY WAY TO THE GYM...
Protest Radio Bigotry!
Sponsored by G.R.O.W.
OF COURSE, I CAN JUST HEAR DUNCAN WARNING ME NOT TO GET SUCKED BACK DOWN INTO MY FORMER MINDSET—
I'm sick of twistos who can't listen to some plain talk about morality without getting their tutus all ruffled!
As far as I'm concerned, we oughta give 'em a year's supply of Crisco and ferry 'em back to whatever sick planet they came from!...
YOUNG FELLOW, I HOPE YOU REALIZE WHAT A BRUTALIZING EFFECT TRIPE LIKE THAT CAN HAVE ON YOUR—
FUCK YOU, FAGGOT! ANIMUS IS COOL!
STERNO!
STERNO!
...STOP HIM!! HE JUST BASHED OLLIE!!
CRUSE
Groan! I CAN'T BELIEVE I'M DOING THIS!...

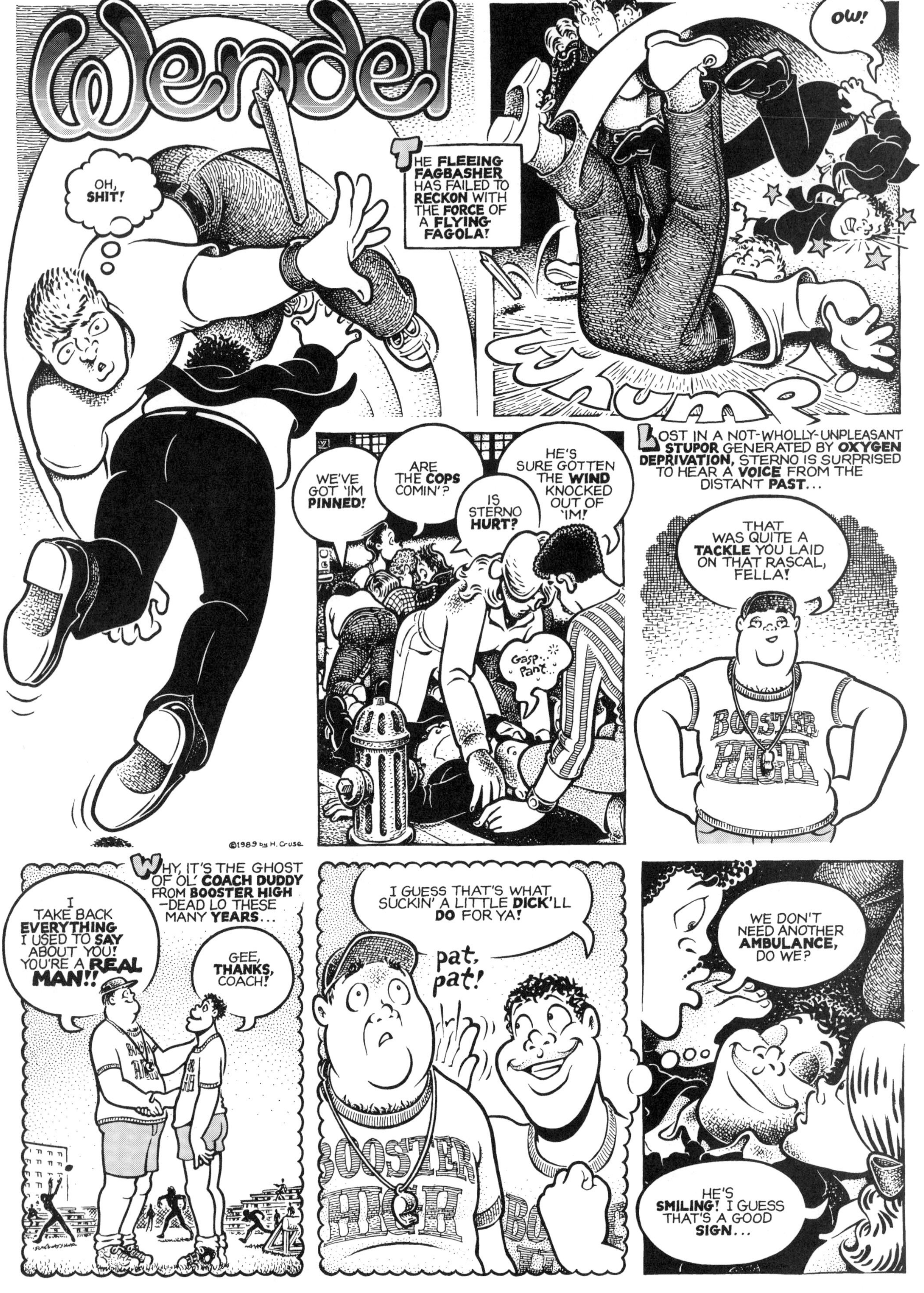

Wendel
OH, SHIT!
THE FLEEING FAGBASHER HAS FAILED TO RECKON WITH THE FORCE OF A FLYING FAGOLA!
OW!
WHUMP!
©1989 by H. Cruse
WE'VE GOT 'IM PINNED!
ARE THE COPS COMIN'?
IS STERNO HURT?
HE'S SURE GOTTEN THE WIND KNOCKED OUT OF 'IM!
Gasp... Pant...
LOST IN A NOT-WHOLLY-UNPLEASANT STUPOR GENERATED BY OXYGEN DEPRIVATION, STERNO IS SURPRISED TO HEAR A VOICE FROM THE DISTANT PAST...
THAT WAS QUITE A TACKLE YOU LAID ON THAT RASCAL, FELLA!
BOOSTER HIGH
WHY, IT'S THE GHOST OF OL' COACH DUDDY FROM BOOSTER HIGH —DEAD LO THESE MANY YEARS...
I TAKE BACK EVERYTHING I USED TO SAY ABOUT YOU! YOU'RE A REAL MAN!!
GEE, THANKS, COACH!
I GUESS THAT'S WHAT SUCKIN' A LITTLE DICK'LL DO FOR YA!
pat, pat!
BOOSTER HIGH
WE DON'T NEED ANOTHER AMBULANCE, DO WE?
HE'S SMILING! I GUESS THAT'S A GOOD SIGN...

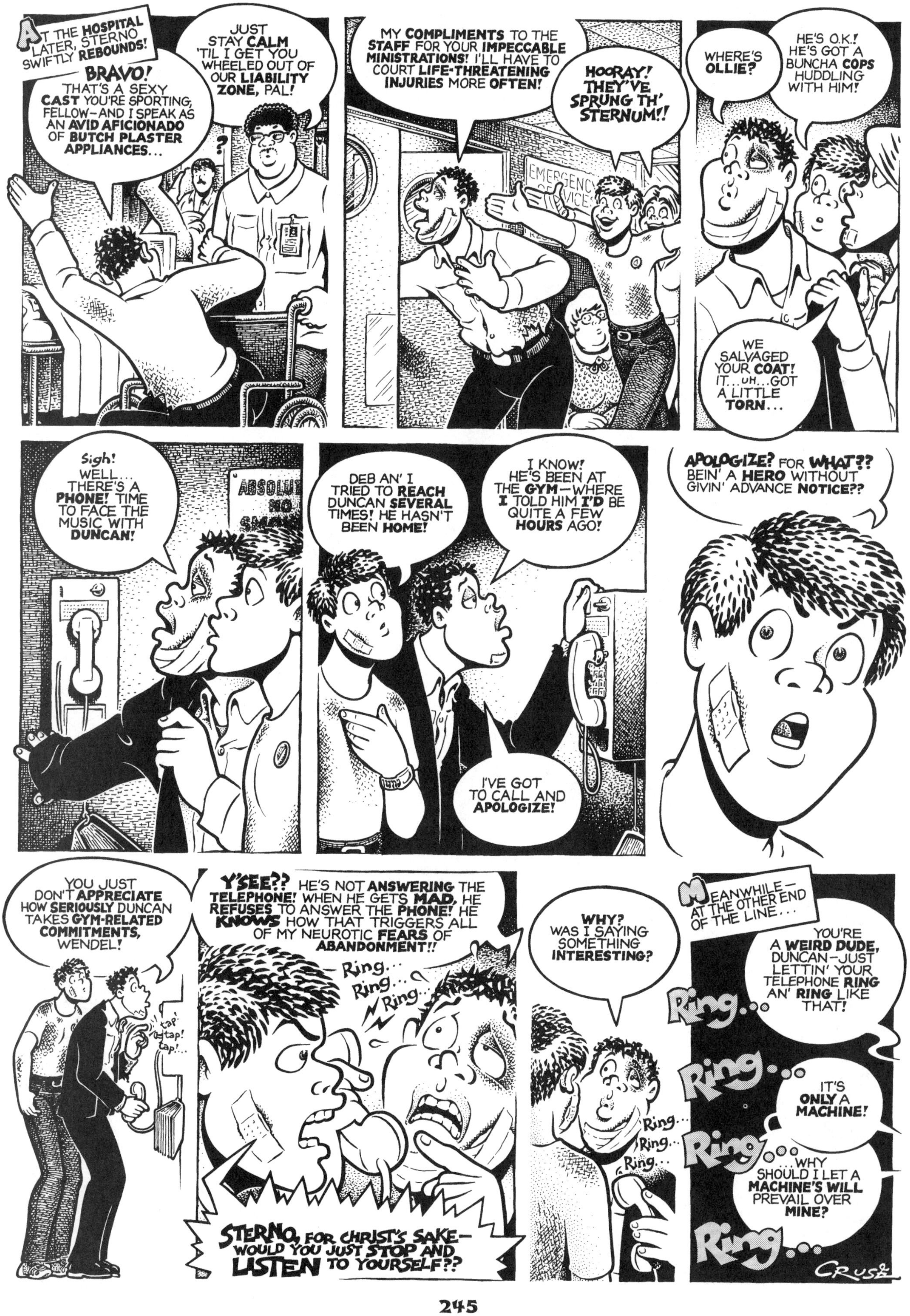

At the hospital later, Sterno swiftly rebounds!
BRAVO! THAT'S A SEXY CAST YOU'RE SPORTING, FELLOW—AND I SPEAK AS AN AVID AFICIONADO OF BUTCH PLASTER APPLIANCES...
JUST STAY CALM 'TIL I GET YOU WHEELED OUT OF OUR LIABILITY ZONE, PAL!
?
MY COMPLIMENTS TO THE STAFF FOR YOUR IMPECCABLE MINISTRATIONS! I'LL HAVE TO COURT LIFE-THREATENING INJURIES MORE OFTEN!
HOORAY! THEY'VE SPRUNG TH' STERNUM!!
EMERGENCY SERVICE
WHERE'S OLLIE?
HE'S O.K.! HE'S GOT A BUNCHA COPS HUDDLING WITH HIM!
WE SALVAGED YOUR COAT! IT...UH...GOT A LITTLE TORN...
Sigh! WELL... THERE'S A PHONE! TIME TO FACE THE MUSIC WITH DUNCAN!
DEB AN' I TRIED TO REACH DUNCAN SEVERAL TIMES! HE HASN'T BEEN HOME!
I KNOW! HE'S BEEN AT THE GYM—WHERE I TOLD HIM I'D BE QUITE A FEW HOURS AGO!
I'VE GOT TO CALL AND APOLOGIZE!
APOLOGIZE? FOR WHAT?? BEIN' A HERO WITHOUT GIVIN' ADVANCE NOTICE??
YOU JUST DON'T APPRECIATE HOW SERIOUSLY DUNCAN TAKES GYM-RELATED COMMITMENTS, WENDEL!
tap! tap! tap!...
Y'SEE?? HE'S NOT ANSWERING THE TELEPHONE! WHEN HE GETS MAD, HE REFUSES TO ANSWER THE PHONE! HE KNOWS HOW THAT TRIGGERS ALL OF MY NEUROTIC FEARS OF ABANDONMENT!!
Ring... Ring... Ring...
STERNO, FOR CHRIST'S SAKE—WOULD YOU JUST STOP AND LISTEN TO YOURSELF??
WHY? WAS I SAYING SOMETHING INTERESTING?
Ring... Ring... Ring...
Meanwhile—at the other end of the line...
YOU'RE A WEIRD DUDE, DUNCAN—JUST LETTIN' YOUR TELEPHONE RING AN' RING LIKE THAT!
Ring...
Ring...
IT'S ONLY A MACHINE!
Ring...
...WHY SHOULD I LET A MACHINE'S WILL PREVAIL OVER MINE?
Ring...
CRUSE

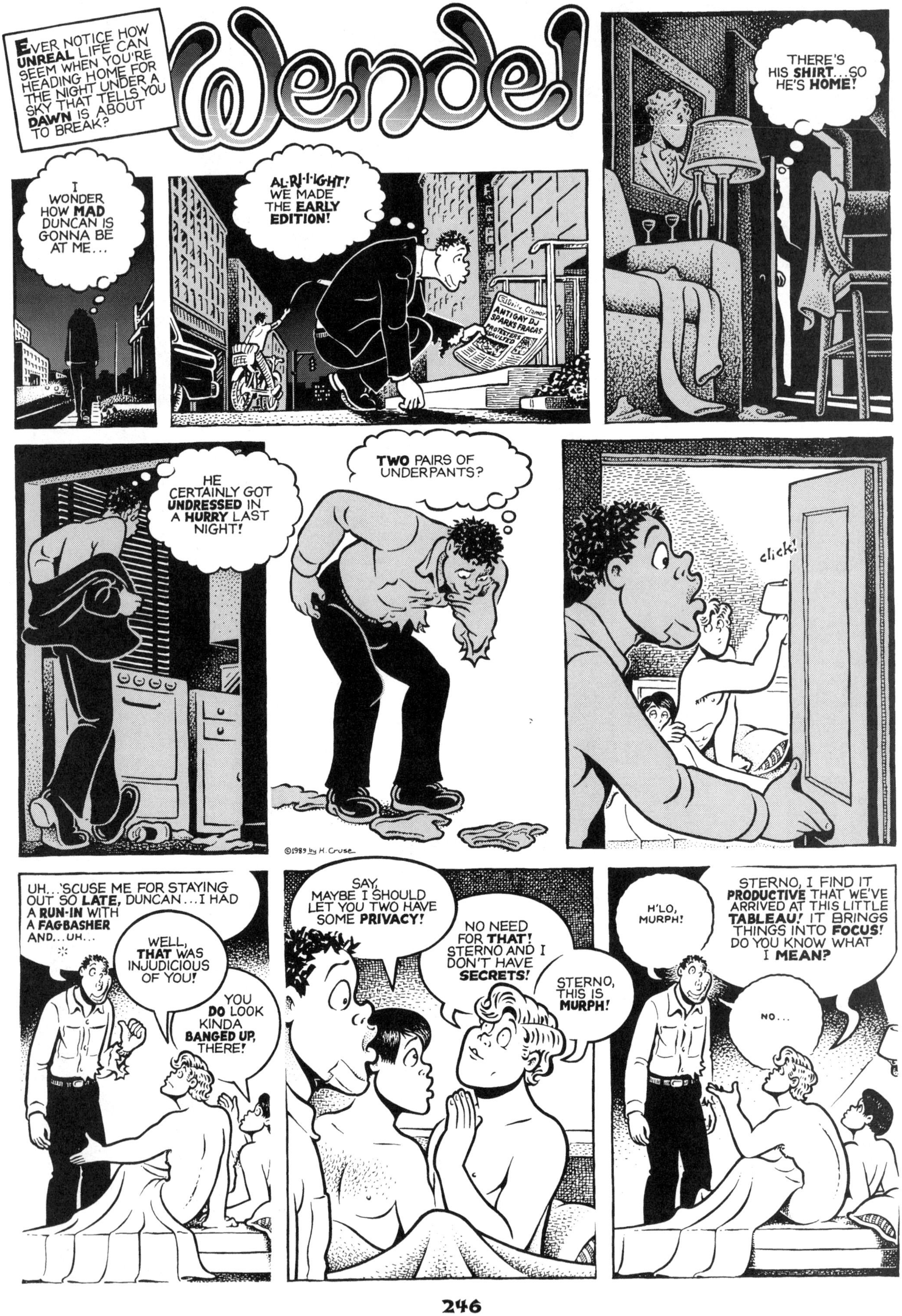
EVER NOTICE HOW UNREAL LIFE CAN SEEM WHEN YOU'RE HEADING HOME FOR THE NIGHT UNDER A SKY THAT TELLS YOU DAWN IS ABOUT TO BREAK?
Wendel
I WONDER HOW MAD DUNCAN IS GONNA BE AT ME...
AL-RI-I-IGHT! WE MADE THE EARLY EDITION!
ANTIGAY DJ SPARKS FRACAS
THERE'S HIS SHIRT... SO HE'S HOME!
HE CERTAINLY GOT UNDRESSED IN A HURRY LAST NIGHT!
TWO PAIRS OF UNDERPANTS?
click!
©1989 by H. Cruse
UH... 'SCUSE ME FOR STAYING OUT SO LATE, DUNCAN... I HAD A RUN-IN WITH A FAGBASHER AND... UH...
WELL, THAT WAS INJUDICIOUS OF YOU!
YOU DO LOOK KINDA BANGED UP, THERE!
SAY, MAYBE I SHOULD LET YOU TWO HAVE SOME PRIVACY!
NO NEED FOR THAT! STERNO AND I DON'T HAVE SECRETS!
STERNO, THIS IS MURPH!
H'LO, MURPH!
STERNO, I FIND IT PRODUCTIVE THAT WE'VE ARRIVED AT THIS LITTLE TABLEAU! IT BRINGS THINGS INTO FOCUS! DO YOU KNOW WHAT I MEAN?
NO...

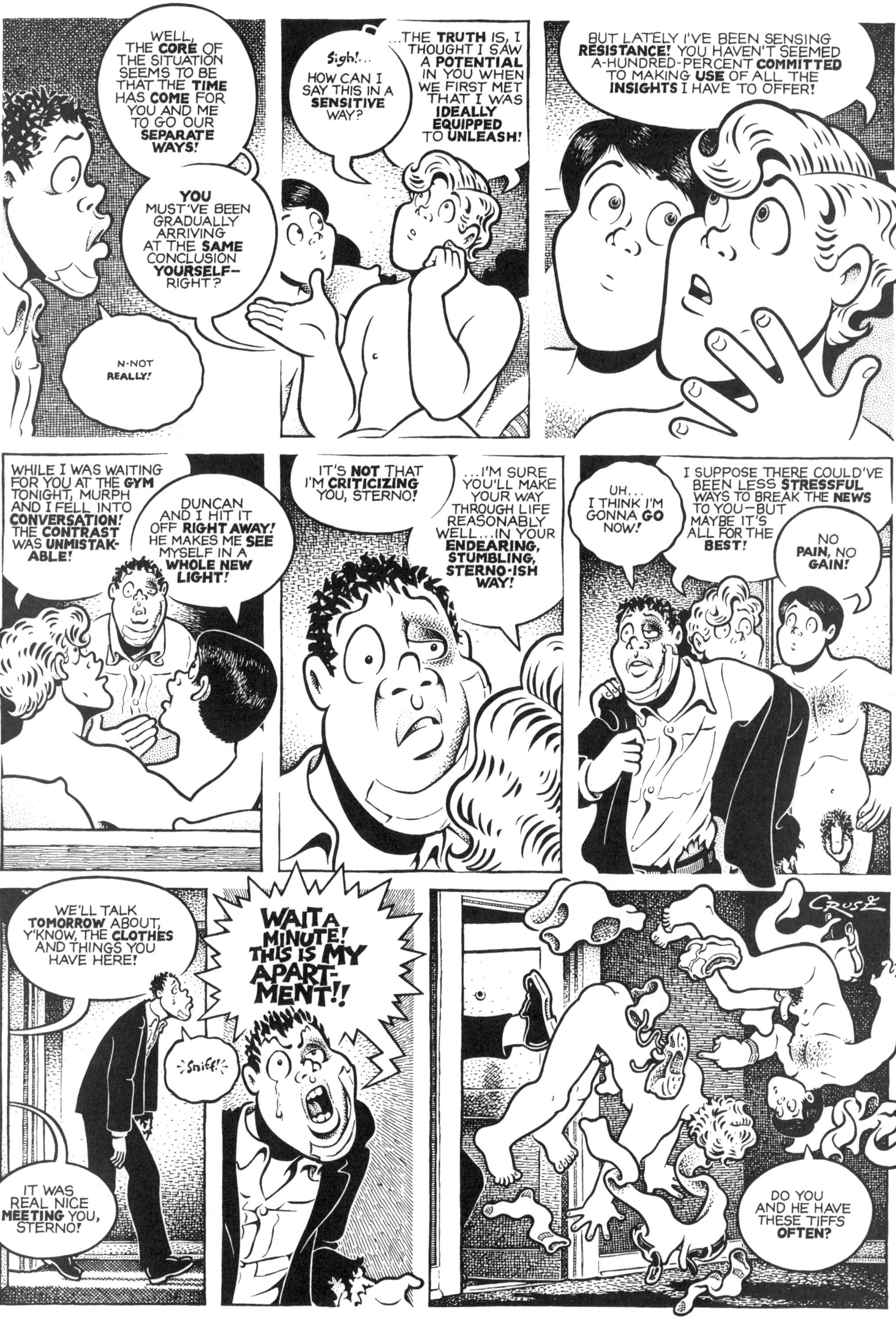
WELL, THE CORE OF THE SITUATION SEEMS TO BE THAT THE TIME HAS COME FOR YOU AND ME TO GO OUR SEPARATE WAYS!
YOU MUST'VE BEEN GRADUALLY ARRIVING AT THE SAME CONCLUSION YOURSELF– RIGHT?
N-NOT REALLY!
Sigh!...
HOW CAN I SAY THIS IN A SENSITIVE WAY?
...THE TRUTH IS, I THOUGHT I SAW A POTENTIAL IN YOU WHEN WE FIRST MET THAT I WAS IDEALLY EQUIPPED TO UNLEASH!
BUT LATELY I'VE BEEN SENSING RESISTANCE! YOU HAVEN'T SEEMED A-HUNDRED-PERCENT COMMITTED TO MAKING USE OF ALL THE INSIGHTS I HAVE TO OFFER!
WHILE I WAS WAITING FOR YOU AT THE GYM TONIGHT, MURPH AND I FELL INTO CONVERSATION! THE CONTRAST WAS UNMISTAKABLE!
DUNCAN AND I HIT IT OFF RIGHT AWAY! HE MAKES ME SEE MYSELF IN A WHOLE NEW LIGHT!
IT'S NOT THAT I'M CRITICIZING YOU, STERNO!
...I'M SURE YOU'LL MAKE YOUR WAY THROUGH LIFE REASONABLY WELL... IN YOUR ENDEARING, STUMBLING, STERNO-ISH WAY!
UH... I THINK I'M GONNA GO NOW!
I SUPPOSE THERE COULD'VE BEEN LESS STRESSFUL WAYS TO BREAK THE NEWS TO YOU–BUT MAYBE IT'S ALL FOR THE BEST!
NO PAIN, NO GAIN!
WE'LL TALK TOMORROW ABOUT, Y'KNOW, THE CLOTHES AND THINGS YOU HAVE HERE!
Sniff!
IT WAS REAL NICE MEETING YOU, STERNO!
WAIT A MINUTE! THIS IS MY APARTMENT!!
CRUSE
DO YOU AND HE HAVE THESE TIFFS OFTEN?

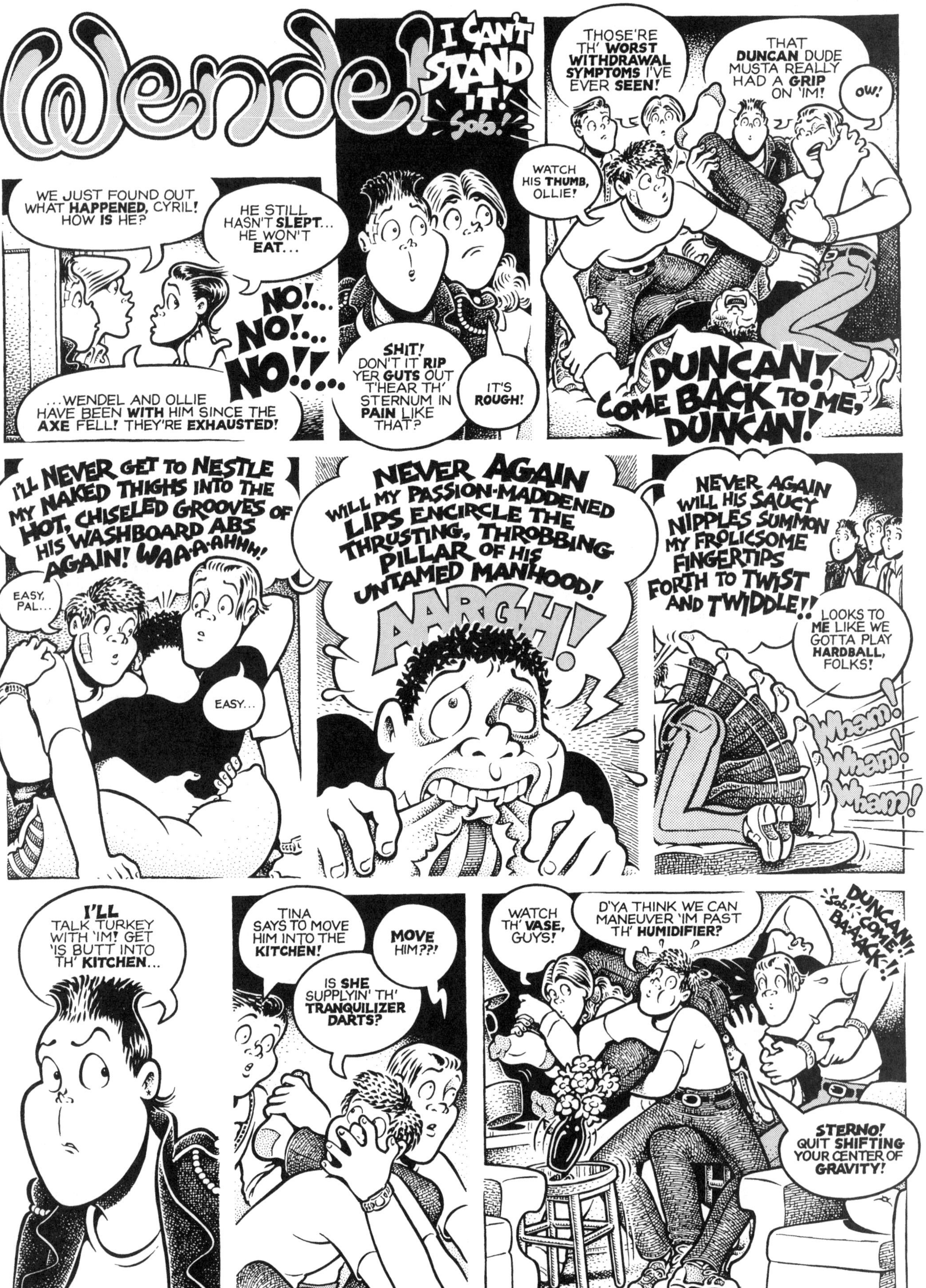
Wendel
I CAN'T STAND IT! Sob!
THOSE'RE TH' WORST WITHDRAWAL SYMPTOMS I'VE EVER SEEN!
THAT DUNCAN DUDE MUSTA REALLY HAD A GRIP ON 'IM!
OW!
WATCH HIS THUMB, OLLIE!
WE JUST FOUND OUT WHAT HAPPENED, CYRIL! HOW IS HE?
HE STILL HASN'T SLEPT... HE WON'T EAT...
NO!... NO!... NO!!...
...WENDEL AND OLLIE HAVE BEEN WITH HIM SINCE THE AXE FELL! THEY'RE EXHAUSTED!
SHIT! DON'T IT RIP YER GUTS OUT T'HEAR TH' STERNUM IN PAIN LIKE THAT?
IT'S ROUGH!
DUNCAN! COME BACK TO ME, DUNCAN!
I'LL NEVER GET TO NESTLE MY NAKED THIGHS INTO THE HOT, CHISELED GROOVES OF HIS WASHBOARD ABS AGAIN! WAA-A-AHHH!
EASY, PAL...
EASY...
NEVER AGAIN WILL MY PASSION-MADDENED LIPS ENCIRCLE THE THRUSTING, THROBBING PILLAR OF HIS UNTAMED MANHOOD!
AARGH!
NEVER AGAIN WILL HIS SAUCY NIPPLES SUMMON MY FROLICSOME FINGERTIPS FORTH TO TWIST AND TWIDDLE!!
LOOKS TO ME LIKE WE GOTTA PLAY HARDBALL, FOLKS!
Wham! Wham! Wham!
I'LL TALK TURKEY WITH 'IM! GET 'IS BUTT INTO TH' KITCHEN...
TINA SAYS TO MOVE HIM INTO THE KITCHEN!
MOVE HIM??!
IS SHE SUPPLYIN' TH' TRANQUILIZER DARTS?
WATCH TH' VASE, GUYS!
D'YA THINK WE CAN MANEUVER 'IM PAST TH' HUMIDIFIER?
DUNCAN!! Sob! COME BA-AACK!!
STERNO! QUIT SHIFTING YOUR CENTER OF GRAVITY!
©1989 by H. Cruse

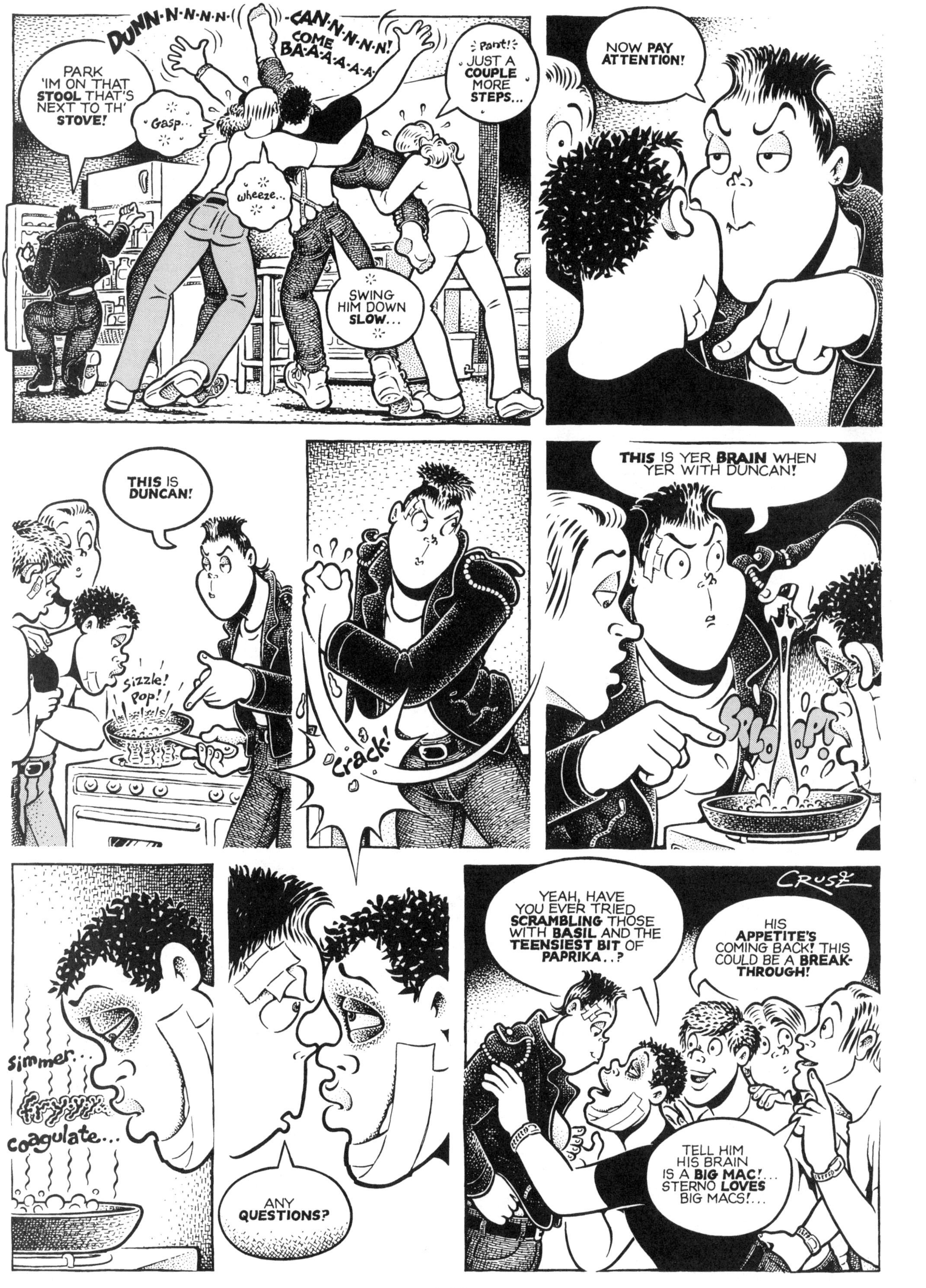
DUNN-N-N-N-N-((-CAN-N-N-N-N!
COME BA-A-A-A-A-A-
PARK 'IM ON THAT STOOL THAT'S NEXT TO TH' STOVE!
Gasp...
wheeze...
Pant! JUST A COUPLE MORE STEPS...
SWING HIM DOWN SLOW...
NOW PAY ATTENTION!
THIS IS DUNCAN!
Sizzle! Pop!
Crack!
THIS IS YER BRAIN WHEN YER WITH DUNCAN!
SPLOOP!
simmer...
fryyy...
coagulate...
ANY QUESTIONS?
CRUSE
YEAH, HAVE YOU EVER TRIED SCRAMBLING THOSE WITH BASIL AND THE TEENSIEST BIT OF PAPRIKA..?
HIS APPETITE'S COMING BACK! THIS COULD BE A BREAK-THROUGH!
TELL HIM HIS BRAIN IS A BIG MAC!... STERNO LOVES BIG MACS!...

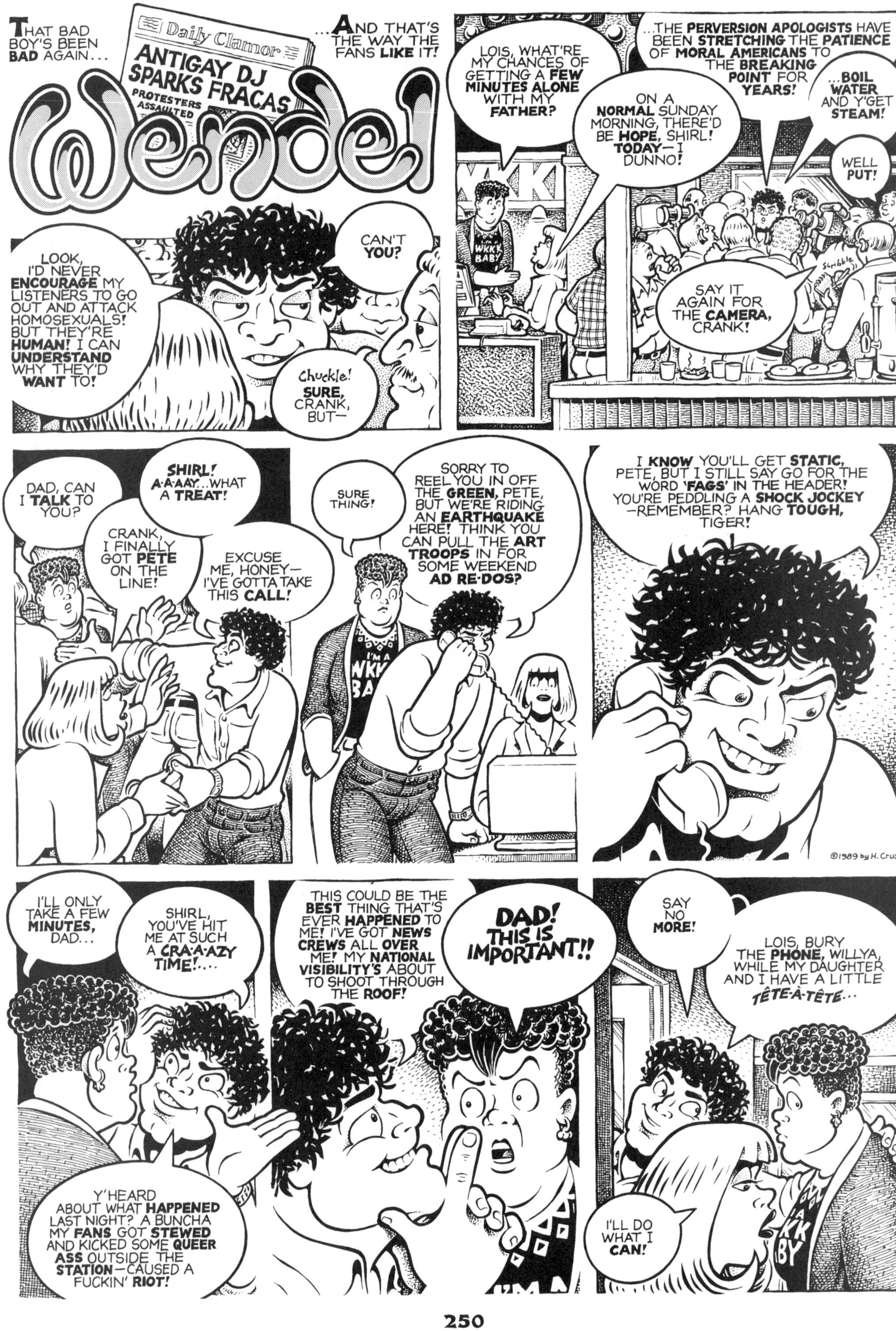

THAT BAD BOY'S BEEN BAD AGAIN...
Daily Clamor
ANTIGAY DJ SPARKS FRACAS
PROTESTERS ASSAULTED
...AND THAT'S THE WAY THE FANS LIKE IT!
Wendel
LOOK, I'D NEVER ENCOURAGE MY LISTENERS TO GO OUT AND ATTACK HOMOSEXUALS! BUT THEY'RE HUMAN! I CAN UNDERSTAND WHY THEY'D WANT TO!
CAN'T YOU?
Chuckle! SURE, CRANK, BUT—
LOIS, WHAT'RE MY CHANCES OF GETTING A FEW MINUTES ALONE WITH MY FATHER?
ON A NORMAL SUNDAY MORNING, THERE'D BE HOPE, SHIRL! TODAY—I DUNNO!
...THE PERVERSION APOLOGISTS HAVE BEEN STRETCHING THE PATIENCE OF MORAL AMERICANS TO THE BREAKING POINT FOR YEARS!
...BOIL WATER AND Y'GET STEAM!
WELL PUT!
SAY IT AGAIN FOR THE CAMERA, CRANK!
Scribble
DAD, CAN I TALK TO YOU?
SHIRL! A-A-AAY...WHAT A TREAT!
CRANK, I FINALLY GOT PETE ON THE LINE!
EXCUSE ME, HONEY—I'VE GOTTA TAKE THIS CALL!
SURE THING!
SORRY TO REEL YOU IN OFF THE GREEN, PETE, BUT WE'RE RIDING AN EARTHQUAKE HERE! THINK YOU CAN PULL THE ART TROOPS IN FOR SOME WEEKEND AD RE-DOS?
I KNOW YOU'LL GET STATIC, PETE, BUT I STILL SAY GO FOR THE WORD 'FAGS' IN THE HEADER! YOU'RE PEDDLING A SHOCK JOCKEY —REMEMBER? HANG TOUGH, TIGER!
©1989 by H. Cruse
I'LL ONLY TAKE A FEW MINUTES, DAD...
SHIRL, YOU'VE HIT ME AT SUCH A CRA-A-AZY TIME!...
Y'HEARD ABOUT WHAT HAPPENED LAST NIGHT? A BUNCHA MY FANS GOT STEWED AND KICKED SOME QUEER ASS OUTSIDE THE STATION—CAUSED A FUCKIN' RIOT!
THIS COULD BE THE BEST THING THAT'S EVER HAPPENED TO ME! I'VE GOT NEWS CREWS ALL OVER ME! MY NATIONAL VISIBILITY'S ABOUT TO SHOOT THROUGH THE ROOF!
DAD! THIS IS IMPORTANT!!
SAY NO MORE!
LOIS, BURY THE PHONE, WILLYA, WHILE MY DAUGHTER AND I HAVE A LITTLE TÊTE-À-TÊTE...
I'LL DO WHAT I CAN!

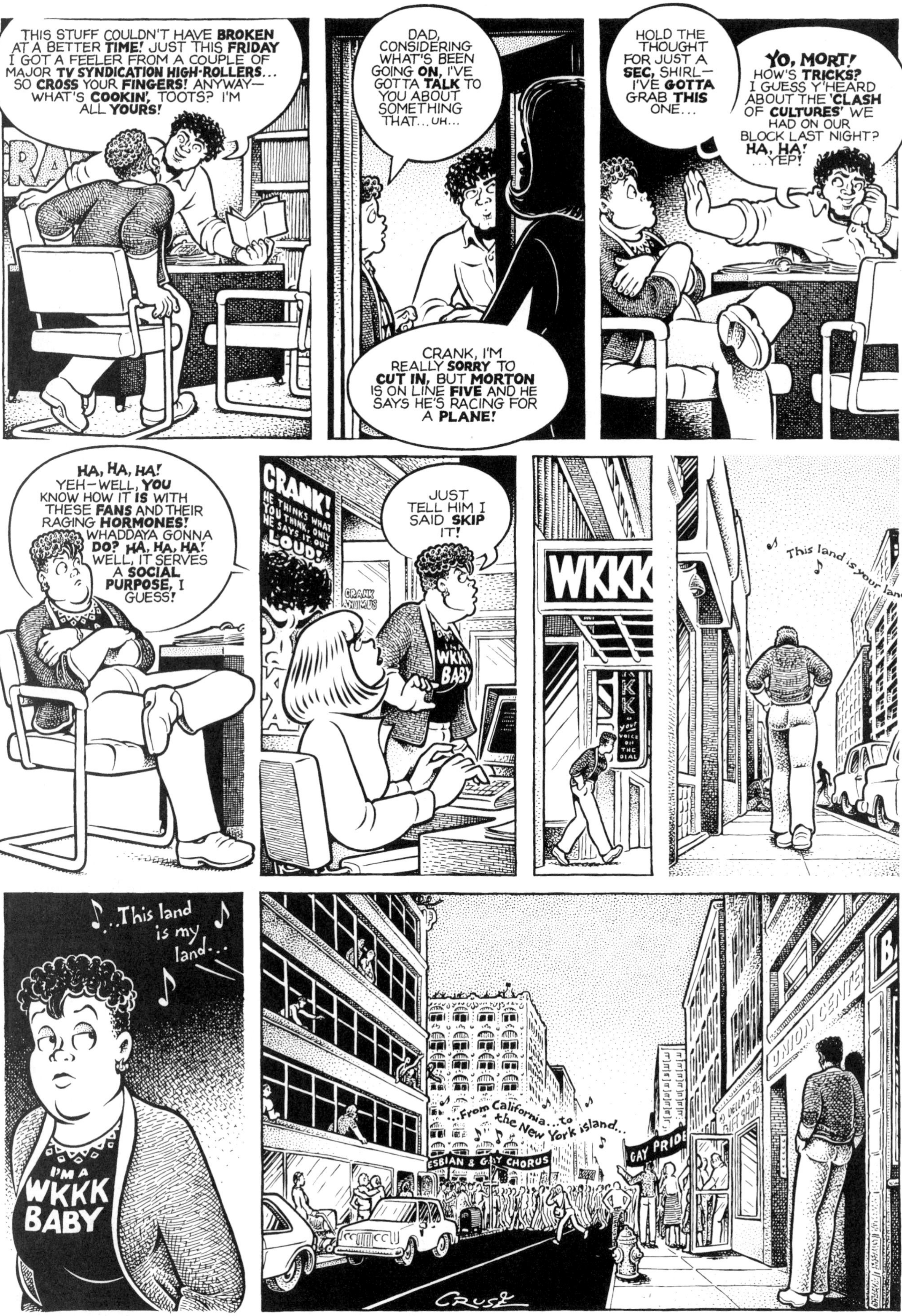
THIS STUFF COULDN'T HAVE BROKEN AT A BETTER TIME! JUST THIS FRIDAY I GOT A FEELER FROM A COUPLE OF MAJOR TV SYNDICATION HIGH-ROLLERS... SO CROSS YOUR FINGERS! ANYWAY— WHAT'S COOKIN', TOOTS? I'M ALL YOURS!
DAD, CONSIDERING WHAT'S BEEN GOING ON, I'VE GOTTA TALK TO YOU ABOUT SOMETHING THAT... UH...
CRANK, I'M REALLY SORRY TO CUT IN, BUT MORTON IS ON LINE FIVE AND HE SAYS HE'S RACING FOR A PLANE!
HOLD THE THOUGHT FOR JUST A SEC, SHIRL— I'VE GOTTA GRAB THIS ONE...
YO, MORT! HOW'S TRICKS? I GUESS Y'HEARD ABOUT THE 'CLASH OF CULTURES' WE HAD ON OUR BLOCK LAST NIGHT? HA, HA! ...YEP!
HA, HA, HA! YEH—WELL, YOU KNOW HOW IT IS WITH THESE FANS AND THEIR RAGING HORMONES! WHADDAYA GONNA DO? HA, HA, HA! WELL, IT SERVES A SOCIAL PURPOSE, I GUESS!
CRANK! HE THINKS WHAT YOU THINK, ONLY HE SAYS IT OUT LOUD!
JUST TELL HIM I SAID SKIP IT!
I'M A WKKK BABY
WKKK
This land is your land...
...This land is my land...
I'M A WKKK BABY
...From California...to the New York island...
LESBIAN & GAY CHORUS
GAY PRIDE
UNION CENTER
CRUSE

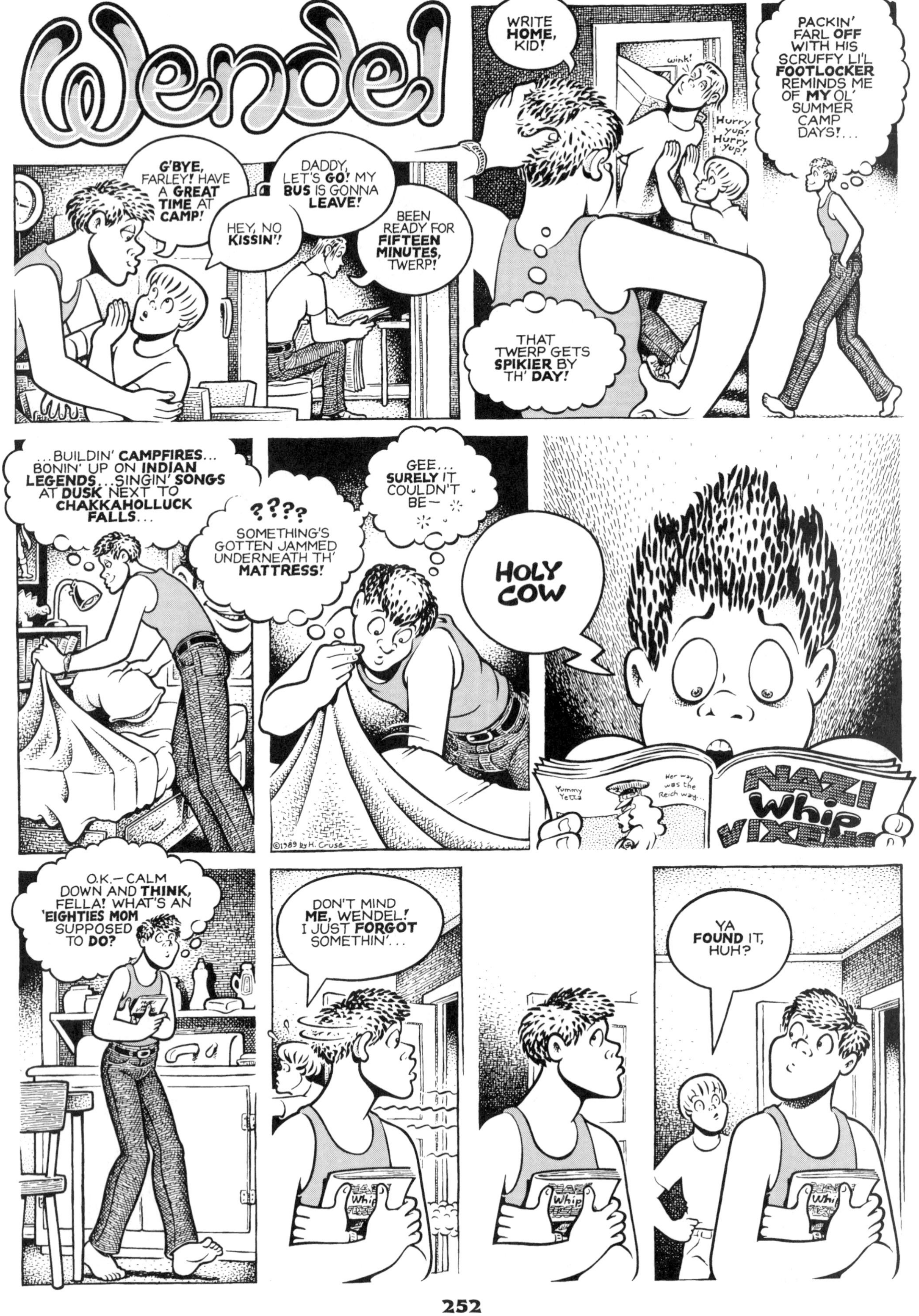

Wendel
G'BYE, FARLEY! HAVE A GREAT TIME AT CAMP!
HEY, NO KISSIN'!
DADDY, LET'S GO! MY BUS IS GONNA LEAVE!
BEEN READY FOR FIFTEEN MINUTES, TWERP!
WRITE HOME, KID!
wink!
Hurry yup! Hurry yup!
THAT TWERP GETS SPIKIER BY TH' DAY!
PACKIN' FARL OFF WITH HIS SCRUFFY LI'L FOOTLOCKER REMINDS ME OF MY OL' SUMMER CAMP DAYS!...
...BUILDIN' CAMPFIRES... BONIN' UP ON INDIAN LEGENDS... SINGIN' SONGS AT DUSK NEXT TO CHAKKAHOLLUCK FALLS...
????
SOMETHING'S GOTTEN JAMMED UNDERNEATH TH' MATTRESS!
GEE... SURELY IT COULDN'T BE—
©1989 by H. Cruse
HOLY COW
Yummy Yetta
Her way was the Reich way...
NAZI Whip VIXENS
O.K.—CALM DOWN AND THINK, FELLA! WHAT'S AN 'EIGHTIES MOM SUPPOSED TO DO?
DON'T MIND ME, WENDEL! I JUST FORGOT SOMETHIN'...
YA FOUND IT, HUH?

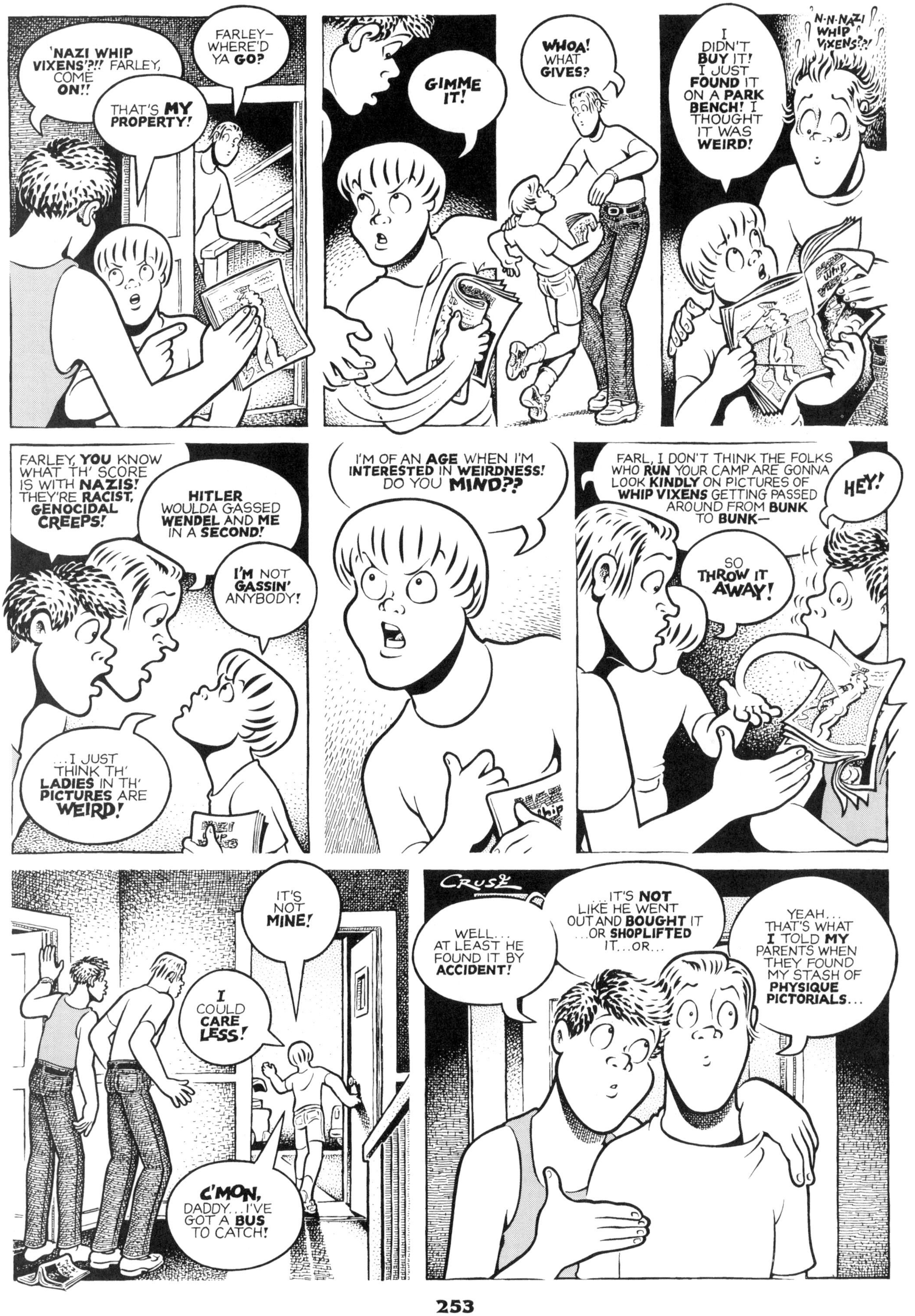
'NAZI WHIP VIXENS'?!! FARLEY, COME ON!!
FARLEY— WHERE'D YA GO?
THAT'S MY PROPERTY!
GIMME IT!
WHOA! WHAT GIVES?
N-N-NAZI WHIP VIXENS?!?!
I DIDN'T BUY IT! I JUST FOUND IT ON A PARK BENCH! I THOUGHT IT WAS WEIRD!
FARLEY, YOU KNOW WHAT TH' SCORE IS WITH NAZIS! THEY'RE RACIST, GENOCIDAL CREEPS!
HITLER WOULDA GASSED WENDEL AND ME IN A SECOND!
I'M NOT GASSIN' ANYBODY!
...I JUST THINK TH' LADIES IN TH' PICTURES ARE WEIRD!
I'M OF AN AGE WHEN I'M INTERESTED IN WEIRDNESS! DO YOU MIND??
FARL, I DON'T THINK THE FOLKS WHO RUN YOUR CAMP ARE GONNA LOOK KINDLY ON PICTURES OF WHIP VIXENS GETTING PASSED AROUND FROM BUNK TO BUNK—
HEY!
SO THROW IT AWAY!
IT'S NOT MINE!
I COULD CARE LESS!
C'MON, DADDY... I'VE GOT A BUS TO CATCH!
CRUSE
WELL... AT LEAST HE FOUND IT BY ACCIDENT!
...IT'S NOT LIKE HE WENT OUT AND BOUGHT IT ...OR SHOPLIFTED IT...OR...
YEAH... THAT'S WHAT I TOLD MY PARENTS WHEN THEY FOUND MY STASH OF PHYSIQUE PICTORIALS...

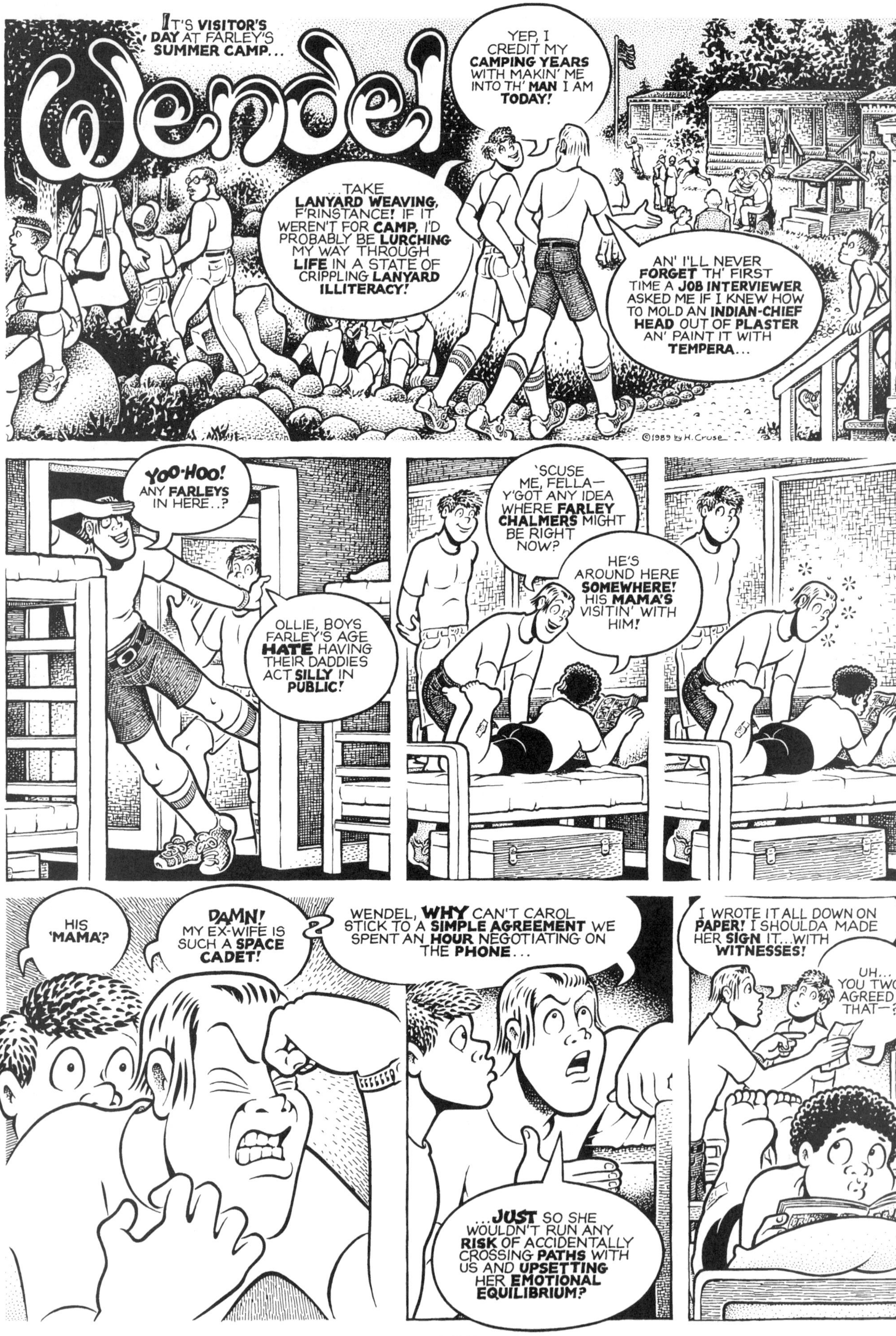
IT'S VISITOR'S DAY AT FARLEY'S SUMMER CAMP...
Wendel
YEP, I CREDIT MY CAMPING YEARS WITH MAKIN' ME INTO TH' MAN I AM TODAY!
...TAKE LANYARD WEAVING, F'RINSTANCE! IF IT WEREN'T FOR CAMP, I'D PROBABLY BE LURCHING MY WAY THROUGH LIFE IN A STATE OF CRIPPLING LANYARD ILLITERACY!
AN' I'LL NEVER FORGET TH' FIRST TIME A JOB INTERVIEWER ASKED ME IF I KNEW HOW TO MOLD AN INDIAN-CHIEF HEAD OUT OF PLASTER AN' PAINT IT WITH TEMPERA...
©1989 by H. Cruse
YOO-HOO! ANY FARLEYS IN HERE..?
OLLIE, BOYS FARLEY'S AGE HATE HAVING THEIR DADDIES ACT SILLY IN PUBLIC!
'SCUSE ME, FELLA— Y'GOT ANY IDEA WHERE FARLEY CHALMERS MIGHT BE RIGHT NOW?
HE'S AROUND HERE SOMEWHERE! HIS MAMA'S VISITIN' WITH HIM!
HIS 'MAMA'?
DAMN! MY EX-WIFE IS SUCH A SPACE CADET!
WENDEL, WHY CAN'T CAROL STICK TO A SIMPLE AGREEMENT WE SPENT AN HOUR NEGOTIATING ON THE PHONE...
...JUST SO SHE WOULDN'T RUN ANY RISK OF ACCIDENTALLY CROSSING PATHS WITH US AND UPSETTING HER EMOTIONAL EQUILIBRIUM?
I WROTE IT ALL DOWN ON PAPER! I SHOULDA MADE HER SIGN IT...WITH WITNESSES!
UH... YOU TWO AGREED THAT—?

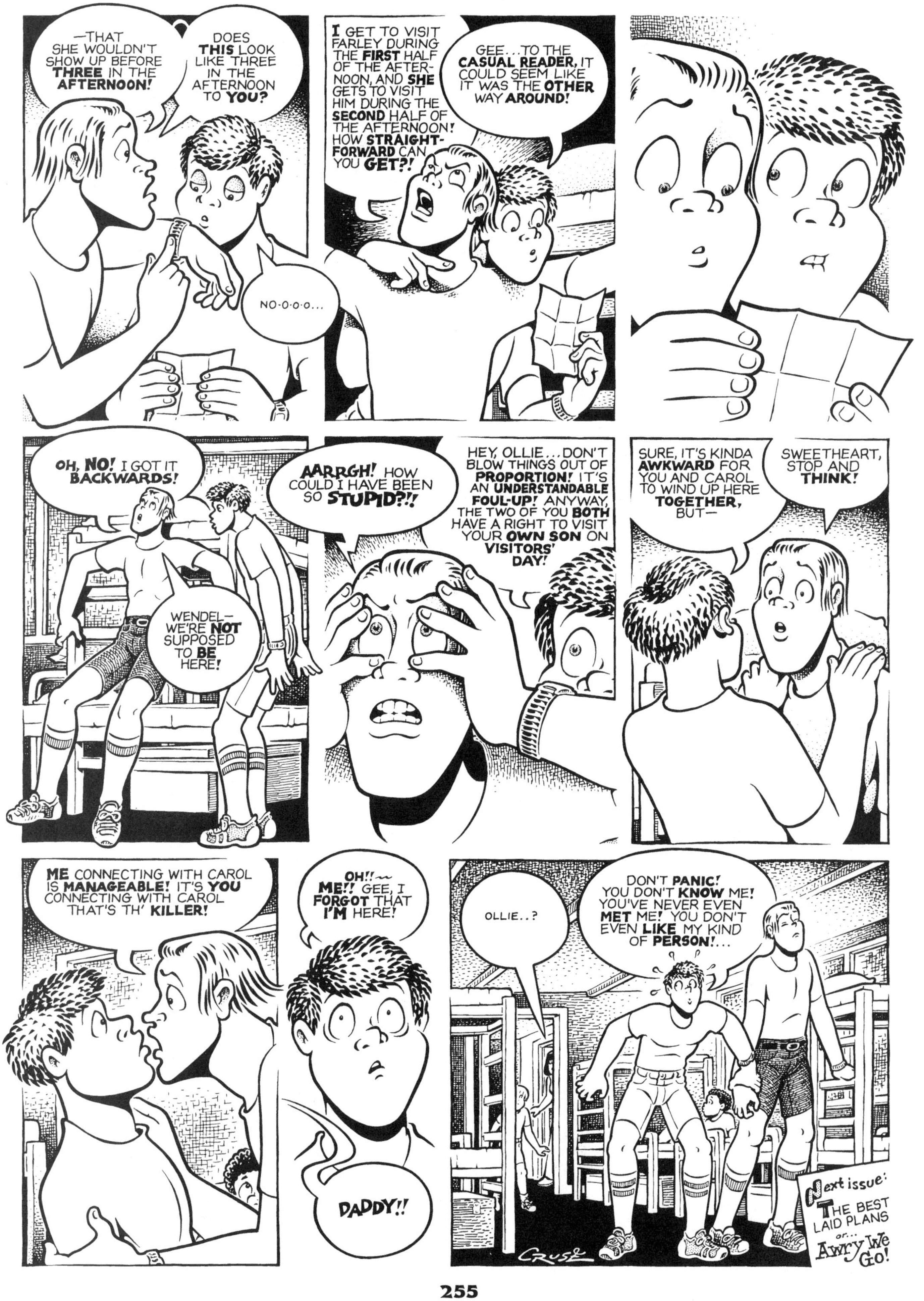
—THAT SHE WOULDN'T SHOW UP BEFORE THREE IN THE AFTERNOON!
DOES THIS LOOK LIKE THREE IN THE AFTERNOON TO YOU?
NO-O-O-O...
I GET TO VISIT FARLEY DURING THE FIRST HALF OF THE AFTERNOON, AND SHE GETS TO VISIT HIM DURING THE SECOND HALF OF THE AFTERNOON! HOW STRAIGHT-FORWARD CAN YOU GET?!
GEE... TO THE CASUAL READER, IT COULD SEEM LIKE IT WAS THE OTHER WAY AROUND!
OH, NO! I GOT IT BACKWARDS!
WENDEL—WE'RE NOT SUPPOSED TO BE HERE!
AARRGH! HOW COULD I HAVE BEEN SO STUPID?!!
HEY, OLLIE... DON'T BLOW THINGS OUT OF PROPORTION! IT'S AN UNDERSTANDABLE FOUL-UP! ANYWAY, THE TWO OF YOU BOTH HAVE A RIGHT TO VISIT YOUR OWN SON ON VISITORS' DAY!
SURE, IT'S KINDA AWKWARD FOR YOU AND CAROL TO WIND UP HERE TOGETHER, BUT—
SWEETHEART, STOP AND THINK!
ME CONNECTING WITH CAROL IS MANAGEABLE! IT'S YOU CONNECTING WITH CAROL THAT'S TH' KILLER!
OH!!~ ME!! GEE, I FORGOT THAT I'M HERE!
DADDY!!
OLLIE..?
DON'T PANIC! YOU DON'T KNOW ME! YOU'VE NEVER EVEN MET ME! YOU DON'T EVEN LIKE MY KIND OF PERSON!...
CRUSE
Next issue: THE BEST LAID PLANS or... Awry We Go!

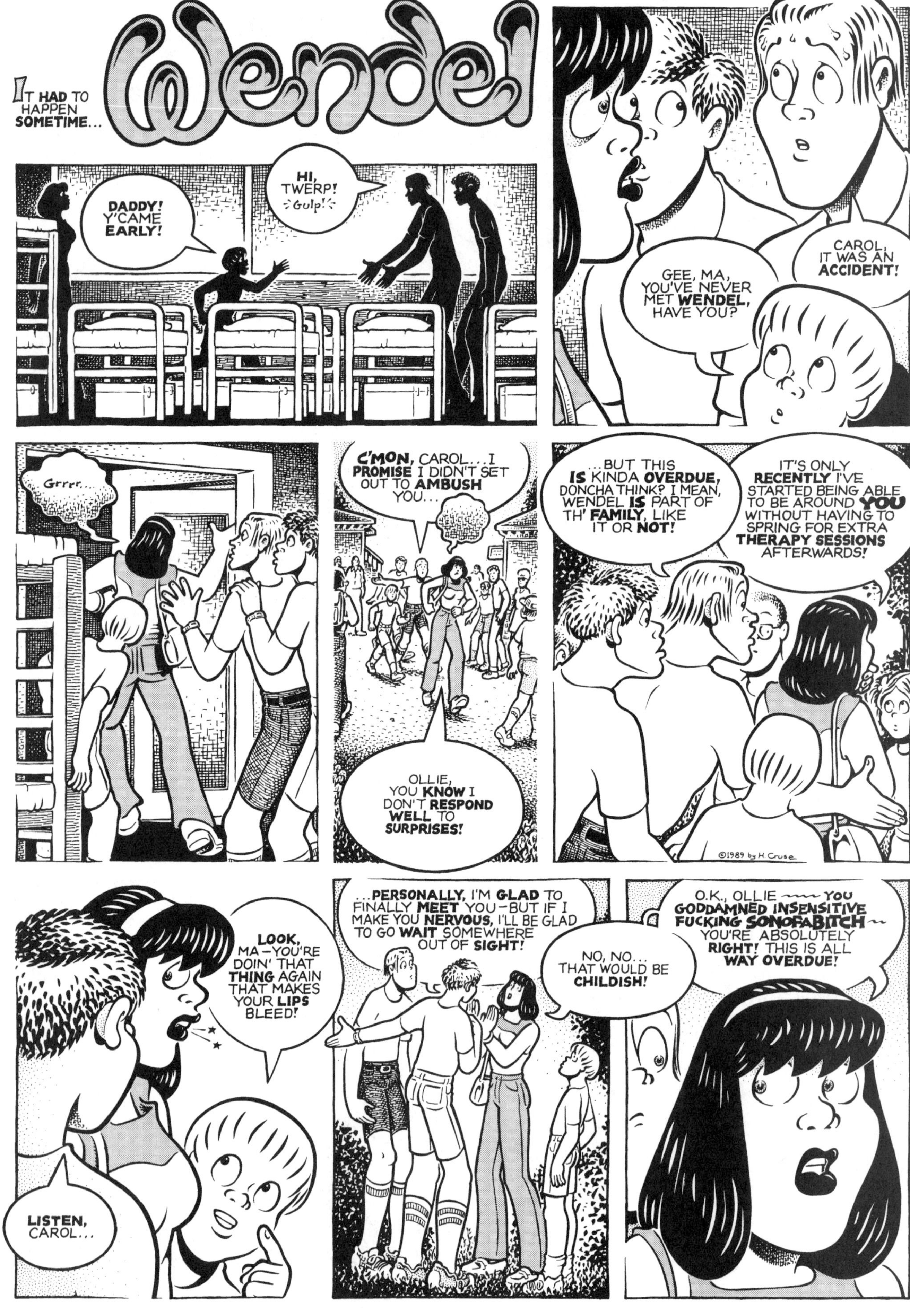
IT HAD TO HAPPEN SOMETIME...
Wendel
DADDY! Y'CAME EARLY!
HI, TWERP! -Gulp!-
GEE, MA, YOU'VE NEVER MET WENDEL, HAVE YOU?
CAROL, IT WAS AN ACCIDENT!
Grrrr...
C'MON, CAROL... I PROMISE I DIDN'T SET OUT TO AMBUSH YOU...
OLLIE, YOU KNOW I DON'T RESPOND WELL TO SURPRISES!
...BUT THIS IS KINDA OVERDUE, DONCHA THINK? I MEAN, WENDEL IS PART OF TH' FAMILY, LIKE IT OR NOT!
IT'S ONLY RECENTLY I'VE STARTED BEING ABLE TO BE AROUND YOU WITHOUT HAVING TO SPRING FOR EXTRA THERAPY SESSIONS AFTERWARDS!
©1989 by H. Cruse
LOOK, MA—YOU'RE DOIN' THAT THING AGAIN THAT MAKES YOUR LIPS BLEED!
LISTEN, CAROL...
...PERSONALLY, I'M GLAD TO FINALLY MEET YOU—BUT IF I MAKE YOU NERVOUS, I'LL BE GLAD TO GO WAIT SOMEWHERE OUT OF SIGHT!
NO, NO... THAT WOULD BE CHILDISH!
O.K., OLLIE ~~ YOU GODDAMNED INSENSITIVE FUCKING SONOFABITCH ~ YOU'RE ABSOLUTELY RIGHT! THIS IS ALL WAY OVERDUE!

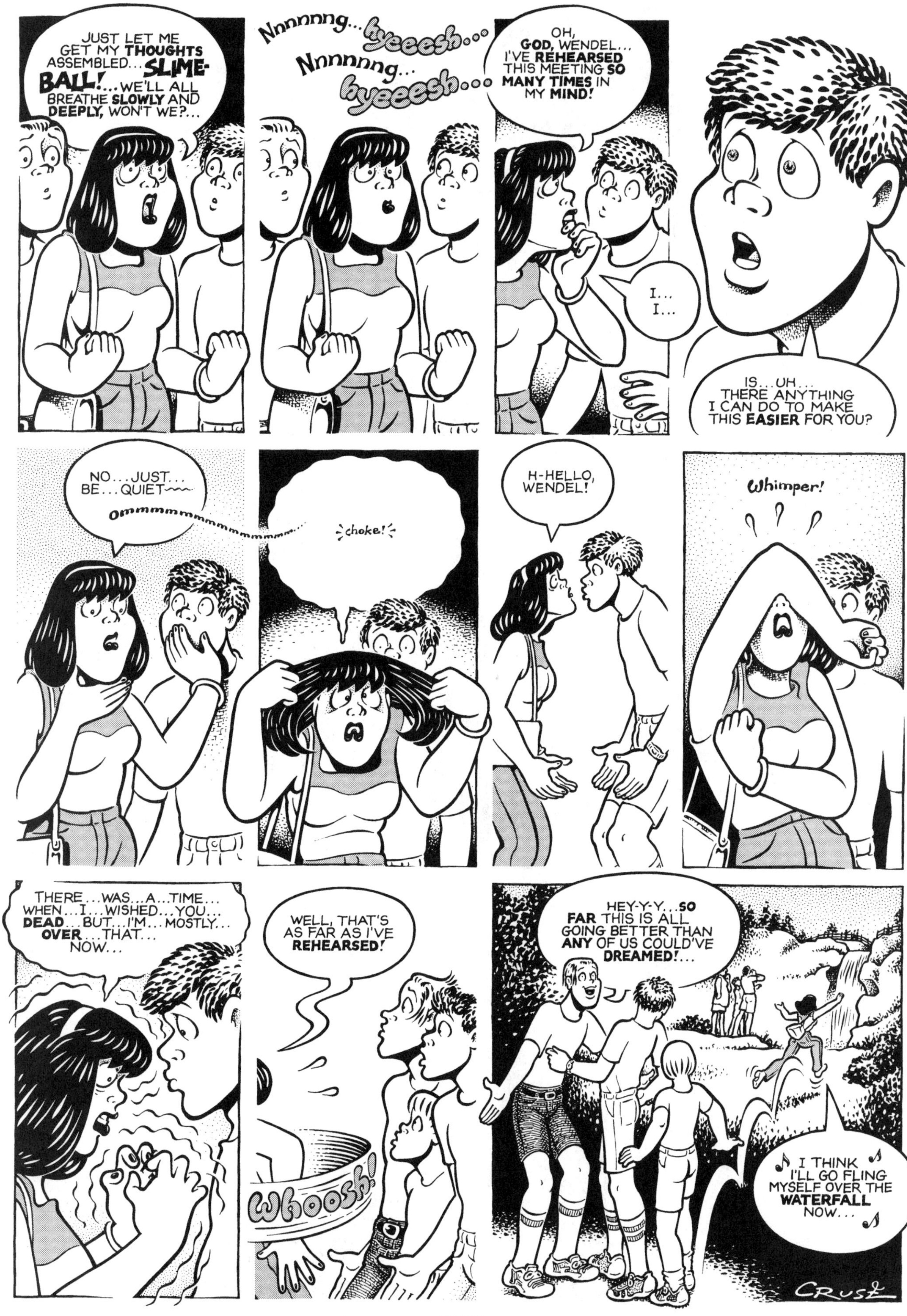
JUST LET ME GET MY **THOUGHTS** ASSEMBLED... **SLIME-BALL!**... WE'LL ALL BREATHE **SLOWLY** AND **DEEPLY**, WON'T WE?...
Nnnnnng... hyeeesh...
Nnnnnng... hyeeesh...
OH, **GOD**, WENDEL... I'VE **REHEARSED** THIS MEETING **SO MANY TIMES** IN MY **MIND!**
I... I...
IS... UH... THERE ANYTHING I CAN DO TO MAKE THIS **EASIER** FOR YOU?
NO... JUST... BE... QUIET~~~
Ommmmmmmmmmmmmmm...
choke!
H-HELLO, WENDEL!
Whimper!
THERE... WAS... A... TIME... WHEN... I... WISHED... YOU... **DEAD**... BUT... I'M... MOSTLY... **OVER**... THAT... NOW...
WELL, THAT'S AS FAR AS I'VE **REHEARSED!**
Whoosh!
HEY-Y-Y... **SO FAR** THIS IS ALL GOING BETTER THAN **ANY** OF US COULD'VE **DREAMED!**...
I THINK I'LL GO FLING MYSELF OVER THE **WATERFALL** NOW...
CRUSE

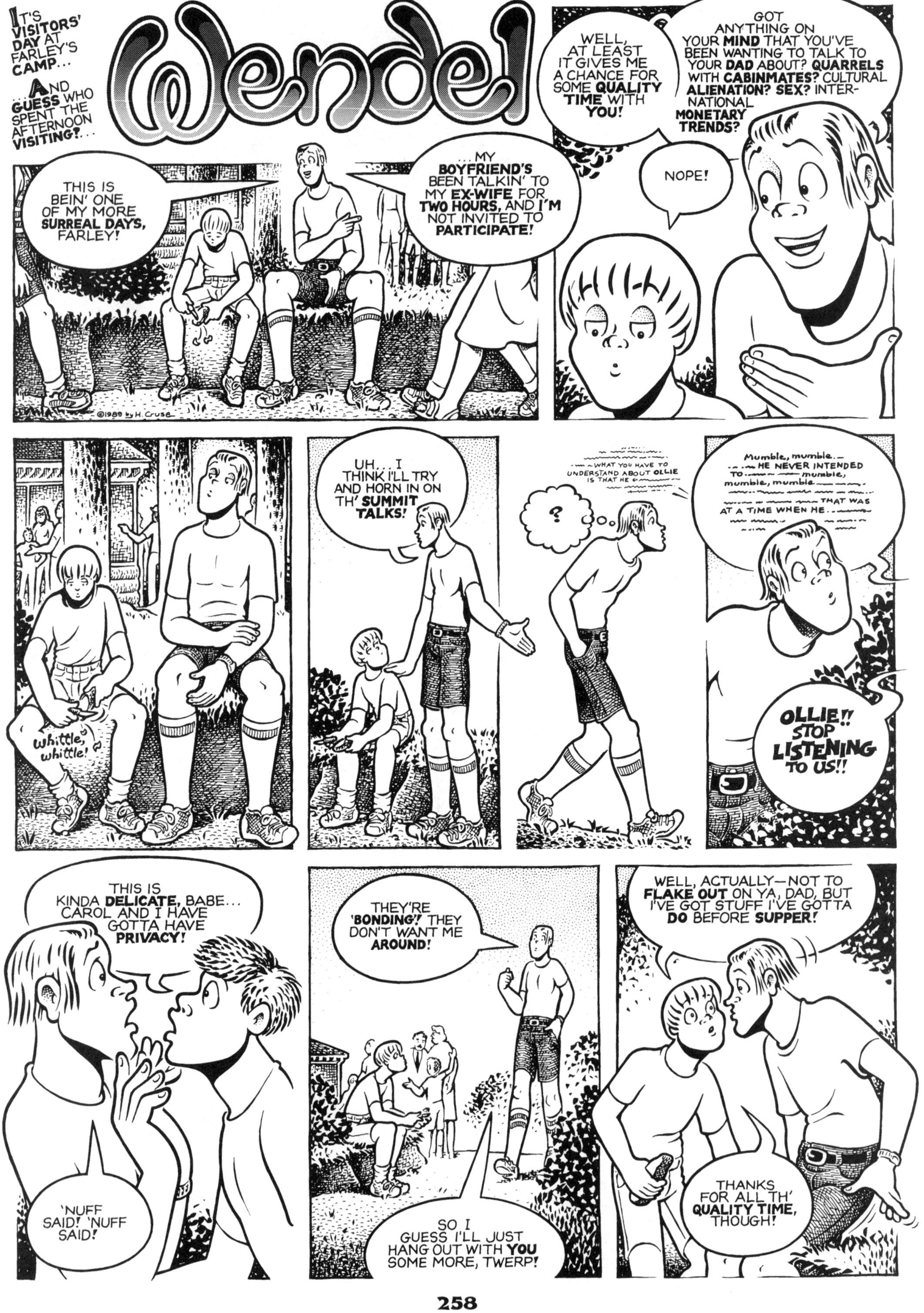

IT'S VISITORS' DAY AT FARLEY'S CAMP...
...AND GUESS WHO SPENT THE AFTERNOON VISITING?...
Wendel
THIS IS BEIN' ONE OF MY MORE SURREAL DAYS, FARLEY!
...MY BOYFRIEND'S BEEN TALKIN' TO MY EX-WIFE FOR TWO HOURS, AND I'M NOT INVITED TO PARTICIPATE!
©1989 by H. Cruse
WELL, AT LEAST IT GIVES ME A CHANCE FOR SOME QUALITY TIME WITH YOU!
GOT ANYTHING ON YOUR MIND THAT YOU'VE BEEN WANTING TO TALK TO YOUR DAD ABOUT? QUARRELS WITH CABINMATES? CULTURAL ALIENATION? SEX? INTER-NATIONAL MONETARY TRENDS?
NOPE!
whittle, whittle!
UH... I THINK I'LL TRY AND HORN IN ON TH' SUMMIT TALKS!
WHAT YOU HAVE TO UNDERSTAND ABOUT OLLIE IS THAT HE
?
Mumble, mumble. HE NEVER INTENDED TO mumble, mumble, mumble THAT WAS AT A TIME WHEN HE.
OLLIE!! STOP LISTENING TO US!!
THIS IS KINDA DELICATE, BABE... CAROL AND I HAVE GOTTA HAVE PRIVACY!
'NUFF SAID! 'NUFF SAID!
THEY'RE 'BONDING!' THEY DON'T WANT ME AROUND!
SO I GUESS I'LL JUST HANG OUT WITH YOU SOME MORE, TWERP!
WELL, ACTUALLY—NOT TO FLAKE OUT ON YA, DAD, BUT I'VE GOT STUFF I'VE GOTTA DO BEFORE SUPPER!
THANKS FOR ALL TH' QUALITY TIME, THOUGH!

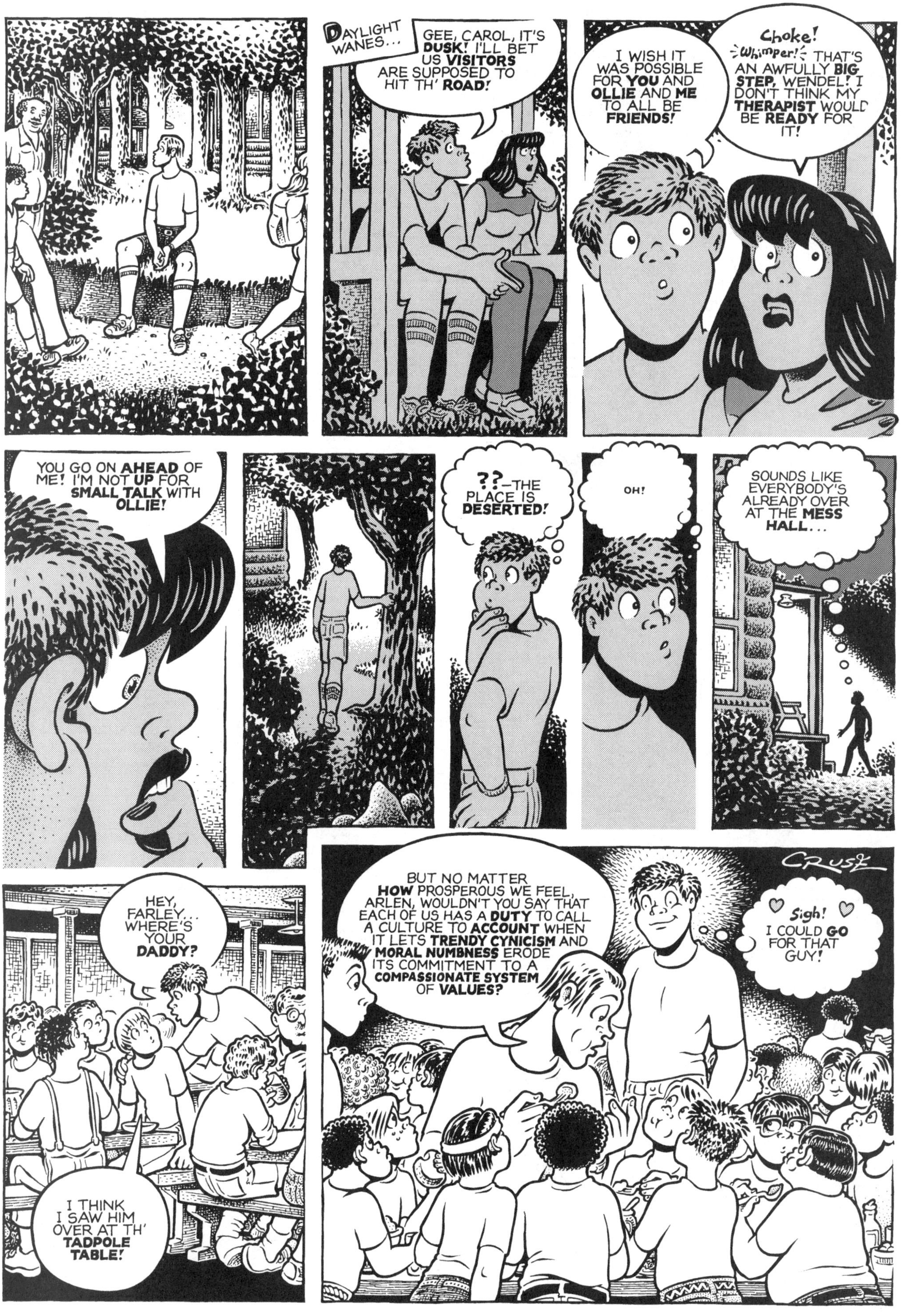
DAYLIGHT WANES...
GEE, CAROL, IT'S DUSK! I'LL BET US VISITORS ARE SUPPOSED TO HIT TH' ROAD!
I WISH IT WAS POSSIBLE FOR YOU AND OLLIE AND ME TO ALL BE FRIENDS!
Choke! Whimper! THAT'S AN AWFULLY BIG STEP, WENDEL! I DON'T THINK MY THERAPIST WOULD BE READY FOR IT!
YOU GO ON AHEAD OF ME! I'M NOT UP FOR SMALL TALK WITH OLLIE!
??—THE PLACE IS DESERTED!
OH!
SOUNDS LIKE EVERYBODY'S ALREADY OVER AT THE MESS HALL...
HEY, FARLEY... WHERE'S YOUR DADDY?
I THINK I SAW HIM OVER AT TH' TADPOLE TABLE!
BUT NO MATTER HOW PROSPEROUS WE FEEL, ARLEN, WOULDN'T YOU SAY THAT EACH OF US HAS A DUTY TO CALL A CULTURE TO ACCOUNT WHEN IT LETS TRENDY CYNICISM AND MORAL NUMBNESS ERODE ITS COMMITMENT TO A COMPASSIONATE SYSTEM OF VALUES?
Sigh! I COULD GO FOR THAT GUY!
CRUSE

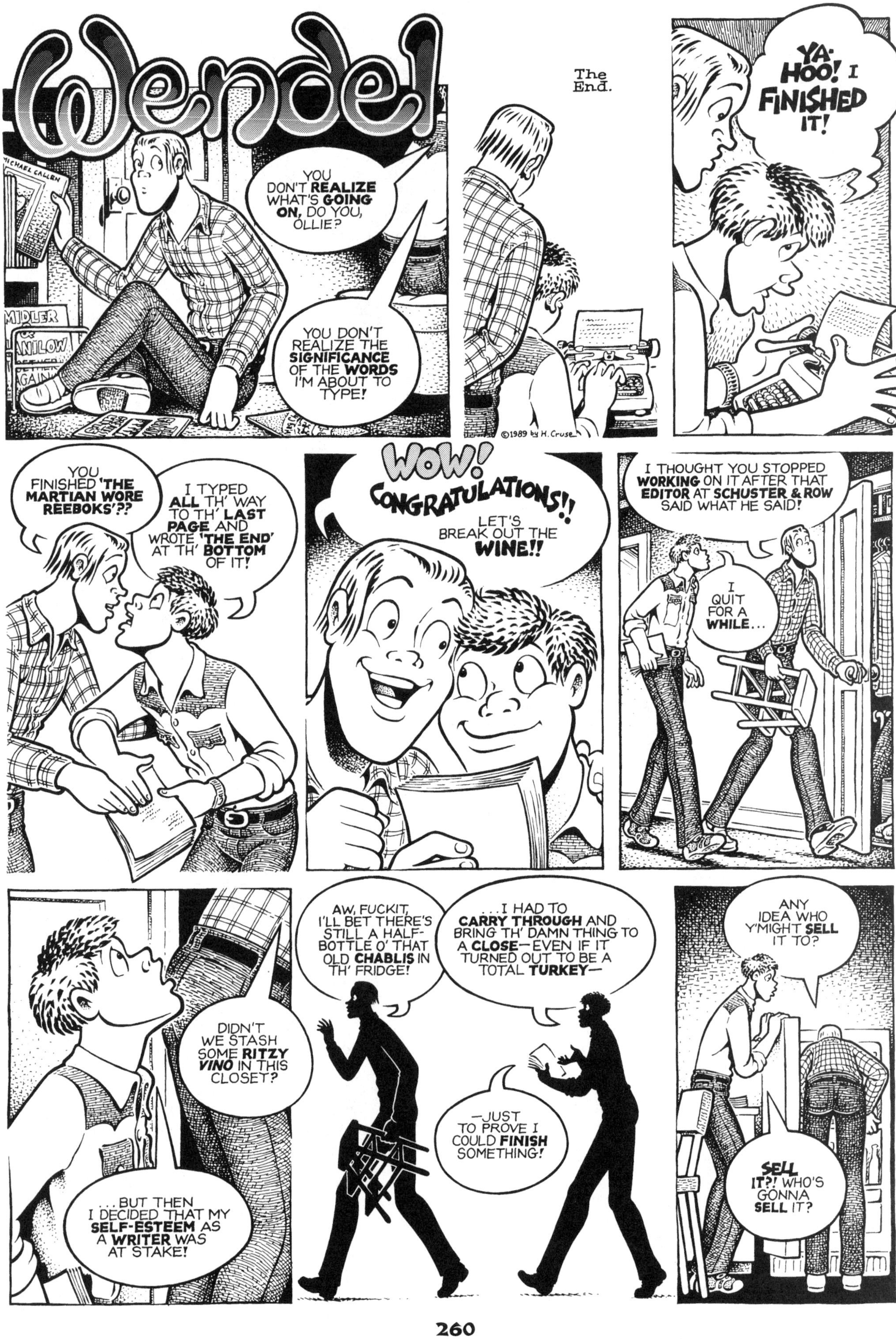
Wendel
The End.
YOU DON'T REALIZE WHAT'S GOING ON, DO YOU, OLLIE?
YOU DON'T REALIZE THE SIGNIFICANCE OF THE WORDS I'M ABOUT TO TYPE!
YA-HOO! I FINISHED IT!
©1989 by H. Cruse
YOU FINISHED 'THE MARTIAN WORE REEBOKS'??
I TYPED ALL TH' WAY TO TH' LAST PAGE AND WROTE 'THE END' AT TH' BOTTOM OF IT!
WOW! CONGRATULATIONS!!
LET'S BREAK OUT THE WINE!!
I THOUGHT YOU STOPPED WORKING ON IT AFTER THAT EDITOR AT SCHUSTER & ROW SAID WHAT HE SAID!
I QUIT FOR A WHILE...
DIDN'T WE STASH SOME RITZY VINO IN THIS CLOSET?
...BUT THEN I DECIDED THAT MY SELF-ESTEEM AS A WRITER WAS AT STAKE!
AW, FUCKIT, I'LL BET THERE'S STILL A HALF-BOTTLE O' THAT OLD CHABLIS IN TH' FRIDGE!
...I HAD TO CARRY THROUGH AND BRING TH' DAMN THING TO A CLOSE—EVEN IF IT TURNED OUT TO BE A TOTAL TURKEY—
—JUST TO PROVE I COULD FINISH SOMETHING!
ANY IDEA WHO Y'MIGHT SELL IT TO?
SELL IT?! WHO'S GONNA SELL IT?

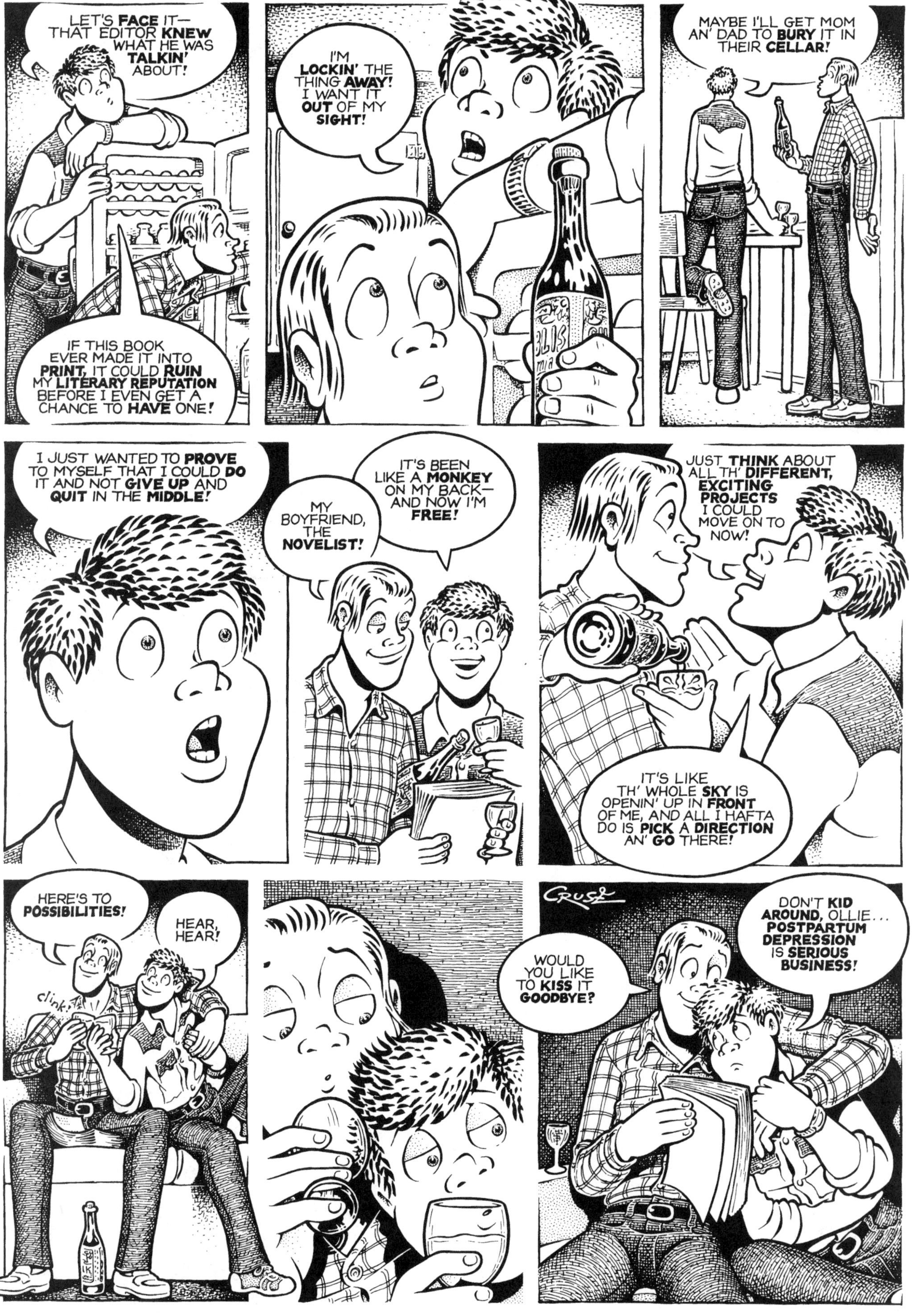
LET'S FACE IT— THAT EDITOR KNEW WHAT HE WAS TALKIN' ABOUT!
IF THIS BOOK EVER MADE IT INTO PRINT, IT COULD RUIN MY LITERARY REPUTATION BEFORE I EVEN GET A CHANCE TO HAVE ONE!
I'M LOCKIN' THE THING AWAY! I WANT IT OUT OF MY SIGHT!
MAYBE I'LL GET MOM AN' DAD TO BURY IT IN THEIR CELLAR!
I JUST WANTED TO PROVE TO MYSELF THAT I COULD DO IT AND NOT GIVE UP AND QUIT IN THE MIDDLE!
IT'S BEEN LIKE A MONKEY ON MY BACK— AND NOW I'M FREE!
MY BOYFRIEND, THE NOVELIST!
JUST THINK ABOUT ALL TH' DIFFERENT, EXCITING PROJECTS I COULD MOVE ON TO NOW!
IT'S LIKE TH' WHOLE SKY IS OPENIN' UP IN FRONT OF ME, AND ALL I HAFTA DO IS PICK A DIRECTION AN' GO THERE!
HERE'S TO POSSIBILITIES!
HEAR, HEAR!
clink!
CRUSE
WOULD YOU LIKE TO KISS IT GOODBYE?
DON'T KID AROUND, OLLIE... POSTPARTUM DEPRESSION IS SERIOUS BUSINESS!

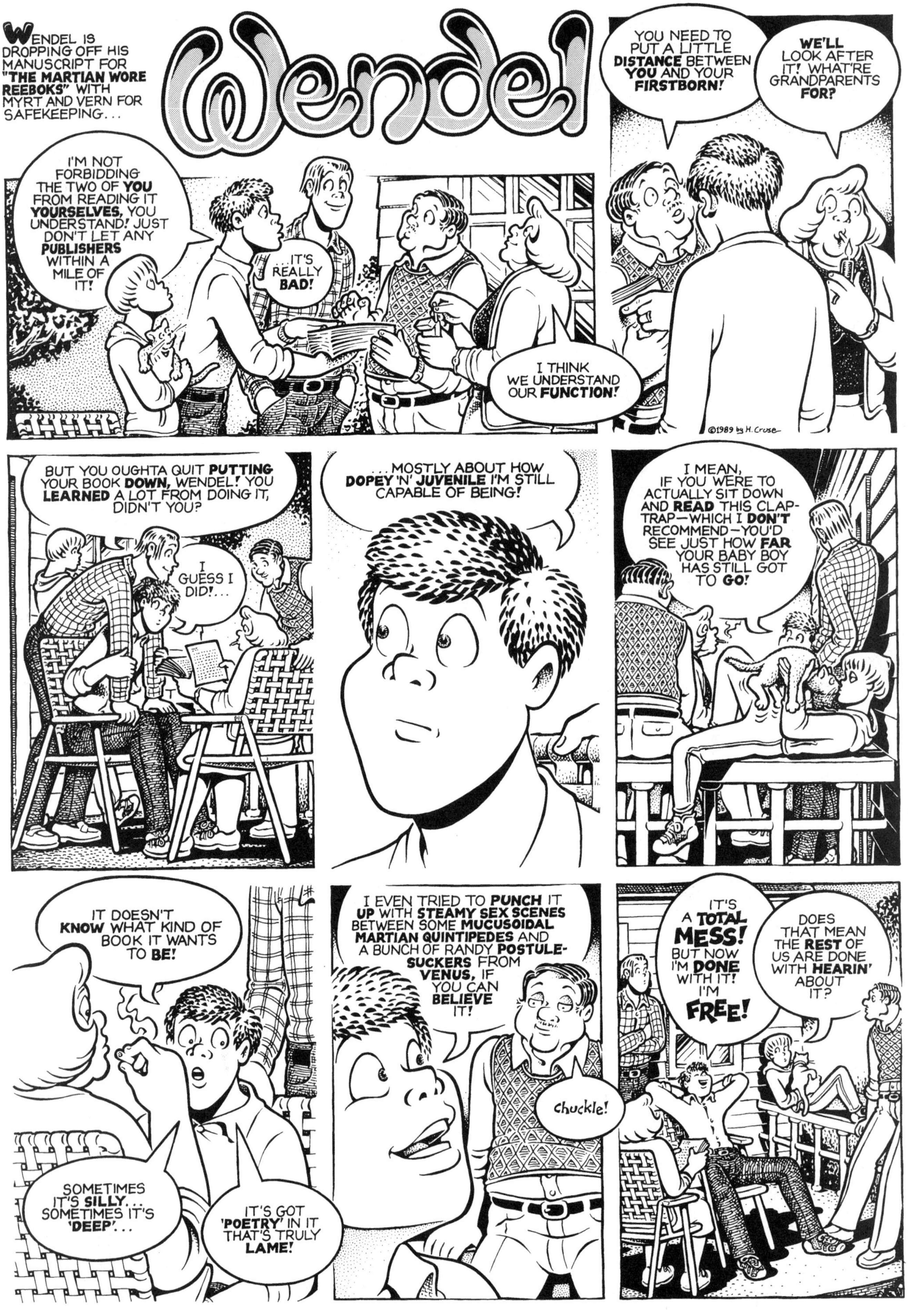
Wendel
WENDEL IS DROPPING OFF HIS MANUSCRIPT FOR "THE MARTIAN WORE REEBOKS" WITH MYRT AND VERN FOR SAFEKEEPING...
I'M NOT FORBIDDING THE TWO OF YOU FROM READING IT YOURSELVES, YOU UNDERSTAND! JUST DON'T LET ANY PUBLISHERS WITHIN A MILE OF IT!
...IT'S REALLY BAD!
I THINK WE UNDERSTAND OUR FUNCTION!
YOU NEED TO PUT A LITTLE DISTANCE BETWEEN YOU AND YOUR FIRSTBORN!
WE'LL LOOK AFTER IT! WHAT'RE GRANDPARENTS FOR?
©1989 by H. Cruse
BUT YOU OUGHTA QUIT PUTTING YOUR BOOK DOWN, WENDEL! YOU LEARNED A LOT FROM DOING IT, DIDN'T YOU?
I GUESS I DID!...
...MOSTLY ABOUT HOW DOPEY 'N' JUVENILE I'M STILL CAPABLE OF BEING!
I MEAN, IF YOU WERE TO ACTUALLY SIT DOWN AND READ THIS CLAP-TRAP—WHICH I DON'T RECOMMEND—YOU'D SEE JUST HOW FAR YOUR BABY BOY HAS STILL GOT TO GO!
IT DOESN'T KNOW WHAT KIND OF BOOK IT WANTS TO BE!
SOMETIMES IT'S SILLY... SOMETIMES IT'S 'DEEP'...
IT'S GOT 'POETRY' IN IT THAT'S TRULY LAME!
I EVEN TRIED TO PUNCH IT UP WITH STEAMY SEX SCENES BETWEEN SOME MUCUSOIDAL MARTIAN QUINTIPEDES AND A BUNCH OF RANDY POSTULE-SUCKERS FROM VENUS, IF YOU CAN BELIEVE IT!
chuckle!
IT'S A TOTAL MESS! BUT NOW I'M DONE WITH IT! I'M FREE!
DOES THAT MEAN THE REST OF US ARE DONE WITH HEARIN' ABOUT IT?

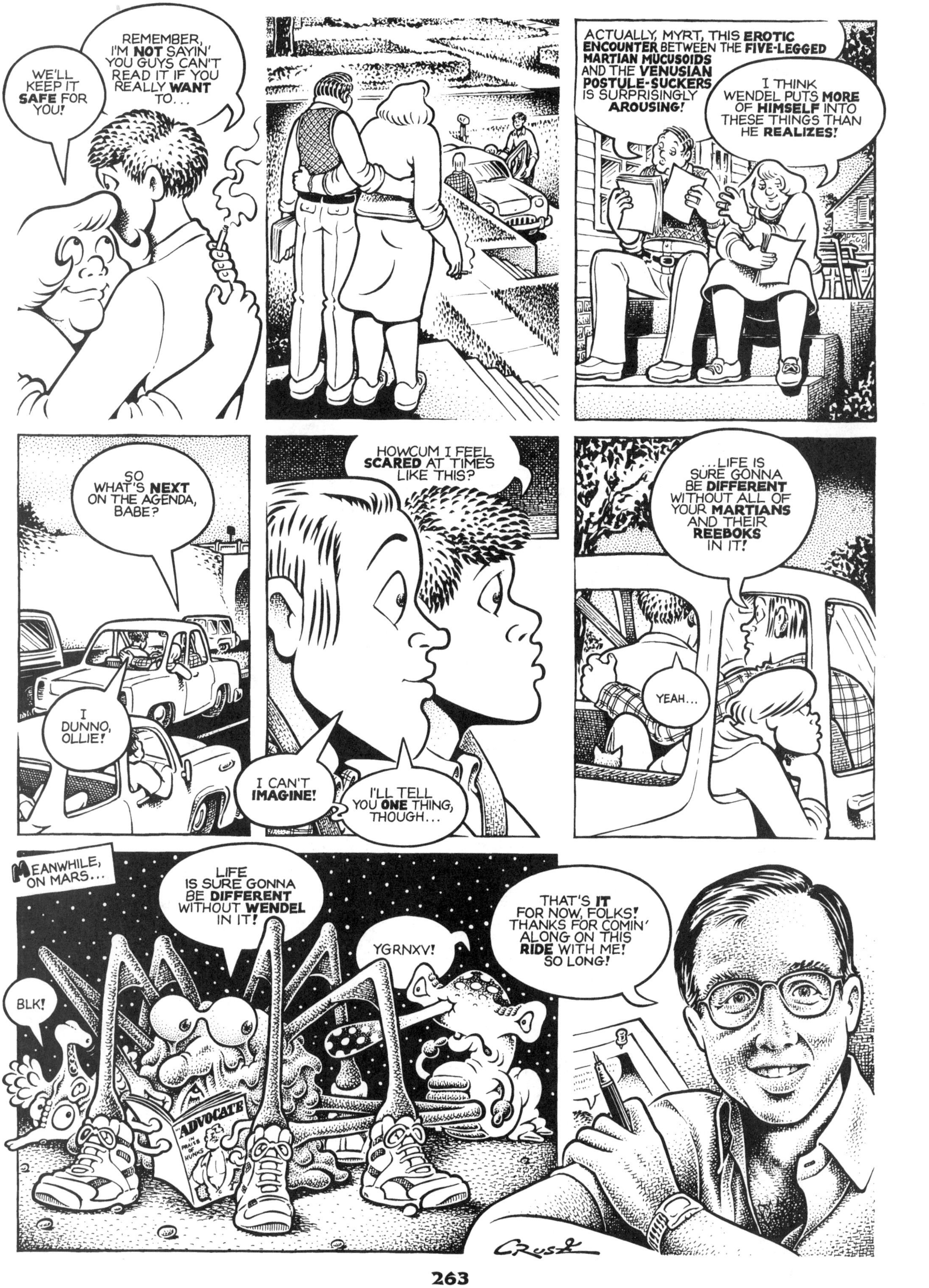
REMEMBER, I'M NOT SAYIN' YOU GUYS CAN'T READ IT IF YOU REALLY WANT TO...
WE'LL KEEP IT SAFE FOR YOU!
ACTUALLY, MYRT, THIS EROTIC ENCOUNTER BETWEEN THE FIVE-LEGGED MARTIAN MUCUSOIDS AND THE VENUSIAN POSTULE-SUCKERS IS SURPRISINGLY AROUSING!
I THINK WENDEL PUTS MORE OF HIMSELF INTO THESE THINGS THAN HE REALIZES!
SO WHAT'S NEXT ON THE AGENDA, BABE?
I DUNNO, OLLIE!
HOWCUM I FEEL SCARED AT TIMES LIKE THIS?
I CAN'T IMAGINE!
I'LL TELL YOU ONE THING, THOUGH...
...LIFE IS SURE GONNA BE DIFFERENT WITHOUT ALL OF YOUR MARTIANS AND THEIR REEBOKS IN IT!
YEAH...
MEANWHILE, ON MARS...
LIFE IS SURE GONNA BE DIFFERENT WITHOUT WENDEL IN IT!
BLK!
YGRNXV!
ADVOCATE
IN PRAISE OF HUNKS
THAT'S IT FOR NOW, FOLKS! THANKS FOR COMIN' ALONG ON THIS RIDE WITH ME! SO LONG!
CRUSE

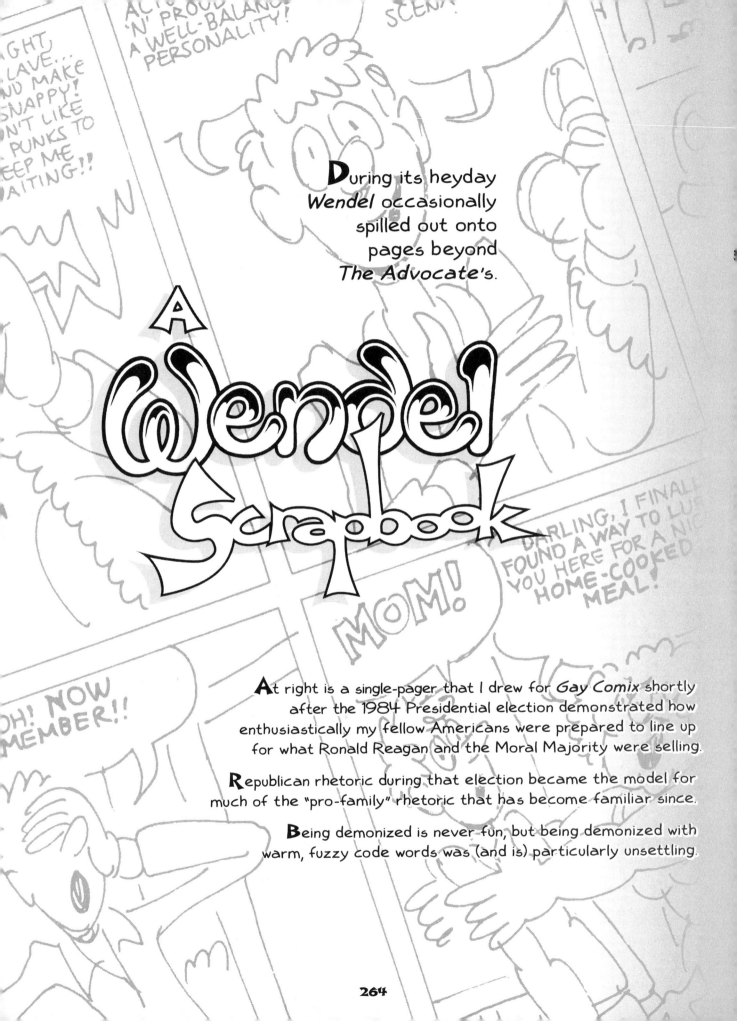

During its heyday *Wendel* occasionally spilled out onto pages beyond *The Advocate*'s.

A Wendel Scrapbook

At right is a single-pager that I drew for *Gay Comix* shortly after the 1984 Presidential election demonstrated how enthusiastically my fellow Americans were prepared to line up for what Ronald Reagan and the Moral Majority were selling.

Republican rhetoric during that election became the model for much of the "pro-family" rhetoric that has become familiar since.

Being demonized is never fun, but being demonized with warm, fuzzy code words was (and is) particularly unsettling.

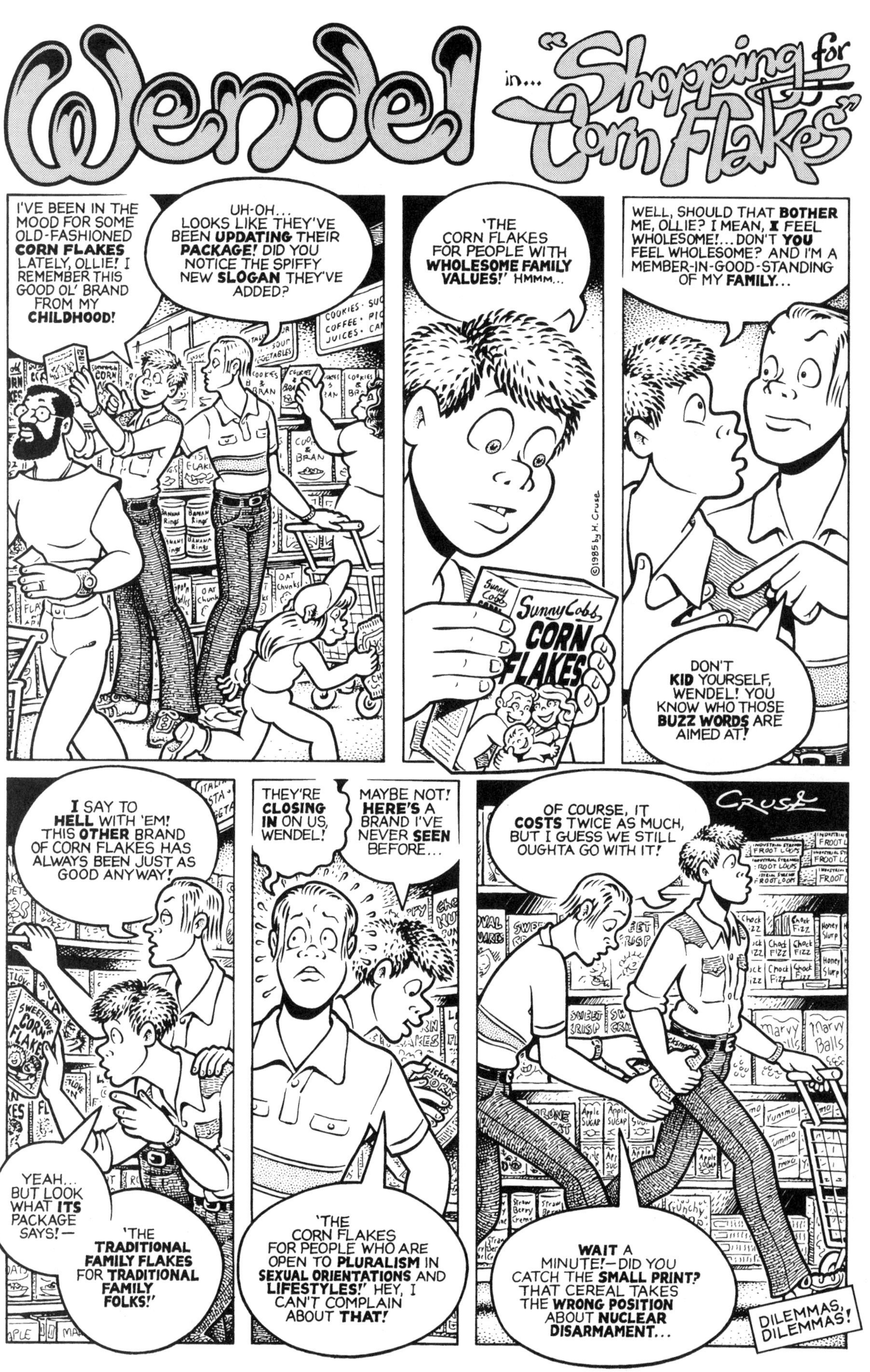
Wendel in... "Shopping for Corn Flakes"
I'VE BEEN IN THE MOOD FOR SOME OLD-FASHIONED **CORN FLAKES** LATELY, OLLIE! I REMEMBER THIS GOOD OL' BRAND FROM MY **CHILDHOOD**!
UH-OH... LOOKS LIKE THEY'VE BEEN **UPDATING** THEIR **PACKAGE**! DID YOU NOTICE THE SPIFFY NEW **SLOGAN** THEY'VE ADDED?
'THE CORN FLAKES FOR PEOPLE WITH **WHOLESOME FAMILY VALUES**!' HMMM...
SunnyCobb CORN FLAKES
©1985 by H. Cruse
WELL, SHOULD THAT **BOTHER** ME, OLLIE? I MEAN, **I** FEEL WHOLESOME!... DON'T **YOU** FEEL WHOLESOME? AND I'M A MEMBER-IN-GOOD-STANDING OF MY **FAMILY**...
DON'T **KID** YOURSELF, WENDEL! YOU KNOW WHO THOSE **BUZZ WORDS** ARE AIMED AT!
I SAY TO **HELL** WITH 'EM! THIS **OTHER** BRAND OF CORN FLAKES HAS ALWAYS BEEN JUST AS GOOD ANYWAY!
YEAH... BUT LOOK WHAT **ITS** PACKAGE SAYS!—
'THE **TRADITIONAL FAMILY FLAKES** FOR **TRADITIONAL FAMILY FOLKS**!'
THEY'RE **CLOSING IN** ON US, WENDEL!
MAYBE NOT! **HERE'S** A BRAND I'VE NEVER **SEEN** BEFORE...
'THE CORN FLAKES FOR PEOPLE WHO ARE OPEN TO **PLURALISM** IN **SEXUAL ORIENTATIONS** AND **LIFESTYLES**!' HEY, I CAN'T COMPLAIN ABOUT **THAT**!
CRUSE
OF COURSE, IT **COSTS** TWICE AS MUCH, BUT I GUESS WE STILL OUGHTA GO WITH IT!
WAIT A MINUTE!—DID YOU CATCH THE **SMALL PRINT**? THAT CEREAL TAKES THE **WRONG POSITION** ABOUT **NUCLEAR DISARMAMENT**...
DILEMMAS, DILEMMAS!

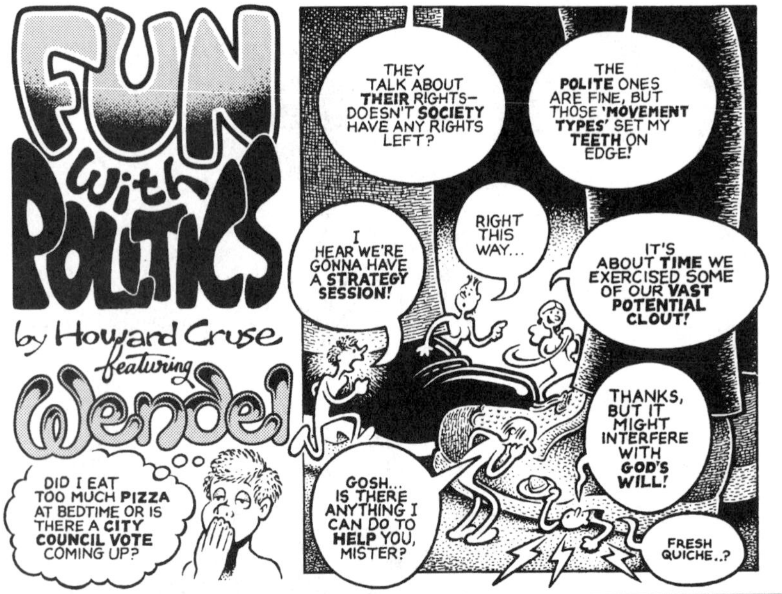
FUN with POLITICS
by Howard Cruse
featuring
Wendel
DID I EAT TOO MUCH PIZZA AT BEDTIME OR IS THERE A CITY COUNCIL VOTE COMING UP?
THEY TALK ABOUT THEIR RIGHTS– DOESN'T SOCIETY HAVE ANY RIGHTS LEFT?
THE POLITE ONES ARE FINE, BUT THOSE 'MOVEMENT TYPES' SET MY TEETH ON EDGE!
I HEAR WE'RE GONNA HAVE A STRATEGY SESSION!
RIGHT THIS WAY...
IT'S ABOUT TIME WE EXERCISED SOME OF OUR VAST POTENTIAL CLOUT!
THANKS, BUT IT MIGHT INTERFERE WITH GOD'S WILL!
GOSH... IS THERE ANYTHING I CAN DO TO HELP YOU, MISTER?
FRESH QUICHE..?

Asked in 1986 by *The Village Voice* to draw a strip reflecting on the New York City Council's impending up-or-down vote on a gay rights law, I temporarily relocated Wendel and Ollie to the Big Apple.

Not knowing while I drew the strip how the vote would go, I used nightmare imagery to comment on the indignity inherent in being forced to beg politicians for one's rights at all.

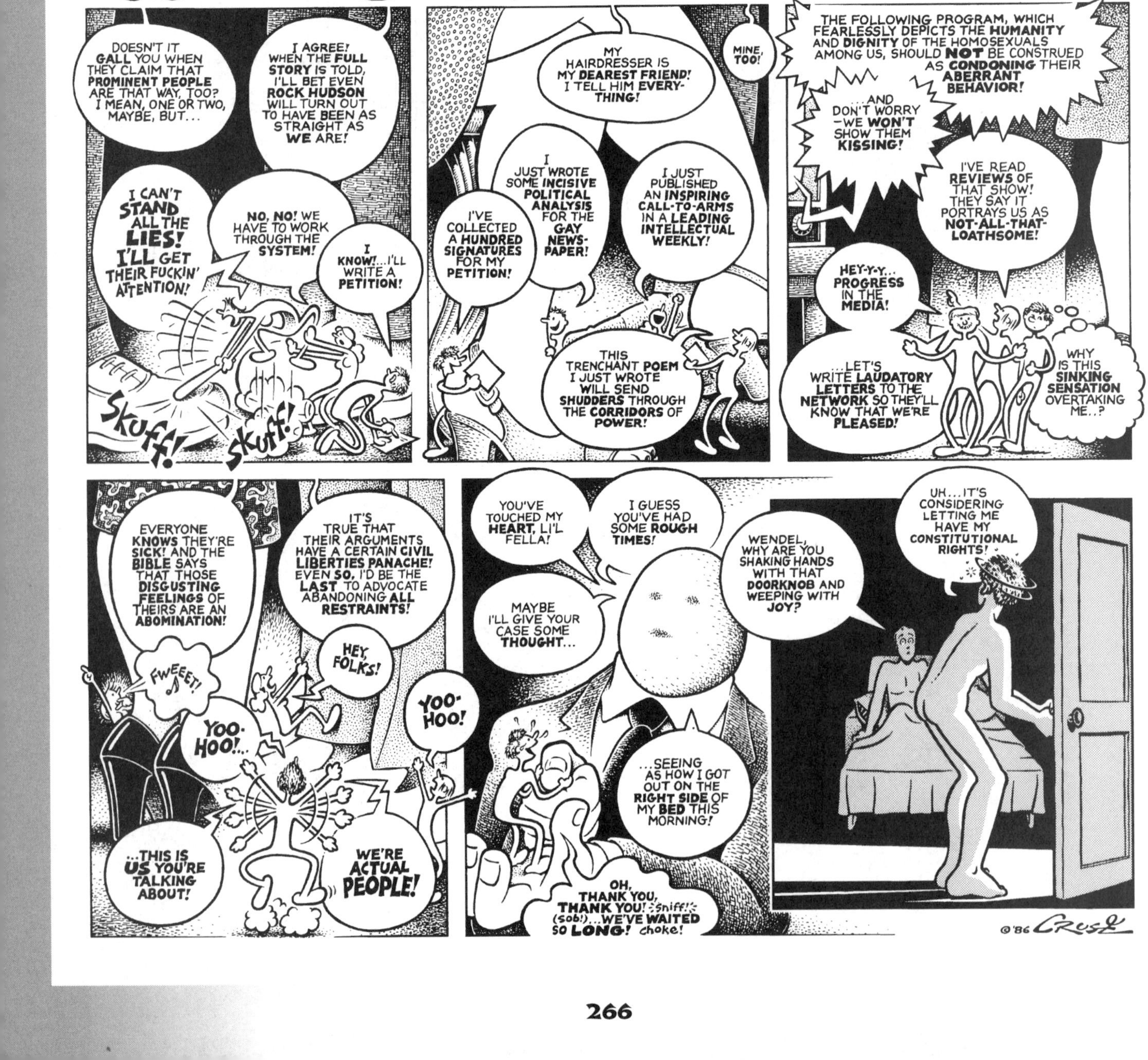
DOESN'T IT GALL YOU WHEN THEY CLAIM THAT PROMINENT PEOPLE ARE THAT WAY, TOO? I MEAN, ONE OR TWO, MAYBE, BUT...
I AGREE! WHEN THE FULL STORY IS TOLD, I'LL BET EVEN ROCK HUDSON WILL TURN OUT TO HAVE BEEN AS STRAIGHT AS WE ARE!
I CAN'T STAND ALL THE LIES! I'LL GET THEIR FUCKIN' ATTENTION!
NO, NO! WE HAVE TO WORK THROUGH THE SYSTEM!
I KNOW!...I'LL WRITE A PETITION!
SKUFF!
SKUFF!
MY HAIRDRESSER IS MY DEAREST FRIEND! I TELL HIM EVERY-THING!
MINE, TOO!
I JUST WROTE SOME INCISIVE POLITICAL ANALYSIS FOR THE GAY NEWS-PAPER!
I JUST PUBLISHED AN INSPIRING CALL-TO-ARMS IN A LEADING INTELLECTUAL WEEKLY!
I'VE COLLECTED A HUNDRED SIGNATURES FOR MY PETITION!
THIS TRENCHANT POEM I JUST WROTE WILL SEND SHUDDERS THROUGH THE CORRIDORS OF POWER!
THE FOLLOWING PROGRAM, WHICH FEARLESSLY DEPICTS THE HUMANITY AND DIGNITY OF THE HOMOSEXUALS AMONG US, SHOULD NOT BE CONSTRUED AS CONDONING THEIR ABERRANT BEHAVIOR!
...AND DON'T WORRY –WE WON'T SHOW THEM KISSING!
I'VE READ REVIEWS OF THAT SHOW! THEY SAY IT PORTRAYS US AS NOT-ALL-THAT-LOATHSOME!
HEY-Y-Y... PROGRESS IN THE MEDIA!
...LET'S WRITE LAUDATORY LETTERS TO THE NETWORK SO THEY'LL KNOW THAT WE'RE PLEASED!
WHY IS THIS SINKING SENSATION OVERTAKING ME..?
EVERYONE KNOWS THEY'RE SICK! AND THE BIBLE SAYS THAT THOSE DISGUSTING FEELINGS OF THEIRS ARE AN ABOMINATION!
IT'S TRUE THAT THEIR ARGUMENTS HAVE A CERTAIN CIVIL LIBERTIES PANACHE! EVEN SO, I'D BE THE LAST TO ADVOCATE ABANDONING ALL RESTRAINTS!
FWEEET!
HEY, FOLKS!
YOO-HOO!...
YOO-HOO!
...THIS IS US YOU'RE TALKING ABOUT!
WE'RE ACTUAL PEOPLE!
YOU'VE TOUCHED MY HEART, LI'L FELLA!
I GUESS YOU'VE HAD SOME ROUGH TIMES!
MAYBE I'LL GIVE YOUR CASE SOME THOUGHT...
...SEEING AS HOW I GOT OUT ON THE RIGHT SIDE OF MY BED THIS MORNING!
OH, THANK YOU, THANK YOU! sniff! (sob!)...WE'VE WAITED SO LONG! choke!
WENDEL, WHY ARE YOU SHAKING HANDS WITH THAT DOORKNOB AND WEEPING WITH JOY?
UH...IT'S CONSIDERING LETTING ME HAVE MY CONSTITUTIONAL RIGHTS!
©'86 CRUSE

Plugging a demonstration, congregating on the cover of the *Gayellow Pages*, or expressing dismay in *Out/Look* magazine over the demise of Andy Lippincott in *Doonesbury*...

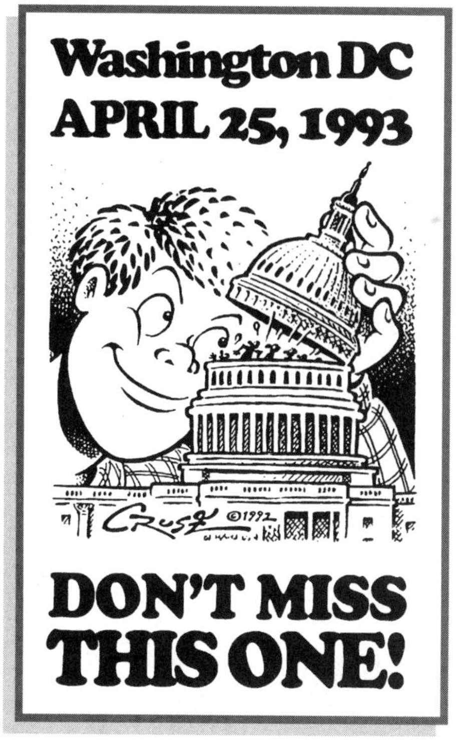

Washington DC
APRIL 25, 1993
©1992 CRUSE
DON'T MISS THIS ONE!

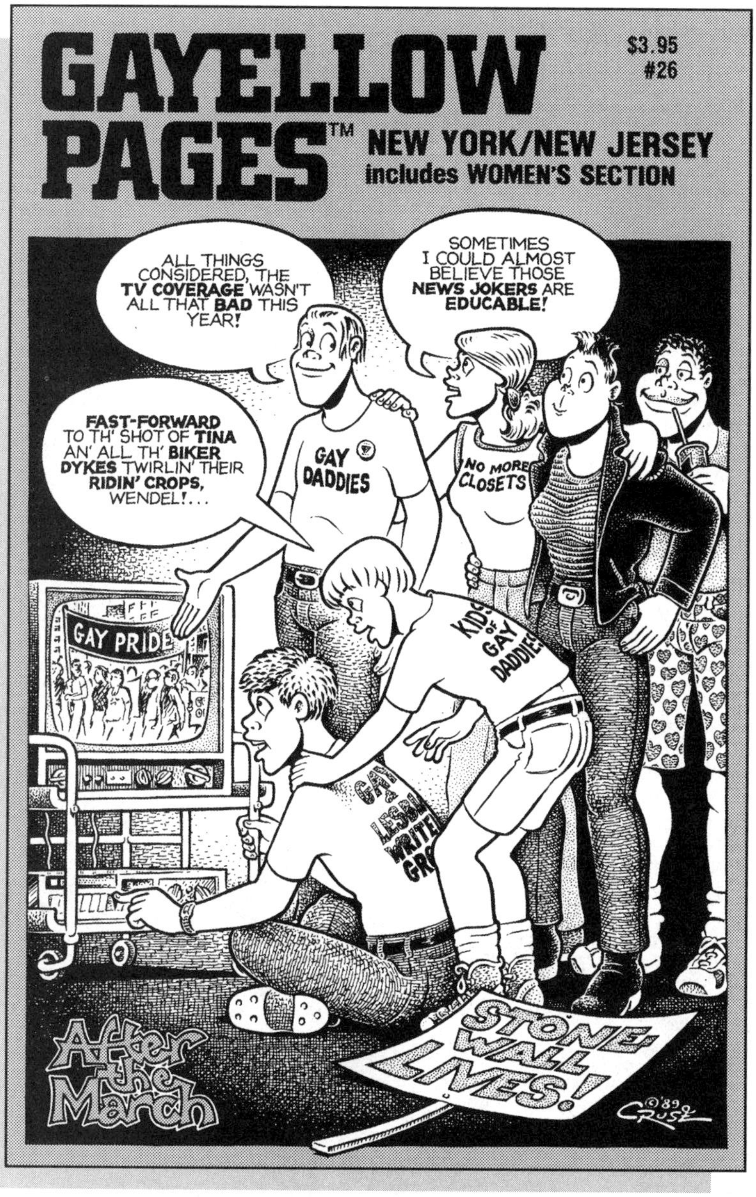

GAYELLOW PAGES™
$3.95
#26
NEW YORK/NEW JERSEY
includes WOMEN'S SECTION
ALL THINGS CONSIDERED, THE TV COVERAGE WASN'T ALL THAT BAD THIS YEAR!
SOMETIMES I COULD ALMOST BELIEVE THOSE NEWS JOKERS ARE EDUCABLE!
FAST-FORWARD TO TH' SHOT OF TINA AN' ALL TH' BIKER DYKES TWIRLIN' THEIR RIDIN' CROPS, WENDEL!...
GAY DADDIES
NO MORE CLOSETS
GAY PRIDE
KIDS OF GAY DADDIES
STONEWALL LIVES!
After the March
©'89 CRUSE

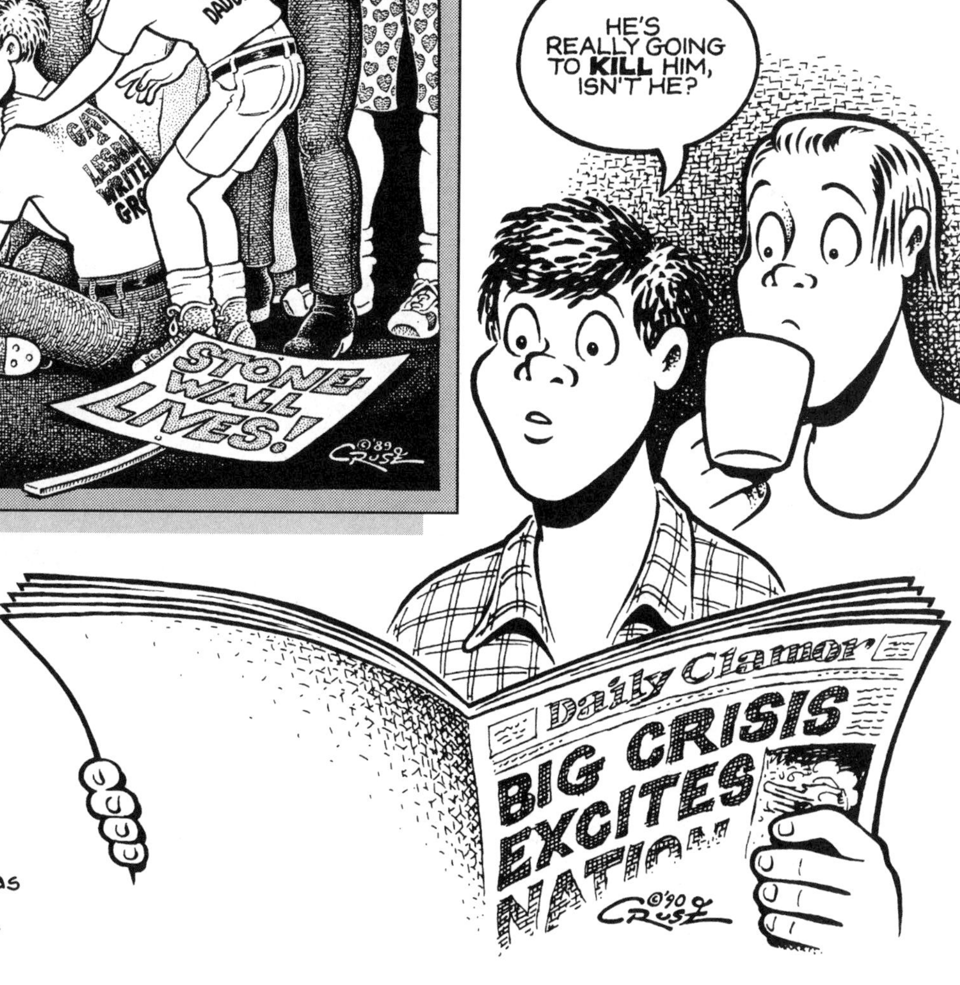

HE'S REALLY GOING TO KILL HIM, ISN'T HE?
Daily Clamor
BIG CRISIS EXCITES NATION
©'90 CRUSE

They all came naturally, since Wendel's world was his readers' world.

Two drawings created for comics fans.

Below is my illustration for "Out of the Closet and into the Comics," a two-part article by Andy Mangels that appeared in *Amazing Heroes* in 1988.

Andy's essay examined both the track record of mainstream comics when it came to depicting homosexuals, and the roles played by the gay creators of mainstream comics. Most such creators were closeted at the time; an encouraging number of them have since come out.

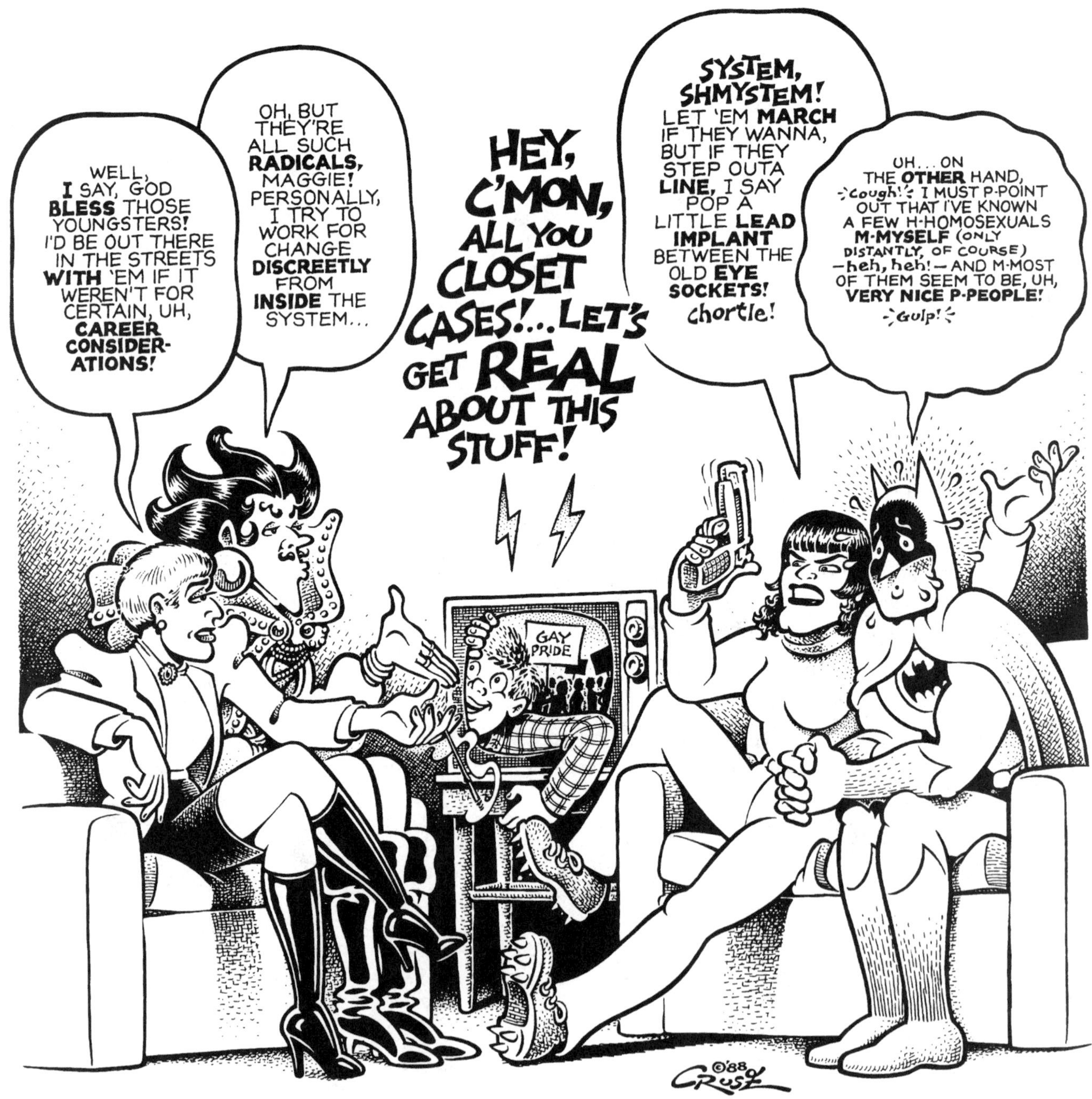
WELL, I SAY, GOD BLESS THOSE YOUNGSTERS! I'D BE OUT THERE IN THE STREETS WITH 'EM IF IT WEREN'T FOR CERTAIN, UH, CAREER CONSIDER-ATIONS!
OH, BUT THEY'RE ALL SUCH RADICALS, MAGGIE! PERSONALLY, I TRY TO WORK FOR CHANGE DISCREETLY FROM INSIDE THE SYSTEM...
HEY, C'MON, ALL YOU CLOSET CASES!... LET'S GET REAL ABOUT THIS STUFF!
SYSTEM, SHMYSTEM! LET 'EM MARCH IF THEY WANNA, BUT IF THEY STEP OUTA LINE, I SAY POP A LITTLE LEAD IMPLANT BETWEEN THE OLD EYE SOCKETS! chortle!
UH... ON THE OTHER HAND, cough! I MUST P-POINT OUT THAT I'VE KNOWN A FEW H-HOMOSEXUALS M-MYSELF (ONLY DISTANTLY, OF COURSE) —heh, heh!— AND M-MOST OF THEM SEEM TO BE, UH, VERY NICE P-PEOPLE! Gulp!
GAY PRIDE
©'88 CRUSE

Here's my program drawing for the 1989 San Diego Comic Con.

The organizers of the popular annual gathering of comics fans (since renamed the San Diego Comic-Con International) broke ground that year by inviting me to be the first openly gay "Special Guest" in the convention's history.

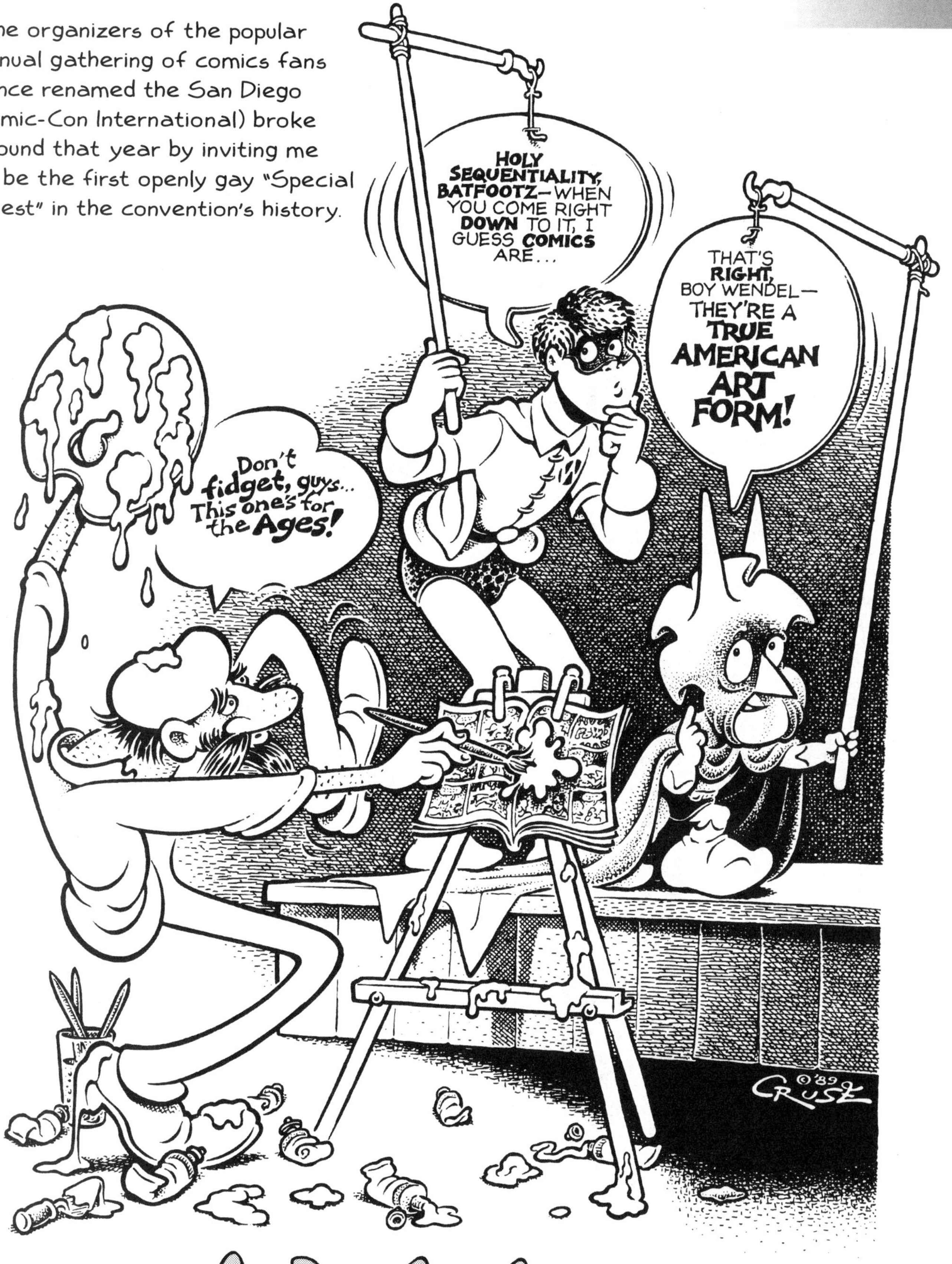

HOLY SEQUENTIALITY, BATFOOTZ—WHEN YOU COME RIGHT DOWN TO IT, I GUESS COMICS ARE...
THAT'S RIGHT, BOY WENDEL—THEY'RE A TRUE AMERICAN ART FORM!
Don't fidget, guys... This one's for the Ages!
©'89 CRUSE

SAN DIEGO COMIC CON ☆ 1989

In 2001 *The Advocate*'s editors asked me to do a comic strip "jam" with Eric Orner, in which Wendel would swap friendly barbs with the title character of Eric's popular syndicated strip *The Mostly Unfabulous Social Life of Ethan Green*.

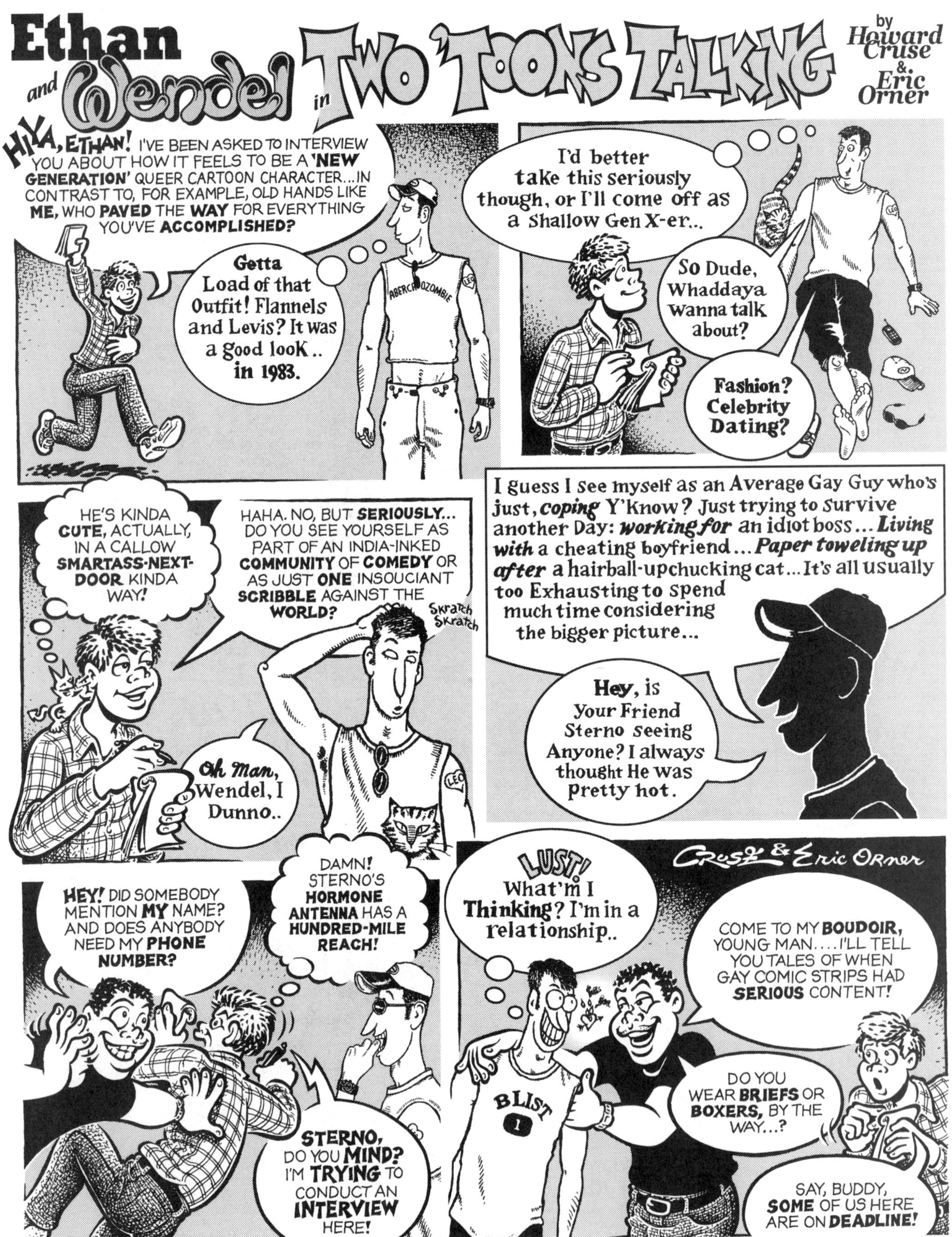

Ethan and Wendel in TWO 'TOONS TALKING
by Howard Cruse & Eric Orner
HIYA, ETHAN! I'VE BEEN ASKED TO INTERVIEW YOU ABOUT HOW IT FEELS TO BE A 'NEW GENERATION' QUEER CARTOON CHARACTER...IN CONTRAST TO, FOR EXAMPLE, OLD HANDS LIKE ME, WHO PAVED THE WAY FOR EVERYTHING YOU'VE ACCOMPLISHED?
Getta Load of that Outfit! Flannels and Levis? It was a good look.. in 1983.
ABERCROZOMBIE
I'd better take this seriously though, or I'll come off as a shallow Gen X-er..
So Dude, Whaddaya wanna talk about?
Fashion? Celebrity Dating?
HE'S KINDA CUTE, ACTUALLY, IN A CALLOW SMARTASS-NEXT-DOOR KINDA WAY!
HAHA. NO, BUT SERIOUSLY... DO YOU SEE YOURSELF AS PART OF AN INDIA-INKED COMMUNITY OF COMEDY OR AS JUST ONE INSOUCIANT SCRIBBLE AGAINST THE WORLD?
SKRATCH SKRATCH
Oh Man, Wendel, I Dunno..
I guess I see myself as an Average Gay Guy who's just, coping Y'Know? Just trying to survive another Day: working for an idiot boss... Living with a cheating boyfriend... Paper toweling up after a hairball-upchucking cat... It's all usually too Exhausting to spend much time considering the bigger picture...
Hey, is Your Friend Sterno seeing Anyone? I always thought He was pretty hot.
HEY! DID SOMEBODY MENTION MY NAME? AND DOES ANYBODY NEED MY PHONE NUMBER?
DAMN! STERNO'S HORMONE ANTENNA HAS A HUNDRED-MILE REACH!
STERNO, DO YOU MIND? I'M TRYING TO CONDUCT AN INTERVIEW HERE!
CRUSE & Eric Orner
LUST! What'm I Thinking? I'm in a relationship..
COME TO MY BOUDOIR, YOUNG MAN.... I'LL TELL YOU TALES OF WHEN GAY COMIC STRIPS HAD SERIOUS CONTENT!
BLIST 1
DO YOU WEAR BRIEFS OR BOXERS, BY THE WAY...?
SAY, BUDDY, SOME OF US HERE ARE ON DEADLINE!

I discovered this forgotten sketch in my files while I was compiling this book.

I'm not sure what occasioned it. I guess I must have been putting in heavy hours at the drawing board.

It seems a pleasant image to leave you with.

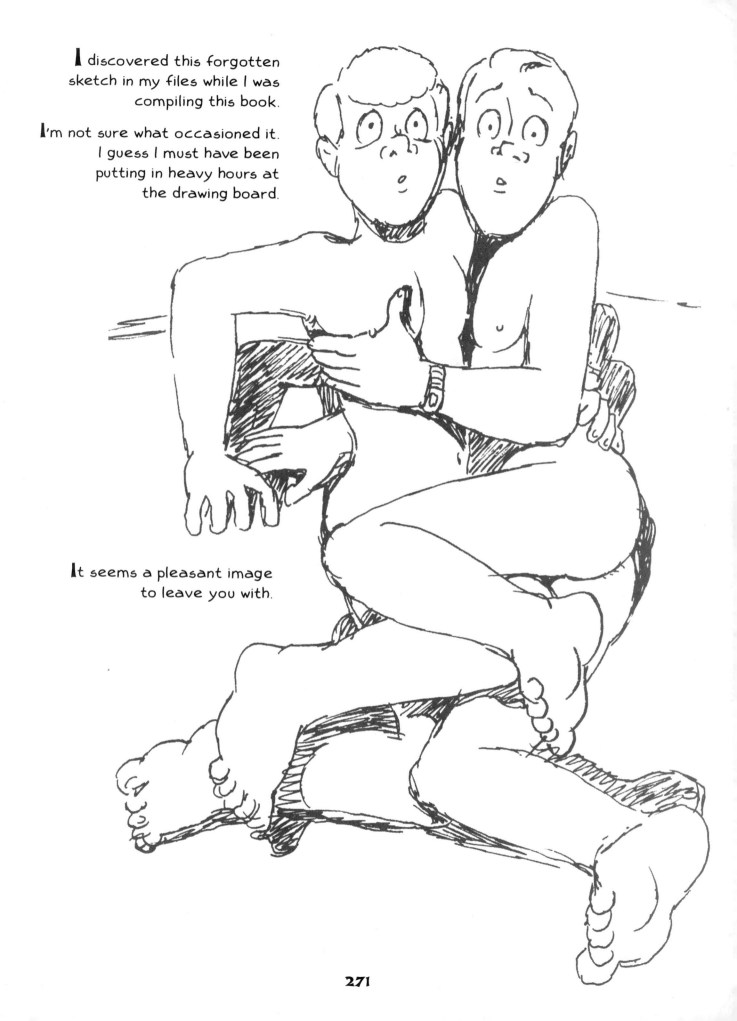

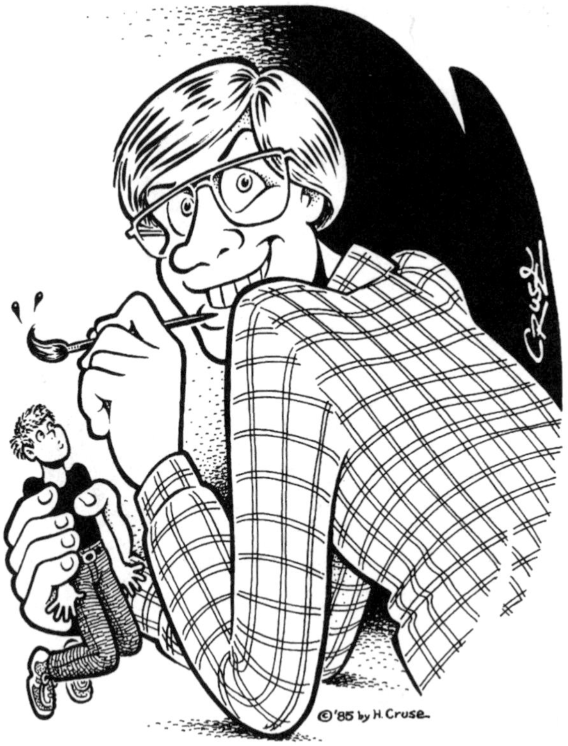
CRUSE
©'85 by H. Cruse

About the Author

Howard Cruse is an Alabama preacher's kid who first attracted national attention as a contributor to underground comic books in the 1970s. He was the founding editor of *Gay Comix* in 1979 and has remained a frequent illustrator for numerous newsstand publications.

His comic strip *Wendel* was regularly featured in *The Advocate,* the national lesbian and gay newsmagazine, first from 1983 through 1985, then again from 1986 through 1989.

Cruse's comic strips have been compiled in four book-length collections. His fifth book, the original graphic novel *Stuck Rubber Baby,* was published by Paradox Press in 1995 and has won awards in the United States, the United Kingdom, and Germany. An Italian-language edition of the novel was published early in 2001 and a French translation is also under way.

Since 1979 Cruse has shared his life in New York City with community organizer Ed Sedarbaum..

Visit Howard's web site, Howard Cruse Central, at www.howardcruse.com